TAKING SIDES

Clashing Views in

United States History, Volume 1, The Colonial Period to Reconstruction

TWELFTH EDITION

Contemporary
Learning Series

A Division of The McGraw-Hill Companies

TAKING SIDES

Clashing Views in

United States History, Volume 1, The Colonial Period to Reconstruction

TWELFTH EDITION

Selected, Edited, and with Introductions by

Larry Madaras
Howard Community College

and

James M. SoRelle
Baylor University

Contemporary Learning Series

A Division of The McGraw-Hill Companies

To Maggie and Cindy

Photo Acknowledgment
Cover image: Library of Congress

Cover Acknowledgment
Maggie Lytle

Copyright © 2008 by McGraw-Hill Contemporary Learning Series
A Division of The McGraw-Hill Companies, Inc., Dubuque, Iowa 52001

Manufactured in the United States of America

Twelfth edition

123456789DOCDOC9876

Library of Congress Cataloging-in-Publication Data
Main entry under title:
Taking sides: clashing views on controversial issues in American history, volume I, the colonial
period to reconstruction/selected, edited, and with introductions by Larry Madaras and James M.
SoRelle.—12th ed.
Includes bibliographical references and index.
1. United States—History. I. Madaras, Larry, *comp.* II. SoRelle, James M., *comp.*
973

0-07-352723-8
978-0-07-352723-9
ISSN: 1091-8833

Printed on Recycled Paper

Preface

The success of the past eleven editions of *Taking Sides: Clashing Views in United States History* has encouraged us to remain faithful to its original objectives, methods, and format. Our aim has been to create an effective instrument to enhance classroom learning and to foster critical thinking. Historical facts presented in a vacuum are of little value to the educational process. For students, whose search for historical truth often concentrates on *when* something happened rather than on *why*, and on specific events rather than on the *significance* of those events, *Taking Sides* is designed to offer an interesting and rewarding departure. The understanding that the reader arrives at based on the evidence that emerges from the clash of views encourages the reader to view history as an *interpretive* discipline, not one of rote memorization.

As in previous editions, the eighteen issues and thirty-six essays that follow are arranged in chronological order and can be incorporated easily into any American history survey course. Each issue has an *introduction*, which sets the stage for the debate that follows in the pro and con selections and provides historical and methodological background to the problem that the issue examines. Each issue concludes with a *postscript*, which ties the readings together, briefly mentions alternative interpretations, and supplies detailed *suggestions for further reading* for the student who wishes to pursue the topics raised in the issue. Also, Internet site addresses (URLs), which should prove useful as starting points for further research, have been provided on the *Internet References* page that accompanies each part opener. At the back of the book is a listing of all the *contributors to this volume* with a brief biographical sketch of each of the authors whose views are debated here.

While we have selected a pair of essays to offer differing points of view in response to each issue question, readers should understand that there are likely many more ways in which these questions can be addressed. Further, the authors of each pair of essays may agree with one another on many historical points and yet still reach opposing conclusions. Readers, therefore, are expected to examine the essays with a critical eye, recognize the strengths and weaknesses of particular arguments, determine which pieces of evidence are most useful in reaching an objective, reasoned conclusion, and consider alternative answers to the questions asked.

Changes to this edition In this edition we have continued our efforts to maintain a balance between traditional political, diplomatic, and cultural issues and the new social history, which depicts a society that benefited from the presence of Native Americans, African Americans, women, and workers of various racial and ethnic backgrounds. With this in mind, we present seven new issues: Was Disease the Key Factor in the Depopulation of Native Americans in the Americas? (Issue 2); Was Colonial Culture Uniquely American? (Issue 3); Did the American Revolution Produce a Christian Nation? (Issue 6);

Was James Madison an Effective Wartime President? (Issue 9); Did the Election of 1828 Represent a Democratic Revolt of the People? (Issue 11); Did the Industrial Revolution Provide More Opportunities for Women in the 1830s? (Issue 12); and Was the Confederacy Defeated Because of Its "Loss of Will"? (Issue 16). In all, there are sixteen new selections.

A word to the instructor   An *Instructor's Manual With Test Questions* (multiple-choice and essay) is available through the publisher for the instructor using *Taking Sides* in the classroom. A general guidebook, *Using Taking Sides in the Classroom*, which discusses methods and techniques for integrating the pro-con approach into any classroom setting, is also available. An online version of *Using Taking Sides in the Classroom* and a correspondence service for *Taking Sides* adopters can be found at http://www.mhcls.com/usingts/.

Acknowledgments   Many individuals have contributed to the successful completion of this edition. We appreciate the evaluations submitted to McGraw-Hill Contemporary Learning Series by those who have used *Taking Sides* in the classroom. Special thanks to those who responded with specific suggestions for the ninth and tenth editions:

Gary Best	**Elliot Pasternack**
University of Hawaii–Hilo	*Middlesex County College (N.J.)*
James D. Bolton	**Robert M. Paterson**
Coastline Community College	*Armstrong State College*
Mary Borg	**Charles Piehl**
University of Northern Colorado	*Mankato State University*
John Whitney	**Ethan S. Rafuse**
Evans College of St. Scholastica	*University of Missouri–Kansas City*
Mark Hickerson	**John Reid**
Chaffey College	*Ohio State University–Lima*
Maryann Irwin	**Murray Rubinstein**
Diablo Valley College	*CUNY Baruch College*
Gordon Lam	**Neil Sapper**
Sierra College	*Amarillo College*
Jon Nielson	**Preston She**
Columbia College	*Plymouth State College*
Andrew O'Shaugnessy	**Tim Koerner**
University of Wisconsin–Oshkosh	*Oakland Community College*
Manian Padma	**Jack Traylor**
DeAnza College	*William Jennings Bryan College*

We are particularly indebted to Maggie Cullen, Cindy SoRelle, the late Barry A. Crouch, Virginia Kirk, Joseph and Helen Mitchell, and Jean Soto, who shared their ideas for changes, pointed us toward potentially useful historical works, and provided significant editorial assistance. Megan Arnold performed indispensable typing duties connected with this project. Susan E. Myers, Ela Ciborowski, and Karen Higgins in the library at Howard Community College provided essential help in acquiring books and articles on interlibrary loan.

Finally, we are sincerely grateful for the commitment, encouragement, and patience provided over the years by David Dean, former list manager for the Taking Sides series; David Brackley, former senior developmental editor; and the entire staff of McGraw-Hill Contemporary Learning Series. Indispensable to this project are Ted Knight, the former list manager, and Jill Peter, the current editor-in-charge of the Taking Sides series.

Larry Madaras
Howard Community College

James M. SoRelle
Baylor University

Contents In Brief

Contents

the Americas. David Hackett Fischer contends that the cultural traditions of colonial America and the United States were derived from English folkways transported by migrants from four different regions in the British Isles.

Professor Edmund S. Morgan argues that Virginia's first decade as a colony was a complete "fiasco" because the settlers were too lazy to engage in the subsistence farming necessary for their survival and failed to abandon their own and the Virginia's company's expectations of establishing extractive industries such as mining, timber, and fishing. According to Professor Russell R. Menard, the indentured servants of seventeenth-century Maryland were hardworking, energetic, and young individuals who went through two stages of history: From 1640 to 1660 servants provided large planters with an inexpensive labor force, but they also achieved greater wealth and mobility in the Chesapeake than if they remained in England; after 1660 opportunities for servants to achieve land, wealth, and status drastically declined.

Gloria Main notes that New England women were highly valued for their labor and relative scarcity in the early colonial period and that their economic autonomy increased in the years during and following the Seven Years War as more women entered the paid labor force and received higher wages for their work. Lyle Koehler contends that Puritan attitudes toward rights of inheritance, as well as the division of labor that separated work into male and female spheres, discouraged productive, independent activity on the part of New England women.

Nathan Hatch argues that by eroding traditional appeals to authority and expanding the number of people who believed they were competent to think for themselves about freedom, equality, and representation, the American Revolution led to an expansion of evangelical Christianity that reinforced the democratic impulses of the new society. Jon Butler insists that men and women seldom referred to America as a "Christian nation" between 1760 and 1790 and that even though Christianity was important, most Americans opposed a Christian national identity enforced by law or governmental action.

Political scientist John P. Roche asserts that the Founding Fathers were not only revolutionaries but also superb democratic politicians who created a constitution that supported the needs of the nation and at the same time was acceptable to the people. According to radical historian Howard Zinn, the Founding Fathers were an elite group of northern money interests and southern slaveholders who used Shay's rebellion in Massachusetts as a pretext to create a strong central government, which protected the property rights of the rich to the exclusion of slaves, Indians, and non-property-holding whites.

Professor Morton Borden argues that President Thomas Jefferson was a moderate and pragmatic politician who placed the nation's best interests above those of the states. History professor Forrest McDonald believes that President Jefferson attempted to replace Hamiltonian Federalist Principles with a Republican ideology in order to restore America's agrarian heritage.

Irving Brant concludes that President James Madison grew into his position as commander in chief during the War of 1812 and set the stage for both land and naval victories at the close of the conflict through his adroit military appointments and skillful diplomacy. Donald Hickey contends that Madison failed to provide the bold and vigorous leadership that was essential to a successful prosecution of the War of 1812 by tolerating incompetence among his generals and cabinet officers and by failing to secure vital legislation from Congress.

According to Professor Dexter, President James Monroe issued his famous declaration of December 2, 1823 to protest Russian expansionism in the Pacific Northwest and to prevent European intervention in South America from restoring to Spain her former colonies. According to Professor Ernest R. May, domestic political considerations brought about the Monroe Doctrine when the major presidential candidates attempted to gain a political advantage over their rivals during the presidential campaign of 1824.

Bancroft Prize winner Sean Wilentz argues that in spite of its vulgarities and slanders, the 1828 election campaign "produced a valediction on the faction-ridden jumble of the Era of Bad Feelings and announced the rough arrival of two distinct national coalitions." Professor Richard P. McCormick believes that voting statistics demonstrate that a genuine political revolution did not take place until the presidential election of 1840, when fairly well-balanced political parties had been organized in virtually every state.

PART 3   ANTEBELLUM AMERICA   257

Professor Thomas Dublin argues that the women who worked in the Lowell mills in the 1830s were a close-knit community who developed bonds of mutual dependence in both their boarding houses and the factory. According to Professor Gerda Lerner, while Jacksonian democracy provided political and economic opportunities for men, both the "lady" and the "mill girl" were equally disenfranchised and isolated from vital centers of economic opportunity.

Professor Wilma A. Dunaway believes that modern historians have exaggerated the amount of control slaves exercised over their lives and underplayed the cruelty of slave experience—family separations, nutritional deficiencies, sexual exploitation, and physical abuse that occurred on the majority of small plantations. Professor Genovese argues that slaves developed their own system of family and cultural values within the Southern paternalistic and pre-capitalistic slave society.

Professor of history Ramón Eduardo Ruiz argues that for the purpose of conquering Mexico's northern territories, the United States waged an aggressive war against Mexico from which Mexico never recovered. Professor of diplomatic history Norman A. Graebner argues that President James Polk pursued an aggressive policy that he believed would force Mexico to sell New Mexico and California to the United States and to recognize the annexation of Texas without starting a war.

C. Vann Woodward depicts John Brown as a fanatic who committed wholesale murder in Kansas in 1856 and whose ill-fated assault on Harpers Ferry, Virginia, in 1859, while admired by his fellow abolitionists and many northern intellectuals, was an irrational act of treason against the United States. Donald G. Mathews describes abolitionists as uncompromising agitators, not unprincipled fanatics, who employed flamboyant rhetoric but who crafted a balanced and thoughtful critique of the institution of slavery as a social evil that violated the nation's basic values.

Professor of history Richard E. Beringer and his colleagues argue that the Confederacy lacked the will to win the Civil War because of an inability to fashion a viable southern nationalism, increasing religious doubts about the Confederate cause, and guilt over slavery. Pulitzer Prize–winning historian James M. McPherson maintains that either side might have emerged victorious in the Civil War but that the Union success was contingent upon winning three major campaigns between 1862 and 1864.

Issue 17.   Did Abraham Lincoln Free the Slaves?   378

Allen Guelzo insists that Abraham Lincoln was committed to freeing the nation's slaves from the day of his inauguration and that, by laying the foundation for liberating some four million African Americans held in bondage, the Emancipation Proclamation represents the most epochal of Lincoln's writings. Vincent Harding credits slaves themselves for engaging in a dramatic movement of self-liberation while Abraham Lincoln initially refused to declare the destruction of slavery as a war aim and then issued the Emancipation Proclamation, which failed to free any slaves in areas over which he had any authority.

Issue 18.   Was Reconstruction a "Splendid Failure"?   399

Eric Foner asserts that although Reconstruction did not achieve radical goals, it was a "splendid failure" because it offered African Americans in the South a temporary vision of a free society. LaWanda Cox explores the hypothetical question of whether Reconstruction would have succeeded had Lincoln lived and concludes that, despite his many talents, not even Lincoln could have guaranteed the success of the full range of reform for African Americans.

Introduction

The Study of History

Larry Madaras

James M. SoRelle

In a pluralistic society such as ours, the study of history is bound to be a complex process. How an event is interpreted depends not only on the existing evidence but also on the perspective of the interpreter. Consequently, understanding history presupposes the evaluation of information, a task that often leads to conflicting conclusions. An understanding of history, then, requires the acceptance of the idea of historical relativism. Relativism means that redefinition of our past is always possible and desirable. History shifts, changes, and grows with new and different evidence and interpretations. As is the case with the law and even with medicine, beliefs that were unquestioned 100 or 200 years ago have been discredited or discarded since.

Relativism, then, encourages revisionism. There is a maxim that "the past must remain useful to the present." Historian Carl Becker argued that every generation should examine history for itself, thus ensuring constant scrutiny of our collective experience through new perspectives. History, consequently, does not remain static, in part because historians cannot avoid being influenced by the times in which they live. Almost all historians commit themselves to revising the views of other historians, synthesizing theories into macro-interpretations, or revising the revisionists.

Schools of Thought

Three predominant schools of thought have emerged in American history since the first graduate seminars in history were given at The Johns Hopkins University in Baltimore in the 1870s. The *progressive* school dominated the professional field in the first half of the twentieth century. Influenced by the reform currents of Populism, progressivism, and the New Deal, these historians explored the social and economic forces that energized America. The progressive scholars tended to view the past in terms of conflicts between groups, and they sympathized with the underdog.

The post–World War II period witnessed the emergence of a new group of historians who viewed the conflict thesis as overly simplistic. Writing against the backdrop of the Cold War, these *neoconservative*, or *consensus*, historians argued that Americans possess a shared set of values and that the areas of agreement within our nation's basic democratic and capitalistic framework are more important than the areas of disagreement.

In the 1960s, however, the civil rights movement, women's liberation, and the student rebellion (with its condemnation of the war in Vietnam) fragmented the consensus of values upon which historians and social scientists of the 1950s had centered their interpretations. This turmoil set the stage for the emergence of another group of scholars. *New Left* historians began to reinterpret the past once again. They emphasized the significance of conflict in American history, and they resurrected interest in those groups ignored by the consensus school. In addition, New Left historians critiqued the expansionist policies of the United States and emphasized the difficulties confronted by Native Americans, African Americans, women, and urban workers in gaining full citizenship status.

Progressive, consensus, and New Left history is still being written. The most recent generation of scholars, however, focuses upon social history. Their primary concern is to discover what the lives of "ordinary Americans" were really like. These new social historians employ previously overlooked court and church documents, house deeds and tax records, letters and diaries, photographs, and census data to reconstruct the everyday lives of average Americans. Some employ new methodologies, such as quantification (enhanced by advancing computer technology) and oral history, while others borrow from the disciplines of political science, economics, sociology, anthropology, and psychology for their historical investigations.

The proliferation of historical approaches, which are reflected in the issues debated in this book, has had mixed results. On the one hand, historians have become so specialized in their respective time periods and methodological styles that it is difficult to synthesize the recent scholarship into a comprehensive text for the general reader. On the other hand, historians know more about the American past than at any other time in history. They dare to ask new questions or ones that previously were considered to be germane only to scholars in other social sciences. Although there is little agreement about the answers to these questions, the methods employed and issues explored make the "new history" a very exciting field to study.

Issue 1 discusses the key element of historical truth and the extent to which historians, applying the technique of empirical research, can determine exactly what happened in the past. Oscar Handlin insists that the truth of past events is absolute and knowable if pursued by historians employing the scientific method of research. William McNeill, however, argues that the absolute truth about human behavior is unattainable because historians do not have all the facts at their disposal and because they tend to organize their evidence and make intellectual choices based on subjective judgments. Consequently, historians' interpretations may be challenged by others who approach the evidence from a different point of view.

The topics that follow represent a variety of perspectives and approaches. Each of these controversial issues can be studied for its individual importance to our nation's history. Taken as a group, they interact with one another to illustrate larger historical themes. When grouped thematically, the issues reveal continuing motifs in the development of American history.

The New Social History

Some of the most innovative historical research over the last forty years reflects the interests of the new social historians. The work of several representatives of this group who treat the issues of race, gender, and class appears in this volume. For example, in Issue 2, Colin Calloway and David Jones discuss the impact of the encounters between Europeans and Native Americans. Calloway says that while Native Americans confronted numerous diseases in the Americas, traditional Indian healing practices failed to offer much protection from the diseases introduced by Europeans beginning in the late-fifteenth century and which decimated the indigenous peoples. Jones recognizes the disastrous impact of European diseases on Native Americans, but he insists that Indian depopulation also was a consequence of the forces of poverty, malnutrition, environmental stress, dislocation, and social disparity.

In Issue 3, Gary Nash suggests that colonial American society must be studied from the perspective of the cultural convergence of three broad cultural traditions in North America—Native American, European, and African. David Hackett Fischer contends that the cultural traditions of colonial America and the United States were derived from English folkways transported by migrants from four different regions in the British Isles.

The impact of the institution of slavery on the African American family is explored in Issue 13. Focusing on harsh realities of the antebellum plantation system in the South, Wilma Dunaway criticizes those historians who have insisted that slaves succeeded in exercising a significant amount of control over their own lives, including the realm of family relations. Eugene Genovese, one of Dunaway's targets, argues that slaves developed their own system of family and cultural values within the southern paternalistic and pre-capitalist slave society.

Two issues explore the field of women's history. The economic status of women in colonial New England is debated in Issue 5. Gloria Main supports the view that white women in colonial America were better off than their European counterparts. In the seventeenth century, women's work was highly valued and not restricted by a clearly defined division of labor; after 1760, more women entered the paid labor force, and their wages rose. Lyle Koehler, on the other hand, emphasizes the subordinate economic status occupied by colonial New England women and concludes that the only way for these women to experience upward mobility was to marry well.

Issue 12 addresses the economic opportunities available to women in the 1830s. Thomas Dublin examines the labor opportunities for women in the Lowell, Massachusetts textile mills and concludes that they benefited from the mutually dependent society that they created within their living quarters and the factories. Gerda Lerner counters this more optimistic view of women's status by concluding that most women in Jacksonian America were disenfranchised and isolated from vital centers of economic opportunity.

Issue 4 debates the work habits of the early settlers in the Chesapeake colonies. Describing the difficulties of Virginia's first European residents, Edmund Morgan blames the colonists themselves for their misfortunes. According to

Morgan, these settlers suffered because they placed the goal of getting rich quick above the basic need of supplying food and shelter for themselves. Russell Menard's essay examines the status of indentured servants in seventeenth-century Maryland. Menard characterizes the members of this labor force as ambitious, energetic, and hardworking.

Revolution, Religion, and Reform in the New Nation

The impact of the American Revolution on religion is considered in Issue 6. Nathan Hatch insists that the American Revolution led to an expansion of evangelical Christianity that reinforced the democratic impulses of the new nation. Jon Butler counters with the argument that, while Christianity was important, most Americans opposed a Christian national identity enforced by law or governmental action.

The major and most controversial reform effort in the pre-Civil War period was the movement to abolish slavery. Issue 15 deals with the motivations of those who became abolitionists. In his profile of John Brown, C. Vann Woodward lends support to the view that abolitionists were "unrestrained fanatics." Brown, says Woodward, was passionately and fanatically dedicated to his war against slavery, and his actions in Kansas and at Harpers Ferry indicated his willingness to go to any lengths, including murder and treason, to emancipate southern slaves. Donald Mathews, however, believes that the abolitionists' flamboyant rhetoric and uncompromising agitation should not be mistaken as evidence of irrational fanaticism. Instead, he portrays the abolitionists as dedicated reformers who crafted a balanced, reasoned critique that defined slavery as a violation of the nation's basic values.

War, Leadership, and Resolution

As a nation committed to peace, the United States has faced some of its sternest tests in times of war. Such conflicts inevitably have challenged the leadership abilities of the commanders in chief, the will of American citizens, and the ideals of the republic founded on democratic principles. Several issues in this volume address the response to war and its aftermath. In Issue 9, Irving Brant and Donald Hickey evaluate the wartime leadership of James Madison in the War of 1812. Brant offers a generally positive portrait of Madison stressing the president's skillful diplomacy and management of the military forces at his disposal. Hickey, in contrast, claims that Madison failed to provide bold and vigorous leadership curing the conflict.

Three issues cover topics relating to the Civil War and its consequences. In Issue 16, Richard E. Beringer et al. argue that a collective guilt over slavery seriously weakened Confederate goals. Hence, despite adequate manpower and weaponry, the South lost because of an insufficient will to win. James M. McPherson focuses more directly upon actual military engagements and concludes that either side might have won the war. The ultimate success of the

Union, he determines, was contingent upon winning three major campaigns between 1862 and 1864.

Abraham Lincoln's image as "the Great Emancipator" is the focus of the essays in Issue 17. Allen Guelzo insists that the Emancipation Proclamation represented a culmination of Lincoln's long-standing commitment to end slavery in the United States. Vincent Harding, however, defends the position that slaves were the agents of their own freedom, while Lincoln was reluctant to make emancipation a war issue.

Perhaps no other period of American history has been subjected to more myths than the era of Reconstruction. Only within the past thirty years has the traditional, pro-southern interpretation been revised in high school and college texts. In Issue 18, Eric Foner concedes that Reconstruction was not very radical, much less revolutionary. It was, nevertheless, a "splendid failure" because it offered the former slaves a vision of what a free society should look like. LaWanda Cox explores the possibility for success of the Reconstruction program from the hypothetical query of whether Abraham Lincoln could have avoided the failures of his successors had he lived. She concludes that, despite Lincoln's unquestionable leadership skills, there is no guarantee that he could have persuaded white southerners to adopt peacefully a program of land reform and political empowerment for their former slaves.

Politics in America

According to the Constitution, an election is held every four years to choose a president. Political scientists have designated those elections, which mark a significant change in the distribution of power, as "key" or "realigning" elections. In Issue 11, Sean Wilentz concludes that the presidential election of 1828 marked a significant victory for the democratization of American society. Richard McCormick, however, believes that a genuine political revolution did not occur until the presidential election of 1840.

The American people gave legitimacy to their revolution through the establishment of a republican form of government. The United States has operated under two constitutions: the first established the short-lived confederation from 1781 to 1789; the second was written in 1787 and remains in effect over 200 years later. In Issue 7, John P. Roche contends that the drafters of the Constitution of the United States were democratic reformers. Howard Zinn describes the founders as an economic elite who desired a stronger central government to protect their property rights.

Issue 8 addresses the presidential leadership of Thomas Jefferson. Although Jefferson was a leader of the Democratic-Republican Party that defeated the Federalists in 1800, Morton Borden does not view Jefferson as a political ideologue. Instead, according to Borden, as president, Jefferson was a pragmatic, moderate politician who placed the nation's best interests above ideological considerations. Forrest McDonald, by contrast, presents Jefferson as a rigid ideologue whose foremost concern was to restore the agrarian heritage idealized by his Republican supporters.

Comparative History: America in a Global Perspective

The role of American history within the larger framework of world history is central to the discussion presented in two of the issues in this volume. Issue 10 addresses the intent of the Monroe Doctrine, which served as the foundation of United States foreign policy through most of the nineteenth century. Dexter Perkins, in one of the earliest scholarly analyses of this policy, argues that President James Monroe hoped to use this doctrine to prevent Spain from restoring control over her former colonies in South America. Ernest May, however, concludes that the Monroe Doctrine was more a consequence of domestic political considerations as presidential hopefuls jockeyed for position in advance of the presidential election of 1824.

A discussion of early nineteenth-century foreign policy in Issue 14 concerns both U.S. diplomatic relations with the rest of the world and America's self-perception within the world of nations. Did the U.S. government conceive of its power as continental, hemispheric, or worldwide? And what were the consequences of these attitudes? Ramón Eduardo Ruiz argues that the United States waged a racist and imperialistic war against Mexico for the purpose of conquering what became the American Southwest. Norman A. Graebner contends that President James K. Polk pursued an aggressive (but not imperialistic) policy that would force Mexico to recognize U.S. annexation of Texas and to sell New Mexico and California to its northern neighbor without starting a war.

Conclusion

The process of historical study should rely more on thinking than on memorizing data. Once the basics of who, what, when, and where are determined, historical thinking shifts to a higher gear. Analysis, comparison and contrast, evaluation, and explanation take command. These skills not only increase our knowledge of the past but also provide general tools for the comprehension of all the topics about which human beings think.

The diversity of a pluralistic society, however, creates some obstacles to comprehending the past. The spectrum of differing opinions on any particular subject eliminates the possibility of quick and easy answers. In the final analysis, conclusions are often built through a synthesis of several different interpretations, but, even then, they may be partial and tentative.

The study of history in a pluralistic society allows each citizen the opportunity to reach independent conclusions about the past. Since most, if not all, historical issues affect the present and future, understanding the past becomes essential to social progress. Many of today's problems have a direct connection with the past. Additionally, other contemporary issues may lack obvious direct antecedents, but historical investigation can provide illuminating analogies. At first, it may appear confusing to read and to think about opposing historical views, but the survival of our democratic society depends on such critical thinking by acute and discerning minds.

Internet References . . .

Institute for the Study of Civic Values

The Institute for the Study of Civic Values is a nonprofit organization established in Philadelphia in 1973 to promote the fulfillment of America's historic civic ideals. At a time when millions of Americans are struggling to identify the values that we share, the institute believes that it is our civic values—the principles embodied in the Declaration of Independence, the Constitution, and the Bill of Rights—that bring us together as a people.

http://www.iscv.org

Virginia's Indians, Past and Present

Drawn from collections at James Madison University, under the Internet School Library Media Center, this site provides links to historical information, lesson plans, and bibliographies as well as links to tribal home pages.

http://falcon.jmu.edu/~ramsoyil/vaindians.htm

13 Originals: Founding the American Colonies

This Web site concerning the 13 original colonies provides a history of the foundation of each colony. On this site, you will find maps of colonial America as well as the text of colonial charters, grants, and related documents. This is a comprehensive site with many links to detailed historical information.

http://www.timepage.org/spl/13colony.html

Labor, Economy, and Slavery in Early America

Link on Discovery, Exploration, Colonies & Revolution Web site; contains information on a wide variety of topics relating to the American colonies.

http://www.teacher02.com/colonies.htm# labor

PART 1

Colonial Society

*C*olonial settlement in British North America took place in the context of regional conditions that varied in time and place. The ethnic identity of the European colonists affected their relations with Native Americans and Africans, as well as with each other. Many of the attitudes, ideals, and institutions that emerged from the colonial experience served the early settlers well and are still emulated today.

- Is History True?

- Was Disease the Key Factor in the Depopulation of Native Americans in the Americas?

- Was Colonial Culture Uniquely American?

- Were the First Colonists in the Chesapeake Region Ignorant, Lazy, and Unambitious?

- Did Colonial New England Women Enjoy Significant Economic Autonomy?

ISSUE 1

Is History True?

YES: Oscar Handlin, from *Truth in History* (The Belknap Press of Harvard University Press, 1979)

NO: William H. McNeill, from "Mythistory, or Truth, Myth, History, and Historians," *The American Historical Review* (February 1986)

ISSUE SUMMARY

YES: Oscar Handlin insists that historical truth is absolute and knowable by historians who adopt the scientific method of research to discover factual evidence that provides both a chronology and context for their findings.

NO: William McNeill argues that historical truth is general and evolutionary and is discerned by different groups at different times and in different places in a subjective manner that has little to do with a scientifically absolute methodology.

The basic premise of this volume of readings is that the study of history is a complex process that combines historical facts and the historian's interpretation of those facts. Underlying this premise is the assumption that the historian is committed to employing evidence that advances an accurate, truthful picture of the past. Unfortunately, the historical profession in the last several years has been held up to close public scrutiny as a result of charges that a few scholars, some quite prominent, have been careless in their research methods, cited sources that do not exist, and reached conclusions that were not borne out by the facts. The result has been soiled or ruined reputations and the revocation of degrees, book awards, and tenure. Certainly, this is not the end to which most historians aspire, and the failures of a few should not cast a net of suspicion on the manner in which the vast majority of historians practice their craft.

In reflecting upon her role as a historian, the late Barbara Tuchman commented, "To write history so as to enthrall the reader and make the subject as captivating and exciting to him as it is to me has been my goal. . . . A prerequisite . . . is to be enthralled one's self and to feel a compulsion to communicate the magic." For Tuchman, it was the historian's responsibility to the reader to conduct thorough research on a particular topic, sort through the mass of facts to determine what was essential and what was not, and to formulate what remained into a dramatic narrative. Tuchman and most practicing historians also agree with the nineteenth-century German historian Leopold von Ranke that the task of the historian is to discover what really happened. In most instances, however, historians write about events at which they were not present. According to Tuchman, "We can never be certain that we have recaptured [the past] as it really was. But the least we can do is to stay within the evidence."

David Hackett Fischer has written about the difficulties confronting historians as they attempt to report a truthful past, and he is particularly critical of what he terms the "absurd and pernicious doctrine" of historical relativism as it developed in the United States in the 1930s under the direction of Charles Beard and Carl Becker. Becker's suggestion that each historian will write a history based upon his or her own values or the climate of opinion in a particular generation strikes Fischer as a slippery slope leading to the loss of historical accuracy. In conclusion, Fischer writes, "The factual errors which academic historians make today are rarely deliberate. The real danger is not that a scholar will delude his readers, but that he will delude himself."

The selections that follow explore the topic of historical truth. In the late 1970s, Oscar Handlin, like Fischer, became extremely concerned about the impact of the historical and cultural relativism of postmodern and deconstructionist approaches to the study of history. For Handlin, historical truth is absolute and knowable if pursued by the historian adopting the scientific method of research. The value of history, he believes, lies in the capacity to advance toward the truth by locating discrete events, phenomena, and expressions in the historical record.

In contrast, William McNeill recognizes a very thin line between fact and fiction. He claims that historians distinguish between the truth of their conclusions and the myth of those conclusions they reject. The result is what he terms "mythistory." Moreover, the arrangement of historical facts involves subjective judgments and intellectual choices that have little to do with the scientific method. Historical truth, McNeill proposes, is evolutionary, not absolute.

YES

Oscar Handlin

The Uses of History

Why resist the temptation to be relevant? The question nags historians in 1978 as it does other scholars. The world is turning; it needs knowledge; and possession of learning carries an obligation to attempt to shape events. Every crisis lends weight to the plea: transform the library from an ivory tower into a fortress armed to make peace (or war), to end (or extend) social inequality, to alter (or preserve) the existing economic system. The thought boosts the ego, as it has ever since Francis Bacon's suggestion that knowledge is power. Perhaps authority really does lie in command of the contents of books!

In the 1960s the plea became an order, sometimes earnest, sometimes surly, always insistent. Tell us what we need to know—straight answers. Thus, students to teachers, readers to authors. The penalties for refusal ranged from mere unpopularity to organized boycotts and angry confrontations—in a few cases even to burning manuscripts and research notes. Fear added to the inducements for pleasing the audience, whether in the classroom or on the printed page.

To aim to please is a blunder, however. Sincere as the supplicants generally are, it is not knowledge they wish. Having already reached their conclusions, they seek only reassuring confirmation as they prepare to act. They already know that a unilateral act of will could stop wars, that the United States is racist, and that capitalism condemns the masses to poverty. The history of American foreign policy, of the failure of post-Civil War Reconstruction, and of industrial development would only clutter the mind with disturbing ambiguities and complexities.

At best, the usable past demanded of history consists of the data to flesh out a formula. We must do something about the war, the cities, pollution, poverty, and population. Our moral sense, group interest, and political affiliation define the goals; let the historian join the other social scientists in telling us how to reach them. At worst, the demand made of the past is for a credible myth that will identify the forces of good and evil and inspire those who fight with slogans or fire on one side of the barricades or the other.

The effort to meet either demand will frustrate the historian true to his or her craft. Those nimble enough to catch the swings of the market in the classroom or in print necessarily leave behind interior standards of what is important and drop by the wayside the burden of scrupulous investigation and rigorous judgment. Demands for relevance distort the story of ethnicity as they corrupt the historical novel.

Whoever yields, forgoes the opportunity to do what scholars are best qualified to do. Those who chase from one disaster to another lose sight of the long-term trend; busy with the bandaids, they have no time to treat the patient's illness. The family did not originate yesterday, or the city, or addiction to narcotics; a student might well pick up some thoughts on those subjects by shifting his sights from the 1970s to Hellenistic society.

Above all, obsession with the events of the moment prevents the historian from exercising the faculty of empathy, the faculty of describing how people, like us, but different, felt and behaved as they did in times and places similar to, but different, from our own. The writer or teacher interested only in passing judgment on the good guys and the bad will never know what it meant to be an Irish peasant during a famine, or the landlord; an Alabama slave in the 1850s, or the master; a soldier at Antietam, or a general.

The uses of history arise neither from its relevance nor from its help in preparing for careers—nor from its availability as a subject which teachers pass on to students who become teachers and in turn teach others to teach.

Nevertheless, again and again former pupils who come back for reunions after twenty-five years or more spontaneously testify to the utility of what they had learned at college in the various pursuits to which life's journey had taken them. Probing usually reveals not bits of information, not a general interpretation, but a vague sense that those old transactions of classroom and library had somehow expanded their knowledge of self. The discipline of history had located them in time and space and had thereby helped them know themselves, not as physicians or attorneys or bureaucrats or executives, but as persons.

These reassuring comments leave in suspense the question of why study of the past should thus help the individuals understand himself or herself. How do those who learn this subject catch a glimpse of the process of which they are part, discover places in it?

Not by relevance, in the competition for which the other, more pliable, social sciences can always outbid history. Nor by the power of myth, in the peddling of which the advantage lies with novelists. To turn accurate knowledge to those ends is, as C. S. Peirce noted, "like running a steam engine by burning diamonds."

The use of history lies in its capacity for advancing the approach to truth.

The historian's vocation depends on this minimal operational article of faith: Truth is absolute; it is as absolute as the world is real. It does not exist because individuals wish it to anymore than the world exists for their convenience. Although observers have more or less partial views of the truth, its actuality is unrelated to the desires or the particular angles of vision of the viewers. Truth is knowable and will out if earnestly pursued; and science is the procedure or set of procedures for approximating it.

What is truth? Mighty above all things, it resides in the small pieces which together form the record.

History is not the past, any more than biology is life, or physics, matter. History is the distillation of evidence surviving from the past. Where there is no evidence, there is no history. Much of the past is not knowable in this way, and about those areas the historian must learn to confess ignorance.

No one can relive the past; but everyone can seek truth in the record. Simple, durable discoveries await the explorer. So chronology—the sequential order of events reaching back beyond time's horizon—informs the viewer of the long distance traversed and of the immutable course of occurrences: no reversal of a step taken; no after ever before. The historian cannot soar with the anthropologists, who swoop across all time and space. Give or take a thousand years, it is all one to them in pronouncements about whether irrigation systems succeeded or followed despotisms, or in linking technology, population, food, and climatic changes. In the end they pick what they need to prop up theory. The discipline of dates rails off the historian and guards against such perilous plunges. No abstraction, no general interpretation, no wish or preference can challenge chronology's dominion, unless among those peoples who, lacking a sense of time, lack also a sense of history. And whoever learns to know the tyranny of the passing hours, the irrecoverable nature of days passed, learns also the vanity of all aspirations to halt the clock or slow its speed, of all irridentisms, all efforts to recapture, turn back, redeem the moments gone by.

Another use of history is in teaching about vocabulary, the basic component of human communication. Words, singularly elusive, sometimes flutter out of reach, hide in mists of ambiguity, or lodge themselves among inaccessible logical structures, yet form the very stuff of evidence. The historian captures the little syllabic clusters only by knowing who inscribed or spoke them—a feat made possible by understanding the minds and hearts and hands of the men and women for whom they once had meaning. Words released by comprehension wing their messages across the centuries. A use of history is to instruct in the reading of a word, in the comprehension of speakers, writers different from the listener, viewer.

And context. Every survival bespeaks a context. Who graved or wrote or built did so for the eyes of others. Each line or shape denotes a relation to people, things, or concepts—knowable. The identities of sender and recipient explain the content of the letter; the mode of transmission explains the developing idea, the passions of employers and laborers, the organization of the factory. A use of history is its aid in locating discrete events, phenomena, and expressions in their universes.

The limits of those universes were often subjects of dispute. Early in the nineteenth century Henry Thomas Buckle complained, in terms still applicable decades thereafter, of "the singular spectacle of one historian being ignorant of political economy; another knowing nothing of law; another nothing of ecclesiastical affairs and changes of opinion; another neglecting the philosophy of statistics, another physical science," so that those important pursuits, being cultivated, "some by one man, and some by another, have been isolated rather than united," with no disposition to concentrate them upon history. He thus echoed Gibbon's earlier injunction to value all facts. A Montesquieu, "from the meanest of them, will draw conclusions unknown to ordinary men" and arrive at "philosophical history."

On the other hand, a distinguished scholar fifty years later pooh-poohed the very idea that there might be a relation among the Gothic style, feudalism, and scholasticism, or a link between the Baroque and Jesuitism. Nevertheless, the dominant thrust of twentieth-century historians has been toward recognition of the broader contexts; in a variety of fashions they have searched for a totality denominated civilization, culture, or spirit of an epoch, and which they have hoped would permit examination of enlightening linkages and reciprocal relations. Even those who deny that history is a single discipline and assert that it is only "congeries of related disciplines" would, no doubt, expect each branch to look beyond its own borders.

In the final analysis, all the uses of history depend upon the integrity of the record, without which there could be no counting of time, no reading of words, no perception of the context, no utility of the subject. No concern could be deeper than assaults upon the record, upon the very idea of a record.

⚬✦⚬

Although history is an ancient discipline, it rests upon foundations laid in the seventeenth century, when a century of blood shed in religious and dynastic warfare persuaded those who wrote and read history to accept a vital difference in tolerance between facts and interpretation. The text of a charter or statute was subject to proof of authenticity and validity, whatever the meanings lawyers or theologians imparted to its terms. The correct date, the precise phrasing, the seal were facts which might present difficulties of verification, but which, nevertheless, admitted of answers that were right or wrong. On the other hand, discussion of opinions and meanings often called for tolerance among diverse points of view, tolerance possible so long as disputants distinguished interpretation from the fact, from the thing in itself. Scholars could disagree on large matters of interpretation; they had a common interest in agreeing on the small ones of fact which provided them grounds of peaceful discourse.

From that seminal insight developed the scientific mechanisms that enabled historians to separate fact from opinion. From that basis came the Enlightenment achievements which recognized the worth of objectivity and asserted the possibility of reconstructing the whole record of the human past.

True, historians as well as philosophers often thereafter worried about the problems of bias and perspective; and some despaired of attaining the ideal of ultimate objectivity. None were ever totally free of bias, not even those like Ranke who most specifically insisted on the integrity of the fact which he struggled to make the foundation of a truly universal body of knowledge. But, however fallible the individual scholar, the historian's, task, Wilhelm von Humboldt explained, was "to present what actually happened."

It may have been a dream to imagine that history would become a science meaningful to all people, everywhere. If so, it was a noble dream.

By contrast, historians in the 1970s and increasingly other scientists regarded the fact itself as malleable. As the distinction between fact and interpretation faded, all became faction—a combination of fact and fiction. The passive acceptance of that illegitimate genre—whatever mixes with fiction ceases to be fact—revealed the erosion of scholarly commitment. More and more often, the factual elements in an account were instrumental to the purpose the author-manipulator wished them to serve. It followed that different writers addressing different readers for different purposes could arrange matters as convenient. In the end, the primacy of the fact vanished and only the authority of the author, the receptivity of the audience, and the purpose intended remained.

Whence came this desertion, this rejection of allegiance to the fact?

Chroniclers of the past always suffered from external pressure to make their findings relevant, that is, to demonstrate or deny the wisdom, correctness, or appropriateness of current policies. They resisted out of dedication to maintaining the integrity of the record; and long succeeded in doing so. In the 1970s, however, the pressures toward falsification became more compelling than ever before.

Although the full fruits of the change appeared only in that decade, its origins reached back a half-century. It was one of Stalin's most impressive achievements to have converted Marxism from its nineteenth-century scientific base to an instrument of state purpose, and it was not by coincidence that history was the first discipline to suffer in the process. The Soviet Union did more than impose an official party line on interpretations of Trotsky's role in the revolution of 1917; it actually expunged the name Trotsky from the record, so that the fact of the commissar's existence disappeared. What started in the domain of history led in time to Lysenko's invasion of the natural sciences. The Nazis, once in power, burned the nonconforming books; and after 1945 the assault spread to all countries subject to totalitarian control. Those developments were neither surprising nor difficult to comprehend; they followed from the nature of the regimes which fostered them.

More surprising, more difficult to comprehend, was the acquiescence by the scholars of free societies in the attack on history, first, insofar as it affected colleagues less fortunately situated, then as it insinuated itself in their own ranks. External and internal circumstances were responsible.

In a sensate society the commercial standards of the media governed the dissemination of information. Since whatever sold was news, the salient consideration was one of attracting attention; factual accuracy receded to the remote background. An affluent and indulgent society also mistook flaccid permissiveness for tolerance. Everything went because nothing was worth defending, and the legitimate right to err became the disastrous obliteration of the difference between error and truth.

Difficult critical issues tempted the weak-minded to tailor fact to convenience. In the United States, but also in other parts of the world, the spread of a kind of tribalism demanded a history unique to and written for the specifications of particular groups. Since knowledge was relative to the knowers, it was subject to manipulation to suit their convenience. The process by which blacks, white ethnics, and women alone were conceded the capability of understanding and writing their own histories wiped out the line between truth and myth.

That much was comprehensible; these forces operated outside the academy walls and were not subject to very much control. More important, more susceptible to control, and less explicable was the betrayal by the intellectuals of their own group interests and the subsequent loss of the will to resist. A variety of elements contributed to this most recent *trahison des clercs*. Exaggerated concern with the problems of bias and objectivity drove some earnest scholars to despair. Perhaps they reacted against the excessive claims of the nineteenth century, perhaps against the inability of historians, any more than other scholars, to withstand the pressures of nationalism in the early decades of the twentieth century. In any case, not a few followed the deceptive path from acknowledgment that no person was entirely free of prejudice or capable of attaining a totally objective view of the past to the conclusion that all efforts to do so were vain and that, in the end, the past was entirely a recreation emanating from the mind of the historian. Support from this point of view came from the philosophers Benedetto Croce in Italy and, later, R. G. Collingwood in England. Support also came from a misreading of anthropological relativism, which drew from the undeniable circumstances that different cultures evolved differently, the erroneous conclusion that judgments among them were impossible.

Perhaps playfully, perhaps seriously, Carl L. Becker suggested that the historical fact was in someone's mind or it was nowhere, because it was "not the past event," only a symbol which enabled later writers to recreate it imaginatively. His charmingly put illustrations deceived many a reader unaware that serious thinkers since Bayle and Hume had wrestled with the problem. "No one could ever object to the factual truth that Caesar defeated Pompey; and whatever the principles one wishes to use in dispute, one will find nothing less questionable than this proposition—Caesar and Pompey existed and were not just simple modification of the minds of those who wrote their lives"—thus Bayle.

The starting point in Becker's wandering toward relativism, as for others among his contemporaries, was the desire to be useful in solving "the everlasting riddle of human experience." Less subtle successors attacked neutrality "toward the main issues of life" and demanded that society organize all its forces in support of its ideals. "Total war, whether it be hot or cold, enlists everyone and calls upon everyone to assume his part. The historian is no freer from this obligation than the physicists." Those too timid to go the whole way suggested that there might be two kinds of history, variously defined: one, for instance, to treat the positive side of slavery to nurture black pride; another, the negative, to support claims for compensation.

Historians who caved in to pressure and ordered the past to please the present neglected the future, the needs of which would certainly change and in unpredictable ways. Scholarship could no more provide the future than the present with faith, justification, self-confidence, or sense of purpose unless it first preserved the record, intact and inviolable.

History does not recreate the past. The historian does not recapture the bygone event. No amount of imagination will enable the scholar to describe exactly what happened to Caesar in the Senate or to decide whether

Mrs. Williams actually lost two hundred pounds by an act of faith. History deals only with evidence from the past, with the residues of bygone events. But it can pass judgment upon documentation and upon observers' reports of what they thought they saw.

Disregarding these constraints, Becker concluded that, since objectivity was a dream, everyman could be his own historian and contrive his own view of the past, valid for himself, if for no one else. He thus breached the line between interpretation, which was subjective and pliable, and fact, which was not.

Internal specialization allowed historians to slip farther in the same direction. The knowledge explosion after 1900 made specialization an essential, unavoidable circumstance of every form of scholarly endeavor. No individual could presume to competence in more than a sector of the whole field; and the scope of the manageable sector steadily shrank. One result was the dissolution of common standards; each area created its own criteria and claimed immunity from the criticism of outsiders. The occupants of each little island fortress sustained the illusion that the dangers to one would not apply to others. Lines of communication, even within a single faculty or department, broke down so that, increasingly, specialists in one area depended upon the common mass media for knowledge about what transpired in another.

The dangers inherent in these trends became critical as scholarship lost its autonomy. Increasingly reliance on support from external sources—whether governments or foundations—circumscribed the freedom of researchers and writers to choose their own subjects and to arrive at their own conclusions. More generally, the loss of autonomy involved a state of mind which regarded the fruits of scholarship as dependent and instrumental—that is, not as worthy of pursuit for their own sake, not for the extent to which they brought the inquirer closer to the truth, but for other, extrinsic reasons. Ever more often, scholars justified their activity by its external results—peace, training for citizenship, economic development, cure of illness, and the like—in other words, by its usefulness. The choice of topics revealed the extent to which emphasis had shifted from the subject and its relation to the truth to its instrumental utility measured by reference to some external standard.

The plea from utility was dangerous. In the 1930s it blinded well-intentioned social scientists and historians to the excesses of totalitarianism. It was inevitable in creating the omelette of a great social experiment that the shells of a few eggs of truth would be broken, so the argument ran. So, too, in the avid desire for peace, in the praiseworthy wish to avoid a second world war, Charles A. Beard abandoned all effort at factual accuracy. Yet the errors to which the plea for utility led in the past have not prevented others from proceeding along the same treacherous path in pursuit of no less worthy, but equally deceptive utilitarian goals.

Finally, the reluctance to insist upon the worth of truth for its own sake stemmed from a decline of faith by intellectuals in their own role as intellectuals. Not many have, in any conscious or deliberate sense, foresworn their allegiance to the pursuit of truth and the life of the spirit. But power tempted them as it tempts other men and women. The twentieth-century intellectual had unparalleled access to those who actually wielded political or military influence. And few could resist the temptation of being listened to by presidents and ministers, of seeing ideas translated into action. Moreover, a more subtle, more insidious temptation nested in the possibility that possession of knowledge may itself become a significant source of power. The idea that a name on the letterhead of an activist organization or in the endorsement of a political advertisement might advance some worthy cause gives a heady feeling of sudden consequence to the no-longer-humble professor. Most important of all is the consciousness that knowledge can indeed do good, that it is a usable commodity, not only capable of bringing fame to its possessor but actually capable of causing beneficent changes in the external world.

All too few scholars are conscious that in reducing truth to an instrument, even an instrument for doing good, they necessarily blunt its edge and expose themselves to the danger of its misuse. For, when truth ceases to be an end in itself and becomes but a means toward an end, it also becomes malleable and manageable and is in danger of losing its character—not necessarily, not inevitably, but seriously. There may be ways of avoiding the extreme choices of the ivory tower and the marketplace, but they are far from easy and call for extreme caution.

In 1679 Jacques Bossuet wrote for his pupil the Dauphin, heir apparent to the throne of France, a discourse on universal history. Here certainly was an opportunity to influence the mind of the future monarch of Europe's most powerful kingdom. Bossuet understood that the greatest service he could render was to tell, not what would be pleasant to hear, but the truth about the past, detached and whole, so that in later years his pupil could make what use he wished of it.

Therein Bossuet reverted to an ancient tradition. The first law for the historian, Cicero had written, "is never to dare utter an untruth and the second, never to suppress anything true." And, earlier still, Polybius had noted that no one was exempt from mistakes made out of ignorance. But "deliberate misstatements in the interest of country or of friends or for favour" reduced the scholar to the level of those who gained "their living by their pens" and weighed "everything by the standard of profit."

In sum, the use of history is to learn from the study of it and not to carry preconceived notions or external objectives into it.

The times, it may be, will remain hostile to the enterprise of truth. There have been such periods in the past. Historians would do well to regard the example of those clerks in the Dark Ages who knew the worth of the task. By retiring from an alien world to a hidden monastic refuge, now and again one of them at least was able to maintain a true record, a chronicle that survived the destructive passage of armies and the erosion of doctrinal disputes and informed the future of what had transpired in their day. That task is ever worthy. Scholars should ponder its significance.

William H. McNeill  **NO**

Mythistory, or Truth, Myth, History, and Historians

Myth and history are close kin inasmuch as both explain how things got to be the way they are by telling some sort of story. But our common parlance reckons myth to be false while history is, or aspires to be, true. Accordingly, a historian who rejects someone else's conclusions calls them mythical, while claiming that his own views are true. But what seems true to one historian will seem false to another, so one historian's truth becomes another's myth, even at the moment of utterance.

A century and more ago, when history was first established as an academic discipline, our predecessors recognized this dilemma and believed they had a remedy. Scientific source criticism would get the facts straight, whereupon a conscientious and careful historian needed only to arrange the facts into a readable narrative to produce genuinely scientific history. And science, of course, like the stars above, was true and eternal, as Newton and Laplace had demonstrated to the satisfaction of all reasonable persons everywhere.

Yet, in practice, revisionism continued to prevail within the newly constituted historical profession, as it had since the time of Herodotus. For a generation or two, this continued volatility could be attributed to scholarly success in discovering new facts by diligent work in the archives; but early in this century thoughtful historians began to realize that the arrangement of facts to make a history involved subjective judgments and intellectual choices that had little or nothing to do with source criticism, scientific or otherwise.

In reacting against an almost mechanical vision of scientific method, it is easy to underestimate actual achievements. For the ideal of scientific history did allow our predecessors to put some forms of bias behind them. In particular, academic historians of the nineteenth century came close to transcending older religious controversies. Protestant and Catholic histories of post-Reformation Europe ceased to be separate and distinct traditions of learning—a transformation nicely illustrated in the Anglo-American world by the career of Lord Acton, a Roman Catholic who became Regius Professor of History at Cambridge and editor of the first *Cambridge Modern History*. This was a great accomplishment. So was the accumulation of an enormous fund of exact and reliable data through painstaking source criticism that allowed the writing of history in the western world to assume a new depth, scope, range, and precision as compared to anything possible in earlier times. No heir of that scholarly tradition should scoff at the faith of our predecessors, which inspired so much toiling in archives.

Yet the limits of scientific history were far more constricting than its devotees believed. Facts that could be established beyond all reasonable doubt remained trivial in the sense that they did not, in and of themselves, give meaning or intelligibility to the record of the past. A catalogue of undoubted and indubitable information, even if arranged chronologically, remains a catalogue. To become a history, facts have to be put together into a pattern that is understandable and credible; and when that has been achieved, the resulting portrait of the past may become useful as well—a font of practical wisdom upon which people may draw when making decisions and taking action.

Pattern recognition of the sort historians engage in is the chef d'oeuvre of human intelligence. It is achieved by paying selective attention to the total input of stimuli that perpetually swarm in upon our consciousness. Only by leaving things out, that is, relegating them to the status of background noise deserving only to be disregarded, can what matters most in a given situation become recognizable. Suitable action follows. Here is the great secret of human power over nature and over ourselves as well. Pattern recognition is what natural scientists are up to; it is what historians have always done, whether they knew it or not.

Only some facts matter for any given pattern. Otherwise, useless clutter will obscure what we are after: perceptible relationships among important facts. That and that alone constitutes an intelligible pattern, giving meaning to the world, whether it be the world of physics and chemistry or the world of interacting human groups through time, which historians take as their special domain. Natural scientists are ruthless in selecting aspects of available sensory inputs to pay attention to, disregarding all else. They call their patterns theories and inherit most of them from predecessors. But, as we now know, even Newton's truths needed adjustment. Natural science is neither eternal nor universal; it is instead historical and evolutionary, because scientists accept a new theory only when the new embraces a wider range of phenomena or achieves a more elegant explanation of (selectively observed) facts than its predecessor was able to do.

No comparably firm consensus prevails among historians. Yet we need not despair. The great and obvious difference between natural scientists and historians is the greater complexity of the behavior historians seek to understand. The principal source of historical complexity lies in the fact that human beings react both to the natural world and to one another chiefly through the mediation of symbols. This means, among other things, that any theory about human life, if widely believed, will alter actual behavior, usually by inducing people to act as if the theory were true. Ideas and ideals thus become self-validating within remarkably elastic limits. An extraordinary behavioral motility results. Resort to symbols, in effect, loosened up the connection between external reality and human responses, freeing us from instinct by setting us adrift on a sea of uncertainty. Human beings thereby acquired a new capacity to err, but also to change, adapt, and learn new ways of doing things. Innumerable errors, corrected by experience, eventually made us lords of creation as no other species on earth has ever been before.

The price of this achievement is the elastic, inexact character of truth, and especially of truths about human conduct. What a particular group of persons understands, believes, and acts upon, even if quite absurd to outsiders, may nonetheless cement social relations and allow the members of the group to act together and accomplish feats otherwise impossible. Moreover, membership in such a group and participation in its sufferings and triumphs give meaning and value to individual human lives. Any other sort of life is not worth living, for we are social creatures. As such we need to share truths with one another, and not just truths about atoms, stars, and molecules but about human relations and the people around us.

Shared truths that provide a sanction for common effort have obvious survival value. Without such social cement no group can long preserve itself. Yet to outsiders, truths of this kind are likely to seem myths, save in those (relatively rare) cases when the outsider is susceptible to conversion and finds a welcome within the particular group in question.

The historic record available to us consists of an unending appearance and dissolution of human groups, each united by its own beliefs, ideals, and traditions. Sects, religions, tribes, and states, from ancient Sumer and Pharaonic Egypt to modern times, have based their cohesion upon shared truths—truths that differed from time to time and place to place with a rich and reckless variety. Today the human community remains divided among an enormous number of different groups, each espousing its own version of truth about itself and about those excluded from its fellowship. Everything suggests that this sort of social and ideological fragmentation will continue indefinitely.

Where, in such a maelstrom of conflicting opinions, can we hope to locate historical truth? Where indeed?

Before modern communications thrust familiarity with the variety of human idea-systems upon our consciousness, this question was not particularly acute. Individuals nearly always grew up in relatively isolated communities to a more or less homogeneous world view. Important questions had been settled long ago by prophets and sages, so there was little reason to challenge or modify traditional wisdom. Indeed there were strong positive restraints upon any would-be innovator who threatened to upset the inherited consensus.

To be sure, climates of opinion fluctuated, but changes came surreptitiously, usually disguised as commentary upon old texts and purporting merely to explicate the original meanings. Flexibility was considerable, as the modern practice of the U.S. Supreme Court should convince us; but in this traditional ordering of intellect, all the same, outsiders who did not share the prevailing orthodoxy were shunned and disregarded when they could not be converted. Our predecessors' faith in a scientific method that would make written history absolutely and universally true was no more than a recent example of such a belief system. Those who embraced it felt no need to pay attention to ignoramuses who had not accepted the truths of "modern science." Like other true believers, they were therefore spared the task of taking others' viewpoints seriously or wondering about the limits of their own vision of historical truth.

But we are denied the luxury of such parochialism. We must reckon with multiplex, competing faiths—secular as well as transcendental, revolutionary as well as traditional—that resound amongst us. In addition, partially autonomous professional idea-systems have proliferated in the past century or so. Those most important to historians are the so-called social sciences—anthropology, sociology, political science, psychology, and economics—together with the newer disciplines of ecology and semeiology. But law, theology, and philosophy also pervade the field of knowledge with which historians may be expected to deal. On top of all this, innumerable individual authors, each with his own assortment of ideas and assumptions, compete for attention. Choice is everywhere; dissent turns into cacaphonous confusion; my truth dissolves into your myth even before I can put words on paper.

The liberal faith, of course, holds that in a free marketplace of ideas, Truth will eventually prevail. I am not ready to abandon that faith, however dismaying our present confusion may be. The liberal experiment, after all, is only about two hundred and fifty years old, and on the appropriate world-historical time scale that is too soon to be sure. Still, confusion is undoubted. Whether the resulting uncertainty will be bearable for large numbers of people in difficult times ahead is a question worth asking. Iranian Muslims, Russian communists, and American sectarians (religious and otherwise) all exhibit symptoms of acute distress in face of moral uncertainties, generated by exposure to competing truths. Clearly, the will to believe is as strong today as at any time in the past; and true believers nearly always wish to create a community of the faithful, so as to be able to live more comfortably, insulated from troublesome dissent.

The prevailing response to an increasingly cosmopolitan confusion has been intensified personal attachment, first to national and then to subnational groups, each with its own distinct ideals and practices. As one would expect, the historical profession faithfully reflected and helped to forward these shifts of sentiment. Thus, the founding fathers of the American Historical Association and their immediate successors were intent on facilitating the consolidation of a new American nation by writing national history in a WASPish mold, while also claiming affiliation with a tradition of Western civilization that ran back through modern and medieval Europe to the ancient Greeks and Hebrews. This version of our past was very widely repudiated in the 1960s, but iconoclastic revisionists felt no need to replace what they attacked with any architectonic vision of their own. Instead, scholarly energy concentrated on discovering the history of various segments of the population that had been left out or ill-treated by older historians: most notably women, blacks, and other ethnic minorities within the United States and the ex-colonial peoples of the world beyond the national borders.

Such activity conformed to our traditional professional role of helping to define collective identities in ambiguous situations. Consciousness of a common past, after all, is a powerful supplement to other ways of defining who "we" are. An oral tradition, sometimes almost undifferentiated from the practical wisdom embodied in language itself, is all people need in a stable social universe where in-group boundaries are self-evident. But with civilization, ambiguities multipled, and formal written history became useful in defining "us" versus "them." At first, the central ambiguity ran between rulers and ruled. Alien conquerors who lived on taxes collected from their subjects were at best a necessary evil when looked at from the bottom of civilized society. Yet in some situations, especially when confronting natural disaster or external attack, a case could be made for commonality, even between taxpayers and tax consumers. At any rate, histories began as king lists, royal genealogies, and boasts of divine favor—obvious ways of consolidating rulers' morale and asserting their legitimacy vis-à-vis their subjects. . . .

All human groups like to be flattered. Historians are therefore under perpetual temptation to conform to expectation by portraying the people they write about as they wish to be. A mingling of truth and falsehood, blending history with ideology, results. Historians are likely to select facts to show that we—whoever "we" may be—conform to our cherished principles: that we are free with Herodotus, or saved with Augustine, or oppressed with Marx, as the case may be. Grubby details indicating that the group fell short of its ideals can be skated over or omitted entirely. The result is mythical: the past as we want it to be, safely simplified into a contest between good guys and bad guys, "us" and "them." Most national history and most group history is of this kind, though the intensity of chiaroscuro varies greatly, and sometimes an historian turns traitor to the group he studies by setting out to unmask its pretensions. Groups struggling toward self-consciousness and groups whose accustomed status seems threatened are likely to demand (and get) vivid, simplified portraits of their admirable virtues and undeserved sufferings. Groups accustomed to power and surer of their internal cohesion can afford to accept more subtly modulated portraits of their successes and failures in bringing practice into conformity with principles.

Historians respond to this sort of market by expressing varying degrees of commitment to, and detachment from, the causes they chronicle and by infusing varying degrees of emotional intensity into their pages through particular choices of words. Truth, persuasiveness, intelligibility rest far more on this level of the historians' art than on source criticism. But, as I said at the beginning, one person's truth is another's myth, and the fact that a group of people accepts a given version of the past does not make that version any truer for outsiders.

Yet we cannot afford to reject collective self-flattery as silly, contemptible error. Myths are, after all, often self-validating. A nation or any other human group that knows how to behave in crisis situations because it has inherited a heroic historiographical tradition that tells how ancestors resisted their enemies successfully is more likely to act together effectively than a group lacking such a tradition. Great Britain's conduct in 1940 shows how world politics can be redirected by such a heritage. Flattering historiography does more than assist a given group to survive by affecting the balance of power among warring peoples, for an appropriately idealized version of the past may also allow a group of human beings to come closer to living up to its noblest ideals. What is can move toward what ought to be, given collective commitment to a flattering self-image. The American civil rights movement of the fifties and sixties illustrates this phenomenon amongst us.

These collective manifestations are of very great importance. Belief in the virtue and righteousness of one's cause is a necessary sort of self-delusion for human beings, singly and collectively. A corrosive version of history that emphasizes all the recurrent discrepancies between ideal and reality in a given group's behavior makes it harder for members of the group in question to act cohesively and in good conscience. That sort of history is very costly indeed. No group can afford it for long.

On the other hand, myths may mislead disastrously. A portrait of the past that denigrates others and praises the ideals and practice of a given group naively and without restraint can distort a people's image of outsiders so that foreign relations begin to consist of nothing but nasty surprises. Confidence in one's own high principles and good intentions may simply provoke others to resist duly accredited missionaries of the true faith, whatever that faith may be. Both the United States and the Soviet Union have encountered their share of this sort of surprise and disappointment ever since 1917, when Wilson and Lenin proclaimed their respective recipes for curing the world's ills. In more extreme cases, mythical, self-flattering versions of the past may push a people toward suicidal behavior, as Hitler's last days may remind us.

More generally, it is obvious that mythical, self-flattering versions of rival groups' pasts simply serve to intensify their capacity for conflict. With the recent quantum jump in the destructive power of weaponry, hardening of group cohesion at the sovereign state level clearly threatens the survival of humanity; while, within national borders, the civic order experiences new strains when subnational groups acquire a historiography replete with oppressors living next door and, perchance, still enjoying the fruits of past injustices.

The great historians have always responded to these difficulties by expanding their sympathies beyond narrow in-group boundaries. Herodotus set out to award a due meed of glory both to Hellenes and to the barbarians; Ranke inquired into what really happened to Protestant and Catholic, Latin and German nations alike. And other pioneers of our profession have likewise expanded the range of their sympathies and sensibilities beyond previously recognized limits without ever entirely escaping, or even wishing to escape, from the sort of partisanship involved in accepting the general assumptions and beliefs of a particular time and place.

Where to fix one's loyalties is the supreme question of human life and is especially acute in a cosmopolitan age like ours when choices abound. Belonging to a tightly knit group makes life worth living by giving individuals something beyond the self to serve and to rely on for personal guidance, companionship, and aid. But the stronger such bonds, the sharper the break with the rest of humanity. Group solidarity is always maintained, at least partly, by exporting psychic frictions across the frontiers, projecting animosities onto an outside foe in order to enhance collective cohesion within the group itself. Indeed, something to fear, hate, and attack is probably necessary for the full expression of human emotions; and ever since animal predators ceased to threaten, human beings have feared, hated, and fought one another.

Historians, by helping to define "us" and "them," play a considerable part in focusing love and hate, the two principal cements of collective behavior known to humanity. But myth making for rival groups has become a dangerous game in the atomic age, and we may well ask whether there is any alternative open to us.

In principle the answer is obvious. Humanity entire possesses a commonality which historians may hope to understand just as firmly as they can comprehend what unites any lesser group. Instead of enhancing conflicts, as parochial historiography inevitably does, an intelligible world history might be expected to diminish the lethality of group encounters by cultivating a sense of individual identification with the triumphs and tribulations of humanity as a whole. This, indeed, strikes me as the moral duty of the historical profession in our time. We need to develop an ecumenical history, with plenty of room for human diversity in all its complexity.

Yet a wise historian will not denigrate intense attachment to small groups. That is essential to personal happiness. In all civilized societies, a tangle of overlapping social groupings lays claim to human loyalties. Any one person may therefore be expected to have multiple commitments and plural public identities, up to and including membership in the human race and the wider DNA community of life on planet Earth. What we need to do as historians and as human beings is to recognize this complexity and balance our loyalties so that no one group will be able to command total commitment. Only so can we hope to make the world safer for all the different human groups that now exist and may come into existence.

The historical profession has, however, shied away from an ecumenical view of the human adventure. Professional career patterns reward specialization; and in all the well-trodden fields, where pervasive consensus on important matters has already been achieved, research and innovation necessarily concentrate upon minutiae. Residual faith that truth somehow resides in original documents confirms this direction of our energies. An easy and commonly unexamined corollary is the assumption that world history is too vague and too general to be true, that is, accurate to the sources. Truth, according to this view, is only attainable on a tiny scale when the diligent historian succeeds in exhausting the relevant documents before they exhaust the historian. But as my previous remarks have made clear, this does not strike me as a valid view of historical method. On the contrary, I call it naive and erroneous.

All truths are general. All truths abstract from the available assortment of data simply by using words, which in their very nature generalize so as to bring order to the incessantly fluctuating flow of messages in and messages out that constitutes human consciousness. Total reproduction of experience is impossible and undesirable. It would merely perpetuate the confusion we seek to escape. Historiography that aspires to get closer and closer to the documents—all the documents and nothing but the documents—is merely moving closer and closer to incoherence, chaos, and meaninglessness. That is a dead end for sure. No society will long support a profession that produces arcane trivia and calls it truth.

Fortunately for the profession, historians' practice has been better than their epistemology. Instead of replicating confusion by paraphrasing the totality of relevant and available documents, we have used our sources to discern, support, and reinforce group identities at national, transnational, and subnational levels and, once in a while, to attack or pick apart a group identity to which a school of revisionists has taken a scunner.

If we can now realize that our practice already shows how truths may be discerned at different levels of generality with equal precision simply because different patterns emerge on different time-space scales, then, perhaps, repugnance for world history might diminish and a juster proportion between parochial and ecumenical historiography might begin to emerge. It is our professional duty to move toward ecumenicity, however real the risks may seem to timid and unenterprising minds.

With a more rigorous and reflective epistemology, we might also attain a better historiographical balance between Truth, truths, and myth. Eternal and universal Truth about human behavior is an unattainable goal, however delectable as an ideal. Truths are what historians achieve when they bend their minds as critically and carefully as they can to the task of making their account of public affairs credible as well as intelligible to an audience that shares enough of their particular outlook and assumptions to accept what they say. The result might best be called mythistory perhaps (though I do not expect the term to catch on in professional circles), for the same words that constitute truth for some are, and always will be, myth for others, who inherit or embrace different assumptions and organizing concepts about the world.

This does not mean that there is no difference between one mythistory and another. Some clearly are more adequate to the facts than others. Some embrace more time and space and make sense of a wider variety of human behavior than others. And some, undoubtedly, offer a less treacherous basis for collective action than others. I actually believe that historians' truths, like those of scientists, evolve across the generations, so that versions of the past acceptable today are superior in scope, range, and accuracy to versions available in earlier times. But such evolution is slow, and observable only on an extended time scale, owing to the self-validating character of myth. Effective common action can rest on quite fantastic beliefs. *Credo quia absurdum* may even become a criterion for group membership, requiring initiates to surrender their critical faculties as a sign of full commitment to the common cause. Many sects have prospered on this principle and have served their members well for many generations while doing so.

But faiths, absurd or not, also face a long-run test of survival in a world where not everyone accepts anyone set of beliefs and where human beings must interact with external objects and nonhuman forms of life, as well as with one another. Such "foreign relations" impose limits on what any group of people can safely believe and act on, since actions that fail to secure expected and desired results are always costly and often disastrous. Beliefs that mislead action are likely to be amended; too stubborn an adherence to a faith that encourages or demands hurtful behavior is likely to lead to the disintegration and disappearance of any group that refuses to learn from experience.

Thus one may, as an act of faith, believe that our historiographical myth making and myth breaking is bound to cumulate across time, propagating mythistories that fit experience better and allow human survival more often, sustaining in-groups in ways that are less destructive to themselves and to their neighbors than was once the case or is the case today. If so, ever-evolving mythistories will indeed become truer and more adequate to public life, emphasizing the really important aspects of human encounters and omitting irrelevant background noise more efficiently so that men and women will know how to act more wisely than is possible for us today.

This is not a groundless hope. Future historians are unlikely to leave out blacks and women from any future mythistory of the United States, and we are unlikely to exclude Asians, Africans, and Amerindians from any future mythistory of the world. One hundred years ago this was not so. The scope and range of historiography has widened, and that change looks as irreversible to me as the widening of physics that occurred when Einstein's equations proved capable of explaining phenomena that Newton's could not.

It is far less clear whether in widening the range of our sensibilities and taking a broader range of phenomena into account we also see deeper into the reality we seek to understand. But we may. Anyone who reads historians of the sixteenth and seventeenth centuries and those of our own time will notice a new awareness of social process that we have attained. As one who shares that awareness, I find it impossible not to believe that it represents an advance on older notions that focused attention exclusively, or almost exclusively, on human intentions and individual actions, subject only to God or to a no less inscrutable Fortune, while leaving out the social and material context within which individual actions took place simply because that context was assumed to be uniform and unchanging.

Still, what seems wise and true to me seems irrelevant obfuscation to others. Only time can settle the issue, presumably by outmoding my ideas and my critics' as well. Unalterable and eternal Truth remains like the Kingdom of Heaven, an eschatological hope. Mythistory is what we actually have—a useful instrument for piloting human groups in their encounters with one another and with the natural environment.

To be a truth-seeking mythographer is therefore a high and serious calling, for what a group of people knows and believes about the past channels expectations and affects the decisions on which their lives, their fortunes, and their sacred honor all depend. Formal written histories are not the only shapers of a people's notions about the past; but they are sporadically powerful, since even the most abstract and academic historiographical ideas do trickle down to the level of the commonplace, if they fit both what a people want to hear and what a people need to know well enough to be useful.

As members of society and sharers in the historical process, historians can only expect to be heard if they say what the people around them want to hear—in some degree. They can only be useful if they also tell the people some things they are reluctant to hear—in some degree. Piloting between this Scylla and Charybdis is the art of the serious historian, helping the group he or she addresses and celebrates to survive and prosper in a treacherous and changing world by knowing more about itself and others.

Academic historians have pursued that art with extraordinary energy and considerable success during the past century. May our heirs and successors persevere and do even better!

POSTSCRIPT

Is History True?

Closely associated to the question of historical truth is the matter of historical objectivity. Frequently, we hear people begin statements with the phrase "History tells us . . ." or "History shows that . . . ," followed by a conclusion that reflects the speaker or writer's point of view. In fact, history does not directly tell or show us anything. That is the job of historians, and as William McNeill argues, much of what historians tell us, despite their best intentions, often represents a blending of historical evidence and myth.

Is there such a thing as a truly objective history? Historian Paul Conkin agrees with McNeill that objectivity is possible only if the meaning of that term is sharply restricted and is not used as a synonym for certain truth. History, Conkin writes, "is a story about the past; it is not the past itself. . . . Whether one draws a history from the guidance of memory or of monuments, it cannot exactly mirror some directly experienced past nor the feelings and perceptions of people in the past." He concludes, "In this sense, much of history is a stab into partial darkness, a matter of informed but inconclusive conjecture. . . . Obviously, in such areas of interpretation, there is no one demonstrably correct 'explanation,' but very often competing, equally unfalsifiable, theories. Here, on issues that endlessly fascinate the historian, the controversies rage, and no one expects, short of a great wealth of unexpected evidence, to find a conclusive answer. An undesired, abstractive precision of the subject might so narrow it as to permit more conclusive evidence. But this would spoil all the fun." For more discussion on this and other topics related to the study of history, see Paul K. Conkin and Roland N. Stromberg, *The Heritage and Challenge of History* (Dodd, Mead & Company, 1971).

The most thorough discussion of historical objectivity in the United States is Peter Novick, *That Noble Dream: The 'Objectivity Question' and the American Historical Profession* (Cambridge University Press, 1988), which draws its title from Charles A. Beard's article in the *American Historical Review* (October 1935) in which Beard reinforced the views expressed in his 1933 presidential address to the American Historical Association. [See "Written History as an Act of Faith," *American Historical Review* (January 1934).] Novick's thorough analysis generated a great deal of attention, the results of which can be followed in James T. Kloppenberg, "Objectivity and Historicism: A Century of American Historical Writing," *American Historical Review* (October 1989), Thomas L. Haskell, "Objectivity Is Not Neutrality: Rhetoric vs. Practice in Peter Novick's *That Noble Dream*," *History & Theory* (1990), and the scholarly forum "Peter Novick's *That Noble Dream*: The Objectivity Question and the Future of the Historical Profession," *American Historical Review* (June 1991). A critique of recent historical writing that closely follows the concerns expressed by Handlin can be found in Keith Windschuttle, *The Killing of History: How Literary Critics and Social Theorists Are Murdering Our Past* (The Free Press, 1996).

Readers interested in this subject will also find the analyses in Barbara W. Tuchman, *Practicing History: Selected Essays* (Alfred A. Knopf, 1981) and David Hackett Fischer, *Historians' Fallacies: Toward a Logic of Historical Thought* (Harper & Row, 1970) to be quite stimulating. Earlier, though equally rewarding, volumes include Harvey Wish, *The American Historian: A Social-Intellectual History of the Writing of the American Past* (Oxford University Press, 1960); John Higham, with Leonard Krieger and Felix Gilbert, *History: The Development of Historical Studies in the United States* (Prentice-Hall, 1965); and Marcus Cunliffe and Robin Winks, eds., *Pastmasters: Some Essays on American Historians* (Harper & Row, 1969).

ISSUE 2

Was Disease the Key Factor in the Depopulation of Native Americans in the Americas?

YES: Colin G. Calloway, from *New Worlds for All: Indians, Europeans, and the Remaking of Early America* (The Johns Hopkins University Press, 1997)

NO: David S. Jones, from "Virgin Soils Revisited," *William and Mary Quarterly* (October 2003)

ISSUE SUMMARY

YES: Colin Calloway says that while Native Americans confronted numerous diseases in the Americas, traditional Indian healing practices failed to offer much protection from the diseases introduced by Europeans beginning in the late-fifteenth century and which decimated the indigenous peoples.

NO: David Jones recognizes the disastrous impact of European diseases on Native Americans, but he insists that Indian depopulation was also a consequence of the forces of poverty, malnutrition, environmental stress, dislocation, and social disparity.

On October 12, 1492, Christopher Columbus, a Genoese mariner sailing under the flag and patronage of the Spanish monarchy, made landfall on a tropical Caribbean island, which he subsequently named San Salvador. This action established for Columbus the fame of having discovered the New World and, by extension, America. Of course, this "discovery" was all very ironic since Columbus and his crew members were not looking for a new world but, instead, a very old one—the much-fabled Orient. By sailing westward instead of eastward, Columbus was certain that he would find a shorter route to China. He did not anticipate that the land mass of the Americas would prevent him from reaching his goal or that his "failure" would guarantee his fame for centuries thereafter.

Moreover, Columbus's encounter with indigenous peoples whom he named "Indians" (*los indios*) presented further proof that Europeans had not discovered America. These "Indians" were descendants of the first people who migrated from Asia at least 30,000 years earlier and fanned out in a southeasterly direction until they populated much of North and South America. By the time Columbus arrived, Native Americans numbered approximately 40 million, 3 million of whom resided in the continental region north of Mexico.

Columbus's arrival (and return on three separate occasions between 1494 and 1502) possessed enormous implications not only for the future development of the United States but also for the Western Hemisphere as a whole, as well as for Europe and Africa. Relations between Native Americans and Europeans were marred by the difficulties that arose from people of very different cultures encountering each other for the first time. These encounters led to inaccurate perceptions, misunderstandings, and failed expectations. While at first the American Indians deified the explorers, experience soon taught them to do otherwise. European opinion ran the gamut from admiration to contempt; for example, some European poets and painters expressed admiration for the Noble Savage, while other Europeans accepted as a rationalization for military aggression the sentiment that "the only good savage is a dead one."

William Bradford's account of the Pilgrims' arrival at Cape Cod describes the insecurity the new migrants felt as they disembarked on American soil. "[T]hey had now no friends to welcome them nor inns to entertain or refresh their weatherbeaten bodies; no houses or much less towns to repair to, to seek for succor. . . . Besides, what could they see but a hideous and deserted wilderness, full of wild beasts and wild men. . . . If they looked behind them there was the mighty ocean which they had passed and was not a main bar and gulf to separate them from all the civil parts of the world." Historical hindsight, however, suggests that if anyone should have expressed fears about the unfolding encounter in the Western Hemisphere, it would be the Native Americans since their numbers declined by as much as 95 percent in the first century following Columbus's arrival. While some of this decline can be attributed to violent encounters with Europeans, there seems to have been a more hostile (and far less visible) force at work. As historian William McNeill has suggested, the main weapon that overwhelmed indigenous peoples in the Americas was the Europeans' breath!

The following essays explore the role played by disease in the depopulation of Native Americans in the Western Hemisphere. Colin G. Calloway makes clear that Indian doctors possessed a sophisticated knowledge of the healing power of plants that they shared with Europeans, but these curatives were insufficient in providing protection against the variety of new diseases introduced into the Americas by European explorers and settlers. The "Columbian exchange" included epidemics that decimated indigenous tribes.

Physician David S. Jones recognizes the consequences of the introduction of European diseases among Native Americans, but he contends that there were other factors at work that explain the drastic loss of life among American Indians. For example, poverty, malnutrition, environmental stress, dislocation, and social disparity exacerbated the conditions within which infectious diseases could spread in such dramatic proportions.

YES

Colin G. Calloway

New Worlds for All: Indians, Europeans, and the Remaking of Early America

Healing and Disease

North American Indians did not inhabit a disease-free paradise prior to European invasion. The great epidemic diseases and crowd infections that ravaged Europe and Asia—smallpox, diphtheria, measles, bubonic and pneumonic plague, cholera, influenza, typhus, dysentery, yellow fever—were unknown in America. Indian peoples faced other, less devastating, problems. Bioarchaeological studies reveal evidence of malnutrition and anemia resulting from dietary stress, high levels of fetal and neonatal death and infant mortality, parasitic intestinal infections, dental problems, respiratory infections, spina bifida, osteomyelitis, nonpulmonary tuberculosis, and syphilis. Indian people also suffered their share of aches and pains, breaks and bruises, digestive upsets, arthritis, wounds, and snakebites. To deal with these things, Indian doctors employed a rich knowledge of the healing properties of plants and what today we would call therapeutic medicine. They combined knowledge of anatomy and medicinal botany with curative rituals and ceremonies.

Traditional Native American and contemporary Western ways of healing are not necessarily in conflict, and are often complementary, as evidenced when Navajo medicine men and Navajo oral traditions helped investigators from the Indian Health Service and the Centers for Disease Control identify deer mice as the source of the "mystery illness" that struck the Southwest in 1993. So too in early America, European and Indian cures could work together. Contrary to the popular modern stereotype that all Indians were and are attuned to plant life, all Europeans totally out of touch with nature, many early explorers and colonists possessed an extensive knowledge of plants and their properties, knowledge that modern urban Americans have lost. Europeans in the seventeenth century generally believed that for every sickness there were natural plant remedies, if one only knew where to find them. Indian healers, many of them women, knew where to find them, and Europeans were receptive to the cures they could provide. . . .

Unfortunately, traditional Indian cures offered little protection against the new diseases that swept the land after Europeans arrived in North America. Separated from the Old World for thousands of years, the peoples of America escaped great epidemics like the Black Death, which killed perhaps a third of the population in fourteenth-century Europe. But they were living on borrowed time. Lack of exposure to bubonic plague, smallpox, and measles allowed Indian peoples no opportunity to build up immunological resistance to such diseases. From the moment Europeans set foot in America, hundreds of thousands of Indian people were doomed to die in one of the greatest biological catastrophes in human history.

Imported diseases accompanied Spanish conquistadors into Central and South America at the beginning of the sixteenth century, wreaking havoc among the great civilizations of Mexico, Peru, and Yucatán, and facilitating their conquest by the invaders. It was not long before the unseen killers were at work among the Indian populations of North America.

Established and well-traveled trade routes helped spread disease. Indians who came into contact with Europeans and their germs often contaminated peoples farther inland who had not yet seen a European; they in turn passed the disease on to more distant neighbors. It is likely that most Indian people who were struck down by European diseases like smallpox died without ever laying eyes on a European. In tracing the course of imported plagues among Indian populations in colonial America, many scholars describe them not as epidemics but as pandemics, meaning that the same disease occurred virtually everywhere.

As many as 350,000 people lived in Florida when the Spaniards first arrived, but the populations of the Calusa, Timucua, and other tribes plummeted after contact. Calusas who canoed to Cuba to trade may have brought smallpox back to the Florida mainland as early as the 1520s. When Hernando de Soto invaded the Southeast in 1539, the Spaniards found that disease had preceded them. In the Carolina upcountry, they found large towns abandoned and overgrown with grass where, said the Indians, "there had been a pest in the land two years before." In 1585, Sir Francis Drake's English crew, returning from plundering Spanish ships in the Cape Verde Islands, brought a disease that was probably typhus to the Caribbean and Florida. Indians around St. Augustine died in great numbers, "and said amongste themselves, it was the Inglisshe God that made them die so faste." The population collapse continued in the seventeenth century. Governor Diego de Rebolledo reported in 1657 that the Guale and Timucua Indians were few "because they have been wiped out with the sickness of the plague and smallpox which have overtaken them in past years." Two years later the new governor of Florida said 10,000 Indians had died in a measles epidemic. According to one scholar, the Timucuans numbered as many as 150,000 people before contact; by the end of the seventeenth century, their population had been cut by 98 percent. The Apalachee Indians of northern Florida numbered 25,000–30,000 in the early seventeenth century; by the end of the century, less than 8,000 survived. Two and a half centuries after contact with the Spaniards, all of Florida's original Indian people were gone.

The pattern repeated itself elsewhere. In 1585, the English established a colony at Roanoke Island in Virginia. Almost immediately, local Indians began to fall ill and die. "The disease was so strange to them," wrote Thomas Hariot, "that they neither knew what it was, nor how to cure it." Across the continent, Pueblo Indians in New Mexico may have suffered from a huge smallpox epidemic that spread as far south as Chile and across much of North America in 1519–24. When they first encountered Europeans in 1539, the Pueblos numbered at least 130,000 and inhabited between 110 and 150 pueblos. By 1706, New Mexico's Pueblo population had dropped to 6,440 people in 18 pueblos. When de Soto's Spaniards passed through the area now known as Arkansas in 1541–43, the region was densely populated. Thousands of people lived in large towns, cultivating extensive cornfields along rich river valleys. One hundred thirty years later, these thriving communities were gone, victims of disease and possibly drought. When French explorers arrived in the mid-seventeenth century, they found Caddoes, Osages, and Quapaws living on the peripheries of the region, but central Arkansas was empty. Epidemic diseases continued their devastation. In 1698, Frenchmen found less than one hundred men in the Quapaw villages after a recent smallpox epidemic killed most of the people. "In the village are nothing but graves," the French chronicler reported.

Indian peoples in eastern Canada who had been in contact with French fur traders and fishermen since early in the sixteenth century experienced the deadly repercussions of such commerce. Jesuit Father Pierre Biard, working among the Micmacs and Maliseets of Nova Scotia in 1616, heard the Indians "complain that since the French mingle and carry on trade with them they are dying fast, and the population is thinning out. For they assert that before this association and intercourse all their countries were very populous and they tell how one by one different coasts, according as they traffic with us, have been reduced more by disease."

Deadly pestilence swept the coast of New England in 1616–17. Indians "died in heapes," and the Massachusett Indians around Plymouth Bay were virtually exterminated. As reported by Governor William Bradford, the Pilgrims found cleared fields and good soil, but few people, the Indians "being dead & abundantly wasted in the late great mortalitiy which fell in all these parts about three years over before the coming of the English, wherin thousands of them dyed, they not being able to burie one another; their sculs and bones were found in many places lying still above ground, where their houses & dwellings had been; a very sad spectacle to behold."

Smallpox was a fact of life—or death—for most of human history. An airborne disease, normally communicated by droplets or dust particles, it enters through the respiratory tract. People can become infected simply by breathing. Not surprisingly, it spread like wildfire through Indian populations. However, because early chroniclers sometimes confused smallpox with other diseases and because the contagions came so quickly, it is difficult to discern which disease was doing the killing at any particular time. By the seventeenth century, smallpox in Europe was a childhood disease: most adults, having been infected as children, had acquired lifelong immunity and were not contagious. The long transatlantic crossings further reduced the chances that European crews could transmit the disease to America. Not until children crossed the Atlantic did smallpox, and the other lethal childhood diseases that plagued Europe, take hold on Native American populations. The Spanish brought children to the Caribbean early, but not until the beginning of the seventeenth century did Dutch and English colonists bring their families to New York and New England. The arrival of sick European children sentenced thousands of Indian people to death.

Smallpox struck New England in 1633, devastating Indian communities on the Merrimack and Connecticut Rivers. Bradford reported how "it pleased God to visit these Indeans with a great sickness, and such a mortalitie that of a 1000 above 900, and a halfe of them dyed, and many of them did rott above ground for want of buriall." The epidemic reduced the Pequots in southern Connecticut from perhaps as many as thirteen thousand people to only three thousand, setting the stage for their defeat by the English in 1637, and it may have reduced the Mohawks in eastern New York from almost eight thousand to less than three thousand. Such mortality rates were not unusual when virulent new diseases cut through previously unexposed populations. Indians from the Hudson River told Adriaen Van der Donck in 1656 "that before the smallpox broke out amongst them, they were ten times as numerous as they are now." John Lawson estimated that in 1701 there was "not the sixth Savage living within two hundred Miles of all our Settlements, as there were fifty Years ago." A recent smallpox epidemic in the Carolina upcountry had "destroy'd whole towns."

At the beginning of the seventeenth century, the Huron Indians numbered as many as 30,000–40,000 people, living in perhaps twenty-eight villages on the northern shores of the Great Lakes in southern Ontario. The French identified them as crucial to their plans for North American empire. The Hurons were the key to extensive trade networks reaching far beyond the Great Lakes, and their villages could also serve as 'jumping-off points" for Jesuit missionary enterprises among more distant tribes. French traders and missionaries arrived in Huronia, and it was not long before the new diseases were reaping a grim harvest among the Hurons. Their longhouses were transformed into death traps. The smallpox epidemic that ravaged New England in 1633 reached Huronia in 1634. Smallpox or measles was thinning Huron numbers in 1635–36. A Huron elder, blaming the epidemic on the Jesuits, said, "The plague has entered every lodge in the village, and has so reduced my family that today there are but two of us left, and who can say whether we two will survive." Influenza struck in 1636–37. Smallpox returned in 1639. Huron population was scythed in half between 1634 and 1640. In 1648–49, famine and the attacks of the Iroquois completed the deadly work the diseases had begun. The Hurons scattered, most of the survivors being absorbed by other tribes.

Smallpox continued throughout the eighteenth century. It killed half the Cherokees in 1738 and returned in 1760; the Catawbas of South Carolina lost half their number to the epidemic of 1759. In 1763, the British doled out blankets from the smallpox hospital at Fort Pitt to visiting Indians; smallpox erupted among the tribes of the Ohio Valley soon thereafter. Outbreaks of smallpox were reported among Indian populations in New Mexico in 1719, 1733, 1738, 1747, and 1749; in Texas recurrently between 1674 and 1802; and in California, where Indian neophytes congregated in Spanish mission villages made easy targets for new crowd-killing diseases.

The massive smallpox epidemic that ravaged western North America between 1779 and 1783 illustrates the speed with which the disease could spread its tentacles throughout Indian country. The epidemic seems to have broken out in Mexico, and it afflicted Indian peoples in Peru and Guatemala. Spreading north to Spanish settlements like San Antonio and Santa Fe, it was picked up by Indians who visited the area to trade for horses. It was then quickly transmitted north and west, through the Rockies and across the plains, slaughtering as it went. It spread into the Canadian forests, killed as many as 90 percent of the Chipewyans in the central subarctic, and by 1783 was killing Cree Indians around Hudson Bay.

Abundant sources of fish and other marine resources supported dense populations on the Northwest Coast before European maritime traders and explorers brought smallpox in the late eighteenth century. When English explorer George Vancouver sailed into Puget Sound in 1793, he met Indian people with pockmarked faces and found human skulls and bones scattered along the beach, a grim reminder of the ravages of an earlier epidemic. These northwestern populations declined dramatically over the next century.

Smallpox was probably the number-one killer of Indian people, but it was by no means the only fatal disease. Epidemics of measles, influenza, bubonic plague, diphtheria, typhus, scarlet fever, yellow fever, and other unidentified diseases also took their toll. Alcoholism added to the list of killer diseases imported from Europe. "A person who resides among them may easily observe the frightful decrease of their numbers from one period of ten years to another," said John Heckewelder, lamenting the impact of alcohol. "Our vices have destroyed them more than our swords."

Recurring epidemics allowed Indian populations no opportunity to bounce back from earlier losses. They cut down economic productivity, generating hunger and famine, which rendered those who survived one disease more vulnerable to affliction by the next. New diseases combined with falling birth rates, escalating warfare, alcoholism, and general social upheaval to turn Indian America into a graveyard. Decreased fecundity hindered population recovery. Nantucket, off the coast of Massachusetts, was once described as "an island full of Indians" and is estimated to have had a population of about 3,000 in the mid-seventeenth century. By 1763, there were 348 people. An epidemic of yellow fever that year left only twenty survivors. Some 3,000 Indians inhabited Martha's Vineyard in 1642; 313 survived in 1764. Mohawk population continued to decline to little more than 600 by the time of the Revolution. At the western door of the Iroquois confederacy, Seneca population remained stable, but this was largely because they adopted captives and immigrants from other communities ravaged by war and disease. The Illinois Indians of the Great Lakes region numbered more than ten thousand people in 1670; by 1800, no more than five hundred survived. On the banks of the

Missouri in present-day Nebraska, the Omaha Indians numbered more than three thousand in the late 1700s; cholera and smallpox cut their population to less than three hundred by 1802. In years when Indian peoples needed all their resources to deal with Europeans and to cope with a world that was changing around them, their numbers were being steadily eroded by disease.

Survivors, many of them disfigured by pockmarks, faced the future bereft of loved ones and without the wisdom of elders to guide them. Societies woven together by ties of kinship and clan were torn apart. After disease struck Martha's Vineyard in 1645–46, one survivor lamented that all the elders who had taught and guided the people were dead, "and their wisdom is buried with them." In 1710, Indians near Charleston, South Carolina, told a settler they had forgotten most of their traditions because "their Old Men are dead." In some cases, power struggles followed the deaths of traditional leaders. Old certainties no longer applied, and long-established patterns of behavior must sometimes have seemed irrelevant. The impact of such losses on Indian minds and souls is incalculable.

Traditional healing practices proved powerless against the onslaught. Fasting, taking a sweat bath, and plunging into an icy river—a common Indian remedy for many ailments—aggravated rather than alleviated the effects of smallpox. Just as some Europeans looked to Indian skills and practices to deal with snakebites and ailments native to North America, so some Indian people looked to Europeans to provide relief from European sicknesses. Some believed that European witchcraft caused the new diseases; so it made sense to combat them with European power and medicine. Others, with their loved ones dying around them, were willing to try anything. Many Hurons accepted baptism from Jesuit priests, regarding it as a curative ritual and hoping it could save their children.

Despite instances of genocide and germ warfare against Indian populations, Europeans frequently provided what help and comfort they could. Dead Indians were of no value to European missionaries seeking converts, European merchants seeking customers, or European ministers seeking allies. Hearing that Massasoit "their friend was sick and near unto death," Governor William Bradford and the Plymouth colonists "sente him such comfortable things as gave him great contente, and was a means of his recovery." French nuns ministered to sick Indians in seventeenth-century Quebec. Most Spanish missions in eighteenth-century California had dispensaries, medical supplies, and medical books, and some padres displayed genuine concern for the health of their mission populations. The state of medical knowledge was still rudimentary in the eighteenth century, but Europeans, motivated by self-interest as much as humanitarian concern, shared with Indians what medical advances there were. British Indian superintendent Sir William Johnson had the Mohawks inoculated against smallpox, and some Indians were vaccinated after Edward Jenner developed the cowpox vaccine in 1796. Many Indian people overcame their suspicion of the white man's medicine to accept the protection it could offer against the white man's diseases.

Nevertheless, the protection was too little and too late to stop demographic disaster. Not all Indian populations suffered 75 percent or 90 percent mortality rates—indeed, in some areas of the country Indian populations were on the rise in the eighteenth century—but the result was a world newly emptied of Indian inhabitants. Europeans arriving in Indian country in the wake of one or more epidemics made inaccurate estimates of precontact Indian population size on the basis of head counts of survivors. Seeing remnant populations, they gained a distorted impression of the size and sophistication of the societies that had once existed—and that distorted impression entered the history books. America, many believed, was an "empty wilderness," a "virgin land." If the country was empty, that was a recent development; it was depopulated rather than unpopulated. The new world of opportunity, which "free lands" opened for Europeans in North America, was in itself a by-product of European invasion.

Historians working to revise the old view of the European settlement of America as a story of progress and triumph have rightly stressed the biological cataclysm that followed European "discovery." But epidemic diseases also plagued European societies and shattered European families. France suffered epidemics and famine with appalling regularity throughout the seventeenth and eighteenth centuries. Recurrent outbreaks of plague devastated overcrowded London in the seventeenth century, sometimes, as in 1625, killing 25 percent of the population. In 1665, London experienced the horror of the Great Plague, which did not end until the Fire of London destroyed much of the city the following year. European immigrants to America did not entirely escape Old World diseases, and they succumbed to some new ones. Malaria wreaked havoc among Spanish expeditions in the sixteenth century. Early settlers at Jamestown, Virginia, suffered high death rates in unfamiliar environments. In 1740, Ephraim and Elizabeth Hartwell of Concord, Massachusetts, watched helplessly as all five of their young children died of the "throat distemper" that ravaged New England. Boston suffered recurrent outbreaks of smallpox in the seventeenth and eighteenth centuries. Yellow fever, imported from the Tropics, killed one out of every ten people in Philadelphia, then the capital of the United States, in 1793. But with less crowded communities, more sanitary conditions, improved diet, and greater economic opportunities, most colonists enjoyed a healthier life and longer life expectancy in their new world than did their contemporaries in Europe.

Though scholars disagree widely in their estimates, it is likely that in what is today the United States, Indian population stood at somewhere between 5 million and 10 million in 1492. By 1800, the figure had fallen to around 600,000. By contrast, the European population of the English colonies in America doubled every twenty-five years in the late eighteenth century. The first U.S. census in 1790 counted a total population of 3.9 million people. By 1800, North America had just under 5 million whites and about 1 million blacks. As James Axtell points out, the Indian people who survived in the eastern United States were being engulfed in a sea of white and black faces. The demographic complexion of the new world created by the interaction of Europeans, Indians, and Africans was very different in 1800 from what it had been three centuries before.

Nevertheless, the American population of 1800 combined Indian and European healing practices. Indians and Europeans alike employed "folk remedies" as well as doctors to cure diseases and injuries. The British lagged behind the Spaniards in establishing hospitals in the New World: Cortez built the first hospital in Mexico City for Indian and Spanish poor in 1521, and by the end of the seventeenth century, there were more than one hundred fifty hospitals in New Spain. In contrast, the first general hospital to care for the sick poor in the British colonies was established in Philadelphia in 1752; Massachusetts General Hospital, not until 1811. The first medical school was established at the University of Pennsylvania in 1765; Harvard Medical School, not until 1783. For most of the eighteenth century, American physicians who wanted a medical education had to go to Europe. With few trained physicians and few medical facilities available, people in rural and small-town communities turned in times of sickness to family, neighbors, clergymen, skilled women, and local healers. In many areas of the country, itinerant Indian physicians remained common well into the twentieth century, providing health care for America's poor, whether Indian, white, or black. Many Indian people preserved their belief in the efficacy of traditional medicine—both herbal and spiritual—even as they benefited from European medicine as practiced by white doctors. False Face societies and curing rituals continued among the Iroquois long after many Iroquois had embraced Christianity. Medicine was power, and Indian people needed to draw on all the power available to them as they struggled to survive in the disease-ridden land that was their new world.

David S. Jones  **NO**

Virgin Soils Revisited

The decimation of American Indian populations that followed European arrival in the Americas was one of the most shocking demographic events of the last millennium. Indian populations declined by as much as 95 percent in the first century after the arrival of Christopher Columbus, prompting one historian to conclude that "early America was a catastrophea—a horror story, not an epic." This collapse established the foundation for the subsequent social and political developments of American history. Since the earliest encounters of colonization, colonists and their descendants have struggled to explain how and why depopulation occurred. They have debated the role of race, politics, and even genocide. All have concluded that infectious diseases, introduced by Europeans and Africans, played a decisive role. American Indians suffered terrible mortality from smallpox, measles, tuberculosis, and many other diseases. Their susceptibility led to American Indian decline even as European populations thrived.

Discussions of the epidemiological vulnerability of American Indians rose to prominence with the work of William McNeill and Alfred W. Crosby in the 1970s. Both argued that the depopulation of the Americas was the inevitable result of contact between disease-experienced Old World populations and the "virgin" populations of the Americas. As Crosby defined them in 1976, "Virgin soil epidemics are those in which the populations at risk have had no previous contact with the diseases that strike them and are therefore immunologically almost defenseless." His theory provided a powerful explanation for the outcomes of encounter between Europeans and indigenous groups, not just in the Americas but throughout the world. Since Crosby's analysis of virgin soil epidemics appeared in the *William and Mary Quarterly*, countless writers have cited his definition and attributed the devastation of American Indian populations to their immunologic inadequacy. As argued in Jared Diamond's Pulitzer Prize-winning *Guns, Germs, and Steel*, "The main killers were Old World germs to which Indians had never been exposed, and against which they therefore had neither immune nor genetic resistance." Such assertions, which apply the intuitive appeal of natural selection to the demographic history of the Americas, dominate academic and popular discussions of depopulation.

From *William & Mary Quarterly,* vol. LX, no. 4, October 2003, pp. 703–705, 734–742. Copyright © 2003 by Omohundro Institute of Early American History & Culture. Reprinted by permission. References omitted.

Even as Crosby's model of virgin soil epidemics remains a central theme of the historiography of the Americas, it has been misunderstood and misrepresented. Crosby actually downplayed the "genetic weakness hypothesis" and instead emphasized the many environmental factors that might have contributed to American Indian susceptibility to Old World diseases, including lack of childhood exposure, malnutrition, and the social chaos generated by European colonization. Subsequent historians, however, have often reduced the complexity of Crosby's model to vague claims that American Indians had "no immunity" to the new epidemics. These claims obscure crucial distinctions between different mechanisms that might have left American Indians vulnerable. Did American Indians lack specific genes that made Europeans and Africans, after generations of natural selection, more resistant to smallpox and tuberculosis? Did they lack antibodies that their Eurasian counterparts acquired during childhood exposure to endemic infections? Were their immune systems compromised by the malnutrition, exhaustion, and stress created by European colonization? These different explanations, blurred within simple claims of no immunity, have very different implications for our understanding of what was responsible for this demographic catastrophe.

It is now possible to revisit the theory of virgin soil epidemics and reassess the many possible causes of American Indian susceptibility to European pathogens. The confusion can be untangled by surveying and resynthesizing diverse research about Indian depopulation. A review of the literature of colonization shows the prevalence of simplistic assertions of no immunity and their possible ideological appeals. It also demonstrates the importance of defining the specific claims contained within the theory of virgin soil epidemics and evaluating each of them separately. Recent immunological research has clarified the different mechanisms that can compromise human immunity. Parallel work by biological anthropologists, archaeologists, and historians has elucidated the details of the mortality of specific Indian populations. Taken together, this work suggests that although Indians' lack of prior exposure might have left them vulnerable to European pathogens, the specific contribution of such genetic or developmental factors is probably unknowable. In contrast, the analyses clearly show that the fates of individual populations depended on contingent factors of their physical, economic, social, and political environments. It could well be that the epidemics among American Indians, despite their unusual severity, were caused by the same forces of poverty, social stress, and environmental vulnerability that cause epidemics in all other times and places. These new understandings of the mechanisms of depopulation require historians to be extremely careful in their writing about American Indian epidemics. If they attribute depopulation to irresistible genetic and microbial forces, they risk being interpreted as supporting racial theories of historical development. Instead, they must acknowledge the ways in which multiple factors, especially social forces and human agency, shaped the epidemics of encounter and colonization. . . .

Taken as a whole, recent immunological research offers many clues about the state of Indian immunity. American Indians could certainly mount immune responses to European pathogens. Perhaps their "naïveté" left them without protective genes, making them incrementally susceptible. Perhaps their homogeneity left them vulnerable to adaptable pathogens. Research about these questions continues on the cutting edge of immunology. It is possible that definitive evidence of demographically significant resistance genes will emerge. The historical experiment, however, has run its course. European and American populations mixed for over five hundred years before scientists could study them adequately. The opportunity for further research on first contact populations remains remote. As a result, the state of virgin immunity will forever remain contested. This leaves the literature on genetics and immunity promising, but unsatisfying. Genetic arguments of population-wide vulnerability must therefore be made with great caution. Other immunological mechanisms remain plausible, but problematic. Initial lack of adaptive immunity likely left American Indian societies vulnerable to certain pathogens, but certainly not to all of them, and adaptive immunity does not seem to have been relevant for the dominant causes of mortality in developing societies.

Furthermore, the mechanisms of adaptive immunity, along with the impact of simultaneous and successive synergistic infections, emphasize the importance of the disease environment, and not only the population itself, in shaping a population's susceptibility to infection. Other features of the environment, defined broadly, also have profound effects on immunity. A population's physical, social, economic, and political environments all interact to create patterns of vulnerability, regardless of its genetic substrate.

Such vulnerabilities have long been recognized. Even as observers began asserting racial arguments of disease susceptibility in the nineteenth century, they saw that a wide range of social factors created susceptibility to epidemic disease. After studying an outbreak of measles among the indigenous populations of Fiji in 1875, W. Squire concluded, "We need invoke no special susceptibility of race or peculiarity of constitution to explain the great mortality." He blamed social conditions, especially "want of nourishment and care." In 1909, anthropologist Aleš Hrdlička reached a similar conclusion about American Indians: "Doubtless much of what now appears to be greater racial susceptibility is a result of other conditions." Sherburne Cook came to believe that disease amongst indigenous populations worldwide "acted essentially as the outlet through which many other factors found expression."

Malnutrition provides the most obvious, and prevalent, demonstration of the links between social conditions, environmental conditions, and disease. In addition to causing deficiency diseases, such as rickets and pellagra, malnutrition increases susceptibility to infection. Some vitamin deficiencies cause skin breakdown, eroding the first barrier of defense against infection. Protein deficiencies impair both cellular and humoral responses. Malnutrition during infancy and childhood has particularly devastating effects on subsequent immune function. Certain diseases have more specific connections to nutrition. Malnutrition, especially vitamin A deficiency, increases mortality from measles. Malnourished children are more likely to die from chicken pox. Such interactions create "a vicious circle. Each episode of infection increases the need for calories and protein and at the same time causes anorexia; both of these aggravate the nutritional deficiency, making the patient even more susceptible to infection." Understanding these relationships, scientists have realized that malnutrition "is the most common cause of secondary immunodeficiency in the world."

Historians have thoroughly documented the impact of malnutrition on disease susceptibility. Such connections have clear importance for American Indians, who faced both disease and social disorder following European colonization. As Cronon describes, villages disrupted by disease and social breakdown "often missed key phases in their annual subsistence cycles—the corn planting, say, or the fall hunt and so were weakened when the next infection arrived." This would have been particularly damaging for the many populations that eked out only a precarious subsistence before European arrival. Although some writers have described American Indians living in bountiful harmony with their environment, archaeologists and physical anthropologists have shown that many groups were terribly malnourished. The accomplishments of the Mayan civilization might have been undone by climate change, crop failures, and famine. Disease, malnutrition, and violence made Mesoamerican cities as unhealthful as their medieval European counterparts, with life expectancies of 21 to 26 years. The Arikaras had life expectancies as low as 13.2 years. Careful study of skeletal remains has found widespread evidence of nutritional deficiencies, with health conditions worsening in the years before contact with Europeans. Baseline malnutrition, especially in the large agricultural societies in Mexico and the Andes, left American Indians vulnerable—at the outset—to European diseases. When the conditions of colonization disrupted subsistence, the situation only grew worse.

Malnutrition may be the most obvious factor, but it was only one of many. Environmental historians have shown how physical environments can leave populations susceptible to disease. Lowland Ecuadorians, weakened by endemic parasites and intestinal diseases, were more vulnerable to European infections than their highland compatriots. After Spanish arrival in Mexico, a "plague of sheep" destroyed Mexican agricultural lands and left Mexicans susceptible to famine and disease. Colonization introduced a host of damaging changes in New England. Deforestation led to wider temperature swings and more severe flooding. Livestock overran Indian crops and required pastures and fences, leading to frequent conflict and widespread seizure of Indian land. Europeans also introduced pests, including blights, insects, and rats. All of these changes fueled rapid soil erosion and undermined the subsistence of surviving Indian populations. More dramatic environmental events also wreaked havoc. Drought, earthquakes, and volcanic eruptions undermined resistance to disease in Ecuador in the 1690s. A devastating hurricane struck Fiji in 1875, exacerbating the measles outbreak there. As one observer commented, "Certainly for the last 16 years there has been experienced no such weather, and nothing could be more fatal to a diseased Fijian than exposure to it."

Historians and anthropologists have also documented many cases in which the varied outcomes of specific populations depended on specific social environments. The Lamanai Mayas, heavily colonized by the Spanish regime, had higher mortality than the more isolated Tipu Mayas. While much of Peru suffered severely, the region of Huamanga lost only 20 percent of its population between 1532 and 1570, the result of "a high birth rate, the relative immunity of remote high-altitude areas to disease, shrewd politics, and good luck." The Pueblos suffered when "the endemic problems of drought and famine were superimposed upon the economic disruption caused by the Spanish drain on food and labor." Severe outbreaks of smallpox and erysipelas in Peru from 1800 to 1805 reflected a combination of drought, crop failures, famines, mining failures, and economic collapse. The introduction of specific epidemics reflected specific historical events. Dauril Alden and Joseph Miller traced outbreaks of smallpox from West African droughts, through the middle passage of the slave trade, to Brazil. Measles raced down the political hierarchy in Fiji in 1875 as a series of conferences carried news of a treaty with the British empire, along with the virus, from the royal family to regional and local leaders throughout the island. Local variability and contingency led Linda Newson to conclude that "levels of decline and demographic trends were influenced by the size, distribution, and character of populations, especially their settlement patterns, social organization, and levels of subsistence." Even in the late twentieth century, specific social factors left isolated indigenous populations vulnerable to European pathogens. Magdalena Hurtado, who has witnessed first-contact epidemics in South America, emphasizes the adverse consequences of "sedentism, poverty, and poor access to health care."

Studies of North American tribes in the nineteenth and twentieth centuries have found similar local variability. Geographer Jody Decker shows how a single epidemic among the northern Plains tribes had disparate effects, "even for contiguous Native groups," depending on "population densities, transmission rates, immunity, subsistence patterns, seasonality and geographic location." Drought and famine left the Hopis particularly susceptible to an epidemic in 1780. The Mandans suffered severely from smallpox in 1837: famine since the previous winter had left them malnourished, and cold, rainy weather confined them to their crowded lodges. When smallpox struck, they had both high levels of exposure and low levels of resistance. As Clyde Dollar concludes, "It is no wonder the death rate reached such tragically high levels." Once North American tribes came under the care of the federal governments in the United States and Canada, they often suffered from malnutrition and poor sanitation. Mary-Ellen Kelm, who has studied the fates of the Indians of British Columbia, concludes that "poor Aboriginal health was not inevitable"; instead, it was the product of specific government policies.

Comparative studies have particular power for demonstrating the local specificity of depopulation. Stephen Kunitz has shown that Hawaiians suffered more severely than Samoans, a consequence of different patterns of land seizure by colonizing Europeans. The Navajo did better than the neighboring Hopi because their pastoral lifestyle adapted more easily to the challenges imposed by American settlers. In these cases similar indigenous populations encountered similar colonizers, with very different outcomes: "The kind of colonial contact that occurred was of enormous importance." Kunitz's cases demonstrate that "diseases rarely act as independent forces but instead are shaped by the different contexts in which they occur."

Paralleling this work, some historians have begun to provide integrated analyses of the many factors that shaped demographic outcomes. Any factor that causes mental or physical stress—displacement, warfare, drought, destruction of crops, soil depletion, overwork, slavery, malnutrition, social and economic chaos—can increase susceptibility to disease. These same social and environmental factors also decrease fertility, preventing a population from replacing its losses. The magnitude of mortality depended on characteristics of precontact American Indian populations (size, density, social structure, nutritional status) and on the patterns of European colonization (frequency and magnitude of contact, invasiveness of the European colonial regime). As anthropologist Clark Spencer Larsen argues, scholars must "move away from monocausal explanations of population change to reach a broad-based understanding of decline and extinction of Native American groups after 1492."

The final evidence of the influence of social and physical environments on disease susceptibility comes from their ability to generate remarkable mortality among even the supposedly disease-experienced Old World populations. Karen Kupperman has documented the synergy of malnutrition, deficiency diseases, and despair at Jamestown, where 80 percent of the colonists died between 1607 and 1625. Smallpox mortality, nearly 40 percent among Union soldiers during the Civil War, reflected living conditions and not inherent lack of innate or adaptive immunity. Mortality among soldiers infected with measles, which exceeded 20 percent during the United States Civil War, reached 40 percent during the siege of Paris in the Franco-Prussian War. Poverty and social disruption continue to shape the distribution of disease, generating enormous global disparities with tuberculosis, HIV, and all other diseases.

Is it possible to quantify the variability, to delineate the relative contribution of potential genetic, developmental, environmental, and social variables? Detailed studies have documented "considerable regional variability" in American Indian responses to European arrival. Many American Indian groups declined for a century and then began to recover. Some, such as the natives of the Bahamas, declined to extinction. Others, such as the Navajo, experienced steady population growth after European arrival. More precise data exist for select groups. Newson, for instance, has compiled data about die-off ratios, the proportion of those who died to those who survived. While die-off ratios were as high as 58:1 along the Peruvian coast, they were lower (3.4:1) in the Peruvian highlands. In Mexico they varied between 47.8:1 and 6.6:1, again depending on elevation. They ranged from 5.1:1 in Chiapas to 24:1 in Honduras and 40:1 in Nicaragua. Mortality rates from European diseases among South Pacific islanders ranged between 3 percent and 25 percent for measles, and 2.5 percent to 25 percent for influenza. Such variability among relatively homogeneous populations, with die-off ratios differing by an order of magnitude, most likely reflects the contingency of social variables. But most of these numbers are, admittedly, enormous: a 4:1 die-off ratio indicates that 75 percent died. Why did so many populations suffer such high baseline mortality? Does this reflect a shared genetic vulnerability, whose final intensity was shaped by social variables? Or does it reflect a shared social experience, of pre-existing nutritional stress exacerbated by the widespread chaos of encounter and colonization? Both positions are defensible.

The variability of outcomes reflected in the different fates of different Indian populations provides powerful evidence against the inevitability of mortality. It undermines popular claims, made most influentially by Henry Dobyns, that American Indians suffered universal mortality from infectious diseases. Noble David Cook, for instance, argues that the vulnerability was so general that Indians died equally whatever the colonial context, "no matter which European territory was involved, regardless of the location of the region. It seemed to make no difference what type of colonial regime was created." Such assertions, which reduce the depopulation of the Americas to an inevitable encounter between powerful diseases and vulnerable peoples, do not match the contingency of the archaeological and historical records. These, instead, tell a story of populations made vulnerable.

One could argue that the differences in American and European disease environments, the nutritional status of precontact Americans, and the disruptions of colonization created conditions in which disease could only thrive. Only a time traveler equipped with a supply of vaccines could have altered the demographic outcomes. But it is also possible that outcomes might have been different. Suppose Chinese explorers, if they did reach the Americas, had introduced Eurasian diseases in the 1420s, leaving American populations two generations to recover before facing European colonization. Suppose smallpox struck Tenochtitlan after Cortés's initial retreat and not during his subsequent siege of the city. An epidemic then might have been better tolerated than during the siege. Or suppose that the epidemics of 1616–1617 and 1633–1634 struck New England tribes during the nutritionally bountiful summers and not during the starving times of winter (or perhaps it was because of those starving times that the epidemics tended to appear in winters). The historic record of epidemic after epidemic suggests that high mortality must have been a likely consequence of encounter. But it does not mean that mortality was the inevitable result of inherent immunological vulnerability.

Consider an analogous case, the global distribution of HIV/AIDS. From the earliest years of the epidemic, HIV has exhibited striking disparities in morbidity and mortality. Its prevalence varies between sub-Saharan Africa and developed countries and between different populations within developed countries. Few scientists or historians would argue that these disparities between African and Europeans or between urban minorities and suburban whites exist because the afflicted populations have no immunity to HIV. Instead, the social contingency of HIV on a local and global scale has long been recognized. We should be just as cautious before asserting that no immunity led to the devastation of the American Indians.

Historians and medical scientists need to reassess their casual deployment of deterministic models of depopulation. The historic record demonstrates that we cannot understand the impact of European diseases on the Americas merely by focusing on Indians' lack of immunity. It is certainly true that epidemics devastated American Indian populations. It is also likely that genetic mechanisms of disease susceptibility exist: they influence the susceptibility of

American Indians—and everyone else—to infectious disease. What remains in doubt is the relative contributions of social, cultural, environmental, and genetic forces. Even when immunologists demonstrate that a wide variety of genes contribute to susceptibility to infectious disease, it will likely remain unknown how these factors played out among American Indians in past centuries. Demographic data, meanwhile, provide convincing evidence of the strong impact of social contingency on human disease. This uncertainty leaves the door open for the debates to be shaped by ideology.

Although unprecedented in their widespread severity, virgin soil epidemics may have arisen from nothing more unique than the familiar forces of poverty, malnutrition, environmental stress, dislocation, and social disparity that cause epidemics among all other populations. Whenever historians describe the depopulation of the Americas that followed European arrival, they should acknowledge the complexity, the subtlety, and the contingency of the process. They need to replace homogeneous and ambiguous claims of no immunity with heterogeneous analyses that situate the mortality of the epidemics in specific social and environmental contexts. Only then can they overcome the widespread public and academic appeal of immunologic determinism and do justice to the crucial events of the encounter between Europeans and Americans.

POSTSCRIPT

Was Disease the Key Factor in the Depopulation of Native Americans in the Americas?

The so-called "Columbian Exchange" involved a reciprocal trade in plants and animals, human beings, and ideas, as well as diseases. With regard to the exchange of diseases, this was not a one-way street. For example, the introduction of destructive microorganisms produced epidemic diseases (smallpox, tuberculosis, measles, typhoid, and syphilis) that decimated human populations on both sides of the Atlantic. On a more positive note, Europeans brought food stuffs such as wheat and potatoes to the New World and carried home maize, beans, and manioc. Native Americans benefited from horses and other farm animals introduced from Europe, but these were offset by the efforts of the Europeans to enslave and kill the indigenous peoples whom they encountered. The best study of these various by-products of European exploration is Alfred W. Crosby, *The Columbian Exchange: Biological and Cultural Consequences of 1492* (Greenwood Press, 1973). Crosby's conclusions are largely shared by William H. McNeill, *Plagues and Peoples* (Doubleday, 1977) and Jared Diamond, *Guns, Germs, and Steel: The Fates of Human Societies* (W. W. Norton, 1997).

The effects of the encounters between Europeans and Native Americans is explored in Gary B. Nash, *Red, White & Black: The Peoples of Early North America*, 3d ed. (Prentice Hall, 1992) and three works by James Axtell, *The European and the Indian: Essays in the Ethnohistory of Colonial North America* (Oxford University Press, 1981), *The Invasion Within: The Contest of Cultures in Colonial North America* (Oxford University Press, 1985), and *Beyond 1492: Encounters in Colonial North America* (Oxford University Press, 1992). Francis Jennings, *The Invasion of America: Indians, Colonialism, and the Cant of Conquest* (University of North Carolina Press, 1975) and David E. Stannard, *American Holocaust: Columbus and the Conquest of the New World* (Oxford University Press, 1992), which accuses Europeans and white Americans of conducting a full-blown campaign of genocide against native peoples in the Americas, offer two of the harshest critiques of European dealings with American Indians. The relationship between disease and environmental conditions is explored in William Cronon, *Changes in the Land: Indians, Colonists, and the Ecology of New England* (Hill & Wang, 1983), Karen Ordahl Kupperman, *Indians and English: Facing Off in Early America* (Cornell University Press, 2000), and Russell Thornton, *American Indian Holocaust and Survival: A Population History Since 1492* (University of Oklahoma Press, 1987). Alvin M. Josephy Jr. examines the pre-Columbian Native Americans in

America in 1492: The World of the Indian Peoples Before the Arrival of Columbus (Alfred A. Knopf, 1992).

The era of European exploration during the fifteenth, sixteenth, and seventeenth centuries is covered in J. H. Parry, *The Age of Reconnaissance: Discovery, Exploration, and Settlement, 1450 to 1650* (Praeger, 1963). Samuel Eliot Morison, *The European Discovery of America: The Northern Voyages* (Oxford University Press, 1971), David Beers Quinn, *England and the Discovery of America, 1481–1620* (Harper & Row, 1974), Wallace Notestein, *The English People on the Eve of Colonization, 1603–1630* (Harper & Brothers, 1954), Charles Gibson, *Spain in America* (Harper & Row, 1966), and W. J. Eccles, *France in America* (Harper & Row, 1972) all discuss European contacts in North America.

ISSUE 3

Was Colonial Culture
Uniquely American?

YES: Gary B. Nash, from Jack Greene and J.R. Pole, eds., *Colonial British America: Essays in the New History of the Early Modern Era* (The Johns Hopkins University Press, 1984)

NO: David Hackett Fischer, from *Albion's Seed: Four British Folkways in America* (Oxford University Press, 1989)

ISSUE SUMMARY

YES: Gary Nash argues that colonial American culture emerged from a convergence of three broad cultural traditions—European, Native American, and African—which produced a unique tri-racial society in the Americas.

NO: David Hackett Fischer contends that the cultural traditions of colonial America and the United States were derived from English folkways transported by migrants from four different regions in the British Isles.

Michel-Guillaume Jean de Crevecoeur was a French immigrant who became a naturalized subject of the Colony of New York in 1764. He married an American woman, and the couple settled on a comfortable estate in New York. In 1782, Crevecoeur published a volume entitled *Letters from an American Farmer* in which he attempted to analyze the culture and national character of his adopted land. In probing the unique quality of the American, Crevecoeur wrote: "What then is the American, this new man? He is either an European, or the descendant of an European, hence that strange mixture of blood, which you will find in no other country. . . . He is an American who, leaving behind him all his ancient prejudices and manners, receives new ones from the new mode of life he has embraced, the new government he obeys, and the new rank he holds. He becomes an American by being received in the broad lap of our great *Alma Mater*. Here individuals of all nations are melted into a new race of men, whose labors and posterity will one day cause great changes in the world." A half century later, another Frenchman, the aristocratic Alexis de Tocqueville, explored the distinctiveness of America by emphasizing the twin components of democracy and equality. But it was an American historian, Frederick Jackson Turner, who captured the attention of generations of scholars and students by characterizing the unique qualities of life in America and distinguishing that life from Old World culture. For Turnerians, it was the American frontier experience that was most responsible for Crevecoeur's "new man."

Historians continue to express interest in the nature of American culture as they explore the Old World and New World roots of the American people and the society they created beginning in the seventeenth century. Just how new was that early American culture? How much did it depart from the cultural heritage of those tens of thousands of immigrants who arrived in England's North American colonies prior to the American Revolution? Modern-day students who are unfamiliar with the writings of Crevecoeur, Tocqueville, and Turner should find it worthwhile to explore the basic components of the American culture that emerged in the colonial period. By understanding the nature of that culture, Americans can better grasp who they are.

For Gary Nash, the main problem in developing a clear picture of colonial American culture has been the tendency of past generations of scholars to operate from a male-dominated and highly ethnocentric framework. In Nash's view, those who ignore important segments of the population that played significant roles in colonial social development fail to describe that development accurately. His essay makes clear that while white male Europeans were prominent in carving a cultural base for the American people, they were assisted by their female counterparts, as well as Native Americans and Africans, male and female. That culture was unique, he suggests, primarily because it was a tri-racial composite, not one simply transferred intact from Europe.

Not all scholars, however, agree with this notion of American distinctiveness. In the nineteenth century, Herbert Baxter Adams and his followers insisted that American culture was best understood as an extension of England or Europe. David Hackett Fischer presents an intriguing modification of this so-called "germ theory." According to Fischer, American society was germinated by four waves of British immigrants, each of which brought with them the shared characteristics of Englishmen as well as the distinctive folkways of their respective regions. These four different sets of folkways, he concludes, account for the distinctiveness of regional cultures in the New World colonies, but each remains a direct product of English culture. In the following selection from Fischer's *Albion's Seed,* the author focuses upon the different ways in which the concept of freedom is defined in American society. These differences, says Fischer, reflect the varying "freedom ways" if immigrants from eastern England, the southern and western counties, the North Midlands, and the borders of North Britain and northern Ireland, who settled in British North America between 1629 and 1775.

YES

Gary B. Nash

Race, Class, and Politics: Essays on American Colonial and Revolutionary Society

The Social Development of Colonial America

The history of social development in colonial America—portrayed in this paper primarily as the history of social relations between groups of people defined by race, gender, and class—is in glorious disarray. Disarray because all of the old paradigms have collapsed under the weight of the last generation of scholarship. Glorious because a spectacular burst of innovative scholarship, the product of those who have crossed disciplinary boundaries, transcended filiopietism, and been inspired in the best sense by the social currents of their own times, has left us with vastly more knowledge of the first century and a half of American history than we ever had before. . . .

So much creative work has been done during the last generation that it may seem that the time has arrived to build new models of social development. Yet this still may be premature because in spite of their many virtues, the innovative studies of the past two decades are so male-centered and oblivious to the black and native American peoples of colonial society that any new synthesis would necessarily be constructed with materials that present a skewed and incomplete picture of the social process in the prerevolutionary period.

If social development is defined as changing social relations between different groups in society, then the foundation of any such study must be rigorous analysis of the structural arrangements that did not strictly govern most human interaction but set the boundaries for it in the preindustrial period, as between masters and slaves, men and women, parents and children, employers and employees. Those relationships, moreover, must be examined within the context of a triracial society. This marks a fundamental difference between social development in England and America or in France and America. Of course other differences existed as well, but perhaps none was so great as that produced by the convergence of three broad cultural groups on the North American coastal plain in the seventeenth and eighteenth centuries. Some of the best work in colonial social history has been unmindful of this, drawing conceptually on European historical studies as if the colonies were pure offshoots

Greene, Jack O., and J.R. Pole. *Colonial British America: Essays in the New History of the Early Modern Era.* pp. 233–261. Copyright © 1983 Johns Hopkins University Press. Reprinted with permission of the Johns Hopkins University Press. References omitted.

of English society. . . . [W]e must regard the social development of colonial America as *sui generis* because of the triracial environment in which most colonists lived their lives. This racial intermingling had profound effects on the social formation of the colonies. . . .

Native Americans

Ideally, a discussion of the role of native American societies in the social development of eastern North America should be regionally organized because there was no unified "Indian" experience and the various tribal histories that ethnohistorians have reconstructed are closely related to the histories of European colonizers in particular areas. But space limitations permit only some general remarks about the underdeveloped field of native American history and its connection to the history of the colonizers. It is important to differentiate between coastal and interior tribes: even though disease and warfare thoroughly ravaged the numerous seaboard tribes by the third generation of settlement in every colony, these small societies profoundly affected the shaping of settler communities.

The process of decimation, dispossession, and decline among the Indian societies of the coastal areas occurred in different ways during the first century of European colonization. Everywhere that Europeans settled, a massive depopulation occurred as the invaders' diseases swept through biologically defenseless native societies. Yet this rarely broke the resistance of the native peoples. In New England that occurred only after the stronger coastal tribes, such as the Wampanoags and Narragansetts, finally succumbed in a long war of attrition to an enemy who sought no genuine accommodation. In Virginia and Maryland the tidewater tribes genuinely strove for accommodation following their unsuccessful resistance movements of 1622 and 1644. But, as in New England, their inability to function in any way that served European society finally led to conflict initiated by whites. Even as friendly colonized people they were obstacles in the path of an acquisitive and expanding plantation society. In South Carolina it was not dead Indians but Indians alive and in chains that benefited the white settlers. The build-up of the colonizer population was slow enough, and the desire among the Indians for trade goods intense enough, that the white Carolinians, most of them transplanted from Barbados, where they had learned to trade in human flesh, could lure the coastal tribes into obliterating each other in the wars for slaves.

The result was roughly the same in all the colonies along the seaboard. By the 1680s in the older colonies and by the 1720s in the new ones the coastal tribes were shattered. Devastated by disease and warfare, the survivors either incorporated themselves as subjects of stronger inland groups or entered the white man's world as detribalized servile dependents. Their desire for European trade goods, which kept them in close contact with European colonizers, and the persistence of ancient intertribal hostilities, which thwarted pan-tribal resistance, sealed their fate once the growth of the settler population made it apparent that their value as trading partners was incidental in comparison with the value of the land that their destruction would convert to European possession.

Although they were defeated, the coastal cultures served a crucial function for tribes farther inland. Their prolonged resistance gave interior societies time to adapt to the European presence and to devise strategies of survival as the white societies grew in size and strength. "People like the Iroquois," T. J. C. Brasser has pointed out, "owed a great deal to the resistance of the coastal Algonkians, and both peoples were well aware of this." The coastal tribes provided a buffer between the interior Indians and the Europeans, and when the coastal tribes lost their political autonomy, their remnants were often incorporated into the larger inland tribes. This was important in the much stronger opposition that the Iroquois, Cherokees, and Creeks offered to European encroachment—a resistance so effective that for the first century and a half of European settlement the white newcomers were restricted to the coastal plain, unable to penetrate the Appalachians, where the interior tribes, often allied with the French, held sway.

During the first half of the eighteenth century the interior Indian societies demonstrated their capacity for adapting to the presence of Europeans and for turning economic and political interaction with them to their own advantage. Drawing selectively from European culture, they adopted through the medium of the fur, skin, and slave trade European articles of clothing, weapons, metal implements, and a variety of ornamental objects. To some extent this incorporation of material objects robbed the Indians of their native skills. But agriculture, fishing, and hunting, the mainstays of Indian subsistence before the Europeans came, remained so thereafter. European implements such as the hoe only made Indian agriculture more efficient. The knife and fishhook enabled the natives to fish and trap with greater intensity in order to obtain the commodities needed in the barter system. However, pottery making declined, and the hunter became more dependent upon the gun.

Yet, interaction with European societies over many generations sowed seeds of destruction within tribal villages. It is not necessary to turn Indians into acquisitive capitalists to explain their desire for trade goods. They did not seek guns, cloth, kettles, and fishhooks out of a desire to become part of bourgeois culture, accumulating material wealth from the fur trade, but because they recognized the advantages, within the matrix of their own culture, of goods fashioned by societies with a more complex technology. The utility of the Europeans' trade goods, not the opportunities for profit provided by the fur trade, drew native Americans into it, and from the Indian point of view, trade was carried on within the context of political and social alliance.

Nonetheless, the fur trade required native Americans to reallocate their human resources and reorder their internal economies. Subsistence hunting turned into commercial hunting, and consequently males spent more time away from the villages trapping and hunting. Women were also drawn into the new economic organization of villages, for the beaver, marten, or fox had to be skinned and the skins scraped, dressed, trimmed, and sewn into robes. Among some tribes the trapping, preparation, and transporting of skins became so time-consuming that food resources had to be procured in trade from other tribes. Ironically, the reorientation of tribal economies toward the fur trade dispersed villages and weakened the localized basis of clans and lineages. Breaking up in order to be nearer the widely dispersed trapping grounds, Indian villagers moved closer to the nomadic woodland existence that Europeans had charged them with at the beginning of contact.

Involvement in the fur trade also altered the relationship of native Americans to their ecosystem. The tremendous destruction of animal life triggered by the advent of European trade undermined the spiritual framework within which hunting had traditionally been carried out and repudiated the ancient emphasis on living in balance with the natural environment. Trade also broadened vastly the scale of intertribal conflict. With Europeans competing for client tribes who would supply furs to be marketed throughout Europe, Indian societies were sucked into the rivalry of their patrons. As furs became depleted in the hunting grounds of one tribe, they could maintain the European trade connection only by conquering more remote tribes whose hunting grounds had not yet been exhausted or by forcibly intercepting the furs of other tribes as they were transported to trading posts. Thus, the Iroquois decimated the Hurons of the Great Lakes region in the mid-seventeenth century as part of their drive for beaver hegemony.

While the interior tribes were greatly affected by contact with the colonizers, they nonetheless rejected much of what the newcomers presented to them as a superior way of life. Tribes such as the Iroquois, Creeks, and Cherokees were singularly unimpressed with most of the institutions of European life and saw no reason to replace what they valued in their own culture with what they disdained in the culture of others. This applied to the newcomers' political institutions and practices, system of law and justice, religion, education, family organization, and childrearing practices. Many aspects of Indian life were marked by cultural persistency in the long period of interaction with Europeans. Indian societies incorporated what served them well and rejected what made no sense within the framework of their own values and modes of existence.

Despite their maintenance of their traditional culture in many areas of life, the native Americans' involvement in the European trade network hastened the spread of epidemic diseases, raised the level of warfare, depleted ecozones of animal life, and drew Indians into a market economy that over a long period of time constricted their economic freedom. The interior tribes reorganized productive relations within their own communities to serve a trading partner who, through the side effects of trade, became a trading master.

Social development within the British mainland colonies proceeded in some unexpected ways because of the Indian presence. Unable to coordinate themselves militarily and politically in the first 150 years of settlement, English colonizers were unable to conquer or dislodge from their tribal homelands—as did their Spanish counterparts to the south—the powerful interior native American societies. Hence, the settlers' societies, restricted to the coastal plain, developed differently than if they had been free to indulge their appetite for land and their westward yearning. Higher mortality rates associated with the spread of epidemic diseases in more densely settled areas, the rise of tenantry in rural areas, underemployment in the cities at the end of the colonial period, the decline of indentured servitude because of the growing pool of landless free laborers, and the rise of class tensions in older seaboard communities are some of the social phenomena that may be attributed in part to the limitations placed upon westward movement by the controlling hand of the major eastern tribes in the trans-Allegheny and even the Piedmont region. The native American was also of primary importance in forging an "American" identity among English, Scotch-Irish, German, and other European immigrants in North America. In their relations with the native people of the land the colonizers in British North American served a long apprenticeship in military affairs. Far more populous than the settlers of New France and therefore much more covetous of Indian land, they engaged in hundreds of military confrontations ranging from localized skirmishes to large-scale regional wars. The allegiance of the diverse immigrants to the land, the annealing of an American as distinct from an English identity, had much to do with the myriad ways in which the colonists interacted with a people who were culturally defined as "the others" but were inextricably a part of the human landscape of North America.

Afro-Americans

Unless we wish to continue picturing some one million Africans brought to or born in America before the Revolution as mindless and cultureless drones, it will be necessary to push forward recent work on the social development of black society and then to incorporate this new corpus of scholarship into an overall analysis of colonial social development. It bears noting that a large majority of the persons who crossed the Atlantic to take up life in the New World in the three hundred years before the American Revolution were Africans. Their history is still largely untold because so much attention has been paid to the kind of slave systems Europeans fashioned in the New World—the black codes they legislated, their treatment of slaves, the economic development they directed—that the slaves themselves, as active participants in a social process, are often forgotten.

In attempting to remedy this gap, historians have borrowed heavily from the work of anthropologists. The encounter model of Sidney Mintz and Richard Price, developed with reference to the Caribbean world, is especially useful because it explores how Africans who found themselves in the possession of white masters five thousand miles from their homeland created institutions and ways of life that allowed them to live as satisfactorily as possible under the slave regimen imposed upon them by the master class. In their New World encounter with European colonizers the problem was not one of merging a West African culture with a European culture, because the human cargoes aboard slave ships were not a single collective African people but rather a culturally heterogeneous people from many tribes and regions. Hence, arriving slaves did not form "communities" of people at the outset but could only become communities through forging a new life out of the fragments of many old cultures combined with elements of the dominant European culture that now bounded their existence. "What the slaves undeniably shared at the outset," according to Mintz and Price, "was their enslavement; all—or nearly all—else had to be created by them."

Major strides have been taken in tracing this process of social adaptation in the Chesapeake region and along the rice coast of South Carolina and

Georgia, though much remains to be done. Already, it is apparent that in this process of adaptation there was a premium on cultural innovation and creativity, both because slaves had to adjust rapidly to the power of the master class and because of the initial cultural heterogeneity of the Africans. Unlike the European colonizers, Africans were immediately obliged "to shift their primary cultural and social commitment from the Old World to the New." This required rapid adaptation, learning new ways of doing things that would ensure survival. It is not surprising, therefore, that Africans developed local slave cultures rather than a unified Afro-American culture. In adapting to North American slavery, they adopted "a general openness to ideas and usages from other cultural traditions, a special tolerance (within the West African context) of cultural differences." Of all the people converging in seventeenth- and eighteenth-century North America, the Africans, by the very conditions of their arrival, developed the greatest capacity for cultural change.

The complexity of black culture in America cannot be understood without considering the evolution of distinct, regional black societies as they developed over the long course of slavery. One of the accomplishments of the new social historians of the colonial South is to have broken much new ground on the life cycle, family formation, and cultural characteristics of the black population, which was increasingly creole, or American-born, as the eighteenth century progressed. This work makes it possible already to go beyond earlier studies of slave life in the colonies, which were based largely on studies of nineteenth-century sources, when discussing the development of Afro-American society in the eighteenth-century colonies.

How much of African culture survived under eighteenth-century slavery is an oft-debated question. There can be little doubt that slave masters were intent on obliterating every Africanism that reduced the effectiveness of slaves as laborers and that they had some success in this. It is also true that slavery eliminated many of the cultural differences among slaves, who came from a wide variety of African cultural groups—Fulanis, Ibos, Yorubas, Malagasies, Ashantis, Mandingos, and others. At the same time, it must be remembered that throughout the eighteenth century, unlike in the nineteenth, large numbers of new Africans arrived each year. Slave importations grew rapidly in the eighteenth century, so that probably never more than half the adult slaves were American-born. This continuous infusion of African culture kept alive many of the elements that would later be transmuted almost beyond recognition. Through fashioning their own distinct culture within the limits established by the rigors of the slave system, blacks were able to forge their own religious forms, their own music and dance, their own family life, and their own beliefs and values. All of these proved indispensable to survival in a system of forced labor. All were part of the social development of black society. And all affected the social development of white society as well.

Women

One final aspect of social development, occasionally alluded to in this essay but indispensable to the work that lies ahead, concerns social relations defined by gender. In the last ten years, and especially in the last four or five, a wave of new work has appeared, some of it defined as women's history and some as demographic or family history. This work shows how rich the possibilities are for those who wish to study the lives of women and female-male relationships. It is crucial to the construction of new paradigms of social development that these studies of women's productive and reproductive lives, which need to be studied with class, racial, and regional differences in mind, be pushed forward at an accelerated pace and then integrated with the studies of the much better understood male half of the population. It is out of the convergence of the already completed demographic and community studies and the studies of women, blacks, and native Americans still remaining to be done that a new understanding of the social development of colonial America will emerge.

Albion's Seed: Four British Folkways in America

In Boston's museum of fine arts, not far from the place where English Puritans splashed ashore in 1630, there is a decidedly unpuritanical painting of bare-breasted Polynesian women by Paul Gauguin. The painting is set on a wooded riverbank. In the background is the ocean, and the shadowy outline of a distant land. The canvas is crowded with brooding figures in every condition of life—old and young, dark and fair. They are seen in a forest of symbols, as if part of a dream. In the corner, the artist has added an inscription: "D'ou venons nous? Qui sommes nous? Ou allons nous?"

That painting haunts the mind of this historian. He wonders how a Polynesian allegory found its way to a Puritan town which itself was set on a wooded riverbank, with the ocean in the background and the shadow of another land in the far distance. He observes the crowd of museumgoers who gather before the painting. They are Americans in every condition of life, young and old, dark and fair. Suddenly the great questions leap to life. Where do *we* come from? Who are we? Where are we going?

The answers to these questions grow more puzzling the more one thinks about them. We Americans are a bundle of paradoxes. We are mixed in our origins, and yet we are one people. Nearly all of us support our republican system, but we argue passionately (sometimes violently), among ourselves about its meaning. Most of us subscribe to what Gunnar Myrdal called the American Creed, but that idea is a paradox in political theory. As Myrdal observed in 1942, America is "conservative in fundamental principles . . . but the principles conserved are liberal and some, indeed, are radical."

We live in an open society which is organized on the principle of voluntary action, but the determinants of that system are exceptionally constraining. Our society is dynamic, changing profoundly in every period of American history; but it is also remarkably stable. The search for the origins of this system is the central problem in American history. . . .

The organizing question here is about what might be called the determinants of a voluntary society. The problem is to explain the origins and stability of a social system which for two centuries has remained stubbornly democratic in its politics, capitalist in its economy, libertarian in its law, individualist in its society and pluralistic in its culture.

Much has been written on this subject—more than anyone can possibly read. But a very large outpouring of books and articles contains a remarkably small number of seminal ideas. Most historians have tried to explain the determinants of a voluntary society in one of three ways: by reference to the European culture that was transmitted to America, or to the American environment itself, or to something in the process of transmission.

During the nineteenth century the first of these explanations was very much in fashion. Historians believed that the American system had evolved from what one scholar called "Teutonic germs" of free institutions, which were supposedly carried from the forests of Germany to Britain and then to America. This idea was taken up by a generation of historians who tended to be Anglo-Saxon in their origins, Atlantic in their attitudes and Whiggish in their politics. Most had been trained in the idealist and institutional traditions of the German historical school.

For a time this Teutonic thesis became very popular—in Boston and Baltimore. But in Kansas and Wisconsin it was unkindly called the "germ theory" of American history and laughed into oblivion. In the early twentieth century it yielded to the Turner thesis, which looked to the American environment and especially to the western frontier as a way of explaining the growth of free institutions in America. This idea appealed to scholars who were middle western in their origins progressive in their politics, and materialist in their philosophy.

In the mid-twentieth century the Turner thesis also passed out of fashion. Yet another generation of American historians became deeply interested in processes of immigration and ethnic pluralism as determinants of a voluntary society. This third approach was specially attractive to scholars who were not themselves of Anglo-Saxon stock. Many were central European in their origin, urban in their residence, and Jewish in their religion. This pluralistic "migration model" is presently the conventional interpretation.

Other explanations have also been put forward from time to time, but three ideas have held the field: the germ theory, the frontier thesis, and the migration model.

This [essay] returns to the first of those explanations, within the framework of the second and third. It argues a modified "germ thesis" about the importance for the United States of having been British in its cultural origins. The argument is complex, and for the sake of clarity might be summarized in advance. It runs more or less as follows.

During the very long period from 1629 to 1775, the present area of the United States was settled by at least four large waves of English-speaking immigrants. The first was an exodus of Puritans from the east of England to Massachusetts during a period of eleven years from 1629 to 1640. The second was the migration of a small Royalist elite and large numbers of indentured servants from the south of England to Virginia (ca. 1642–75). The third was a movement from the North Midlands of England and Wales to the Delaware Valley (ca. 1675–1725). The fourth was a flow of English-speaking people from the borders of North Britain and northern Ireland to the Appalachian backcountry mostly during the half-century from 1718 to 1775.

These four groups shared many qualities in common. All of them spoke the English language. Nearly all were British Protestants. Most lived under British laws and took pride in possessing British liberties. At the same time, they also differed from one another in many other ways: in their religious denominations, social ranks, historical generations, and also in the British regions from whence they came. They carried across the Atlantic four different sets of British folkways which became the basis of regional cultures in the New World.

By the year 1775 these four cultures were fully established in British America. They spoke distinctive dialects of English, built their houses in diverse ways, and had different methods of doing much of the ordinary business of life. Most important for the political history of the United States, they also had four different conceptions of order, power and freedom which became the cornerstones of a voluntary society in British America.

Today less than 20 percent of the American population have any British ancestors at all. But in a cultural sense most Americans are Albion's seed, no matter who their own forebears may have been. Strong echoes of four British folkways may still be heard in the major dialects of American speech, in the regional patterns of American life, in the complex dynamics of American politics, and in the continuing conflict between four different ideas of freedom in the United States. The interplay of four "freedom ways" has created an expansive pluralism which is more libertarian than any unitary culture alone could be. That is the central thesis of this [essay]: the legacy of four British folkways in early America remains the most powerful determinant of a voluntary society in the United States today. . . .

✦

Massachusetts Freedom Ways: The Puritan Idea of Ordered Liberty

The public life of New England was . . . shaped by an idea of liberty which was peculiar to the Puritan colonies. To understand its nature, one might begin with the word itself. From the generation of John Winthrop (1558-1649) to that of Samuel Adams (1722-1803), the noun "liberty" was used throughout New England in at least four ways which ring strangely in a modern ear.

First, "liberty" often described something which belonged not to an individual but to an entire community. For two centuries, the founders and leaders of Massachusetts wrote of the "liberty of New England," or the "liberty of Boston" or the "liberty of the Town." This usage continued from the great migration to the War of Independence and even beyond. Samuel Adams, for example, wrote more often about the "liberty of America" than about the liberty of individual Americans.

This idea of collective liberty, or "publick liberty" as it was sometimes called, was thought to be consistent with close restraints upon individuals. In Massachusetts these individual restrictions were numerous, and often very confining. During the first generation, nobody could live in the colony without approval of the General Court. Settlers even of the highest rank were sent prisoners to England for expressing "divers dangerous opinion," or merely because the Court judged them to be "persons unmeet to inhabit here." Others were not allowed to move within the colony except by special permission of the General Court. For a time, the inhabitants of Dedham, Sudbury and Concord were forbidden to move out of their towns, because the General Court believed that those frontier settlements were dangerously under-populated. . . .

New Englanders also used the word "liberty" in a second way which is foreign to our own time. When it referred to individuals, it often became a plural noun—"liberties" rather than "liberty." These plural liberties were understood as specific exemptions from a condition of prior restraint—an idea which had long existed in East Anglia and in many other parts of the western world. In the manor of Hengrave (Suffolk), for example, tenants were granted a specific "liberty" of fishing in the river Lark. Such a liberty was not universal or absolute; the river was closed to all other people. There were a great many of these liberties in East Anglian communities during the early seventeenth century. A person's status was defined by the number and nature of liberties to which he was admitted.

The idea of plural liberties as specific exemptions from a condition of prior constraint was carried to Massachusetts. The General Court, for example, enacted laws which extended "liberties and privileges of fishing and fowling" to certain inhabitants, and thereby denied them to everyone else. One person's "liberty" in this sense became another's restraint. In Massachusetts, as in England, a person's rank was defined by the liberties that he possessed, and vice versa.

The laws of the Bay Colony granted some liberties to all men, others to all free men, and a few only to gentlemen. For example, a "true gentleman" and "any man equal to a gentleman," was granted the liberty not to be punished by whipping "unless his crime be very shameful, and his course of life vicious and profligate." Other men had a lesser liberty, not to be whipped more than forty stripes. Other liberties were assigned not to individuals at all, but to churches and towns and other social groups. . . .

New England Puritans also used the word "liberty" in a third meaning, which became urgently important to the founders of Massachusetts. This was the idea of "soul liberty," or "Christian liberty," an idea of high complexity. Soul liberty was freedom to serve God in the world. It was freedom to order one's own acts in a godly way—but not in any other. It made Christian freedom into a form of obligation.

The founding generation in Massachusetts often wrote of "soul liberty," "Christian liberty" or "liberty of conscience." Many moved to the New World primarily in hopes of attaining it. What they meant was not a world of religious freedom in the modern sense, or even of religious toleration, but rather of freedom for the true faith. In their minds, this idea of religious liberty was thought to be consistent with the persecution of Quakers, Catholics, Baptists, Presbyterians, Anglicans and indeed virtually everyone except those within a very narrow spectrum of Calvinist orthodoxy. Soul liberty also was thought to be consistent with compulsory church attendance and rigorous Sabbath laws. Even the Indians were compelled to keep the Puritan Sabbath in Massachusetts. To the founders of that colony, soul freedom meant that they were free to persecute others in their own way. . . . To others of different persuasions, the Puritans' paradoxical idea of "soul freedom" became a cruel and bloody contradiction. But to the Puritans themselves "soul liberty" was a genuinely libertarian principle which held that a Christian community should be free to serve God in the world. Here was an idea in which the people of Massachusetts deeply believed, and the reason why their colony was founded in the first place.

The words "liberty" and also "freedom" were used in yet a fourth way by the builders of the Bay Colony. Sometimes, the people of Massachusetts employed the word "freedom" to describe a collective obligation of the "body politicke," to protect individual members from the tyranny of circumstance. This was conceived not in terms of collective welfare or social equality but of individual liberty. It was precisely the same idea that a descendant of the Massachusetts Puritans, Franklin Roosevelt, conceived as the Four Freedoms. That way of thinking was not his invention. It appeared in Massachusetts within a few years of its founding. The Massachusetts poor laws, however limited they may have been, recognized every individual should be guaranteed a freedom from want in the most fundamental sense. The General Court also explicitly recognized even a "freedom from fear." Its language revealed a libertarian conception of social problems (and solutions) that was characteristic of English-speaking people as early as the seventeenth century.

These four libertarian ideas—collective liberty, individual liberties, soul liberty and freedom from the tyranny of circumstance—all had a common denominator. They were aspects of a larger conception which might be called ordered liberty. This principle was deeply embedded in Puritan ideas and also in East Anglian realities. It came to be firmly established in Massachusetts even before the end of the great migration. For many years it continued to distinguish the culture of New England from other parts of British America. Even today, in much modified forms, it is still a living tradition in parts of the United States. But this principle of "ordered liberty" is also opposed by other libertarian ideas, which were planted in different parts of British America. . . .

Virginia Freedom Ways:
The Anglican Idea of Hegemonic Liberty

"How is it," Dr. Samuel Johnson asked, "that we hear the loudest yelps for liberty among the drivers of negroes?" That famous question captured a striking paradox in the history of Virginia. Like most other colonists in British America, the first gentlemen of Virginia possessed an exceptionally strong consciousness of their English liberties, even as they took away the liberty of others. Governor William Berkeley himself, notwithstanding his reputation for tyranny, wrote repeatedly of "prized liberty" as the birthright of an Englishman.

The first William Fitzhugh often wrote of Magna Carta and the "fundamental laws of England," with no sense of contradiction between his Royalist politics and libertarian principles. Fitzhugh argued that Virginians were both "natural subjects to the king" and inheritors of the "laws of England," and when they ceased to be these things, "then we are no longer freemen but slaves."

Similar language was used by many English-speaking people in the seventeenth and eighteenth century. The fine-spun treatises on liberty which flowed so abundantly from English pens in this era were rationales for political folkways deeply embedded in the cultural condition of Englishmen.

These English political folkways did not comprise a single libertarian tradition. They embraced many different and even contradictory conceptions of freedom. The libertarian ideas that took root in Virginia were very far removed from those that went to Massachusetts. In place of New England's distinctive idea of ordered liberty, the Virginians thought of liberty as a hegemonic condition of dominion over others and—equally important—dominion over oneself. . . .

Virginia ideas of hegemonic liberty conceived of freedom manly as the power to rule, and not to be overruled by others. Its opposite was "slavery," a degradation into which true-born Butons descended when they lost their power to rule. . . .

It never occurred to most Virginia gentlemen that liberty belonged to everyone. It was thought to be the special birthright of free-born Englishmen—a property which set this "happy breed" apart from other mortals, and gave them a right to rule less fortunate people in the world. Even within their own society, hegemonic liberty was a hierarchical idea. One's status in Virginia was defined by the liberties that one possessed. Men of high estate were thought to have more liberties than others of lesser rank. Servants possessed few liberties, and slaves none at all. This libertarian idea had nothing to do with equality. Many years later, John Randolph of Roanoke summarized his ancestral creed in a sentence: "I am an aristocrat," he declared, "I love liberty; I hate equality."

In Virginia, this idea of hegemonic liberty was thought to be entirely consistent with the institution of race slavery. A planter demanded for himself the liberty to take away the liberties of others—a right of *laisser asservir*, freedom to enslave. The growth of race slavery in turn deepened the cultural significance of hegemonic liberty, for an Englishman's rights became his rank, and set him apart from others less fortunate than himself. The world thus became a hierarchy in which people were ranked according to many degrees of unfreedom, and they received their rank by the operation of fortune, which played so large a part in the thinking of Virginians. At the same time, hegemony over others allowed them to enlarge the sphere of their own personal liberty, and to create the conditions within which their special sort of libertarian consciousness flourished. . . .

Hegemonic liberty was a dynamic tradition which developed through at least three historical stages. In the first it was linked to Royalist cause in the English Civil War. The Virginia gentleman Robert Beverley boasted that the colony "was famous, for holding out the longest for the Royal Family, of any of the English Dominions." Virginia was the last English territory to relinquish its allegiance to Charles I, and the first to proclaim Charles II king in 1660 even before the Restoration in England. Speeches against the Stuarts were ferociously punished by the county courts. The Assembly repeatedly expressed its loyalty to the Crown, giving abundant thanks for "his Majesty's most gracious favors towards us, and Royal Condescensions to anything requisite."

In the second stage, hegemonic liberty became associated with Whiggish politics, and with an ideology of individual independence which was widely shared throughout the English-speaking world. In Virginia, many families who had been staunch Royalists in the seventeenth century became strong Whigs in eighteenth century; by the early nineteenth century they would be Jeffersonian Republicans. Their principles throughout tended to be both elitist and libertarian—a clear expression of a cultural ethic which was capable of continuing expansion. . . .

In the nineteenth and twentieth centuries, the tradition of hegemonic liberty entered a third stage of development, in which it became less hierarchical and more egalitarian. Such are the conditions of modern life that this idea is no longer the exclusive property of a small elite, and the degradation of others is no longer necessary to their support. The progress of political democracy has admitted everyone to the ruling class. In America and Britain today, the idea of an independent elite, firmly in command of others, has disappeared. But the associated idea of an autonomous individual, securely in command of self, is alive and flourishing. . . .

❧

. . . Quakers believed in an idea of reciprocal liberty that embraced all humanity, and was written in the golden rule.

This Christian idea was reinforced in Quaker thinking by an exceptionally strong sense of English liberties. As early as 1687, William Penn ordered the full text of the Magna Carta to be reprinted in Philadelphia, together with a broad selection of other constitutional documents. His purpose was to remind the freeholders of Pennsylvania to remember their British birthright. . . .

On the subject of liberty, the people of Pennsylvania needed no lessons from their Lord Proprietor. Few public questions were introduced among the colonists without being discussed in terms of rights and liberties. On its surface, this libertarian rhetoric seemed superficially similar to that of Massachusetts and Virginia. But the founders of Pennsylvania were a different group of Englishmen—a later generation, from another English region, with a special kind of Christian faith. Their idea of liberty was not the same as that which came to other parts or British America.

The most important of these differences had to do with religious freedom— "liberty of conscience." William Penn called it. This was not the conventional Protestant idea of liberty to do only that which is right. The Quakers believed that liberty of conscience extended even to ideas that they believed to be wrong. Their idea of "soul freedom" protected every Christian conscience.

The most articulate spokesman for this idea was William Penn himself. Of nearly sixty books and pamphlets that Penn wrote before coming to America, half were defenses of liberty of conscience. Some of these works were among the most powerful statements ever written on this subject. One ended with a revealing personal remark: ". . . tis a matter of great satisfaction to the author that he has so plainly cleared his conscience in pleading for the liberty of other men's." . . .

William Penn's personal experience of religious persecution gave him other reasons for believing in religious liberty. His own sufferings convinced him that the coercion of conscience was not merely evil but futile, and deeply dangerous to true faith. "They subvert all true religion," Penn wrote, ". . . where men believe not because 'tis false, but so commanded by their superiors."

These memories and experiences were not Penn's alone. In the period from 1661 to 1685, historians estimate that at least 15,000 Quakers were imprisoned in England, and 450 died for their beliefs. As late as the year 1685, more than 1,400 Quakers were still languishing in English jails. Most "books of sufferings" recorded punishments that continued well into the eighteenth century—mostly fines and seizures for nonpayment of tithes. . . .

Many Quaker immigrants to Pennsylvania had experienced this religious persecution; they shared a determination to prevent its growth in their own province. The first fundamental law passed in Pennsylvania guaranteed liberty of conscience for all who believed in "one Almighty God," and established complete freedom of worship. It also provided penalties for those who "derided the religion of others." The Quaker founders of Pennsylvania were not content merely to restrain government from interfering with rights of conscience. They also made it an instrument of positive protection. Here was a reciprocal idea of religious liberty which they actively extended to others as well as themselves.

Liberty of conscience was one of a large family of personal freedoms which Quakers extended equally to others. William Penn recognized three secular "rights of an Englishman": first, a "right and title to your own lives, liberties and estates: second, representative government; third, trial by jury." In Pennsylvania, these liberties went far beyond those of Massachusetts, Virginia and old England itself. . . .

The Quakers of the Delaware Valley also differed from other English-speaking people in regard to race slavery. The question was a difficult one for them. The first generation of Quakers had been deeply troubled by slavery, but many were not opposed outright. The problem was compounded in the Delaware Valley by the fact that slavery worked well as an economic institution in this region. Many Quakers bought slaves. Even William Penn did so. Of the leaders of the Philadelphia Yearly Meeting for whom evidence survives, 70 percent owned slaves in the period from 1681 to 1705.

But within the first decade of settlement a powerful antislavery movement began to develop in the Delaware Valley. As early as 1688, the Quakers of Germantown issued a testimony against slavery on the ground that it violated the golden rule. In 1696, two leading Quakers, Cadwalader Morgan and William Southeby, urged the Philadelphia Yearly Meeting to forbid slavery and slave trading. The meeting refused to go that far, but agreed to advise Quakers "not to encourage the bringing in of any more Negroes." As antislavery feeling expanded steadily among Friends, slaveowning declined among leaders of the Philadelphia yearly meeting—falling steadily from 70 percent before 1705, to only 10 percent after 1756.

The Pennsylvania legislature took action in 1712, passing a prohibitive duty on the importation of slaves. This measure was disallowed by the English Crown, which had a heavy stake in the slave trade. In 1730 the Philadelphia yearly meeting cautioned its members, but still a few Friends continued to buy slaves. Other Quaker antislavery petitions and papers followed in increasing number. . . . The argument came down to the reciprocal principle of the golden rule. Quakers argued that if they did not wish to be slaves themselves, they had no right to enslave others. . . .

The Quakers radically redefined the "rights of Englishmen" in terms of their Christian beliefs. But they never imagined that they were creating something new. Penn and others in the colony wrote always of their rights as "ancient" and "fundamental" principles which were rooted in the immemorial customs of the English-speaking people and in the practices of the primitive church.

In the conservative cast of their libertarian thinking, the Quakers were much the same as Puritans and Anglicans. But in the substance of their libertarian thought they were very different. In respect to liberty of conscience, trial by jury, the rights of property, the rule of representation, and race slavery, Quakers genuinely believed that every liberty demanded for oneself should also be extended to others. . . .

Backcountry Freedom Ways: The Border Idea of Natural Liberty

The backsettlers, no less than other colonists in every part of British America, brought with them a special way of thinking about power and freedom, and a strong attachment to their liberties. As early as the middle decades of the eighteenth century their political documents contained many references to liberty as their British birthright. In 1768, the people of Mecklenberg County, North Carolina, declared, "We shall ever be more ready to support the government under which we find the most liberty."

No matter whether they came from . . . England or Scotland or Ireland, their libertarian ideas were very much alike—and profoundly different from notions of liberty that had been carried to Massachusetts, Virginia and Pennsylvania. The traveler Johann Schoepf was much interested in ideas of law and liberty which he found in the backcountry. "They shun everything which appears to demand of them law and order, and anything that preaches constraint," Schoepf wrote of the backsettlers. "They hate the name of a justice, and yet they are not transgressors. Their object is merely wild. Altogether, natural freedom . . . is what pleases them."

This idea of "natural freedom" was widespread throughout the southern back settlements. But it was not a reflexive response to the "frontier" environment, not was it "merely wild." as Schoepf believed. The backcountry idea of natural liberty was created by a complex interaction between the American environment and a European folk culture. It derived in large part from the British border country, where anarchic violence had long been a condition of life. The natural liberty of the borderers was an idea at once more radically libertarian, more strenuously hostile to ordering institutions than were the other cultures of British America. . . .

A leading advocate of natural liberty in the eighteenth century was Patrick Henry, a descendant of British borderers, and also a product of the American backcountry. Throughout his political career, Patrick Henry consistently defended the principles of minimal government, light taxes, and the right of armed resistance to authority in all cases which infringed liberty. . . .

Patrick Henry's principles of natural liberty were drawn from the political folkways of the border culture in which he grew up. He embibed them from his mother, a lady who described the American Revolution as merely another set of "lowland troubles." The libertarian phrases and thoughts which echoed so strongly in the backcountry had earlier been heard in the borders of North Britain. When the backcountry people celebrated the supremacy of private interests they used the same thoughts and words as William Cotesworth, an English borderer who in 1717 declared: ". . . you know how natural it is to pursue private interest even against that Darling principle of a more general good. . . . It is the interest of the Public to be served by the man that can do it cheapest, though several private persons are injured by it."

This idea of natural liberty was not a reciprocal idea. It did not recognize the right of dissent or disagreement. Deviance from cultural norms was rarely tolerated: opposition was suppressed by force. One of Andrew Jackson's early biographers observed that "It appears to be more difficult for a North-of-Irelander than for other men to allow an honest difference of opinion in an opponent, so that he is apt to regard the terms opponent and enemy as synonymous.

When backcountrymen moved west in search of that condition of natural freedom which Daniel Boone called "elbow room," they were repeating the thought of George Harrison, a North Briton who declared in the borderlands during the seventeenth century that "every man at nature's table has a right to elbow room." The southern frontier provided space for the realization of this ideal, but it did not create it.

This libertarian idea of natural freedom as "elbow room" was very far from the ordered freedom of New England towns, the hegemonic freedom of Virginia's county oligarchs, and the reciprocal freedom of Pennsylvania Quakers. Here was yet another freedom way which came to be rooted in the Culture of an American region, where it flourished for many years to come.

POSTSCRIPT

Was Colonial Culture Uniquely American?

Although Nash and Fischer approach the issue of American exceptionalism from different perspectives, both recognize uniqueness in American society. Fischer's America is obviously a product of an Old World English cultural heritage. By emphasizing the impact on America of the distinct folkways of peoples migrating from four different geographical regions in the British Isles, however, Fischer reinforces the notion of a unique quality to American culture, one grounded in British folkways. Unfortunately, this Anglocentric argument leaves no room for cultural contributions from Native Americans and Africans, or Germans, Dutch, and Swedes. Nash, on the other hand, suggests that we examine the numerous non-English and non-European elements of American culture. His appreciation of cultural pluralism is developed in greater detail in *Red, White, and Black: The Peoples of Early America*, 3d ed. (Prentice Hall, 1992).

Another significant issue in the study of our cultural origins is the question of their impact on the American character. Frederick Jackson Turner's "The Significance of the Frontier in American History," a paper read at the annual meeting of the American Historical Association in 1893, reflects the views of Crevecoeur and Tocqueville by asserting that a unique national character developed out of America's frontier experience. The Turner thesis remained a hot topic of historical debate for three-quarters of a century as Turnerians and anti-Turnerians discussed the fine details of the impact of the frontier on American national character. The staunchest disciple of Turner was Ray Allen Billington, whose *The Far Western Frontier, 1830–1860* (Harper & Row, 1956), *The Frontier Heritage* (Holt, Rinehart, 1966), and *Frederick Jackson Turner* (Oxford University Press, 1973) should be examined by interested students. An important extension of the Turner thesis is offered in David M. Potter, *People of Plenty: Economic Abundance and the American Character* (University of Chicago, 1954), which identifies another factor contributing to a distinctive American character. Michael Kammen's *People of Paradox: An Inquiry Concerning the Origins of American Civilization* (Knopf, 1972) argues that American distinctiveness derives from the contradiction produced by a culture created from an interaction of Old and New World patterns. Students interested in pursuing these questions of culture and character should examine Michael McGiffert, ed., *The Character of Americans: A Book of Readings*, rev. ed. (Dorsey Press, 1970) and David Stannard, "American Historians and the Idea of National Character," *American Quarterly* (May 1971).

Finally, on the topic of American exceptionalism, students should consult Seymour Martin Lipset, *The First New Nation: The United States in Historical and Comparative Perspective* (Basic Books, 1963) and *American Exceptionalism: A*

Double-Edged Sword (W. W. Norton, 1996). Critics of exceptionalism are represented in Daniel Bell's "The End of American Exceptionalism," *Public Interest* (Fall 1975) and Laurence Veysey, "The Autonomy of American History Reconsidered," *American Quarterly* (Fall 1979). Michael Kammen's "The Problem of American Exceptionalism: A Reconsideration," *American Quarterly* (March 1993) presents a valuable summary of both sides of the debate.

ISSUE 4

Were the First Colonists in the Chesapeake Region Ignorant, Lazy, and Unambitious?

YES: Edmund S. Morgan, from *American Slavery, American Freedom: The Ordeal of Colonial Virginia* (W. W. Norton, 1975)

NO: Russell R. Menard, from "From Servant to Freeholder: Status Mobility and Property Accumulation in Seventeenth-Century Maryland," *William and Mary Quarterly* (January 1973)

ISSUE SUMMARY

YES: Professor Edmund S. Morgan argues that Virginia's first decade as a colony was a complete "fiasco" because the settlers were too lazy to engage in the subsistence farming necessary for their survival and failed to abandon their own and the Virginia's company's expectations of establishing extractive industries such as mining, timber, and fishing.

NO: According to Professor Russell R. Menard, the indentured servants of seventeenth-century Maryland were hardworking, energetic, and young individuals who went through two stages of history: From 1640 to 1660 servants provided large planters with an inexpensive labor force, but they also achieved greater wealth and mobility in the Chesapeake than if they remained in England; after 1660 opportunities for servants to achieve land, wealth, and status drastically declined.

Until the 1970s American history textbooks ignored the seventeenth century once the colonies were founded. The new social history that has incorporated ordinary people—not just elite white males, but common white males, females, African-Americans, women, and Indians—has added a whole new dimension to the colonial period. Racial, class, gender, and sectional differences emerge, and for the first time historians clearly distinguished the seventeenth and eighteenth centuries.

The English were latecomers in colonizing the new world. Earlier voyages by John Cabot in 1497 and 1498 around Canada were not followed up in the same way the Spaniards established colonies in Latin America. Before Jamestown there were notable failures at colonization.

The first permanent English settlements were established in the Chesapeake Bay region—Virginia in 1607 and Maryland in 1634. There were many similarities between the two colonies. Both colonies started out with charters granted by the British monarchy. Both experienced economic hardships in the beginning. Relations with the Indians were strained. Mortality rates were higher in New England because of the hot climates and concomitant rampant diseases so few lived past the age of 45. Combined with late marriages, the population growth was low. Only sustained immigration from England prevented the two colonies from collapsing in their first two decades.

One major difference between Virginia and Maryland was the fact that Virginia was the first "successful" English colony. It became the model for the mistakes that other colonies tried to avoid. The Jamestown settlement, which the 105 colonists (39 died at sea) had established in May 1607, bartered with the Indians for corn, but even Captain John Smith could not trade for enough food or force the settlers to stop arguing among themselves and plant crops. Only 38 of the original settlers survived until January 1608 when a fresh supply of food and 120 new settlers arrived from England. Still the experiences of the first year did not prevent the "starving time" of the winter of 1609–1610 when several of the inhabitants resorted to eating their deceased family members.

In the first selection, Professor Edmund Morgan is highly critical of the first settlers of Virginia. Others have pointed out that the earliest immigrants came from the "gentlemen" class and lacked the farming skills necessary for survival. But Morgan puts as much of the blame on the policies of the Virginia company and the London government as he does on the settlers. Even after the "starving time," the survivors and the new immigrants continued to pursue extraction industries such as gold, silver, iron mining, fishing, and lumber and silk binding at the expense of subsistence agriculture.

In the second selection, Professor Russell R. Menard describes the indentured servants who came to Maryland in the years from 1640 to 1690 to make up for the shortage of labor in the Chesapeake Bay until slave labor filled this void in the eighteenth century. Because land and jobs were scarce, many English migrants indentured their services to a ships' captain for passage to the New World. The captain in turn sold the contract to a craftsman or farmer, which bound over the servant for a term that lasted around five years. Upon completion of the contract, these servants would receive their "freedom dues"—usually three barrels of corn, a suit of clothes, and access to 50 acres of land if they could fulfill the requirements.

How well did the servants fare after they were freed? According to Professor Menard, there were two periods for Maryland's indentured servants. In the years from 1640 to 1660, servants were treated well and upon completion of their indentures moved from renters to landowners and often attained positions of wealth and power. After 1660 the dramatic rise in the population accompanied by increasing land prices and falling tobacco prices made it harder for the newly freed indentured servants to achieve land ownerships, power, and status. In the eighteenth century, the Chesapeake became a less egalitarian and more stratified society.

YES

Edmund S. Morgan

The Jamestown Fiasco

The first wave of Englishmen reached Virginia at Cape Henry, the southern headland at the opening of Chesapeake Bay, on April 26, 1607. The same day their troubles began. The Indians of the Cape Henry region (the Chesapeakes), when they found a party of twenty or thirty strangers walking about on their territory, drove them back to the ships they came on. It was not the last Indian victory, but it was no more effective than later ones. In spite of troubles, the English were there to stay. They spent until May 14 exploring Virginia's broad waters and then chose a site that fitted the formula Hakluyt had prescribed. The place which they named Jamestown, on the James (formerly Powhatan) River, was inland from the capes about sixty miles, ample distance for warning of a Spanish invasion by sea. It was situated on a peninsula, making it easily defensible by land; and the river was navigable by oceangoing ships for another seventy-five miles into the interior, thus giving access to other tribes in case the local Indians should prove as unfriendly as the Chesapeakes.

Captain Christopher Newport had landed the settlers in time to plant something for a harvest that year if they put their minds to it. After a week, in which they built a fort for protection, Newport and twenty-one others took a small boat and headed up the river on a diplomatic and reconnoitering mission, while the settlers behind set about the crucial business of planting corn. Newport paused at various Indian villages along the way and assured the people, as best he could, of the friendship of the English and of his readiness to assist them against their enemies. Newport gathered correctly from his attempted conversations that one man, Powhatan, ruled the whole area above Jamestown, as far as the falls at the present site of Richmond. His enemies, the Monacans, lived above the falls (where they might be difficult to reach if Powhatan proved unfriendly). Newport also surmised, incorrectly, that the Chesapeake Indians who had attacked him at Cape Henry were not under Powhatan's dominion. He accordingly tried to make an alliance against the Chesapeakes and Monacans with a local chief whom he mistook for Powhatan. At the same time, he planted a cross with the name of King James on it (to establish English dominion) and tried to explain to the somewhat bewildered and justifiably suspicious owners of the country that one arm of the cross was Powhatan, the other himself, and that the fastening of them together signified the league between them.

If the Indians understood, they were apparently unimpressed, for three days later, returning to Jamestown, Newport found that two hundred of Powhatan's warriors had attacked the fort the day before and had only been prevented from destroying it by fire from the ships. The settlers had been engaged in planting and had not yet unpacked their guns from the cases in which they were shipped. That was a mistake they were not likely to repeat. But for the next ten years they seem to have made nearly every possible mistake and some that seem almost impossible. It would take a book longer than this to recount them all, and the story has already been told many times. But if we are to understand the heritage of these ten disastrous years for later Virginia history, we should look at a few of the more puzzling episodes and then try to fathom the forces behind them.

Skip over the first couple of years, when it was easy for Englishmen to make mistakes in the strange new world to which they had come, and look at Jamestown in the winter of 1609–10. It is three planting seasons since the colony began. The settlers have fallen into an uneasy truce with the Indians, punctuated by guerrilla raids on both sides, but they have had plenty of time in which they could have grown crops. They have obtained corn from the Indians and supplies from England. They have firearms. Game abounds in the woods; and Virginia's rivers are filled with sturgeon in the summer and covered with geese and ducks in the winter. There are five hundred people in the colony now. And they are starving. They scour the woods listlessly for nuts, roots, and berries. And they offer the only authentic examples of cannibalism witnessed in Virginia. One provident man chops up his wife and salts down the pieces. Others dig up graves to eat the corpses. By spring only sixty are left alive.

Another scene, a year later, in the spring of 1611. The settlers have been reinforced with more men and supplies from England. The preceding winter has not been as gruesome as the one before, thanks in part to corn obtained from the Indians. But the colony still is not growing its own corn. The governor, Lord De la Warr, weakened by the winter, has returned to England for his health. His replacement, Sir Thomas Dale, reaches Jamestown in May, a time when all hands could have been used in planting. Dale finds nothing planted except "some few seeds put into a private garden or two." And the people he finds at "their daily and usuall workes, bowling in the streetes."

It is evident that the settlers, failing to plant for themselves, depend heavily on the Indians for food. The Indians can finish then off at any time simply by leaving the area. And the Indians know it One of them tells the English flatly that "we can plant any where . . . and we know that you cannot live if you want [i.e., lack] our harvest, and that reliefe we bring you." If the English drive out the Indians, they will starve. . . .

It is not easy to make sense out of the behavior displayed in these episodes. How to explain the suicidal impulse that led the hungry English to destroy the corn that might have fed them and to commit atrocities upon the people who grew it? And how to account for the seeming unwillingness or incapacity of the English to feed themselves? Although they had invaded Indian territory and quarreled with the owners, the difficulty of obtaining land was not great. The Indians were no match for English weapons. Moreover, since the Indians could afford to give up the land around Jamestown as well as Henrico without seriously endangering their own economy, they made no concerted effort to drive the English out. Although Indian attacks may have prevented the English from getting a crop into the ground in time for a harvest in the fall of 1607, the occasional Indian raids thereafter cannot explain the English failure to grow food in succeeding years. How, then, can we account for it?

The answer that comes first to mind is the poor organization and direction of the colony. The government prescribed by the charter placed full powers in a council appointed by the king, with a president elected by the other members. The president had virtually no authority of his own; and while the council lasted, the members spent most of their time bickering and intriguing against one another and especially against the one man who had the experience and the assurance to take command. The names of the councillors had been kept secret (even from themselves) in a locked box, until the ships carrying the first settlers arrived in Virginia. By that time a bumptious young man named John Smith had made himself unpopular with Captain Christopher Newport (in command until their arrival) and with most of the other gentlemen of consequence aboard. When they opened the box, they were appalled to find Smith's name on the list of councillors. But during the next two years Smith's confidence in himself and his willingness to act while others talked overcame most of the handicaps imposed by the feeble frame of government. It was Smith who kept the colony going during those years. But in doing so he dealt more decisively with the Indians than with his own quarreling countrymen, and he gave an initial turn to the colony's Indian relations that was not quite what the company had intended. . . .

In their relations to the Indians, as in their rule of the settlers, the new governing officers of the colony were ruthless. The guerrilla raids that the two races conducted against each other became increasingly hideous, especially on the part of the English. Indians coming to Jamestown with food were treated as spies. Gates had them seized and killed "for a Terrour to the Reste to cawse them to desiste from their subtell practyses." Gates showed his own subtle practices by enticing the Indians at Kecoughtan (Point Comfort) to watch a display of dancing and drumming by one of his men and then "espyeinge a fitteinge oportunety fell in upon them putt fyve to the sworde wownded many others some of them beinge after fownde in the woods with Sutche extreordinary Lardge and mortall wownds that itt seemed strange they Cold flye so far." It is possible that the rank and file of settlers aggravated the bad relations with the Indians by unauthorized attacks, but unauthorized fraternization seems to have bothered the governors more. The atrocities committed against the queen of the Paspaheghs, though apparently demanded by the men, were the work of the governing officers, as were the atrocities committed against the Englishmen who fled to live with the Indians.

John Smith had not had his way in wishing to reduce the Indians to slavery, or something like it, on the Spanish model. But the policy of his successors, though perhaps not with company approval made Virginia look far more like the Hispaniola of Las Casas that it did when Smith was in charge.

And the company and the colony had few benefits to show for all the rigor. At the end of ten years, in spite of the military discipline of work gangs, the colonists were still not growing enough to feed themselves and were still begging, bullying, and buying corn from the Indians whose lands they scorched so deliberately. We cannot, it seems, blame the colony's failures on lax discipline and diffusion of authority. Failures continued and atrocities multiplied after authority was made absolute and concentrated in one man.

Another explanation, often advanced, for Virginia's early troubles, and especially for its failure to feed itself, is the collective organization of labor in the colony. All the settlers were expected to work together in a single community effort, to produce both the food and the exports that would make the company rich. Those who held shares would ultimately get part of the profits, but meanwhile the incentives of private enterprise were lacking. The work a man did bore no direct relation to his reward. The laggard would receive as large a share in the end as the man who worked hard.

The communal production of food seems to have been somewhat modified after the reorganization of 1609 by the assignment of small amounts of land to individuals for private gardens. It is not clear who received such allotments, perhaps only those who came at their own expense. Men who came at company expense may have been expected to continue working exclusively for the common stock until their seven-year terms expired. At any rate, in 1614, the year when the first shipment of company men concluded their service, Governor Dale apparently assigned private allotments to them and to other independent "farmers." Each man got three acres, or twelve acres if he had a family. He was responsible for growing his own food plus two and a half barrels of corn annually for the company as a supply for newcomers to tide them over the first year. And henceforth each "farmer" would work for the company only one month a year.

By this time Gates and Dale had succeeded in planting settlements at several points along the James as high up as Henrico, just below the falls. The many close-spaced tributary rivers and creeks made it possible to throw up a palisade between two of them to make a small fortified peninsula. Within the space thus enclosed by water on three sides and palisaded on the fourth, the settlers could build their houses, dig their gardens, and pasture their cattle. It was within these enclaves that Dale parceled out private allotments. Dignified by hopeful names like "Rochdale Hundred" or "Bermuda City," they were affirmations of an expectation that would linger for a century, that Virginia was about to become the site of thriving cities and towns. In point of fact, the new "cities" scarcely matched in size the tiny villages from which Powhatan's people threatened them. And the "farmers" who huddled together on the allotments assigned to them proved incapable of supporting themselves or the colony with adequate supplies of food.

At first it seemed to sympathetic observers that they would. Ralph Hamor, in an account of the colony published in 1615, wrote, "When our people were fedde out of the common store and laboured jointly in the manuring of the ground and planting corne, glad was that man that could slippe from his labour, nay the most honest of them in a generall businesse, would not take so much faithfull and true paines in a weeke, as now he will doe in a day, neither cared they for the increase, presuming that howsoever their harvest prospered, the generall store must maintain them, by which meanes we reaped not so much corne from the labours of 30 men, as three men have done for themselves."

According to John Rolfe, a settler who had married John Smith's fair Pocahontas, the switch to private enterprise transformed the colony's food deficit instantly to a surplus: instead of the settlers seeking corn from the Indians, the Indians sought it from them. If so, the situation did not last long. Governor Samuel Argall, who took charge at the end of May, 1617, bought 600 bushels from the Indians that fall, "which did greatly relieve the whole Colonie." And when Governor George Yeardley relieved Argall in April, 1619, he found the colony "in a great scarcity for want of corn" and made immediate preparations to seek it from the Indians, If, then, the colony's failure to grow food arose from its communal organization of production, the failure was not overcome by the switch to private enterprise.

Still another explanation for the improvidence of Virginia's pioneers is one that John Smith often emphasized, namely, the character of the immigrants. They were certainly an odd assortment, for the most conspicuous group among them was an extraordinary number of gentlemen. Virginia, as a patriotic enterprise, had excited the imagination of England's nobility and gentry. The shareholders included 32 present or future earls, 4 countesses, and 3 viscounts (all members of the nobility) as well as hundreds of lesser gentlemen, some of them perhaps retainers of the larger men. Not all were content to risk only their money. Of the 105 settlers who started the colony, 36 could be classified as gentlemen. In the first "supply" of 120 additional settlers, 28 were gentlemen, and in the second supply of 70, again 28 were gentlemen. These numbers gave Virginia's population about six times as large a proportion of gentlemen as England had.

Gentlemen, by definition, had no manual skill, nor could they be expected to work at ordinary labor. They were supposed to be useful for "the force of knowledge, the exercise of counsell"; but to have ninety-odd wise men offering advice while a couple of hundred did the work was inauspicious, especially when the wise men included "many unruly gallants packed thether by their friends to escape il destinies" at home.

What was worse, the gentlemen were apparently accompanied by the personal attendants that gentlemen thought necessary to make life bearable even in England. The colony's laborers "were for most part footmen, and such as they that were Adventurers brought to attend them, or such as they could perswade to goe with them, that never did know what a dayes worke was." Smith complained that he could never get any real work from more than thirty out of two hundred, and he later argued that of all the people sent to Virginia, a hundred good laborers "would have done more than a thousand of those that went." Samuel Argall and John Rolfe also argued that while a few gentlemen would have been useful to serve as military leaders, "to have more to wait and play than worke, or more commanders and officers than industrious labourers was not so necessarie."

The company may actually have had little choice in allowing gentlemen and their servants to make so large a number of their settlers. The gentlemen were paying their own way, and the company perhaps could not afford to deny them. But even if unencumbered by these volunteers, the colony might have foundered on the kind of settlers that the company itself did want to send. What the company wanted for Virginia was a variety of craftsmen. Richard Hakluyt had made up a list for Walter Raleigh that suggests the degree of specialization contemplated in an infant settlement: Hakluyt wanted both carpenters and joiners, tallow chandlers and wax chandlers, bowstave preparers and bowyers, fletchers and arrowhead makers, men to rough-hew pikestaffs and other men to finish them. In 1610 and again in 1611 the Virginia Company published lists of the kind of workers it wanted. Some were for building, making tools, and other jobs needed to keep the settlers alive, but the purpose of staying alive would be to see just what Virginia was good for and then start sending the goods back to England. Everybody hoped for gold and silver and jewels, so the colony needed refiners and mineral men. But they might have to settle for iron, so send men with all the skills needed to smelt it. The silk grass that Hariot described might produce something like silk, and there were native mulberry trees for growing worms, so send silk dressers. Sturgeon swam in the rivers, so send men who knew how to make caviar. And so on. Since not all the needed skills for Virginia's potential products were to be found in England, the company sought them abroad: glassmakers from Italy, millwrights from Holland, pitch boilers from Poland, vine dressers and salt-makers from France. The settlers of Virginia were expected to create a more complex, more varied economy than England itself possessed. As an extension of England, the colony would impart its variety and health to the mother country.

If the company had succeeded in filling the early ships for Virginia with as great a variety of specialized craftsmen as it wanted, the results might conceivably have been worse than they were. We have already noticed the effect of specialization in England itself, where the division of labor had become a source not of efficiency but of idleness. In Virginia the effect was magnified. Among the skilled men who started the settlement in 1607 were four carpenters, two bricklayers, one mason (apparently a higher skill than bricklaying), a blacksmith, a tailor, and a barber. The first "supply" in 1608 had six tailors, two goldsmiths, two refiners, two apothecaries, a blacksmith, a gunner (i.e., gunsmith?), a cooper, a tobacco pipe maker, a jeweler, and a perfumer. There were doubtless others, and being skilled they expected to be paid and fed for doing the kind of work for which they had been hired. Some were obviously useful. But others may have found themselves without means to use their special talents. If they were conscientious, the jeweler may have spent some time looking for jewels, the goldsmiths for gold, the perfumer for something to make perfume with. But when the search proved futile, it did not follow that they should or would exercise their skilled hands at any other tasks. It was not suitable for a perfumer or a jeweler or a goldsmith to put his hand to the hoe. Rather, they could join the gentlemen in genteel loafing while a handful of ordinary laborers worked at the ordinary labor of growing and gathering food.

The laborers could be required to work at whatever they were told to; but they were, by all accounts, too few and too feeble. The company may have rounded them up as it did in 1609 when it appealed to the mayor of London to rid the city of its "swarme of unnecessary inmates" by sending to Virginia any who were destitute and lying in the streets.

The company, then, partly by choice, partly by necessity, sent to the colony an oversupply of men who were not prepared to tackle the work essential to settling in a wilderness. In choosing prospective Virginians, the company did not look for men who would be particularly qualified to keep themselves alive in a new land. The company never considered the problem of staying alive in Virginia to be a serious one. And why should they have? England's swarming population had had ample experience in moving to new areas and staying alive. The people who drifted north and west into the pasture-farming areas got along, and the lands there were marginal, far poorer than those that awaited the settlers of tidewater Virginia. Though there may have been some farmers among the early settlers, no one for whom an occupation is given was listed as a husbandman or yeoman. And though thirty husbandmen were included in the 1611 list of men wanted, few came. As late as 1620 the colony reported "a great scarcity, or none at all" of "husbandmen truely bred," by which was meant farmers from the arable regions. In spite of the experience at Roanoke and in spite of the repeated starving times at Jamestown, the company simply did not envisage the provision of food as a serious problem. They sent some food supplies with every ship but never enough to last more than a few months. After that people should be able to do for themselves.

The colonists were apparently expected to live from the land like England's woodland and pasture people, who gave only small amounts of time to their small garden plots, cattle, and sheep and spent the rest in spinning, weaving, mining, handicrafts, and loafing. Virginians would spend their time on the more varied commodities of the New World. To enable them to live in this manner, the company sent cattle, swine, and sheep: and when Dale assigned them private plots of land, the plots were small, in keeping with the expectation that they would not spend much time at farming. The company never intended the colony to supply England with grain and did not even expect that agricultural products might be its principal exports. They did want to give sugar, silk, and wine a try, but most of the skills they sought showed an expectation of setting up extractive industries such as iron mining, smelting, saltmaking, pitch making, and glassmaking. The major part of the colonists' work time was supposed to be devoted to processing the promised riches of the land for export; and with the establishment of martial law the company had the means of seeing that they put their shoulders to the task.

Unfortunately, the persons charged with directing the motley work force had a problem, quite apart from the overload of gentlemen and specialized craftsmen they had to contend with. During the early years of the colony they could find no riches to extract. They sent back some cedar wood, but lumber was too bulky a product to bear the cost of such long transportation to market. Sassafras was available in such quantities that the market for it quickly collapsed. The refiners found no gold or silver or even enough iron to be worth mining. Silk grass and silk proved to be a will-o'-the-wisp.

The result was a situation that taxed the patience both of the leaders and of the men they supervised. They had all come to Virginia with high expectations. Those who came as servants of the company had seven years in which to make their employers rich. After that they would be free to make themselves rich. But with no prospect of riches in sight for anybody, it was difficult to keep them even at the simple tasks required for staying alive or to find anything else for them to do.

The predicament of those in charge is reflected in the hours of work they prescribed for the colonists, which contrast sharply with those specified in the English Statute of Artificers. There was no point in demanding dawn-to-dusk toil unless there was work worth doing. When John Smith demanded that men work or starve, how much work did he demand? By his own account, "4 hours each day was spent in worke, the rest in pastimes and merry exercise." The governors who took charge after the reorganization of 1609 were equally modest in their demands. William Strachey, who was present, described the work program under Gates and De la Warr in the summer of 1610:

> It is to be understood that such as labor are not yet so taxed but that easily they perform the same and ever by ten of the clock they have done their morning's work: at what time they have their allowances [of food] set out ready for them, and until it be three of the clock again they take their own pleasure, and afterward, with the sunset, their day's labor is finished.

The Virginia Company offered much the same account of this period. According to a tract issued late in 1610, "the setled times of working (to effect all themselves, or the Adventurers neede desire) [require] no more pains then from six of clocke in the morning untill ten and from two of the clocke in the afternoone till foure." The long lunch period described here was spelled out in the *Lawes Divine, Morall and Martiall.* If we calculate the total hours demanded of the work gangs between the various beatings of the drum, they come to roughly five to eight hours a day in summer and three to six hours in winter. And it is not to be supposed that these hours refer only to work done in the fields and that the men were expected to work at other tasks like building houses during the remainder of the day. The *Laws* indicate that at the appointed hours every laborer was to repair to his work "and every crafts man to his occupation, Smiths, Joyners, Carpenters, Brick makers, etc." Nor did military training occupy the time not spent in working. The *Laws* provided for different groups to train at different times and to be exempt from work during the training days. Although colonists and historians alike have condemned the *Laws* as harsh, and with reason, the working hours that the code prescribed sound astonishingly short to modern ears. They certainly fell way below those demanded at the time in English law; and they seem utterly irrational in a chronically starving community.

To have grown enough corn to feed the colony would have required only a fraction of the brief working time specified, yet it was not grown. Even in their free time men shunned the simple planting tasks that sufficed for the Indians.

And the very fact that the Indians did grow corn may be one more reason why the colonists did not. For the Indians presented a challenge that Englishmen were not prepared to meet, a challenge to their image of themselves, to their self-esteem, to their conviction of their own superiority over foreigners, and especially over barbarous foreigners like the Irish and the Indians.

If you were a colonist, you knew that your technology was superior to the Indians'. You knew that you were civilized, and they were savages. It was evident in your firearms, your clothing, your housing, your government, your religion. The Indians were supposed to be overcome with admiration and to join you in extracting riches from the country. But your superior technology had proved insufficient to extract anything. The Indians, keeping to themselves, laughed at your superior methods and lived from the land more abundantly and with less labor than you did. They even furnished you with the food that you somehow did not get around to growing enough of yourselves. To be thus condescended to by heathen savages was intolerable. And when your own people started deserting in order to live with them, it was too much. If it came to that, the whole enterprise of Virginia would be over. So you killed the Indians, tortured them, burned their villages, burned their cornfields. It proved your superiority in spite of your failures. And you gave similar treatment to any of your own people who succumbed to the savage way of life. But you still did not grow much corn. That was not what you had come to Virginia for.

By the time the colony was ten years old and an almost total loss to the men who had invested their lives and fortunes in it, only one ray of hope had appeared. It had been known, from the Roanoke experience, that the Indians grew and smoked a kind of tobacco; and tobacco grown in the Spanish West Indies was already being imported into England, where it sold at eighteen shillings a pound. Virginia tobacco had proved, like everything else, a disappointment; but one of the settlers, John Rolfe, tried some seeds of the West Indian variety, and the result was much better. The colonists stopped bowling in the streets and planted tobacco in them—and everywhere else that they could find open land. In 1617, ten years after the first landing at Jamestown, they shipped their first cargo to England. It was not up to Spanish tobacco, but it sold at three shillings a pound.

To the members of the company it was proof that they had been right in their estimate of the colony's potential. But the proof was bitter. Tobacco had at first been accepted as a medicine, good for a great variety of ailments. But what gave it its high price was the fact that people had started smoking it for fun. Used this way it was considered harmful and faintly immoral. People smoked it in taverns and brothels. Was Virginia to supplement England's economy and redeem her rogues by pandering to a new vice? The answer, of course, was yes. But the men who ran the Virginia Company, still aiming at ends of a higher nature, were not yet ready to take yes for an answer.

Russell R. Menard

 **NO**

From Servant to Freeholder: Status Mobility and Property Accumulation in Seventeenth-Century Maryland

. . . Miles Gibson, Stephen Sealus, and William Scot all arrived in Maryland as indentured servants in the 1660s. They completed their terms and soon accumulated enough capital to purchase land. Thereafter, their careers diverged sharply. Gibson, aided by two good marriages, gained a place among the local gentry and served his country as justice of the peace, burgess, and sheriff. At his death in 1692, he owned more than two thousand acres of land and a personal estate appraised at over six hundred pounds sterling, including nine slaves. Sealus's career offers a sharp contrast to that of his highly successful contemporary. He lost a costly court case in the mid-1670s and apparently was forced to sell his plantation to cover the expenses. He spent the rest of his days working other men's land. By 1691, Sealus was reduced to petitioning the county court for relief. He was "both weake and lame," he pleaded, "and not able to worke whereby to maintaine himselfe nor his wife." His petition was granted, but the Sealus family remained poor. Stephen died in 1696, leaving an estate appraised at £18 6s. William Scot did not approach Gibson's success, but he did manage to avoid the dismal failure of Sealus. He lived on his small plantation for nearly forty years, served his community in minor offices, and slowly accumulated property. In his will, Scot gave all seven of his sons land of their own and provided his three daughters with small dowries. Although interesting in themselves, these brief case histories do not reveal very much about the life chances of servants in the seventeenth century. They do suggest a range of accomplishment, but how are we to tell whether Scot, Sealus, or Gibson is most typical, or even if any one of them represents the position that most servants attained? Did servitude offer any hard-working Englishman without capital a good chance of becoming, like Miles Gibson, a man of means and position in a new community? Or did servitude only offer, as it finally offered Stephen Sealus, a chance to live in poverty in another place? Perhaps Scot was more typical. Did servitude promise poor men a chance to obtain moderate prosperity and respectability for themselves and their families? How much property and status mobility did most servants manage to

From *William & Mary Quarterly*, 3rd ser. XXX (1973), by Russell R. Menard. Copyright © 1973 by Omohundro Institute of Early American History & Culture. Reprinted by permission.

achieve in the seventeenth century? This essay examines the careers of a group of men who immigrated to Maryland in the seventeenth century in order to provide some of the data needed for answers to such questions.

The study of mobility requires an assessment of a man's position in society for at least two points in his career, a task that the general absence of census materials, tax lists, and assessment records makes difficult. Nevertheless, a study of mobility among servants is possible because we know their place in the social structure at the beginning of their careers in the New World. Servants started at the bottom of white society: they entered the colonies with neither freedom nor capital. Since we can define their position on arrival, measuring the degree of success they achieved is a fairly simple task. We can, as the capsule biographies of Gibson, Sealus, and Scot demonstrate, describe their progress in the New World. A study of the fortunes of indentured servants and the way those fortunes changed over time provides a sensitive indicator of the opportunities available within colonial society.

The broadest group under study in this essay consists of 275 men who entered Maryland as servants before the end of 1642, although the main concern is with 158 for whom proof exists that they survived to be freemen. Not all the men who came into Maryland as servants by 1642 are included in the 275. No doubt a few servants escape any recorded mention, while others appear who are not positively identified as servants. One large group falling into this latter category included 66 men, not specifically called servants, who were listed in the proofs of headrights as having been transported into the colony at the expense of someone else to whom they were not related. It is probable that all of these men emigrated under indentures, but since proof was lacking they have been excluded from the study.

The mortality rate among these servants was probably high. One hundred and seventeen of the 275—more than 40 percent—did not appear in the records as freemen. The deaths of 14 of the missing are mentioned, but we can only speculate on the fate of most of the servants who disappeared. Some may have been sold out of the province before their terms were completed, and some may have run away, while others may have left Maryland immediately after becoming freemen. A majority probably died while still servants, victims of the unusual climate, poor food, ill housing, hard work, or an occasional cruel master, before they had a chance to discover for themselves if America was a land of opportunity.

For the 158 who definitely survived the rigors of servitude, opportunity was abundant. Seventy-nine to 81 (identification is uncertain in two cases) of the survivors, about 50 percent, eventually acquired land in Maryland. To be properly interpreted, however, this figure must be understood within the context of the careers of those who failed to acquire land. Fourteen of those who survived servitude but did not acquire land in Maryland died within a decade of completing their terms. Another 25 left before they had lived in the colony for ten years as freemen. These figures are conservative, for they include only those for whom death or migration can be proven. Twenty-five of the 158 survivors appear only briefly in the records and then vanish without a trace, presumably among the early casualties or emigrants. Furthermore, there is no reason to believe that those who left were any less successful than those who remained. At least 11 of the 25 known emigrants became landowners in Virginia. Only 13 to 15 of the 158 servants who appeared in the records as freemen (less than 10 percent) lived for more than a decade in Maryland as freemen without becoming landowners.

Those who acquired land did so rapidly. The interval between achieving freedom and acquiring land, which was discovered in forty-six cases, ranged from two years for Richard Nevill and Phillip West to twelve for John Norman and Walter Walterlin. Francis Pope, for whom the interval was seven years, and John Maunsell, who took eight, came closer to the median of seven and one-half years.

The holdings of the vast majority of those who acquired land were small. Most lived as small planters on tracts ranging in size from fifty acres to four hundred acres, although fourteen former servants managed to become large landowners, possessing at least one thousand acres at one time in their lives. Zachary Wade, who owned over four thousand acres at his death in 1678 and about five thousand acres in the early 1670s, ranked with the largest landowners in Maryland.

Inventories of personal estates, taken at death, have survived for 31 of the 158 former servants. Analysis of the inventories reinforces the conclusion that most of these men became small planters. About 60 percent of the inventories show personal property appraised at less than one hundred pounds sterling. Men whose estates fell into this range led very simple lives. In most cases, livestock accounted for more than half the total value of their personal possessions. At best their clothing and household furnishings were meager. They either worked their plantations themselves or with the help of their wives and children, for few of these small planters owned servants and even fewer owned slaves. In Aubrey Land's apt phrase, they led lives of "rude sufficiency." But they fared no better than if they had remained in England.

Not all former servants remained small planters. Twelve of the thirty-one left estates appraised at more than one hundred pounds. Men such as John Halfhead, Francis Pope, and James Walker could be described as substantial planters. Their life style was not luxurious, but their economic position was secure and their assets usually included a servant or two and perhaps even a slave. Two men, Zachary Wade and Henry Adams, gained entry into the group of planter-merchants who dominated the local economy in the seventeenth century. Wade, whose estate was appraised at just over four hundred pounds, was wealthier than 95 percent of his contemporaries, while Adams left an estate valued at £569 15s. 1d. when he died in 1686.

There are still other measures of mobility which confirm the picture of abundant opportunity for ex-servants that the study of property accumulation has indicated. Abbot E. Smith has estimated that only two of every ten servants brought to America in the seventeenth century became stable and useful members of colonial society, but if we take participation in government as indicative of stability and usefulness, the careers of the 158 men who survived servitude demonstrate that Smith's estimates are much too low, at least for the earlier part of the century.

Former servants participated in the government of Maryland as jurors, minor office holders, justices of the peace, sheriffs, burgesses, and officers in the militia. Many also attended the Assembly as freemen at those sessions at which they were permitted. The frequency with which responsible positions were given to ex-servants testifies to the impressive status mobility they achieved in the mid-seventeenth century. Seventy-five or seventy-six of the survivors—just under 50 percent—sat on a jury, attended an Assembly session, or filled an office in Maryland. As was the case with landholding, this figure must be understood in light of the careers of those who failed to participate. Fourteen of the nonparticipants died within a decade of becoming freemen; another twenty-seven left the province within ten years of completing their terms. There is no reason to assume that those who left did not participate in their new homes—two of the twenty-seven, John Tue and Mathew Rhodan, became justices of the peace in Virginia, while two others, Thomas Yewell and Robert Sedgrave, served as militia officer and clerk of a county court respectively. If we eliminate the twenty-five who appeared but fleetingly in the records, only sixteen or seventeen (slightly more than 10 percent) lived for more than a decade in the province as freemen without leaving any record of contribution to the community's government.

For most former servants participation was limited to occasional service as a juror, an appointment as constable, or service as a sergeant in the militia. Some compiled remarkable records in these minor positions. William Edwin, who was brought into the province in 1634 by Richard Gerard and served his time with the Jesuits, sat on nine provincial court juries and served a term as constable. Richard Nevill, who also entered Maryland in 1634, served on six provincial court juries and was a sergeant in the militia. A former servant of Gov. Leonard Calvert, John Halfhead, served on eleven juries and attended two sessions of the Assembly. John Robinson managed, in five years before his death in 1643, to attend two Assemblies, sit on three provincial court juries, and serve as constable and coroner of St. Clement's Hundred.

A high percentage of the 158 survivors went beyond service in these minor posts to positions of authority in the community. Twenty-two of them served the province as justice of the peace, burgess, sheriff, councillor, or officer in the militia. They accounted for four of Maryland's militia officers, twelve burgesses, sixteen justices, seven sheriffs, and two members of the Council.

For nine of the twenty-two former servants who came to hold major office in Maryland, tenure was brief. They served for a few years as an officer in the militia or as a county justice, or sat as burgess in a single session of the Assembly. . . .

Although the personal history of each of these 158 men is unique, common patterns may be discerned. We can construct a career model for indentured servants in Maryland in the middle of the seventeenth century which should reveal something about the way opportunity was structured and what options were open to men at various stages in their lives. We can also identify some of the components necessary for constructing a successful career in Maryland.

As a group, the indentured servants were young when they emigrated. While they ranged in age from mere boys such as Ralph Hasleton to the "old and decripit" Original Browne, the great majority were in their late teens and early twenties. Age on arrival was determined in thirty-six cases with a median of nineteen. Probably most were from English families of the "middling sort," yeomen, husbandmen, and artisans, men whose expectations might well include the acquisition of a freehold or participation in local government.

The careers of these men suggest that a few had formal education. Robert Vaughan and Robert Sedgrave both served as clerks in county court, a position requiring record-keeping skills. Cuthbert Fenwick was attorney to Thomas Cornwallis, who was probably the wealthiest man in Maryland in the 1630s and 1640s. It seems unlikely that Cornwallis would have allowed a man without education to manage his estate during his frequent absences from the province. These men were, however, not at all typical, for most of the 158 survivors were without education. Total illiterates outnumbered those who could write their names by about three to two, and it is probable that many who could sign their names could do little more.

A servant's life was not easy, even by seventeenth-century standards. Probably they worked the ten to fourteen hours a day, six days a week, specified in the famous Elizabethan Statute of Artificers. Servants could be sold, and there were severe penalties for running away. They were subject to the discipline of their masters, including corporal punishment within reason. On the other hand, servants had rights to adequate food, clothing, shelter, and a Sunday free from hard labor. Servants could not sue at common law, but they could protest ill-treatment and receive a hearing in the courts. Cases in this period are few, but the provincial court seems to have taken seriously its obligation to enforce the terms of indentures and protect servants' rights. No instances of serious mistreatment of servants appear in the records in the late 1630s and early 1640s. Servants were worked long and hard, but they were seldom abused. Moreover, the servant who escaped premature death soon found himself a free man in a society that offered great opportunities for advancement.

None of the indentures signed by these servants has survived, but it is possible to offer some reasonable conjecture concerning the terms of their service. John Lewger and Jerome Hawley, in their *Relation of Maryland,* offered some advice to men thinking of transporting servants into the province and they also printed a model indenture. A servant was to work at whatever his master "shall there imploy him, according to the custome of the Countrey." In return, the master was to pay his passage and provide food, lodging, clothing, and other "necessaries" during the servant's term "and at the end of the said term, to give him one whole yeeres provision of Corne, and fifty acres of Land, according to the order of the countrey." The order or custom of the country was specified in an act passed by the October 1640 session of the Assembly. Upon completion of his term the servant was to receive "one good Cloth Suite of Keirsey or Broadcloth a Shift of white linen one new pair of Stockins and Shoes two hoes one axe 3 barrels of Corne and fifty acres of land five whereof at least to be plantable." The land records make it clear that the requirement that masters give their former servants fifty acres of land cannot be taken literally.

In practice, custom demanded only that a master provide a servant with the rights for fifty acres, an obligation assumed by the proprietor in 1648. If a servant wished to take advantage of this right and actually acquire a tract, he had to locate some vacant land and pay surveyor's and clerk's fees himself.

The usual term of service, according to Lewger and Hawley, was five years. However, they suggested, "for any artificer, or one that shall deserve more than ordinary, the Adventurer shall doe well to shorten that time . . . rather then to want such usefull men." A bill considered but not passed by the 1639 Assembly would have required servants arriving in Maryland without indentures to serve for four years if they were eighteen years old or over and until the age of twenty-four if they were under eighteen. The gap between time of arrival and first appearance in the records as freemen for the men under study suggests that the terms specified in this rejected bill were often followed in practice.

Servants were occasionally able to work out arrangements with their masters which allowed them to become freemen before their terms were completed. John Courts and Francis Pope purchased their remaining time from Fulke Brent, probably arranging to pay him out of whatever money they could earn by working as freemen. Thomas Todd, a glover, was released from servitude early by his master, John Lewger. In return, Todd was to dress a specified number of skins and also to make breeches and gloves to Lewger. George Evelin released three of his servants, Philip West, William Williamson, and John Hopson, for one year, during which they were to provide food, clothing, and lodging for themselves and also pay Evelin one thousand pounds of tobacco each. Such opportunities were not available to all servants, however, and most probably served full terms.

On achieving freedom there were three options open to the former servant: he could either hire out for wages, lease land and raise tobacco on his own, or work on another man's plantation as a sharecropper. Although custom demanded that servants be granted the rights to fifty acres of land on completing their terms, actual acquisition of a tract during the first year of freedom was simply impracticable, and all former servants who eventually became freeholders were free for at least two years before they did so. To acquire land, one had to either pay surveyor's and clerk's fees for a patent or pay a purchase price to a landholder. The land then had to be cleared and housing erected. Provisions had to be obtained in some way until the crop was harvested, for a man could not survive a growing season on a mere three barrels of corn. Tools, seed, and livestock were also necessary. All this required capital, and capital was precisely what servants did not have. Wage labor, sharecropping, and leaseholding all offered men a chance to accumulate enough capital to get started on their own plantations and to sustain themselves in the meantime.

Wages were high in mid-seventeenth-century Maryland, usually fifteen to twenty pounds of tobacco per day for unskilled agricultural labor and even higher for those with much needed skills. These were remarkable rates given the fact that a man working alone could harvest, on the average, no more than fifteen hundred to two thousand pounds of tobacco a year. Thirty-two of the

158 survivors were designated artisans in the records: 11 carpenters, 4 black-smiths, 5 tailors, 4 sawyers, 2 millwrights, a brickmason, mariner, cooper, glover, and barber-surgeon. These men probably had little trouble marketing their skills. At a time when labor was scarce, even men who had nothing but a strong back and willing hands must have found all the work they wanted. However, few of the 158 men devoted themselves to full time wage labor for extended periods. Instead, most worked their own crop and only hired out occasionally to supplement their planting income.

Nevertheless, some men did sign contracts or enter into verbal agree-ments for long-term wage labor. There were some differences between their status and that of indentured servants. They probably could not be sold, they could sue at common law for breach of covenant, and they may have possessed some political privileges. There were severe restrictions on their personal free-dom, however, and their daily life must have been similar to a servant's. Wages ranged from eleven hundred to fifteen hundred pounds of tobacco a year plus shelter, food, and clothing. Ex-servants occasionally hired out for long terms, perhaps because of heavy indebtedness or lack of alternative opportunities, or perhaps because of the security such contracts afforded. Recently freed ser-vants may have found long-term wage contracts an attractive means of making the transition from indentured laborer to free colonist. While long-term wage labor was, in a sense, a prolongation of servitude, it could also serve as a means of capital accumulation and an avenue of mobility.

The records reveal little of the extent or conditions of sharecropping in the 1640s, but it is clear that several of the 158 former servants did work on another man's plantation for a share of the crop. By the 1660s—and there seems no reason to assume that this was not also the case in the earlier period—working for a "share" meant that a man joined other workers on a plantation in making a crop, the size of his share to be determined by dividing the total crop by the number of laborers. Contracts often required the planta-tion owner to pay the cropper's taxes and provide diet, lodging, and washing, while obliging the cropper to work at other tasks around the plantation. The status of such sharecroppers seems indistinguishable from that of wage laborers on long-term contracts.

Most of the 158 former servants established themselves as small planters on leased land immediately after they had completed their terms. There were two types of leases available to ex-servants, leaseholds for life or for a long term of years and short-term leaseholds or tenancies at will. Although these forms of leaseholding differed in several important respects, both allowed the tenant to become the head of a household. As householders, former bonds-men achieved a degree of independence and a measure of responsibility denied to servants, wage laborers, and sharecroppers. Heads of households were masters in their own families, responsible for the discipline, education, and maintenance of their subordinates. They formed the backbone of the political community, serving on juries, sitting in Assembly, and filling the minor offices. The favorable man/land ratio in early Maryland made the for-mation of new households a fairly easy task and servants usually became householders soon after completing their terms.

In many ways there was little difference between land held in fee simple and a lease for life or for a long term of years. Such leases were inheritable and could be sold; they were usually purchased for a lump sum and yearly rents were often nominal. Terms varied considerably, but all long-term leaseholds provided the tenant a secure tenure and a chance to build up equity in his property. Such leases were not common in seventeenth-century Maryland, although a few appear on the private manors in St. Mary's County in the 1640s. Probably men were reluctant to purchase a lease when they could acquire land in fee simple for little additional outlay.

Tenancies at will or short-term leaseholds, usually running for no more than six or seven years, were undoubtedly the most common form of tenure for recently freed servants. In contrast to long-term leases, short-term leaseholds offered little security, could not be sold or inherited, and terminated at the death of either party to the contract. Their great advantage was the absence of an entry fee, a feature particularly attractive to men without capital. Since land was plentiful and labor scarce, rents must have been low, certainly no higher than five hundred pounds of tobacco a year for a plantation and perhaps as low as two hundred pounds. Rent for the first year, furthermore, was probably not demanded until after the crop was in. No contracts for the 1640s have survived, but later in the century tenants were often required to make extensive improvements on the plantation. Although tenure was insecure, short-term leaseholding afforded ample opportunity for mobility as long as tobacco prices remained high. In the 1640s and 1650s, leaseholding benefited both landlord and tenant. Landlords had their land cleared, housing erected, and orchards planted and fenced while receiving a small rental income. Tenants were able to accumulate the capital necessary to acquire a tract of their own.

Prior to 1660, small planters, whether leaseholders or landowners, frequently worked in partnership with another man when attempting to carve new plantations out of the wilderness. Much hard work was involved in clearing land, building shelter, and getting in a crop; men who could not afford to buy servants or pay wages often joined with a mate. Partners Joseph Edlow and Christopher Martin, John Courts and Francis Pope, John Shirtcliffe and Henry Spinke, and William Brown and John Thimbelly were all former servants who arrived in Maryland before the end of 1642. They must have found their "mateships" mutually beneficial, since, except for Martin who died in 1641, all eventually became landowners.

Some men—about 10 percent of those former servants who lived in Maryland for more than a decade as freemen—did not manage to escape tenancy. Rowland Mace, for example, was still a leaseholder on St. Clement's Manor in 1659, after which he disappeared from the records. The inventory of the estate of Charles Steward, who lived on Kent Island as a freeman for more than forty years and was frequently called planter, indicates that he was operating a plantation when he died in 1685, but Steward failed to acquire freehold title to a tract of his own. A few others acquired land, held it briefly, and then returned to leaseholding arrangements. John Maunsell had some prosperous years in Maryland. He arrived in the province in 1638 as a servant to William Bretton and served about four years. He patented one hundred acres in 1649 and added five hundred more in 1651, but he could not hold the land and in 1653 sold it all to William Whittle. He then moved to St. Clement's Manor, where he took up a leasehold, and was still a tenant on the manor when he died in 1660. John Shanks, although he too suffered fluctuations in prosperity, ended his career on a more positive note. Entering Maryland in 1640 as a servant to Thomas Gerard, he must have been quite young when he arrived, for he did not gain his freedom until 1648. In 1652 he patented two hundred acres and also purchased the freedom of one Abigail, a servant to Robert Brooke, whom he soon married. He sold his land in 1654, and, following Maunsell's path, took up a leasehold on St. Clement's Manor. Shanks, however, managed to attain the status of a freeholder again, owning three hundred acres in St. Mary's County when he died in 1684. His inventory—the estate was appraised at just under one hundred pounds—indicates that Shanks ended life in Maryland as a fairly prosperous small planter.

Most of the 158 former servants, if they lived in Maryland for more than ten years as freemen, acquired land and held it for as long as they remained in the province. Almost any healthy man in Maryland in the 1640s and 1650s, if he worked hard, practiced thrift, avoided expensive lawsuits, and did not suffer from plain bad luck, could become a landowner in a short time. Tobacco prices were relatively high, and, while living costs may also have been high, land was not expensive. Even at the highest rates a one hundred-acre tract could be patented for less than five hundred pounds of tobacco, and even the lowest estimates indicate that a man could harvest twelve hundred pounds in a year. Again barring ill-health and misfortune, retaining land once acquired must not have been too difficult a task, at least before tobacco prices fell after the Restoration.

Hard work and thrift were, of course, not the only paths to landownership. For some the fruits of office cleared the way. William Empson, for example, was still a tenant to Thomas Baker in 1658, after ten years of freedom. In 1659, Nicholas Gwyther employed him as deputy sheriff, and in the next year Empson was able to purchase a plantation from his former landlord. Others charmed their way to the status of freeholder. Henry Adams married Mary Cockshott, daughter of John Cockshott and stepdaughter of Nicholas Causine, both of whom were substantial Maryland planters. To the historian, though perhaps not to Adams, Miss Cockshott's most obvious asset was twelve hundred acres of land which her mother had taken up for her and her sister Jane in 1649.

For most former servants progress stopped with the acquisition of a small plantation. Others managed to go beyond small planter status to become men of wealth and power. What was it that distinguished the 13 former servants who became men of importance in Maryland politics from the other 145 who survived servitude?

Education was one factor. We have already seen that a few of the 158 probably possessed some formal training. Early colonial Maryland did not have enough educated men to serve as justices or sheriffs, perform clerical and surveying functions, or work as attorneys in the courts. Under such conditions, a man proficient with the pen could do quite well for himself. Men such as Cuthbert Fenwick, Robert Vaughan, and Robert Sedgrave found their education valuable in making the transition from servant to man of consequence. While approximately 60 percent of the 158 who survived servitude were totally illiterate, only 2 of the 13 who came to exercise real power in Maryland and only 7 of the 22 who held major office were unable to write their names.

Marriage played a role in some of the most impressive success stories. Henry Adams's marriage has already been mentioned. Zachary Wade married a niece of Thomas Hatton, principal secretary of Maryland in the 1650s. James Langsworth married a Gardiner thereby allying himself with a very prominent southern Maryland family. Cuthbert Fenwick married at least twice. We know nothing of his first wife, but Fenwick found fame and fortune by marrying in 1649 Jane Moryson, widow of a prominent Virginian, a niece of Edward Eltonhead, one of the masters of chancery, and a sister of William Eltonhead, who sat on the Maryland Council in the 1650s.

It would be a mistake, however, to overestimate the significance of education and marriage in the building of a successful career. Certainly they helped, but they were not essential ingredients. Nicholas Gwyther became a man of consequence in Maryland, but married a former servant. John Warren served as justice of St. Mary's County for nine years, but could not write his name. Daniel Clocker and John Maunsell both held major office in Maryland. Both were illiterate and both married former servants. Clearly, Maryland in the middle of the seventeenth century was open enough to allow a man who started at the bottom without special advantages to acquire a substantial estate and a responsible position.

It seems probable that Maryland continued to offer ambitious immigrants without capital a good prospect of advancement throughout the 1640s and 1650s. But there is evidence to suggest that opportunities declined sharply after 1660. True, the society did not become completely closed and some men who started life among the servants were still able to end life among the masters. Miles Gibson is a case in point, and there were others. Philip Lynes emigrated as a servant in the late 1660s and later became a member of the Council and a man of considerable wealth. Christopher Goodhand, who also entered Maryland as a servant in the late 1660s, later served as justice of Kent County and left an estate appraised at nearly six hundred pounds. However, in the latter part of the century men such as Gibson, Goodhand, and Lynes were unusual; at mid-century they were not. . . .

This reduction in the proportion of former servants among Maryland's rulers is directly related to basic demographic processes that worked fundamental changes in the colony's political structure. The rapid growth in the population of the province during the seventeenth century affected the life chances of former servants in at least two ways. First, there was a reduction in the number of offices available in proportion to the number of freemen, resulting in increased competition for positions of power and profit. Secondly, there was an increase in the number of men of wealth and status available to fill positions of authority. In the decades immediately following the founding of the province there were simply not enough men who conformed to the standards people expected their rulers to meet. As a consequence, many uneducated small planters of humble origins were called upon to rule. Among the immigrants to Maryland after the Restoration were a number of younger sons of English gentry families and an even larger number of merchants, many of whom were attracted to the Chesapeake as a result of their engagement in the tobacco trade. By the late seventeenth century, these new arrivals, together with a steadily growing number of native gentlemen, had created a ruling group with more wealth, higher status, and better education than the men who had ruled earlier in the century. As this group grew in size, poor illiterate planters were gradually excluded from office. . . .

Former servants also found that their chances of acquiring land and of serving as jurors and minor office holders were decreasing. Probably the movement of prices for tobacco and land was the most important factor responsible for this decline of opportunity. During the 1640s and 1650s, the available evidence—which, it must be admitted, is not entirely satisfactory—indicates that farm prices for Chesapeake tobacco fluctuated between one and one-half and three pence per pound. After 1660, prices declined due to overproduction, mercantilist restrictions, and a poorly developed marketing system that allowed farm prices to sink far below those justified by European price levels. . . .

One consequence of these price changes was a change in the nature and dimensions of short-term leaseholding. In the 1640s and 1650s, tenancy was a typical step taken by a man without capital on the road to land acquisition. However, falling tobacco prices and rising land prices made it increasingly difficult to accumulate the capital necessary to purchase a freehold. In the 1660s fragmentary results suggest that only 10 percent of the householders in Maryland were established on land they did not own. By the end of the century the proportion of tenants had nearly tripled. Tenancy was no longer a transitory status; for many it had become a permanent fate.

A gradual constriction of the political community paralleled the rise *in* tenancy. In years immediately following settlement, all freemen, whether or not they owned land, regularly participated in government as voters, jurors and minor office holders. At the beginning of the eighteenth century a very different situation prevailed. In a proclamation of 1670, Lord Baltimore disfranchised all freemen who possessed neither fifty acres of land nor a visible estate worth forty pounds sterling. This meant, in effect, that short-term leaseholders could no longer vote, since few could meet the forty pounds requirement. Furthermore, by the early eighteenth century landowners virtually monopolized jury duty and the minor offices. In the middle of the seventeenth century, most freemen in Maryland had an ample opportunity to acquire land and participate in community government; by the end of the century a substantial portion of the free male heads of households were excluded from the political process and unable to become landowners. . . .

From 1662 to 1672, 179 servants were brought into the Charles County Court to have their ages judged. Only 58 of the 179 definitely appeared in the records as freemen, a fact which in itself suggests declining opportunities, since there does seem to be a relationship between a man's importance in the community and the frequency of his appearance in the public records. Of the

58 of whom something could be learned, only 13 to 17—22 to 29 percent— eventually became landowners. Furthermore, none acquired great wealth. Mark Lampton, who owned 649 acres in the early 1690s, was the largest land- owner in the group and the only one who owned more than 500 acres. Robert Benson, whose estate was appraised at just over two hundred pounds, left the largest inventory. Lampton was the only other one of the 58 whose estate was valued at more than one hundred pounds.

A study of the participation of these men in local government indicates that opportunities in this field were also declining. Only twenty-three to twenty-five of the fifty-eight sat on a jury or filled an office, and the level at which they participated was low. Only one, Henry Hardy, who was appointed to the Charles County bench in 1696, held major office. A few others com- piled impressive records as minor office holders. Mathew Dike, for example, sat on eight juries and served as overseer of the highways and constable, while Robert Benson was twice a constable and fourteen times a juryman. For most of these men, however, occasional service as a juror was the limit of their par- ticipation. Five of the twenty-three known participants served only once as a juror, while another six only sat twice.

The contrast between the careers of these 58 men and the 158 who entered Maryland before 1642 is stark. At least 46 of the 58 lived in the prov- ince as freemen for over a decade. In other words, 50 to 57 percent lived in Maryland as freemen for more than ten years and did not acquire land, while 36 to 40 percent did not participate in government. Only about 10 percent of the 158 who arrived in the earlier period and lived in the colony for a decade as freemen failed to become landowners and participants.

How successful, then, in the light of these data, was the institution of servitude in seventeenth-century Maryland? The answer depends on perspec- tive and chronology. Servitude had two primary functions. From the master's viewpoint its function was to supply labor. From the point of view of the pro- spective immigrant without capital, servitude was a means of mobility, both geographic and social; that is, it was a way of getting to the New World and, once there, of building a life with more prosperity and standing than one could reasonably expect to attain at home. Its success in performing these two quite different functions varied inversely as the century progressed. Prior to 1660, servitude served both purposes well. It provided large planters with an inexpensive and capable work force and allowed poor men entry into a soci- ety offering great opportunities for advancement. This situation in which the two purposes complemented each other did not last, and the institution grad- ually became more successful at supplying labor as it became less so at provid- ing new opportunities. Some men were always able to use servitude as an avenue of mobility, but, over the course of the century, more and more found that providing labor for larger planters, first as servants and later as tenants, was their permanent fate.

POSTSCRIPT

Were the First Colonists in the Chesapeake Region Ignorant, Lazy, and Unambitious?

Professor Edmund S. Morgan is the preeminent colonial American historian who has trained three generations of scholars at Yale University. Now in his eighties, Morgan is still a productive scholar writing books and review essays for the *New York Review of Books* on the latest output of scholarship in the field. For a convenient compilation of Morgan's essays, see *The Genuine Article: A Historian Looks at Early America* (Norton, 2004).

Morgan's chapter on the "Jamestown Fiasco" is important for several reasons. First of all, he rejects the New England model of colonization as being typical. Earlier generations of colonial historians wrote a lot about the Puritans because they kept extensive written legal and church records as well as diaries—all of which provided historians with an abundance of traditional historical sources. Morgan anticipated the framework of Jack P. Greene, *Pursuits of Happiness: The Social Development of Early Modern British Colonies and the Formation of American Culture* (University of North Carolina Press, 1988) and others who see the Chesapeake settlements (and not New England) as typical of the expansionist policies of the British empire in Ireland and the West Indies. He also implies that the original colonists were trying to imitate the Spaniards to the extent that they hoped to extract mineral wealth from the colonists for export such as iron ore, salt making, glass making, silk making, and pitch. Unfortunately these resources were not available in the original Virginia settlements.

Professor Morgan also dispatches the romantic view that many historians attributed to the colonists. He discusses in other parts of his book the "guerilla warfare" that existed between the first European settlers and the Indians. Though earlier historians have focused on the hardships of the first Virginians and the starving time of the winter of 1609–1610 that led to cannibalism. Morgan blames the colonists themselves for their plight. The colonists did not take advantage of the abundance of fish and game in Virginia nor did they plant enough grain and corn to feed themselves. Why this occurred was partly due to the social backround of the earliest settlers—too many "gentlemen" and not enough farmers. But Morgan extends his argument even further. The colonists modeled themselves after their English kin and hoped to set up small industries producing exports with agriculture as only a minor part of the economy. As previously mentioned the mineral resources did not exist. Ironically Virginia became a productive colony in later decades when tobacco became the export of salvation.

Professor Russell R. Menard is part of the group of Chesapeake scholars who have mined the records of the Maryland archives, which contain county records of land deeds, land sales, slave transactions, indentured servant contracts, marriages, probation of wills, and contested court cases. Because the population of seventeenth century Maryland was relatively small, increasing from 4,018 in 1660 to 34,172 in 1700, quantitative historians can study large aggregates of the seventeenth century population and get answers to questions about average family sizes, mortality rates, trade patterns, consumption habits, economic wealth, and mobility patterns.

Menard's study of the social mobility in seventeenth century Maryland employs modern sociological concepts in studying the records of the indentured servants found in the Maryland archives. By studying the land records and indentured contracts for the various southern and eastern shore Maryland counties found in the Maryland archives, Menard argues that the first generation of the newly freed indentured servants were upwardly mobile, and achieved land ownership, and sizeable amounts of wealth and political offices.

But Menard argues that the second generations of servants freed in the 1660s and thereafter achieved limited success due to the lack of good cheap land, fluctuating and often downward tobacco prices, and the inability to achieve political offices.

Professors Morgan and Menard disagree on the quality and backgrounds of the earliest settlers to Virginia and Maryland, respectively. Perhaps Maryland's indentured servants were better because the founders of Maryland profited from the mistakes of England's first successful colony. Perhaps the traditional sources used by Morgan and the quantitative by Menard lend themselves to differing interpretations. But both historians agree that by 1700 both Virginia and Maryland created a more stratified society with a wealthy planter class tied into tobacco growing where slave labor replaced the indentured servants as the major workforce.

The starting point for the modern study of *Seventeenth Century America: Essays in Colonial History,* ed. by James Norton Smith (University of North Carolina Press, 1959), are the essays by Bernard Bailyn, "Politics and Social Structure in Virginia" and Mildred Campbell's "Social Origins of Some Early Americans," the latter's middle-class origins challenged by David Galenson's books and articles. See for example "'Middling People' or 'Common Sort'? The Social Origins of Some Early Americans Reexamined . . ." with Campbell's rebuttal in the *William and Mary Quarterly* xxxv/3 (July 1978), pp. 499–540. Both views are challenged by Lorena S. Walsh's study of servants. See "Servitude and Opportunity in Charles County, Maryland, 1658–1705."

Walsh's essay and those of many seventeenth century "cliometricians" can be found in Aubrey C. Land, Lois Green Carr, and Edward C. Papenfuse, *Law, Society and Politics in Early Maryland* (John Hopkins University Press, 1977). See the introductions and the essays in two other important collections: Thad W. Tate and David L. Ammerman, eds., *The Chesapeake in the Seventeenth Century: Essays on Anglo-American Society* (University of North Carolina Press, 1979) and Lois Green Carr, Philip D. Morgan and Jean B. Russo, eds., *Colonial Chesapeake Society* (University of North Carolina Press, 1988).

ISSUE 5

Did Colonial New England Women Enjoy Significant Economic Autonomy?

YES: Gloria L. Main, from "Gender, Work, and Wages in Colonial New England," *The William and Mary Quarterly* (January 1994)

NO: Lyle Koehler, from *A Search for Power: The "Weaker Sex" in Seventeenth-Century New England* (University of Illinois Press, 1980)

ISSUE SUMMARY

YES: Gloria Main notes that New England women were highly valued for their labor and relative scarcity in the early colonial period and that their economic autonomy increased in the years during and following the Seven Years War as more women entered the paid labor force and received higher wages for their work.

NO: Lyle Koehler contends that Puritan attitudes toward rights of inheritance, as well as the division of labor that separated work into male and female spheres, discouraged productive, independent activity on the part of New England women.

Students in American history classes have for generations read of the founding of the colonies in British North America, their political and economic development, and the colonists' struggles for independence, without ever being confronted by a female protagonist in this magnificent historical drama. The terms "sons of liberty" and "founding fathers" reflect the end result of a long tradition of gender-specific myopia. In fact, only in the last generation have discussions of the role of women in the development of American society made their appearance in standard textbooks. Consequently, it is useful to explore the status of women in colonial America.

The topic, of course, is quite complex. The status of colonial women was determined by cultural attitudes that were exported to the New World from Europe, by the specific conditions confronting successive waves of settlers—male and female—in terms of labor requirements, and by changes produced by colonial maturation over time. It would be impossible to pinpoint a single, static condition in which *all* colonial women existed.

What was the status of women in the British North American colonies? To what degree did the legal status of women differ from their *de facto* status? A half-century of scholarship has produced the notion that colonial women enjoyed a more privileged status than either their European contemporaries or their nineteenth-century descendants. In the 1970s John Demos and Roger Thompson reinforced this view developed earlier in the writings of Richard B. Morris, Elizabeth Dexter, and Mary Beard. For example, Demos contends that despite the fact that Plymouth Colony was based on a patriarchal model in which women were expected to subordinate themselves to men, women still shared certain responsibilities with their husbands in some business activities and in matters relating to their children. They not only performed all the household duties but also assisted the men with agricultural duties outside the home when the necessity arose.

Women were closed off from any formal public power in the colony even when they performed essential economic functions within the community. In colonial America and during the American Revolution, they practiced law, pounded iron as blacksmiths, trapped for furs and tanned leather, made guns, built ships, and edited and printed newspapers. At the same time, however, colonial society viewed women as subordinate beings. They held no political power within the individual colonies and still were suspect as the transmitters of evil, simply because they were women. Nor was it a coincidence that most suspected witches were female. Many of those accused of witchcraft in late-seventeenth-century New England were older women who had inherited land that traditionally would have gone to males. Such patterns of inheritance disrupted the normative male-dominated social order. Witchcraft hysteria in colonial America, then, was a by-product of economic pressures *and* gender exploitation.

The following essays explore the economic status of women in colonial New England. Gloria Main compares types of work, pay scales, and trends in wages in the seventeenth and eighteenth centuries and discovers that the division of labor between men and women was less clearly defined than traditionally assumed. Because they were relatively scarce, she concludes, women were valued for their labor and, as time passed, New England women developed a significant degree of economic autonomy.

Lyle Koehler insists that economic and social factors discouraged productive, independent activity on the part of New England women. Given limited opportunities for occupational training and denied access to public schools, most women were resigned to poorly paid jobs. Rarely did they inherit enough to start their own businesses. The only way for most women to experience upward economic mobility, Koehler claims, was to marry well.

YES

Gloria L. Main

Gender, Work, and Wages in Colonial New England

. . . Historians of colonial women . . . tend to ignore economic issues when debating trends in women's status and condition. Most believe that white women were more highly regarded in the colonies than at home, because of the higher value of their labor and their relative scarcity, at least in the seventeenth century in regions such as the Chesapeake. Others posit that economic opportunities for women narrowed as colonial society developed beyond primitive conditions in which women shouldered burdens customarily borne by men. Data presented below lend support to the first proposition but dispute the second.

This article examines the types of work women in early New England did compared to men, weighs relative pay scales, and explores trends in the wages of both sexes. Evidence comes from two types of sources: wage ceilings discussed or imposed by governments in 1670 and 1777 and pay rates found in account books, diaries, and probate records. These sources also supply the basis for estimating women's rates of participation in the paid labor force and for tabulating the types of work women performed for pay. All of this material can be conveniently summarized by dividing the colonial period into four phases: initial growth (1620–1674), crisis and recovery (1675–1714), stability (1715–1754), and expansion (1755–1774). The sequence, however, defies simple linear interpretations of progression, either from good conditions to bad, declension, or from bad conditions to good, progress. Both the status of women and the region's economy experienced cycles of good and bad times, but the closing decades of the period saw real improvement for both. Perhaps the most important lesson of this investigation is that even relatively modest economic changes can, by their cumulative actions, significantly alter family relations and living standards. . . .

Settlers in a new land must find ways to acquire the goods they want and cannot make for themselves. For New Englanders, this proved a major challenge. Probably the most notable characteristic of the economy that is evident in probate inventories was the economy's dependence on England for manufactures of all sorts, including textiles. In the first generation after settlement, few women could have engaged in spinning, weaving, or dyeing simply because

From *William & Mary Quarterly*, vol. LI no. 1, January 1994, by Gloria Main, pp. 41–42, 52–66. Copyright © 1994 by Omohundro Institute of Early American History & Culture. Reprinted by permission.

unprocessed textile fibers were in short supply. "Farmers deem it better for their profit to put away [sell] their cattel and corn for cloathing, then to set upon making of cloth." Flax production was labor intensive, and sheep did not thrive under pioneering conditions: wolves found them easy prey, and the woodland underbrush tore away their wool. By the 1670s these conditions had changed. An aggressive bounty system and the spread of settlements into the interior gradually exterminated the wolves and cleared enough pastureland so that sheep became a more familiar sight on mainland farms. Spinning wheels, mentioned in Plymouth Colony inventories as early as 1644, gradually became common, and most mid-century householders' inventories in Plymouth and neighboring colonies listed wool and flax, and some mention sheep, cotton, and even homemade cloth. Still, textile production must have continued to fall short of potential demand, because few people chose to invest their time in weaving. Of roughly 1,500 inventories dating from before 1675, only thirty, all for men, list looms. Similarly, when Carl Bridenbaugh recorded the occupations of men in the early volumes of Rhode Island land evidences, he identified only one weaver and one cloth worker out of forty-two artisans before 1670.

Nor did many early households possess the tools for such women's tasks as brewing, baking, or dairying. Only a few women appear anywhere in John Pynchon's Connecticut Valley accounts. Of the four women he mentioned in the 1640s, one received pay for chickens and eggs, one for weeding, one for making hay, and the fourth for domestic service. There is no mention of brewing, baking, or butter making, although in 1648 Pynchon paid Henry Burt for making malt, probably from the barley mowed by Richard Excell that year, and Pynchon paid another man for milking his cows in 1666–1667. The first reference to spinning appears in 1663, to knitting in 1668, and to sewing in 1669.

Most of New England's people were farmers. Women who were not tied down by young children probably spent their time outdoors working in gardens or with their men in the fields. Although English women did not customarily do heavy field work, they did garden with hoes, and in the colonies the hoe played a major role wherever families could use existing Indian fields. In early Saybrook Alice Apsley marketed medicinal herbs and onions from her garden. Goody Macksfield supplied a Boston shopkeeper with apples, squashes, beans, cucumbers, carrots, and cabbages, as well as honey, butter, cheese, and eggs. C. Dallett Hemphill examined the work activities of Salem women recorded in testimony before the Essex County court between 1636 and 1683 and found them engaged in men's work or working with men: servant Ann Knight winnowed corn, another woman carried grain to the mill, and others milked cows and branded steers in the company of men; a witness in one case remembered seeing the wife of Joseph Dalaber working alongside her husband planting and covering corn.

. . . [T]he ratio of women's pay to men's pay was at its highest point in this early period when the division of labor between men and women was less clearly defined than in contemporary England or as it later came to be in New England. Women could hoe in already-cleared Indian fields, and meadows and salt marshes supplied their small herds of animals with forage. When these sites filled up and the numbers of livestock expanded, newcomers had to break new ground and create meadows planted with English grasses. Inventories record the gradual advent of a more English farming style using heavy plows drawn by teams of oxen, while tax lists and town genealogies trace the growing supply of sturdy young sons. Similarly, the appearance of spinning wheels, firkins, brewing vats, and dye pots attests to the kinds of activities that came to employ women. The division of labor between the sexes widened and, as it did so, separated them physically.

The use of ox teams, restricted to older men, effectively segregated family members into field and home workers. Men and older boys also did the sowing and harrowing at the beginning of the farm year and the reaping and mowing at harvest. In early spring they planted and pruned orchards and carted and spread dung. In June they washed and sheared sheep. In fall they pressed cider and slaughtered hogs. In the slack seasons men cut and dragged timber, built and maintained fences, cleared underbrush, ditched bogs, and dug out stones. In most of these activities, handling draft animals was essential and was work for males only. The men used oxen to remove stumps and boulders, drag timber, cart dung, and haul hay and horses to drive cider presses. Only men and older boys paddled canoes, steered scows, piloted "gundalows" (gondolas), or rowed boats.

Women participated in none of these activities except at harvest time, when their help was welcomed. Even then, they did not mow grass or grain, because most did not have the height or upper body strength to handle scythes. Diaries after 1750 show them helping with the reaping, probably binding sheaves and sickling wheat and rye. Young Jabez Fitch of Norwich, Connecticut, reported enthusiastically in his diary on July 24, 1759, "there was a great Reeping[;] we Liv'd very well[;] we had Women anough & Some more." A story related in a town history about one woman's feat is no doubt apocryphal but interesting for its celebration of women's physical achievements in a less genteel age: a Mrs. Brown of Chester, New Hampshire, around the year 1800 or earlier, with others had sowed rye for its seed. At harvest time she prepared breakfast, nursed her child, walked five or six miles to the field, reaped her rye (finishing before any of the men), and walked back home.

Men's diaries also describe both sexes and all ages gathering corn by day and husking together at night, making the work an occasion for a frolic. Both sexes and all ages went berrying and nutting together. Young people often turned such occasions to their own devices, especially when gathering strawberries on long June evenings. The excitement these occasions could create is recorded in the diary of a Harvard undergraduate, who, with other young men, succeeded in transforming a quilting party into a late night gala.

Many farm tasks fell more or less exclusively to the female members of the household. Girls and women tended the fowl and small animals. They milked the cows at dawn and dusk, separated the cream, churned the butter, and made the cheese. They planted and hoed kitchen gardens in plots men had prepared by plowing and harrowing. Women boiled the offal for such by-products as sausage casings, head cheese, calf's foot jelly, and rennet after men killed, cleaned, and butchered animals. Gender-based assignment of many farm chores centered on objective differences in body height and strength rather than on what was deemed culturally appropriate to one sex or the other. Females carried out some of the same tasks as younger boys—they helped hay, hoe, weed, harvest crops, and husk corn.

Yet gender ordered male and female spheres in ways that went beyond obvious physical distinctions. For instance, men and older boys not only cut timber but operated sawmills, erected buildings, dug wells and cellars, laid stone, pointed chimneys, and shaved shingles and staves. Men tanned and curried hides, made saddles or gloves, and bound shoes. Older boys got the bark for tanning, shaved it, ground it, and laid the leather away. . . . [S]killed craftsmen in these trades earned substantially more than farm laborers. Females never participated in these activities. Nor did girls drive cattle or carry grain on horseback to the mill, as boys did. Women did not thresh grain, even though boys of thirteen or fourteen did so. Although men and boys traveled abroad freely in their duties, women's work more often kept them inside or near their own home or those of kinsmen or employers. In and around the home they earned income from tasks that males assiduously avoided: cleaning, cooking, sewing, spinning, washing clothes, nursing, and caring for children.

Thus, people allocated work among themselves based on physical capacity but also on gender. The advent of English-style agriculture, involving large draft animals and deep plowing, helped fix many boundaries between the sexes. The case of John Graves II of East Guilford is illustrative. Five daughters and four sons survived infancy; all of them appear in his accounts at one time or another credited for a day's or a week's work. Of the eighty-nine work occasions he recorded between 1703 and 1726 (the year he died), he identified daughters on twenty-one occasions and sons on sixty-eight. Thus, sons appeared more than three times as often. Graves hired occasional male help in addition to his sons and kept a young servant named Thome for two years when his younger boys were too small to hoe, make fences, or mow hay. Meanwhile, his girls did chores—but never farm work—for his neighbors. They sewed, spun, nursed, and kept house.

An account book of great interest because of the economic activities of women that it records is that of merchant Elisha Williams of Wethersfield, Connecticut, a commercial farm town situated on the Connecticut River just south of Hartford. Williams's ledger begins in 1738, and its pages are filled with references to women credited for onions. A bunch of roped onions weighed about three or four pounds, and Williams bought them for 5d. per bunch in 1738. Women earned a penny per bunch for tying them in the early 1740s. They generally took their pay in the form of store merchandise, mostly luxury imports such as sugar, chocolate, pepper, rum, cotton lace, and silk romall, a silken handkerchief used as a head covering. Other goods paid for by women's onions included medicine, a pair of spectacles, and a copy of Homer's *Iliad.*

So far, the evidence from account books and diaries has helped locate the boundaries demarcating women's work from men's work. Those boundaries, however, were permeable. Men could and did cross into women's domain when the size of the market justified a larger scale of operations than the home could provide. For example, baking and brewing were normally women's work, but men in port towns also made their living by these activities. Men in New England did not lose self-respect if they milked cows, but they did not normally make cheese or churn cream into butter.

If, however, the family began to specialize in dairying for sale, the men might take part. Matthew Patten of New Hampshire mentioned husbands as well as wives buying and selling butter. Thus, when nominally feminine tasks became important to household income, men undertook a share of the responsibility, even if only to keep track of the profits. Male account keepers commonly listed payments due from boarders and lodgers but never credited the work by their wives that made the hospitality possible. On the other hand, some male-dominated occupations were always open to women. Retail trade was perhaps the most common, although before 1740 such opportunities arose in only a few commercial areas. Most women in retailing were widows who had taken over a deceased husband's shop, although one Mary Johnson of Boston, who was not identified as a widow, owned shop goods worth over two hundred pounds, according to the 1669 inventory of her estate. Helen Hobart ran a shop in Hingham in 1682 with her husband's approval. By the late colonial period, such opportunities had spread deeper into the interior. In Worcester County in 1760, for instance, twelve out of 267 licensed dispensers of spirituous liquors (4.5 percent) were women.

Though women had always acted as midwives, nursed the sick, and disbursed homemade remedies, a few also "doctored." The administrator of the estate of David Clark of Wrentham listed payment to Mary Johnson, "Doctoress" for "Physick and Tendance." William Corbin, minister of the Anglican church in Boston, willed his medical books to Jane Allen of Newbury, spinster and daughter of the Honorable Samuel Allen, Esquire. In 1758 the Reverend Ebenezer Parkman went to see the widow Ruhamah Newton, who had broken her leg in a fall. Friends had called a Mrs. Parker to set the leg, and the time it took her to get her apparatus in order and carry out the operation delayed the diarist's return home "till night."

Women taught school, as did men. Generally speaking, women taught young pupils of both sexes to read and spell, and men instructed more advanced classes in writing and arithmetic. Seventeenth-century records occasionally identify "school dames" who took students for fees, but they do not seem to have been common outside the largest settlements.

In the eighteenth century, women usually taught the younger children and girls during the summer, often for only half the wages of the young male college graduates who took the older children the rest of the year. The town of Amesbury, Massachusetts, voted in 1707 that the selectmen "hire four or five school Dames for the town to teach children to read" and allowed five pounds to two men "to keep a school to teach young parsons to write and sifer two months this year." Most towns seem to have found the two-tier system a cheap and efficient way to comply with the provincial school laws. The town meeting of Hingham instructed its selectmen to "hire a schoolmaster as cheap as they can get one, provided they shall hire a single man and not a man that have a family."

There was also a two-tier system in making apparel. Men normally tailored coats and breeches, and women sewed shirts and gowns; however, women in the eighteenth century also engaged in tailoring to a limited extent. In 1708, the estate of Simon Gross, deceased mariner of Hingham, paid for forty weeks of training as a tailor for his daughter Allis. John Ballantine, minister at Westfield, Massachusetts, mentioned two occasions in 1768 when Ruth Weller came for a week to make garments; in 1773 he noted that "Sally Noble, Tailer" was working at his house.

Gender distinctions were very clear in the processing of textiles. Females did not comb worsted or hackle flax, which was men's work, although women, along with boys, pulled flax, carded wool, and picked seeds out of cotton. Girls and women spun, dyed, and knitted yarn, but few engaged in weaving, traditionally a male occupation in England. Women did take up the craft in the eighteenth century, doing simple weaves while men concentrated on more complex patterns.

Few inventoried estates mention looms in the seventeenth century, and only 6 percent in Essex County, Massachusetts, list them around 1700. By 1774, the proportion of inventories with looms in Alice Hanson Jones's New England sample ranged from a low of 17 percent in Essex County to a high of 37.5 percent in Plymouth County. The spread of looms did not mean that the region's textile industry was in the throes of protoindustrialization. Rather, households in less commercial areas were producing more cloth for home use in order to spend their cash and vendible products on new consumer goods like tea and sugar. The newer weavers included women who took up weaving as a nearly full-time activity in the years before marriage or during widowhood. Growing numbers of married women also wove part time to conserve or expand family income.

Weaving may be the only occupation in the colonial period for which there is sufficient documentation to compare men's and women's pay for the same type of work. Women weavers appear in account books as early as 1704 in Norwich, Connecticut, and in 1728, when Mary Stodder purchased a loom from John Marsh of Litchfield. Altogether, eighteen women weavers appear in the diaries, probate records, and account books consulted for this study, of whom just four are identified as "widow." Of those for whom pay rates are available, comparisons with contemporary male weavers show that the sexes earned similar rates per yard for common kinds of cloth. We can conclude that, in this instance, women did earn equal pay for equal work. However, only two women weavers in the sample, Mary Parker and Hannah Smith of Hingham, received credit for weaving more than the common fabrics— "plain," drugget, shirting, linen, tow, and "blanketing." Men produced a much wider variety, including relatively fancy weaves. Judging from these examples, an expanding demand for domestic cloth created opportunities for women to do simple weaving. They could do so without driving down piece rates, which rose by a third between the 1750s and the 1770s; from 4.1d. to 5.4d. and then to 5.5d. in the early 1770s. Although the sources do not reveal great numbers of women working at looms, women's growing presence in the late colonial period signals a trend that accelerated during the Revolution.

The history of weaving and tailoring in New England illustrates the flexibility inherent in the region's gender-based work roles. The further removed the activity was from hard-core masculine tasks associated with oxen, plows, and heavy equipment, the more likely that respectable women did it. The history of work and gender in New England during the colonial years divides readily into four periods of unequal duration. In the earliest period, before the 1670s, the economy simplified compared to England's economy, and the variety of occupations open to either sex contracted sharply. Women spent more time outdoors and working alongside men. The second period came with the proliferation of activities by which men habitually and strictly segregated themselves from women, and women undertook domestic manufacturing tasks with which historians have so often associated them: brewing beer, baking bread, churning butter, making cheese, spinning yarn, and knitting stockings and mittens. Not every housewife practiced all these arts, and specialization encouraged exchange between them.

The third period, beginning about 1715, constituted the farm maintenance stage in older settlements during which demand for unskilled labor declined relative to skilled labor. Increasing population densities created exchange opportunities that encouraged both men and women to specialize and invest more time in nonfarm occupations. This stage might have continued indefinitely, with population growth putting continuous downward pressure on wages, but outside forces intervened, creating the fourth and final phase of New England's colonial development. Beginning in 1739, wars and their aftermaths administered a succession of shocks to the system, creating sudden demands for men and provisions and putting large amounts of money into circulation. The conclusion to the Seven Years' War opened up northern New England and Nova Scotia to British settlement, and the treaty that ended the War for Independence swung open the gates to Iroquoia in New York, as did the Battle of Fallen Timbers (1794) for the Ohio Valley. Much of the labor supply that might have depressed wage rates emigrated instead; in New England, it was not replaced by immigrants.

Despite New England's limited resources and the absence of technological change, demand generated by war and export markets drove the region's economy at a faster rate than its population grew. Evidence for economic expansion appears in both account books and probate inventories. First, stores with new consumer wares appeared. Storekeepers began moving into the rural interior during the 1740s, and their numbers grew dramatically in the ensuing decades. Proportionately, there were nearly as many retailers in Massachusetts in 1771 as there were in the United States in 1929. Many hopeful young businessmen were assisted by merchants in port cities who had advanced their wares on credit to the neophytes.

The lure was the money jingling in farmers' pockets from increasing prices for their products, beginning with the preparations against Louisbourg in 1744–1745. Prices for livestock began to soar faster than inflation, offering strong inducements to farmers to expand their herds. The sterling equivalent of Connecticut inventory values of oxen, for instance, jumped 19 percent in the 1740s, continued to rise in the 1750s, and by the early 1760s reached 80 percent above levels of the 1730s. During the height of the Seven Years' War, Connecticut prices for cows and barreled pork climbed 50 percent, while prices for sheep doubled. After dropping modestly in the late 1760s, prices for oxen and cows rose sharply in the early 1770s, attaining levels not seen since the 1640s. Livestock values in Massachusetts did not keep up with this torrid pace, but the cost of oxen ballooned by more than 70 percent in 1758–1763 and grew again in the early 1770s. Connecticut wheat prices ascended a bit more demurely: 43 percent in the 1750s and 48 percent in 1772–1774. Farmers in newer settlements sent off, besides barreled meat and draft animals, loads of lumber products, such as staves and shingles, potash, tar, turpentine, and maple syrup. New Englanders also shipped thousands of pounds of well-preserved butter and cheese every year.

For men with resources, the rational reaction to such prices would have been to devote more of their own and their sons' time to farming and less time to crafts such as weaving. To raise and feed more livestock, farmers had to create more pasture and mowing lands, plant more timothy and clover, maintain longer fence lines, and store many more tons of hay in their newly erected barns. Winter chores expanded, cutting the time available for craft activities.

When farmers endeavored to raise more livestock and the grass to feed them, and when farm wives found themselves milking more cows, churning more butter, and making more cheese, men and women were putting pressure on a labor force that in the short run could expand only by crossing the gender division of labor. Every attempt by the colonial governments during the Seven Years' War to recruit soldiers for the summer campaigns further reduced the available pool of young men, and farmers found themselves engaged in a bidding war that raised wages and bounties. According to Fred Anderson, men in military service during these years could earn far more than a fully employed farm laborer. With an eight-month enlistment, plus bounty, minimum income for soldiers in Massachusetts rose from £10.1 sterling in 1755 to £13.9 in 1757, and bounced between a high of £21.75 and a low of £15.75 thereafter. When bounties for reenlistment are figured in, estimated maximum incomes reached £32.3 in 1760 and £29.2 in 1762. Anywhere from one-fourth to one-third of men aged sixteen to twenty-nine served with Massachusetts forces at some point during the war.

The rise in wages beginning in the 1740s at first touched only men but in the long term affected everyone by loosening the bonds between parents and their grown children as daughters found work outside the home and sons joined the military or emigrated. The account books show that men abruptly began employing greater numbers of women in the final two decades of the colonial period. Women had already begun moving into tailoring and weaving, but the labor shortages of the Seven Years' War boosted demand for their services, and the migration out of southern New England in the 1760s apparently worked to cushion the postwar depression in farm wages and prices.

Rising wages and expanding employment meant higher incomes for those who did not emigrate. The probate inventories of the late colonial period show that most New England families were prospering. The estimated sterling value per capita of consumer goods in 1774 was 10 percent higher than in the middle colonies, for instance, and an index of amenities in probate inventories from rural New England registered substantial gains in the decades before 1774, catching up and then keeping pace with Chesapeake households that had long been engaged in a commercial economy.

The New England economy took time to recover from the crises of war and destruction in 1675–1694; it grew only slowly for a long period before heating up during the Seven Years' War. That war accelerated economic change, bringing more women into the paid labor force and expanding the penetration of the market into the rural interior. The growing proportion of young women working outside the home in the final decades of the colonial period accompanied a rise in their wages, which no doubt helped attract them. When combined with evidence that increasing numbers of country girls were attending school and learning how to write, the growing ability of women to earn money and conduct business at the local store can be viewed as a positive good, giving them greater control over their own lives. Furthermore, the addition of tea, sugar, and spices to their diets, painted earthenware to their tables, featherbeds to sleep on, and greater privacy, all surely added pleasures to generally hard lives. Although marriage still meant coverture, more women chose to remain single and access to divorce became easier. There is also a demographic indicator that women's lot was improving: life expectancy of married women rose. Mean age at death increased from sixty-two to sixty-six for women marrying between 1760 and 1774 and to sixty-eight for those marrying between 1775 and 1800. On balance, these changes appear beneficial. Women would not gain politically or legally from American Independence, and equality was never even a prospect, but in the decades before 1776 they had won a little liberty, and comfort is no mean thing.

Women in Work and Poverty: The Difficulties of Earning a Living

For some time now, many scholars of early American history have asserted that the absence of sufficient manpower resulted in extensive economic freedom for the "weaker sex." As Page Smith puts it, "There were, in the early years, very few negative definitions—that this or that activity was unsuitable or inappropriate for a woman to engage in. In consequence colonial women moved freely into most occupations in response to particular needs and opportunities rather than abstract theories of what was proper." Eleanor Flexner has more emphatically concluded, "In a struggling society in which there was a continuous labor shortage, no social taboos could keep a hungry woman idle." Barbara Mayer Wertheimer enthusiastically catalogues many of the jobs held by colonial women, and asserts that the earliest female settlers possessed "power and responsibility such as they had never known in seventeenth-century England or on the European continent . . . [They labored at] many kinds of work outside the home from which they were later barred."

Despite such assertions, there has been no systematic effort to determine the exact occupations available to women, and the extent to which these utilized skills *not* focused strictly around the domesticity and nurturance of the conventional female role. Moreover, we do not know how many women worked at some occupation other than that of housewife and mother, or how much they earned. Because the characterization of woman as the weaker sex affected Puritan views of sexual behavior, intelligence, and social privilege, we might suspect that it also deterred women from supporting themselves. In fact, as we shall see, economic factors discouraged productive, independent activity on the part of women.

Limitations on Searching Out a Calling

Puritans certainly believed in the efficacy of work. Detesting those who lived "idle like swine," they felt that labor brought "strength to the body, and vigour to the mynde," thereby providing an outlet for energies which could otherwise lead one to sin. The authorities encouraged each person to search out a suitable calling through apprenticeship, self-training, or hiring out. Boys had considerably more options than girls; apprenticeship contracts

From A SEARCH FOR POWER: THE WEAKER SEX IN SEVENTEENTH-CENTURY NEW ENGLAND by Lyle Koehler, pp. 108–129. Copyright © 1980 by Lyle Koehler.

specified that the latter be taught only housewifely duties like cooking and sewing, while boys could learn the "secrets" of any number of trades, including blacksmithing, husbandry, shop management, milling, carpentry, and seamanship. It is unlikely that those daughters who never served as apprentices learned any of the male occupational "secrets," because limited opportunities for occupational training, as well as denial of access to public schools, put at a disadvantage any "strong-minded" woman who wished to advance in the world of work. Even if she could overcome the limits of her socialization for domesticity, or use that training to hire herself out in a female vocation, a young woman still could not readily accrue the funds necessary to set herself up in a business or trade; besides, she was unable to earn very much at women's jobs.

Moreover, fathers neglected to give their daughters a portion of the family estate as a nest egg, while they did sometimes convey realty to sons. . . . The daughter who inherited very much from her father's estate was quite a rarity in seventeenth-century Connecticut; only the daughter of a very wealthy man could actually have taken steps to become economically self-sufficient after her father's demise. Furthermore, daughters tended to receive their share in personalty, not in realty which could be converted into a permanent productive income, whereas for sons the reverse was true. In fact, daughters inherited proportionally smaller legacies than had been customary in late medieval England.

The mean and median (£22) values of daughters' inheritances yielded some immediate purchasing power, but did little to increase their occupational possibilities. The average inheritance did not allow a daughter money enough to purchase a home lot near the town's center, which sold for £80 or £100. Nor could she rent a shop and stock it with goods. While the young man could work at a trade and save a tidy sum by his late twenties, the young woman possessed no similar option. Hartford County records indicate that seventeenth-century inheritance patterns made it virtually impossible for a maiden, whose access to employment was already limited by her training and lack of education, to become part of the property-holding group which ran New England affairs.

The Single Woman as Servant

While her parents were still alive, or after she inherited too little to buy her own financial independence, a single woman could strive to earn money at only one occupation before 1685. Domestic servitude did little more than insure that the young woman would continue to exist as a member of the submissive, inferior, financially dependent class. Female servants assisted with household duties, child care, and garden maintenance—but always under the supervision of a "mistress" or "master," whose orders had to be obeyed unless they violated criminal law. Servants received meals, clothing, and a place to sleep, but generally earned no financial remuneration in return for their valuable work. The few women who hired themselves out (unlike those invariably single ones who served as apprentices, redemptioners, indentured domestics, and even slaves) enjoyed a small measure of economic reward. Their typical annual salary was just £3 or £4, only 50 to 60 percent of the male hired servant's wage. Even with the addition of a sum for the room and board furnished by the master, the female domestic drew one of the lowest annual incomes of any working person.

Since before 1650 domestic servitude was considered an honorable occupation for a woman, some newly arrived single women sought employment in that capacity. These females, whose mean age was 20.7 years, often lived briefly in Puritan households under conditions of relative equality, and then married into the best families. Still, their actual numbers were few; in addition, male domestic migrating to New England outnumbered females three to one. . . .

In the first three decades of settlement, then, a handful of women used servitude as a vehicle for marital advancement, although not as a means to accumulate money for future investment. Since such women labored as indentured servants or redemptioners (usually for seven years, in return for the cost of their passage), before 1650 there is no instance of a female hiring out her own time. After that date, however, the image of the servant deteriorated so remarkably that only a severely impoverished single woman would want to become a domestic. Scottish, Irish, Indian, black, and poor English servants soon replaced the earlier "most honourable" English. . . .

The deterioration of servant status after 1650 made domestic work no longer a realistic option for the "middling" and "better sorts." Because women of those classes no longer became servants, opportunities for them to leave home and hire out their labor decreased. Nor did the poor English, Scottish, Irish, black, and Indian women who became servants and slaves gain even a small measure of control over their own lives. For sustenance, every woman had to rely on a father, master, or husband; marriage became literally basic to survival for many New England women.

As a result, housewifery served as the chief "occupation" for almost all New England women, and it no more facilitated financial independence than had other forms of domestic servitude. Women certainly contributed to the productivity of the family farm. Although they did not often work outdoors planting and harvesting crops, as English farm wives did, many spent a good deal of time cleaning house, spinning flax, dipping candles, canning preserves, roasting meat, caring for children, and performing untold other tasks. Some spun and made stockings, shirts, or breeches, which they sold to neighbors for an occasional shilling. Goodwives also sold poultry, butter, cheese, and garden produce, or bartered such items for desired commodities in the informal village trade networks. However, woman's work in the home was assumed to be less dangerous and time-consuming than men's—a conclusion which may have rankled Puritan women as much as it has irritated housewives in more modern times. Above all else, the wife was not to use her presumed "free time" to exceed her ordained station by taking an interest in commercial activities or any other "outward matters." She could contract for rents and wages, sell goods, and collect debts only when her husband had so authorized. The records from seventeenth-century civil cases reveal that New England husbands granted their wives such privileges in only 6 or 7 percent of all families.

The wife's access to experience in "outward matters" which could have provided her with some income in either marriage or widowhood was, therefore, much circumscribed.

The Nurturant Callings of Wet Nurse, Teacher, Doctor, and Midwife

Of course, Puritans did allow married women to labor at activities other than housewifery; but those activities also centered around the female's assumed nurturance, and were unremunerative and part-time. Serving as a wet nurse was one such activity, even though its short-term and low-demand characteristics made it a very insubstantial "occupation." Wet nurses enjoyed some popularity because, despite the strong cultural ideal affirming maternal breast-feeding, Puritan mothers sometimes found it impossible to perform that "duty." Puerperal fever or other serious illnesses incapacitated mothers and, it was believed, could be transmitted through the milk. Sore or inverted nipples, breast inflammations, and scanty milk also necessitated the occasional use of a wet nurse. Fear of the presumed toxic effects of colostrum caused mothers to observe a taboo on suckling infants for three or four days after delivery, which increased possibilities for wet nursing. Still, wet nurses rarely received more than temporary employment, and the payment for that service was probably never very great. In fact, such short-term help may have been freely given, much the way neighboring wives helped out during measles or other epidemics. There is no record of New Englanders "farming out" babies to wet nurses for anywhere from ten to nineteen months, as was common in England. Indeed, Puritan women who wet nursed infants probably did not even think of themselves as being employed at an occupation.

Like wet nurses, teachers maternally provided for the needs of the young. At dame schools, where a wife or "poor patient widow sits/And awes some twenty infants as she knits," the female teacher instructed her neighbor's younger offspring for 10s to £2 per year, 1/10th to 1/120th of the salary for male teachers in the public schools. As early as 1639 Mistress Jupe taught pupils at the Ipswich dame school; before the century's end, twenty-three or twenty-four other women assisted young scholars in reading, writing, and religion at fourteen different New England locales. These schoolmarms were expected to rely upon their husbands' or ex-husbands' estates for sustenance, not upon any salary for their own work. Moreover, they were barred from working with the upper grades (over age nine or ten), lest the difficulty of the material studied at those levels overtax a woman's "weak" intellectual ability. They constituted only 12.6 percent (25 of 199) of all school-teachers this researcher could locate in the seventeenth-century Puritan records.

The practice of medicine was another nurturant occupational activity open to married women. Many English housewives and their American counterparts learned "chirurgery"—the use of herbs, potions, and poultices to cure any number of maladies. Knowledge of the medicinal properties of wild herbs passed through the female line in some families for generations. Alice Apsley, Lady Fenwick, one of the first women to settle at Ft. Saybrook, Connecticut, distributed homegrown herbs to sick callers at her residence from 1639 until her departure from the colony in 1645. Mistress Field of Salem prepared a green "sympathetic oynment" which purportedly healed sprains, aches, cramps, scaldings, cuts, mange in cattle, stench blood, tumors, the bites of "Venomous Beasts," and "old Rotten Sores." Doctor Margaret Jones of Charlestown, Massachusetts, secured some reputation as a witch because the aniseed, liquors, and small doses of herbs she administered produced "extraordinary violent effects." Hannah Bradford of Windsor, Connecticut, was such a capable physician that she reputedly "taught the first male doctor much of his medical lore." At least three women proved to be able surgeons. Henry Winthrop's widow reportedly "hath very good successe" in her "Surgerye"; Mistress Allyn patched up wounded soldiers as an army surgeon during King Philip's War; and, on Martha's Vineyard, Mistress Blande dispensed "Phisicke and Surgery" to many sick Indians.

Altogether, women comprised 24 percent (N = 42 of 175) of New England's medical practitioners. These female doctors, nurses, and midwives earned the respect of their neighbors, but evidence suggests that they received little income from their services. Medicine in the seventeenth century lacked the financial advantages of ministry, governorship, or commerce; not until the 1690s did physicians begin to achieve some recognition as highly paid, self-conscious professionals. Before that, almost all doctors practiced medicine as a second profession, spending the bulk of their working hours in the ministry, the magistracy, husbandry, or housewifery. . . .

In the 1690s, the professionalization of medicine had severe consequences for female physicians. Men trained through apprenticeship to male doctors began displacing local female chirurgeons. One can search the colonial records in vain for some mention of female physicians during that decade. For the first time, particularly in urban areas, Puritans began distinguishing between male "doctors" and female "nurses," even though such "nurses" assisted Boston wives in recovering from childbirth, cared for infants' ailments, and treated cases of smallpox. Sam Sewall mentions seven different male physicians in his diary for the years 1674 to 1699, but all women who treat illnesses are referred to either as midwives or as nurses.

Throughout the seventeenth century both sexes dispensed medical advice, but one realm of expertise, midwifery, remained the exclusive province of women. (In fact, the York County authorities fined one man fifty shillings "for presumeing to Act the Part of a Midwife.") Women learned midwifery from personal experience, from other midwives, or from standard obstetrical texts like Nicholas Culpeper's *Directory for Midwives* (1651). There were no medical examinations to pass in New England, nor did a prospective midwife take out a license to practice, as was required in England and in nearby New Amsterdam.

Midwives occupied a position of some influence. They were given the important function of examining women accused of premarital pregnancy, infanticide, or witchcraft; often the guilt or innocence of the accused rested on the findings of these female juries. In return for this necessary service, the town selectmen sometimes issued grants of land to widowed midwives.

However, that happened only in a few instances, and it is significant that this researcher has found no account book or other record which mentions a midwife receiving any reward for her services. . . .

Women in Business

Limitations on daughters' inheritances and the lack of remunerative work for single women meant that few could join the property-holding group which controlled capital investment in land. So, too, did the paltry wages of midwives, physicians, teachers, and wet nurses, along with husbandly control over their incomes, prevent working wives from acquiring the economic security which would have enabled them to become property owners. As urbanization increased, especially late in the century, working women were generally unable to accumulate the capital necessary to participate in the Commercial Revolution enveloping New England.

Of course, some women who possessed both money and prestige also maintained small-scale businesses. As early as 1640 Philippa Hammond operated a shop at Boston. So did Widow Howdin (1645), Alice Thomas (before 1672), Ann Carter (1663), Jane Bernard (1672–76), Abigail Johnson (1672–73), Mistress Gutteridge (1690), Elizabeth Connigrave (1672–74), Rebecca Windsor (1672–74), and Mary Castle (1690). Almost all of these women ran coffee or cook shops, thereby utilizing their domestic training. Mary Avery and Susanna Jacob kept shop between 1685 and 1691, but whether they were owners or merely employees is unknown. Esther Palmer, a merchant, located in the metropolis in 1683, and Florence Mackarta, in partnership with two men, constructed a slaughterhouse on Peck's Wharf in 1693. A 1687 Boston tax list gives the names of forty-eight different women who derived some income from a trade or their estates—11.4 percent of all such persons rated. But businesswomen were rarer than the initial impression suggests. For example, it is not actually specified how many of the women on the 1687 list owned businesses and how many merely drew income from the estates of their deceased husbands. What *is* clear is that fully 85.4 percent of these women were widows.

Businesswomen, whether married or widowed, were few throughout New England. The paucity of early businesswomen can be readily demonstrated by searching through transcriptions of courtroom proceedings, town records, and other sources. . . . In all of New England outside Boston there are records of only nine women who worked at a trade or who ran a business other than innkeeping. By late century Margaret Barton of Salem, a chair frame maker, had accrued a fortune in "ventures at sea." In Hartford County, Elizabeth Gardner, Mary Phelps, and Mary Stanly owned interests in (respectively) an iron mill, a grist mill, and a shop. Jane Stolion appeared in court in 1645–46, accused of charging excessive prices at her New Haven dress and cloth shop. Mistress Jenny came before the Plymouth General Court in 1644 for not keeping the mortars at her mill clean, nor the bags of corn there from spoiling. Elizabeth Cadwell operated her husband's ferry across the Connecticut River at Hartford after his death in 1695. One Maine widow, Elizabeth Rowdan, maintained a blacksmith shop and mill. Other women may have worked in their husbands' bakery, cook, or apparel shops, or may have tailored clothing for sale; but the records observe a rigorous silence on that score, mentioning only one female baker at Salem (1639). Altogether, only 2.3 percent (N = 23 of 988) of all tradespeople-merchants (again excluding innkeepers) were members of the "weaker sex."

An examination of those licensed to keep inns or sell alcoholic beverages indicates that few women supported themselves in this occupation, at least before the 1690s. Since all innkeepers had to secure licenses from the authorities, the records are quite complete. The first female innkeeper does not appear until 1643. Between 1643 and 1689 at least fifty-seven other women operated inns; however, they constituted but 18.9 percent of Boston's innkeepers and only 5 percent of those in the remainder of New England. On Ebenezer Peirce's *Civil, Military, and Professional Lists of Plymouth and Rhode Island Colonies* just three of seventy Plymouth innkeepers are female. In the 1690s, with large numbers of men away fighting in the Maine Indian wars, the New England total increased sharply, to eighty-four women—eight in Maine, twenty-four in New Hampshire, and fifty-two in the Bay Colony. Women then comprised over half of the tavernkeepers in Boston and approximately 20 percent of those in other locales. . . .

Although innkeeping or some other business may have given the individual woman some measure of personal satisfaction and self-sufficiency, the Boston tax list of 1687 suggests that businesswomen fared less well than businessmen. An occasional woman like the Widow Kellond might derive an annual income as high as £80 from her trade and estates, but she was much the exception. Only nineteen members of the "weaker sex"—39.6 percent of all tradeswomen—earned £10 or more from their trades and estates, while 74 percent of all tradesmen earned that much. The forty-eight female traders made £580 over the previous year, an average of £12, whereas the 373 male traders made £7,383, or £20 each.

There were several reasons why tradeswomen, when they managed to open shops, earned only 60 percent as much as tradesmen. Since the women possessed little training, their businesses tended to accent service in a way that was compatible with female sex-role stereotyping. Distributing beer, maintaining a cook shop, keeping an inn, and operating a millinery shop utilized talents common to housewives, but ones which returned little profit. Women in such businesses could not easily attract customers on the open market, for they lacked the mobility of carpenters, bricklayers, blacksmiths, and coopers. They could not advertise in newspapers, for none existed. They could not reap the benefits of an international trade, since they lacked ties to the great English trading houses and familiarity with foreign markets. Even credit was a problem. As milliner Hannah Crowell complained in 1696, "being a Woman [I] was not able to ride up and down to get in debts."

Women also lacked the capital necessary to establish large scale businesses. Only after her husband died did the typical woman strike out on her own, with the help of her widow's portion. Of all women who were licensed to sell spirituous liquors, some 71.1 percent were widows. Innkeeping was a ready source of sustenance for any widow whose husband left her their house and little else. Working at a trade became an acceptable means of support for widows of artisans, but even they could only rarely increase the net value of their estates over the amounts they inherited. Age, decreased mobility, and a lack of appropriate training or education each took a toll. Moreover, husbands were often reluctant to provide for their wives by leaving them a full or part interest in their trade tools or their shops. Only two of fifty-seven Hartford County artisans, merchants, and shopkeepers bequeathed their widows interest in their businesses. Another man left a shop at Hartford to his sister.

Even those few widows who enjoyed some occupational independence were expected to restrict their activities to nurturant, housewifely, and comparatively low-status occupations. Highstatus positions such as public grammar-school teaching, the ministry, and major public offices were limited to men. Elizabeth Jones, appointed the Boston poundkeeper in 1670, 1676, and 1689, was the only woman to serve as a public official on even a minor level.

The woman who wished to work "by her own hand," whether widowed, married, or single, faced still other disadvantages. Before 1647 the Maine General Court forbade any woman from inhabiting the Isles of Shoales, thereby making it impossible for females to help out with the fishing or to operate stores at which the fishermen might buy provisions. Perhaps deterred by the sentiment expressed in Maine law, no woman of record ever fished at sea for a profit. Nor could women become sailors—when one dressed as a man and left Massachusetts on a vessel, her fellow seamen, upon discovering her sex, tarred and feathered her in a nearly fatal maltreatment. The presence of working women on the Atlantic was so inconceivable to Puritans that when a mysterious "Shallop at Sea man'd with women" was reported, men attributed the phenomenon to witchcraft.

Wealth and Poverty

The limited, poorly paid, comparatively low status employment opportunities available to early New England women meant that they could not really participate in the expanding possibilities opened by the Commercial Revolution. Despite such disabilities, some observers might argue that dependent wives were rewarded in the end, by inheriting sizable properties (although not businesses) from their deceased husbands. Such widows could enjoy some independence in their later years. The tax lists seem to provide some evidence for this view; women appear as heads of families approximately 6 percent of the time, and fare well when their estates are compared to those of male family heads. . . .

It would be incorrect to assume, however, that as a group widows in Puritan New England were comparatively well-to-do, for most never appeared on a tax list. . . . Many husbands, well aware that their wives might have difficulty maintaining an estate, specified that their widows live with one or more sons in the family dwelling unit. Such men usually reserved one room, a garden, a cow, and some household goods for their widow's use. In one-tenth of all wills (N = 30 of 282) fathers directed children to maintain their mother with annual supplies or a monetary allotment. The annual maintenance payment rarely amounted to much, however, averaging £9 13s.; most widows received less than £7. . . .

Although one-sixth or one-fifth of all widows (those of the middling and better sorts) enjoyed limited affluence, many more suffered poverty. . . . The appointment of "keepers" for the indigent, or lodging them in the almshouse under a male attendant's supervision, blatantly reinforced female dependence. Such control angered some poor women, and at least two of them entirely rejected the dependence entailed in any form of relief. Mary Webster, a "wretched woman" of Hadley, Massachusetts, protested the efforts of church deacon Philip Smith to mitigate her indigence, expressing herself so sharply "that he declared himself apprehensive of receiving mischief at her hands" (ca. 1684). Jane Bourne of Cambridge refused to accept an allotment from the town for her food and lodging, instead moving out of town to secure employment elsewhere as a servant (1663). A third woman, Abigail Day, was "full of Discontent" and "Impatience under her Afflictions" while at the Boston almshouse. She would "thank neither God nor man" for the objectionable diet there, and she complained that her keeper "had several times made attempts upon her chastity" (1697).

The dissatisfaction of poor women like Abigail Day, Jane Bourne, and Mary Webster is readily understandable, for the paternalism of the Puritan system of poor relief too easily reflected women's difficulties in searching for gainful employment or starting businesses. Wherever they turned, women encountered the fruits of Puritan sexism—in low pay, lack of education and job training, decreased opportunities to secure the funds needed to open a business, and limitations on the kinds of employment available. . . . The great majority of women in early New England worked under a condition of dependence, whether as servants under the control of masters, poor women under the control of almshouse attendants or other keepers, widows under the relative control of their children, or (in the most common occupation of all) housewives under the control of their husbands.

The circumstances of life in seventeenth-century Puritan New England hardly had an emancipating effect. New England wives sometimes maintained family businesses in their husband's absence, or occasionally ran shops of their own; but so did English women. In fact, Alice Clark's research indicates that English women, as members of a more urbanized society, labored at many more occupations than did their New England counterparts. . . . While all of the information is not yet in, it is striking that 40 percent of New England's adult population comprised just 25 percent of all servants, 24 percent of all medical practitioners (if nurses and midwives are subtracted, the percentage drops to 9.6), 12.6 percent of all schoolteachers, 18 percent of all innkeepers, and 2.3 percent of all tradespeople-merchants. Moreover, these women received much less remuneration than their male counterparts. Although labor shortages were frequent in the first few decades of settlement, such times did not lead to more women on the job market, or to women doing men's work. Inheritance patterns in agrarian locales made it virtually impossible for daughters and wives to exercise much control over capital investment in land. All but a few urban women were similarly unable to acquire real estate or capital which would have enabled them to expand their incomes. The only way for women to experience any upward mobility was to marry well. Seventeenth-century New England was a "Garden of Eden" only for the woman who pursued economic opportunity dependently, as the rib of a (hopefully) prospering and generous Adam.

POSTSCRIPT

Did Colonial New England Women Enjoy Significant Economic Autonomy?

Students wishing to explore further the status of women in colonial British North America should read the classic essay by Lois Green Carr and Lorena S. Walsh, "The Planter's Wife: The Experience of White Women in Seventeenth-Century Maryland," *The William and Mary Quarterly* (October 1977) and Mary Beth Norton's "The Evolution of White Women's Experience in Early America," *American Historical Review* (June 1984). Norton's research on this topic is extended further in her *Founding Mothers & Fathers: Gendered Power and the Forming of American Society* (Knopf, 1996).

Surveys of American women's history that address the colonial period include June Sochen, *Herstory: A Woman's View of American History* (Alfred, 1974); Mary P. Ryan, *Womanhood in America: From Colonial Times to the Present* (New Viewpoints, 1974); and Nancy Woloch, *Women and the American Experience* (Knopf, 1984). Support for the view that women experienced significant upward mobility by migrating to the American colonies can be found in Richard B. Morris, *Studies in the History of American Law*, 2d ed. (Octagon Books, 1964); Elizabeth Anthony Dexter, *Colonial Women of Affairs*, 2d ed. (Houghton Mifflin, 1931); Mary Ritter Beard, *Woman as Force in History* (Macmillan, 1946); Eleanor Flexner, *Century of Struggle* (Belknap Press, 1959); Roger Thompson, *Women in Stuart England and America: A Comparative Study* (Routledge and Kegan, 1974); and Page Smith, *Daughters of the Promised Land: Women in American History* (Little, Brown, 1977).

Many of the scholarly monographs that include discussions of colonial women focus disproportionately on New England. For example, Edmund S. Morgan, *The Puritan Family: Religion and Domestic Relations in Seventeenth-Century New England* (Boston Public Library, 1944) and John Demos, *A Little Commonwealth: Family Life in Plymouth Colony* (Oxford, 1970) both discuss the status of women within the context of the New England family. N. E. H. Hull's *Female Felons: Women and Serious Crime in Colonial Massachusetts* (Illinois, 1987) and Cornelia Hughes Dayton's *Women Before the Bar: Gender, Law, and Society in Connecticut, 1639–1789* (University of North Carolina Press, 1995) treat the legal status of female New Englanders. For the relationship between women and witchcraft, see John Putnam Demos, *Entertaining Satan: Witchcraft and the Culture of Early New England* (Oxford, 1982) and Carol F. Karlsen, *The Devil in the Shape of a Woman: Witchcraft in Colonial New England* (Random House, 1987). Also of interest is Laurel Thatcher Ulrich, *Good Wives: Image and Reality in the Lives of Women in Northern New England, 1650–1750* (Knopf, 1980).

Women in colonial Virginia are treated in Darrett B. Rutman and Anita H. Rutman, *A Place in Time: Middlesex County, Virginia, 1650–1750* (W. W. Norton, 1984) and Kathleen M. Brown, *Good Wives, Nasty Wenches, and Anxious Patriarchs: Gender, Race, and Power in Colonial Virginia* (University of North Carolina Press, 1996).

Women in the age of the American Revolution are the focus of Carol Ruth Berkin, *Within the Conjurer's Circle: Women in Colonial America* (General Learning Press, 1974), Linda Grant DePauw and Conover Hunt, *"Remember the Ladies": Women in America, 1750–1815* (Viking Press, 1976), Mary Beth Norton, *Liberty's Daughters: The Revolutionary Experience of American Women, 1750–1800* (Little, Brown, 1980), Linda Kerber, *Women of the Republic: Intellect and Ideology in Revolutionary America* (North Carolina, 1980), Charles W. Akers, *Abigail Adams: An American Woman* (Little, Brown, 1980), and Joy Day Buel and Richard Buel, Jr., *The Way of Duty: A Woman and Her Family in Revolutionary America* (W. W. Norton, 1984). For the conclusion that the American Revolution failed to advance women's status, see Joan Hoff Wilson's "The Illusion of Change: Women and the American Revolution" in Alfred F. Young, ed., *The American Revolution: Explorations in the History of American Radicalism* (Northern Illinois University Press, 1976).

Internet References . . .

Virtual Marching Tour of the American Revolution

Sponsored by the Independence Hall Association in Philadelphia, this site is a promising work in progress. Its goal is to provide information about Revolutionay times through text and images.

http://www.ushistory.org/march/

The Constitution of the United States

Sponsored by the National Archives and Records Administration, this site presents a wealth of informaiton on the U.S. Constitution. From here you can link to the biographies of the 55 delegates to the Constitutional Convention, take an in-depth look at the convention and the ratification process, read a transcription of the complete text of the Constitution, and view high-resolution images of each page of the Constitution.

http://www.nara.gov/exhall/charters/constitution/conmain.html

Thomas Jefferson Papers: Home Page

The Thomas Jefferson Papers: Home Page site consists of the complete Thomas Jefferson Papers from the Manuscript Division at the Library of Congress. This collection of 27,000 documents is the largest collection of original Jefferson documents in the world. Organized into nine series, this collection includes correspondence, manuscripts, and miscellaneous bound volumes. Also provided on this site are selected quotations of Thomas Jefferson and essays written about him.

http://memeory.loc.gov/ammem/mtjhtml/mtjhome.html

Andrew Jackson: "Champion of the Kingly Commons"

Collection of the Jacksonian era, including discussion of the myth and image of Andrew Jackson and his times.

http://xroads.virginia.edu/~CAP/jackson/jackson.html

PART 2

Revolution and the New Nation

*T*he American Revolution led to independence from England and to the establishment of a new nation. As the United States matured, its people and leaders struggled to implement fully the ideals that had sparked the Revolution. What had been abstractions before the formation of the new government had to be applied and refined in day-to-day practice. The nature of post-revolutionary America, government stability, the transition of power against the backdrop of political factionalism, the extension of democracy, and the international role of the new United States had to be worked out.

- Did the American Revolution Produce a Christian Nation?

- Were the Founding Fathers Democratic Reformers?

- Was Thomas Jefferson a Political Compromiser?

- Was James Madison an Effective Wartime President?

- Was the Monroe Doctrine of 1823 Designed to Protect the Latin American Countries from European Intervention?

- Did the Election of 1828 Represent a Democratic Revolt of the People?

ISSUE 6

Did the American Revolution Produce a Christian Nation?

YES: Nathan O. Hatch, from "The Democratization of Christianity and the Character of American Politics," in Mark A. Noll, ed., *Religion and American Politics* (Oxford University Press, 1990)

NO: Jon Butler, from "Why Revolutionary America Wasn't a 'Christian Nation'," in James H. Hutson, ed., *Religion and the New Republic: Faith in the Founding of America* (Rowman & Littlefield, 2000)

ISSUE SUMMARY

YES: Nathan Hatch argues that by eroding traditional appeals to authority and expanding the number of people who believed they were competent to think for themselves about freedom, equality, and representation, the American Revolution led to an expansion of evangelical Christianity that reinforced the democratic impulses of the new society.

NO: Jon Butler insists that men and women seldom referred to America as a "Christian nation" between 1760 and 1790 and that even though Christianity was important, most Americans opposed a Christian national identity enforced by law or governmental action.

Although generations of American schoolchildren have been taught that the British colonies in North America were founded by persons fleeing religious persecution in England, the truth is that many of those early settlers were motivated by other factors, some of which had little to do with theological preferences. To be sure, the Pilgrims and Puritans of New England sought to escape the proscriptions established by the Church of England. Many New Englanders, however, did not adhere to the precepts of Calvinism and, therefore, were viewed as outsiders. The Quakers who populated Pennsylvania were mostly fugitives from New England, where they had been victims of religious persecution. But to apply religious motivations to the earliest settlers of Virginia, South Carolina, or Georgia is to engage in a serious misreading of the historical record. Even in New England the religious mission of (the first governor of Massachusetts Bay Colony) John Winthrop's "city upon a hill" began to erode as the colonial settlements matured and stabilized.

Although religion was a central element in the lives of the seventeenth- and eighteenth-century Europeans who migrated to the New World, proliferation of religious sects and denominations, emphasis upon material gain in all parts of the colonies, and the predominance of reason over emotion that is associated with the Deists of the Enlightenment period all contributed to a gradual but obvious movement of the colonists away from the church and clerical authority. William Bradford (the second governor of Plymouth Colony), for example, expressed grave concern that many Plymouth residents were following a path of perfidy, and William Penn (founder of Pennsylvania) was certain that the "holy experiment" of the Quakers had failed. Colonial clergy, fearful that a fall from grace was in progress, issued calls for a revival of religious fervor. The spirit of revivalism that spread through the colonies in the 1730s and 1740s, therefore, was an answer to these clerical prayers.

The episode known as the First Great Awakening coincided with the Pietistic movement in Europe and England and was carried forward by dynamic preachers such as Gilbert Tennant, Theodore Frelinghuysen, and George Whitefield. They promoted a religion of the heart, not of the head, in order to produce a spiritual rebirth. These revivals, most historians agree, reinvigorated American Protestantism. Many new congregations were organized as a result of irremediable schisms between "Old Lights" and "New Lights." Skepticism about the desirability of an educated clergy sparked a strong strain of anti-intellectualism. Also, the emphasis on conversion was a message to which virtually everyone could respond, regardless of age, sex, or social status. For some historians, the implications of the Great Awakening extended beyond the religious sphere into the realm of politics and were incorporated into the American Revolution. To what extent was the cause of religion, especially Protestant Christianity, advanced by the revolutionary era? Did the United States become a Christian nation in the wake of the Revolution?

In the following selections, Nathan O. Hatch points out that the most dynamic popular movements in the new republic were religious in nature. The American Revolution, he argues, broke down traditional appeals to authority, and the democratization of American society went hand-in-hand with the expansion of Protestant Christianity. Ordinary people, not elites, took the lead in applying the new political ideals of freedom and equality to evangelical Christian commitments to popular sovereignty.

Jon Butler recognizes that throughout the eighteenth century the British North American colonies established governmentally supported religion, but he sees this as a product the colonists' weak adherence to Christianity in that only about 20 percent of the colonists were church members. After the Revolution, Butler says that most states reduced or withdrew their involvement with religion. This process culminated with the ratification of the First Amendment prohibiting government activity in religion generally.

YES

Nathan O. Hatch

The Democratization of Christianity and the Character of American Politics

This essay will argue that at the very inception of the American republic the most dynamic popular movements were expressly religious. However powerful working-class organizations became in cities such as New York and Baltimore, their presence cannot compare with the phenomenal growth, and collective elán, of Methodists, Baptists, Christians, Millerites, and Mormons. It was lay preachers in the early republic who became the most effective agents in constructing new frames of reference for people living through a profoundly transitional age. Religious leaders from the rank and file were phenomenally successful in reaching out to marginal people, in promoting self-education and sheltering participants from the indoctrination of elite orthodoxies, in binding people together in supportive community, and in identifying the aspirations of common people with the will of God.

The vitality of these religious ideologies and mass movements has had a considerable long-term effect upon the character and limits of American politics. Churches, after all, came to serve as competing universes of discourse and action. And the political implications of mass movements that were democratic and religious at the same time are far more profound than merely predisposing members to vote Federalist or Republican, Democrat or Whig. As mass popular movements, churches came to be places in which fundamental political assumptions were forged: ideas about the meaning of America, the priority of the individual conscience, the values of localism, direct democracy, and individualism, and the necessity of dynamic communication, predicated on the identification of speaker or author with an audience.

This paper will suggest that to understand the democratization of American society, one must look at what happened to Protestant Christianity in the years 1780–1830. In an age when people expected almost everything from religion (and churches) and almost nothing from politics (and the state), the popular churches are essential to comprehending the enduring shape of American democracy....

The American Revolution is the single most crucial event in American history. The generation overshadowed by it and its counterpart in France stands at the fault line that separates an older world, premised on standards of deference, patronage, and ordered succession, from a newer one to which we are attuned since it continues to shape our values. The American Revolution and the beliefs flowing from it created a cultural ferment over the meaning of freedom, a debate that brought to the fore crucial issues of authority, organization, and leadership.

Above all, the Revolution dramatically expanded the circle of people who considered themselves capable of thinking for themselves about issues of freedom, equality, sovereignty, and representation; and it eroded traditional appeals to the authority of tradition, station, and education. Ordinary people moved towards these new horizons as they gained access to a powerful new vocabulary, a rhetoric of liberty that would not have occurred to people were it not for the Revolution. In time, the well-being of ordinary people edged closer to the center of what it means to be American, public opinion came to assume normative significance, and leaders could not survive who would not, to use Patrick Henry's phrase, "bow with utmost deference to the majesty of the people." The correct solution to any important problem, political, legal, or religious, would have to appear as the people's choice.

The profoundly transitional age between 1776 and 1830 left the same kind of indelible imprint upon the structures of American Christianity as it did upon those of American political life. Only land, Robert Wiebe has noted, could compete with Christianity as the pulse of a new democratic society. The age of the democratic revolutions unfolded with awesome moment for people in every social rank. Amidst such acute uncertainty, many humble Christians in America began to redeem a dual legacy. They yoked together strenuous demands for revivals, in the name of Whitefield, and calls for the expansion of popular sovereignty, in the name of the Revolution. It is the linking of these equally potent traditions that sent American Christianity cascading in so many creative directions in the early republic. Church authorities had few resources to restrain these movements fed by the passions of ordinary people. American Methodism, for example, under the tutelage of Francis Asbury, veered sharply from the course of British Methodism from the time of Wesley's death until the end of the Napoleonic Wars. The heavy, centralizing hand of Jabez Bunting kept England's potent evangelical tradition firmly grounded in traditional notions of authority and leadership. After 1800, the leaders of British Methodism were able to bar the eccentric American revivalist Lorenzo Dow from contaminating their meetings. In America, however, Dow took the camp meeting circuit by storm despite periodic censure from bishops and presiding elders. Given his effectiveness and popular support, they were unable to mount a direct challenge to his authority.

A diverse array of evangelical firebrands went about the task of movement-building in the generation after the Revolution. While they were intent on bringing evangelical conversion to the mass of ordinary Americans, rarely could they divorce that message from contagious new vocabularies and impulses that swept through American popular cultures in an era of democratic revolution: an appeal to class as the fundamental problem of society, a refusal to recognize the cultural authority of elites, a disdain for the supposed lessons of history and tradition, a call for reform using the rhetoric of the

Revolution, a commitment to turn the press into a sword of democracy, and an ardent faith in the future of the American republic.

At the same time, Americans who espoused evangelical and egalitarian convictions, in whatever combination, were left free to experiment with abandon, unopposed by civil or religious authority. Within a few years of Jefferson's election in 1800, it became anachronistic to speak of dissent in America—as if there were still a commonly recognized center against which new or emerging groups had to define themselves. There was little to restrain a variety of new groups from vying to establish their identity as a counterestablishment. The fundamental history of this period, in fact, may be a story of things left out, as Roland Berthoff has recently suggested. Churches and religious movements after 1800 operated in a climate in which ecclesiastical establishments had withered, in which the federal government had almost no internal functions—a "midget institution in a giant land"—and in which a rampant migration of people continued to snap old networks of personal authority. American churches did not face the kind of external social and political pressures which in Great Britain often forced Christianity and liberty to march in opposite directions. Such isolation made it possible for religious "outsiders" to see their own destiny as part and parcel of the meaning of America itself. If the earth did belong to the living, as President Jefferson claimed, why should the successful newcomer defer to the claims of education, status, and longevity.

The reality of a nonrestrictive environment permitted an unexpected and often explosive conjunction of evangelical fervor and popular sovereignty. It was this engine that greatly accelerated the process of Christianization with America popular culture, allowing indigenous expressions of faith to take hold among ordinary people, both white and black. This expansion of evangelical Christianity did not proceed primarily from the nimble response of religious elites meeting the challenge before them. Rather, Christianity was effectively reshaped by ordinary people who molded it in their own image and threw themselves into expanding its influence. Increasingly assertive common people wanted their leaders unpretentious, their doctrines self-evident and down-to-earth, their music lively and singable, their churches in local hands. It was this upsurge of democratic hope that characterized so many religious cultures in the early republic and brought Baptists, Methodists, Disciples, and a host of other insurgent groups to the fore. The rise of evangelical Christianity in the early republic is, in some measure, a story of the success of common people in shaping the culture after their own priorities rather than the priorities outlined by gentlemen, such as the Founding Fathers. A style of religious leadership that the public had deemed "untutored" and "irregular" as late as the First Great Awakening became overwhelmingly successful, even normative, in the first decades of the new nation.

It is easy to miss the profoundly democratic character of the early republic's insurgent religious movements. The Methodists, after all, retained power in a structured hierarchy under the control of bishops; the Mormons reverted to rule by a single religious prophet and revelator; and groups such as the Disciples of Christ, despite professed democratic structures, came to be controlled by powerful individuals such as Alexander Campbell, who had little patience with dissent. As ecclesiastical structures, these movements often turned out to be less democratic than the congregational structure of the New England Standing Order.

The democratization of Christianity, then, has less to do with the specifics of polity and governance and more with the very incarnation of the church into popular culture. In at least three respects the popular religious movements of the early republic articulated a profoundly democratic spirit. First, they denied the age-old distinction that set the clergy apart as a separate order of men and they refused to defer to learned theologians and received orthodoxies. All were democratic or populist in the way their instinctively associated virtue with ordinary people rather than with elites, exalted the vernacular in word and song as the hallowed channel for communicating with and about God, and freely turned over the reigns of power. These groups also shared with the Jeffersonian Republicans an overt rejection of the past as a repository of wisdom. By redefining leadership itself, these movements were instrumental in shattering the centuries-old affinity between Christianity and the norms of high culture. They reconstructed the foundations of religion fully in keeping with the values and priorities of ordinary people.

Second, these movements empowered ordinary people by taking their deepest spiritual impulses at face value rather than subjecting them to the scrutiny of orthodox doctrine and the frowns of respectable clergymen. In the last two decades of the century, preachers from a wide range of new religious movements openly fanned the flames of religious ecstasy. Rejecting in 1775 the Yankee Calvinism of his youth, Henry Alline found that his soul was transported with divine love, "ravished with a divine ecstasy beyond any doubts or fears, or thoughts of being then deceived." What had been defined as "enthusiasm" increasingly became advocated from the pulpit as an essential part of Christianity. Such a shift in emphasis, accompanied by rousing gospel singing rather than formal church music, reflected the success of common people in defining for themselves the nature of faith. In addition, an unprecedented wave of religious leaders in the last quarter of the century expressed their own openness to a variety of signs and wonders—in short, an admission of increased supernatural involvement in everyday life. Scores of preachers' journals, from Methodists and Baptists, from North and South, from white and black, indicated a ready acceptance to interpret dreams and visions as inspired by God, normal manifestations of divine guidance and instruction. "I know the word of God is our infallible guide, and by it we are to try all our dreams and feelings," conceded the Methodist stalwart Freeborn Garrettson." But, he added, "I also know, that both sleeping and waking, things of a divine nature have been revealed to me." Those volatile aspects of popular religion, long held in check by the church, came to be recognized and encouraged from the pulpit. It is no wonder that a dismayed writer in the *Connecticut Evangelical Magazine* countered in 1805: "No person is warranted from the word of God to publish to the world the discoveries of heaven or hell which he supposes he has had in a dream, or trance, or vision."

The early republic was also a democratic moment in a third sense. Religious outsiders were flushed with confidence about their prospects and had little sense of their own limitations. They dreamed that a new age of religious and social harmony would spring up naturally out of their own efforts to overthrow coercive and authoritarian structures. This upsurge of democratic hope, this passion for equality, led to a welter of diverse and competing forms, many of them structured in highly undemocratic ways. The Methodists under Francis Asbury, for instance, used authoritarian means to build a church that would not be a respecter of persons. This church faced the curious paradox of gaining phenomenal influence among laypersons with whom it would not share ecclesiastical authority. Similarly, the Mormons used a virtual religious dictatorship as the means to return power to illiterate men. Yet, despite these authoritarian structures, the fundamental impetus of these movements was to make Christianity a liberating force, giving people the right to think and act for themselves rather than being forced to rely upon the mediations of an educated elite. The most fascinating religious story of the early republic is the signal achievements of these and other populist religious leaders, outsiders who brought to bear the full force of democratic persuasions upon American culture.

The wave of popular religious movements that broke upon the United States in the half-century after independence did more to Christianize American society than anything before or since. Nothing makes that point clearer than the growth of Methodists and Baptists as mass movements among white and black Americans. Starting from scratch just prior to the Revolution, the Methodists in America grew at a rate that terrified other denominations, reaching a quarter of a million members by 1820 and doubling again by 1830. Baptist membership multiplied tenfold in the three decades after the Revolution, the number of churches increasing from 500 to over 2500. The black church in America was born amidst the crusading vigor of these movements and quickly assumed its own distinct character and broad appeal among people of color. By the middle of the nineteenth century, Methodist and Baptist churches had splintered into more different denominational forms than one cares to remember. Yet together these movements came to constitute nearly 70 percent of Protestant church members in the United States and twothirds of its ministers.

This essay grows out of research on five distinct traditions or mass movements that came to the fore early in the nineteenth century: the Christian movement, the Methodists, the Baptists, the black churches, and the Mormons. Each was led by young men of relentless energy who went about movement-building as self-conscious outsiders. They shared an ethic of unrelenting labor, a passion for expansion, a hostility to orthodox belief and style, a zeal for religious reconstruction, and a systematic plan to labor on behalf of their ideals. However diverse their theologies and church organizations, they were able to offer common people, especially the poor, compelling visions of individual self-respect and collective self-confidence. . . .

In passing, it is instructive to suggest at least four reasons that historians have failed to explore the dynamics of popular religion in this era. First, during the last three decades the quickened interest in religion as a cultural force emerged within a broader historiographical tendency to downplay the social impact of the Revolution. Second, historians have interpreted the Second Great Awakening as an attempt by traditional religious elites to impose social order upon a disordered and secularized society—revivalism as an attempt to salvage Protestant solidarity. A third reason is that church historians from the more popular denominations have had reasons to sanitize their own histories. Modern church historians have chosen to focus on those dimensions of their own heritage that point to cultural enrichment, institutional cohesion, and intellectual respectability. William Warren Sweet, for instance, was committed to a vision of Methodists and Baptists as bearers of civilization to the uncouth and unretrained society of the frontier. Churches were instruments of order, education, and moral discipline.

A fourth reason that popular religious movements remain unexplored is surprising given the deep commitment by a new generation of social historians to understand the lives of common people in the age of capitalist transformation. While considerable attention has been focused on the changing nature of markets, on the decline of independent artisans and farmers and the rise of the American working class, surprisingly little energy has gone into exploring the dynamics of insurgent religious movements. This neglect stems both from the neo-Marxist preoccupation with the formation of social classes and the assumption that religion is generally a conservative force and a pernicious one. What these studies fail to take into account is that, for better or worse, the most dynamic popular movements in the early republic were expressly religious. . . .

An additional benefit of piecing together the story of these democratic religious movements is new insight into crucial questions about how America became a liberal society, individualistic, competitive, and market driven. In an age when most ordinary Americans expected almost nothing from government institutions and almost everything from religious ones, popular religious ideologies were perhaps the most important bellwethers of shifting worldviews. The passion for equality that came to the fore in these years decisively rejected the past as a repository of wisdom. Far from looking backward and clinging to an older moral economy, insurgent religious leaders espoused convictions that were essentially modern and individualistic. These persuasions defied elite privilege and vested interests, and anticipated the dawn of a millennial age of equality and justice. Yet, to achieve these visions of the common good, they espoused means inseparable from the individual pursuit of one's own spiritual and temporal well-being. They assumed that the leveling of aristocracy, root and branch, in all areas of human endeavor would naturally draw people together in harmony and equality. In this way, religious movements fervent about preserving the supernatural in everyday life had the ironic effect of accelerating the breakup of traditional society and the advent of a social order given over to competition, self-expression, and free enterprise. In this moment of fervent democratic aspiration, insurgent religious leaders had no way to foresee that their own assault upon mediating structures could lead to a society in which grasping entrepreneurs could erect new forms of tyranny in religious, political, or economic institutions. The individ-ualization of conscience, which they so greatly prized, moved them to see the very hand of providence in a social order of free and independent persons with interests to promote. Nothing better shows this process than the tumul-tuous career of John Leland, a career illustrating dramatically the ties in the early republic between popular religion, democratic politics, and liberal individualism.

In 1814 Leland was one of the most popular and controversial Baptists in America. He was most famous as a protagonist of religious freedom. As a leader among Virginia Baptists in the 1780s, Leland had been influential in petitioning the legislature on behalf of Jefferson's bill for religious freedom and for the bill to end the incorporation of the Protestant Episcopal Church. There is strong evidence that James Madison personally sought his support for the federal constitution, which Leland had first opposed. At the same time, Leland also marshalled Baptist opposition to slavery in Virginia. After returning to New England in 1791, he became the outstanding proponent of religious freedom as preacher, lecturer, and publicist and served two terms in the Massachusetts legislature representing the town of Cheshire.

On a national level Leland was best known for the 1,235-pound "Mam-moth Cheese" he had presented to President Thomas Jefferson. In New York and Baltimore crowds flocked to see this phenomenal creation, molded in a cider press supposedly from the milk of 900 cows and bearing the motto "Rebellion to tyrants is obedience to God." Leland made the presentation to Mr. Jefferson at the White House on New Year's Day 1802 as a token of esteem from the staunchly republican citizens of Cheshire. Two days later, at the pres-ident's invitation, he preached before both houses of Congress on the text "And behold a greater than Solomon is here." One congressman who heard that sermon, Manasseh Cutler, a Massachusetts Federalist and Congregational-ist clergyman, had few kind words to say about Leland's politics or his reli-gion, dismissing "the cheesemonger" as a "poor ignorant, illiterate, clownish creature." "Such a farrago, bawled with stunning voice, horrid tone, frightful grimaces, and extravagant gestures, I believe, was never heard by any decent auditory before. . . . Such an outrage upon religion, the Sabbath, and common decency, was extremely painful to every sober, thinking person present."

Leland's political notoriety has often masked the fact that fundamen-tally he was a preacher and itinerant evangelist. In 1824 he confessed that he had preached 8,000 times, had baptized over 1,300 persons, had known almost 1,000 Baptist preachers, and had traveled an equivalent of three times round the world. Given Leland's stature and connections, it is not at all surprising that he attended the Baptists' first Triennial Convention in Philadelphia and preached at William Staughton's church the night before the first session. That sermon sounded a sharp alarm for Baptists who were hun-gry for respectability. Even before any decision had been made about forming a missions organization, Leland warned against the danger of "Israel" insist-ing on having a king so that they could be like other nations: "like the people now-a-days; they form societies, and they must have a president and two or three vice-presidents, to be like their neighbors around them." After Baptists joined the Protestant quest for voluntary association, Leland stepped up his attacks upon missionary agencies and the clerical elites that stood behind them. For the next decade and a half, he went on the offensive against the organizational schemes and clerical professionalism at the core of American Protestant denominations. Leland ridiculed the mercenary foundation of foreign and domestic missions, the oppression of "a hierarchical clergy— despotic judiciary—[and] an aristocratic host of lawyers," the mechanical operations of theological seminaries, the tyranny of formal structures, and the burden of creedalism—"this Virgin Mary between the souls of men and the Scriptures." In a letter to John Taylor, the stalwart foe of mission activity in Kentucky, Leland confessed in 1830 that his calling had been "to watch and check *clerical hierarchy,* which assumes as many shades as a chameleon."

John Leland had every reason to take up the path of order and decorum that appealed to other Baptist leaders. Yet he seemed to come out of Revolutionary times with a different set of impulses stirring within. Rather than looking for ways to instill energy in government and to promote vigorous central policies, Leland sought at every step to restrain the accumulation of power. "I would as soon give my vote to a wolf to be a shepherd," he said in an oration celebrating American independence in 1802, "as to a man, who is always contending for the energy of government, to be a ruler." John Leland's dissent flowed out of a passion for religious liberty that exalted the individual conscience over creedal systems, local control over powerful ecclesiastical structures, and popular sensibility over the instincts of the educated and powerful. As prolific publicist, popular hymnwriter, amusing and satirical preacher, Leland strongly advocated freedom in every sphere of life. Self-reliant to an eccentric degree, Leland is fascinating and important in his own right. He also stands as an important bridge between the Revolutionary era and the quest for localism and independence that confounded Baptist history through the Jacksonian period. The importance of this story, played out on the fringes of denominational life, is not fully appreciated given its lack of coherence and the orientation of early denominational historians to celebrate the opposite, the growth of respectability and organizational coherence.

Brought up as a fervent New Light, John Leland found resources to accept, even defend, his own "rusticity of manners." Chief among these was a Jeffersonian view of conscience that championed intellectual selfreliance. In a pamphlet published in 1792 attacking the New England Standing Order, Leland explained how he came to trust his own reasoning rather than the conclusions of great men. Having once had "profound reverence" for leading civic figures, Leland discovered that in reality "not two of them agreed.". . .

Leland hammered out his view of conscience as he battled the state-church tradition of Virginia during the 1780s and of New England thereafter. In over thirty pamphlets and regular contributions to Phinehas Allen's staunchly Jeffersonian *Pittsfield Sun,* Leland spelled out a vision of personal autonomy that colored his personal life, his theological views, and his conception of society.

As early as 1790 Leland began to sound his clarion call that conscience should be "free from human control." His passion was to protect the "empire of conscience," the court of judgment in every human soul, from the inevitable encroachments of state-church traditions, oppressive creeds, ambitious and greedy clergymen—even from family tradition. "For a man to contend for religious liberty on the court-house green, and deny his wife, children and servants, the liberty of conscience at home, is a paradox not easily reconciled. . . . each one must give an account of himself to God." Upon returning to New England in 1791, Leland assailed the Standing Order in a pamphlet entitled *The Rights of Conscience Inalienable . . . or, The High-flying Churchman, Stripped of his Legal Robe, Appears a Yaho* (New London, 1791). With language borrowed directly from Jefferson's *Notes on the State of Virginia*, he argued that truth can stand on its own without the props of legal or creedal defense. He reiterated the theme that "religion is a matter between God and individuals." In addition to repeating his warning to parents that it was "iniquitous to bind the consciences" of children, Leland clarified his explicitly democratic view of conscience: that the so-called wise and learned were actually less capable of mediating truth than were common people. Leland dismissed the common objection that "the ignorant part of the community are not capacited to judge for themselves":

> Did many of the rulers believe in Christ when he was upon earth? Were not the learned clergy (the scribes) his most inveterate enemies? Do not great men differ as much as little men in judgment? Have not almost all lawless errors crept into the world through the means of wise men (so called)? Is not a simple man, who makes nature and reason his study, a competent judge of things? Is the Bible written (like Caligula's laws) so intricate and high, that none but the letter learned (according to the common phrase) can read it? Is not the vision written so plain that he that runs may read it?

In an 1801 sermon, *A Blow at the Root*, published in five editions in four different states from Vermont to Georgia, Leland continued to project an image of the autonomous person besieged by the coercive forces of state, creed, tradition, and clerical hierarchy. The political triumph of Jeffer son , the *"Man of the People,"* convinced Leland that the "genius of America," which had been slumbering, had finally "arisen, like a lion, from the swelling of Jordon, and roared like thunder in the states, 'we will be free; we will rule ourselves; our officers shall be honorable servants, but not mean masters.'"

Leland's legacy is an exaggerated opposition to official Christianity. He articulated a twofold persuasion that operated powerfully in the hinterland of Baptist church life: an aversion to central control and a quest for self-reliance. One reason that it is so difficult to write Baptist history in the early republic is that centrifugal forces were so powerfully at work, giving free reign to regional distinctives and take-charge entrepreneurs. Whatever success cosmopolitan leaders like Richard Furman or Francis Wayland had in building central institutions, their way was dogged at very step: by serious defections to the antiformalist appeals of Alexander Campbell and, later, William Miller, by the rise of significant Antimission Baptist associations in regions as diverse as New York, Pennsylvania, Illinois, Kentucky, and North Carolina; and by the appearance of charismatic dissenters such as J. R. Graves and his Landmark

Baptists. Equally important was the entrenched opposition to central authority among those who remained within the regular Baptist fold. The Triennial Convention, after all, had never represented Baptist churches themselves, but only individuals and societies willing to pay appropriate dues to the organization. After 1826 it was virtually dismembered when its champions from different regions locked horns over issues of authority and control.

John Leland is also important because of the way he turned a quest for self-reliance into a godly crusade. Like Elias Smith, James O'Kelly, Lorenzo Dow, Barton Stone, and William Miller, he fervently believed that individuals had to make a studied effort to prune away natural authorities: church, state, college, seminary, even family. Leland's message carried the combined ideological leverage of evangelical urgency and Jeffersonian promise. Choosing simple language and avoiding doctrinal refinements, he proclaimed a divine economy that was atomistic and competitive rather than wholistic and hierarchical. The triumph of liberal individualism, in this form at least, was not something imposed upon the people of America from above. They gladly championed the promise of personal autonomy as a message they could understand and a cause to which they could subscribe—in God's name no less.

Jon Butler  **NO**

Why Revolutionary America Wasn't a "Christian Nation"

Was America a "Christian nation" on the eve of the Revolution? Colonial law certainly would have made it appear so throughout most of the eighteenth century. Indeed, one of the great transformations of the eighteenth century centered on the renewal, not the decline, of the state church tradition in colonial America. Between 1690 and 1710 the colonial legislatures in South Carolina, North Carolina, Maryland, and New York effectively established the Church of England as the governmentally supported religion in their colonies, and the Virginia Burgesses thoroughly reworked the feeble Anglican establishment of the early seventeenth century. To the north, the old Puritan order in Massachusetts and Connecticut not only survived what contemporaries and historians have, rightly or wrongly, long described as "declension" or, put differently, the creation of a new, more diverse, more commercial, and more secular society. The state church apparatus found itself strengthened, not weakened. It became more elastic, and unlike the Anglican establishments to the south, it survived into the nineteenth century. In all, then, seven of the thirteen colonies gave legal support to a single expression of Protestant Christianity for 60 to 150 years before the Revolution.

Even where the law did not establish a single church, it usually upheld Protestant Christianity. Above all, the law punished. In colonies with church establishments, the law may have tolerated religious activity by dissenters, but it did not always do so, and it sometimes made that activity difficult. In colonies without establishments, the law customarily penalized a wide variety of settlers who may not have upheld Protestant Christianity in at least some perfunctory fashion. It openly discriminated against Catholics and Jews, denying them the right to own property or to vote, sometimes both, in different colonies. The law penalized blasphemers who spoke ill of Protestant Christianity. Long after the Salem witch trials of 1692 the law outlawed magic and witchcraft, Perhaps the situation in Pennsylvania, usually regarded as the most tolerant of all the colonies, expressed the legal situation well. Throughout the pre-Revolutionary period, Pennsylvania forced officeholders to swear to their belief in the divinity of Jesus, banned blasphemy, forbade Sunday labor, and urged all settlers to at- 'tend Christian services on the Sabbath so "looseness, irreligion, and Atheism may not creep in under the pretense of conscience."

From RELIGION AND THE NEW REPUBLIC: FAITH IN THE FOUNDING OF AMERICA, James Houston, ed., 2000, pp. 189–198. Copyright © 2000 by Rowman & Littlefield. Reprinted by permission. References omitted.

The eighteenth century also witnessed an explosion of congregational expansion that substantially increased church participation and membership in ways that might give life to the laws' strictures. Fully 85 percent of the colonial congregations that existed at the beginning of the American Revolution had been formed after 1700 and no less than 60 percent of these congregations had been formed after 1740. This expansion occurred in two waves, the first between 1680 and 1710, and the second between 1740 and 1770. The expansion came primarily from two causes. The first was revivalism, meaning the growth of evangelical, born-again Christianity in its rudimentary modern sense. The second was denominational expansion, meaning the systematic provision of leadership and ministry by ever more religious organizations, often headquartered in Philadelphia (not Boston), including Quakers, Presbyterians, Baptists, German Lutheran, and German Reformed, among others.

Thus, where we think of the early seventeenth century, and especially early New England, as the preeminent period of religious activity in colonial America, the eighteenth century dwarfed that activity and expansion many times over. It contributed crucial new forms of ministry, especially revivalism, and it bolstered new models of denominational leadership central to American religion in the next two centuries.

Were we to stop here, perhaps the answer to our question "Was late eighteenth-century America a Christian nation" might be yes. But as lawyers and mathematicians know, if the law and statistics are not funny things, they are at least arguable. This is particularly true when the facts turn out to be more complicated than they seem, not merely in the courtroom but in life, and when these complications occurred long before the relationship between religion and government changed after American independence.

One complication centered on the people. Put simply, whatever the law required or demanded, and however much congregational expansion Skyrocketed in the eighteenth century, the people by no means either responded or followed. Though historians do indeed argue about these things, it is all but impossible to calculate church membership at more than 20 percent of colonial adults before the American Revolution, a figure that would only decline further when the enslaved population is added, given the overwhelming failure of Christian proselytizing among the half-million Africans forcibly transported to the mainland colonies after 1680. In short, surprising as it may seem, church membership was far lower on the eve of independence—about 80 percent of adults did not belong—than it is at the end of the twentieth century, when it runs about 60 percent of adults.

Nor does computing attendance improve the situation. In fact, very few congregations recorded attendance, and when clergymen bragged about it, as Anglican ministers did in reports to the Bishop of London in 1724, their facts often seemed contradictory, to put it generously. Something seems suspicious when, for example, the minister in Virginia's Henrico Parish reported "sometimes 100 or 200 attend" but "20 is the greatest number that do [take communion] at one time," or when the minister of St. Paul's church in Narragansett, Rhode Island, reported congregations of 150 to 270 on Sundays but only 17 communicants. If these figures are accurate, these allegedly numerous listeners evinced a spiritual shyness that could have made even Puritans blush.

In this light, we might rethink the eighteenth-century colonial congregational expansion. Rather than seal the identity of the colonies as "Christian," congregational growth mainly helped to keep Christianity's head above the waters of the public indifference to Christian practice and belief that concerned Crèvecoeur and Woodmason. This in itself was no mean accomplishment, and it bore immense significance for Christianity's fate during and after the Revolution and for Christianity's expansion in the early national and antebellum periods, when techniques devised in the pre-Revolutionary era made powerful contributions to religious and social reform before the Civil War.

Ironically, perhaps, both the revivalism and proliferation of institutional formation and leadership that escalated congregational growth in the four score years before the Revolution cast the "Christian nation" question into doubt. Perhaps an oxymoron will help. We might say that, on the surface, the pre-Revolutionary "colonial nation" was nominally or even formally Christian. The law demanded adherence to a rudimentary Christianity and seven colonies established state churches. But these laws made sense precisely because actual Christian adherence in the population was relatively weak— perhaps no more so than it was in contemporary Europe, including Britain— not because attachment to Christianity was strong and overwhelming. In short, the law existed to compel Christian attachment. The law did not measure the Christian commitment of the people.

The proliferation of congregations, combined with Enlightenment doubts about coercion in religion generally, threw into doubt even the old minimal or formal pattern of Christian church establishment. In the aftermath of the Revolution, this led most states to withdraw from or greatly reduce government involvement with religion and culminated in the First Amendment to the Federal Constitution.

The remarkable proliferation of congregations between 1680 and 1770 led settlers in many places to ask the question that Charles Woodmason heard in the Carolina backcountry in the 1760s: "Whose Christianity?" The post-1680 congregational growth was not monochromatic. Instead, it introduced a religious pluralism unprecedented in Western society. Numbers alone tell part of the story. About 75 percent of all seventeenth-century churches were Congregational (in New England) or Anglican (Church of England and largely in Virginia). By the Revolution, however, Congregational and Anglican churches formed only about 35 percent of all colonial congregations. Now, 65 percent of the congregations were Presbyterian, Baptist, Quaker, German Reformed, Lutheran, Dutch Reformed, Methodist, Catholic, Moravian, Separatist-Congregational, German Baptist, Mennonite, French Protestant, Sandemanian, Jewish, and Rogerene, many of which had only been thinly visible or could not even be found in the colonies as late as 1700.

This vigorous pluralism never produced the religious antagonism and violence that characterized nineteenth- and twentieth-century America, to say nothing of the world in the 1990s. But it produced substantial tensions and arguments that unsettled familiar patterns of government aid to Christianity.

In New England, the arguments prospered during a revivalism of the 1740s and 1750s among both Congregationalists and Baptists that produced so-called "separatist" congregations of "born-again" or "revived" believers. Many arguments centered on theology, and some were inevitably personal. But many others focused on the spoils of government support for local religion or involved new government activity in religion. When a congregation split between "Old Lights" and "New Lights," who retained monies levied for Christianity's support in the town?

The arguments among the disputing Congregationalists joined those of Baptists, who generally objected to paying levies for religion at all. In turn, traditional Congregationalists turned up coercive legislation surrounding religion. In 1742, for example, the Connecticut assembly passed an "Act for Regulating Abuses and Correcting Disorders in Ecclesiastical Affairs," clearly directed against Congregational and Baptist revivalists. The act effectively banned unapproved itinerant preaching, ordered ministerial associations not to "meddle" in affairs outside their own jurisdiction, and allowed magistrates to eject nonresidents from the colony if they preached without the permission of the local clergymen and a majority of his congregation.

In Virginia, Anglicans, Presbyterians, and Baptists quickly fell out into disputes about the liberty of dissenters to preach and thereby contest the Anglicans' domination of Virginia's public religious life. As Thomas Jefferson rightly remembered the situation, the Anglican attack on Presbyterians and Baptists in the 1750s and 1760s had been preceded by efforts to curtail Quakers in the seventeenth century, "driving them from the colony by the severest penalties." (In fact, Virginia also chased Puritans from Nansemond County to Maryland in 1647–1648, which Jefferson did not know about.) In the late 1740s Virginia officials sought to inhibit the Presbyterian leader, Samuel Davies, by denying him a license to preach beyond his congregation. The Board of Trade in London, not American politicians, settled the matter, reminding Virginia's government in 1751 that "Toleration and a Free Exercise of Religion . . . should ever be held sacred in His Majesties Colonies."

Baptists received even rougher treatment because their preaching combined social, legal, and theological challenges to the Anglicans' status in Virginia. John Williams described the physical attack on "Brother Waller," a Caroline County Baptist preacher, in 1771, only five years before the Revolution. Coercion here was not mild or merely irritating but physical and violent.

> The Parson of the Parish would keep running the end of his horsewhip in [Waller's] mouth, laying his whip across the hymn book, etc. When done singing, [Waller] proceeded to prayer. In it he was violently jerked off the stage; [the parson and sheriff] caught him by the back part of his neck, beat his head against the ground, sometimes up, sometimes down, they carried him through a gate that stood some considerable distance, where a gentleman gave him . . . twenty lashes with his horsewhip.

Certainly, Anglicans had much to defend, from their social status to the political power held by their members, to their control of local and provincial government, to their power to tax, and to their church buildings, which represented the finest widespread domestic public architecture in the colony and, perhaps, in the colonies generally.

Even in places where there was no establishment, as in Pennsylvania, or where the establishment was weak, as in New York, eighteenth-century pluralism and revivalism brought difficulty rather than repose. Presbyterians who had fought Anglicans in Virginia had been well trained by their own internal disputing in the middle colonies. The arguments over revivalism produced innumerable personal confrontations in the 1740s and a fifteen-year schism in the Synod of Philadelphia from 1743 to 1758. George Whitefield caused dissension up and down the colonies as he drew listeners from clergymen jealous of his charismatic preaching. The combination of pluralism, lack of coercion, and lethargic ministerial leadership induced nominally German Lutheran and Reformed immigrants to Pennsylvania into utter spiritual indifference, the kind about which Crèvecoeur complained. Taken together, then, the specter of religious turmoil caused by pluralism, revivalism, and the bitterness engendered by government partiality in religion left the question of a colonial "Christian nation" increasingly open as the Revolution began.

A question not left open was that of church establishment. The experience of colonial religious diversity, the failures of the old religious establishments, the association of the Church of England with king and parliament, and the principles of the Declaration of Independence all encouraged many Americans to rethink the relationship between government and religion as the Revolution proceeded. The old Church of England lost most in this reevaluation. Between 1776 and 1785 the legal establishments that the Church of England had won eighty years earlier collapsed everywhere from New York to South Carolina. As this occurred, even Connecticut relieved "separates," including Episcopalians, Baptists, Quakers, "or any other Denomination," from church taxes. Only Massachusetts held out firmly, continuing to collect taxes for the local ministry. Although the new state distributed the church funds by local vote, this was majoritarianism, not democracy; it effectively funneled aid only to traditional Congregational churches except in a few towns.

The most important contest over religious identity and government occurred in Virginia. It merged growing colonial doubt about the wisdom of government involvement in religion with the narrower question of a single church establishment. The result proved dramatic. The Virginia debate stimulated a remarkable movement away from any substantial government aid for religious activity and directly shaped the religion clause in the First Amendment.

The Virginia debate, which occurred between 1779 and 1785, centered on two issue—general support for religion by aiding numerous Christian denominations and complete disestablishment. Proponents of aid to many denominations, including some Presbyterians and Patrick Henry, backed freedom of worship for all religious groups but advocated government support and tax funds for several if not all Protestant groups. In contrast, Thomas Jefferson, later supported by James Madison, offered a bill "for Establishing Religious Freedom." It prohibited tax levies for "any religious worship, place, or ministry whatsoever" and also upheld freedom of worship for all religious groups. Both sides struggled over these issues from 1779 to 1785 without any resolution.

A crucial debate during elections for the Virginia Burgesses in 1785 completely altered public opinion on the religion question. George Washington's turnaround symbolized the process. At first, Washington supported multiple establishment; he thought it was a fine idea to give government aid to several Protestant groups. But as the debate proceeded and stimulated increasing rancor, Washington turned against the proposal. Multiple establishment, Washington commented, seemed innocuous and natural, but it clearly would "rankle, and perhaps convulse the state."

As a result, in 1786 the Virginia legislature turned down Patrick Henry's bill for multiple establishment. Overwhelming opposition to it came from Baptists, Methodists, Episcopalians, and some Presbyterians. The legislature then approved by a vote of 74 to 20 Thomas Jefferson's bill "for Establishing Religious Freedom." It outlawed government aid to religion and guaranteed freedom of worship to all religions in the state, not just Protestants or even merely to Christians.

The Virginia debate renewed discussions in other states, and then with regard to the new federal government, about the relationship between America's religious identity and its relationship to government. In the states, it produced a rush of sentiment against a single establishment and against government aid to denominations generally. South Carolina's 1778 constitution had authorized government aid to several Protestant groups. But its 1790 constitution abandoned multiple establishment and guaranteed a broad freedom of worship. Multiple establishment bills failed in Georgia in 1782 and 1784, and in 1789 a new Georgia constitution eliminated multiple religious establishment entirely. The post-Revolutionary Maryland constitution permitted multiple establishment. But the Maryland assembly rejected funding for several Protestant groups by a two-to-one margin in 1785, and in 1810 a constitutional amendment eliminated multiple establishment in Maryland.

In New Hampshire, government aid to local Protestant congregations slowly collapsed, and in 1819 the legislature repealed the statute permitting the collection of local church taxes. Only Connecticut and Massachusetts held out, Connecticut until 1818 and Massachusetts until 1833; tellingly, these establishments fell in large measure because citizens of both states tired of the incessant bickering about church taxes, especially as they watched tax-supported congregations split over the doctrine of Unitarianism and lawsuits over the tax revenues belonging to the now divided congregations increase.

The First Amendment to the Federal Constitution passed in 1791 reflected this dual trend of eschewing a single church establishment and of prohibiting governmental activity in religion generally. The First Amendment prohibited a federal "establishment of religion," not merely of churches. Many commentators routinely describe the First Amendment as being about "church and state," following Jefferson in his famous 1802 letter to the Danbury Baptist Association where he backed a "wall of separation between church and state" in America. But the First Amendment banned government activity in religion generally and did not mention the narrower issue of church.

In its breadth, the First Amendment confirmed the eighteenth-century colonial American experience that religion increasingly took many forms, and complex ones, in this extraordinarily compound society. In this multifarious society, government should refrain from activity in religion. Congress specifically rejected wording that would have limited the First Amendment to narrower issues, such as prohibiting government support for a specific "religious doctrine," for "articles of faith or modes of worship," to protect only the "rights of conscience," to prohibit aid to "one religious sect or society in preference to others," or to establish a national church. All this language was deemed too narrow.

The amplitude of the First Amendment and the debates surrounding its wording help answer our question about late eighteenth-century America as a "Christian nation." It is surprising—or perhaps it is not surprising at all—how seldom, if ever, men and women referred to America as a "Christian nation" between 1760 and 1790. Indeed, such a phrase would have puzzled or even alarmed advocates of church establishment, whether traditional single establishments or more general government aid to religion or multiple denominations. When Yale president Ezra Stiles supported the continuation of Connecticut's Congregational establishment in 1783, he did so precisely because he believed Connecticut—indeed, America—was not a Christian nation. Too much atheism, too much indifference, too much heterodoxy, and too much immorality made that phrase meaningless. Indeed, for Stiles, Connecticut's church establishment had a simple attraction: it coerced men and women to support Christianity in at least some rudimentary fashion when they would otherwise ignore it. Government tax revenues could guarantee the modicum of "religion" that might keep a sinful, spiritually indifferent society afloat.

The Virginia Baptist John Leland agreed with Stiles's diagnosis of America's spiritual malaise but disputed Stiles's prescription. Leland likewise ridiculed the notion that a "Christian commonwealth" could or did exist in either Virginia or even the nation. Virginia and the nation needed saving, not praising. But unlike Stiles, Leland denied the government's right to engage the religious enterprise, and he did so on religious grounds, indeed, on specifically Christian grounds. As other Virginia opponents of general aid to religion put it in 1785, Christ "not only maintained and supported his gospel in the world for several hundred years without the aid of civil power, but against all the powers of the earth." To Leland, if not to Stiles, the contrast between early Christian practice and modern governmental aid to religion was stark and negative. If Christ did not use or want government aid, why did modern Christians?

The debate about America's religious identity and about government involvement with religion changed after passage of the Bill of Rights and the First Amendment in 1791 and especially after the 1810s. America's attraction as a field for Christian proselytizing only increased as American power and vibrancy became more obvious. The lure of the new public schools as a vehicle for Christian, or at least Protestant, instruction proved irresistible. Protestants increasingly attached providence to American purposes, especially in foreign affairs. Few heeded Lincoln's caution when, after ministers assured him that God was on the North's side in the Civil War, he replied that he was more concerned that the North was on God's side. Fewer still observed even the least caution when the federal government began to mold American Indians into "Christian nations" in the 1870s and when, to aid the effort, the War Department assigned reservations to specific denominations—Presbyterian, Methodist, Episcopal, Catholic, and even Quaker. These denominations then excluded competing missionaries, sometimes by force. They taught Christian doctrine in government-funded schools. They openly, vigorously, and sometimes violently suppressed traditional Indian religion and ceremonies, including most notoriously the Ghost Dance, a campaign capped but not ended by the massacre at Wounded Knee in South Dakota in December 1890. And they did so unashamedly for over sixty years with the support of many religious groups and Indian "reformers" from the advent of President Grant's ill-named "Peace Policy" in 1869 until 1933, when the New Deal Indian commissioner John Collier abolished these policies.

This struggle to shape America as a Christian nation after 1790 also frequently used "history" as a proselytizing instrument. Backers of such efforts rewrote a complex and often ambiguous eighteenth-century past to recast Revolutionary America as a "Christian nation," a phraseology that has appeared episodically in American history at crucial intervals down to the present.

Yet however politically useful in either the nineteenth century or in our own times, the concept of the "Christian nation" does not resonate well with the facts of eighteenth-century colonial and American history. Both before and after the American Revolution most, if not all, observers understood America as a society where Christianity was important yet not ubiquitous. In it, a partially Christian people imbibed multifarious religions—innumerable versions of Christianity plus Judaism, traditional African religious expression, native American religions, even notions of magic and occultism (to the chagrin of many). The capacity of all these religions to uplift and inspire was tempered by an often equally strong propensity to divide, anger, and demean. In the 1780s this complexity and energy increasingly prompted Americans to distrust governmental involvement in religion. At the founding of the republic they moved to protect the civil peace and spiritual renewal simultaneously by withdrawing from specific and general establishments of Christianity everywhere except Connecticut and Massachusetts, by prohibiting the federal government from "an establishment of religion," not merely an establishment of Christianity, and by requiring that the federal government never breach the "free exercise of religion." In short, although the people should or might become "Christian," such a national identity would best remain a matter of practice, not law or governmental encouragement.

This was not a unanimous construction, though unwittingly it might have been elegant. Certainly it was not easy. But it was the unique late-eighteenth-century construction that made the relationship between religion and the formation of the American republic so remarkable, so compelling, and so important. No other Western society knew it. And no other Western society ever wrote so bold, so novel, and so successful a prescription for religion's role in a nation's destiny.

POSTSCRIPT

Did the American Revolution Produce a Christian Nation?

In his book *Religion in America: Past and Present* (Prentice-Hall, 1961), Clifton E. Olmstead argues for a broader application of religious causes to the origins of the American Revolution. First, Olmstead contends that the First Great Awakening fostered a sense of community among American colonists, thus providing the unity required for an organized assault on English control. Moreover, the Awakening further weakened existing ties between colonies and Mother Country by drawing adherents of the Church of England into the evangelical denominations that expanded as a result of revivalistic Protestantism. Second, tensions were generated by the demand that an Anglican bishop be established in the colonies. Many evangelicals found in this plan evidence that the British government wanted further control over the colonies. Third, the Quebec Act, enacted by Parliament in 1774, not only angered American colonists by nullifying their claims to western lands, but also heightened religious prejudice in the colonies by granting tolerance to Roman Catholics. Fourth, ministers played a significant role in encouraging their parishioners to support the independence movement. Olmstead claims that this revolutionary movement in the colonies was defended overwhelmingly by Congregationalist, Presbyterian, Dutch Reform, and Baptist ministers. Finally, many of the revolutionaries, imbued with the American sense of mission, believed that God was ordaining their revolutionary activities.

In his famous revolutionary-era pamphlet *Common Sense*, Thomas Paine formulated a rationale for the American colonies to declare their independence from England. In one passage, Paine employed a form of geographical predestination by stressing the differences between England and America. "[E]ven the distance at which the Almighty hath placed England and America is a strong and natural proof that the authority of the one over the other was never the design of heaven." In other words, if God had wanted the colonies to remain part of the British Empire, he would not have placed such a wide expanse of ocean between them; hence, God favored American independence. While many Americans today would use the above passage to conclude that the Revolution was divinely ordained, it does not necessarily follow that the American revolutionaries conceived of their conflict with England as an opportunity to create a godly republic. They may have invoked the guidance of a Supreme Being, but seldom did these expressions emanate from a devoutly Christian faith. For a discussion of the role of Christianity in the Revolutionary era and beyond, see Mark A. Noll, Nathan O. Hatch, and George M. Marsden, *The Search for Christian America* (Crossway Books, 1983).

Further support for these views can be found in Alan Heimert, *Religion and the American Mind from the Great Awakening to the Revolution* (Cambridge University Press, 1966), Cedric B. Cowing, *The Great Awakening and the American Revolution: Colonial Thought in the Eighteenth Century* (University of Chicago, 1971), Richard Hofstadter, *America at 1750: A Social Portrait* (Knopf, 1973), Rhys Isaac, *The Transformation of Virginia, 1740–1790* (University of North Carolina Press, 1982), Ruth H. Bloch, *Visionary Republic* (Cambridge University Press, 1985), and Harry S. Stout, *The New England Soul: Preaching and Religious Culture in Colonial New England* (Oxford University Press, 1986). Alan Heimert's views have been challenged by Sidney Mead and Bernard Bailyn. Students interested in further analyses of the Great Awakening should consult Edwin Scott Gaustad, *The Great Awakening in New England* (Harper & Brothers, 1957), David S. Lovejoy, *Religious Enthusiasm and the Great Awakening* (Prentice-Hall, 1969), and Marilyn J. Westerkamp, *Triumph of the Laity: Scots-Irish Piety and the Great Awakening, 1625–1760* (Oxford University Press, 1987).

ISSUE 7

Were the Founding Fathers Democratic Reformers?

YES: John P. Roche, from "The Founding Fathers: A Reform Caucus in Action," *American Political Science Review* (December 1961)

NO: Howard Zinn, from *A People's History of the United States* (Harper Collins, 1999)

ISSUE SUMMARY

YES: Political scientist John P. Roche asserts that the Founding Fathers were not only revolutionaries but also superb democratic politicians who created a constitution that supported the needs of the nation and at the same time was acceptable to the people.

NO: According to radical historian Howard Zinn, the Founding Fathers were an elite group of northern money interests and southern slaveholders who used Shay's Rebellion in Massachusetts as a pretext to create a strong central government, which protected the property rights of the rich to the exclusion of slaves, Indians, and non-property-holding whites.

The United States possesses the oldest written constitution of any major power. The 55 men who attended the Philadelphia Convention of 1787 could scarcely have dreamed that 200 years later the nation would venerate them as the most "enlightened statesmen" of their time. James Madison, the principal architect of the document, may have argued that the Founding Fathers had created a system that might "decide forever the fate of Republican Government which we wish to last for ages," but Madison also told Thomas Jefferson in October 1787 that he did not think the document would be adopted, and if it was, it would not work.

The enlightened statesmen view of the Founding Fathers, presented by nineteenth-century historians like John Fiske, became the accepted interpretation among the general public until the Progressive Era. In 1913 Columbia University professor Charles A. Beard's *An Economic Interpretation of the Constitution of the United States* (Free Press, 1913, 1986) caused a storm of controversy because it questioned the motivations of the Founding Fathers. The

Founding Fathers supported the creation of a stronger central government, argued Beard, not for patriotic reasons but because they wanted to protect their own economic interests.

Beard's research method was fairly simple. Drawing upon a collection of old, previously unexamined treasury records in the National Archives, he discovered that a number of delegates to the Philadelphia Convention and, later, to the state ratifying conventions held substantial amounts of continental securities that would sharply increase in value if a strong national government were established. In addition to attributing economic motives to the Founding Fathers, Beard included a Marxist class conflict interpretation in his book. Those who supported the Constitution, he said, represented "personalty interests which hamd been adversely affected under the Articles of Confederation: money, public securities, manufactures, and trade and shipping." Those who opposed ratification of the Constitution were the small farmers and debtors.

Beard's socioeconomic conflict interpretation of the supporters and opponents of the Constitution raised another issue: How was the Constitution ratified if the majority of Americans opposed it? Beard's answer was that most Americans could not vote because they did not own property. Therefore, the entire process, from the calling of the Philadelphia Convention to the state ratifying conventions, was nonrepresentative and nondemocratic.

An economic interpretation was a product of its times. Economists, sociologists, and political scientists had been analyzing the conflicts that resulted from the Industrial Revolution, which America had been experiencing at the turn of the twentieth century. Beard joined a group of progressive historians who were interested in reforming the society in which they lived and who also shared his discontent with the old-fashioned institutional approach. The role of the new historians was to rewrite history and discover the real reason why things happened. For the progressive historians, reality consisted of uncovering the hidden social and economic conflicts within society.

In the years between the world wars, the general public held steadfastly to the enlightened statesmen view of the Founding Fathers, but Beard's thesis on the Constitution became the new orthodoxy in most college texts on American history and government. The post–World War II period witnessed the emergence of the neoconservative historians, who viewed the Beardian approach to the Constitution as overly simplistic.

In the first of the following selections, which is a good example of consensus history, John P. Roche contends that although the Founding Fathers may have been revolutionaries, they were also superb democratic politicians who framed a Constitution that supported the needs of the nation and at the same time was acceptable to the people. A good example of Beard's lasting influence can be found in the second selection in which radical historian Howard Zinn argues from the Beardian perspective. The Founding Fathers, he argues, were an elite group of northern money interests and southern slaveholders who used Shay's Rebellion in Massachusetts as a pretext to create a strong central government, which protected the property rights of the rich to the exclusion of slaves, Indians, and non-property-holding whites.

YES

John P. Roche

The Founding Fathers: A Reform Caucus in Action

The work of the Constitutional Convention and the motives of the Founding Fathers have been analyzed under a number of different ideological auspices. To one generation of historians, the hand of God was moving in the assembly; under a later dispensation, the dialectic (at various levels of philosophical sophistication) replaced the Deity: "relationships of production" moved into the niche previously reserved for Love of Country. . . . The Framers have undergone miraculous metamorphoses: at one time acclaimed as liberals and bold social engineers, today they appear in the guise of sound Burkean conservatives, men who in our time would subscribe to *Fortune*. . . .

The "Fathers" have thus been admitted to our best circles; the revolutionary ferocity which confiscated all Tory property in reach . . . has been converted . . . into a benign dedication to "consensus" and "prescriptive rights." . . . It is not my purpose here to argue that the "Fathers" were, in fact, radical revolutionaries; that proposition has been brilliantly demonstrated. . . . My concern is with the further position that not only were they revolutionaries, but also they were democrats. Indeed, in my view, there is one fundamental truth about the Founding Fathers . . . : They were first and foremost superb democratic politicians. . . . As recent research into the nature of American politics in the 1780s confirms, they were committed (perhaps willy-nilly) to working within the democratic framework, within a universe of public approval. . . . The Philadelphia Convention was not a College of Cardinals or a council of Platonic guardians working within a manipulative, pre-democratic framework; it was a nationalist reform caucus which had to operate with great delicacy and skill in a political cosmos full of enemies to achieve the one definitive goal—popular approbation. . . .

What they did was to hammer out a pragmatic compromise which would both bolster the "national interest" and be acceptable to the people. What inspiration they got came from their collective experience as professional politicians in a democratic society. As John Dickinson put it to his fellow delegates on August 13, "Experience must be our guide. Reason may mislead us."

In this context, let us examine the problems they confronted and the solutions they evolved. The Convention has been described picturesquely as a counter-revolutionary junta and the Constitution as a coup d'état, but this

From John P. Roche, "The Founding Fathers: A Reform Caucus in Action," *American Political Science Review*, vol. 55, no. 4 (December 1961). Copyright © 1961 by The American Political Science Association. Reprinted by permission of Cambridge University Press.

has been accomplished by withdrawing the whole history of the movement for constitutional reform from its true context. No doubt the goals of the constitutional elite were "subversive" to the existing political order, but it is overlooked that their subversion could only have succeeded if the people of the United States endorsed it by regularized procedures. . . .

I

When the Constitutionalists went forth to subvert the Confederation, they utilized the mechanisms of political legitimacy. And the roadblocks which confronted them were formidable. At the same time, they were endowed with certain potent political assets. The history of the United States from 1786 to 1790 was largely one of a masterful employment of political expertise by the Constitutionalists as against bumbling, erratic behavior by the opponents of reform. Effectively, the Constitutionalists had to induce the states, by democratic techniques of coercion, to emasculate themselves. . . . And at the risk of becoming boring, it must be reiterated that the only weapon in the Constitutionalist arsenal was an effective mobilization of public opinion.

The group which undertook this struggle was an interesting amalgam of a few dedicated nationalists with the self-interested spokesmen of various parochial bailiwicks. The Georgians, for example, wanted a strong central authority to provide military protection for their huge, underpopulated state against the Creek Confederacy; Jerseymen and Connecticuters wanted to escape from economic bondage to New York; the Virginians hoped to establish a system which would give that great state its rightful place in the councils of the republic. The dominant figures in the politics of these states therefore cooperated in the call for the Convention. In other states, the thrust towards national reform was taken up by opposition groups who added the "national interest" to their weapons system; in Pennsylvania, for instance, the group fighting to revise the Constitution of 1776 came out four-square behind the Constitutionalists, and in New York, [Alexander] Hamilton and the Schuyler [family] ambiance took the same tack against George Clinton. There was, of course, a large element of personality in the affair: there is reason to suspect that Patrick Henry's opposition to the Convention and the Constitution was founded on his conviction that Jefferson was behind both, and a close study of local politics elsewhere would surely reveal that others supported the Constitution for the simple (and politically quite sufficient) reason that the "wrong" people were against it. . . .

What distinguished the leaders of the Constitutionalist caucus from their enemies was a "Continental" approach to political, economic and military issues. To the extent that they shared an institutional base of operations, it was the Continental Congress (thirty-nine of the delegates to the Federal Convention had served in Congress), and this was hardly a locale which inspired respect for the state governments. . . . Membership in the Congress under the Articles of Confederation worked to establish a continental frame of reference, that a Congressman from Pennsylvania and one from North Carolina would share. . . . This was particularly true with respect to external affairs: the average state legislator was probably about as concerned with foreign policy than as he is today, but Congressmen were constantly forced to take the broad view of American prestige, were compelled to listen to the reports of Secretary John Jay and to the dispatches and pleas from their frustrated envoys in Britain, France and Spain. From considerations such as these, a "Continental" ideology developed which seems to have demanded a revision of our domestic institutions primarily on the ground that only by invigorating our general government could we assume our rightful place in the international arena. . . .

Note that I am not endorsing the "Critical Period" thesis; on the contrary, Merrill Jensen seems to me quite sound in his view that for most Americans, engaged as they were in self-sustaining agriculture, the "Critical Period" was not particularly critical. In fact, the great achievement of the Constitutionalists was their ultimate success in convincing the elected representatives of a majority of the white male population that change was imperative. A small group of political leaders with a Continental vision and essentially a consciousness of the United States' international impotence, provided the matrix of the movement. To their standard other leaders rallied with their own parallel ambitions. Their great assets were (1) the presence in their caucus of the one authentic American "father figure," George Washington, whose prestige was enormous; (2) the energy and talent of their leadership (in which one must include the towering intellectuals of the time, John Adams and Thomas Jefferson, despite their absence abroad), and their communications "network," which was far superior to anything on the opposition side; (3) the preemptive skill which made "their" issue The Issue and kept the locally oriented opposition permanently on the defensive; and (4) the subjective consideration that these men were spokesmen of a new and compelling credo: American nationalism, that ill-defined but nonetheless potent sense of collective purpose that emerged from the American Revolution. . . .

The Constitutionalists got the jump on the "opposition" (a collective noun: oppositions would be more correct) at the outset with the demand for a Convention. Their opponents were caught in an old political trap: they were not being asked to approve any specific program of reform, but only to endorse a meeting to discuss and recommend needed reforms. If they took a hard line at the first stage, they were put in the position of glorifying the status quo and of denying the need for any changes. Moreover, the Constitutionalists could go to the people with a persuasive argument for "fair play"—"How can you condemn reform before you know precisely what is involved?" Since the state legislatures obviously would have the final say on any proposals that might emerge from the Convention, the Constitutionalists were merely reasonable men asking for a chance. Besides, since they did not make any concrete proposals at that stage, they were in a position to capitalize on every sort of generalized discontent with the Confederation.

Perhaps because of their poor intelligence system, perhaps because of over-confidence generated by the failure of all previous efforts to alter the Articles, the opposition awoke too late to the dangers that confronted them in 1787. Not only did the Constitutionalists manage to get every state but Rhode Island . . . to appoint delegates to Philadelphia, but when the results were in, it appeared that they dominated the delegations. Given the apathy of the opposition, this was a natural phenomenon: in an ideologically nonpolarized political atmosphere those who get appointed to a special committee are likely to be the men who supported the movement for its creation. . . . Much has been made of the fact that the delegates to Philadelphia were not elected by the people; some have adduced this fact as evidence of the "undemocratic" character of the gathering. But put in the context of the time, this argument is wholly specious: the central government under the Articles was considered a creature of the component states and in all the states but Rhode Island, Connecticut and New Hampshire, members of the national Congress were chosen by the state legislatures. This was not a consequence of elitism or fear of the mob; it was a logical extension of states'-rights doctrine to guarantee that the national institution did not end-run the state legislatures and make direct contact with the people.

II

With delegations safely named, the focus shifted to Philadelphia. While waiting for a quorum to assemble, James Madison got busy and drafted the so-called Randolph or Virginia Plan with the aid of the Virginia delegation. This was a political master-stroke. Its consequence was that once business got under way, the framework of discussion was established on Madison's terms. There was no interminable argument over agenda; instead the delegates took the Virginia Resolutions—"just for purposes of discussion"—as their point of departure. And along with Madison's proposals, many of which were buried in the course of the summer, went his major premise: a new start on a Constitution rather than piecemeal amendment. . . .

Standard treatments of the Convention divide the delegates into "nationalists" and "states'-righters" with various improvised shadings ("moderate nationalists," etc.), but these are a posteriori categories which obfuscate more than they clarify. What is striking to one who analyzes the Convention as a case-study in democratic politics is the lack of clear-cut ideological divisions in the Convention. Indeed, I submit that the evidence—Madison's Notes, the correspondence of the delegates, and debates on ratification—indicates that this was a remarkably homogeneous body on the ideological level. [Robert] Yates and [John] Lansing [of New York], who favored the New Jersey Plan] . . . left in disgust on July 10. . . . Luther Martin, Maryland's bibulous narcissist, left on September 4 in a huff when he discovered that others did not share his selfesteem; others went home for personal reasons. But the hard core of delegates accepted a grinding regimen throughout the attrition of a Philadelphia summer precisely because they shared the Constitutionalist goal.

Basic differences of opinion emerged, of course, but these were not ideological; they were structural. If the so-called "states'-rights" group had not accepted the fundamental purposes of the Convention, they could simply have pulled out and by doing so have aborted the whole enterprise. Instead of bolting, they returned day after day to argue and to compromise. An interesting symbol of this basic homogeneity was the initial agreement on secrecy: these professional politicians did not want to become prisoners of publicity; they wanted to retain that freedom of maneuver which is only possible when men are not forced to take public stands in the preliminary stages of negotiation. There was no legal means of binding the tongues of the delegates: at any stage in the game a delegate with basic principled objections to the emerging project could have taken the stump (as Luther Martin did after his exit) and denounced the convention to the skies. Yet . . . the delegates generally observed the injunction. Secrecy is certainly uncharacteristic of any assembly marked by strong ideological polarization. . . .

Commentators on the Constitution who have read *The Federalist* in lieu of reading the actual debates have credited the Fathers with the invention of a sublime concept called "Federalism." . . . Federalism, as the theory is generally defined, was an improvisation which was later promoted into a political theory. Experts on "federalism" should take to heart the advice of David Hume, who warned . . . "there is no subject in which we must proceed with more caution than in [history], lest we assign causes which never existed and reduce what is merely contingent to stable and universal principles." In any event, the final balance in the Constitution between the states and the nation must have come as a great disappointment to Madison. . . .

It is indeed astonishing how those who have glibly designated James Madison the "father" of Federalism have overlooked the solid body of fact which indicates that he shared Hamilton's quest for a unitary central government. To be specific, they have avoided examining the clear import of the Madison-Virginia Plan, and have disregarded Madison's dogged inch-by-inch retreat from the bastions of centralization. The Virginia Plan envisioned a unitary national government effectively freed from and dominant over the states. The lower house of the national legislature was to be elected directly by the people of the states with membership proportional to population. The upper house was to be selected by the lower and the two chambers would elect the executive and choose the judges. The national legislature was to be empowered to disallow the acts of state legislatures, and the central government was vested, in addition to the powers of the nation under which the Articles of Confederation, with plenary authority wherever ". . . the separate States are incompetent or in which the harmony of the United States may be interrupted by the exercise of individual legislation." Finally, just to lock the door against state intrusion, the national Congress was to be given the power to use military force on recalcitrant states. This was Madison's "model" of an ideal national government, though it later received little publicity in *The Federalist*.

The interesting thing was the reaction of the Convention to this militant program for a strong autonomous central government. Some delegates were startled, some obviously leery of so comprehensive a project of reform, but nobody set off any fireworks and nobody walked out. Moreover, in the two weeks that followed, the Virginia Plan received substantial endorsement *en principe;* the initial temper of the gathering can be deduced from the approval "without debate or dissent," on May 31, of the Sixth Resolution which granted Congress the authority to disallow state legislation ". . . contravening in its opinion the Articles of Union." Indeed, an amendment was included to bar states from contravening national treaties.

The Virginia Plan may therefore be considered, in ideological terms, as the delegates' Utopia, but as the discussions continued and became more specific, many of those present began to have second thoughts. . . . They were practical politicians in a democratic society, and no matter what their private dreams might be, they had to take home an acceptable package and defend it—and their own political futures—against predictable attack. On June 14 the breaking point between dream and reality took place. Apparently realizing that under the Virginia Plan, Massachusetts, Virginia and Pennsylvania could virtually dominate the national government—and probably appreciating that to sell this program to "the folks back home" would be impossible—the delegates from the small states dug in their heels and demanded time for a consideration of alternatives. . . .

Now the process of accommodation was put into action smoothly—and wisely, given the character and strength of the doubters. Madison had the votes, but this was one of those situations where the enforcement of mechanical majoritarianism could easily have destroyed the objectives of the majority: the Constitutionalists were in quest of a qualitative as well as a quantitative consensus; . . . it was a political imperative if they were to attain ratification.

III

According to the standard script, at this point the "states'-rights" group intervened in force behind the New Jersey Plan, which has been characteristically portrayed as a revision to the status quo under the Articles of Confederation with but minor modifications. A careful examination of the evidence indicates that only in a marginal sense is this an accurate description. It is true that the New Jersey Plan put the states back into the institutional picture, but one could argue that to do so was a recognition of political reality rather than an affirmation of states'-rights. A serious case can be made that the advocates of the New Jersey Plan, far from being ideological addicts of states'-rights, intended to substitute for the Virginia Plan a system which would both retain strong national power and have a chance of adoption in the states. The leading spokesman for the project asserted quite clearly that his views were based more on counsels of expediency than on principle. . . . In his preliminary speech on June 9, Paterson had stated ". . . to the public mind we must accommodate ourselves," and in his notes for this and his later effort as well, the emphasis is the same. The structure of government under the Articles should be retained:

> 2. Because it accords with the Sentiments of the People
>
> > [Proof:] 1. Coms. [Commissions from state legislatures defin-
> > ing the jurisdiction of the delegates]
> > 2. News-papers—Political Barometer. Jersey never would have
> > sent Delegates under the first [Virginia] Plan—
>
> Not here to sport Opinions of my own. Wt. [What] can be done. A little
> practicable Virtue preferable to Theory.

This was a defense of political acumen, not of states'-rights. . . .

In other words, the advocates of the New Jersey Plan concentrated their fire on what they held to be the political liabilities of the Virginia Plan—which were matters of institutional structure—rather than on the proposed scope of national authority. Indeed, the Supremacy Clause of the Constitution first saw the light of day in Paterson's Sixth Resolution; the New Jersey Plan contemplated the use of military force to secure compliance with national law; and finally Paterson made clear his view that under either the Virginia or the New Jersey systems, the general government would ". . . act on individuals and not on states." From the states'-rights viewpoint, this was heresy: the fundament of that doctrine was the proposition that any central government had as its constituents the states, not the people, and could only reach the people through the agency of the state government.

Paterson then reopened the agenda of the Convention, but he did so within a distinctly naturalist framework. Paterson's position was one of favoring a strong central government in principle, but opposing one which in fact put the big states in the saddle.

How attached would the Virginians have been to their reform principles if Virginia were to disappear as a component geographical unit (the largest) for representational purposes? Up to this point, the Virginians had been in the happy position of supporting high ideals with that inner confidence born of knowledge that the "public interest" they endorsed would nourish their private interest. Worse, they had shown little willingness to compromise. Now the delegates from the small states announced that they were unprepared to be offered up as sacrificial victims to a "national interest" which reflected Virginia's parochial ambition. Caustic Charles Pinckney was not far off when he remarked sardonically that ". . . the whole [conflict] comes to this: Give N. Jersey an equal vote, and she will dismiss her scruples, and concur in the Natil. system." What he rather unfairly did not add was that the Jersey delegates were not free agents who could adhere to their private convictions; they had to take back, sponsor and risk their reputations on the reforms approved by the Convention—and in New Jersey, not in Virginia. . . .

IV

On Tuesday morning, June 19, . . . James Madison led off with a long, carefully reasoned speech analyzing the New Jersey Plan which, while intellectually vigorous in its criticisms, was quite conciliatory in mood. "The great difficulty," he observed, "lies in the affair of Representation; and if this could be adjusted, all others would be surmountable." (As events were to demonstrate, this diagnosis was correct.) When he finished, a vote was taken on whether to continue with the Virginia Plan as the nucleus for a new constitution: seven states voted "Yes"; New York, New Jersey, and Delaware voted "No"; and Maryland, whose position often depended on which delegates happened to be on the floor, divided. Paterson, it seems, lost decisively; yet in a fundamental sense he and his allies had achieved their purpose: from that day onward, it could never be forgotten that the state governments loomed ominously in the background. . . . Moreover, nobody bolted the convention: Paterson and his colleagues took their defeat in stride and set to work to modify the Virginia Plan, particularly with respect to its provisions on representation in the national legislature. Indeed, they won an immediate rhetorical bonus; when Oliver Ellsworth of Connecticut rose to move that the word "national" be expunged from the Third Virginia Resolution ("Resolved that a national Government ought to be established consisting of a supreme Legislative, Executive and Judiciary"), Randolph agreed and the motion passed unanimously. The process of compromise had begun.

For the next two weeks, the delegates circled around the problem of legislative representation. The Connecticut delegation appears to have evolved a possible compromise quite early in the debates, but the Virginians and particularly Madison (unaware that he would later be acclaimed as the prophet of "federalism") fought obdurately against providing for equal representation of states in the second chamber. . . . On July 2, the ice began to break when through a number of fortuitous events—and one that seems deliberate—the majority against equality of representation was converted into a dead tie. The Convention had reached the stage where it was "ripe" for a solution (presumably all the therapeutic speeches had been made), and the South Carolinians proposed a committee. Madison and James Wilson wanted none of it, but with only Pennsylvania dissenting, the body voted to establish a working party on the problem of representation.

The members of this committee, one from each state, were elected by the delegates—and a very interesting committee it was. Despite the fact that the Virginia Plan had held majority support up to that date, neither Madison nor Randolph was selected (Mason was the Virginian) and Baldwin of Georgia, whose shift in position had resulted in the tie, was chosen. From the composition, it was clear that this was not to be a "fighting" committee: the emphasis in membership was on what might be described as "second-level political entrepreneurs." On the basis of the discussions up to that time, only Luther Martin of Maryland could be described as a "bitter-ender." Admittedly, some divination enters into this sort of analysis, but one does get a sense of the mood of the delegates from these choices—including the interesting selection of Benjamin Franklin, despite his age and intellectual wobbliness, over the brilliant and incisive Wilson or the sharp, polemical Gouverneur Morris, to represent Pennsylvania. His passion for conciliation was more valuable at this juncture than Wilson's logical genius, or Morris' acerbic wit. . . .

It would be tedious to continue a blow-by-blow analysis of the work of the delegates; the critical fight was over representation of the states and once the Connecticut Compromise was adopted on July 17, the Convention was over the hump. Madison, James Wilson, and Gouverneur Morris of New York (who was there representing Pennsylvania!) fought the compromise all the way in a last-ditch effort to get a unitary state with parliamentary supremacy. But their allies deserted them. . . . Moreover, once the compromise had carried (by five states to four, with one state divided), its advocates threw themselves vigorously into the job of strengthening the general government's substantive powers—as might have been predicted, indeed, from Paterson's early statements. It nourishes an increased respect for Madison's devotion to the art of politics, to realize that this dogged fighter could sit down six months later and prepare essays for *The Federalist* in contradiction to his basic convictions about the true course the Convention should have taken.

V

Two tricky issues will serve to illustrate the later process of accommodation. The first was the institutional position of the Executive. Madison argued for an executive chosen by the National Legislature and on May 29 this had been adopted with a provision that after his seven-year term was concluded, the chief magistrate should not be eligible for reelection. In late July this was reopened and for a week the matter was argued from several different points of view. . . . One group felt that the states should have a hand in the process; another small but influential circle urged direct election by the people. There were a number of proposals: election by the people, election by state governors, by electors chosen by state legislatures, by the National legislature, . . . and there was some resemblance to three-dimensional chess in the dispute because of the presence of two other variables, length of tenure and reeligibility. Finally, after opening, reopening, and re-reopening the debate, the thorny problem was consigned to a committee for resolution.

The Brearley Committee on Postponed Matters was a superb aggregation of talent and its compromise on the Executive was a masterpiece of political improvisation. (The Electoral College, its creation, however, had little in its favor as an institution—as the delegates well appreciated.) The point of departure for all discussion about the presidency in the Convention was that in immediate terms, the problem was non-existent; in other words, everybody present knew that under any system devised, George Washington would be President. Thus they were dealing in the future tense and to a body of working politicians the merits of the Brearley proposal were obvious: everybody got a piece of cake. (Or to put it more academically, each viewpoint could leave the Convention and argue to its constituents that it had really won the day.) First, the state legislatures had the right to determine the mode of selection of the electors; second, the small states received a bonus in the Electoral College in the form of a guaranteed minimum of three votes while the big states got acceptance of the principle of proportional power; third, if the state legislatures agreed (as six did in the first presidential election), the people could be involved directly in the choice of electors; and finally, if no candidate received a majority in the College, the right of decision passed to the National Legislature with each state exercising equal strength. (In the Brearley recommendation, the election went to the Senate, but a motion from the floor substituted the House; this was accepted on the ground that the Senate already had enough authority over the executive in its treaty and appointment powers.)

This compromise was almost too good to be true, and the Framers snapped it up with little debate or controversy. No one seemed to think well of the College as an institution; indeed, what evidence there is suggests that there was an assumption that once Washington had finished his tenure as President, the electors would cease to produce majorities and the chief executive would usually be chosen in the House. George Mason observed casually that the selection would be made in the House nineteen times in twenty and no one seriously disputed this point. The vital aspect of the Electoral College was that it got the Convention over the hurdle and protected everybody's interests. . . .

In short, the Framers did not in their wisdom endow the United States with a College of Cardinals—the Electoral College was neither an exercise in applied Platonism nor an experiment in indirect government based on elitist distrust of the masses. It was merely a jerry-rigged improvisation which has subsequently been endowed with a high theoretical content. . . .

The second issue on which some substantial practical bargaining took place was slavery. The morality of slavery was, by design, not at issue; but in its other concrete aspects, slavery colored the arguments over taxation, commerce, and representation. The "Three-Fifths Compromise," that three-fifths of the slaves would be counted both for representation and for purposes of direct taxation (which was drawn from the past—it was a formula of Madison's utilized by Congress in 1783 to establish the basis of state contributions to the Confederation treasury) had allayed some Northern fears about Southern over-representation. . . . The Southerners, on the other hand, were afraid that Congressional control over commerce would lead to the exclusion of slaves or to their excessive taxation as imports. Moreover, the Southerners were disturbed over "navigation acts," i.e., tariffs or special legislation providing, for example, that exports be carried only in American ships; as a section depending upon exports, they wanted protection from the potential voracity of their commercial brethren of the Eastern states. To achieve this end, Mason and others urged that the Constitution include a proviso that navigation and commercial laws should require a two-thirds vote in Congress.

These problems came to a head in late August and, as usual were handed to a committee in the hope that, in Gouverneur Morris' words, ". . . these things may form a bargain among the Northern and Southern states." The Committee reported its measures of reconciliation on August 25, and on August 29 the package was wrapped up and delivered. What occurred can best be described in George Mason's dour version (he anticipated Calhoun in his conviction that permitting navigation acts to pass by majority vote would put the South in economic bondage to the North—it was mainly on this ground that he refused to sign the Constitution):

> The Constitution as agreed to till a fortnight before the Convention rose was such a one as he would have set his hand and heart to. . . . [Until that time] The 3 New England States were constantly with us in all questions . . . so that it was these three States with the 5 Southern ones against Pennsylvania, Jersey and Delaware. With respect to the importation of slaves, [decision-making] was left to Congress. This disturbed the two Southernmost States who knew that Congress would immediately suppress the importation of slaves. Those two States therefore struck up a bargain with the three New England States. If they would join to admit slaves for some years, the two Southern-most States would join in changing the

clause which required the 2/3 of the Legislature in any vote [on navigation acts]. It was done.

On the floor of the Convention there was a virtual love-feast on this happy occasion. Charles Pinckney of South Carolina attempted to overturn the committee's decision, when the compromise was reported to the Convention, by insisting that the South needed protection from the imperialism of the Northern states. But his Southern colleagues were not prepared to rock the boat and General C. C. Pinckney arose to spread oil on the suddenly ruffled waters; he admitted that:

> It was in the true interest of the S[outhern] States to have no regulation of commerce; but considering the loss brought on the commerce of the Eastern States by the Revolution, their liberal conduct towards the views of South Carolina [on the regulation of the slave trade] and the interests the weak Southn. States had in being united with the strong Eastern states, he thought it proper that no fetters should be imposed on the power of making commercial regulations; and that his constituents, though prejudiced against the Eastern States, would be reconciled to this liberality. He had himself prejudices against the Eastern States before he came here, but would acknowledge that he had found them as liberal and candid as any men whatever.

Pierce Butler took the same tack, essentially arguing that he was not too happy about the possible consequences, but that a deal was a deal. . . .

VI

Drawing on their vast collective political experience, utilizing every weapon in the politician's arsenal, looking constantly over their shoulders at their constituents, the delegates put together a Constitution. It was a makeshift affair; some sticky issues (for example, the qualification of voters) they ducked entirely; others they mastered with that ancient instrument of political sagacity, studied ambiguity (for example, citizenship), and some they just overlooked. In this last category, I suspect, fell the matter of the power of the federal courts to determine the constitutionality of acts of Congress. When the judicial article was formulated (Article III of the Constitution), deliberations were still in the stage where the legislature was endowed with broad power under the Randolph formulation, authority which by its own terms was scarcely amenable to judicial review. In essence, courts could hardly determine when ". . . the separate States are incompetent or . . . the harmony of the United States may be interrupted"; the National Legislature, as critics pointed out, was free to define its own jurisdiction. Later the definition of legislative authority was changed into the form we know, a series of stipulated powers, but the delegates never seriously reexamined the jurisdiction of the judiciary under this new limited formulation. All arguments on the intention of the Framers in this matter are thus deductive and a posteriori, though some obviously make more sense than others.

The Framers were busy and distinguished men, anxious to get back to their families, their positions, and their constituents. . . . They were trying to do an important job, and do it in such a fashion that their handiwork would be acceptable to very diverse constituencies. No one was rhapsodic about the final document, but it was a beginning, a move in the right direction, and one they had reason to believe the people would endorse. In addition, since they had modified the impossible amendment provisions of the Articles . . . to one demanding approval by only three-quarters of the states, they seemed confident that gaps in the fabric which experience would reveal could be rewoven without undue difficulty.

So with a neat phrase introduced by Benjamin Franklin (but devised by Gouverneur Morris) which made their decision sound unanimous, and an inspired benediction by the Old Doctor urging doubters to doubt their own infallibility, the Constitution was accepted and signed. Curiously, Edmund Randolph, who had played so vital a role throughout, refused to sign, as did his fellow Virginian George Mason and Elbridge Gerry of Massachusetts. Randolph's behavior was eccentric; . . . the best explanation seems to be that he was afraid that the Constitution would prove to be a liability in Virginia politics, where Patrick Henry was burning up the countryside with impassioned denunciations. Presumably, Randolph wanted to check the temper of the populace before he risked his reputation, and perhaps his job, in a fight with both Henry and Richard Henry Lee. Events lend some justification to this speculation: after much temporizing . . . Randolph endorsed ratification in Virginia and ended up getting the best of both worlds. . . .

The Constitution, then, was an apotheosis of "constitutionalism," a triumph of architectonic genius; it was a patchwork sewn together under the pressure of both time and events by a group of extremely talented democratic politicians. They refused to attempt the establishment of a strong, centralized sovereignty on the principle of legislative supremacy for the excellent reason that the people would not accept it. They risked their political fortunes by opposing the established doctrines of state sovereignty because they were convinced that the existing system was leading to national impotence and probably foreign domination. For two years, they worked to get a convention established. For over three months, in what must have seemed to the faithful participants an endless process of give-and-take, they reasoned, cajoled, threatened, and bargained amongst themselves. The result was a Constitution which the people, in fact, by democratic processes, did accept, and a new and far better national government was established. . . .

To conclude, the Constitution was neither a victory for abstract theory nor a great practical success. Well over half a million men had to die on the battlefields of the Civil War before certain constitutional principles could be defined—a baleful consideration which is somehow overlooked in our customary tributes to the farsighted genius of the Framers and to the supposed American talent for "constitutionalism." The Constitution was, however, a vivid demonstration of effective democratic political action, and of the forging of a national elite which literally persuaded its countrymen to hoist themselves by their own boot straps.

Howard Zinn

A People's History of the United States

To many Americans over the years, the Constitution drawn up in 1787 has seemed a work of genius put together by wise, humane men who created a legal framework for democracy and equality. This view is stated, a bit extravagantly, by the historian George Bancroft, writing in the early nineteenth century:

> The Constitution establishes nothing that interferes with equality and individuality. It knows nothing of differences by descent, or opinions, of favored classes, or legalized religion, or the political power of property. It leaves the individual alongside of the individual. . . . As the sea is made up of drops, American society is composed of separate, free, and constantly moving atoms, ever in reciprocal action . . . so that the institutions and laws of the country rise out of the masses of individual thought which, like the waters of the ocean, are rolling evermore.

Another view of the Constitution was put forward early in the twentieth century by the historian Charles Beard (arousing anger and indignation, including a denunciatory editorial in the *New York Times*). He wrote in his book *An Economic Interpretation of the Constitution:*

> Inasmuch as the primary object of a government, beyond the mere repression of physical violence, is the making of the rules which determine the property relations of members of society, the dominant classes whose rights are thus to be determined must perforce obtain from the government such rules as are consonant with the larger interests necessary to the continuance of their economic processes, or they must themselves control the organs of government.

In short, Beard said, the rich must, in their own interest, either control the government directly or control the laws by which government operates.

Beard applied this general idea to the Constitution, by studying the economic backgrounds and political ideas of the fifty-five men who gathered in Philadelphia in 1787 to draw up the Constitution. He found that a majority of them were lawyers by profession, that most of them were men of wealth, in land, slaves, manufacturing, or shipping, that half of them had money loaned out at interest, and that forty of the fifty-five held government bonds, according to the records of the Treasury Department.

Thus, Beard found that most of the makers of the Constitution had some direct economic interest in establishing a strong federal government: the manufacturers needed protective tariffs; the moneylenders wanted to stop the use of paper money to pay off debts; the land speculators wanted protection as they invaded Indian lands; slaveowners needed federal security against slave revolts and runaways; bondholders wanted a government able to raise money by nationwide taxation, to pay off those bonds.

Four groups, Beard noted, were not represented in the Constitutional Convention: slaves, indentured servants, women, men without property. And so the Constitution did not reflect the interests of those groups.

He wanted to make it clear that he did not think the Constitution was written merely to benefit the Founding Fathers personally, although one could not ignore the $150,000 fortune of Benjamin Franklin, the connections of Alexander Hamilton to wealthy interests through his father-in-law and brother-in-law, the great slave plantations of James Madison, the enormous landholdings of George Washington. Rather, it was to benefit the groups the Founders represented, the "economic interests they understood and felt in concrete, definite form through their own personal experience."

Not everyone at the Philadelphia Convention fitted Beard's scheme. Elbridge Gerry of Massachusetts was a holder of landed property, and yet he opposed the ratification of the Constitution. Similarly, Luther Martin of Maryland, whose ancestors had obtained large tracts of land in New Jersey, opposed ratification. But, with a few exceptions, Beard found a strong connection between wealth and support of the Constitution.

By 1787 there was not only a positive need for strong central government to protect the large economic interests, but also immediate fear of rebellion by discontented farmers. The chief event causing this fear was an uprising in the summer of 1786 in western Massachusetts, known as Shays' Rebellion.

In the western towns of Massachusetts there was resentment against the legislature in Boston. The new Constitution of 1780 had raised the property qualifications for voting. No one could hold state office without being quite wealthy. Furthermore, the legislature was refusing to issue paper money, as had been done in some other states, like Rhode Island, to make it easier for debt-ridden farmers to pay off their creditors.

Illegal conventions began to assemble in some of the western counties to organize opposition to the legislature. At one of these, a man named Plough Jogger spoke his mind:

> I have been greatly abused, have been obliged to do more than my part in the war; been loaded with class rates, town rates, province rates, Continental rates and all rates . . . been pulled and hauled by sheriffs, constables and collectors, and had my cattle sold for less than they were worth. . . .
> . . . The great men are going to get all we have and I think it is time for us to rise and put a stop to it, and have no more courts, nor sheriffs, nor collectors nor lawyers. . . .

The chairman of that meeting used his gavel to cut short the applause. He and others wanted to redress their grievances, but peacefully, by petition to the General Court (the legislature) in Boston.

However, before the scheduled meeting of the General Court, there were going to he court proceedings in Hampshire County, in the towns of Northampton and Springfield, to seize the cattle of farmers who hadn't paid their debts, to take away their land, now full of grain and ready for harvest. And so, veterans of the Continental army, also aggrieved because they had been treated poorly on discharge—given certificates for future redemption instead of immediate cash—began to organize the farmers into squads and companies. One of these veterans was Luke Day, who arrived the morning of court with a fife-and-drum corps, still angry with the memory of being locked up in debtors' prison in the heat of the previous summer.

The sheriff looked to the local militia to defend the court against these armed farmers. But most of the militia was with Luke Day. The sheriff did manage to gather five hundred men, and the judges put on their black silk robes, waiting for the sheriff to protect their trip to the courthouse. But there at the courthouse steps, Luke Day stood with a petition, asserting the people's constitutional right to protest the unconstitutional acts of the General Court, asking the judges to adjourn until the General Court could act on behalf of the farmers. Standing with Luke Day were fifteen hundred armed farmers. The judges adjourned.

Shortly after, at courthouses in Worcester and Athol, farmers with guns prevented the courts from meeting to take away their property, and the militia were too sympathetic to the farmers, or too outnumbered, to act. In Concord, a fifty-year-old veteran of two wars, Job Shattuck, led a caravan of carts, wagons, horses, and oxen onto the town green, while a message was sent to the judges:

> The voice of the People of this county is such that the court shall not enter this courthouse until such time as the People shall have redress of the grievances they labor under at the present.

A county convention then suggested the judges adjourn, which they did.

At Great Barrington, a militia of a thousand faced a square crowded with armed men and boys. But the militia was split in its opinion. When the chief justice suggested the militia divide, those in favor of the court's sitting to go on the right side of the road, and those against on the left, two hundred of the militia went to the right, eight hundred to the left, and the judges adjourned. Then the crowd went to the home of the chief justice, who agreed to sign a pledge that the court would not sit until the Massachusetts General Court met. The crowd went back to the square, broke open the county jail, and set free the debtors. The chief justice, a country doctor, said: "I have never heard anybody point out a better way to have their grievances redressed than the people have taken."

The governor and the political leaders of Massachusetts became alarmed. Samuel Adams, once looked on as a radical leader in Boston, now insisted people act within the law. He said "British emissaries" were stirring up the farmers. People in the town of Greenwich responded: You in Boston have the money, and we don't. And didn't you act illegally yourselves in the Revolution? The insurgents were now being called Regulators. Their emblem was a sprig of hemlock.

The problem went beyond Massachusetts. In Rhode Island, the debtors had taken over the legislature and were issuing paper money. In New Hampshire, several hundred men, in September of 1786, surrounded the legislature in Exeter, asking that taxes be returned and paper money issued; they dispersed only when military action was threatened.

Daniel Shays entered the scene in western Massachusetts. A poor farm hand when the revolution broke out, he joined the Continental army, fought at Lexington, Bunker Hill, and Saratoga, and was wounded in action. In 1780, not being paid, he resigned from the army, went home, and soon found himself in court for nonpayment of debts. He also saw what was happening to others: a sick woman, unable to pay, had her bed taken from under her.

What brought Shays fully into the situation was that on September 19, the Supreme Judicial Court of Massachusetts met in Worcester and indicted eleven leaders of the rebellion, including three of his friends, as "disorderly, riotous and seditious persons" who "unlawfully and by force of arms" prevented "the execution of justice and the laws of the commonwealth." The Supreme Judicial Court planned to meet again in Springfield a week later, and there was talk of Luke Day's being indicted.

Shays organized seven hundred armed farmers, most of them veterans of the war, and led them to Springfield. There they found a general with nine hundred soldiers and a cannon. Shays asked the general for permission to parade, which the general granted, so Shays and his men moved through the square, drums banging and fifes blowing. As they marched, their ranks grew. Some of the militia joined, and reinforcements began coming in from the countryside. The judges postponed hearings for a day, then adjourned the court.

Now the General Court, meeting in Boston, was told by Governor James Bowdoin to "vindicate the insulted dignity of government." The recent rebels against England, secure in office, were calling for law and order. Sam Adams helped draw up a Riot Act, and a resolution suspending habeas corpus, to allow the authorities to keep people in jail without trial. At the same time, the legislature moved to make some concessions to the angry farmers, saying certain old taxes could now be paid in goods instead of money.

This didn't help. In Worcester, 160 insurgents appeared at the courthouse. The sheriff read the Riot Act. The insurgents said they would disperse only if the judges did. The sheriff shouted something about hanging. Someone came up behind him and put a sprig of hemlock in his hat. The judges left.

Confrontations between farmers and militia now multiplied. The winter snows began to interfere with the trips of farmers to the courthouses. When Shays began marching a thousand men into Boston, a blizzard forced them back, and one of his men froze to death.

An army came into the field, led by General Benjamin Lincoln, on money raised by Boston merchants. In an artillery duel, three rebels were killed. One soldier stepped in front of his own artillery piece and lost both arms. The winter grew worse. The rebels were outnumbered and on the run. Shays took refuge in Vermont, and his followers began to surrender. There were a few more deaths in battle, and then sporadic, disorganized, desperate acts of violence against authority: the burning of barns, the slaughter of a general's horses. One government soldier was killed in an eerie night-time collision of two sleighs.

Captured rebels were put on trial in Northampton and six were sentenced to death. A note was left at the door of the high sheriff of Pittsfidd:

> I understand that there is a number of my countrymen condemned to die because they fought for justice. I pray have a care that you assist not in the execution of so horrid a crime, for by all that is above, he that condemns and he that executes shall share alike. . . . Prepare for death with speed, for your life or mine is short. When the woods are covered with leaves, I shall return and pay you a short visit.

Thirty-three more rebels were put on trial and six more condemned to death. Arguments took place over whether the hangings should go forward. General Lincoln urged mercy and a Commission of Clemency, but Samuel Adams said: "In monarchy the crime of treason may admit of being pardoned or lightly punished, but the man who dares rebel against the laws of a republic ought to suffer death." Several hangings followed; some of the condemned were pardoned. Shays, in Vermont, was pardoned in 1788 and returned to Massachusetts, where he died, poor and obscure, in 1825.

It was Thomas Jefferson, in France as ambassador at the time of Shays' Rebellion, who spoke of such uprisings as healthy for society. In a letter to a friend he wrote: "I hold it that a little rebellion now and then is a good thing. . . . It is a medicine necessary for the sound health of government. . . . God forbid that we should ever be twenty years without such a rebellion. . . . The tree of liberty must be refreshed from time to time with the blood of patriots and tyrants. It is its natural manure."

But Jefferson was far from the scene. The political and economic elite of the country were not so tolerant. They worried that the example might spread. A veteran of Washington's army, General Henry Knox, founded an organization of army veterans, "The Order of the Cincinnati," presumably (as one historian put it) "for the purpose of cherishing the heroic memories of the struggle in which they had taken part," but also, it seemed, to watch out for radicalism in the new country. Knox wrote to Washington in late 1786 about Shays' Rebellion, and in doing so expressed the thoughts of many of the wealthy and powerful leaders of the country:

> The people who are the insurgents have never paid any, or but very little taxes. But they see the weakness of government; they feel at once their own poverty, compared with the opulent, and their own force, and they are determined to make use of the latter, in order to remedy the former. Their creed is "That the property of the United States has been protected from the confiscations of Britain by the joint exertions of all, and therefore ought to he the common properly of all. And he that attempts opposition to this creed is an enemy to equity and justice and ought to be swept from off the face of the earth."

Alexander Hamilton, aide to Washington during the war, was one of the most forceful and astute leaders of the new aristocracy. He voiced his political philosophy:

> All communities divide themselves into the few and the many. The first are the rich and well-horn, the other the mass of the people. The voice of the people has been said to be the voice of God; and however generally this maxim has been quoted and believed, it is not true in fact. The people are turbulent and changing; they seldom judge or determine right. Give therefore to the first class a distinct permanent share in the government. . . . Can a democratic assembly who annually revolve in the mass of the people be supposed steadily to pursue the public good? Nothing but a permanent body can check the imprudence of democracy. . . .

At the Constitutional Convention, Hamilton suggested a President and Senate chosen for life.

The Convention did not take his suggestion. But neither did it provide for popular elections, except in the case of the House of Representatives, where the qualifications were set by the state legislatures (which required property-holding for voting in almost all the states), and excluded women, Indians, slaves. The Constitution provided for Senators to be elected by the state legislators, for the President to be elected by electors chosen by the state legislators, and for the Supreme Court to be appointed by the President.

The problem of democracy in the post-Revolutionary society was not, however, the Constitutional limitations on voting. It lay deeper, beyond the Constitution, in the division of society into rich and poor. For if some people had great wealth and great influence; if they had the land, the money, the newspapers, the church, the educational system—how could voting, however broad, cut into such power? There was still another problem: wasn't it the nature of representative government, even when most broadly based, to be conservative, to prevent tumultuous change?

It came time to ratify the Constitution, to submit to a vote in state conventions, with approval of nine of the thirteen required to ratify it. In New York, where debate over ratification was intense, a series of newspaper articles appeared, anonymously, and they tell us much about the nature of the Constitution. These articles, favoring adoption of the Constitution, were written by James Madison, Alexander Hamilton, and John Jay, and came to be known as the *Federalist Papers* (opponents of the Constitution became known as anti-Federalists).

In *Federalist Paper #10*, James Madison argued that representative government was needed to maintain peace in a society ridden by factional disputes. These disputes came from "the various and unequal distribution of property. Those who hold and those who are without property have ever formed distinct interests in society." The problem, he said, was how to control the factional struggles that came from inequalities in wealth. Minority factions could be controlled, he said, by the principle that decisions would be by vote of the majority.

So the real problem, according to Madison, was a majority faction, and here the solution was offered by the Constitution, to have "an extensive republic," that is, a large nation ranging over thirteen states, for then "it will be more difficult for all who feel it to discover their own strength, and to act in unison with each other. . . . The influence of factious leaders may kindle a flame within their particular States, but will be unable to spread a general conflagration through the other States."

Madison's argument can be seen as a sensible argument for having a government which can maintain peace and avoid continuous disorder. But is it the aim of government simply to maintain order, as a referee, between two equally matched fighters? Or is it that government has some special interest in maintaining a certain kind of order, a certain distribution of power and wealth, a distribution in which government officials are not neutral referees but participants? In that case, the disorder they might worry about is the disorder of popular rebellion against those monopolizing the society's wealth. This interpretation makes sense when one looks at the economic interests, the social backgrounds, of the makers of the Constitution.

As part of his argument for a large republic to keep the peace, James Madison tells quite clearly, in *Federalist #10*, whose peace he wants to keep: "A rage for paper money, for an abolition of debts, for an equal division of property, or for any other improper or wicked project, will be less apt to pervade the whole body of the Union than a particular member of it."

When economic interest is seen behind the political clauses of the Constitution, then the document becomes not simply the work of wise men trying to establish a decent and orderly society, but the work of certain groups trying to maintain their privileges, while giving just enough rights and liberties to enough of the people to ensure popular support.

In the new government, Madison would belong to one party (the Democrat-Republicans) along with Jefferson and Monroe. Hamilton would belong to the rival party (the Federalists) along with Washington and Adams. But both agreed—one a slaveholder from Virginia, the other a merchant from New York—on the aims of this new government they were establishing. They were anticipating the long-fundamental agreement of the two political parties in the American system. Hamilton wrote elsewhere in the *Federalist Papers* that the new Union would be able "to repress domestic faction and insurrection." He referred directly to Shays' Rebellion: "The tempestuous situation from which Massachusetts has scarcely emerged evinces that dangers of this kind are not merely speculative."

It was either Madison or Hamilton (the authorship of the individual papers is not always known) who in *Federalist Paper #63* argued the necessity of a "well-constructed Senate" as "sometimes necessary as a defense to the people against their own temporary errors and delusions" because "there are particular moments in public affairs when the people, stimulated by some irregular passion, or some illicit advantage, or misted by the artful misrepresentations of interested men, may call for measures which they themselves will afterwards be the most ready to lament and condemn." And: "In these critical moments, how salutary will be the interference of some temperate and respectable body of citizens in order to check the misguided career, and to suspend the blow meditated by the people against themselves, until reason, justice, and truth can regain their authority over the public mind?"

The Constitution was a compromise between slaveholding interests of the South and moneyed interests of the North. For the purpose of uniting the thirteen states into one great market for commerce, the northern delegates wanted laws regulating interstate commerce, and urged that such laws require only a majority of Congress to pass. The South agreed to this, in return for allowing the trade in slaves to continue for twenty years before being outlawed.

Charles Beard warned us that governments—including the government of the United States—are not neutral, that they represent the dominant economic interests, and that their constitutions are intended to serve these interests. One of his critics (Robert E. Brown, *Charles Beard and the Constitution*) raises an interesting point. Granted that the Constitution omitted the phrase "life, liberty and the pursuit of happiness," which appeared in the Declaration of Independence, and substituted "life, liberty, or property"—well, why shouldn't the Constitution protect property? As Brown says about Revolutionary America, "practically everybody was interested in the protection of property" because so many Americans owned property.

However, this is misleading. True, there were many property owners. But some people had much more than others. A few people had great amounts of property; many people had small amounts; others had none. Jackson Main found that one-third of the population in the Revolutionary period were small fanners, while only 3 percent of the population had truly large holdings and could be considered wealthy.

Still, one-third was a considerable number of people who felt they had something at stake in the stability of a new government. This was a larger base of support for government than anywhere in the world at the end of the eighteenth century. In addition, the city mechanics had an important interest in a government which would protect their work from foreign competition. As Staughton Lynd puts it: "How is it that the city workingmen all over America overwhelmingly and enthusiastically supported the United States Constitution?"

This was especially true in New York. When the ninth and tenth states had ratified the Constitution, four thousand New York City mechanics marched with floats and banners to celebrate. Bakers, blacksmiths, brewers, ship joiners and shipwrights, coopers, cartmen and tailors, all marched. What Lynd found was that these mechanics, while opposing elite rule in the colonies, were nationalist. Mechanics comprised perhaps half the New York population. Some were wealthy, some were poor, but all were better off than the ordinary laborer, the apprentice, the journeyman, and their prosperity required a government that would protect them against the British hats and shoes and other goods that were pouring into the colonies after the Revolution. As a result, the mechanics often supported wealthy conservatives at the ballot box.

The Constitution, then, illustrates the complexity of the American system: that it serves the interests of a wealthy elite, but also does enough for small property owners, for middle-income mechanics and farmers, to build a broad base of support. The slightly prosperous people who make up this base of support are buffers against the blacks, the Indians, the very poor whites. They enable the elite to keep control with a minimum of coercion, a maximum of law—all made palatable by the fanfare of patriotism and unity.

The Constitution became even more acceptable to the public at large after the first Congress, responding to criticism, passed a series of amendments known as the Bill of Rights. These amendments seemed to make the new government a guardian of people's liberties: to speak, to publish, to worship, to petition, to assemble, to be tried fairly, to be secure at home against official intrusion. It was, therefore, perfectly designed to build popular backing for the new government. What was not made clear—it was a time when the language of freedom was new and its reality untested—was the shakiness of anyone's liberty when entrusted to a government of the rich and powerful.

Indeed, the same problem existed for the other provisions of the Constitution, like the clause forbidding states to "impair the obligation of contract," or that giving Congress the power to tax the people and to appropriate money. They all sound benign and neutral until one asks: Tax who, for what? Appropriate what, for whom? To protect everyone's contracts seems like an act of fairness, of equal treatment, until one considers that contracts made between rich and poor, between employer and employee, landlord and tenant, creditor and debtor, generally favor the more powerful of the two parties. Thus, to protect these contracts is to put the great power of the government, its laws, courts, sheriffs, police, on the side of the privileged—and to do it not, as in premodern times, as an exercise of brute force against the weak but as a matter of law.

The First Amendment of the Bill of Rights shows that quality of interest hiding behind innocence. Passed in 1791 by Congress, it provided that "Congress shall make no law . . . abridging the freedom of speech, or of the press. . . ." Yet, seven years after the First Amendment became part of the Constitution, Congress passed a law very clearly abridging the freedom of speech.

This was the Sedition Act of 1798, passed under John Adams's administration, at a time when Irishmen and Frenchmen in the United States were looked on as dangerous revolutionaries because of the recent French Revolution and the Irish rebellions. The Sedition Act made it a crime to say or write anything "false, scandalous and malicious" against the government, Congress, or the President, with intent to defame them, bring them into disrepute, or excite popular hatreds against them.

This act seemed to directly violate the First Amendment. Yet, it was enforced. Ten Americans were put in prison for utterances against the government, and every member of the Supreme Court in 1798–1800, sitting as an appellate judge, held it constitutional.

There was a legal basis for this, one known to legal experts, but not to the ordinary American, who would read the First Amendment and feel confident that he or she was protected in the exercise of free speech. That basis has been explained by historian Leonard Levy. Levy points out that it was generally understood (not in the population, but in higher circles) that, despite the First Amendment, the British common law of "seditious libel" still ruled in America. This meant that while the government could not exercise "prior restraint"— that is, prevent an utterance or publication in advance—it could legally punish the speaker or writer afterward. Thus, Congress has a convenient legal basis for the laws it has enacted since that time, making certain kinds of speech a crime. And, since punishment after the fact is an excellent deterrent to the exercise of free expression, the claim of "no prior restraint" itself is destroyed. This leaves the First Amendment much less than the stone wall of protection it seems at first glance.

Are the economic provisions in the Constitution enforced just as weakly? We have an instructive example almost immediately in Washington's first administration, when Congress's power to tax and appropriate money was immediately put to use by the Secretary of the Treasury, Alexander Hamilton.

Hamilton, believing that government must ally itself with the richest elements of society to make itself strong, proposed to Congress a series of laws, which it enacted, expressing this philosophy. A Bank of the United States was set up as a partnership between the government and certain banking interests. A tariff was passed to help the manufacturers. It was agreed to pay bondholders—most of the war bonds were now concentrated in a small group of wealthy people—the full value of their bonds. Tax laws were passed to raise money for this bond redemption.

One of these tax laws was the Whiskey Tax, which especially hurt small farmers who raised grain that they converted into whiskey and then sold. In 1794 the farmers of western Pennsylvania took up arms and rebelled against the collection of this tax. Secretary of the Treasury Hamilton led the troops to put them down. We see then, in the first years of the Constitution, that some of its provisions—even those paraded most flamboyantly (like the First Amendment)—might be treated lightly. Others (like the power to tax) would be powerfully enforced.

Still, the mythology around the Founding Fathers persists. To say, as one historian (Bernard Bailyn) has done recently, that "the destruction of privilege and the creation of a political system that demanded of its leaders the responsible and humane use of power were their highest aspirations" is to ignore what really happened in the America of these Founding Fathers.

Bailyn says:

> Everyone knew the basic prescription for a wise and just government. It was so to balance the contending powers in society that no one power could overwhelm the others and, unchecked, destroy the liberties that belonged to all. The problem was how to arrange the institutions of government so that this balance could be achieved.

Were the Founding Fathers wise and just men trying to achieve a good balance? In fact, they did not want a balance, except one which kept things as they were, a balance among the dominant forces at that time. They certainly did not want an equal balance between slaves and masters, propertyless and property holders, Indians and white.

As many as half the people were not even considered by the Founding Fathers as among Bailyn's "contending powers" in society. They were not mentioned in the Declaration of Independence, they were absent in the Constitution, they were invisible in the new political democracy. They were the women of early America.

POSTSCRIPT

Were the Founding Fathers Democratic Reformers?

Roche stresses the political reasons for writing a new Constitution. In a spirited essay that reflects great admiration for the Founding Fathers as enlightened politicians, Roche describes the Constitution as "a triumph of architectonic genius; it was a patch-work sewn together under the pressure of both time and events by a group of extremely talented democratic politicians."

Roche narrates the events of the convention of 1787 with a clarity rarely seen in the writings on this period. He makes the telling point that once the dissenters left Philadelphia, the delegates were able to hammer out a new Constitution. All the Founding Fathers agreed to create a stronger national government, but differences centered around the shape the new government would take. The delegates' major concern was to create as strong a national government as possible that would be acceptable to all the states. Had the ratifying conventions rejected the new Constitution, the United States might have disintegrated into 13 separate countries.

An avowed Marxist and radical leftist, Howard Zinn is a political activist who served in a bombing squadron in the Army Air Corps in World War II, was an early member of the Student Non-Violent Coordinating Committee (SNCC), which was the most vocal civil rights group in the 1960s, and a staunch peace activist against our wars in Vietnam, Central America, and the Middle East. He believes that history should be studied and written primarily for the purpose of eliminating America's violent past and moving it in a more peaceful, equitable direction.

Zinn's *A People's History of the United States* (Harper Collins, 1999) has sold over a million copies since it was first published in 1980. His critique of the Founding Fathers draws upon the scholarship of Charles Beard's *An Economic Interpretation of the Constitution* (Free Press, 1913, 1986), which argued that the Founding Fathers were primarily interested in protecting their property rights. He believes that Shay's Rebellion, an uprising of western Massachusetts farmers who were unable to pay their taxes to the Massachusetts government, was the catalyst that inspired the men at Philadelphia in 1787 to write a new constitution. He quotes from James Madison's *Federalist Paper #10* that it will be easier to keep order in a large nation of 13 states where minority factions could be controlled by a vote of the majority. He admits that one-third of the population were small farmers, "a considerable number of people who felt that they had something at stake in the new society."

Zinn believes that there were structural difficulties with the Constitution. For example, representative government was designed to prevent tumultuous change and therefore was inherently conservative. He also argues that the major problem in American society—the division into rich and poor—transcended constitutional problems.

How does Zinn explain the support for the new government if it favored the well-to-do? "The Constitution," he says, "illustrates the complexity of the American system; that it serves the interests of a wealthy elite, but also does enough for small property owners, for middle-income mechanics and farmers, to build a broad base of support. The slightly prosperous people who make up this base of support are buffers against the blacks, the Indians, the very poor whites. They enable the elite to keep control with a minimum of coercion, a maximum of law—all made palatable by the fanfare of patriotism and unity."

The enlightened statemen's views reasserted itself during the cold war in the 1950s and 1960s with the methodological critiques of Charles Beard's *An Economic Interpretation of the Constitution* (Macmillan, 1913) by Robert E. Brown, *Charles Beard and the Constitution* (Princeton University Press, 1956) and Forrest McDonald's many works, the earliest *We the People* (University of Chicago Press, 1958), which argued that numerous interest groups in the states ratified the Constitution for a variety of political and economic reasons. The best summary of this scholarship is the widely reprinted article by Stanley Elkins and Eric McKitrick, "The Founding Fathers: Young Men of the Revolution," in Jack P. Greene, ed., *The Reinterpretation of the American Revolution 1763–1789* (Harper & Row, 1968), pp. 378–395, which argues that the Federalists were broad-minded nationalists and the less organized anti-Federalists were small-minded localists, an interpretation influenced by Cecilia Kenyon, "Men of Little Faith: the Anti-Federalists on the Nature of Representative Government," *William and Mary Quarterly* 12 (1955), pp. 3–43.

Historian Gordon S. Wood changed the focus of the debate by trying to recapture the conflicting views of politics in the eighteenth century in *The Creation of the American Republic, 1776–1787* (University of North Carolina Press, 1969), a seminal work that has replaced Beard as the starting point for scholarship on this topic. A devastating critique of the methodological fallacies of Wood and other intellectual writers on this period can be found in Ralph Lerner's "The Constitution of the Thinking Revolutionary," in Richard Beeman et al., eds., *Beyond Confederation: Origins of the Constitution and American National Identity* (University of North Carolina Press, 1987). See other essays in *Beyond Confederation* including Wood's response, "Interests and Disinterestedness in the Making of the Constitution," pp. 69–109. The bicentennial produced an explosion of scholarship by historians and law professors. For overviews, see Peter S. Onof, "Reflections on the Founding: Constitutional Historiography in Bicentennial Perspective," *William and Mary Quarterly*, 30 Ser., XLVI (1989), pp. 341–375), and Richard D. Bernstein, "Charting the Bicentennial," *Columbia Law Review*, LXXXVII (1987), 1565–1624.

In recent years the anti-Federalists have received positive evaluations from both conservatives and leftists who reject the excessive accumulation of power by the national government. See conservative Herbert J. Storing, *What the Anti-Federalists Were For* (University of Chicago Press, 1981), an influential effort to analyze anti-Federalist ideas and Alfred F. Young, "The Framers of the Constitution and the 'Genius' of the People," *Radical History Review* (Vol. 42, 1988). Earlier, Jackson Turner Main revived the Beardian conflict interpretations between agrarian localists and cosmopolitan elitists in "The Anti-Federalists," *Critics of the Constitution, 1781–1788* (University of North Carolina Press, 1961), which has been superseded by Saul Cornell, *The Other Founders: Anti-Federalism and the Dissenting Tradition in America, 1788–1828* (University of North Carolina Press, 1999), a sympathetic and comprehensive analysis buttressed by research into the primary writings and secondary accounts of the anti-Federalists critically evaluated by the author.

Readers can gain a sense of the debates over ratification of the Constitution by reading some of the original texts. Two of the most convenient anthologies are Michael Kammen, ed., *The Origins of the American Constitution: A Documentary History* (New York, 1986) and Bernard Bailyn, ed., *The Debate on the Constitution,* 2 vols. (New York, 1993).

ISSUE 8

Was Thomas Jefferson a Political Compromiser?

YES: Morton Borden, from *America's Eleven Greatest Presidents,* 2d ed. (Rand McNally, 1971)

NO: Forrest McDonald, from *The Presidency of Thomas Jefferson* (The University Press of Kansas, 1976)

ISSUE SUMMARY

YES: Professor Morton Borden argues that President Thomas Jefferson was a moderate and pragmatic politician who placed the nation's best interests above those of the states.

NO: History professor Forrest McDonald believes that President Jefferson attempted to replace Hamiltonian Federalist Principles with a Republican ideology in order to restore America's agrarian heritage.

Jefferson still lives, stated John Adams on July 4, 1826, the 50th anniversary of Independence Day. Unknown to Adams, Jefferson had indeed passed away a few hours earlier the same day. But Jefferson never really died. He was one of the few heroes of history to become a living legend. According to recent biography Joseph J. Ellis, Jefferson is the *American Sphinx* (Random House, 1997).

There are many Jeffersons. One was the true Renaissance man who knew a little about everything. "Not a sprig of grass shoots uninteresting to me," he once wrote to his daughter. As a philosopher who spoke to posterity, he waxed eloquent in his letters about civil liberties, the rights of man, states' rights, strict construction of the Constitution, and the virtues of the agrarian way of life. A practical man, he was an architect of the nation's capital, the University of Virginia, and his own home. Visitors to his Monticello plantation are amazed by the elaborate pulley and drainage systems that he devised. A respected member of the Virginia aristocracy who owned about 10,000 acres and from 100 to 200 slaves, Jefferson ran his farm in a self-sufficient manner and carefully studied the efficiency of employing slave labor. When he traveled, he recorded everything he observed in detailed journals. The newest inventions—steam engines, thermometers, elevators—fascinated him.

Another Jefferson was the man who has been ranked among the top half-dozen U.S. presidents in every major poll taken by historians in the last 35 years. Does Jefferson deserve such an honor? It depends on how the functions of the presidency are perceived. One role that Jefferson disdained more than any other president in our history was the function of chief of state. So important to the modern presidency, the ceremonial role could have been played by the tall, dignified Virginia aristocrat as well as it was by George Washington, had he so desired. But Jefferson hated formalities. He walked to his inauguration and refused to wear a hat. Because he was a widower, he abandoned the practice of holding large, formal parties. He also felt they smacked too much of monarchy. He preferred small, intimate dinners with his intellectual friends and political cronies. A shy, soft-spoken individual with a slight speech impediment, the author of the Declaration of Independence did not campaign for office. He also refused to deliver an annual address to Congress, preferring to send them a written message. In short, if one uses modern terminology, Jefferson was not "mediagenic." In 2004, Jefferson might not have even been nominated by his party, much less elected to the presidency. Considering the vitriolic fights over Hamilton's economic policies, Washington's foreign policy of neutrality as well as the fiasco in the 1800 election that resulted in an electoral college tie, Jefferson's presidency was remarkable for the smooth transition in which the opposition party took power. As Professor Richard Hofstadter points out in *The Idea of a Party System: The Rise of Legitimate Opposition in the United States, 1780-1840* (University of California Press, 1969), Jefferson's pragmatic "disposition dictated an initial strategy of conciliation toward the Federalist which led to a basic acceptance of the Hamiltonian fiscal system, including even the bank, to a patronage policy which Jefferson considered to be fair and compromising and hoped would appease moderate Federalists, and to an early attempt to pursue neutrality and to eschew aggravating signs of that Francophia and Anglophobia with which the Federalists so obsessively and hyperbolically charged him." His first term was more successful than his second. He waged a winning war against the Barbary pirates in the Mediterranean and took advantage of Napoleon's offer to purchase the Louisiana territory, thereby nearly doubling the size of the United States. His second term, however, was consumed with a failed embargo.

In the first of the following selections, Professor Morton Borden substantiates the views of moderate Federalists who believed that Jefferson was a practical politician and, above all, a nationalist who incorporated Federalist policies with traditional Republican views in running his presidency. Forrest McDonald, in the second selection, sees Jefferson as a backward-looking agrarian ideologue staunchly opposed to Alexander Hamilton's Federalist programs and his philosophy of government. In the author's view, Jefferson wanted to take government away from the mercantile classes and return it to the masses.

YES

Morton Borden

Thomas Jefferson

For twelve years the Constitution worked, after a fashion. From its inception the new document had been subjected to severe trials and divisive strains. A rebellion in Pennsylvania, a naval war with France, a demand for states' rights from Virginia and Kentucky, and various Western schemes of disunion—all had been surmounted. Had it not been for the great prestige of George Washington and the practical moderation of John Adams, America's second attempt at a federal union might have failed like the first. Partisan passions had run high in the 1790's, and any single factor on which men disagreed—Hamilton's financial plans or the French Revolution or the Sedition Act—might easily have caused a stoppage of the nation's political machinery.

The two-party system emerged during this decade, and on each important issue public opinion seemed to oscillate between Federalist and Democratic-Republican. Perhaps this was to be expected of a young nation politically adolescent. Year by year Americans were becoming more politically alert and active; if there was little room for middle ground between these two factions, yet opinions were hardly fixed and irrevocable. The culmination of partisan controversy and the test of respective strengths took place in the monumental election of 1800.

Jefferson was feared, honestly feared, by almost all Federalists. Were he to win the election, so they predicted, all the hard constructive gains of those twelve years would be dissipated. Power would be returned to the individual states; commerce would suffer; judicial power would be lessened; and the wonderful financial system of Hamilton would be dismantled and destroyed. Jefferson was an atheist, and he would attack the churches. Jefferson was a hypocrite, an aristocrat posing as democrat, appealing to the baser motives of human beings in order to obtain votes. Jefferson was a revolutionary, a Francophile and, after ruining the army and navy under the guise of economy measures, might very well involve the nation in a war with England. In short, it was doubtful if the Constitution could continue its successful course under such a president.

In like manner the Republicans feared another Federalist victory. To be sure, John Adams had split with Hamilton and had earned the enmity of the Essex Junto. But would he not continue Hamilton's "moneyed system"? Did not Adams share the guilt of every Federalist for the despicable Alien and

Sedition Acts? Was it not true that "His Rotundity" so admired the British system that he was really a monarchist at heart? Republicans were not engaging in idle chatter, nor were they speaking solely for effect, when they predicted many dire consequences if Adams were elected. A typical rumor had Adams uniting "his house to that of his majesty of Britain" and "the bridegroom was to be king of America."

Throughout the country popular interest in the election was intense, an intensity sustained over months of balloting. When the Republicans carried New York City, Alexander Hamilton seriously suggested that the results be voided. And when the breach between Adams and Hamilton became public knowledge, Republicans nodded knowingly and quoted the maxim: "When thieves fall out, honest men come by their own."

The Federalists were narrowly defeated. But the decision was complicated by a result which many had predicted: a tied electoral vote between the two Republican candidates, Aaron Burr and Thomas Jefferson. (Indeed, the Twelfth Amendment was adopted in 1804 to avoid any such recurrence.) A choice between the two would be made by the House of Representatives. At this moment, February, 1801, the Constitution seemed on the verge of collapse. Federalist members of the lower house united in support of Burr; Republicans were just as adamant for Jefferson. After thirty-five ballots, neither side had yet obtained the necessary majority. The issue seemed hopelessly deadlocked. What would happen on March 4, inauguration day?

One representative from Maryland sick with a high fever, was literally carried into Congress on a stretcher to maintain the tied vote of his state. The Republican governor of Pennsylvania, Thomas McKean, threatened to march on Washington with troops if the Federalists persisted in thwarting the will of the people. Hamilton was powerless; his advice that Jefferson was the lesser evil went unheeded. So great was their hatred of the Virginian that most Federalists in Congress would have opposed him regardless of the consequences. After all, they reasoned, Jefferson would dismantle the federal government anyway. In the end, however, patriotism and common sense prevailed. For the choice was no longer Jefferson or Burr, but Jefferson or no president at all. A few Federalists, led by James A. Bayard of Delaware, could not accept the logic of their party, and threw the election to Jefferson.

What a shock it was, then, to read Jefferson's carefully chosen words in his inaugural address:

> But every difference of opinion is not a difference of principle. We have called by different names brethren of the same principle. We are all republicans—we are all federalists. If there be any among us who would wish to dissolve this Union or to change its republican form, let them stand undisturbed as monuments of the safety with which error of opinion may be tolerated where reason is left free to combat it. I know, indeed, that some honest men fear that a republican government cannot be strong; that this government is not strong enough. But would the honest patriot, in the full tide of successful experiment, abandon a government which has so far kept us free and firm, on the theoretic and visionary fear that this government, the world's best hope, may by possibility want energy to preserve itself? I trust

not. I believe this, on the contrary, the strongest government on earth. I believe it is the only one where every man, at the call of the laws, would fly to the standard of the law, and would meet invasions of the public order as his own personal concern. Sometimes it is said that man cannot be trusted with the government of himself. Can he, then, be trusted with the government of others? Or have we found angels in the form of kings to govern him? Let history answer this question.

The words were greeted with applause—and confusion. It was obvious that Jefferson wanted to salve the wounds of bitter factionalism. While many Federalists remained distrustful and some even regarded it as hypocritical, most men approved the tone of their new president's message.

But what did Jefferson mean? Were there no economic principles at stake in his conflicts with Hamilton? Were there no political and constitutional principles implicit in the polar views of the respective parties? And, in the last analysis, did not these differences reflect a fundamental philosophical quarrel over the nature of human beings? Was not the election of 1800 indeed a revolution? If not, then what is the meaning of Jeffersonianism?

For two terms Jefferson tried, as best he could, to apply the standards of his inaugural address. Naturally, the Alien and Sedition Acts were allowed to lapse. The new secretary of the treasury, Albert Gallatin, was instructed to devise an easily understood program to erase the public debt gradually. Internal taxes were either abolished or reduced. Frugality and economy were emphasized to an extreme. Elegant and costly social functions were replaced by simple and informal receptions. The expense of maintaining ambassadors at the courts of Portugal, Holland, and Prussia was erased by withdrawing these missions. The army and navy were pared down to skeleton size. To be sure, Jefferson had to reverse himself on the matter of patronage for subordinate government posts. Originally he planned to keep these replacements to a minimum, certainly not to permit an individual's partisan opinions to be a basis for dismissal unless the man manifestly used his office for partisan purposes. This position was politically untenable, according to Jefferson's lieutenants, and they pressed him to accept a moderate number of removals. Indeed, Jefferson's handling of patronage is symbolic of what Hamilton once called his "ineradicable duplicity."

The Federalist leaders cried out in anguish at every one of these policy changes. The lowering of the nation's military strength would increase the danger of invasion. It was a rather risky gamble to assume that peace could be maintained while European war was an almost constant factor, and the United States was the major neutral carrier. The abolition of the excises, especially on distilled spirits, would force the government to rely on tariffs, on unpredictable source of revenue depending on the wind and waves. It was charged that several foreign ambassadors were offended by Jefferson's rather affected and ultrademocratic social simplicity. Most important, the ultimate payment of the public debt would reduce national power.

This time, however, the people did not respond to the Federalist lament of impending anarchy. After all, commerce prospered throughout most of Jefferson's administration. Somehow the churches remained standing. No bloodbaths took place. The Bank of the United States still operated. Peace was maintained. Certainly, some Federalist judges were under attack, but the judicial power passed through this ordeal to emerge unscathed and even enhanced. Every economic indicator—urban growth, westward expansion, agricultural production, the construction of canals, turnpikes and bridges—continued to rise, undisturbed by the political bickering in Washington.

At first the Federalists were confident that they would regain power. Alexander Hamilton's elaborate scheme for an organization to espouse Christianity and the Constitution, as the "principal engine" to restore Federalist power, was rejected out of hand. He was told that "our adversaries will soon demonstrate to the world the soundness of our doctrines and the imbecility and folly of their own." But hope changed to despair as the people no longer responded; no "vibration of opinion" took place as in the 1790's. Federalism was the party of the past, an antiquated and dying philosophy. "I will fatten my pigs, and prune my trees; nor will I any longer . . . trouble to govern this country," wrote Fisher Ames: "You federalists are only lookers-on." Jefferson swept the election of 1804, capturing every state except Connecticut and Delaware from the Federalist candidate, Charles C. Pinckney. "Federalism is dead," wrote Jefferson a few years later, "without even the hope of a day of resurrection. The quondam leaders indeed retain their rancour and principles; but their followers are amalgamated with us in sentiment, if not in name."

⋅⟨◉⟩⋅

It is the fashion of some historians to explain the Federalist demise and Republican ascendancy in terms of a great change in Jefferson. A radical natural law philosopher when he fought as minority leader, he became a first-rate utilitarian politician as president. The Virginian became an American. Revolutionary theory was cast aside when Jefferson faced the prosaic problem of having to run the country. He began to adopt some of the techniques and policies of the Federalists. Indeed, it is often observed that Jefferson "outfederalized the Federalists."

There is much to be said for this view. After all, less than three months after he assumed the presidency, Jefferson dispatched a naval squadron to the Mediterranean on a warlike mission, without asking the permission of Congress. Two members of his Cabinet, Levi Lincoln and Albert Gallatin, thought the action unconstitutional, and so advised the President. Almost from the moment of its birth the young nation had paid tribute, as did every European power, rather than risk a war with the Barbary pirates. But Jefferson could not abide such bribery. No constitutional scruples could delay for a moment his determination to force the issue. Later, Congress declared war, and in four years Barbary power was shattered. The United States under Jefferson accomplished an object that England, France, Spain, Portugal, and Holland had desired for more than a century—unfettered commerce in the Mediterranean. Here, then, in this episode, is a totally different Jefferson—not an exponent of states' rights and strict interpretation of the Constitution, but an American nationalist of the first order.

Perhaps the most frequently cited example of Jefferson's chameleon quality, however, was on the question of whether the United States should or should not purchase the Louisiana Territory from France. On this question the fundamental issue was squarely before Jefferson, and a choice could not be avoided. The purchase would more than double the size of the United States. Yet the Constitution did not specifically provide for such acquisition of foreign territory. Further, the treaty provided that this area would eventually be formed into states, full partners in the Union. Again, the Constitution did not specifically cover such incorporation. A broad interpretation of Article IV, Section III, however, might permit United States' ratification of the treaty. Should theory be sacrificed and an empire gained? Or were the means as important as the ends?

Broad or loose construction of the Constitution was the key to the growth of federal power. Federalists had argued in this vein to justify most of their legislation in the 1790's. To Jefferson, individual liberty and governmental power were on opposite ends of a seesaw, which the Federalists had thrown off balance. He believed that government, especially the central government, must be restricted within rather narrow and essential limits. Only by continually and rigidly applying strict construction to the Constitution could this tendency to overweening power be controlled and individual liberty be safeguarded. As early as 1777, Jefferson, then governor of Virginia, had warned that constitutions must be explicit, "so as to exclude all possible doubt; . . . [lest] at some future day . . . power[s] should be assumed."

On the other hand, the purchase of Louisiana would fulfill a dream and solve a host of problems. Jefferson envisioned an American empire covering "the whole northern, if not the southern continent, with a people speaking the same language, governed in similar forms, and by similar laws." The purchase would be a giant step in the direction of democracy's inevitable growth. "Is it not better," asked Jefferson, "that the opposite bank of the Mississippi should be settled by our own brethren and children, than by strangers of another family?"

Of more immediate interest, westerners would be able to ship their goods down the Mississippi without fear that New Orleans might be closed. Indian attacks undoubtedly would taper off without the Spanish to instigate them. Uppermost in Jefferson's mind, however, was the freedom from England that the purchase would assure. He did not fear Spanish ownership. A feeble; second-rate nation like Spain on the frontier offered little threat to America's future security. The continued possession of Louisiana by an imperialistic France led by the formidable Napoleon, however, might force the United States into an alliance with England. At first Jefferson thought a constitutional amendment specifically permitting the purchase might solve the dilemma. But Napoleon showed signs of wavering. The treaty had to be confirmed immediately, with no indication of constitutional doubt. Jefferson asked the Republican leaders in the Senate to ratify it "with as little debate as possible, and particularly so far as respects the constitutional difficulty."

In still other ways Jefferson's presidency was marked by Federalist policies which encouraged the growth of central power. Internal improvements loomed large in Jefferson's mind. While many turnpikes and canals were financed by private and state capital, he realized that federal support would be necessary, especially in the western part of the nation. With the use of federal money obtained from the sale of public lands, and (later) aided by direct congressional appropriations, the groundwork for the famous Cumberland road was established during Jefferson's administration. He enthusiastically supported Gallatin's plan to spend twenty million dollars of federal funds on a network of national roads and canals. Other more pressing problems intervened, however, and it was left to later administrations to finance these local and interstate programs. If Hamilton had pressed for internal improvements in the 1790's (he suggested them in the *Report on Manufactures*), Jefferson probably would have raised constitutional objections.

Finally, is not Jefferson's change of tack further reflected in the political history of that era? Over the span of a few years it seemed as if each party had somehow reversed directions. In 1798–99 Jefferson and Madison penned the Virginia and Kentucky Resolutions as an answer to the Federalists' infamous Alien and Sedition Acts. In 1808–9 more radical but comparable rumblings of dissatisfaction emanated from some New England Federalists over Jefferson's Embargo Act. For the embargo, says one of Jefferson's biographers, was "the most arbitrary, inquisitorial, and confiscatory measure formulated in American legislation up to the period of the Civil War." Further, both parties splintered during Jefferson's administration. Many moderate Federalists, like John Quincy Adams, found themselves in closer harmony with administration policy than with Essex Junto beliefs. And Jefferson's actions alienated old comrades, like John Randolph, Jr., whose supporters were called the Tertium Quids. It is interesting to note that there is no historical consensus of why, when, how, or what precipitated the break between Randolph and Jefferson. Randolph is always referred to as brilliant but erratic; and whatever immediate reason is alleged, the cause somehow has to do with Randolph's personality and Jefferson's betrayal of the true doctrines.

⚬◑⚬

It is part of Jefferson's greatness that he could inspire a myth and project an image. But one must not confuse myth and reality, shadow and substance. Thomas Jefferson as he was, and Thomas Jefferson as people perceived him, are quite different. While both concepts of course, are of equal value in understanding our past, it is always the historian's task to make the distinction. Too often, in Jefferson's case, this has not been done. Too often the biographers have described the myth—have taken at face value the popular view of Jefferson and his enemies, contained in the vitriolic newspaper articles and pamphlets, the passionate debates and fiery speeches of that period—and missed or misconstrued the reality.

This is understandable. Even the principals inevitably became involved and helped to propagate the exaggerated images of the 1790's and thus misunderstood one another's aims and motives. Jefferson, according to his grandson, never considered Federalist fulminations "as abusing him; they had never known him. They had created an imaginary being clothed with odious attributes, to whom they gave his name; and it was against that creature of their imaginations they had levelled their anathemas." John Adams, reminiscing in a letter to Jefferson, wrote: "Both parties have excited artificial terrors and if I were summoned as a witness to say upon oath, which party had excited . . . the most terror, and which had really felt the most, I could not give a more sincere answer, than in the vulgar style 'Put them in a bag and shake them, and then see which comes out first.'"

On March 4, 1801, following a decade of verbal violence, many Americans were surprised to hear that "We are all republicans—we are all federalists." Some historians act as if they, too, are surprised. These historians then describe Jefferson's administration as if some great change took place in his thinking, and conclude that he "outfederalized the Federalists." This is a specious view, predicated on an ultraradical Jefferson of the 1790's in constant debate with an ultraconservative Hamilton. Certainly Jefferson as president had to change. Certainly at times he had to modify, compromise, and amend his previous views. To conclude, however, that he outfederalized the Federalists is to miss the enormous consistency of Jefferson's beliefs and practices.

Jefferson was ever a national patriot second to none, not even to Hamilton. He always conceived of the United States as a unique experiment, destined for greatness so long as a sharp line isolated American civilization from European infection. Thus he strongly advised our youth to receive their education at home rather than in European schools, lest they absorb ideas and traits he considered "alarming to me as an American." From "Notes on Virginia" to his advice at the time of Monroe's doctrine, Jefferson thought of America first. It matters not that Hamilton was the better prophet; Jefferson was the better American. The French minister Adet once reported: "Although Jefferson is the friend of liberty . . . although he is an admirer of the efforts we have made to cast off our shackles . . . Jefferson, I say, is an American, and as such, he cannot sincerely be our friend. An American is the born enemy of all the peoples of Europe."

Jefferson's nature was always more practical than theoretical, more commonsensical than philosophical. Certainly the essence of his Declaration of Independence is a Lockean justification of revolution; but, said Jefferson, "It was . . . an expression of the American mind," meant "to place before mankind the common sense of the subject." Jefferson always preferred precision to "metaphysical subtleties." The Kentucky and Virginia Resolutions can be understood only as a specific rebuttal of the Sedition Act. "I can never fear that things will go far wrong," wrote Jefferson, "where common sense has fair play."

One must also remember that Hamilton's power lessened considerably in the last four years of Federalist rule. He had a strong coterie of admirers, but the vast body of Federalists sided with John Adams. Despite all Hamilton did to insure Adams' defeat, and despite the split in Federalist ranks, the fact that Jefferson's victory in 1801 was won by a narrow margin indicated Federalist approval of Adams' actions. Certainly the people at that time—Jefferson and Adams included—regarded 1801 as the year of revolution. But if historians must have a revolution, perhaps Adams' split with the Hamiltonians is a better date.

"The mid-position which Adams desired to achieve," writes Manning Dauer, "was adopted, in the main, by Jefferson and his successors."

To be sure, the two men disagreed on many matters of basic importance. Jefferson placed his faith in the free election of a virtuous and talented natural aristocracy; Adams did not. Within the constitutional balance, Jefferson emphasized the power of the lower house; Adams would give greater weight to the executive and judiciary. Jefferson, as a general rule, favored a strict interpretation of the Constitution; Adams did not fear broad construction. Both believed that human beings enjoyed inalienable rights, but only Jefferson had faith in man's perfectability. Jefferson could say, "I like a little rebellion now and then. It is like a storm in the atmosphere"; Adams had grown more conservative since 1776. Jefferson always defended and befriended Thomas Paine; Adams found Edmund Burke's position on the French Revolution more palatable.

Yet, the sages of Quincy and Monticello were both moderate and practical men. Despite the obvious and basic contrasts, both Adams and Jefferson stood side by side on certain essentials: to avoid war, to quiet factionalism, to preserve republican government. Their warm friendship, renewed from 1812 to 1826 in a remarkable and masterful correspondence, was based on frankness, honesty, and respect. "About facts," Jefferson wrote, "you and I cannot differ, because truth is our mutual guide; And if any opinions you may express should be different from mine, I shall receive them with the liberality and indulgence which I ask for my own." Jefferson and Adams represent, respectively, the quintessence of the very best in American liberalism and conservatism. Their indestructible link, then, was "a keen sense of national consciousness," a realization that America's destiny was unique. This is the meaning of Jefferson's words: "We are all republicans—we are all federalists."

Forrest McDonald  **NO**

The Faithful and The Crisis of Faith

By most objective criteria, the Americans of 1800 had abundant cause to be proud, confident, even smug. . . .

And yet a sense of decadence had plagued the land for five years and, more. From the pulpit rang cries of despair and doom; dishonesty as well as panic had invaded the marketplace; liars and libelers made a travesty of freedom of the press; violence, hysteria, and paranoia infested the public councils. Those Americans who called themselves Federalists felt betrayed by an ungrateful people for whom they had labored long and well, and feared that the horrors of Jacobinism and anarchy were hourly imminent. Those who called themselves Republicans felt betrayed by the twin evils of money and monarchy, and feared that liberty was about to breathe its last. Many who embraced neither political sect, whether from apathy or disgust, nonetheless shared the general feeling that the nation was in an advanced state of moral rot.

What the Federalists thought was actually of little consequence, for they were soon to expire, in what Thomas Jefferson called the Revolution of 1800. Almost miraculously, with their demise—though not because of it—despair suddenly gave way to euphoria. The new optimism, like the pervasive gloom and the defeat of Federalism that preceded it, stemmed from an interplay of social, religious, ideological, and economic forces and institutions, and from certain ingrained American characteristics. If one would understand the Jeffersonian revolution—how it happened and how it affected the nation's destiny—one must seek first to understand those forces, institutions, and characteristics.

One of the tenets of Republicanism in America was that, contrary to the teachings of Montesquieu and other theorists, republican government was best adapted to large territories, since in an area as vast as the United States the very diversity of the people would prevent an accumulation of power inimical to liberty. If the principle, was sound, the Americans were truly blessed, for their culture was nothing if not plural. At first blush that generalization might appear strong, or indeed entirely unfounded. Overwhelmingly, Americans were farmers or traders of British extraction and the Protestant faith; and even in politics, as Jefferson said in his inaugural address, "we are all republicans, we are all federalists." But the mother country itself was scarcely homogeneous, despite the amalgamation that financial and governmental power had brought to Great Britain in the eighteenth century; it comprised a host of different Celtic peoples—the Irish, the Welsh, the Cornish, and three distinct varieties of Scots—as well as Englishmen who differed from

From THE PRESIDENCY OF THOMAS JEFFERSON by Forrest McDonald. Copyright © 1976 by University Press of Kansas. Reprinted by permission.

one another from north to south and east to west. Americans had proved slow to cast off the cultural baggage that they or their ancestors had brought with them; and a generation of independence, though building some sense of nationhood, had erased neither their original ethnic traits nor the intense localism that complemented and nourished those traits. As to differences in political principles, Jefferson was right in regarding them as largely superficial; yet they were substantive enough to lead many men to fight, and some to kill, one another. . . .

It should not be surprising that those who were saved through revivalism were also supporters of Jeffersonian Republicanism, for the theology of the one was psychologically akin to the ideology of the other. In part, to be sure, religious dissenters supported Jefferson because of his well-known championship of the cause of religious liberty. New England Baptists, for instance, having fought long and vainly for disestablishment, virtually idolized Jefferson. South and west of New England, however, establishment had long since ceased to be a live issue, and in much of that area Jefferson's religious views, to the extent that they were fully known, were if anything a political handicap. Rather, it was the compatibility of outlooks that made it possible for southern and western revivalists simultaneously to embrace evangelical Arminianism in religion and Republican ideology in politics.

Anglo-Americans, like the English themselves, were by and large non-ideological people, but in 1800 the country was divided into two fiercely antagonistic ideological camps. In a loose, general sort of way, and with allowance for a number of exceptions, it can be said that the revival ideologies derived from contrasting views of the nature of man. The first view, that associated with the Hamiltonian Federalists, was premised upon the belief that man, while capable of noble and even altruistic behavior, could never entirely escape the influence of his inborn baser passions—especially ambition and avarice, the love of power and the love of money. The second, that espoused by the Jeffersonian Republicans, held that man was born with a tabula rasa, with virtually boundless capacity for becoming good or evil, depending upon the wholesomeness of the environment in which he grew. From the premise of the first it followed that government should recognize the evil drives of men as individuals, but check them and even harness them in such a way that they would work for the general good of society as a whole. From the premise of the second it followed that government should work to rid society of as many evils as possible—including, to a very large extent, the worst of evils, government itself. The one was positive, the other negative; the one sought to do good, the other to eradicate evil.

But the ideological division was more specifically focused than that. The High Federalists believed in and had fashioned a governmental system modeled upon the one that began to emerge in England after the Glorious Revolution of 1688 and was brought to maturity under the leadership of Sir Robert Walpole during the 1720s and 1730s. In part the system worked on the basis of what has often, simple-mindedly, been regarded as the essence of Hamiltonianism: tying the interests of the wealthy to those of the national government, or more accurately, inducing people of all ranks to act in the general interest by making it profitable for them to do so. But the genius of Hamilton's system ran much deeper. He erected a complex set of interrelated institutions, based upon the monetization of the public debt, which made it virtually impossible for anyone to pursue power and wealth successfully except through the framework of those institutions, and which simultaneously delimited and dictated the possible courses of government activity, so that government had no choice but to function in the public interest as Hamilton saw it. For instance, servicing the public debt, on which the whole superstructure rested, required a regular source of revenue that was necessarily derived largely from duties on imports from Great Britain. For that reason the United States could not go to war with Britain except at the risk of national bankruptcy, but could fight Revolutionary France or France's ally Spain, which were owners of territories that the United States avidly desired. Hamilton regarded this as the proper American foreign policy, at least for a time; and should circumstances change, he was perfectly capable of redefining the rules and rerigging the institutions so as to dictate another policy. In domestic affairs, a wide range of implications of his system was equally inescapable.

The Jeffersonian Republicans regarded this scheme of things as utterly wicked, even as the English opposition had regarded Walpole's system. Indeed, though the Jeffersonians borrowed some of their ideas from James Harrington and other seventeenth-century writers and some from John Locke, their ideology was borrowed *in toto* from such Oppositionists as Charles Davenant, John Trenchard, Thomas Gordon, James Burgh, and most especially Henry St. John, First Viscount Bolingbroke. As a well-rounded system, it is all to be found in the pages of the *Craftsman,* an Oppositionist journal that Bolingbroke published from 1726 to 1737. The Republicans adjusted the ideology to fit the circumstances, to fit the United States Constitution and the "ministry" of Alexander Hamilton rather than the British constitution and the ministry of Robert Walpole; but that was all, and astonishingly little adjustment was necessary.

The Bolingbroke-Oppositionist *cum* Jeffersonian Republican ideology ran as follows. Corruption was everywhere, it was true; but given a proper environment, that need not be the way of things. Mankind could be rejuvenated through education and self-discipline, but that was possible only in the context of a life style that exalted living on, owning, and working the land. Only the land could give people the independence and unhurried existence that were prerequisite to self-improvement.

In some Edenic past, "the people"—which both Bolingbroke and Jefferson understood to mean the gentry and the solid yeomanry, and not to include aristocrats, money jobbers, priests, or the scum in the cities—had enjoyed the proper atmosphere, and therefore had been happy. Relationships were based upon agriculture and its "handmaiden" commerce, upon ownership of land, honest labor in the earth, craftsmanship in the cities, and free trade between individuals. All men revered God, respected their fellows, deferred to their betters, and knew their place. Because they were secure in their sense of place, they were also secure in their identities and their sense of values; and manly virtue, honor, and public spirit governed their conduct.

Then a serpent invaded the garden. To Bolingbroke, the evil started with the Glorious Revolution, which begat two bastard offspring: the Financial Revolution and the system of government by ministry, rather than the system of separation of powers that had been embodied in the ancient English constitution. To Jefferson, things were slightly more complex. America had been spared the corruption that had poisoned England until the accession of George III, and when it began to infest America, the spirit of 1776 had saved the day. Yet the American Revolution, because of the Hamiltonians, was ultimately undermined in just the way the English revolution had been: both were waged to check executive power, and both ended in the worst form of executive tyranny, ministerial government. The instrument of corruption in both instances was money—not "real" money, gold and silver, but artificial money in the form of public debt, bank notes, stocks, and other kinds of paper—the acquisition of which had nothing to do with either land or labor. Government ministers assiduously encouraged people to traffic in such paper, and with that stimulus the pursuit of easy wealth proved irresistible. A frenzy for gambling, stock-jobbing, and paper shuffling permeated the highest councils of state and spread among the people themselves. Manly virtue gave way to effeminacy and vice; public spirit succumbed to extravagance, venality, and corruption.

Jefferson never tired of telling a story which, to him, epitomized what had gone wrong. Early in Washington's first administration, Jefferson recalled, he had been engaged in a friendly discussion of political principles with Hamilton and Vice-President Adams. Jefferson had maintained that an agrarian republic was most conducive to human happiness. Adams disagreed and, to Jefferson's horror, said that monarchy was better, that if the British government were purged of corruption it would be the best system ever devised. Hamilton, to the astonishment of both his listeners, declared that if the British system were urged of corruption it would not work: it was, he said, the most perfect system of government as it stood, for corruption was the most suitable engine of effective government.

In the matter of foreign relations, Republicans opposed the corrupt new order on two interrelated sets of grounds, with the same logic and often the same language that the Oppositionists had used earlier. One was that it entangled the nation with foreign powers, making independent, self-determined action impossible. Not only had Hamilton's system prevented the United States from siding with Revolutionary France against Britain in the early 1790s—which the Republicans believed to be the moral course, as well as the one most advantageous to the country—but it continually subjected America to alien influences because foreigners owned a large percentage of the public debt and the stock of the Bank of the United States. This involvement, in turn, gave rise to the second set of grounds for objection: foreign entanglements necessitated standing armies and navies, the support of which added to an already oppressive tax burden. The gentry and yeomanry, the Republicans believed, had been carrying more than their share of the tax load, even when taxes had been mainly in the form of import duties; and when excise taxes were levied specifically to support the military during the quasi war with

France in 1798, the new burden fell almost exclusively on the landed. Taxes to support standing armies and navies were doubly galling because a professional military corps, as a class distinct from the people, was a threat to liberty in its own right, and it could also be unleashed to collect taxes by force, thus making the people pay for their own oppression. (English Oppositionists had been afraid of standing armies, but not of navies, for they had regarded a strong naval establishment as necessary for the protection of British commerce. The American Republicans' fear of standing armies was largely abstract, since they believed that the traditional American reliance on militias would prevent the rise of dangerous armies; but their hostility to navies was immediate and strong, for navies seemed most likely to involve the United States in fighting, and besides, navies cost a lot of money for upkeep even when they were not actively employed.)

Given all that, a revolution in the form of a return to first principles was called for. The several branches of government must be put back into constitutional balance, the moneychangers must be ousted from the temples, the gentry and yeomanry must be restored to supremacy, commerce must be returned to its subordinate role as agriculture's handmaiden, and the values of the agrarian way of life must be cherished anew. In the undertaking, the Republicans had reason for hope—as, in reality, Bolingbroke and his circle had not—for it could all be done within the framework of the Constitution. The Constitution made it possible for the Republicans to gain control of the national government, and should they prove able to do so, only two major tasks needed to be done. The first was to purge government of extreme, irreconcilable monarchists. Jefferson believed that this could be done quickly and easily, for he thought that all but a handful of the people in government were men of sound and honorable principles. The second was to pay off the public debt as rapidly as possible, since that was the wellspring of the whole system of corruption. This would not be easy; but with good management, honest administration, and rigid economy, Jefferson believed that it could be accomplished within sixteen years.

That was the Republicans' ideology and the essence of their program: restore the separation of powers through the voluntary restraint of virtuous officials, cast out the monarchists and the money men, repeal the most oppressive of taxes, slash expenses, pay off the public debt, and thus restore America to the pristine simplicity of an Arcadian past.

It is to be observed that nothing has been said of strict construction of the Constitution and the extreme states'-rights doctrine of interposition, with which Jefferson was associated in his argument against the constitutionality of the Bank in 1791 and in his authorship of the Kentucky Resolutions against the Alien and Sedition Acts in 1798 and 1799. The fact is that only a handful of people knew of those documents or knew that Jefferson had written them; they were not a part of his public identity. Moreover, they were arguments that had been coined in the first instance as matters of political expediency— as means of heading off what Jefferson regarded as dangerous activity by the Federalists—and he never thought of them as sacred principles of constitutional government.

It is also to be observed that nothing has been said of the federal judiciary or of territorial expansion, two matters that consumed much of the energy and attention of the Jeffersonians when they came to power. The judiciary was of merely tangential consequence in the Jeffersonians' thinking; it became important to them only when it loomed as an unexpected stumbling block. Territorial expansion was an integral part of their program, but only implicitly: it went without saying that the nation should expand as the opportunity arose, to make room for generations of farmers yet unborn.

The Republicans gained control of the national government, after twelve years of Federalist domination, in a bitterly contested election that began in April of 1800 and was not completed until February of 1801. Their triumph was not a popular mandate for the implementation of the Republican ideology, nor was it a popular mandate for anything else. The presidential electors were, for the most part, chosen by the state legislatures, who also chose all the members of the United States Senate. The decision was in the hands of no more than a thousand men, and for practical purposes it turned on the activities of two or three dozen factional leaders. The supporters of Thomas Jefferson proved to be more skillful as political manipulators and masters of intrigue than were the supporters of President John Adams—they had already proved, in capturing majorities in most legislatures, that they were better organized and more artful in arousing the voters—and that was the key to their success.

Nonetheless, their program had a broad basis of popular support, for it was peculiarly suited to the genius of the American people, and it appealed to their prejudices and interests as well. Moreover, there was no doubt that the Republicans had the talent, the energy, and the determination to carry the program into execution. But there was a question, a very large one. Republican theory was wondrous potent as an ideology of opposition. It remained to be seen whether it was a sound basis for administration.

Jeffersonian Republicanism was an ideology and an idea, a system of values and a way of looking at things; and as the aphorism goes, ideas and ideals have consequences. But it was also a program of action, carefully crafted and methodically executed; and as we are sometimes wont to forget, actions have consequences, too. To appraise Jefferson's presidency, it is therefore necessary to take both sets of criteria into account.

In the realm of ideas and ideology, Jeffersonian Republicanism was a body of thought that had been taken largely from the Oppositionist tradition of eighteenth-century England, principally as incorporated in the writings of Charles Davenant, John Trenchard, Thomas Gordon, James Burgh, and most particularly Henry St. John, Viscount Bolingbroke. This system of thought is explicated rather fully in the text, and it would be pointless to reiterate the effort here. It is useful, however, to remember that we are speaking of *oppositionist* thought: Bolingbroke and his predecessors and followers (whether calling themselves Tories or Commonwealthmen or Real Whigs) were condemning and seeking to undo the Financial Revolution and its attendant political corruption, as epitomized by the ministry of Sir Robert Walpole, In its stead, they proposed to restore a pristine and largely imaginary past in which life was rural, relationships were personal, the gentry ruled as a natural aristocracy, the main corpus of the citizenry was an honest yeomanry, commerce and craft-manufacturing existed only as handmaidens to agriculture, standing armies and privileged monopolies and fictitious paper wealth were all unknown, and government was limited—limited to an essentially passive function as impartial arbiter and defender of the existing social order, and limited by the unwritten but inviolable Constitution, dividing power among three separate, distinct, and coequal branches. In other words, the Jeffersonians' ideological forebears were reactionaries, swimming against the tide of history, for the world aborning was the depersonalized world of money, machines, cities, and big government.

The Jeffersonians, though castigated by their enemies as dangerous innovators and radicals, were likewise resisting the emergence of the modern world. They had seen the Hamiltonian Federalists attempting to transform and corrupt America, even as the Oppositionists had seen Walpole and the new monied classes transform and corrupt England, and they swallowed the Oppositionists' ideas and ideology whole. The Jeffersonians republicanized Bolingbroke, to be sure, developing the doctrine that absolute separation of powers, with a strictly limited presidency, was guaranteed by the written Constitution. In their hearts, however, they did not trust paper constitutions, and their view of Jefferson's mission as president did not differ substantively and significantly from Bolingbroke's idea of a Patriot King: a head of state who would rally the entire nation to his banner, and then, in an act of supreme wisdom and virtue, voluntarily restrain himself and thus give vitality and meaning to the constitutional system. The Republicans also added the doctrine of states' rights, but that was mainly a tactical position which most of them abandoned—except rhetorically—once they came into control of the national government. The only genuine changes they brought to the ideology were two. One was to relocate its social base, from that of an Anglican gentry to that of southern slaveholders, Celtic-American back-country men, and evangelical Protestants. The other was to put the ideology into practice.

If who they were and what they were seeking are thus understood, it is evident that they remained remarkably true to their principles throughout Jefferson's presidency—despite charges to the contrary by a host of critics, ranging from Alexander Hamilton to Henry Adams to Leonard Levy. Moreover, they were remarkably successful in accomplishing what they set out to do. They set out to destroy the complex financial mechanism that Hamilton had built around the public debt, and they went a long way toward that goal—so close that if war could have been avoided for another eight years, their success might have been total. They also set out to secure the frontiers of the United States by expanding the country's territorial domain into the vast wilderness, and they succeeded so well that it became possible to dream that the United States could remain a nation of uncorrupted farmers for a thousand years to come.

And yet on the broader scale they failed, and failed calamitously—not because of their own shortcomings, but because their system was incompatible with the immediate current of events, with the broad sweep of history, and with the nature of man and society. As an abstract idea, Bolingbrokism *cum*

Jeffersonian Republicanism may have been flawless, and it was certainly appealing. In the real world, it contradicted and destroyed itself.

At the core of the Republicans' thinking lay the assumption, almost Marxian in its naïveté, that only two things must be done to remake America as an ideal society and a beacon unto mankind. First, the public debt must be extinguished, for with it would die stock-jobbing, paper-shuffling, "monopoly" banking, excisemen, placemen, and all the other instrumentalities of corruption that the Walpole/Hamilton system "artificially" created. Second, governmental power must be confined to its constitutional limits, which implied reduction of the functions of government but also, and more importantly, meant adherence to the rules of the separation of powers—that being the only legitimate method, in their view, whereby a free government could exercise its authority. If ancient ways were thus restored, the Jeffersonians believed, liberty and independence would inevitably follow. In turn, liberty and independence—by which they meant the absence of governmental restraint or favor and the absence of effective interference from foreign powers—would make it possible for every man, equal in rights but not in talents, to pursue happiness in his own way and to find his own "natural" level in the natural order.

Things did not work out that way, especially in regard to relations with foreign powers: far from freeing the country from foreign interference, Republican policy sorely impaired the nation's ability to determine its own destiny. In their eagerness to retire the public debt, the Jeffersonians tried diligently to economize. Toward that end they slashed military and naval appropriations so much as to render the United States incapable of defending itself at a time when the entire Western world was at war. Simultaneously, in their haste to destroy all vestiges of the Hamiltonian system, the Jeffersonians abolished virtually all internal taxes. This relieved the farmers and planters of an onerous tax burden and arrested the proliferation of hated excisemen, but it also made national revenues almost totally dependent upon duties on imports—which meant dependent upon the uninterrupted flow of international commerce, which in turn depended upon the will of Napoleon Bonaparte and the ministers of King George III.

For two or three years the Jeffersonians were extremely lucky. That is to say, during that period the kaleidoscope of events in Europe turned briefly and flukishly in their favor. They obtained Louisiana as a result of a concatenation of circumstances that was wildly improbable and was never to be repeated. They were able to pay off much of the public debt and to accumulate sizable treasury surpluses because Great Britain, out of consideration for its own interests, allowed the Americans to engage in a trade of debatable legality, thus swelling the volume of American imports and, concomitantly, the revenues flowing into the United States Treasury.

From 1803 onward, however, each turn of the international wheel was less favorable to the United States. By 1805 it was apparent that West Florida—for which the Jeffersonians hungered almost obsessively, since its strategic and economic value was considerably greater than that of all Louisiana excepting New Orleans—would not become American in the way that Louisiana had. In the same year it began to be clear that the British would not long continue to allow the United States to grow wealthy by trading with Britain's mortal enemies.

But for their ideology, the Jeffersonians could have reversed their earlier policy stance, embraced Britain, and become hostile toward France and Spain, thus enabling the nation to continue to prosper and expand. Given their ideological commitment, they could not do so. Moreover, given the consequences of their actions so far, they lacked the strength to make even a token show of force against Great Britain. Thus in 1807, when both Britain and France forbade the United States to engage in international commerce except as tributaries to themselves, the embargo—a policy of pusillanimity and bungling, billed as a noble experiment in peaceful coercion—was the only course open to them.

At home, as they became ever more deeply impaled upon the horns of their self-created international dilemma, the Jeffersonians became progressively less tolerant of opposition or criticism. From the beginning they had shown considerable disdain for the federal courts; as Jefferson's second term wore on, this disdain degenerated into contempt for due process of law and for law itself. Thus the embargo became a program of domestic tyranny in inverse ratio to its ineffectiveness as an instrument of international policy: the more the policy was found wanting, the more rigorously was it enforced.

The embargo, then, both as a bankrupt foreign policy and as a reign of domestic oppression, was not a sudden aberration but the logical and virtually certain outcome of the Jeffersonian ideology put into practice: the ideology's yield was dependence rather than independence, oppression rather than liberty.

One other aspect of the Jeffersonian experience wants notice, and that concerns the Republicans' conception of the presidency as a limited branch of government, absolutely separate from the legislative branch. In practice, adherence to that ideal was impossible because of the very nature of the presidential office. For one thing, though some presidential powers are relatively independent, others are intermeshed with those of Congress. For another, the American executive branch is "republicanized," or kept from being monarchical, by being made elective for a fixed term of years. To be sure, the Republicans' political machinery was so effective that Jefferson could doubtless have been elected to a third and even a fourth term, had he chosen. But Washington's two-term precedent was strong, and, what was more telling, the psychic cost of the presidential office was and is frightful; by the seventh or eighth year Jefferson, like Washington before him and like most two-term presidents who followed him, was physically, emotionally, and spiritually exhausted. The second term was therefore a lame-duck term, and that fact subtly but significantly altered the relationship between the president and Congress. Pure though Jefferson's motives and the motives of many Republican congressmen were, it was important to them that his popularity would cease to be of use to them in seeking reelection, and it was important to him that he would not need their political support in 1808. In the circumstances, Jefferson did what lame-duck presidents normally do—that is, he gravitated toward the arena in which he had less to do with Congress, the area of foreign relations; and Congress, and especially the Senate, also followed the norm by rising at the end to regain powers that it believed had been more or less usurped from it.

Still another crucial aspect of the American presidency, one with which the Republicans were not at all prepared to cope, is that the Constitution vests in one office and one person two distinct and nearly incompatible roles which under the British system had come to be divided between the king and his ministers. One is the truly monarchical function, that of serving as the ritualistic symbol of the nation. The other is the purely executive function, that of fashioning policy and directing its implementation. Success in the one hinges upon the president's charisma, his leadership, and his abstract appeal to the whole people; success in the other hinges upon the president's skill in tangible dealings with small groups and individual human beings. The Republicans' conception of the presidency was, in these terms, entirely unrealistic: they disavowed the first role and wanted the president to fill the second by standing as aloof from Congress as a proper king stands from his subjects.

Jefferson was superbly gifted at playing both roles, and he was able to play them without offending Republican sensibilities or prejudices. He ostentatiously disdained the pomp and pageantry that had marked the presidencies of Washington and Adams, but all the while he assiduously and effectively courted popularity. Foreign ministers and Federalist critics alike commented upon his inordinate love of popularity, and marked it as a weakness of character; perhaps it was, but it was also true wisdom, for reverence toward the Crown was a deeprooted habit in the English-speaking world, and love of the president as king-surrogate was a crucial social adhesive for the diffuse and pluralistic infant United States. Indeed, in this respect Jefferson made a profound contribution toward the perdurance of the republic. Washington had been a veritable demigod and a symbol of the nation, and thus provided a sort of half-way house between monarchy and republicanism; Jefferson humanized the presidency and served as a symbol, not of the nation, but of the people, and thus made the transition complete.

In the role of policy-maker and administrator, Jefferson was even more skilled. After his inaugural he abandoned the monarchical practice of appearing in person before Congress; he never held court or levees, but invited congressmen in small groups for dinner, where he word homespun and hosted them in the manner of a country squire; he never openly initiated legislation, and only deferentially suggested that Congress might look into one subject or another; he never vetoed a bill on policy grounds and would not have dreamed of doing so. In sum, he allowed Congress to function with no overt presidential direction and with only the gentlest of presidential guidance. As to cabinet meetings, he conducted them as a democracy of equals. And yet, almost until the end, he ran Congress more successfully and more thoroughly than did any preceding president and precious few succeeding presidents, and the cabinet always reflected his will except when he had no firm opinions on a matter. Moreover, he did so without the use of bribery, patronage, corruption or coercion: it all flowed from the force of his intellect, his character, and his personality.

But, perversely, that too was a weakness of the Jeffersonian scheme of things: the system could be made to work only with a Thomas Jefferson at the helm. When Jefferson himself faltered, as he did on several occasions during his presidency, the government almost stopped functioning except in the routine operations of Galatin's Treasury machinery. When Jefferson left the office, all the shortcomings of his method of administration became manifest. The cabinet became a center of petty bickering and continuous cabalizing, and Congress split into irreconcilable factions and repeatedly asserted its will against the president.

For all these reasons, Jefferson's legacy to his successor was a can of serpents. Jefferson's second term was merely a calamity; Madison's first would be a disaster.

There is more to a presidency than the tangible events that happen during and in consequence of it: there are also the myths it inspires. For a time, of course, memories were too fresh, feelings were too strong, and events were too unpleasant to admit of the kind of romanticization that is a necessary prelude to myth-making. By 1826, however—when Jefferson along with John Adams died on the fiftieth anniversary of the Declaration of Independence—memories had mellowed, new rivalries had replaced the old, and artful and designing men were looking to the past for heroes whose lives could be used or misused to justify their own doings. Jefferson was admirably suited for such use and misuse, for he had written and acted in a greater variety of ways on a greater variety of subjects than any of the other Founding Fathers, and he was more quotable than any of them save possibly Adams alone.

But the Jefferson legend developed along curiously divided lines. In the realm of formal historical writing, he fared poorly until well into the twentieth century. . . .

Meanwhile, in the realm of folklore and political rhetoric, which ordinary Americans heard and heeded more frequently and more trustingly than they did the staid pronouncements of historians, Jefferson was exalted as the patron saint of all good things. The range of causes for which his name was invoked is staggering: democracy and partisanship, states' rights and nationalism, slavery and abolitionism, egalitarianism and racism, imperialism and isolationism, populism and laissez-faire capitalism, the planned and the decentralized society. In the nineteenth century, so long as rural values continued to prevail in America despite the relentless march of industrialization, Jefferson continued to be identified with the agrarian tradition; in the twentieth, when the center of American life and values became the city, his connection with that ideal was all but forgotten, and instead he came to be regarded as the champion of the "have-nots" against the "haves," of the "common man" (or the "forgotten man" or the "little fellow") against aristocrats and plutocrats.

In the 1920s and 1930s the two strands of the legend began to come together. The Democratic politician-historian Claude G. Bowers and the more scholarly Gilbert Chinard began the process of beatification through the written word, and though the Jefferson they described was one he would scarcely have recognized, the process has continued. Franklin Roosevelt's New Deal depicted itself as thoroughly Jeffersonian, though given to the use of "Hamiltonian means to accomplish Jeffersonian ends"—and while building a federal bureaucracy almost as large as the population of the entire country had been during Jefferson's time and while extending its regulatory power apace, it built Jefferson a monument which declared his true mission to have been as a libertarian. In time, and in our own time, "Jefferson" and "Jeffersonian" came to mean merely "good," or "that which the nation aspires to be."

The real Jefferson—the one who once lived in Virginia and once worked in the President's House—was lost in the shuffle. So, too, was the America he wanted his country to become; and in a nation of crime-ridden cities and poisoned air, of credit cards and gigantic corporations, of welfare rolls and massive bureaucracies, of staggering military budgets and astronomical public debts, of corruption and alienation, that loss is the more poignant. He and his followers set out to deflect the course of History, and History ended up devouring them and turning even their memory to its own purposes. History has a way of doing that.

POSTSCRIPT

Was Thomas Jefferson a Political Compromiser?

Professor Borden seems to approve of Jefferson's pragmatic, commonsense and moderate approach to politics. Rejecting many of the differences between Federalists and Republicans as mere political rhetoric, Borden maintains that "Jefferson was ever a national patriot . . . [who] always conceived of the United States as a unique experiment, destined for greatness so long as sharp line isolated American civilization from European infection." Jefferson became a proponent of strong executive power, he argues, because he believed such measures as the Louisiana Purchase and the embargo furthered the nation's best interests.

Professor Forrest McDonald rejects the consensus view of American politics held by Professor Borden that there are little ideological differences between the opposition political parties. He believes there were philosophical differences between Hamilton and Jefferson that effected public policies. Hamilton believed that men were motivated by ambition, avarice, and a lust for power. Jefferson believed human beings were born with a blank slate and were capable of becoming good or evil, "depending upon the wholesomeness of the environment." Drawing upon the political theories of the British Opportunists of the early eighteenth century, the Republican ideology consisted in getting rid of extreme, irreconcilable monarchists and paying off the debt as quickly as possible and "thus restore America to the pristine simplicity of an Arcadian past." Unfortunately, the policies didn't always work. Reduction in land taxes meant the government became excessively dependent upon tariffs for their revenue. The failed embargo against England and France in Jefferson's second term not only created a nationwide economic depression, "the embargo also became a program of domestic tyranny in inverse ratio to its effectiveness as an instrument of international policy: the more the policy was found wanting, the more rigorously it was enforced."

It is not surprising that Jefferson's two major biographers, both professors at the University of Virginia for many years, have written sympathetic portraits. Dumas Malone's magisterial *Jefferson and His Times,* 6 volumes (Little, Brown, 1948–1981) and Merrill Peterson's 900-page opus *Thomas Jefferson and the New Nation: A Bibliography* (Oxford, 1970) contain detailed accounts of most facets of his life and are very useful as reference works. Peterson's *The Jeffersonian Images in the American Mind* (Oxford, 1960) is a wonderful account of the use and misuse of Jefferson's image in American politics since his death up to 1960.

Recent writings on Jefferson reflect a more critical tone. One reason is Jefferson's views on slavery and race. William Cohen in "Thomas Jefferson and the Problem of Slavery," *The Journal of American History* (December, 1969) believes Jefferson was a typical Virginia planter committed to protecting his chattel property. Fawn M. Brodie's psychobiography *Thomas Jefferson: An Intimate History* (Norton, 1974) was one of the first to accept as true the liaison between Jefferson and Sally Hemings that led to five unacknowledged sons and daughters. A shorter version can be found in Brodie's "The Great Taboo," *American Heritage* (June 1972). More recently, DNA tests have confirmed that Jefferson fathered the youngest of Sally's children. See the article by Eric S. Lander and Joseph J. Ellis et. al., "DNA Analysis: Founding Father," *Nature* (November 5, 1998, pp. 13–14, 27–28). A layperson's explanation of the DNA article is "Jefferson's Secret Life" by Barbara Murray and Brian Duffy in *U.S. News and World Report* (November 9, 1998). The controversy is fully examined with a complete bibliography and a critical discussion of Jefferson's earlier biographers who refused to consider the possibility of a Jefferson–Hemings liaison in Annette Gordon-Reed, *Thomas Jefferson and Sally Hemings: An American Controversy* (The University Press of Virginia, 1997).

The most recent analysis of *Jeffersonian America* (Blackwell Publishers, 2002) with the most complete bibliography is by Peter S. Onuf and Leonard Sadorsky. Two collections of essays in the 1990s reflect a more critical tone than the very sympathetic works of Malone and Peterson. See Peter S. Onuf, eds., *Jeffersonian Legacies* (The University of Virginia Press, 1993) and James Horn and Peter S. Onuf, eds., *The Revolution of 1800: Democracy, Race and the New Republic* (The University of Press of Virginia, 2002).

ISSUE 9

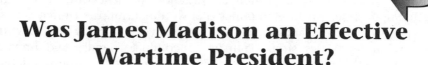

Was James Madison an Effective Wartime President?

YES: Irving Brant, from *James Madison: Commander in Chief, 1812–1836* (Bobbs-Merrill, 1961)

NO: Donald R. Hickey, from *The War of 1812: A Forgotten Conflict* (University of Illinois Press, 1989)

ISSUE SUMMARY

YES: Irving Brant coonconcludes that President James Madison grew into his position as commander in chief during the War of 1812 and set the stage for both land and naval victories at the close of the conflict through his adroit military appointments and skillful diplomacy.

NO: Donald Hickey contends that Madison failed to provide the bold and vigorous leadership that was essential to a successful prosecution of the War of 1812 by tolerating incompetence among his generals and cabinet officers and by failing to secure vital legislation from Congress.

With the signing of the Treaty of Paris in 1783, the American Revolution came to an end, and the United States entered the family of nations as an independent and sovereign state. While some diplomatic historians have insisted that the United States immediately became a major player on the world stage, clearly independence did not automatically bring into being a strong nation capable of competing effectively with the major European powers. Despite having defeated the British, the new country possessed only marginal army and naval forces and no income to support the military. Moreover, the central government under the Articles of Confederation was simply too weak to enforce wide-reaching foreign interests. John Adams, the American minister to England, shouldered most of the diplomatic burden for the United States in the years immediately following the Revolution, and Adams realized from the outset that until the United States possessed a stronger national government that it would not be able to enforce its will on other countries. A remedy for this situation, therefore, was accomplished at the Constitutional Convention.

With the French Revolution and, subsequently, the outbreak of a general European conflict culminating in the Napoleonic Wars, American leaders were forced to determine what, if any, role the United States should play in the European struggles, especially when the nations involved in those conflicts called upon the fledgling nation for assistance. President George Washington insisted upon a flexible foreign policy that would permit the United States to pursue its own interests and issued a Proclamation of Neutrality in 1793 stating that the United States should pursue "a conduct friendly and impartial toward the belligerent powers." John Adams, as president, witnessed deteriorating relations with France in the wake of the XYZ affair but responded to his own party's call for war by concluding that such action was not in the security interests of the United States. Later, Adams viewed this decision to avoid war as the capstone of his political career.

As relations with England over American shipping and trade rights declined during the presidency of Thomas Jefferson, the United States found itself once again moving toward armed conflict with the former Mother Country. Following the 1807 attack on the American frigate *Chesapeake* by the British vessel *Leopard*, Jefferson sought to protect the national interest short of going to war by imposing economic sanctions through the Embargo Act. The measure delayed the war but also crippled American shipping interests, and when James Madison succeeded Jefferson as president in 1809, he faced several perplexing problems. After all, England's maritime practice of impressment and further harassment of American shipping on the high seas violated the United States' national honor, wreaked economic havoc in the West and South whose farmers depended upon exporting their surplus agricultural goods to Europe, and threatened the young nation's rightful claims to neutrality. When he failed to persuade the British to halt their attacks on American shipping, President Madison requested from Congress a declaration of war against Great Britain, which Congress provided on June 18, 1812.

In the essays that follow, Madison's execution of the war as commander-in-chief is evaluated. Irving Brant presents a generally sympathetic appraisal of Madison's wartime leadership. Despite early difficulties in which U.S. military forces faced defeat after defeat, Madison ultimately exercised the reigns of power quite skillfully in both military and diplomatic decision making. Regardless of the fact that the war failed to resolve either nation's specific goals, Andrew Jackson's stunning land victory at New Orleans (concluded two weeks after the Treaty of Ghent had been signed) led to the popular conclusion that "Mr. Madison's War" represented a second successful war for independence from England.

Donald Hickey is far less enthusiastic about Madison's performance as wartime president. In fact, he believes that the general lack of attention given to the War of 1812 by scholars stems from the fact "that no great president is associated with the conflict." To his critics, Madison, like Nero, fiddled while the nation's capital burned. The president's overly cautious leadership, his inability to command influence in Congress, and his failure to appoint effective military and administrative leaders to prosecute the war seriously undermined the effort and brought the United States perilously close to defeat.

YES

Irving Brant

James Madison: Commander in Chief, 1812–1836

Peace Ratified by Victory

The clock ticked off Friday, January 13, 1815, with suspense heightened by nonarrival of the New Orleans mail. Baton Rouge reported that the Tennessee and Kentucky militia had gone by on the river. General Jackson had proclaimed martial law in New Orleans and made a mass levy of its militia. The stringent restraints stirred Federalists to frenzy.

President Madison began the war, cried their *Federal Republican,* by stimulating mobs to violence and assassination, and now it was seen "in what manner his favorite General is about to close it." From what source did a military officer derive the power of forcing all ages into military service and forbidding civilians to leave without a permit? Subjugation by a foreign foe would be better than such a loss of rights. More days passed. The Tennessee River was in raging flood, holding back the New Orleans mails, but the Georgetown paper had a different explanation:

> "The suspicion gains ground that the government is in possession of the official account of the capture of this important city. . . . An inquiry by Congress . . . will fix the blame upon the Executive."

Delayed a week, a carrier struggled through with news of indecisive fighting seven miles south of New Orleans, after which Jackson took a strong position nearer the city. The next evening (January 21) the President's twenty dinner guests included twenty-three-year-old George Ticknor of Boston. A servant called Madison out and word went around that the New Orleans mail had arrived. Wrote Ticknor:

> "The President soon returned with added gravity and said that there was no news! Silence ensued. No man seemed to know what to say at such a crisis . . . and said nothing at all."

When dinner was announced, modest young Ticknor went to the foot of the table. "The President desired me to come round to him, and seeing me

From JAMES MADISON: COMMANDER IN CHIEF, 1812–1836, 1961, pp. 363–365, 367–371, 377–380. Copyright © 1961 by Simon & Schuster. Reprinted by permission. References omitted.

hesitate . . . fairly seated me between himself and Mrs. Madison." Ticknor continued:

> "I found the President more free and open than I expected, starting subjects of conversation and making remarks that sometimes savored of humor and levity . . . but his face was always grave. He talked of religious sects and parties and was curious to know how the cause of liberal Christianity stood with us, and if the Athanasian creed was well received by our Episcopalians. He pretty distinctly intimated to me his own regard for the Unitarian doctrines."

They talked of education and internal improvements, but when the President mentioned the *Edinburgh Review* he fell into so sudden a silence that Ticknor decided not to reveal his acquaintance with Editor Jeffrey. The precaution was wasted, for Madison undoubtedly .was thinking of the magazine's prewar friendliness. Yet unknown was its declaration of November 1812 that the war was the end-result of a preposterous policy that produced beggary, disorder and wretchedness in Great Britain, culminating in a conflict that would remain an "everlasting stain on the character of our country."

Waiting for tidings from New Orleans, the President found items of cheer or concern from other quarters. The Boston *Yankee* reported agitation among the people of Maine "to free themselves from the base thraldom of *traitors* and *cowards*" by obtaining separate statehood. The New York *Columbian* predicted that the great warships building on Lake Ontario would gain control by summer. Through a pilot's error Decatur's frigate, the *President,* pounded for ninety minutes on the Sandy Hook bar, suffering damage that prevented escape from four heavy warships. She dismantled the *Endymion* but was overtaken and captured by the others.

At the end of January, Jackson's report of a December 23 battle came through—a night attack in which the enemy camp was penetrated but fog halted the operation. Jackson next morning placed his army behind a dry canal twenty feet wide, running half a mile from a cypress swamp to the Mississippi. Here he repulsed a frontal attack and forced the enemy to fall back. "Generals Jackson, Carroll and Coffee," wrote a colonel, "are worth more than their weight in gold."

By this time the British had a new commander, Major General Sir Edward Pakenham, Wellington's brother-in-law. Three fourths of his 8,000 men . . . were Peninsular veterans, including the army that captured Washington.

Facing the British between swamp and river were 5,500 American troops, mostly Tennessee and Kentucky militiamen, with a core of regulars and a supplement of French Louisianans, sailors, "free men of color" and several hundred pirates and smugglers from the lower delta. On the west shore were 4,500 Americans, chiefly untried Kentucky militia. Congressman Hanson's newspaper appraised the situation and prescribed the remedy:

> "The only measure for the preservation of the country which is likely to produce any lasting beneficial results, would be the impeachment and punishment of James Madison. While this man, if he deserves the name, is at the head of affairs . . . there can be nothing but dishonor, disappointment and

disaster. . . . Turn your eyes to New Orleans. . . . The same contemptible force that retired before the Maryland militia at Baltimore, with the addition, perhaps, of a few black regiments, are about to cut off, at one slice, a whole state from the union."

Federalist apprehensions or hopes turned to certainty when the semi-official *Intelligencer* reported Jackson in bad health (from fatigue and exposure), still short of ammunition; and that the President intended to call out 5,000 more Kentuckians (actually 6,500 from Kentucky and Tennessee, already summoned). These disclosures inspired a Federalist congressman to say, "absolutely, that government was in possession of information that the British had taken New Orleans." Instead of letting the facts ooze out by drops, jeered the *Federal Republican,* "Mr. Madison may as well lift the gate and let the flood through." Why was not New Orleans properly defended?

> "Go ask the winds. You might as well attempt to reanimate the clay cold tenants of a churchyard, as hope to make any impression on Mr. Madison. His heart is petrified and hard as marble. His body is torpid, and he is without feeling."

Twenty-four hours later Washington was wild with joy. The invading British veterans were utterly defeated on January 8, with the most amazing disparity of losses in the annals of modern war. Of the enemy, 700 killed (including Pakenham), 1,400 wounded, 500 captured. American losses: seven killed, six wounded. . . .

For ten days after Jackson's great victory the two armies remained within cannon shot, each deterred from assault by the narrowness of the front between river and morass. Then, at midnight, the British spiked their artillery and returned to their ships. The President reduced his call for western militia. It was confidently believed, Governor Shelby was told, that the war could be converted to an offensive one and brought to an early termination.

A few hours after that was written, southbound expresses raced through Washington. One rider was to receive a thousand dollars if he reached Charleston within a given time. The purpose was obvious, to enable speculators to buy tobacco and cotton before news of peace shot prices up. But was the report thus carried genuine? A speeding messenger paused long enough to hand a letter to a member of Congress. Henry Clay's secretary, it said, had brought the preliminaries of peace. A rumor that the President's house was illuminated set off a far-spreading celebration, but the government newspaper next morning advised readers to suspend their opinions.

That evening (February 14) Madison found Monroe at the door, the treaty in his hands. The official view was planted instantly in the *National Intelligencer.* "The general principle of the treaty is a restitution and recognition of the rights and possessions of each party, as they stood before the war." Disputed boundary points would be settled by joint commissions, with disagreements referred to a friendly sovereign. Hostilities would cease upon the exchange of ratifications *in Washington*—a speed-up arrangement. Both sides would make peace with the Indians. No grievance was rectified and no concession made.

The Prince Regent already had ratified the treaty and the *Intelligencer* was happy to add that "the President will, probably, lay it before the Senate this day." He did so, and it was unanimously ratified twenty-four hours later. Anthony St. John Baker came in from Norfolk next day with the British ratification. On February 17—two years and eight months after war was declared—the President proclaimed the conflict ended.

On the initiative of Senator Bibb of Georgia, administration floor leader, the documents accompanying the treaty were kept secret. The American *projet,* submitted by joint agreement on November 10, included for the record all of the original American demands—on impressment, blockade and ship seizures. To publish these with the British notation "inadmissible" would have created an impression of lengthy controversy and defeat on issues rendered noncrucial by European peace and barely mentioned in the negotiations. Pertinent material actually kept from the public covered the struggle in the final weeks over the British right to navigate the Mississippi and American rights in the Newfoundland fisheries. Airing those issues would make it harder to settle them in a treaty of commerce.

To the Senate the President confidentially revealed the final American moves on those two points. The envoys gave Great Britain the choice of having Mississippi and fishery rights (as of 1783) confirmed or of omitting both from the treaty. London countered by asking that each be confirmed in exchange for a boundary concession. Staking the fate of the treaty on their move, the Americans rejected the proposals and reaffirmed their claims but offered to omit settlement of fisheries, boundaries and Mississippi navigation. To their surprise the cabinet agreed. That left the American claims unaccepted but formally asserted and supported by the still-valid treaty of 1783. Later diplomatic events justified the American strategy.

Madison's conjectures about the evil influence of Federalist noncooperation were confirmed both by Gallatin and by John Quincy Adams, who wrote to his father: "Had Massachusetts been true to herself and to the Union, Great Britain would not have dared to hinge the question of peace or war upon Moose Island, or upon the privileges of Massachusetts fishermen." He regarded Gallatin "as having contributed the largest and most important share to the conclusion of the peace." There had been sharp minor disagreements, yet Adams reported basic harmony "as great and constant as perhaps ever existed between five persons employed together upon so important a trust."

Transmitting the ratification, President Madison congratulated congressmen and the people on an event highly honorable to the nation, terminating "with peculiar felicity a campaign signalized by the most brilliant successes." The late war, reluctantly declared, had been necessary to assert the rights and independence of the country:

> "It has been waged with a success which is the natural result of the wisdom of the legislative councils, of the patriotism of the people, of the public spirit of the militia, and of the valor of the military and naval forces of the country. Peace, at all times a blessing, is peculiarly welcome, therefore, at a period when the causes of the war have ceased to operate, when the Government has demonstrated the efficiency of its powers of defense, and

when the nation can review its conduct without regret and without reproach."

The reference to legislative wisdom differed a trifle from Private Secretary Coles's late remark that the oscillating and inefficient measures of Congress "so completely disgusted and sickened me that I cannot bear to think of them." The President expressed private confidence that the resources and spirit of the nation were adequate to the war's successful continuance. But he rejoiced that peace came "at a time and on terms which could not but render it truly welcome."

In the public celebration, the *Intelligencer* noted, "the star spangled banner of America and the red cross flag of Britain were displayed together." Thus Key's triumphal phrase entered the American vernacular. Coming on the heels of the New Orleans victory, Sérurier commented, the news from Ghent carried public intoxication to its height. "Peace could not come at a happier moment to crown the courageous constancy of these people and their councillors." In Canada, England's failure to adhere to her original demands was taken as a portent of future conquest. Said the Montreal *Herald:*

> "It is inconceivable to see to what a pitch illuminations and rejoicings are carried throughout the United States. . . . What a contrast is exhibited in this country! You scarcely meet a cheerful countenance from one end of the province to the other when you speak of the peace."

In the United States national pride extended well into the ranks of the Federalists. But their leaders, though welcoming peace, wept buckets of tears over its ignoble quality. The New York *Evening Post,* informed of the treaty's terms by London newspapers but pretending ignorance, was ready to hazard its reputation that the government had not "obtained one single avowed object, for which they involved the country in this bloody and expensive war." By means of it Madison had obtained the Presidency for a second term, with a salary of $25,000 and a gorgeous marble palace, "yet LET THE NATION REJOICE, WE HAVE ESCAPED RUIN."

With as little subtlety and more malice the *Federal Republican* hammered day after day upon the President's alleged failure to rescue the 6,257 impressed American seamen held in British captivity. "We have no knowledge of human nature if this wretched man is not, ere long, hunted down by the blood-hounds of his own rearing." Mobs would soon be in a temper "to tear his majesty's heart out, if he had one." In reality, as the editors well knew, these seamen were classed as prisoners of war, whose release was required by the treaty. The reference of boundary disputes to commissioners was described by Federalists as a deceptive cover for the surrender of territory. Let the dispatches be submitted to Congress and "the humiliation of our cabinet and the war party will be complete."

Stalking silently through jubilant Washington were three figures of gloom— Harrison Gray Otis, opium-trader Thomas H. Perkins and William Sullivan. Sent to place the demands of the Hartford Convention before President Madison, they made no effort to perform their outdated mission. "Their position," wrote

Sérurier, "was awkward, embarrassing, and lent itself cruelly to ridicule." Two of them appeared Wednesday night in the drawing room of the President, "presented their respects to him, and talked of nothing."

Otis did not go to this place where "all was tinsel and vulgarity" (he wrote to his wife) because "we have received no [dinner] invitation from Mr. Madison. What a mean and contemptible little blackguard." It suited Madison's purpose, said Otis, to spread the belief that the mission would have failed in any circumstances. "I believe however we should have succeeded and that the little pigmy shook in his shoes at our approach."

Senator Barry of Kentucky saw no vulgarity in the levee. Queen Dolley was in high spirits, needing only a new palace, and the President "much elated. The glad tidings of peace, procured by the glory of the American arms under his management, has inspired him with new life and vigor."

Republican leaders and presses rallied to the President's defense against the torrent of invective. Why, asked the Boston *Chronicle,* was "the illustrious Madison" personally calumniated? Because he "stands elevated on the mountain of patriotism, unshaken amid the storms and tempests of an infuriated faction." Massachusetts Republican legislators gloried in the personal intrepidity and magnanimity with which Madison led the nation to triumph "while assailed by the artillery of personal detraction." The tremendous uplift of the long-repressed New England minority was evident in a Boston toast:

> "The Commander in Chief of the Army and Navy of the United States—His patriotism and undaunted perseverance in a season of darkness and difficulty have been to his friends in the East like the shadow 'of a great rock in a weary land.'"

Throughout the country addresses to the President mixed the themes of heightened national honor and (as phrased by former Attorney General Pinkney) "admiration of the enlightened wisdom and patriotic firmness by which your conduct has been distinguished." Pinkney's successor Richard Rush addressed him more intimately: "Your anxious moments sir will now be fewer; your labors abridged; your friends more than ever gratified; an unmanly opposition more than ever confounded; the nation in your day advanced anew in prosperity and glory," The nationwide acclaim was gall to the bitter-end Federalists, whose vexation was put into words by the New York *Courier:*

> "Our conflict with England, has resulted in total discomfiture—in the abandonment of every object sought by It; and we are doomed to hear the names of Madison and Monroe resounding in reiterate and tumultuous shouts to the heavens!"

There was ample scope for debate over objectives won, lost, or actually nonexistent. But two facts could not be gainsaid: the treaty, as the *National Intelligencer* observed, was denounced most bitterly by writers whose pens were "scarcely nibbed" since they were employed in advocating peace on British terms; and, except by American Federalists, the outcome was construed throughout the world as a triumph for the United States. . . .

If the treaty had settled the issues that produced the war, the public reaction to it would have had little permanent significance. But because it ended without a decision of grievances, the true measuring factors were the resultant public policies on both sides of the Atlantic. In that respect the trend of the war counted for a great deal more than the early course of it.

Among most Americans, the miserable failures of overage generals and untrained troops were almost blotted out of mind by the shining achievements of the final year. With contrary emotions the same was true in England. Measured by its immediate impact and lasting influence, the victory at New Orleans was no meaningless bloody postlude to the war. In America the news of this victory preceded and dramatized the peace; to Europe it was the riveting hammer blow of the builders of a new world power. To all alike it was the climax of the war, doubling the effect of the triumph on Lake Champlain, acting as a galvanizing agent on public opinion around the world.

One of the first to sense this truth was Louis Sérurier. He not only repeated but enlarged his assertion of January 1814 that, come what might of the peace negotiations, the results of the war were immutable; the United States henceforth would be a great naval and manufacturing power. The treaty, he wrote, returned the two countries to their point of departure in only one respect—the restitution of possessions and prewar rights. "In all other regards, all is loss for England; all is gain for the United States." American naval victories were "a prelude to the lofty destiny to which they are called on that element." On land they had made rapid progress in discipline, fought with valor, and "in three great attacks saw Wellington's best corps flee before their militia." With this had come a revolution in political thinking:

> "These three years of warfare have been a trial of the capacity of their institutions to sustain a state of war, a question . . . now resolved to their advantage. It has moreover had the good effect of destroying the illusions, the prejudices and the mental habits of too prolonged peace; of familiarizing the people with the carrying of arms, of reconciling them to the idea of taxes and the sacrifices necessary to their defense."

The war had produced an expansion of manufactures that could not be achieved in twenty years of peace. It had proved that the attempt so often made to dissolve the Union was impossible to execute. "Finally the war has given the Americans what they so essentially lacked, a national character founded on a glory common to all." Out of this had come a development of world-wide importance. It had established a new equilibrium on the sea, due to the reconciling of the two American political parties on the subject of a Navy, to which the Republicans were once opposed:

> "Glory has dissipated this prejudice and united all minds. You will notice that the President in his message has recommended [the Navy's] progressive enlargement. . . . England will perhaps shudder at this, but Europe and France especially will applaud it. . . . The United States . . . are at this moment, in my eyes, a naval power. . . . Within ten years they will be masters in their waters and upon their coasts."

Former President John Adams reached similar conclusions. Madison had proved that an administration under the present Constitution could declare war and make peace; that Great Britain never could conquer the country; that American officers and men were equal to England's Peninsular veterans, that the Navy was equal, ship for ship, to any that ever floated. In full accord and of broader range was Justice Story's rejoicing reaction. Current appraisal blended into a picture of the American future:

> "Peace has come in a most welcome time to delight and astonish us. Never did a country occupy more lofty ground; we have stood the contest, single-handed, against the conqueror of Europe; and we are at peace, with all our blushing victories thick crowding on us. If I do not much mistake, we shall attain to a very high character abroad as well as crush domestic faction."

Still ardent in party matters, Story saw a most "glorious opportunity for the Republican party to place themselves permanently in power." He prayed to God that the golden moment would not be thrown away:

> "Let us extend the national authority over the whole extent of power given by the Constitution. Let us have great military and naval schools; an adequate regular army; the broad foundations laid of a permanent navy; a national bank; a national system of bankruptcy; a great navigation act; . . . judicial courts which shall embrace the whole constitutional power; . . . national justices of the peace for the commercial and national concerns of the United States."

By such enlarged and liberal institutions, said this jurist, the government "will be endeared to the people and the factions of the great states will be rendered harmless. Let us prevent the possibility of a division by creating great national interests which shall bind us in an indissoluble chain."

Here was a nationalism so high and sweeping as to beggar the supposition that Chief Justice Marshall dragged Story into the centralizing policies about to burgeon in the Supreme Court. Rather it suggests that the war itself intensified the judicial as well as the political trend toward federal power in an expanding nation.

James Madison's attitude toward these developments was yet to be revealed. Carried far enough they would violate his concept of a federal republic. But his contribution to them was not open to question. In the Continental Congress, the Virginia legislature and the Federal Convention of 1787, he had worked to build a strong general government. In the Congress of the United States, as Secretary of State and as President he was unremitting in stirring national resistance to maritime aggressions. As Commander in Chief he bore the fundamental responsibility and shared the actual blame for the early deficiencies in military leadership. But more and more he became commander in fact as well as name. His personal promotion of Generals Brown and Jackson, foiling the adroit maneuvers of Secretary Armstrong against them, set the stage for the land victories that redeemed the initial disgraces. Again over cabinet Opposition, he brought about the naval supremacy on Lake Champlain that operated with the New Orleans victory to furnish the contemporaneous verdict on the war.

Beyond all this, and no less essential to the development of strength through trial, were the fortitude with which Madison met the early campaign disasters, his ceaseless endeavors to obtain more and yet more support from Congress, his calmness in the face of Federalist sedition, his imperviousness to personal diatribes, his astute handling of the diplomatic preliminaries to peace. These coalesced with the naval and late military operations, in a war that became single combat with the world's foremost power, to produce the outburst of jubilation in America and amazement in Europe that marked its ending.

"Mr. Madison's War"—called so in reproach at its onset—had become at its close a determinant of the nation's destiny. Madison's own appraisal of it was made with modesty and analytical insight:

> "Whatever be the light in which any individual actor on the public theater may appear, the contest exhibited in its true features can not fail to do honor to our country; and in one respect particularly to be auspicious to its solid and lasting interest. If our first struggle was a war of our infancy, this last was that of our youth; and the issue of both, wisely improved, may long postpone if not forever prevent a necessity for exerting the strength of our manhood."

Donald R. Hickey  **NO**

The War of 1812:
A Forgotten Conflict

Introduction

The war of 1812 is probably our most obscure war. Although a great deal has been written about the conflict, the average American is only vaguely aware of why we fought or who the enemy was. Even those who know something about the contest are likely to remember only a few dramatic moments, such as the Battle of New Orleans, the burning of the nation's capital, or the writing of "The Star-Spangled Banner."

Why is this war so obscure? One reason is that no great president is associated with the conflict. Although his enemies called it "Mr. Madison's War," James Madison hardly measures up to such war leaders as Abraham Lincoln, Woodrow Wilson, or Franklin Roosevelt. Moreover, the great generals in this war—Andrew Jackson and Winfield Scott—were unable to turn the tide because each was confined to a secondary theater of operations. No one like George Washington, Ulysses Grant, or Dwight Eisenhower emerged to put his stamp on the war and to carry the nation to victory. . . .

The campaign of 1812 was both disappointing and embarrassing to Republicans. The string of defeats on the Canadian frontier had dashed all hopes for a quick and an easy victory and had exposed the administration to criticism. The war had never lost its political character, and Republican leaders had hoped that triumphs on the battlefield would disarm their critics and enhance their chances at the polls. "[A] little success," said one Republican, "would silence many who are clamerous." "[I]f our government does not look sharp," said another, "the Federalists will come in again." But except for the naval victories, there was little to cheer about, and the result was growing disillusionment with the management of the war. "Our affairs," Senator Thomas Worthington of Ohio scrawled in his diary on December 1, "is [in] a miserable way[,] defeated and disgraced[,] the revenue extravagantly expended[,] the war not man[a]ged at all."

Although voters usually rally around a wartime president, Madison fared worse in 1812 than he had in 1808. A split in the Republican party and charges of mismanagement very nearly cost him his office. In addition, the Federalists

From THE WAR OF 1812: A FORGOTTEN CONFLICT, 1990, pp. 1, 100–106, 232–233, 301–302, 308–309. Copyright © 1990 by University of Illinois Press. Reprinted by permission. References omitted.

made significant gains in the congressional and state elections. Although the Republicans retained control over the national government and a majority of the state governments, the election results showed that many questioned not only the administration's handling of the war but the wisdom of the war itself.

The presidential campaign opened in February of 1812 when Republicans in the Virginia legislature nominated electors committed to Madison. In the ensuing months Republican caucuses in seven other states followed suit. The regular Republicans in Congress added their endorsement in May of 1812. At a widely publicized meeting (which most people considered the official Republican caucus), eighty-three members of Congress promised to support Madison for the presidency and seventy-one-year-old John Langdon of New Hampshire for the vice presidency. (Langdon declined because of age, which necessitated substituting Elbridge Gerry of Massachusetts.) Nine other members of Congress later added their endorsements, so Madison ended up with the avowed support of about two-thirds of the Republican membership. Most Republican congressmen from New York and other northern states, however, withheld their support because they preferred a northern candidate.

Shortly after the Washington caucus, Republicans in the New York state legislature met to nominate their own candidate. The favorite was De Witt Clinton, the mayor of New York City. Known as the "Magnus Apollo," Clinton was a handsome, popular, and talented statesman from a family long active in politics. Although some New Yorkers were fearful of splitting the party, Clinton won the legislature's endorsement when congressmen returning from Washington brought stories of growing disillusionment with Madison and letters from Postmaster General Gideon Granger urging support for a northern candidate.

Clinton's friends put his case before the people in an address published in the summer of 1812. The address attacked the congressional nominating system and the Virginia Dynasty and charged the administration with mismanaging the war. Virginia's domination of the presidency, the address said, had given rise to charges of *"Virginia influence,"* pitting the agricultural states against the commercial ones. To put an end to this divisiveness, the address recommended Clinton as a man who would provide "vigor in war, and a determined character in the relations of peace."

Clinton's nomination posed a dilemma for Federalists. Should they maintain their purity by supporting a Federal candidate—a course sure to lead to defeat—or should they vote for Clinton, a man long associated with the Republican party but considered friendly to commerce and anxious for peace? In New York and Virginia, the prevailing sentiment was for a Federal candidate, the favorites being Rufus King, John Marshall, and Charles Cotesworth Pinckney. Elsewhere there was considerable support for Clinton because, as one Federalist put it, he "wd. engage, if chosen President, to make immediate Peace with England." The sentiment for Clinton was particularly strong among Federalists in Pennsylvania and Massachusetts. In mid-summer a Philadelphia committee of correspondence sent out a circular recommending Clinton because of "his residence and attachments, his asserted freedom from foreign influence, his avowed hostility to the anti-commercial system, . . . combined with the positive declarations which have been made that he is desirous of the restoration of peace."

To fix their election strategy, Federalists held a convention in New York City in September of 1812. Seventy delegates from eleven states attended, though most were from New York, Pennsylvania, and New Jersey. Rufus King spearheaded the opposition to Clinton, believing that he was nothing more than the "Leader of a Faction." King thought "it was of less importance that the Federalists should acquire a temporary ascendency by the aid of a portion of the Repubs. than that their reputation and integrity shd. be preserved unblemished." Many of the delegates disagreed, not because they had any great confidence in Clinton but because they saw him as the lesser of two evils. As Timothy Pickering of Massachusetts put it, "I am far enough from desiring Clinton for President . . . but I would vote for any man in preference to Madison."

Harrison Gray Otis delivered an impassioned appeal on behalf of Clinton. According to one observer, "Mr. Otis arose, apparently much embarrassed, holding his hat in his hand, and seeming as if he were almost sorry he had arisen. Soon he warmed with his subject, his hat fell from his hand, and he poured forth a strain of eloquence that chained all present to their seats." Otis's appeal carried the day, but the convention stopped short of formally endorsing Clinton, fearing that this would undermine his Republican support. Instead, the delegates simply urged Federalists to support presidential electors "most likely by their votes to effect a change in the present course of measures." The convention made no provision for the vice presidency, but Jared Ingersoll became the accepted candidate when he was nominated by Federalists in Lancaster County, Pennsylvania.

None of the candidates openly campaigned for office, but the followers of each were busy, particularly in the middle states. "Never did I witness a more spirited preparation for an election," said a New Yorker. The answer was the principal issue in the campaign. Madison's supporters insisted that the contest was necessary to vindicate the nation's rights and to uphold its independence. "It is a war of right against lawless aggression," said a South Carolina campaign document, "of Justice against perfidy and violence." Republicans also argued that the president could not be blamed for setbacks in the field, that it was unfair "to impute to Mr. Madison the failure of every military expedition, or the defection of every military chief." In response to this, the Clintonians accused Madison's followers of embracing "the British maxim—*the king can do no wrong*," and of applying it "to the President in its full force."

The Clintonians sought to win northern support by portraying their candidate as a bold and energetic leader who was friendly to commerce and the navy and in no way tied to France. In pro-war states, Clinton's followers emphasized that he would shorten the war by prosecuting it more vigorously, while in anti-war states he was portrayed as a man who would achieve this end by negotiating with the British. Friends of the administration were quick to exploit this inconsistency. "In the west," said one critic, "Mr. Clinton is recommended as a friend of war . . . in the East he is presented as a friend of peace." A character in a contemporary play echoed this sentiment: "He cannot have *war* and *peace at the same time.*"

The Clintonians claimed that there had been a breakdown in presidential leadership, a charge that some of Madison's followers privately conceded. According to a New Hampshire War Hawk, "many of the friends of the Administration believe, that the Executive are not disposed to prosecute the war with vigor, provided they can find any *hole* through which they can creep out, and avoid the contest." Even in Madison's home state a "horrible spirit of disaffection or distrust" was said to be afoot. "[A]ll the misfortunes of our arms," reported a Virginia Republican, "are here Publicly ascribed to the mismanagement of the Genl Government." Many people wondered whether "Little Jemmy" (who was only five feet four inches tall) was big enough for the job. "Mr. Madison is wholly unfit for the storms of War," Henry Clay confided to a friend. "Nature has cast him in too benevolent a mould."

The Republicans sought to counter charges of Madison's weakness by attacking Clinton's character. One called him "the modern *Cromwell*," a second described him as a "sprig of upstart nobility," while a third compared him to "*Judas Iscariot.*" The Republicans also tried to discredit Clinton by focusing on his alliance with the Federalists. According to a Philadelphia campaign document, this alliance was "unanswerable evidence, that Mr. Clinton has sacrificed his democratic principles on the altar of his ambition." "[C]ourting the interest and votes of the *Essex Junto,*" said another Republican, "ought forever [to] damn him with Democrats."

The means of selecting presidential electors varied from state to state. Half of the states chose their electors by popular vote, while the rest left the decision to the legislature. Each state followed its own timetable, and the results drifted in over a two-month period in the fall of 1812. The outcome was by no means certain. According to congressman Samuel Latham Mitchill, November was "a dark and dismal month" in the White House because news of election defeats coupled with military reverses rolled in "[day] after day, like the tidings of Job's disasters."

The voting followed the same sectional pattern as the vote on the declaration of war. Clinton fared best in the North, Madison in the South and West. The outcome hinged on the results in New York and Pennsylvania, the two populous middle Atlantic states. Clinton needed both to win. He had no trouble in New York, winning all of that state's twenty-nine electoral votes. This result was due mainly to shrewd maneuvering in the legislature by twenty-nine-year-old Martin Van Buren, who henceforth would be known as the "Little Magician." Madison, however, prevailed in Pennsylvania, winning all twenty-five electoral votes and proving again that this state was the "Keystone in the Democratic Arch." The election was "pretty close work," concluded Richard Rush, "and Pennsylvania, as usual, carries the union on her back." Madison was aided in no small degree by Pennsylvania's booming prosperity, which was based on military spending and an extensive overseas trade. "Never did the abundant harvests of Pennsylvania find a quicker or a better market," crowed a Republican campaign document. In all, Madison won 128 electoral votes to Clinton's 89. (By contrast, Madison had defeated Charles Cotesworth Pinckney in 1808 by a margin of 122 to 47.)

The Republicans also lost ground in the congressional elections. The proportion of seats they held fell from 75 to 63 percent in the House and from 82 to

78 percent in the Senate. Their losses were particularly heavy in New York, Massachusetts, and New Hampshire. The Republicans lost control of several states, too. In 1811 they had won every state except Connecticut, Rhode Island, and Delaware. In 1812 they lost these states as well as Massachusetts, New Jersey, and Maryland. They also lost their majority in the New York assembly and suffered small or moderate losses in almost every other state east of the Appalachian Mountains. Although the Republicans remained in charge of the nation's destinies, their popularity appeared to be waning. The Federalists, on the other hand, had every reason to be pleased. By capitalizing on the mismanagement and unpopularity of the war and by exploiting the gruesome violence at Baltimore, they had achieved their most impressive electoral gains since the 1790s.

❧❦❧

With the elections safely behind them, Republican leaders urged President Madison to strengthen his cabinet. Ever since the previous spring, Secretary of War William Eustis and Secretary of the Navy Paul Hamilton had been under heavy fire. By the end of the year this criticism had reached such a torrent that it threatened to engulf the president himself. "Our executive officers are most incompetent men," said John C. Calhoun. "We are literally boren down under the effects of errors and mismanagement." "The clamor against the gentlemen who are at the head of the War and Navy Departments," said another congressman, "is loud & very general." If these men are not removed, added a Georgia senator, the president "must be content, with defeat, and disgrace in all his efforts, during the war." Although Madison was reluctant to act, he finally accepted the resignations of both men in December .

To replace Hamilton, Madison chose William Jones, a Philadelphia merchant and former congressman who had fought at Trenton and Princeton and served on a privateer during the Revolution. Though later discredited for mismanaging the national bank, Jones had considerable ability. With some justice, Madison later claimed that he was "the fittest minister who had ever been charged with the Navy Department." Far more knowledgeable about naval affairs than his predecessor, he was a good administrator who brought energy and efficiency to the department and won the admiration of his contemporaries. "I know of Some," said Nathaniel Macon in 1814, "who once thought little of his talents, [but] now consider him, the most useful member of the administration."

It was much harder to find a new secretary of war because this office was such an administrative nightmare. "[W]ith all its horrors & perils," said Gallatin, the office "frightens those who know best its difficulties." Finding a candidate who is "qualified, popular, and willing to accept is extremely difficult." Secretary of State James Monroe agreed to serve temporarily but refused to take the office permanently because he was hoping for a command in the field. Senator William H. Crawford and General Henry Dearborn also declined.

The president finally settled on John Armstrong of New York. Although knowledgeable about military affairs, Armstrong was abrasive and indolent and a known enemy of the Virginia Dynasty. In 1783 he had written the Newurgh Letters inciting the Continental Army to mutiny, and many people considered this "an indelible stain" upon his character. He also had a reputation for intrigue, a reputation that was largely justified. Given his liabilities, his confirmation in the Senate was doubtful. "Armstrong will rub hard, if he gets through at all," said one Republican. Though the Senate finally approved him, the vote was 18–15, with both Virginia senators abstaining.

The new appointments improved the efficiency of the administration but not without a price. Armstrong lived up to his reputation for intrigue and alienated his colleagues. Monroe saw him as a rival for the presidential succession and was constantly at odds with him. Monroe finally told Madison that if Armstrong were not removed he would "ruin not you and the admn. only, but the whole republican party and cause." Gallatin also despised him. Armstrong sided with Gallatin's enemies (particularly in Pennsylvania) and distributed his patronage accordingly. The crowning insult came when he awarded an army staff position to William Duane, the editor of the virulently anti-Gallatin Philadelphia *Aurora*. "The appointment of Duane," lamented Gallatin, "has appeared to me so gross an outrage on decency and self respect . . . that I felt no wish to remain associated with an administration which would employ such a miscreant." By the summer of 1813, William Jones had lost confidence in Armstrong, too. "[M]any begin to believe," he said, "that the 'Old Soldier' [Armstrong's nom de plume] is not a legitimate son of Mars." . . .

Throughout the war the Republicans had hoped that favorable election results would shore up their majorities and silence the opposition, but their hopes were never fulfilled. In the elections of 1812, the Federalists had gained control of six of the eighteen states (Massachusetts, Connecticut, Rhode Island, New Jersey, Delaware, and Maryland). The following year they lost New Jersey but won Vermont and New Hampshire, which gave them control over all of New England. In 1814 they retained control of these same seven states.

The Republicans fared no better in congressional elections. Most states held their elections for the Fourteenth Congress in 1814 even though this Congress did not convene until the end of 1815. In the House, Republican strength, which had declined from 75 percent in the Twelfth Congress to 63 percent in the Thirteenth, rose slightly to 65 percent in the Fourteenth Congress. In the Senate, however, Republican strength continued to slide: from 82 percent in the Twelfth Congress to 78 percent in the Thirteenth, to 67 percent in the Fourteenth. Although the leading Senate "Invisibles"—Samuel Smith, William Branch Giles, and Michael Leib—were not returned to the Fourteenth Congress, the regular Republicans were little better off than they had been in the Thirteenth Congress.

Thus in neither Congress nor the country were the Republicans able to win the decisive majorities they sought. Although they counted on the war to enhance their popularity and silence the Federalists, the effect of the conflict was just the opposite. In New England especially, the war served as a catalyst for a Federalist revival. As a result, Federalists achieved a more commanding position in this region than at any time since the 1790s.

It was not only the Federalists who opposed the administration. Many Republicans did, too. The Clintonians and "Invisibles" disliked the administration's management of the war, and the Old Republicans objected to the war itself. The election of 1812 had revealed deep-seated hostility to the Virginia Dynasty, and by 1814 even regular Republicans had become disillusioned with the party's leadership. "If we have another disastrous campaign in Canada," said George Hay of Virginia, "the republican cause is ruined, and Mr. M[adison] will go out covered with the Scorn of one party, and the reproaches of the other." "Without a change in the management of the war on the Canadian frontier," added Nathaniel Macon, "the republican party must go down[.] The people of every part of the Nation, will be disgusted with an administration, who have declared war, without ability to conduct it, to a favorable issue."

With the disasters of 1814—particularly the burning of Washington—the president and his advisors suffered a further loss in public esteem. "The President is much railed at by many of the Democrats," said a Philadelphia merchant. "The whole administration is blamed for the late disastrous occurrences at Washington," declared a Virginia Republican. "Without money, without soldiers & without courage," said Rufus King, "the President and his Cabinet are the objects of very general execration."

The War of 1812 lasted only two years and eight months—from June 18, 1812, to February 17, 1815. Though the war was not long, the United States was beset by problems from the beginning. Many of the nation's military leaders were incompetent, and enlistments in the army and navy lagged behind need. The militia were costly and inefficient and repeatedly refused to cross into Canada or to hold their positions under enemy fire. It was difficult to fill the war loans, and the nation's finances became increasingly chaotic. There was also extensive trade with the enemy—trade that Federalists and republicans alike freely took part in. A combination of Federalist opposition, Republican factionalism, and general public apathy undermined the entire war effort.

Congress was partly responsible for this state of affairs. Endless debate and deep divisions delayed or prevented the adoption of much-needed legislation. Congress was particularly negligent on financial matters. Hoping for a quick war and fearing the political consequences of unpopular measures, Republicans postponed internal taxes and delayed a national bank. As a result, public credit collapsed in 1814, and a general suspension of specie payments ensued. By the end of the war, the administration had to rely on depreciated bank paper and treasury notes. If the contest had continued much longer, the Revolutionary War phrase "not worth a continental" might have been replaced by "not worth a treasury note."

A strong president might have overcome some of these problems, but Madison was one of the weakest war leaders in the nation's history. Although his opponents called the contest "Mr. Madison's War," it never bore his stamp. Cautious, shy, and circumspect, Madison was unable to supply the bold and vigorous leadership that was needed. In some respects, to be sure, his caution served the nation well. Unlike other war presidents, he showed remarkable respect for the civil rights of his domestic foes. Despite pleas from other Republicans, he refused to resort to a sedition law. Thus, even though Federalists had to face mob violence (particularly at the beginning of the war), they never had to contend with government repression. Madison's treatment of enemy aliens and prisoners of war was also commendably humane, and his circumspect policy toward New England disaffection was undoubtedly well judged, too.

In other ways, however, Madison's cautious brand of leadership undermined the nation's war effort. He allowed incompetents like Eustis and Hamilton to hold key positions, he tolerated Armstrong's intrigues and Monroe's backbiting in the cabinet, and he retained Gideon Granger as postmaster general long after his hostility to the administration had become notorious. Madison was also slow to get rid of incompetent generals in the field or to promote officers who had proven themselves in battle. Because he lacked a commanding influence in Congress, he was unable to secure vital legislation, and because he lacked a strong following in the country, he was unable to inspire people to open their hearts and purses.

Contemporaries were aware of Madison's shortcomings, and even Republicans criticized his leadership. "Our President," said John C. Calhoun in 1812, "has not . . . those commanding talents, which are necessary to controul those about him." "[H]is spirit and capacity for a crisis of war," declared a Pennsylvania congressman in 1814, "are very generally called in question." "Mr. Madison," added a western congressman in 1815, "is perhaps 'too good' a man for the responsible office he holds. He does not like to offend his fellow men for any cause." Even Virginia Republicans considered Madison "*too tender* of the feelings of other people." "The amiable temper and delicate sensibility of Mr Madison," declared one Virginian, "are the real sources of our embarrassments."

No doubt poor leadership in Washington and in the field drove up the cost of this war. At the beginning of the contest, a Federalist newspaper predicted that the war would cost 30,000 lives and $180,000,000 and lead to a French-style conscription. This prediction was close to the mark. Official sources, which are not entirely reliable, indicate that the total number of American troops engaged in the contest was 528,000: 57,000 regulars, 10,000 volunteers, 3,000 rangers, and 458,000 militia. Another 20,000 served in the navy and marines. The battle casualties were comparatively light. The official figures are 2,260 killed and 4,505 wounded.

There is no record of how many soldiers died from disease, but before the advent of modern medicine, deaths from disease invariably exceeded those from enemy fire. Epidemics were common, and field commanders sometimes reported 30, 40, or even 50 percent of their troops on the sick list. There were numerous reports of multiple deaths from dysentery, typhoid fever, pneumonia, malaria, measles, typhus, and smallpox. In 1812, a soldier at Buffalo said: "Every day three or four are carried off to their Graves." In 1813, Governor Isaac Shelby said: "They are dying more or less every day on our March." And in 1814, General George Izard called the mortality rate from disease and exposure among his troops "prodigious."

After sampling army record, one scholars has concluded that two and a half times as many soldiers died from disease or accident as were killed or wounded in battle. If this sample is representative, the total number of non-battle military deaths must have been about 17,000. The army executed an additional 205 men, mainly for repeated desertion, and the navy executed a few men, too. Some privateersmen also died in the war, primarily from disease in British prisons. There were a few civilian casualties as well—mostly victims of Indian raids in the West. Adding all the pertinent figures together suggests that the total number of deaths attributable to the war must have been about 20,000.

The cost of the war (excluding property damage and lost economic opportunities) was $158,000,000. This includes $93,000,000 in army and navy expenditures, $16,000,000 for interest on the war loans, and $49,000,000 in veterans' benefits. (The last veteran died in 1905, the last pensioner—the daughter of a veteran—in 1946.) The government also awarded land bounties to some 224,000 people who had served in the war. The national debt, which Republicans had reduced from $83,000,000 in 1801 to $45,000,000 in 1812, rose to $127,000,000 by the end of 1815. The government borrowed $80,000,000 during the war, but because of discounts offered and paper money received, it got only $34,000,000 specie value.

What did the war accomplish? Although militarily the conflict ended in a draw, in a larger sense it represented a failure or Republican policy makers. The nation was unable to conquer Canada or to achieve any of the maritime goals for which it was contended. Indeed, these issues were not even mentioned in the peace treaty, which merely provided for restoring all conquered territory and returning to the *status quo ante bellum*. . . .

The Battle of New Orleans, though fought after Great Britain had signed and ratified the peace treaty, played a particularly important role in forging the myth of American victory. Even before the peace terms were known, Republicans were touting this battle as a decisive turning point in the war. "The terms of the treaty are yet unknown to us," said Congressman Charles J. Ingersoll in early 1815. "But the victory at Orleans has rendered them glorious and honorable, be they what they may. . . . Who is not proud to feel himself an American—our wrongs revenged—our rights recognized!"

Republicans boasted of how they had defeated "the heroes of Wellington," "Wellington's *invincibles*," and "the conquerors of the conquerors of Europe." "[W]e have unqueened the self-stiled Queen of the Ocean," crowed the Boston *Yankee*, and "we have beaten at every opportunity, *Wellington's Veterans!*" The myth of American victory continued to grow so that by 1816 *Niles' Register* could unabashedly claim that "we did virtually dictate the treaty of Ghent." Several months later a Republican congressman declaimed on the nation's triumph. "The glorious achievements of the late war," said Henry Southard of New Jersey, "have sealed the destinies of this country, perhaps for centuries to come, and the Treaty of Ghent has secured our liberties, and established our national independence, and placed this nation on high and honorable ground."

As the years slipped by, most people forgot the causes of the war. They forgot the defeats on land and sea and lost sight of how close the nation had come to military and financial collapse. According to the emerging myth, the United States had won the war as well as the peace. Thus the War of 1812 passed into history not as a futile and costly struggle in which the United States had barely escaped dismemberment and disunion, but as a glorious triumph in which the nation has single-handedly defeated the conqueror of Napoleon and the Mistress of the Seas.

POSTSCRIPT

Was James Madison an Effective Wartime President?

This issue lends itself to a comparative approach by which James Madison's leadership can be viewed alongside that of other American commanders-in-chief. Hickey argues that Madison compares unfavorably to Abraham Lincoln, Woodrow Wilson, and Franklin Roosevelt, but even those great presidents faced serious criticism. One might expand the comparison by assessing the responses to war by presidents James Polk, William McKinley, John Kennedy, Lyndon Johnson, Richard Nixon, and both George Bushes.

A broad historical context for the War of 1812 can be found in Marshall Smelser, *The Democratic Republic, 1801–1815* (Harper & Row, 1968) and John Mayfield, *The New Nation, 1800–1845* (Hill & Wang, 1982). Early American diplomacy is effectively covered in Lawrence S. Kaplan, *Colonies into Nation: American Diplomacy, 1763–1801* (Macmillan, 1972), Paul A. Varg, *Foreign Policies of the Founding Fathers* (Michigan State University Press, 1963), and Reginald Horsman, *The Diplomacy of the New Republic, 1776–1815* (Harlan Davidson, 1985) but should be complemented by the following monographs: Samuel Flagg Bemis, *Pinckney's Treaty: America's Advantage from Europe's Distress, 1783–1800* (The Johns Hopkins Press, 1926), Harry Ammon, *The Genet Mission* (W. W. Norton, 1973), and Alexander DeConde, *The Quasi-War: the Politics and Diplomacy of the Undeclared War with France, 1797–1801* (Charles Scribner's Sons, 1966).

The critical events leading up to the War of 1812 are covered in Bradford Perkins, *Prologue to War, 1805–1812: England and the United States* (University of California Press, 1961); Louis M. Sears, *Jefferson and the Embargo* (Reprint Services, 1967); and Clifford L. Egan, *Neither Peace nor War: Franco-American Relations, 1803–1812* (Louisiana State University Press, 1983). Clashing interpretations on the causes of the war are presented in Julius W. Pratt, *Expansionists of 1812* (Macmillan, 1925), which focuses on the "War Hawks" and the dream to gain control of Canada; and Roger H. Brown, *The Republic in Peril: 1812* (W. W. Norton, 1964), which describes the American preoccupation with national honor and the protection of republican institutions. Fuller explorations of causation can be found in Reginald Horsman, *The Causes of the War of 1812* (University of Pennsylvania Press, 1962); Harry Lewis Coles, *The War of 1812* (University of Chicago Press, 1965); and Patrick C. T. White, *The Nation on Trial: America and the War of 1812* (John Wiley & Sons, 1965).

James Madison's wartime leadership is discussed in Ralph Ketchum, *James Madison* (American Politcal Biography Press, 2003); J. C. A. Stagg, *Mr. Madison's War: Politics, Diplomacy, and Warfare in the Early Republic, 1783–1830* (Princeton University Press, 1983); and Jack Rakove, *James Madison and the Creation of the American Republic* (Scott Forsman/Little, Brown, 1990).

The last crucial military victory for the United States receives scholarly treatment in Robert V. Remini, *The Battle of New Orleans: Andrew Jackson and America's First Military Victory* (Viking Adult, 1999). James M. Banner, Jr. discusses the Federalist opposition to the War of 1812 and the consequences of the Hartford Convention in *To the Hartford Convention: The Federalists and the Origins of Party Politics in Massachusetts, 1789-1815* (Random House, 1970).

ISSUE 10

Was the Monroe Doctrine of 1823 Designed to Protect the Latin American Countries from European Intervention?

YES: Dexter Perkins, from *The Monroe Doctrine: 1823–1826* (Harvard University Press, 1927)

NO: Ernest R. May, from *The Making of the Monroe Doctrine* (Harvard University Press, 1975)

ISSUE SUMMARY

YES: According to Professor Dexter Perkins, President James Monroe issued his famous declaration of December 2, 1823 to protest Russian expansionism in the Pacific Northwest and to prevent European intervention in South America from restoring to Spain her former colonies.

NO: According to Professor Ernest R. May, domestic political considerations brought about the Monroe Doctrine when the major presidential candidates attempted to gain a political advantage over their rivals during the presidential campaign of 1824.

The American government in the early 1800s greatly benefitted from the fact that European nations generally considered what was going on in North America of secondary importance to what was happening in their own countries. In 1801 President Thomas Jefferson became alarmed when he learned that France had acquired the Louisiana territory from Spain. He realized that western states might revolt if the government did not control the city of New Orleans as a seaport for shipping their goods. Jefferson pulled off the real estate coup of the nineteenth century when his diplomats caught Napoleon in a moment of despair. With a stroke of the pen and $15 million, the Louisiana Purchase of 1803 nearly doubled the size of the country. The exact northern, western, and southeastern boundaries were not clearly defined. "But," as diplomatic historian Thomas Bailey has pointed out, "the American negotiators knew that they had bought the western half of perhaps the most valuable river valley on the face of the globe . . ."

After England fought an indecisive war with the United States from 1812 to 1815, she realized that it was to her advantage to maintain peaceful relations with her former colony. In 1817 the Great Lakes, which border on the United States and Canada, were mutually disarmed. Over the next half-century, the principle of demilitarization was extended to the land, resulting in an undefended frontier line that stretched for more than 3,000 miles. The Convention of 1818 clarified the northern boundary of the Louisiana Purchase and ran a line along the 49th parallel from Lake of the Woods in Minnesota to the Rocky Mountains. Beyond that point there was to be a 10-year joint occupancy in the Oregon Territory. In 1819 Spain sold Florida to the United States after Secretary of State John Quincy Adams sent a note telling the Spanish government to keep the Indians on their side of the border or else to get out of Florida. A few years later, the Spanish Empire crumbled in the New World, and a series of Latin American republics emerged.

Afraid the European powers might attack the newly independent Latin American republics and that Russia might expand south into the Oregon Territory, Adams convinced President James Monroe to reject a British suggestion for a joint declaration and to issue instead a unilateral policy statement. The Monroe Doctrine, as it was called by a later generation, had three parts. First, it closed the Western Hemisphere to any further colonization. Second, it forbade, "any interposition" by the European monarchs that would "extend their system to any portion of this hemisphere as dangerous to our peace and safety." And third, the United States pledged to abstain from any involvement in the political affairs of Europe. Viewed in the context of 1823, it is clear that Monroe was merely restating the principles of unilateralism and nonintervention. Both of these were at the heart of American isolationism.

While Monroe renounced the possibility of American intervention in European affairs, he made no such disclaimer toward Latin America, as was originally suggested by Great Britain. It would be difficult to colonize in South America, but the transportation revolution, the hunger for land, which created political turmoil in Texas, and the need for ports on the Pacific to increase American trade in Asia encouraged the acquisition of new lands contiguous to the southwestern boundaries. In the 1840s, journalists and politicians furnished an ideological rationale for this expansion and said it was the Manifest Destiny of Americans to spread democracy, freedom, and white American settlers across the entire North American continent, excluding Canada because it was a possession of Great Britain. Blacks and Indians were not a part of this expansion.

Was the original Monroe Doctrine of 1823 an attempt to establish a coherent long-term policy towards Latin America? In the first selection Professor Dexter Perkins answers yes. President James Monroe, with a push from his Secretary of State John Quincy Adams, issued his statements to protest Russian expansion in the Pacific Northwest and to prevent the European nations from intervening in South America for the purpose of restoring to Spain her former colonies. But Professor Ernest May disagrees. Domestic political considerations, he argues, brought about the Monroe Doctrine, as the major presidential candidates attempted to gain a political advantage over their rivals during the presidential campaign of 1824.

YES

Dexter Perkins

The Northwest Boundary Controversy and the Non-Colonization Principle. 1823–1824

The famous declaration of December 2, 1823, which has come to be known as the Monroe Doctrine, had a dual origin and a dual purpose. On the one hand, it was the result of the advance of Russia on the northwest coast of America, and was designed to serve as a protest against this advance and to establish a general principle against Russian expansion. Referring to this question of the northwest, President Monroe laid down the principle in his message to Congress that "the American continents, by the free and independent condition which they have assumed and maintain, are henceforth not to be considered as subjects for future colonization by any European powers." On the other hand, the message was provoked by the fear of European intervention in South America to restore to Spain her revolted colonies, and was intended to give warning of the hostility of the United States to any such intervention. "With the governments [that is, of the Spanish-American republics] who have declared their independence, and maintained it," wrote the President, "and whose independence we have, on great consideration and just principles, acknowledged, we could not view any interposition for the purpose of oppressing them, or controlling in any other manner their destiny, by any European power, in any other light than as the manifestation of an unfriendly disposition toward the United States." . . .

Russian interest in the northwest coast of America goes back to the second quarter of the eighteenth century, to the days of the renowned navigator Vitus Behring, who discovered in 1727 the Straits that now bear his name, and fourteen years later the Alaskan coast in the neighborhood of latitude 58. Behring's explorations were followed by the voyages of fur traders and by the establishment of trading posts on the islands off the American mainland. After years of demoralizing competition on the part of private individuals, the Tsar determined to create a commercial monopoly for the exploitation of the rich fisheries to be found in that part of the world. By the ukase of July 8, 1799, the Russian-American Company was constituted, and to this company

Reprint by permission of the publisher from THE MONROE DOCTRINE, 1823–1826 by Dexter Perkins, pp. 3–5, 7–8, 16–19, 40–43, 80–81, 85, Cambridge, Mass.: Harvard University Press, Copyright © 1927 by the President and Fellows of Harvard College.

were granted exclusive trading rights and jurisdiction along the coast as far south as latitude 55, and the right to make settlements on either side of that line in territory not occupied by other powers.

From an early date the operations of this Russian corporation were impeded by interlopers, very largely American. American vessels sold arms and ammunition to the natives, and secured a considerable part of the fur trade. As early as 1808 and 1810 complaints on the part of the Russian government began to be made to the government at Washington. There was, obviously enough, a situation that might lead to serious friction. . . .

On September 4/16, 1821, the Tsar Alexander I, acting at the instigation of the Russian monopoly, promulgated an imperial decree which renewed its privileges and confirmed its exclusive trading rights. This time the southern limit of these rights on the American coast was set, not at 55, but at 51 degrees. And in addition, all foreign vessels were forbidden, between Behring Straits and 51 degrees, to come within 100 Italian miles of the shore, on pain of confiscation. A Russian warship was dispatched to the northwest coast to enforce this remarkable decree, and every intention was manifested of barring all other nations from any participation whatever in the trade or fisheries of the region. Such a course of action very naturally provoked a protest, not only on the part of the United States, but also on the part of Great Britain. At this time the two Anglo-Saxon powers had joint ownership, under the convention of 1818, of the territory north from 42 degrees to a line yet to be determined, and the Russian claims of exclusive jurisdiction as far south as 51 degrees could hardly fail to be disquieting. Both from London and from Washington, therefore, came strong diplomatic remonstrance, and thus began a controversy which was to have the closest relationship to the famous pronouncement of 1823.

It is neither necessary nor desirable, in connection with this narrative, to trace the negotiations on the northwest question in all their details. What is of special interest here is the evolution of the non-colonization principle in the course of the discussions, the reception which it met at the hands of the interested powers, and the effect which it produced upon the diplomatic interchanges themselves. . . .

These discussions, begun in 1822, assumed little importance till the late spring of 1823. By that time it had been agreed that the question should be threshed out at St. Petersburg. In June the cabinet discussed the instructions which were to be sent to Mr. Middleton, American minister at the court of the Tsar. The Secretary of State declared it to be his conviction that the United States ought to contest the right of the Russian government to any territorial establishment on the American continents. Apparently this point of view did not pass unchallenged. It was pointed out that Russia would have little reason to accept such drastic doctrine. The United States, in maintaining it, would be asking everything, and conceding virtually nothing. A compromise was suggested and agreed upon by which this country would recognize the territorial claims of the Tsar north of 55 degrees. On this basis, the negotiations were actually to be conducted.

But Adams, with a curious inconsistency, did not on this account surrender the principle which was taking shape in his mind. At the very moment when he was perfecting the instructions to Middleton along the lines agreed upon in the cabinet, he declared himself to Tuyll, the Russian minister at Washington, in language very much more sweeping.

> I told him specially [he writes in his diary, alluding to an interview of July 17, 1823], that we should contest the right of Russia to *any* territorial establishment on this continent, and that we should assume distinctly the principle that the American continents are no longer subjects for *any* new European colonial establishments.

In this statement, almost five months before the appearance of the President's message, we have the non-colonization principle full-fledged, no longer merely a subject of cabinet debate, but explicitly put forward to the minister of another power, to the minister of the power perhaps most concerned in denying it. One might expect that such a declaration would have been most distasteful to Tuyll. But such evidence as we have leads to a contrary conclusion. There are no indications that the Russian minister challenged or controverted Adams. In his dispatch to St. Petersburg reporting the conversation of July 17, he contented himself with the following allusion to the matter: "The American government will avail itself of the present occasion to ask the acceptance of a general principle by which foreign powers will definitely and finally renounce the right of establishing new colonies in either of the Americas." This is underlined in the text itself, but the Russian minister goes on to say that he sees no great difficulty in the way of a settlement of the northwest question. He clearly did not regard the language of Adams as a serious obstacle to understanding. There was nothing in his attitude which might lead the Secretary of State to modify his position.

We have another statement of the non-colonization dogma almost contemporaneous with the interview with Tuyll. This is found in the instructions to Richard Rush, American minister at the Court of Saint James's. As England had an interest in the northwest controversy, it was obviously desirable that the diplomatic representative of the United States at London should be informed of the views of his government on the subject. Accordingly, on July 22, Adams sent forward a long and careful dispatch, in which he set forth his new theory in greater detail than at any other time. That dispatch will claim our special attention later. . . .

Adams secured Monroe's assent to his new principle in July, at the time of sending the dispatches just alluded to. Whether that assent was cordial and positive, or whether it was given as a mere matter of routine, we have no way of knowing. The President may have warmly approved the non-colonization doctrine; he may, on the other hand, have been little aware of its significance or its implications. On this point his writings provide us with no illumination. But at any rate, he *did* accept it. When, therefore, the Secretary of State drew up in November, the customary sketch of the topics of foreign policy which might interest the President in connection with the preparation of the forthcoming message, he naturally included in the paragraph on the Russian negotiations a reference to the new dogma. That paragraph was taken over almost without verbal change by Monroe, and thus it appeared in his communication to the Congress. These facts are clear, for we have the actual manuscript of Adams's outline of the diplomatic matters which he wished to draw to the attention of the President, and the language of that outline, so far as the non-colonization principle is concerned, corresponds almost exactly with the language of the message itself.

There was, apparently, no consideration of the principle in the cabinet discussion preceding the publication of the President's declaration. On this point Calhoun, then Secretary of War, was to testify many years later, and the silence of Adams's diary at the time confirms this testimony. There is, after all, nothing strange in such a circumstance. For the question of the hour, in November, 1823, was not the dispute with Russia, but the menace offered by the Holy Alliance to the independence of the States of South America. It was on these problems that all the debates turned; so, very naturally, the other problem was crowded out. . . .

Having thus examined the origins of the non-colonization clause in the message of 1823, we must now turn back to discuss the viewpoint and the reasoning which lay behind it. What was the motive in promulgating such a sweeping theory? What was the logic by which it might be supported?

In later interpretations of this part of the President's declaration, the emphasis has frequently been laid on the dangers involved in bringing the intrigues and conflicting territorial ambitions of Europe across the seas and into the New World. The United States, the argument has run, would thus be swept into the vortex of European politics, and exposed to the wicked influences for which those politics are notorious. Or it has been maintained that new European territorial establishments would endanger American security, and ought to be opposed on these grounds.

These were not the bases, however, on which John Quincy Adams, in 1823, rested his opposition to colonization. The territorial aspects of colonization were not uppermost in his mind. He was thinking (and the point has been all too little emphasized) primarily of the commercial interests of the United States. In the history of American diplomacy, the principle of non-colonization has a certain affinity with the principle of the open door, asserted three quarters of a century later. It was based on immediate economic factors, not on vague fears of the future. It was because the colonial system meant commercial exclusion that the Secretary of State proclaimed its banishment from the American continents.

A close examination of Adams's point of view makes this clear. The principle of equality of commercial opportunity was one for which he contended with the utmost vigor, not only in the northwest controversy, but in other fields. He fought vigorously against the narrow policy of Great Britain in the British West Indies. He instructed the ministers to the South American states, when they set out in 1823, to contend for the principle that the new republics should treat all nations on the same footing, and that they should give no preferences, not even to their former mother country. The right to which he held most tenaciously in the dispute with Russia was not the right to full possession of the territory on the northwest (on this, as we have seen, it had been agreed to compromise on the line of 55 degrees); the right which he deemed of most importance was the right to trade, and this Middleton was instructed stoutly to maintain. In Adams's opinion the notion of European colonization was flatly opposed to the maintenance of these economic interests. The colonizing methods of the Old World, he told Stratford Canning in November, 1822, had always involved a more or less complete commercial monopoly. "Spain had set the example. She had forbidden foreigners from setting a foot in her Colonies, upon pain of death, and the other colonizing states of Europe had imitated the exclusion, though not the rigor of the penalty." From the very beginning, therefore, the Adams doctrine was knit up with the commercial interests of the United States. And so it remained throughout this early period of its development. Nothing shows this more clearly than the important dispatch of July 22, 1823, to Richard Rush, in which the whole theory of the doctrine found most careful expression. After declaring that the American continents will henceforth no longer be subjects for colonization, the American Secretary of State goes on to say:

> Occupied by civilized independent nations, they will be accessible to Europeans and to each other on that footing alone, and the Pacific Ocean in every part of it will remain open to the navigation of all nations, in like manner with the Atlantic. . . . The application of colonial principles of exclusion, therefore, cannot be admitted by the United States as lawful upon any part of the northwest coast of America, or as belonging to any European nation.

In these clear-cut and precise phrases, the innermost connection of the new dogma with American trading rights stands revealed.

It need not be contended, of course, that there was no more to it than this. It would be a clear exaggeration to say that Adams was contending for trading rights alone. He was thinking also of territorial settlement, as the very dispatch just quoted helps to make clear.

> It is not imaginable [he declared] that, in the present condition of the world, *any* European nation should entertain the project of settling a *colony* on the northwest coast of America. That the United States should form establishments there, with views of absolute territorial right and inland communication, is not only to be expected, but is pointed out by the finger of nature.

But these comments were made with an eye to the future. What was interesting in the immediate sense, "the only useful purpose to which the northwest coast of America" had been or could be made "subservient to the settlement of civilized men," was that of trade and of the fishery. The rights of the United States in this regard it was vital to maintain. On the territorial question there might be compromise; this we have already seen. But on the commercial question there ought to be none. "The right of carrying on trade with the natives throughout the northwest coast they [the United States] cannot renounce." Clearly, it was antagonism to commercial restriction that lay at the basis of the Secretary of State's famous dictum. . . .

The Spanish-American Phase of the Message—The Prelude

The revolt of the Spanish-American colonies followed hard upon the Napoleonic conquest of Spain. From the very beginning, the sympathies of the United States appear to have been engaged upon the side of the revolutionists. American sentiment was distinctly favorable to a movement for independence which had at least a superficial resemblance to that of 1776, and which could easily be regarded as an effort to throw off an odious tyranny and establish throughout the greater part of the New World the blessings of republican government. Fellow feeling in a struggle for liberty and independence was an essential element in forming the policy of the United States with regard to South America.

It was indeed, to all appearances, a far more important element than any hope of material gain. In the formative period of this country's relations with the new states of South America, certainly down to 1822, there is little evidence of the working of economic interest. In the absence of exact statistics for much of the period, and in view of the paucity of references to trade with the Spanish colonies, it is difficult to speak with precision. But certain general observations may safely be made. In the first place, the trade with Cuba and with Spain itself was far more important than the trade with the new republics of the South. A diplomatic policy favorable to the South-American states might jeopardize or even sacrifice commercial interests superior to those which it would promote. If economic reasons were to be regarded as shaping political developments, there were more reasons for a cautious than for an active line of policy. In the second place, there was not, as in the case of Great Britain, any powerful pressure from the commercial classes in favor of colonial independence. The evidence on this point is partly negative, it is true, but it is negative evidence of the strongest kind. One can hardly imagine that the existence of such pressure would pass unnoticed in the debates in Congress, and in such contemporary records as the diary and writings of Adams, and the correspondence of Monroe. But it is not necessary to depend upon this fact alone. Statistics indicate that as late as 1821 only 2.3 percent of American exports and 1.6 percent of American imports were South American in destination or origin. In March of the same year Adams could tell Henry Clay that he had little expectation of any commercial advantages from the recognition of the new states. And even later, in 1823, the Secretary of State speaks of commercial development as a matter of hope for the future rather than a present accomplishment. That hope may, of course, have counted for something from the beginning. But, all things considered, it seems highly probable that political sympathy, not economic self-interest, lay at the root of American policy so far as it revealed itself as favorable to the new states of South America.

From the very beginnings of the South American struggle this sympathy asserts itself. As early as 1810, the American government, then headed by

Madison, sent agents to South America—Joel R. Poinsett to La Plata and Chile, and Robert Lowry to Venezuela. At the end of 1811, James Monroe, then Secretary of State, thought seriously of raising the question of the recognition of the new states, and of exerting American influence in Europe to secure like action from the principal European powers. He also entered into informal relations with agents from at least one of the revolted provinces. And in Congress, at the same time, in response to the sympathetic language of the President's message, a resolution was passed, expressing a friendly solicitude in the welfare of these communities, and a readiness, when they should become nations by a just exercise of their rights, to unite with the Executive in establishing such relations with them as might be necessary. Thus, very early in the course of the colonial struggle, the general bent of American policy was made plain.

But it was some time before the South-American question became a matter of really first-rate importance. In the years 1810 to 1815, the prime concern of the administration at Washington lay in the preservation of American neutral rights, and, from 1812 to 1814, in the prosecution of the war with Great Britain. Moreover, the course of events in the overseas dominions of Spain was for some time hardly favorable to the revolutionists. In 1814 and 1815, indeed, it seemed entirely possible that the revolutionary movements might be snuffed out. In the north, in Venezuela and Colombia, the army of the Spanish general, Morillo, won victory on victory, and drove the leader of the revolutionists, Bolívar, into exile. In the south, in Chile, Osorio reëstablished the power of the mother country, and in Buenos Aires the struggles of contending factions weakened the new government that had been set up. Under such circumstances, prudence would have dictated a policy of reserve on the part of the United States, even if its government had not been preoccupied with other and more pressing matters.

With the year 1817, however, a change takes place in the status of the colonial question. In the case of one, at any rate, of the new states, the struggle was virtually over. The republic of La Plata had declared its independence and successfully maintained it, so that not a Spanish soldier remained upon its territory; even more, it had dispatched its great general, San Martín, across the Andes, and, with the victory of Chacabuco, taken a great step toward the final liberation of Chile. Perhaps as a result of these developments, interest in favor of the recognition of the new state began to develop in the United States; there were numerous newspaper articles in the summer of 1817, notably the discussions of Lautaro in the Richmond *Enquirer;* and the affairs of South America became a matter of debate both in the councils of the administration and in the halls of Congress.

It is interesting, in the light of later events, to examine these developments. So far as the administration was concerned, the point especially to be emphasized is the warm sympathy of the President himself with the South American cause. There has been a tendency in some quarters, in connection with the evolution of the Monroe Doctrine, to ascribe a very slight importance to the views of the very man who promulgated it. Mr. Monroe has been pictured as "slow-moving and lethargic," as prodded forward only by the more vigorous mind and more determined will of John Quincy Adams, his

Secretary of State. But as a matter of fact, Monroe was at all times quite as much interested in the colonial cause, and in as full sympathy with it, as Adams. From the very beginning of his presidency, he showed his concern with regard to it. As early as May, 1817, some months before Adams took office, the President had determined upon a mission of inquiry to the provinces of La Plata, and as early as October he questioned his cabinet on the expediency of recognizing the government of that region. He raised the problem again in the succeeding May, even suggesting the possibility of sending an armed force to the coast of South America, to protect American commerce, "and to countenance the patriots." His views, it is true, were to be overruled or modified by his advisers. But his interest in positive action was very real, and is quite consistent with the character of the man whose flaming sympathy with French republicanism had been so obvious in his earlier career. . . .

In the summer and fall of 1821, however, there occurred events of high importance. Henry Clay, still ardent for the colonial cause, brought up a new resolution in the House of Representatives. It declared that "the House join with the people of the United States in their sympathy with the South Americans; and that it was ready to support the President whenever he should think it expedient to recognize their governments." The first part of this resolution passed by a vote of 134 to 12; and the second, by a vote of 86 to 68. The trend of opinion in Congress was clearly for action, and the hands of the administration were strengthened by this expression of opinion. Meanwhile, events of the greatest importance occurred in South America. In June, Bolívar inflicted a severe defeat upon the army of Morillo at Carabobo. In July, his great rival and associate, San Martín, had entered Lima, bringing the revolution to Peru, the last and most faithful of Spain's American provinces. In August, the Spanish acting viceroy in Mexico, General O'Donoju, signed a treaty with the revolutionary forces in that province on the basis of independence. The facts of the situation pointed toward the complete success of the revolutionists. In March, 1822, the President finally sent to Congress a message recommending that the independence of the new states be acknowledged, and that provision for the sending of ministers be made.

In a sense, the policy of the American government had been prudence itself. Yet in another sense, the recognition of colonial independence was a bold and decisive act, when considered in relation to the past policy of the United States, and to the political situation in 1822. In the earlier period of the discussion of the South American question there was a distinct desire to conciliate European opinion, and even to strengthen the position of the government by active coöperation with European powers. This attitude was never carried to the point of subserviency. The American government never concealed its sympathy with the colonial cause, or its conviction that the only solution of the colonial question lay in the recognition of colonial independence. The language of Adams on this point is unequivocal. "We can neither accede to nor approve of any interference to restore any part of the Spanish supremacy in any of the Spanish American provinces," he wrote to Gallatin, the minister of the United States at Paris, in his instructions of May, 1818, with the pending Congress of Aix-la-Chapelle in mind. "We cannot approve any interposition of other powers, unless it be to promote the total independence, political and commercial, of the colonies," he declared to Campbell, American minister at St. Petersburg, at about the same time. There is nothing of the tone of undue deference in such declarations. But, although the United States thus clearly avowed its views, there was, none the less, great reluctance on the part of the administration to act alone, and in opposition to Europe. In May, 1818, Monroe suggested to his cabinet the possibility of a concert of action with Great Britain to promote the independence of the new states, and he renewed the proposal to Adams two months later. His point of view in regard to the matter had the ardent support of Calhoun. As for Adams himself, his first instincts were to oppose such a policy. The American Secretary of State was not by instinct a coöperator. And yet, despite his temperamental preference for independent action, his policy in 1818 was not based on that preference. His instructions to Gallatin and Campbell professed a desire to act in harmony with the allied powers. In December, 1818, he directly suggested to Bagot, the British minister, concerted action for the recognition of La Plata; at about the same time he told Hyde de Neuville that he hoped France would be prepared to move with the United States; and considerably later, toward the end of 1819, he assured the Russian minister, Poletica, that his desire in these earlier overtures had been to lay the foundations of a general understanding on the colonial question.

When these facts are considered in their entirety, the recognition of the colonies in 1822 assumes a new significance. It required a considerable alteration of American policy to ignore the attitude of the powers of the Old World, and base American action on American interests and sympathies, and nothing else.

This is particularly true when the general European situation is considered. The tendencies of European politics at the close of the Napoleonic wars are too well known to require more than the briefest summary here. They were characterized by the efforts of the Tsar Alexander to found a world alliance for the maintenance of European order. They were characterized by the effort to transact European business in congresses dominated by the great powers. They were characterized by a strong attachment to order, and a strong aversion to revolution. From the time of the Congress of Vienna, the tide of events in the Old World flowed strongly toward reaction. But the events of 1820 and 1821 accentuated that tendency. It needed the actual outbreak of revolution in Spain and in Naples and in Piedmont to develop the new gospel of order to its full. In the Troppau protocol of October, 1820, the three Eastern courts, Russia, Prussia, and Austria, committed themselves to the doctrine that it was the sacred duty of the great states of Europe, in case of danger, to put down pernicious uprisings by force of arms. In the course of the next year, the constitutional movements in Naples and Piedmont were snuffed out summarily, and there was already talk of similar action in Spain. At a time when, in the Old World, the detestation of revolution was finding deeper and deeper expression, it was an act of no equivocal character on the part of the United States to proclaim to the world its recognition of the republics of South America, and to set the seal of its approval on governments which in Continental Europe were regarded by the constituted authorities as fit subjects of moral odium.

Moreover, the administration, when it acted, acted with the most striking independence. It consulted with no European power; it gave no warning to any European chancellery of what was coming; and it paid no attention whatsoever to the situation which existed in Spain. It reckoned not at all with the fact that Ferdinand was in the power of his revolutionary subjects, and that recognition under such circumstances would be particularly distasteful to the legitimists of the Old World; it reckoned no more with the fact that the Spanish constitutionalists were making, or at least professing to make, new efforts at the reconciliation of the colonies with the mother country. Its action was taken on a purely American basis, and from a purely American point of view. It is thus inevitably a fact of profound significance; and its whole character makes it a fitting presage for the still more striking declaration of 1823. . . .

In the discussions upon the northwest controversy, as has been seen, trading influences contributed very materially to the stand which was taken by the administration. But it would be difficult to prove anything of the kind with regard to the warning given to Europe against intervention in South America. This is not to say that such influences necessarily played no rôle at all. John Quincy Adams, of course, came from the great shipping section of the Union. In his instructions to the American ministers sent out to Colombia and La Plata in the spring of 1823, he had laid a very considerable emphasis upon freedom of commercial opportunity, though he was by no means exuberantly optimistic as to the possibilities of the South American trade. In the cabinet discussions of November, he had, on one occasion, brought forward as a reason for action the fact that if the United States stood aside and Great Britain alone vetoed the designs of the Continental powers, the latter country would gain great commercial advantages. It is worth noting, too, that our commerce with the Spanish-American states was considerably more important in 1823 than it had been two or three years before. But these facts would be a slender foundation on which to base an "economic interpretation" of the Monroe Doctrine. And they are offset by many others. Whoever reads the pages of Adams's diary will find it hard to believe that trading considerations played a very considerable rôle in his mind. The distaste produced by the homilies of the Tsar, a genuine and robust disapproval of the trend of European politics, a desire to set forth the political doctrines of the United States in opposition to those of the Alliance, these are the factors that bulked largest in his thought. Economic considerations there may have been in the background. But it was a profound political antagonism that gave force to the action which he advocated in the councils of President Monroe.

With the President himself, this antagonism was even more keenly felt. The letter to Jefferson, written early in June, seems to express his point of view pretty accurately. He was anxious to strike a blow for liberty, and the situation in the fall of 1823 offered him an excellent opportunity. To this must be added the fact that Monroe, like Calhoun, feared that an assault upon the liberties of the Spanish Americans would be dangerous to the safety of the United States itself. It was these considerations, beyond a doubt, that sharpened his pen as he wrote the declaration of December 2. . . .

Monroe's belief in the superiority of American institutions, his conviction that the extension of European dominion would be dangerous to our peace and safety—these are propositions that are hardly capable of rigorous demonstration. Perhaps their strength lies in just that fact. Yet there is, I think, one thing more to be said for them. In resting his opposition to European intermeddling in Spanish America on the "peace and safety" of the United States, the President was taking up a strong position from the legal and moral point of view. For he was basing American policy on the right of self-preservation, a right that is and always has been recognized as fundamental in international law. If in very truth the interposition of the Holy Alliance in South America imperilled the peace and safety of the United States, then the President's right to protest against it was obvious. Nor was it to be expected that as to the reality of the peril he would accept the conclusions of European statesmen. He stood secure in his own conviction and on his own ground. . . .

Ernest R. May  **NO**

The Making of the Monroe Doctrine

... Books on the [Monroe] doctrine analyzed the principles which had been announced: European powers should not help Spain regain her former colonies; European monarchies should not impose their ideology on nations in the New World; and there should be no future European colonization in the Americas. Dexter Perkins made a convincing case that the dangers envisioned had been unreal. To the extent that statesmen on the continent contemplated aiding Spain, overturning American republics, or establishing new colonies in the Western Hemisphere, they were deterred by fear of Britain, not by concern about the United States.

It was clear from the record, however, that the American doctrine had been developed in large part because Monroe and his advisers faced issues which seemed to require decisions. They had an invitation to join Britain in resisting the alleged European threat to Latin America. Everyone recognized that acceptance would mean abandonment of the posture previously held and, as Monroe put it, entanglement "in European politicks, & wars." On the other hand, Monroe, and most of those whom he consulted, saw the offer as so advantageous that it should not be turned down. Except for the maxim that there should be no future colonization, the Monroe Doctrine expressed general agreement with British positions.

Coincidentally, the administration faced the question of whether to recognize or aid Greeks who were fighting for independence from the Ottoman Empire. There was loud public demand to do so. The argument for resisting this demand was again to avoid entanglement in European politics. Daniel Webster summarized a popular view, however, when he asked how the United States could defend liberty in Latin America and ignore the same cause in Europe.

In the upshot, the British alliance did not materialize, and the United States did not lead in recognizing Greece. These decisions, even more than the rhetoric that accompanied them, reaffirmed a policy of nonentanglement. But why?

The literature on the Monroe Doctrine did not answer this question—at least not to my satisfaction. Among those who knew of the British alliance overture, everyone except Secretary of State Adams favored acceptance. Adams was the only member of the administration consistently to oppose recognition of Greece. Explaining why the outcomes were victories for Adams, Bemis says simply that his "views by the force of their reason had prevailed over everybody." (p. 390) The same explanation appears in other accounts. In

Reprinted by permission of the publisher from THE MAKING OF THE MONROE DOCTRINE by Ernest R. May, pp. vii–viii, ix–xi, 132, 181, 183–189, 254–255, Cambridge, Mass.: Harvard University Press, Copyright © 1975, 1992 by the President and Fellows of Harvard College.

fact, however, there is no evidence that Adams changed anyone's opinion. His own diary records that his colleagues held much the same views at the end as at the beginning. Yet Adams got what he wanted.

When puzzling about what besides Adams's persuasive powers might have produced this outcome, I remembered what had struck me when poring through his manuscripts—the quantity of diary entries and especially correspondence that had to do with the approaching presidential election. It was a preoccupation in his household. His wife characterized the coming contest as "a mighty struggle which arouses alike all the passions and most ardent feelings of mankind." And, as it happened, most of his rivals were in one way or another participants in the foreign debate. William H. Crawford and John C. Calhoun were fellow members of Monroe's cabinet. Henry Clay was the speaker of the house. Andrew Jackson, who had just begun to be talked of as a candidate, was a newly elected member of the Senate. None of the existing accounts of the Monroe Doctrine makes more than passing reference to the "mighty struggle" which filled the mind of Mrs. Adams. Yet the more I thought about it, the more I became convinced that the struggle for the presidency might provide a key to understanding why the foreign policy debates came out as they did.

. . . I explore three hypotheses. The first is that the positions of the various policymakers were largely determined by their ideas of national interest and their personal interplay—in other words, that Adams's convictions were more definite and firm and he more stubborn and forceful than the others. The second is that the outcomes are best understood as products of international politics. The hypothesis is that, in view of what other governments were doing, the range of options open to Americans was very narrow, and the choices actually made were those which would have been made in the same circumstances by almost any reasonable men. The third hypothesis is that the whole process was governed by domestic politics. The positions of the policymakers were determined less by conviction than by ambition. They had different stakes riding on the outcomes, and Adams had a greater stake than the others.

No one of these hypotheses seems to me inherently the more plausible. In a study of American foreign policy during and after World War II, I concluded that convictions about "lessons" of history were a controlling force. Examining in more detail the China policy of that period, I found the strength of character of Secretary of State Marshall a critical determinant. In analyzing American policy during World War I, I was most impressed by the extent to which international politics constrained decision-makers in Washington. In the case of the Monroe Doctrine, however, my conclusion is that the outcomes are best ex-plained in terms of domestic politics. . . .

◦◉◦

Domestic Politics

. . . The men who constructed the Monroe Doctrine were all deeply interested in the approaching presidential election. Indeed, it is not too much to say that this subject preoccupied most of them. Mrs. Adams's diary and letters testify that this was the case for her husband, and his own diary suggests the same. Calhoun's nonofficial correspondence for the period dealt with little else. The same is true of Crawford and Clay. We should therefore examine the stakes for which these men were competing and the strategies which they had adopted, for it seems likely that expectations and fears related to the election could well have influenced their reasoning about the pressing issues of foreign policy. . . .

Throughout, Clay's chief target was Adams. In the summer of 1822, probably with Clay's knowledge if not connivance, a document was issued that accused Adams of having truckled to the British during the peace negotiations at Ghent and having shown a willingness to sacrifice the interests of westerners to those of New England fishermen. The author was Jonathan Russell of Rhode Island who, along with Clay and Adams, had been a member of the delegation at Ghent. All the while, newspapers supporting Clay emphasized Adams's Federalist past, his possible pro-British inclinations, and the likelihood that he represented narrow sectional interests.

The logic of this campaign was self-evident. If Clay could make it appear that he alone was the nationalist candidate, he might rally to himself western and northern Republicans whose concern was to prevent the election of Crawford, the triumph of the Radicals, and the preservation of a southern dynasty.

Adams's strategy was partly dictated by these attacks from Clay, some of which were echoed by supporters of Crawford and Calhoun. He had the advantage of being the only prominent candidate who was not a slaveholder. He thus had some chance of capitalizing on the antislavery sentiment that had manifested itself in the North, parts of the West, and even parts of the South during the controversy of 1819–1820 over the admission of Missouri as a state. He had the disadvantages of being his father's son, a former Federalist, and a citizen of a state that was viewed as having interests adverse to those of many other states. Adams needed to establish his credentials as a Republican, a patriot, and a man with a national and not just sectional perspective. . . .

Like Clay, Adams set forth a foreign policy platform. He did so in 1821 in a Fourth of July speech delivered in Washington and subsequently published not only in pro-Adams newspapers but as a pamphlet. Much of his speech simply attacked Britain. Poletica, then the Russian minister to the United States, characterized it as "from one end to the other nothing but a violent diatribe against England, intermingled with republican exaggerations." Also, however, the speech included a prophecy that colonialism would not survive anywhere. Giving more than an intimation of the forthcoming administration decision to recognize some of the Latin American republics, these passages answered Clay's implied accusation that Adams lacked sympathy for people struggling for independence. Also, Adams's speech countered Clay's appeal for a counterpoise to the Holy Alliance by calling in strident language for America to avoid involvement in European politics and to guard above all her own security and peace. "Wherever the standard of freedom or independence has been or shall be unfurled, there will her heart, her benedictions, and her prayers be," said Adams in the lines best to be remembered later. "But she goes not abroad in search of monsters to destroy. She is the well-wisher to the freedom and independence of all. She is the champion and vindicator only of her own."

Characterizing his speech variously as a direct reply to Clay's Lexington speech and as an address "to and for *man,* as well as to and for my country," Adams emphasized to various correspondents how plainly it demonstrated his hostility to the British. To a friendly Philadelphia editor, he wrote that he had meant to warn the British against yielding to their "malignant passions." To another prominent Philadelphian, he explained, "I thought it was high time that we should be asking ourselves, where we were in our relations with that country." Adams manifestly hoped that his Fourth of July oration would put to rest any suspicion that he was an Anglophile.

In the following year, when there appeared Jonathan Russell's indictment of his conduct at Ghent, Adams set aside all but the most imperative business and employed the better part of his summer composing a book-length answer. Being diligent enough and lucky enough to find the originals of some documents that Russell had misquoted and misused, Adams succeeded in demolishing Russell's case. The episode, had, however, demonstrated that the charge of partiality to Britain was a hydra he would have to fight as long as he remained a candidate, and thereafter he continually hacked at it. The *National Journal,* a newspaper started in Washington in November 1823 as a personal organ for Adams, asserted that independence of Britain and the rest of the Old World would remain the chord of its editorial policy.

In campaigning for the presidency, Adams faced problems that did not face Clay, for he was responsible for what happened as well as for what was said. Apparently, he felt that mere rhetoric would have little practical effect on the policies of other governments toward the United States. Otherwise he would not have drafted the notes and dispatches which Crawford criticized and Monroe fretfully modified nor would he have assailed Great Britain in a public speech. On the other hand, he showed keen concern lest the Monroe administration *do* something that would provoke anger or reprisals abroad. After recognition of the Latin American republics, he counseled Monroe to postpone actually sending envoys until reactions had been reported from London and the continental capitals. He fought in the cabinet against any encouragement of an independence movement in Cuba. The prospect that independence might be followed by American annexation, he argued, could lead the British to take preemptive action and seize the island. Similarly, though publicly declaring himself sympathetic with the Greeks, Adams was emphatic in cabinet in opposing any official encouragement. He protested even the proposal that a fact-finding commission be dispatched, as had been done early on for some of the Latin American states. Both the British and the Holy Allies, he warned, could take offense.

The contrast between the boldness of Adams's language and the cautiousness of his actions was due in part, of course, to differences between his role as candidate and his role as responsible statesman. But Adams's efforts to avoid actual trouble with England or the continental powers also served his interests as a candidate. In the first place, he had to be aware that any real trouble with a foreign nation would be blamed on him. If the trouble were with England, the result could be fatally to weaken Adams's base of support in the sea-dependent New England states and among Anglophiles and former

Federalists who, while they were sure to deplore his campaign oratory, might nevertheless vote for him as a lesser evil. In the second place, Adams could not ignore the fact that, if war began to seem imminent, public attention would shift away from the accomplishments for which he could claim credit, such as the annexation of Florida, and focus instead on the probable demands of the conflict to come. Notice, publicity, and interest would go to Calhoun, the secretary of war, who had been a clamorous advocate of preparedness, or perhaps to the military hero, Jackson. Reasons of politics as well as reasons of state could have led Adams to the positions he took within the cabinet.

Adams's optimum strategy thus involved preserving relative tranquility in the nation's international relations while at the same time persuading the doubtful that he was as patriotic and anti-British as any dyed-in-the-wool Jeffersonian and as much a nationalist and as much a partisan of the frontiersmen as was Clay. It was not a strategy easily pursued, especially by a man who felt compelled to explain to a diary the highmindedness of his every action.

Calhoun's task was simpler despite the fact that he, too, held a responsible office. The basis for his campaign was an assumption that none of the other candidates could win. He discounted Clay on the ground that no westerner could receive the votes of the North and South. Crawford would fail, he believed, because his Georgia base and Virginian support would arouse hostility in northern states where electors were chosen by popular ballot and because his advocacy of states rights would alienate people who wanted federal aid for canals, roads, and manufacturing establishments. Adams's disabilities were his identification with New England, his Federalist past, and his lack of experience on domestic issues. Calhoun thought that his own championing of internal improvements, a protective tariff, and frontier defense would capture some of Clay's constituents; his South Carolina background would bring him support in the South; and his nationalistic policies plus his Connecticut ties would allow him to win over some of Adams's partisans.

Calhoun's strategy thus involved out-Claying Clay on internal issues while seeking to chop away at Adams's credibility as a candidate. Through his Federalist allies, the newspapers established by his friends, and Pennsylvania organs controlled by the "Family Party," Calhoun advertised his positions and sounded the refrain that, if neither Clay nor Adams could win, then all opponents of Crawford and the Radicals should rally in his camp. At first, this campaign avoided direct attacks on either Clay or Adams. By 1823, however, Calhoun had become more confident. Late that summer, he directed a change in policy, writing confidentially to his lieutenants that they and the pro-Calhoun press should begin to emphasize policy differences with Adams and to call attention to the fact that Adams's onetime Federalism so compromised him that he would never win the votes of true Republicans outside New England and might even fail to win their votes there. Calhoun's strategy was thus in part complementary to Clay's. It aimed at discrediting Adams and driving him out of the race.

Crawford, too, had a simpler problem that Adams. He had to take blame or credit for what he did as secretary of the treasury, and he and his friends had continually to fight unfounded charges of misuse of funds or patronage.

At least by 1823, however, he had less answerability for other activities of the administration, for it has become notorious that he opposed not only Adams and Calhoun but also Monroe on almost every domestic issue.

Crawford campaigned as, in effect, the leader of an old Jeffersonian party whose principles had been deserted by the Monroe administration. His managers branded all other candidates as actual or potential tools of the Federalists. They contended that the whole Missouri question had been gotten up by Federalists as a device for disrupting Republican unity, and they labeled the domestic programs espoused by Clay and Calhoun as Hamilton's programs in new disguise. They said and for the most part believed that, in any case, these two renegade Republicans would eventually drop out. The ultimate contest would be between Crawford and Adams. Hence they persistently voiced the theme that Adams, the ex-Federalist, was in fact the Federalist candidate.

Until late in 1823, there was no Jackson strategy, for Jackson himself was not yet committed to running, and the men urging him to do so took no action except to disparage other candidates and stimulate signs of the general's personal popularity.

As of the autumn of 1823, Adams was therefore the central figure in the presidential campaign. Clay, Calhoun, and Crawford were all concentrating on undermining him, and he was battling their efforts to tar him as a lukewarm friend of liberty, an Anglophile, a Federalist, and a candidate with a hopelessly narrow electoral base. In view of the small numbers of legislators and voters whose shifts in opinion could transform the prospects for 1824, the contest was carried on relentlessly by all parties.

Knowing the stakes and strategies of the candidates, a detached observer aware of the pressing foreign policy issues might well have made the following predictions:

- That Adams would oppose acceptance of the proffered informal alliance with England. Likely to get most of the credit or blame for anything the administration did in foreign affairs, he would be held to have been its author. Those voters disposed to worry about his possible Federalist or Anglophile proclivities might feel that their fears had been confirmed. Furthermore, Adams would be open to fresh attack from Clay for failing to maintain America's independence. The result would be to cost him important marginal votes in the West, erode his support in the Middle States, and perhaps even lose him influential backers in Vermont, New Hampshire, and Maine. Adams's political interests would be best served if the British offer were spurned.
- That Adams would also oppose actual recognition of Greece. In the first place, he was likely to fear trouble with the continental powers, producing the domestic effects that he had tried to avert by counseling Monroe to be forceful in language but cautious in deed. In the second place, he had to anticipate embarrassment from the fact that the logical person to be envoy or commissioner to Greece was Edward Everett of Harvard, who had composed the pro-Greek manifesto in the *North American Review,* made no secret of his desire to have the job, and expected Adams's help in getting it. Since Everett was a Federalist, Adams had reason to expect that the appointment would fuel Republican

prejudices. On the other hand, to deny Everett the post would be to offend Federalists in New England and elsewhere who might otherwise go to the polls for Adams and who seemed almost certain to do so if Calhoun fell out of the race. It was in Adams's interest as a candidate that any change in American posture toward Greece be postponed until after the election.

- That Crawford and Calhoun and their adherents would favor both alliance with England and recognition of Greece if Adams could be made to seem the sponsor of these acts because of the harm they might work on his election prospects.
- That Calhoun would advocate these steps with special vehemence because they promised him the added benefit of arousing public concern about a possible war and hence turning public attention to his department and to the preparedness measures which he had all along been advocating.

The test of what was and what was not in the personal political interest of the various candidates would have yielded much more specific predictions than any test based on suppositions about their ideological positions or about conditions in the politics of other countries. Moreover, most of these predictions would have been right on the nose. . . .

⋅⟨⊙⟩⋅

Implications

In the instance of the Monroe Doctrine, the positions adopted by American policymakers seem to me to be best explained as functions of their domestic ambitions—Monroe's, to leave the presidency without being followed by recrimination and to be succeeded by someone who would not repudiate his policies; Adams's, Calhoun's, and Clay's, to become President; Jefferson's, Gallatin's, and perhaps Madison's, to see Crawford succeed. Consistently with their fundamental beliefs, any of these men could have taken different positions. Adams, for example, could have reasoned just as easily as Jefferson that concert with England would guarantee America's independence, security, and peace. He actually said as much not long before the specific issues materialized. The processes producing the actual foreign policy decisions are better understood as bargaining encounters among men with differing perspectives and ambitions than as debates about the merits of different policies. And the outcomes are most explicable as ones that equilibrated the competing or conflicting interests of men with differing political assets.

This conclusion may seem cynical. It is not meant to be. For it is in fact an affirmation that foreign policy can be determined less by the cleverness or wisdom of a few policymakers than by the political structure which determines their incentives. . . .

POSTSCRIPT

Was the Monroe Doctrine of 1823 Designed to Protect the Latin American Countries from European Intervention?

The Monroe Doctrine, as it was later called, was really three paragraphs of President Monroe's annual message of December 2, 1823 to Congress. In *The Creation of a Republican Empire 1776–1865*, Volume I of *The Cambridge History of American Foreign Relations* (Cambridge University Press, 1993), Professor Bradford Perkins describes the message as "either a dreadful summary of events over the preceding year—he was perhaps the worst stylist among our early presidents—or a series of recommendations on domestic policy. But one paragraph an-nounced the non-Colonization doctrine, and another section devoted a paragraph each to nonintervention and to isolation."

Professor Dexter Perkins was the leading expert on the Monroe Doctrine. The first of his three volumes on the subject was printed in 1927 and remains the classic work. Though other historians have differed with some of Professor Perkins interpretations, scholars still respect his multi-archival research.

Perkins argues that John Quincy Adams was the architect of the non-colonization principle. This stemmed from his negotiations with the Russians concerning the trade boundaries dominated by Russia in the Pacific Northwest. While Adams was willing to negotiate allowing Russia to extend its trade monopoly from the 55th to the 51st parallel, he convinced President Monroe to include the non-colonization principle in his annual message.

Adams was also responsible for Monroe's assertion of the principle of nonintervention into his annual message. He was afraid that the Holy Alliance of Russia, Prussia, and Austria was committed to putting down revolutions in Europe. Russia and France had already helped restore the powers of Spain's reactionary king, Ferdinand VII. Did they intend to help Spain recover her empire in Latin America?

British diplomats approached the United States with offers to issue a joint statement condemning the intervention of any European powers in Latin America to restore Spain's empire. But Adams felt that the crisis had passed by 1823 and convinced Monroe to issue a unilateral pronouncement rather than a joint one with Congress.

Finally Adams convinced Monroe to restate the principles of isolationism and the two Americas when the president eliminated from his message condemnation of French intervention in Spain and support for the Greek struggle for independence from the Ottoman Empire. The secretary of state believed it was too risky and also illogical for the United States to intervene in European affairs if we expected the European nations to stay out of Latin America.

Some historians think that Perkins' interpretation of the events is incomplete. His discussion of the economic interests of the United States is non-existent. In the late 1950s William Appleman Williams reoriented the framework for writing diplomatic history. *The Tragedy of American History,* revised and enlarged (Delta Books, 1962) and *The Contours of American History* (World Publishing Co., 1961) emphasized the themes of "Open Door Imperialism" in the "Creation of an American Empire." William Earl Weeks has pursued these themes in his books on John Quincy Adams and American Global Empire (University of Kentucky Press, 1992) and *Building the Continental Empire: American Expansion from the Revolution to the Civil War* (Ivan R. Dee, 1996).

Perkins also neglected to study how the Latin American republics responded to the Monroe Doctrine. In 1824 Columbia suggested an alliance based on the principle of non-intervention but it was turned down. A similar request by Brazil the next year was also rejected. In 1826 when President John Quincy Adams proposed sending delegates to an inter-American Conference at Panama, it created a furor in Congress, and our delegates arrived too late to participate. Research on U.S. relations with Latin America is sketchy and outdated. Some of the best books were written in the 1930s: Gaston Nerval, *Autopsy of the Monroe Doctrine* (Macmillan Co., 1934) and Lius Quintanilla, *A Latin Speaks* (The Macmillan Co., 1934).

Professor Ernest May emphasizes the political considerations surrounding *The Making of the Monroe Doctrine* (The Belknap Press, 1985). Neither Dexter Perkins nor the writers with economic viewpoints talk about the foreign policy views of the major candidates who hope to succeed Monroe as president in 1825. By looking at the campaign for president in 1824, according to Professor May, John Quincy Adams trashes England in his speeches and convinces President Monroe to issue a unilateral rather than a joint pronouncement. This makes the future president appear to be much less pro-British than his father, President John Adams, had been in the 1790s.

May's interpretation of the electioneering politics surrounding the Monroe Doctrine has been questioned in an earlier biography of *John Quincy Adams and the Foundations of American Foreign Policy* (Harcourt, Brace, & Co., 1949) and Harry Ammon, *James Monroe* (McGraw Hill, 1971). Both authors believe that Adams and Monroe were motivated by considerations of national interest. International rather than domestic political considerations motivated Adams who believed that the Holy Alliance was not a threat to Latin America, that England had economic reasons for keeping Latin America independent, and that Monroe should assert his non-colonization and non-intervention policies unilaterally.

For a sustained critique of May's book, see Harry Ammon, "Monroe Doctrine: Domestic Politics or National Decision?" *Diplomatic History,* v (Winter, 1981). The best collection of essays on *The Monroe Doctrine,* though old, remains edited by Armon Rappaport (D.C. Health and Co., 1964). Two recent biographies deserve notice: Noble E. Cunningham, Jr., *The Presidency of James Monroe* (University Press of Kansas, 1996) and Paul C. Nagel, *John Quincy Adams: A Public Life, A Private Life* (Knopf, 1998).

ISSUE 11

Did the Election of 1828 Represent a Democratic Revolt of the People?

YES: Sean Wilentz, from *The Rise of American Democracy: Jefferson to Lincoln* (Norton, 2005)

NO: Richard P. McCormick, from "New Perspectives on Jacksonian Politics," *The American Historical Review* (January 1960)

ISSUE SUMMARY

YES: Bancroft Prize winner Sean Wilentz argues that in spite of its vulgarities and slanders, the 1828 election campaign "produced a valediction on the faction-ridden jumble of the Era of Bad Feelings and announced the rough arrival of two district national coalitions."

NO: Professor Richard P. McCormick believes that voting statistics demonstrate that a genuine political revolution did not take place until the presidential election of 1840, when fairly well-balanced political parties had been organized in virtually every state.

According to the conventional wisdom, Andrew Jackson's election to the presidency in 1828 began the era of the common man in which the mass of voters, no longer restrained from voting by property requirements, rose up and threw the elite leaders out of our nation's capital. While recent historians are not quite sure what constituted Jacksonian democracy or who supported it, and they question whether there ever existed such an era of egalitarianism, American history textbooks still include the obligatory chapter on the age of Jackson.

There are several reasons the old-fashioned view of this period still prevails. In spite of the new scholarly interest in social history, it is still easier to generalize about political events. Consequently, most texts continue to devote the major portion of their pages to detailed examinations of the successes and failures of various presidential administrations. Whether Jackson was more significant than other presidents is difficult to assess because "Old Hickory's" forceful personality, compounded with his use of strong executive authority, engendered constant controversy in his eight years in office.

Another reason the traditional concept of Jacksonian democracy has not been abandoned is because critics of the progressive interpretation have not been able to come up with an acceptable alternative view. Culminating with Arthur Schlesinger, Jr.'s Pulitzer Prize–winning and beautifully written *The Age of Jackson* (Little, Brown, 1945), the progressive historians viewed Jackson's election in 1828 as the triumph of the common man in politics. Oversimplified as this interpretation may be, there is little doubt that a major change was taking place in our political system during these years. The death of both Thomas Jefferson and John Adams on July 4, 1826, the fiftieth anniversary of our Declaration of Independence from England, signified the end of the revolutionary generation's control over American politics. The first six presidents had been leaders or descendants of leaders in the revolutionary movement. At the Constitutional Convention in 1787, most of the time was spent discussing the powers of the presidency. Because of the recent experience with the British king, the Founding Fathers were fearful of strong executive authority. Therefore, the presidency was entrusted only to those individuals whose loyalty remained unquestioned. Jackson was the first president of the United States who did not come from either Virginia or Massachusetts. Though Jackson was only a teenager at the time of the American Revolution, his career was similar to those of the early Founding Fathers. Like Washington and Jefferson, Jackson became a living legend before he was 50 years old. His exploits as an Indian fighter and the military hero of the Battle of New Orleans in the War of 1812 were more important than his western background in making him presidential material.

During the past two decades, a number of historians have studied the effects of our presidential elections on the development and maintenance of our two-party system. Borrowing concepts and analytical techniques from political scientists and sociologists, the "new political" historians have demonstrated the effectiveness of our parties in selecting candidates, running campaigns, developing legislation, and legitimizing conflicts within our democratic system. By 1815, the first-party system of competition between the Federalists and the Republican-Democrats had broken down, in part because the Federalists had refused to become a legitimate opposition party. A second-party system developed during the Jackson era between Old Hickory's Democratic party and his Whig opponents. It lasted until the 1850s when the slavery issue led to the formation of a new system of party competition between Republicans and Democrats.

The following selections disagree on the significance of the 1828 presidential race as a critical election in the development of the second-party system. Professor Sean Wilentz has won the Pulitzer Prize for his massive tome on *The Rise of American Democracy* (Norton, 2005). He synthesizes the "new political history" with the more favorable earlier interpretation of Andrew Jackson as the champion of the masses. In spite of its vulgarities and slanders, says Wilentz, the 1828 election campaign "pronounced a valediction on the faction-ridden jumble of the Era of Bad Feelings and announced the rough arrival of two distinct national coalitions," But historian Richard P. McCormick revises the traditional interpretation. His analysis of the voting statistics, he argues, demonstrates that a genuine political revolution did not take place until the presidential election of 1840 when fairly well-balanced parties had been organized in virtually every state.

YES

Sean Wilentz

The Rise of American Democracy: Jefferson to Lincoln

"Under Whip & Spur": Politics, Propaganda, and the 1828 Campaign

Although he looked like a distinguished old warrior, with flashing blue eyes and a shock of whitening steely gray hair, Andrew Jackson was by now a physical wreck. Years of ingesting calomel and watered gin to combat his chronic dysentery had left him almost toothless. (In 1828, he obtained an ill-fitting set of dentures, but he often refused to wear them). An irritation of his lungs, caused by a bullet he had caught in one of his early duels, had developed into bronchiectasis, a rare condition causing violent coughing spells that would bring up what he called "great quantities of slime." The bullet itself remained lodged in his chest, and another was lodged in his left arm, where it accelerated the onset of osteomyelitis. Rheumatism afflicted his joints, and his head often ached, the effect of a lifetime of chewing and smoking tobacco. He had survived near-total collapse of his health in 1822 and 1825, but for the rest of his life, he enjoyed few days completely free of agony. His outbursts of irascible fury, which sometimes shocked even his old friends and allies, owed partly to his suffering and to his efforts to suppress it. But after the debacle of 1825, they also owed to his determination to vindicate not just his own honor but that of the American people. For Jackson and his admirers, the two had become identical.

Willfulness did not mean rashness. In preparing to wreak his vengeance on Adams (whom he respected) and Clay (whom he despised), Jackson took care not to violate the accepted etiquette of presidential campaigning and appeal directly for the job. He was available to serve his country once more, but to look or sound less elevated than that would have been dishonorable (as well as onerous, given the state of his health). Jackson made only one major public appearance over the months before the election, at a public festivity in New Orleans on January 8, commemorating his great victory thirteen years earlier—an invitation, issued by the Louisiana legislature, that he could not refuse without seeming churlish. Yet while he stuck close to the Hermitage, Jackson threw himself into the fray as no other previous presidential candidate before him had, making himself available for visiting delegations of congress-men, giving interviews to interested parties, and writing letters for newspaper publication. When personal attacks on his character began, he became even more active, his sense of honor on the line. Some of his chief supporters, including Van Buren, asked that "we be let alone" and that Jackson "be *still*," but Jackson would command this campaign just as surely as he had any of his military exploits.

His positions on several key issues were moderate and flexible, replicat-ing much of what he had said in 1824, in generalities that would not upset the national coalition his agents were assembling. On the tariff, the primary polit-ical issue in 1828, Jackson remained blandly middle-of-the-road, repeated his support for a "judicious" tariff, and allowed men of different views to imagine that his sympathies lay with them. On internal improvements, Jackson modi-fied his stance somewhat to support a distribution of surplus federal monies to the states for any road and canal projects they wished to undertake, but generally he restated his cautious support for projects that were genuinely national in scope. On the Indian question, he remained persuaded that, for the good of white settlers and natives alike, orderly removal was the only sound solution, but he refrained from saying anything that might be interpreted as an endorsement of the more extreme state-rights removal position.

Instead of a long list of positions and proposals, Jackson's campaign revolved around calls for "reform," a theme broad enough to unite a disparate coalition without merely resorting to platitudes. At one level, "reform" meant undoing what Jackson considered the theft of the presidency in 1825, and end-ing the political climate that had permitted it. Sometimes, Jackson and his supporters proposed specific changes. Jackson himself said he would exclude from his cabinet any man who sought the presidency—one obvious way to help prevent any future "corrupt bargain." He also called for a constitutional amendment to bar any member of Congress from eligibility for any other federal office (except in the judiciary) for two years beyond his departure from office. Other Jacksonians spoke of the candidate's support for the princi-ple of rotation in office, for limiting presidents to a single term, and for ban-ning the executive from appointing congressmen to civil posts—all means to disrupt insider exclusivity and what Jackson called the "intrigue and manage-ment" that had corrupted the government. Otherwise, the Jackson campaign simply reminded the voters of what had happened in 1825—and went further, to charge that "Lucifer" Clay had, during the House negotiations, offered to throw his support to Jackson if Jackson promised he would name him secre-tary of state.

At another level, "reform" meant returning American government to Jeffersonian first principles and halting the neo-Federalist revival supposedly being sponsored under the cover of the American System. President Adams, Jackson and his men charged, had made the mistake of following his father's footsteps, balancing a "hypocritical veneration for the great principles of republicanism" with artful manipulation of political power. All of "the asperity which marked the struggle of 98 & 1800," Jackson wrote, had returned. Having "gone into power contrary to the voice of the nation," the administration had claimed a mandate it did not possess, and then tried to expand its authority even further. Illegitimate from the start, the new Adams regime raised what Jackson called the fundamental question at stake in the election: "[S]hall the government or the people rule?"

While Jackson and his closest advisors refined this message and called the shots from Nashville, his supporters built a sophisticated campaign apparatus unlike any previously organized in a presidential election, a combination so effective that it obviated the need for either a congressional caucus nomination or a national convention. At the top, Jackson's most capable Tennessee operatives, including John Overton, William Lewis, and John Eaton, concentrated their efforts in a central committee headquarters established in Nashville, where decisions about strategy and tactics could be taken efficiently, in rapid response to continuing events and with Jackson's approval. (A similar, smaller Jackson committee headquarters was established in Washington, to work closely with the pro- Jackson caucus in Congress that met regularly under Van Buren's aegis.) The central committee in turn dispatched its messages to (and received intelligence from) Jackson campaign committees established in each state. Finally, the Jacksonians responded to the reforms in presidential voting around the country—reforms that, by 1828, had included, in all but two states, giving the power to choose presidential electors directly to the voters—by coordinating activities at the local level. The state pro-Jackson committees linked up with local Jackson committees, sometimes called Hickory Clubs, that stirred up enthusiasm with rallies and parades and made sure that their supporters arrived at the polls.

Even more extraordinary than the campaign committees was the dense network of pro-Jackson newspapers that seemed to arise out of nowhere beginning in the spring of 1827. Early in the campaign, Jackson's congressional supporters had caucused and pledged to establish "a chain of newspaper posts, from the New England States to Louisiana, and branching off through Lexington to the Western States." In North Carolina alone, nine new Jacksonian papers had appeared by the middle of 1827, while in Ohio, eighteen new papers supplemented the five already in existence in 1824. In each state, the Jackson forces arranged for one newspaper to serve as the official organ of their respective state committees, refining the broadcast of an authoritative message while promoting a cadre of prominent loyal editors, including Ritchie at the *Enquirer*, Amos Kendall at the *Argus of Western America*, Edwin Croswell at the *Albany Argus*, Isaac Hill at the New Hampshire *Patriot*, and, above all, in Washington, Calhoun's friend Duff Green at the anti-administration *United States Telegraph*.

Funding (as well as copy) for the campaign sheets came directly from Jackson's congressional supporters and their friends, who pioneered numerous fund-raising gimmicks, including five-dollar-a-plate public banquets and other ticketed festivities. More substantial sums, including money raised from local bankers and businessmen in the New York–Philadelphia region, were collected and disbursed by Martin Van Buren, who served as the campaign's de facto national treasurer. Some of these monies went to the newspaper editors; others were spent on printing campaign books and pamphlets and producing paraphernalia such as campaign badges. Much of this material made its way to supporters at government cost, thanks to Jacksonian congressmen's liberal partisan use of their personal postal franking privileges.

Jackson's friends made special efforts to solidify their connections to various popular democratic movements, urban and rural, while also winning over more established and politically influential men. The alliances ranged from complete mergers to testy but effective ententes. Kentucky was a special prize for the Jacksonians, having cast its congressional vote for Adams in 1825 at Henry Clay's insistence. The 1828 tariff's high protective rates for hemp growers and manufacturers helped Van Buren offset Clay's advantage among the Kentucky elite, recently aligned with the Old Court Party—but the Jacksonians mainly pinned their hopes on Amos Kendall, Francis Blair, and the revitalized New Court Party machine. In protection-mad Pennsylvania, where the tariff proved extremely popular among the state's ironmongers, the Jacksonians appealed to all of the elements of the old Jeffersonian coalition—including manufacturers, western farmers, and rural Germans—with a propaganda effort headed by the papermaking magnate Congressman Samuel Ingham. In Philadelphia, the presence of numerous New School candidates for state and local office on the Jacksonian ticket alienated the new Working Men's Party, but Jackson's friends reached out to the labor insurgents in various ways, including a direct fifteen-hundred-dollar, I contribution to rescue Stephen Simpson's financially strapped paper, the *Columbian Observer.* Ultimately, the Workies devised their own Jackson ticket, picking and choosing among the official nominees, offering joint nominations to those they deemed reliable, but running their own candidates for the other slots.

New York, which Jackson had lost in 1824, was a different and, as ever, more difficult story. Under the revised state constitution, voters now chose the state's presidential electors. Unlike in most other states, however, New York's electoral votes would be apportioned on a district-by-district basis, meaning that even if Van Buren's agents carried the overall popular vote, Adams was bound to win a portion of the state's Electoral college total. DeWitt Clinton's death resolved much of the early bickering within the New York pro-Jackson camp, leaving Van Buren in control, but it also raised the possibility that some pro-Clinton Jackson men, who had supported the Tennessean chiefly to promote Clinton, might now drift over to Adams. And then there was the perplexing Anti-Masonic uprising in western New York, an outburst of democratic outrage that could never be won over to Grand Master Mason Andrew Jackson. Even with all of the southern states plus Pennsylvania likely to support Jackson, it would not be enough to elect him president. New York's result would be crucial.

The outlook for Jackson improved when political operatives determined that the Anti-Masonic movement remained, for the moment, localized, and that its chief advocates, Thurlow Weed and William Henry Seward, were having difficulty merging it with the Adams campaign. The outlook improved even more when Jackson's operatives confirmed that Henry Clay was not only a Mason but, as one delighted Manhattan pol put it, "a Mason of rank." Van Buren, meanwhile, decided to make the most of his New York strongholds, above all New York City, where the old Tammany Society, after a history of recurrent factionalism, turned into one of the most united and reliable pro-Jackson organizations in the state. As early as January, Tammany began hosting giant public events touting Jackson, and after the death of DeWitt Clinton—who was hated by the Tammany braves—the way was cleared for an all-out effort to spike the city's vote. Hickory Clubs appeared in every ward, sponsoring hickory tree–planting ceremonies and barroom gatherings to toast the general's success. A clutch of partisan editors in the already well-established New York press churned out reams of pro-Jackson material. "The more he is known," one pro-Jackson paper boasted of its man, "the less and less the charges against him seem to be true."

Against this juggernaut, Adams's supporters—their candidate an awkward public figure who spurned involvement in campaign organization—were badly overmatched. But they tried their best and performed credibly as organizers. Henry Clay, ignoring advice that he resign and let Adams bear the full brunt of defeat, took charge of creating a national campaign and of stumping at dinners and celebrations around the country to make the administration's case. Daniel Webster pitched in as well, overseeing the canvassing of potential financial backers (fully exploiting his ample personal connections to New England capitalists), collecting substantial sums, and keeping track of accounts. Although they could not equal the Jacksonians, the Adamsites created a substantial pro-administration press, headed in Washington by Joseph Gales and William Seaton's *National Intelligencer* and Peter Force's *National Journal*. The Adamsites printed forests' worth of pamphlets, leaflets, and handbills, organized their own state central committees, and sponsored countless dinners and commemorations. In at least one state, New Jersey, the Adamsites probably outorganized their opponents. And everywhere outside of Georgia, where Jackson ran unopposed, there was a genuine contest under way, with both parties, as one Marylander wrote, "fairly in the field, under *whip & spur.*"

Adamsite strategic and tactical errors at the state and local level repeatedly undermined whatever enthusiasm the administration's loyalists generated. High-minded stubbornness, linked to an aversion to what looked to some National Republicans like Van Buren–style wheeling and dealing, killed Adams's chances of carrying the middle Atlantic states. In upstate New York, the National Republicans insulted the Anti-Masons by rejecting their nominee for governor, a close friend of Thurlow Weed's, and then bidding the insurgents to show their good faith by adopting the pro-administration slate, ruining any chance of an alliance. In New York City, a protectionist movement, geared to halting the dumping of foreign manufactures on the New York market, arose in the spring; and, by autumn, it had gained a sizable following that cut across class and party lines. But the Adamsites, seemingly unable to believe that their protectionism might appeal to urban workers, held back from the movement. The protectionists ran their own ticket, and the opportunity was wasted. Similar shortsightedness prevailed in Philadelphia, where the Adamsites refused to make common cause with the surviving Federalist establishment, encouraging Jacksonian hopes of taking the city.

The Adamsites did excel in one area, the dark art of political slander. In 1827, a Cincinnati editor and friend of Clay's named Charles Hammond took a fact-finding tour into Kentucky and Tennessee, and unearthed some old stories about alleged legal irregularities in Jackson's marriage (supposedly he was a bigamist), along with charges that Jackson's wife, Rachel, was an adulteress and his mother a common prostitute. The charges were not simply mean-spirited: they evoked broader cultural presumptions that stigmatized Jackson as a boorish, lawless, frontier lowlife, challenging the Christian gentleman, John Quincy Adams. Clay immediately recommended his mudslinger friend to Webster, calling Hammond's paper "upon the whole, the most efficient and discreet gazette that espouses our cause," and suggested that the editor get direct financial support. Hammond, meanwhile, became a fountain of wild and inflammatory charges—that Jackson's mother had been brought to America by British soldiers, that she married a mulatto who was Jackson's father—all of which found their way into what may have been the lowest production of the 1828 campaign, a new journal entitled *Truth's Advocate and Monthly Anti-Jackson Expositor.* Jackson, enraged to the point of tears, held Clay responsible and sent John Eaton to confront the Kentuckian. Clay vehemently denied the charges, though his private correspondence with Hammond contains hints he was lying. Jackson continued to blame everything on Clay.

Character assassination in presidential politics was hardly invented in 1828—recall, for example, the lurid attacks on Thomas Jefferson and "Dusky Sally" Hemings—and Clay could easily and rightly complain of the Jackson campaign's unceasing attacks about the corrupt bargain as the basest sort of slander. But the Hammond affair, beginning more than a year before the 1828 electioneering commenced in earnest, marked the arrival of a new kind of calculated, mass cultural politics, pitting a fervent sexual moralism against a more forgiving, secularist, laissez-faire ethic. Hammond's attacks also ensured that a great deal of the campaign would be fought out in the sewer. The Jacksonians spread sensational falsehoods that President Adams was a secret aristocratic voluptuary who, while minister to Russia, had procured an innocent American woman for the tsar. Clay came in for merciless attacks as an embezzler, gambler, and brothel habitué. The Adamsites responded with a vicious handbill, covered with coffins, charging Jackson with the murder of six innocent American militamen during the Creek War, and labeling him "a wild man under whose charge the Government would collapse." The competition turned largely into a propaganda battle of personalities and politically charged cultural styles instead of political issues. A campaign slogan from four years earlier, coined in support of a possible Adams-Jackson ticket, assumed completely new meaning and summed up the differences, contrasting the nominees as "Adams who can write/Jackson who can fight."

And yet, for all of the vulgarities and slander, the campaign of 1828 was not an unprincipled and demagogic theatrical. Neither was it a covert sectional battle between a pro-slavery southerner and an antislavery New Englander; nor was it a head-on clash between pro-development Adamsite capitalists and antidevelopment Jacksonian farmers and workers, although strong views about slavery and economic development certainly came into play. The campaign pronounced a valediction on the faction-ridden jumble of the Era of Bad Feelings and announced the rough arrival of two distinct national coalitions, divided chiefly over the so-called corrupt bargain and the larger political implications of the American System. It was, above all, a contest over contrasting conceptions of politics, both with ties to the ideals of Thomas Jefferson.

For all of his setbacks and suffering, John Quincy Adams had never abandoned his moral vision of energetic government and national uplift. Protective tariffs, federal road and canal projects, and the other mundane features of the American System were always, to him, a means to that larger end. A fugitive from Federalism, Adams embodied one part of the Jeffersonian legacy, devoted to intellectual excellence, rationality, and government by the most talented and virtuous—those whom Jefferson himself, in a letter to Adams's father, had praised as "the natural aristoi." The younger Adams took the legacy a large step further, seeing the federal government as the best instrument for expanding the national store of intelligence, prosperity, beauty, and light.

Objections to the political ramifications of that vision united the opposition—objections rooted in another part of the Jeffersonian legacy, a fear of centralized government linked to a trust in the virtue and political wisdom of ordinary American voters. Jackson and his polyglot coalition contended that human betterment meant nothing without the backing of the people themselves. Lacking that fundamental legitimacy, Adams, Clay, and their entire administration had, the Jacksonians contended, been engaged from the start in a gigantic act of fraud—one that, to succeed, required shifting as much power as possible to Washington, where the corrupt few might more easily oppress the virtuous many, through unjust tariffs, costly federal commercial projects, and other legislative maneuvers. Were the Adamsites not removed as quickly as possible, there was no telling how far they might go in robbing the people's liberties, under the guise of national improvement, the American System, or some other shibboleth. Hence, the opposition's slogan: "Jackson and Reform."

Jackson himself laid out the stakes in a letter to an old friend, on the omens in what he called the Adamsites' exercise of "patronage" (by which he simply meant "power"):

> The present is a contest between the virtue of the people, & the influence of patronage[. S]hould patronage prevail, over virtue, then indeed "the safe precedent," will be established, that the President, appoints his successor in the person of the sec. of state—Then the people may prepare themselves to become "hewers of wood & drawers of water," to those in power, who with the Treasury at command, will wield by its corrupting influence a majority to support it—The present is an important struggle, for the perpetuity of our republican government, & I hope the virtue of the people may prevail, & all may be well.

Or as one of his New York supporters put it (presuming to speak on behalf of "the sound planters, farmers & mechanics of the country"), the Jacksonians beheld the coming election as "a great contest between the aristocracy and democracy of America."

The balloting began in September and, because of widely varying state polling laws, continued until November. Early returns from New England unsurprisingly gave Adams the lead, although not quite the clean sweep he had expected. (In Maine, a hardy band of ex–Crawford Radicals in and around Portland managed to win one of the state's electoral votes for Jackson.) The trend shifted heavily in mid-October, when Pennsylvania (overwhelmingly, including a strong plurality in Philadelphia) and Ohio (narrowly) broke for Jackson. It remains a matter of speculation how much this news affected the vote in other states, where the polls had not yet opened, but the Jacksonians took no chances, especially in New York, where the three days of voting did not commence until November 3. Holding back until the moment was ripe, the New York Jackson committee suddenly spread the word in late October that Jackson's election was virtually assured, in order to demoralize the opposition. In the end, Jackson carried the state's popular vote, although only by about 5,000 ballots out of 275,000 cast.

The state-by-state reporting of the vote, with news of one Jackson victory after another rolling in, heightened the impression that a virtual revolution was underway. The final tallies showed a more complicated reality. As expected, Adams captured New England, and Jackson swept the South below Maryland. But apart from Jackson's lopsided victory in Pennsylvania, the returns from the key battleground states were remarkably even.[1] If a mere 9,000 votes in New York, Ohio, and Kentucky had shifted from one column to the other, and if New York, with an Adams majority, had followed the winner-takes-all rule of most other states, Adams would have won a convincing 149 to 111 victory in the Electoral College. In other races for federal office the Adamsites actually improved their position. Above all, in the U.S. Senate, what had been a strong six-vote opposition majority in the Twentieth Congress would be reduced to a Jacksonian majority of two when the new Congress assembled in December 1829. Despite all their blunders, and despite Adams's unpopularity, the friends of the administration had not lost future political viability.

These wrinkles in the returns were lost amid Jackson's overwhelming victory nationwide. Jackson won 68 percent of the electoral vote and a stunning 56 percent of the popular vote—the latter figure representing a margin of victory that would not be surpassed for the rest of the nineteenth century. The totals came from a vastly larger number of voters than ever before in a presidential election, thanks to the adoption of popular voting for electors in four states and the bitterness of the one-on-one contest in the middle Atlantic states. More than a million white men voted for president in 1828, roughly four times the total of 1824. Jackson alone won three times as many votes as the total cast for all candidates four years earlier. The magnitude of it all left Adamsites, including the normally sanguine Henry Clay, miserable, and Jacksonians jubilant.

Perhaps the only Jacksonian not thoroughly overjoyed was Jackson himself. Well before the voting was over, he had understood what the outcome would be, and the news confirming his election caused no particular stir at the Hermitage. After all the months of campaigning behind the scenes, and now faced with actually assuming the presidency, the victor reported that "my mind is depressed." Sadness turned to panic and then grief in mid-December, when Rachel Jackson, preparing for the move to Washington, suddenly collapsed and, after five days of violent heart seizures, died. Her husband, who sat up with her throughout her ordeal, would never really recover from the shock. His great biographer James Parton wrote that it henceforth "subdued his spirit and corrected his speech," except on rare occasions when, in a calculated effort to intimidate his foes or inspire his allies, he would break into his customary fits of table pounding and swearing. Yet Rachel's death also steeled Jackson for the political battles to come. Her health had been precarious for several years before she died. Jackson was absolutely certain that the slanders of the 1828 campaign had finally broken her. And for that cruel and unforgivable blow, he would forever blame, above all others, his nemesis, Henry Clay.

Note

1. The final results from the key states were as follows:

	Popular Vote		Electoral Vote	
States	Jackson	Adams	Jackson	Adams
New York	140,763	135,413	20	16
Ohio	67,597	63,396	16	—
Kentucky	39,397	31,460	14	—

Figures from S&I, 2: 492.

Richard P. McCormick  **NO**

New Perspectives on Jacksonian Politics

The historical phenomenon that we have come to call Jacksonian democracy has long engaged the attention of American political historians, and never more insistently than in the past decade. From the time of Parton and Bancroft to the present day scholars have recognized that a profoundly significant change took place in the climate of politics simultaneously with the appearance of Andrew Jackson on the presidential scene. They have sensed that a full understanding of the nature of that change might enable them to dissolve some of the mysteries that envelop the operation of the American democratic process. With such a challenging goal before them, they have pursued their investigations with uncommon intensity and with a keen awareness of the contemporary relevance of their findings.

A cursory view of the vast body of historical writing on this subject suggests that scholars in the field have been largely preoccupied with attempts to define the content of Jacksonian democracy and identify the influences that shaped it. What did Jacksonian democracy represent, and what groups, classes, or sections gave it its distinctive character? The answers that have been given to these central questions have been—to put it succinctly—bewildering in their variety. The discriminating student, seeking the essential core of Jacksonianism, may make a choice among urban workingmen, southern planters, venturous conservatives, farm-bred *nouveaux riches,* western frontiersmen, frustrated entrepreneurs, or yeoman farmers. Various as are these interpretations of the motivating elements that constituted the true Jacksonians, the characterizations of the programmatic features of Jacksonian democracy are correspondingly diverse. Probably the reasonable observer will content himself with the conclusion that many influences were at work and that latitudinarianism prevailed among the Jacksonian faithful.

In contrast with the controversy that persists over these aspects of Jacksonian democracy, there has been little dissent from the judgment that "the 1830's saw the triumph in American politics of that democracy which has remained preeminently the distinguishing feature of our society." The consensus would seem to be that with the emergence of Jackson, the political pulse of the nation quickened. The electorate, long dormant or excluded from the polls by suffrage barriers, now became fired with unprecedented political excitement. The result was a bursting forth of democratic energies, evidenced by a marked upward surge in voting. Beard in his colorful fashion gave expression to the common viewpoint when he asserted that "the roaring flood of the new democracy was . . . [by 1824] foaming perilously near the crest. . . ." Schlesinger, with his allusion to the "immense popular vote" received by Jackson in 1824, creates a similar image. The Old Hero's victory in 1828 has been hailed as the consequence of a "mighty democratic uprising."

That a "new democracy, ignorant, impulsive, irrational" entered the arena of politics in the Jackson era has become one of the few unchallenged "facts" in an otherwise controversial field. Differences of opinion occur only when attempts are made to account for the remarkable increase in the size of the active electorate. The commonest explanations have emphasized the assertion by the common man of his newly won political privileges, the democratic influences that arose out of the western frontier, or the magnetic attractiveness of Jackson as a candidate capable of appealing with singular effectiveness to the backwoods hunter, the plain farmer, the urban working-man, and the southern planter.

Probably because the image of a "mighty democratic uprising" has been so universally agreed upon, there has been virtually no effort made to describe precisely the dimensions of the "uprising." Inquiry into this aspect of Jacksonian democracy has been discouraged by a common misconception regarding voter behavior before 1824. As the authors of one of our most recent and best textbooks put it: "In the years from the beginning of the government to 1824, a period for which we have no reliable election statistics, only small numbers of citizens seemed to have bothered to go to the polls." Actually, abundant data on pre-1824 elections is available, and it indicates a far higher rate of voting than has been realized. Only by taking this data into consideration can voting behavior after 1824 be placed in proper perspective.

The question of whether there was indeed a "mighty democratic uprising" during the Jackson era is certainly crucial in any analysis of the political character of Jacksonian democracy. More broadly, however, we need to know the degree to which potential voters participated in elections before, during, and after the period of Jackson's presidency as well as the conditions that apparently influenced the rate of voting. Only when such factors have been analyzed can we arrive at firm conclusions with respect to the dimensions of the political changes that we associate with Jacksonian democracy. Obviously in studying voter participation we are dealing with but one aspect of a large problem, and the limitations imposed by such a restrictive focus should be apparent.

In measuring the magnitude of the vote in the Jackson elections it is hardly significant to use the total popular vote cast throughout the nation. A comparison of the total vote cast in 1812, for example, when in eight of the seventeen states electors were chosen by the legislature, with the vote in 1832, when every state except South Carolina chose its electors by popular vote, has limited meaning. Neither is it revealing to compare the total vote in 1824 with that in 1832 without taking into consideration the population increase during the interval. The shift from the legislative choice of electors to their election by popular vote, together with the steady population growth, obviously swelled the presidential vote. But the problem to be investigated is whether the Jackson elections brought voters to the polls in such enlarged or unprecedented proportions as to indicate that a "new democracy" had burst upon the political scene.

The most practicable method for measuring the degree to which voters participated in elections over a period of time is to relate the number of votes cast to the number of potential voters. Although there is no way of calculating precisely how many eligible voters there were in any state at a given time, the evidence at hand demonstrates that with the exception of Rhode Island, Virginia, and Louisiana the potential electorate after r824 was roughly equivalent to the adult white male population. A meaningful way of expressing the rate of voter participation, then, is to state it in terms of the percentage of the adult white males actually voting. This index can be employed to measure the variations that occurred in voter participation over a period of time and in both national and state elections. Consequently a basis is provided for comparing the rate of voting in the Jackson elections with other presidential elections before and after his regime as well as with state elections.

Using this approach it is possible, first of all, to ascertain whether or not voter participation rose markedly in the three presidential elections in which Jackson was a candidate. Did voter participation in these elections so far exceed the peak participation in the pre-1824 elections as to suggest that a mighty democratic uprising was taking place? The accompanying data (Table 1) provides an answer to this basic question.

In the 1824 election not a single one of the eighteen states in which the electors were chosen by popular vote attained the percentage of voter participation that had been reached before r824. Prior to that critical election, fifteen of those eighteen states had recorded votes in excess of 50 per cent of their adult white male population, but in 1824 only two states—Maryland and Alabama—exceeded this modest mark. The average rate of voter participation in the election was 26.5 per cent. This hardly fits the image of the "roaring flood of the new democracy . . . foaming perilously near the crest. . . ."

There would seem to be persuasive evidence that in 1828 the common man flocked to the polls in unprecedented numbers, for the proportion of adult white males voting soared to 56.3 per cent, more than double the 1824 figure. But this outpouring shrinks in magnitude when we observe that in only six of the twenty-two states involved were new highs in voter participation established. In three of these—Maryland, Virginia, and Louisiana—the recorded gain was inconsiderable, and in a fourth—New York—the bulk of the increase might be attributed to changes that had been made in suffrage qualifications as recently as 1821 and 1826. Six states went over the 70 per cent mark, whereas ten had bettered that performance before 1824. Instead of a "mighty democratic uprising" there was in 1828 a voter turnout that approached—but in only a few instances matched or exceeded—the maximum levels that had been attained before the Jackson era.

The advance that was registered in 1828 did not carry forward to 1832. Despite the fact that Jackson was probably at the peak of his personal popularity, that he was engaged in a campaign that was presumably to decide issues of great

Table 1

Percentages of Adult White Males Voting in Elections

State	Highest Known % AWM Voting before 1824		Presidential Elections					
	Year	% AWM	1824	1828	1832	1836	1840	1844
Maine	1812[g]	62.0	18.9	42.7	66.2*	37.4	82.2	67.5
New Hampshire	1814[g]	80.8	16.8	76.5	74.2	38.2	86.4*	65.6
Vermont	1812[g]	79.9	—	55.8	50.0	52.5	74.0	65.7
Massachusetts	1812[g]	67.4	29.1	25.7	39.3	45.1	66.4	59.3
Rhode Island	1812[g]	49.4	12.4	18.0	22.4	24.1	33.2	39.8
Connecticut	1819[1]	54.4	14.9	27.1	45.9	52.3	75.7*	76.1
New York	1810[g]	41.5	—	70.4*	72.1	60.2	77.7	73.6
New Jersey	1808[p]	71.8	31.1	70.9	69.0	69.3	80.4*	81.6
Pennsylvania	1808[g]	71.5	19.6	56.6	52.7	53.1	77.4*	75.5
Delaware	1804[g]	81.9	—	—	67.0	69.4	82.8*	85.0
Maryland	1820[1]	69.0	53.7	76.2*	55.6	67.5	84.6	80.3
Virginia	1800[p]	25.9	11.5	27.6*	30.8	35.1	54.6	54.5
North Carolina	1823[c]	70.0#	42.2	56.8	31.7	52.9	83.1*	79.1
Georgia	1812[c]	62.3	—	35.9	33.0	64.9*	88.9	94.0
Kentucky	1820[g]	74.4	25.3	70.7	73.9	61.1	74.3	80.3*
Tennessee	1817[g]	80.0	26.8	49.8	28.8	55.2	89.6*	89.6
Louisiana	1812[g]	34.2	—	36.3*	24.4	19.2	39.4	44.7
Alabama	1819[g]	96.7	52.1	53.6	33.3	65.0	89.8	82.7
Mississippi	1823[g]	79.8	41.6	56.6	32.8	62.8	88.2*	89.7
Ohio	1822[g]	46.5	34.8	75.8*	73.8	75.5	84.5	83.6
Indiana	1822[g]	52.4	37.5	68.3*	61.8	70.1	86.0	84.9
Illinois	1822[g]	55.8	24.2	51.9	45.6	43.7	85.9*	76.3
Missouri	1820[g]	71.9	20.1	54.3	40.8	35.6	74.0*	74.7
Arkansas		—	—	—	—	35.0	86.4	68.8
Michigan		—	—	—	—	35.7	84.9	79.3
National Average			26.5	56.3	54.9	55.2	78.0	74.9

* Exceeded pre-1824 high # Estimate based on incomplete returns
g Gubernatorial election c Congressional election
p Presidential election 1 Election of legislature

magnitude, and that in the opinion of some authorities a "well-developed two party system on a national scale" had been established, there was a slight decline in voter participation. The average for the twenty-three states participating in the presidential contest was 54.9 per cent. In fifteen states a smaller percentage of the adult white males went to the polls in 1832 than in 1828. Only five states bettered their pre-1824 highs. Again the conclusion would be that it was essentially the pre-1824 electorate—diminished in most states and augmented in a few—that voted in 1832. Thus, after three Jackson elections, sixteen states had not achieved the proportions of voter participation that they had reached before 1824. The "new democracy" had not yet made its appearance.

A comparison of the Jackson elections with earlier presidential contests is of some interest. Such comparisons have little validity before 1808 because few states chose electors by popular vote, and for certain of those states the complete returns are not available. In 1816 and 1820 there was so little opposition to Monroe that the voter interest was negligible. The most relevant elections, therefore, are those of 1808 and 1812. The accompanying table (Table 2) gives the percentages of adult white males voting in 1808 and 1812 in those states for which full returns could be found, together with the comparable percentages for the elections of 1824 and 1828. In 1824 only one state—Ohio—surpassed the highs established in either 1808 or 1812. Four more joined this list in 1828—Virginia, Maryland, Pennsylvania, and New Hampshire—although the margin in the last case was so small as to be inconsequential. The most significant conclusion to be drawn from this admittedly limited and unrepresentative data is that in those states where there was a vigorous two-party contest in 1808 and 1812 the vote was relatively high. Conversely, where there was little or no contest in 1824 or 1828, the vote was low.

Table 2

Percentages of Adult White Males Voting in Presidential Elections

State	1808	1812	1824	1828
Maine	Legis.	50.0	18.9	42.7
New Hampshire	62.1	75.4	16.8	76.5
Massachusetts	Legis.	51.4	29.1	25.7
Rhode Island	37.4	37.7	12.4	18.0
New Jersey	71.8	Legis.	31.1	70.9
Pennsylvania	34.7	45.5	19.6	56.6
Maryland	48.4	56.5	53.7	76.2
Virginia	17.7	17.8	11.5	27.6
Ohio	12.8	20.0	34.8	75.8

Note: No complete returns of the popular vote cast for electors in Kentucky or Tennessee in 1808 and 1812 and in North Carolina in 1808 could be located.

When an examination is made of voting in other than presidential elections prior to 1824, the inaccuracy of the impression that "only small numbers of citizens" went to the polls becomes apparent. Because of the almost automatic succession of the members of the "Virginia dynasty" and the early deterioration of the national two-party system that had seemed to be developing around 1800, presidential elections did not arouse voter interest as much as did those for governor, state legislators, or even members of Congress. In such elections at the state level the "common man" was stimulated by local factors to cast his vote, and he frequently responded in higher proportions than he did to the later stimulus provided by Jackson.

The average voter participation for all the states in 1828 was 56.3 per cent. Before 1824 fifteen of the twenty-two states had surpassed that percentage. Among other things, this means that the 1828 election failed to bring to the polls the proportion of the electorate that had voted on occasion in previous elections. There was, in other words, a high potential vote that was frequently realized in state elections but which did not materialize in presidential elections. The unsupported assumption that the common man was either apathetic or debarred from voting by suffrage barriers before 1824 is un- tenable in the light of this evidence.

In state after state (see Table I) gubernatorial elections attracted 70 per cent or more of the adult white males to the polls. Among the notable highs recorded were Delaware with 81.9 per cent in 1804, New Hampshire with 80.8 per cent in 1814, Tennessee with 80.0 per cent in 1817, Vermont with 79.9 per cent in 1812, Mississippi with 79.8 per cent in 1823, and Alabama with a highly improbable 96.7 per cent in its first gubernatorial contest in 1819. There is reason to believe that in some states, at least, the voter participation in the election of state legislators was even higher than in gubernatorial elections. Because of the virtual impossibility of securing county-by-county or district-by-district returns for such elections, this hypothesis is difficult to verify.

Down to this point the voter turnout in the Jackson elections has been compared with that in elections held prior to 1824. Now it becomes appropriate to inquire whether during the period 1824 through 1832 voters turned out in greater proportions for the three presidential contests than they did for the contemporary state elections. If, indeed, this "new democracy" bore some special relationship to Andrew Jackson or to his policies, it might be anticipated that interest in the elections in which he was the central figure would stimulate greater voter participation than gubernatorial contests, in which he was at most a remote factor.

Actually, the election returns show fairly conclusively that throughout the eight-year period the electorate continued to participate more extensively in state elections than in those involving the presidency. Between 1824 and 1832 there were fifty regular gubernatorial elections in the states that chose their electors by popular vote. In only sixteen of these fifty instances did the vote for President surpass the corresponding vote for governor. In Rhode Island, Delaware, Tennessee, Kentucky, Illinois, Mississippi, Missouri, and Georgia the vote for governor consistently exceeded that for President. Only in Connecticut was the reverse true. Viewed from this perspective, too, the remarkable feature of the vote in the Jackson elections is not its immensity but rather its smallness.

Finally, the Jackson elections may be compared with subsequent presidential elections. Once Jackson had retired to the Hermitage, and figures of less dramatic proportions took up the contest for the presidency, did voter participation rise or fall? This question can be answered by observing the percentage of adult white males who voted in each state in the presidential elections of 1836 through 1844 (Table .1). Voter participation in the 1836 election remained near the level that had been established in 1828 and 1832, with 55.2 percent of the adult white males voting. Only five states registered percentages in excess of their pre-1824 highs. But in 1840 the "new democracy" made its appearance with explosive suddenness.

In a surge to the polls that has rarely, if ever, been exceeded in any presidential election, four out of five (78.0 per cent) of the adult white males cast their votes for Harrison or Van Buren. This new electorate was greater than that of the Jackson period by more than 40 per cent. In all but five states— Vermont, Massachusetts, Rhode Island, Kentucky, and Alabama—the peaks of voter participation reached before 1824 were passed. Fourteen of the twenty-five states involved set record highs for voting that were not to be broken throughout the remainder of the ante bellum period. Now, at last, the common man—or at least the man who previously had not been sufficiently aroused to vote in presidential elections—cast his weight into the political balance. This "Tippecanoe democracy," if such a label is permissible, was of a different order of magnitude from the Jacksonian democracy. The elections in which Jackson figured brought to the polls only those men who were accustomed to voting in state or national elections, except in a very few states. The Tippecanoe canvass witnessed an extraordinary expansion of the size of the presidential electorate far beyond previous dimensions. It was in 1840, then, that the "roaring flood of the new democracy" reached its crest. And it engulfed the Jacksonians.

The flood receded only slightly in 1844, when 74.9 per cent of the estimated , potential dectorate went to the polls. Indeed, nine states attained their record highs for the period. In 1848 and 1852 there was a general downward trend in voter participation, followed by a modest upswing in 1856 and 1860. But the level of voter activity remained well above that of the Jackson elections. The conclusion to be drawn is that the "mighty democratic uprising" came after the period of Jackson's presidency.

Now that the quantitative dimensions of Jacksonian democracy as a political phenomenon have been delineated and brought into some appropriate perspective, certain questions still remain to be answered. Granted that the Jacksonian electorate—as revealed by the comparisons that have been set forth—was not really very large, how account for the fact that voter participation doubled between the elections of 1824 and 1828? It is true that the total vote soared from around 359,000 to 1,155,400 and that the percentage of voter participation more than doubled. Traditionally, students of the Jackson period have been impressed by this steep increase in voting and by way of explanation have identified the causal factors as the reduction of suffrage qualifications, the democratic influence of the West, or the personal magnetism of Jackson. The validity of each of these hypotheses needs to be reexamined.

In no one of the states in which electors were chosen by popular vote was any significant change made in suffrage qualifications between 1824 and 1828. Subsequently, severe restrictions were maintained in Rhode Island until 1842, when some liberalization was effected, and in Virginia down to 1850. In Louisiana, where the payment of a tax was a requirement, the character of the state tax system apparently operated to restrict the suffrage at least as late as 1845. Thus with the three exceptions noted, the elimination of suffrage barriers was hardly a factor in producing an enlarged electorate during the Jackson and post-Jackson periods. Furthermore, all but a few states had extended the privilege of voting either to all male taxpayers or to all adult male citizens by 1810. After Connecticut eliminated its property qualification in 1818, Massachusetts in 1821, and New York in 1821 and 1826, only Rhode Island, Virginia, and Louisiana were left on the list of "restrictionist" states. Neither Jackson's victory nor the increased vote in 1828 can be attributed to the presence at the polls of a newly enfranchised mass of voters.

Similarly, it does not appear that the western states led the way in voter participation. Prior to 1824, for example, Ohio, Indiana, and Illinois had never brought to the polls as much as 60 per cent of their adult white males. Most of the eastern states had surpassed that level by considerable margins. In the election of 1828 six states registered votes in excess of 70 per cent of their adult white male populations. They were in order of rank: New Hampshire, Maryland, Ohio, New Jersey, Kentucky, and New York. The six leaders in 1832 were: New Hampshire, Kentucky, Ohio, New York, New Jersey, and Delaware. It will be obvious that the West, however that region may be defined, was not leading the "mighty democratic uprising." Western influences, then, do not explain the increased vote in 1828.

There remains to be considered the factor of Jackson's personal popularity. Did Jackson, the popular hero, attract voters to the polls in unprecedented proportions? The comparisons that have already been made between the Jackson elections and other elections—state and national—before, during, and after his presidency would suggest a negative answer to the question. Granted that a majority of the voters in 1828 favored Jackson, it is not evident that his partisans stormed the polls any more enthusiastically than did the Adams men. Of the six highest states in voter participation in 1828, three favored Adams and three were for Jackson, which could be interpreted to mean that the convinced Adams supporters turned out no less zealously for their man than did the ardent Jacksonians. When Van Buren replaced Jackson in 1836, the voting average increased slightly over 1832. And, as has been demonstrated, the real manifestation of the "new democracy" came not in 1828 but in 1840.

The most satisfactory explanation for the increase in voter participation between 1824 and 1828 is a simple and obvious one. During the long reign of the Virginia dynasty, interest in presidential elections dwindled. In 1816 and 1820 there had been no contest. The somewhat fortuitous termination of the Virginia succession in 1824 and the failure of the congressional caucus to solve the problem of leadership succession threw the choice of a President upon the electorate. But popular interest was dampened by the confusion of choice presented by the multiplicity of candidates, by the disintegration of the old national parties, by the fact that in most states one or another of the candidates was so overwhelmingly popular as to forestall any semblance of a contest, and possibly by the realization that the election would ultimately be decided by the House of Representatives. By 1828 the situation had altered. There were but two candidates in the field, each of whom had substantial sectional backing. A clear-cut contest impended, and the voters became sufficiently aroused to go to the polls in moderate numbers.

One final question remains. Why was the vote in the Jackson elections relatively low when compared with previous and contemporary state elections and with presidential votes after 1840? The answer, in brief, is that in most states either Jackson or his opponent had such a one-sided advantage that the result was a foregone conclusion. Consequently there was little incentive for the voters to go to the polls.

This factor can be evaluated in fairly specific quantitative terms. If the percentage of the total vote secured by each candidate in each state in the election of 1828 is calculated, the difference between the percentages can be used as an index of the closeness, or one-sidedness, of the contest. In Illinois, for example, Jackson received 67 per cent of the total vote and Adams, 33; the difference—thirty-four points—represents the margin between the candidates. The average difference between the candidates, taking all the states together, was thirty-six points. Expressed another way this would mean that in the average state the winning candidate received more than twice the vote of the loser. Actually, this was the case in thirteen of the twenty-two states (see Table 3). Such a wide margin virtually placed these states in f the "no contest" category.

A remarkably close correlation existed between the size of the voter turnout and the relative closeness of the contest. The six states previously listed as having the greatest voter participation in 1828 were among the seven states with the smallest margin of difference between the candidates. The exception was Louisiana, where restrictions on the suffrage curtailed the vote. Even in this instance, however, it is significant that voter participation in Louisiana reached a record high. In those states, then, where there was a close balance of political forces the vote was large, and conversely, where the contest was very one sided, the vote was low.

Most of the states in 1828 were so strongly partial to one or another of the candidates that they can best be characterized as one-party states. Adams encountered little opposition in New England, except in New Hampshire, and Jackson met with hardly any resistance in the South. It was chiefly in the middle states and the older West that the real battle was waged. With the removal of Adams from the scene after 1828, New England became less of a one-party section, but the South remained extremely one sided. Consequently it is not surprising that voter participation in 1832 failed even to match that of 1828.

Here, certainly, is a factor of crucial importance in explaining the dimensions of the voter turnout in the Jackson elections. National parties were still in a rudimentary condition and were highly unbalanced from state to state. Indeed, a two-party system scarcely could be said to exist in more than half of the

Table 3

Differential between Percentages of Total Vote Obtained by Major Presidential Candidates, 1828–1844

State	1828	1832	1836	1840	1844
Maine	20	10	20	1	13
New Hampshire	7	13	50	11	19
Vermont	50	10	20	29	18
Massachusetts	66	30	9	16	12
Rhode Island	50	14	6	23	20
Connecticut	50	20	1	11	5
New York	2	4	9	4	1
New Jersey	4	1	1	4	1
Pennsylvania	33	16	4	1	2
Delaware	—	2	6	10	3
Maryland	2	1	7	8	5
Virginia	38	50	13	1	6
North Carolina	47	70	6	15	5
Georgia	94	100	4	12	4
Kentucky	1	9	6	29	8
Tennessee	90	90	16	11	1
Louisiana	6	38	3	19	3
Alabama	80	100	11	9	18
Mississippi	60	77	2	7	13
Ohio	3	3	4	9	2
Indiana	13	34	12	12	2
Illinois	34	37	10	2	12
Missouri	41	32	21	14	17
Arkansas	—	—	28	13	26
Michigan	—	—	9	4	6
Average Differential	36	36	11	11	9

states until after 1832. Where opposing parties had been formed to contest the election, the vote was large, but where no parties, or only one, took the field, the vote was low. By 1840, fairly well-balanced parties had been organized in virtually every state. In only three states did the margin between Harrison and Van Buren exceed twenty points, and the average for all the states was only eleven points. The result was generally high voter participation.[1]

When Jacksonian democracy is viewed from the perspectives employed in this analysis, its political dimensions in so far as they relate to the behavior of the electorate can be described with some precision. None of the Jackson elections involved a "mighty democratic uprising" in the sense that voters were drawn to the polls in unprecedented proportions. When compared with the peak participation recorded for each state before 1824, or with contemporaneous gubernatorial elections, or most particularly with the vast outpouring of the electorate in 1840, voter participation in the Jackson elections was unimpressive. They key to the relatively low presidential vote would seem to be the extreme political imbalance that existed in most states as between the Jacksonians and their opponents. Associated with this imbalance was the immature development of national political parties. Indeed, it can be highly misleading to think in terms of national parties in connection with the Jackson elections. As balanced, organized parties subsequently made their appearance from state to state, and voters were stimulated by the prospect of a genuine contest, a marked rise in voter participation occurred. Such conditions did not prevail generally across the nation until 1840, and then at last the "mighty democratic uprising" took place.

Note

1.   Careful analysis of the data in Table 3 will suggest that there were three fairly distinct stages in the emergence of a nationally balanced two-party system. Balanced parties appeared first in the middle states between 1824 and 1828. New England remained essentially a one-party section until after Adams had passed from the scene; then competing parties appeared. In the South and the newer West, a one-party dominance continued until divisions arose over who should succeed Jackson. Sectional loyalties to favorite sons obviously exerted a determining influence on presidential politics, and consequently on party formation, in the Jackson years.

POSTSCRIPT

Did the Election of 1828 Represent a Democratic Revolt of the People?

The two essays in this issue discuss the presidential election of 1828 from different approaches. Professor Richard McCormick, a veteran analyzer of nineteenth-century politics, views the 1828 election through the lens of quantitative history. He uses statistics to break down a number of generalizations about the significance of Jackson's election. The Rutgers University professor discounts the removal of property qualifications for voting, the influence of the western states, and the charisma of Jackson as the major reasons why twice as many voters turned out in the 1828 presidential race than they did four years earlier. He argues that in spite of such statistics, a higher percentage of voters had turned out for earlier gubernatorial and legislative elections in most states than for the 1828 presidential election. In McCormick's view, the key election was 1840, not 1828. Why? Because by this time, the two parties—Whigs and Democrats—were equally balanced in all sections of the country, and voters turn out in larger numbers when they perceive a closely contested presidential race.

McCormick's article raises a number of questions. Is he comparing apples and oranges in contrasting local and national elections? Using McCormick's data, is it possible for other historians to reach different conclusions? How does one explain a 50 percent increase in voter turnout between 1824 and 1828?

In the second selection from his Pulitzer Prize–winning book on *The Rise of American Democracy* (W.W. Norton & Co., 2005), Professor Sean Wilentz restores Jackson to the center of the era. He disagrees with McCormick and other historians such as Lee Benson whose *Concept of Jacksonian Democracy: New York as a Test Case* (Princeton Paperback, 1970) stressed ethno-cultural factors in determining voting patterns and removed Jackson from the center of the era. Wilentz disagrees with McCormick and argues that the second-party system started with the presidential election of 1828 when Jackson's personality enabled state coalitions in New York, Ohio, and Kentucky, among others, to organize a national presidential campaign in support of Jackson. McCormick is correct in arguing that some state and local elections prior to 1828 had a larger proportional turnout of voters. But local elections and issues were far more important to a nation barely unified in its transportation and economic systems. Jackson's election and presidency shifted the locus of power to Washington, D.C.

Wilentz's 1,000-page book, which weighs more than *Webster's dictionary,* is especially strong on the development and mobilization of political organizations in the years from Jefferson through Lincoln. His description of the campaign with its sloganeering, mobilization of voters, and mudslinging (Jackson's wife was called a "harlot" and Adams a "pimp), set the tone for the way presidential elections would be run in the future. Contemporaries realized the shift when on inauguration day, March 4, 1829, twenty thousand people from all parts of the country converged on Washington, broke into the White House reception, and cheered wildly for Jackson. Wrote one sour contemporary: "It was like the inundation of the northern barbarians into Rome, save that the tumultuous tide came in from all parts of the compass."

Finally, Wilentz points out that the democratic triumphs led to the rise of "interest group" politics. Men and women, who were outside the normal political process, could use the "new tools" of "a mass press, popular conventions, petition campaigns, and other means to rouse support for . . . such outlandish things as granting women the vote, banning liquor, restricting immigration, and abolishing slavery."

Richard P. McCormick has a full-length study of *The Second American Party System: Party Formation in the Jacksonian Era* (University of North Carolina Press, 1966). A shorter version, "Political Development and the Second Party System" along with other important essays by historians and political scientists, is in William Nisbet Chambers and Water Dean Burnham, eds., *The American Party Systems: Stages of Political Development* (New York, 1967). The fullest account of *The Presidential Election of 1828* (J.P. Lippincott, 1963) is by Jackson's best-known biographer Robert V. Remini. See his shorter version of the "Election of 1828" in Arthur M. Schlesinger, Jr., ed., *The Coming to Power: Critical Presidential Elections in American History* (Chelsea House Publishers, 1971, 1972).

On the political culture of the 1820s and 1830s, see the classic *Andrew Jackson: Symbol for an Age* (Oxford University Press, 1955, 1983) by the late John William Ward. Influencing Wilentz's work were two books on Michigan and Massachusetts politics by Ronald P. Formisano. The first chapter of *The Transformation of Political Culture: Massachusetts Parties, 1790–1840* (Oxford University Press, 1983) talks about how divisions between the "Core and Periphery" destroyed the older form of deferential politics. Daniel Howe's *The Political Culture of American Wings* (University of Chicago Press, 1979) examines the party's pro-business and moralistic outlook.

Useful review essays on the politics of the Jacksonian era are Ronald Formisano, "Toward a Reconstruction of Jacksonian Politics: A Review of the Literature, 1959–1975," *Journal of American History* 63 (1976); Sean Wilentz, "On Class and Politics in Jacksonian America," *Reviews in American History* 10 (1982); Daniel Feller, "Politics and Society: Toward a Jacksonian Synthesis," *Journal of the Early American Republic* 10 (1990); the most recent are the essays by Jonathan Atkins," The Jacksonian Era, 1825–1844" and Jon Ashworth, "The Sectionalization of American Politics, 1845–1860" in *A Companion to 19th-Century America* (Blackwell Publishers, 2001).

Internet References . . .

Birth of a Nation & Antebellum America

This site, maintained by Mike Madin, provides links to a wide assortment of topics from the early national and antebellum eras.

http://www.academicinfo.net/usindnew.html

The Descendants of Mexican War Veterans

An excellent source for the history of the Mexican-American War (1846–1848), which includes images, primary documents, and maps.

http://www.dmwv.org/mexwar/mexwar1.htm

The Atlantic Slave Trade and Slave Life in the Americas: A Visual Record

This site, maintained by Jerome S. Handler and Michael L. Tuite, Jr., is a project of the Virginia Foundation for the Humanities and the Digital Media Lab at the University of Virginia Library. The site includes information and images on various aspects of slave life, including family organization.

http://hitchcock.itc.virginia.edu/Slavery/

Abolitionism, 1830–1850

Another outstanding site from the collections housed at the University of Virginia, which highlights the antislavery protest and includes a number of important abolitionist tracks.

http://www.iath.virginia.edu/utc/abolitn/abhp.html

PART 3

Antebellum America

*P*ressures and trends that began building in the early years of the American nation continued to gather momentum until conflict was almost inevitable. Population growth and territorial expansion brought the country into conflict with other nations. The United States had to respond to challenges from Americans who felt alienated from or forgotten by the new nation because the ideals of human rights and democratic participation that guided the founding of the nation had been applied only to selected segments of the population.

- Did the Industrial Revolution Provide More Economic Opportunities for Women in the 1830s?

- Did Slavery Destroy the Black Family?

- Was the Mexican War an Exercise in American Imperialism?

- Were the Abolitionists "Unrestrained Fanatics"?

ISSUE 12

Did the Industrial Revolution Provide More Economic Opportunities for Women in the 1830s?

YES: Thomas Dublin, from "Women, Work, and Protest in the Early Lowell Mills: 'The Oppressing Hand of Avarice Would Enslave Us'," *Labor History* (Winter 1975)

NO: Gerda Lerner, from "The Lady and the Mill Girl: Changes in the Status of Women in the Age of Jackson," *American Studies* (Spring 1969)

ISSUE SUMMARY

YES: Professor Thomas Dublin argues that the women who worked in the Lowell mills in the 1830s were a close-knit community who developed bonds of mutual dependence in both their boarding houses and the factory.

NO: According to Professor Gerda Lerner, while Jacksonian democracy provided political and economic opportunities for men, both the "lady" and the "mill girl" were equally disenfranchised and isolated from vital centers of economic opportunity.

In 1961 President John F. Kennedy established the Commission on the Status of Women to examine "the prejudice and outmoded customs that act as barriers to the full realization of women's basic rights." The roots of Friedan's "feminine mystique" go back much earlier than the post–World War II "baby boom" generation of suburban America. Women historians have traced the origins of the modern family to the early nineteenth century. As the nation became more stable politically, the roles of men, women, and children became segmented in ways that still exist today.

In nineteenth-century America, most middle-class white women stayed home. Those who entered the workforce as teachers or became reformers were usually extending the values of the Cult of True Womanhood to the outside world. This was true of the women reformers in the Second Great Awakening and the peace, temperance, and abolitionist movements before the Civil War. The first real challenge to the traditional values system occurred when a handful of women showed up at Seneca Falls, New York, in 1848 to sign the Women's Declaration of Rights.

It soon became clear that if they were going to pass reform laws, women would have to obtain the right to vote. After an intense struggle the Nineteenth Amendment was ratified on August 26, 1920. Once the women's movement obtained the vote, there was no agreement on future goals. The problems of the Great Depression and World War II overrode women's issues.

World War II brought about major changes for working women. Six million women entered the labor force for the first time, many of whom were married. "The proportion of women in the labor force," writes Lois Banner, "increased from 25 percent in 1940 to 36 percent in 1945." Many women moved into high-paying, traditionally men's jobs as policewomen, firefighters, and precision toolmakers. The federal government also erected federal child-care facilities, but when the war ended in 1945 many working women lost their nontraditional jobs. The federal day-care program was eliminated, and the government told women to go home even though a 1944 study by the Women's Bureau concluded that 80 percent of working women wanted to continue in their jobs after the war. Most history texts emphasized that women did return home, moved to the suburbs, and created a baby boom generation, which reversed the downward size of families between 1946 and 1964. What is lost in this description is the fact that after 1947 the number of working women again began to rise. By 1951 the proportion had reached 31 percent. Twenty-two years later, at the height of the women's liberation movement, it reached 42 percent.

Ironically modern feminists were unaware of their past. But the situation changed rapidly. The women's movement brought a new wave of female scholars into the profession who were interested in researching and writing about their past.

Issue 12 brings us back to the 1830s when the textile mills along the river systems of Rhode Island, Connecticut, and Massachusetts created the first factory system. Did this "market revolution," a term now favored by current historians, help or hinder the economic opportunities for women?

In the first selection, Professor Thomas Dublin sees positive changes taking place in the lives of the mill girls. He maintains that the girls who worked in the Lowell, Massachusetts factories in the 1830s were a close-knit community of young women who developed bonds of mutual dependence in both their boarding houses and the factory. But Professor Gerda Lerner disagrees. The Jacksonian era may have provided political and economic opportunities for men, but it was different for women. By the 1850s, immigrant women from Ireland had replaced the native-born Lowell females in the low-wage factories while middle-class women were excluded from the medical, legal, and business professions.

YES

Thomas Dublin

Women, Work, and Protest in the Early Lowell Mills: "The Oppressing Hand of Avarice Would Enslave Us"

In the years before 1850 the textile mills of Lowell, Massachusetts were a celebrated economic and cultural attraction. Foreign visitors invariably included them on their American tours. Interest was prompted by the massive scale of these mills, the astonishing productivity of the power-driven machinery, and the fact that women comprised most of the workforce. Visitors were struck by the newness of both mills and city as well as by the culture of the female operatives. The scene stood in sharp contrast to the gloomy mill towns of the English industrial revolution.

Lowell, was, in fact, an impressive accomplishment. In 1820, there had been no city at all—only a dozen family farms along the Merrimack River in East Chelmsford. In 1821, however, a group of Boston capitalists purchased land and water rights along the river and a nearby canal, and began to build a major textile manufacturing center. Opening two years later, the first factory employed Yankee women recruited from the nearby countryside. Additional mills were constructed until, by 1840, ten textile corporations with thirty-two mills valued at more than ten million dollars lined the banks of the river and nearby canals. Adjacent to the mills were rows of company boarding houses and tenements which accommodated most of the eight thousand factory operatives.

As Lowell expanded, and became the nation's largest textile manufacturing center, the experiences of women operatives changed as well. The increasing number of firms in Lowell and in the other mill towns brought the pressure of competition. Overproduction became a problem and the prices of finished cloth decreased. The high profits of the early years declined and so, too, did conditions for the mill operatives. Wages were reduced and the pace of work within the mills was stepped up. Women operatives did not accept these changes without protest. In 1834 and 1836 they went on strike to protest wage cuts, and between 1843 and 1848 they mounted petition campaigns aimed at reducing the hours of labor in the mills.

From *History Labor*, Vol. 16, no. 1, Winter 1975, pp. 99–116. Copyright © 1975 by Taylor & Francis, Ltd. Reprinted by permission.

These labor protests in early Lowell contribute to our understanding of the response of workers to the growth of industrial capitalism in the first half of the nineteenth century. They indicate the importance of values and attitudes dating back to an earlier period and also the transformation of these values in a new setting.

The major factor in the rise of a new consciousness among operatives in Lowell was the development of a close-knit community among women working in the mills. The structure of work and the nature of housing contributed to the growth of this community. The existence of community among woman, in turn, was an important element in the repeated labor protests of the period.

The organization of this paper derives from the logic of the above argument. It will examine the basis of community in the experiences of women operatives and then the contribution that the community of women made to the labor protests in these years as well as the nature of the new consciousness expressed by these protests.

The pre-conditions for the labor unrest in Lowell before 1850 may be found in the study of the daily worklife of its operatives. In their everyday, relatively conflict-free lives, mill women created the mutual bonds which made possible united action in times of crisis. The existence of a tight-knit community among them was the most important element in determining the collective, as opposed to individual, nature of this response.

Before examining the basis of community among women operatives in early Lowell, it may be helpful to indicate in what sense "community" is being used. The women are considered a "community" because of the development of bonds of mutual dependence among them. In this period they came to depend upon one another and upon the larger group of operatives in very important ways. Their experiences were not simply similar or parallel to one another, but were inextricably intertwined. Furthermore, they were conscious of the existence of community, expressing it very clearly in their writings and in labor protests. "Community" for them had objective and subjective dimensions and both were important in their experience of women in the mills.

The mutual dependence among women in early Lowell was rooted in the structure of mill work itself. Newcomers to the mills were particularly dependent on their fellow operatives, but even experienced hands relied on one another for considerable support.

New operatives generally found their first experiences difficult, even harrowing, though they may have already done considerable hand-spinning and weaving in their own homes. The initiation of one of them is described in fiction in the *Lowell Offering:*

> The next morning she went into the Mill; and at first the sight of so many bands, and wheels, and springs in constant motion, was very frightful. She felt afraid to touch the loom, and she was almost sure she could never learn to weave . . . the shuttle flew out, and made a new bump on her head; and the first time she tried to spring the lathe, she broke out a quarter of the treads.

While other accounts present a somewhat less difficult picture, most indicate that women only became proficient and felt satisfaction in their work after several months in the mills.

The textile corporations made provisions to ease the adjustment of new operatives. Newcomers were not immediately expected to fit into the mill's regular work routine. They were at first assigned work as sparehands and were paid a daily wage independent of the quantity of work they turned out. As a sparehand, the newcomer worked with an experienced hand who instructed her in the intricacies of the job. The sparehand spelled her partner for short stretches of time, and occasionally took the place of an absentee. One woman described the learning process in a letter reprinted in the *Offering*:

> Well, I went into the mill, and was put to learn with a very patient girl. . . . You cannot think how odd everything seems. . . . They set me to threading shuttles, and tying weaver's knots, and such things, and now I have improved so that I can take care of one loom. I could take care of two if only I had eyes in the back part of my head. . . .

After the passage of some weeks or months, when she could handle the normal complement of machinery—two looms for weavers during the 1830s—and when a regular operative departed, leaving an opening, the sparehand moved into a regular job.

Through this system of job training, the textile corporations contributed to the development of community among female operatives. During the most difficult period in an operative's career, the first months in the mill, she relied upon other women workers for training and support. And for every sparehand whose adjustment to mill work was aided in this process, there was an experienced operative whose work was also affected. Women were relating to one another during the work process and not simply tending their machinery. Given the high rate of turnover in the mill workforce, a large proportion of women operatives worked in pairs. At the Hamilton Company in July 1836, for example, more than a fifth of all females on the Company payroll were sparehands. Consequently, over forty per cent of the females employed there in this month worked with one another. Nor was this interaction surreptitious, carried out only when the overseer looked elsewhere; rather it was formally organized and sanctioned by the textile corporations themselves.

In addition to the integration of sparehands, informal sharing of work often went on among regular operatives. A woman would occasionally take off a half or full day from work either to enjoy a brief vacation or to recover from illness, and fellow operatives would each take an extra loom or side of spindles so that she might continue to earn wages during her absence. Women were generally paid on a piece rate basis, their wages being determined by the total output of the machinery they tended during the payroll period. With friends helping out during her absence, making sure that her looms kept running, an operative could earn almost a full wage even though she was not physically present. Such informal work-sharing was another way in which mutual dependence developed among women operatives during their working hours.

Living conditions also contributed to the development of community among female operatives. Most women working in the Lowell mills of these years were housed in company boarding houses. In July 1836, for example, more than 73 percent of females employed by the Hamilton Company resided in company housing adjacent to the mills. Almost three-fourths of them, therefore, lived and worked with each other. Furthermore, the work schedule was such that women had little opportunity to interact with those not living in company dwellings. They worked, in these years, an average of 73 hours a week. Their work day ended at 7:00 or 7:30 P.M., and in the hours between supper and the 10:00 curfew imposed by management on residents of company boarding houses there was little time to spend with friends living "off the corporation."

Women in the boarding houses lived in close quarters, a factor that also played a role in the growth of community. A typical boarding house accommodated twenty-five young women, generally crowded four to eight in a bedroom. There was little possibility of privacy within the dwelling, and pressure to conform to group standards was very strong (as will be discussed below). The community of operatives which developed in the mills it follows, carried over into life at home as well.

The boarding house became a central institution in the lives of Lowell's female operatives in these years, but it was particularly important in the initial integration of newcomers into urban industrial life. Upon first leaving her rural home for work in Lowell, a woman entered a setting very different from anything she had previously known. One operative, writing in the *Offering*, described the feelings of a fictional character: ". . . the first entrance into a factory boarding house seemed something dreadful. The room looked strange and comfortless, and the women cold and heartless; and when she sat down to the supper table, where among more than twenty girls, all but one were strangers, she could not eat a mouthfull."

In the boarding house, the newcomer took the first steps in the process which transformed her from an "outsider" into an accepted member of the community of women operatives.

Recruitment of newcomers into the mills and their initial hiring was mediated through the boarding house system. Women generally did not travel to Lowell for the first time entirely on their own. They usually came because they knew someone—an older sister, cousin, or friend—who had already worked in Lowell. The scene described above was a lonely one—but the newcomer did know at least one boarder among the twenty seated around the supper table. The Hamilton Company Register Books indicated that numerous pairs of operatives, having the same surname and coming from the same town in northern New England, lived in the same boarding houses. If the newcomer was not accompanied by a friend or relative, she was usually directed to "Number 20, Hamilton Company," or to a similar address of one of the other corporations where her acquaintance lived. Her first contact with fellow operatives generally came in the boarding houses and not in the mills. Given the personal nature of recruitment in this period, therefore, newcomers usually had the company and support of a friend or relative in their first adjustment to Lowell.

Like recruitment, the initial hiring was a personal process. Once settled in the boarding house a newcomer had to find a job. She would generally go to the mills with her friend or with the boarding house keeper who would introduce her to an overseer in one of the rooms. If he had an opening, she might start work immediately. More likely, the overseer would know of an opening elsewhere in the mill, or would suggest that something would probably develop within a few days. In one story in the *Offering*, a newcomer worked on some quilts for her house keeper, thereby earning her board while she waited for a job opening.

Upon entering the boarding house, the newcomer came under pressure to conform with the standards of the community of operatives. Stories in the *Offering* indicate that newcomers at first stood out from the group in terms of their speech and dress. Over time, they dropped the peculiar "twang" in their speech which so amused experienced hands. Similarly, they purchased clothing more in keeping with urban than rural styles. It was an unusual and strong-willed individual who could work and live among her fellow operatives and not conform, at least outwardly, to the customs and values of this larger community.

The boarding houses were the centers of social life for women operatives after their long days in the mills. There they ate their meals, rested, talked, sewed, wrote letters, read books and magazines. From among fellow workers and boarders they found friends who accompanied them to shops, to Lyceum lectures, to church and church-sponsored events. On Sundays or holidays, they often took walks along the canals or out into the nearby countryside. The community of women operatives, in sum, developed in a setting where women worked and lived together, twenty-four hours a day.

Given the all-pervasiveness of this community, one would expect it to exert strong pressures on those who did not conform to group standards. Such appears to have been the case. The community influenced newcomers to adopt its patterns of speech and dress as described above. In addition, it enforced an unwritten code of moral conduct. Henry Miles, a minister in Lowell, described the way in which the community pressured those who deviated from accepted moral conduct:

> A girl, suspected of immoralities, or serious improprieties, at once loses caste. Her fellow boarders will at once leave the house, if the keeper does not dismiss the offender. In self-protection, therefore, the patron is obliged to put the offender away. Nor will her former companions walk with her, or work with her; till at length, finding herself everywhere talked about, and pointed at, and shunned, she is obliged to relieve her fellow-operatives of a presence which they feel brings disgrace.

The power of the peer group described by Miles may seem extreme, but there is evidence in the writing of women operatives to corroborate his account. Such group pressure is illustrated by a story (in the *Offering*)—in which, operatives in a company boarding house begin to harbor suspicions about a fellow boarder, Hannah, who received repeated evening visits from a man whom she does not introduce to the other residents. Two boarders declare that they will leave if she is allowed to remain in the household. The house keeper finally informed Hannah that she must either depart or not see the man again. She does not accept the ultimatum, but is promptly discharged after the overseer is informed, by one of the boarders, about her conduct. And, only one of Hannah's former friends continues to remain on cordial terms.

One should not conclude, however, that women always enforced a moral code agreeable to Lowell's clergy, or to the mill agents and overseers for that matter. After all, the kind of peer pressure imposed on Hannah could be brought to bear on women in 1834 and 1836 who on their own would not have protested wage cuts. It was much harder to go to work when one's room-mates were marching about town, attending rallies, circulating strike petitions. Similarly, the ten-hour petitions of the 1840s were certainly aided by the fact of a tight-knit community of operatives living in a dense neighborhood of boarding houses. To the extent that women could not have completely private lives in the boarding houses, they probably had to conform to group norms, whether these involved speech, clothing, relations with men, or attitudes toward the ten-hour day. Group pressure to conform, so important to the community of women in early Lowell, played a significant role in the collective response of women to changing conditions in the mills.

In addition to the structure of work and housing in Lowell, a third factor, the homogeneity of the mill workforce, contributed to the development of community among female operatives. In this period the mill workforce was homogeneous in terms of sex, nativity, and age. Payroll and other records of the Hamilton Company reveal that more than 85 per cent of those employed in July, 1836, were women and that over 96 per cent were native-born. Furthermore, over 80 per cent of the female workforce was between the ages of 15 and 30 years old; and only ten per cent was under 15 or over 40.

Workforce homogeneity takes on particular significance in the context of work structure and the nature of worker housing. These three factors combined meant that women operatives had little interaction with men during their daily lives. Men and women did not perform the same work in the mills, and generally did not even labor in the same rooms. Men worked in the picking and initial carding processes, in the repair shop and on the watchforce, and filled all supervisory positions in the mills. Women held all sparehand and regular operative jobs in drawing, speeding, spinning, weaving and dressing. A typical room in the mill employed eighty women tending machinery, with two men overseeing the work and two boys assisting them. Women had little contact with men other than their supervisors in the course of the working day. After work, women returned to their boarding houses, where once again there were few men. Women, then, worked and lived in a predominantly female setting.

Ethnically the workforce was also homogeneous. Immigrants formed only 3.4 per cent of those employed at Hamilton in July, 1836. In addition, they comprised only 3 per cent of residents in Hamilton company housing. The community of women operatives was composed of women of New England stock drawn from the hill-country farms surrounding Lowell. Consequently, when experienced hands made fun of the speech and dress of newcomers, it was understood that they, too, had been "rusty" or "rustic" upon first coming to Lowell. This common background was another element shared by women workers in early Lowell.

The work structure, the workers' housing, and workforce homogeneity were the major elements which contributed to the growth of community among Lowell's women operatives. To best understand the larger implications of community it is necessary to examine the labor protests of this period. For in these struggles, the new values and attitudes which developed in the community of women operatives are most visible.

II

In February, 1834, 800 of Lowell's women operatives "turned-out"—went on strike—to protest a proposed reduction in their wages. They marched to numerous mills in an effort to induce others to join them; and, at an outdoor rally, they petitioned others to discontinue their labors until terms of reconciliation are made. Their petition concluded:

> Resolved, That we will not go back into the mills to work unless our wages are continued . . . as they have been.
> Resolved, That none of us will go back, unless they receive us all as one.
> Resolved, That if any have not money enough to carry them home, they shall be supplied.

The strike proved to be brief and failed to reverse the proposed wage reductions. Turning-out on a Friday, the striking women were paid their back wages on Saturday, and by the middle of the next week had returned to work or left town. Within a week of the turn-out, the mills were running near capacity.

This first strike in Lowell, is important not because it failed or succeeded, but simply because it took place. In an era in which women had to overcome opposition simply to work in the mills, it is remarkable that they would further overstep the accepted middle-class bounds of female propriety by participating in a public protest. The agents of the textile mills certainly considered the turn-out unfeminine. William Austin, agent of the Lawrence Company, described the operatives' procession as an "amizonian [sic] display." He wrote further, in a letter to his company treasurer in Boston: "This afternoon we have paid off several of these Amazons & presume that they will leave town on Monday." The turn-out was particularly offensive to the agents because of the relationship they thought they had with their operatives. William Austin probably expressed the feelings of other agents when he wrote: ". . . notwithstanding the friendly and disinterested advice which has been on all proper occassions [sic] communicated to the girls of the Lawrence mills a spirit of evil omen . . . has prevailed, and overcome the judgement and discretion of too many, and this morning a general turn-out from most of the rooms has been the consequence."

Mill agents assumed an attitude of benevolent paternalism toward their female operatives, and found it particularly disturbing that the women paid such little heed to their advice. The strikers were not merely unfeminine, they were ungrateful as well.

Such attitudes not withstanding, women chose to turn-out. They did so for two principal reasons. First, the wage cuts undermined the sense of dignity and social equality which was an important element in their Yankee heritage. Second, these wage cuts were seen as an attack on their economic independence.

Certainly a prime motive for the strike was outrage at the social implications of the wage cuts. In a statement of principles accompanying the petition which was circulated among operatives, women expressed well the sense of themselves which prompted their protest of these wage cuts:

Union Is Power

Our present object if to have union and exertion, and we remain in possession of our unquestionable rights. We circulate this paper wishing to obtain the names of all who imbibe the spirit of our Patriotic Ancestors, who preferred privation to bondage, and parted with all that renders life desirable—and even life itself—to procure independence for their children. The oppressing hand of avarice would enslave us, and to gain their object, they gravely tell us of the pressure of the time, this we are already sensible of, and deplore it. If any are in want of assistance, the Ladies will be compassionate and assist them; but we prefer to have the disposing of our charities in our own hands; and as we are free, we would remain in possession of what kind Providence has bestowed upon us; and remain daughters of freemen still.

At several points in the proclamation the women drew on their Yankee heritage. Connecting their turn-out with the efforts of their "Patriotic Ancestors" to secure independence from England, they interpreted the wage cuts as an effort to "enslave" them—to deprive them of their independent status as "daughters of freemen."

Though very general and rhetorical, the statement of these women does suggest their sense of self, of their own worth and dignity. Elsewhere, they expressed the conviction that they were the social equals of the overseers, indeed of the mill-owners themselves. The wage cuts, however struck at this assertion of social equality. These reductions made it clear that the operatives were subordinate to their employers, rather than equal partners in a contract binding on both parties. By turning-out the women emphatically denied that they were subordinates; but by returning to work the next week, they demonstrated that in economic terms they were no match for their corporate superiors.

In point of fact, these Yankee operatives were subordinate in early Lowell's social and economic order, but they never consciously accepted this status. Their refusal to do so became evident whenever the mill owners attempted to exercise the power they possessed. This fundamental contradiction between the objective status of operatives and their consciousness of it was at the root of the 1834 turn-out and of subsequent labor protests in Lowell before 1850. The corporations could build mills, create thousands of jobs, and recruit women to fill them. Nevertheless, they bought only the workers' labor power, and then only for as long as these workers chose to stay. Women could always return to their rural homes, and they had a sense of their own worth and dignity, factors limiting the actions of management.

Women operatives viewed the wage cuts as a threat to their economic independence. This independence had two related dimensions. First, the women were self-supporting while they worked in the mills and, consequently, were independent of their families back home. Second, they were able to save out of their monthly earnings and could then leave the mills for the old homestead whenever they so desired. In effect, they were not totally dependent upon mill work. Their independence was based largely on the high level of wages in the mills. They could support themselves and still save enough to return home periodically. The wage cuts threatened to deny them this outlet, substituting instead the prospect of total dependence on mill work. Small wonder, then, there was alarm that "the oppressing hand of avarice would enslave us." To be forced, out of economic necessity, to lifelong labor in the mills would have indeed seemed like slavery. The Yankee operatives spoke directly to the fear of a dependency based on impoverishment when offering to assist any women workers who "have not money enough to carry them home." Wage reductions, however, offered only the *prospect* of a future dependence on mill employment. By striking, the women asserted their actual economic independence of the mills and their determination to remain "daughters of freemen still."

While the women's traditional conception of themselves as independent daughters of freemen played a major role in the turn-out, this factor acting alone would not necessarily have triggered the 1834 strike. It would have led women as individuals to quit work and return to their rural homes. But the turn-out was a collective protest. When it was announced that wage reductions were being considered, women began to hold meetings in the mills during meal breaks in order to assess tactical possibilities. Their turn-out began at one mill when the agent discharged a woman who had presided at such a meeting. Their procession through the streets passed by other mills, expressing a conscious effort to enlist as much support as possible for their cause. At a mass meeting, the women drew up a resolution which insisted that none be discharged for their participation in the turn-out. This strike, then, was a collective response to the proposed wage cuts—made possible because women had come to form a "community" of operatives in the mill, rather than simply a group of individual workers. The existence of such a tight-knit community turned individual opposition of the wage cuts into a collective protest.

In October, 1836, women again went on strike. This second turn-out was similar to the first in several respects. Its immediate cause was also a wage reduction; marches and a large outdoor rally were organized; again, like the earlier protest, the basic goal was not achieved; the corporations refused to restore wages; and operatives either left Lowell or returned to work at the new rates.

Despite these surface similarities between the turn-outs, there were some real differences. One involved scale: over 1500 operatives turned out in 1836, compared to only 800 earlier. Moreover, the second strike lasted much longer than the first. In 1834 operatives stayed out for only a few days; in 1836, the mills ran far below capacity for several months. Two weeks after the second turn-out began, a mill agent reported that only a fifth of the strikers had returned to work: "The rest manifest *good 'spunk'* as they call it." Several days later he described the impact of the continuing strike on operations in his mills: "we must be feeble for months to come as probably not less than 250 of our former scanty supply of help have left town." These lines read in sharp contrast to the optimistic reports of agents following the turnout in February, 1834.

Differences between the two turn-outs were not limited to the increased scale and duration of the later one. Women displayed a much higher degree of organization in 1836 than earlier. To co-ordinate strike activities, they formed a Factory Girls' Association. According to one historian, membership in the short-lived association reached 2500 at its height. The larger organization among women was reflected in the tactics employed. Strikers, according to one mill agent, were able to halt production to a greater extent than numbers alone could explain; and, he complained, although some operatives were willing to work, "it has been impossible to give employment to many who remained." He attributed this difficulty to the strikers' tactics: "This was in many instances no doubt the result of calculation and contrivance. After the original turn-out they, [the operatives] would assail a particular room—as for instance, all the warpers, or all the warp spinners, or all the speeder and stretcher girls, and this would close the mill as effectually as if all the girls in the mill had left."

Now giving more thought than they had in 1834 to the specific tactics of the turn-out, the women made a deliberate effort to shut down the mills in order to win their demands. They attempted to persuade less committed operatives, concentrating on those in crucial departments within the mill. Such tactics anticipated those of skilled mulespinners and loomfixers who went out on strike in the 1880s and 1890s.

In their organization of a Factory Girl's Association and in their efforts to shut down the mills, the female operatives revealed that they had been changed by their industrial experience. Increasingly, they acted not simply as "daughters of freemen" offended by the impositions of the textile corporations, but also as industrial workers intent on improving their position within the mills.

There was a decline in protest among women in the Lowell mills following these early strike defeats. During the 1837–1843 depression, textile corporations twice reduced wages without evoking a collective response from operatives. Because of the frequency of production cutbacks and lay-offs in these years, workers probably accepted the mill agents' contention that they had to reduce wages or close entirely. But with the return of prosperity and the expansion of production in the mid-1840's, there were renewal labor protests among women. Their actions paralleled those of working men and reflected fluctuations in the business cycle. Prosperity itself did not prompt turn-outs, but it evidently facilitated collective actions by women operatives.

In contrast to the protests of the previous decade, the struggles now were primarily political. Women did not turn-out in the 1840s; rather, they mounted annual petition campaigns calling on the State legislature to limit the hours of labor within the mills. These campaigns reached their height in 1845 and 1846, when 2,000 and 5,000 operatives respectively signed petitions. Unable to curb the wage cuts, or the speed-up and stretch-out imposed by mill owners, operatives sought to mitigate the consequences of these changes by reducing the length of the working day. Having been defeated earlier in economic struggles, they now sought to achieve their new goal through political action. The Ten Hour Movement, seen in these terms, was a logical outgrowth of the unsuccessful turn-outs of the previous decade. Like the earlier struggles, the Ten Hour Movement was an assertion of the dignity of operatives and an attempt to maintain that dignity under the changing conditions of industrial capitalism.

The growth of relatively permanent labor organizations and institutions among women was a distinguishing feature of the Ten Hour Movement of the 1840s. The Lowell Female Labor Reform Association was organized in 1845 by women operatives, It became Lowell's leading organization over the next three years, organizing the city's female operatives and helping to set up branches in other mill towns. The Association was affiliated with the New England Workingmen's Association and sent delegates to its meetings. It acted in concert with similar male groups, and yet maintained its own autonomy. Women elected their own officers, held their own meetings, testified before a state legislative committee, and published a series of "Factory Tracts" which exposed conditions within the mills and argued for the ten-hour day.

An important educational and organizing tool of the Lowell Female Labor Reform Association was the *Voice of Industry*, a labor weekly published in Lowell between 1845 and 1848 by the New England Workingmen's Association. Female operatives were involved in every aspect of its publication and used the *Voice* to further the Ten Hour Movement among women. Their Association owned the press on which the *Voice* was printed. Sarah Bagley, the Association president, was a member of the three-person publishing committee of the *Voice* and for a time served as editor. Other women were employed by the paper as travelling editors. They wrote articles about the Ten Hour Movement in other mill towns, in an effort to give ten-hour supporters a sense of the larger cause of which they were a part. Furthermore, they raised money for the *Voice* and increased its circulation by selling subscriptions to the paper in their travels about New England. Finally, women used the *Voice* to appeal directly to their fellow operatives. They edited a separate "Female Department," which published letters and articles by and about women in the mills.

Another aspect of the Ten Hour Movement which distinguished it from the earlier labor struggles in Lowell was that it involved both men and women. At the same time that women in Lowell formed the Female Labor Reform Association, a male mechanics' and laborers' association was also organized. Both groups worked to secure the passage of legislation setting ten hours as the length of the working day. Both groups circulated petitions to this end and when the legislative committee came to Lowell to hear testimony, both men and women testified in favor of the ten-hour day.

The two groups, then, worked together, and each made an important contribution to the movement in Lowell. Women had the numbers, comprising as they did over eighty per cent of the mill workforce. Men, on the other hand, had the votes, and since the Ten Hour Movement was a political struggle, they played a crucial part. After the State committee reported unfavorably on the ten-hour petitions, the Female Labor Reform Association denounced the committee chairman, a State representative from Lowell, as a corporation "tool." Working for his defeat at the polls, they did so successfully and then passed the following post-election resolution: "*Resolved,* That the members of this Association tender their grateful acknowledgments to the voters of Lowell, for consigning William Schouler to the obscurity he so justly deserves. . . ." Women took a more prominent part in the Ten Hour Movement in Lowell than did men, but they obviously remained dependent on male voters and legislators for the ultimate success of their movement.

Although co-ordinating their efforts with those of working men, women operatives organized independently within the Ten Hour Movement. For instance, in 1845 two important petitions were sent from Lowell to the State legislature. Almost ninety per cent of the signers of one petition were females, and more than two-thirds of the signers of the second were males. Clearly the separation of men and women in their daily lives was reflected in the Ten Hour petitions of these years.

The way in which the Ten Hour Movement was carried from Lowell to other mill towns also illustrated the independent organizing of women within the larger movement. For example, at a spirited meeting in Manchester, New Hampshire in December, 1845—one presided over by Lowell operatives—more than a thousand workers, two-thirds of them women, passed resolutions calling for the ten-hour day. Later, those in attendance divided along male-female lines each meeting separately to set up parallel organizations. Sixty women joined the Manchester Female Labor Reform Association that evening, and by the following summer it claimed over three hundred members. Female operatives met in company boarding houses to involve new women in the movement. In their first year of organizing, Manchester workers obtained more than 4,000 signatures on ten-hour petitions. While men and women were both active in the movement, they worked through separate institutional structures from the outset.

The division of men and women within the Ten Hour Movement also reflected their separate daily lives in Lowell and in other mill towns. To repeat, they held different jobs in the mills and had little contact apart from the formal, structured overseer-operative relation. Outside the mill, we have noted, women tended to live in female boarding houses provided by the corporations and were isolated from men, Consequently, the experiences of women in 'these early' mill towns were different from those of men, and in the course of their daily lives they came to form a close-knit community. It was logical that women's participation in the Ten Hour Movement mirrored this basic fact.

The women's Ten Hour Movement, like the earlier turnouts, was based in part on the participants' sense of their own worth and dignity as daughters of freemen. At the same time, however, also indicated the growth of a new consciousness. It reflected a mounting, feeling of community among women operatives and a realization that their interests and those of their employers were not identical, that they had to rely on themselves and not on corporate benevolence to achieve a reduction in the hours of labor. One woman, in an open letter to a State legislator, expressed this rejection of middle-class paternalism: "Bad as is the condition of so many women, it would be much worse if they had nothing but your boasted protection to rely upon; but they have at last learnt the lesson which a bitter experience teaches, that not to those who style themselves their "natural protectors" are they to look for the needful help, but to the strong and resolute of their own sex. Such an attitude, underlying the self-organizing of women in the ten-hour petition campaigns, was clearly the product of the industrial experience in Lowell.

Both the early turn-outs and the Ten Hour Movement were, as noted above, in large measure dependent upon the existence of a close-knit community of women operatives. Such a community was based on the work structure, the nature of worker housing, and workforce homogeneity. Women were drawn together by the initial job training of newcomers; by the informal work sharing among experienced hands, by living in company boarding houses, by sharing religious, educational, and social activities in their leisure hours. Working and living in a new and alien setting, they came to rely upon one another for friendship and support. Understandably, a community feeling developed among them.

This evolving community as well as the common cultural traditions which Yankee women carried into Lowell were major elements that governed their response to changing mill conditions. The pre-industrial tradition of independence and self-respect made them particularly sensitive to management labor policies. The sense of community enabled them to transform their individual opposition to wage cuts and to the increasing pace of work into public protest. In these labor struggles women operatives expressed a new consciousness of their rights both as workers and as women. Such a consciousness, like the community of women itself, was one product of Lowell's industrial revolution.

The experiences of Lowell women before 1850 present a fascinating picture of the contradictory impact of industrial capitalism. Repeated labor protests reveal that female operatives felt the demands of mill employment to be oppressive. At the same time, however, the mills, provided women with work outside of the home and family, thereby offering them an unprecedented. That they came to challenge employer paternalism was a direct consequence of the increasing opportunities offered them in these years. The Lowell mills both exploited and liberated women in ways unknown to the preindustrial political economy.

Gerda Lerner

The Lady and the Mill Girl: Changes in the Status of Women in the Age of Jackson

The period 1800–1840 is one in which decisive changes occurred in the status of American women. It has remained surprisingly unexplored. With the exception of a recent, unpublished dissertation by Keith Melder and the distinctive work of Elisabeth Dexter, there is a dearth of descriptive material and an almost total absence of interpretation. Yet the period offers essential clues to an understanding of later institutional developments, particularly the shape and nature of the woman's rights movement. This analysis will consider the economic, political, and social status of women and examine the changes in each area. It will also attempt an interpretation of the ideological shifts which occurred in American society concerning the "proper" role for women.

Periodization always offers difficulties. It seemed useful here, for purposes of comparison, to group women's status before 1800 roughly under the "colonial" heading and ignore the transitional and possibly atypical shifts which occurred during the American Revolution and the early period of nationhood. Also, regional differences were largely ignored. The South was left out of consideration entirely because its industrial development occurred later.

The status of colonial women has been well studied and described and can briefly be summarized for comparison with the later period. Throughout the colonial period there was a marked shortage of women, which varied with the regions and always was greatest in the frontier areas. This (from the point of view of women) favorable sex ratio enhanced their status and position. The Puritan world view regarded idleness as sin; life in an underdeveloped country made it absolutely necessary that each member of the community perform an economic function. Thus work for women, married or single, was not only approved, it was regarded as a civic duty. Puritan town councils expected single girls, widows, and unattached women to be self-supporting and for a long time provided needy spinsters with parcels of land. There was no social sanction against married women working; on the contrary, wives were expected to help their husbands in their trade and won social approval for doing extra work in or out of the home. Needy children, girls as well as boys, were indentured or apprenticed and were expected to work for their keep.

The vast majority of women worked within their homes, where their labor produced most articles needed for the family. The entire colonial production of cloth and clothing and in part that of shoes was in the hands of women. In addition to these occupations, women were found in many different kinds of employment. They were butchers, silversmiths, gunsmiths, upholsterers. They ran mills, plantations, tan yards, shipyards, and every kind of shop, tavern and boarding house. They were gate keepers, jail keepers, sextons, journalists, printers, "doctoresses," apothecaries, midwives, nurses, and teachers. Women acquired their skills the same way as did the men, through apprenticeship training, frequently within their own families.

Absence of a dowry, ease of marriage and remarriage, and a more lenient attitude of the law with regard to women's property rights were manifestations of the improved position of wives in the colonies. Under British common law, marriage destroyed a woman's contractual capacity; she could not sign a contract even with the consent of her husband. But colonial authorities were more lenient toward the wife's property rights by protecting her dower rights in her husband's property, granting her personal clothing, and upholding pre-nuptial contracts between husband and wife. In the absence of the husband, colonial courts granted women "femme sole" rights, which enabled them to conduct their husband's business, sign contracts, and sue. The relative social freedom of women and the esteem in which they were held was commented upon by most early foreign travelers in America.

But economic, legal, and social status tells only part of the story. Colonial society as a whole was hierarchical, and rank and standing in society depended on the position of the men. Women did not play a determining role in the ranking pattern; they took their position in society through the men of their own family or the men they married. In other words, they participated in the hierarchy only as daughters and wives, not as individuals. Similarly, their occupations were, by and large, merely auxiliary, designed to contribute to family income, enhance their husbands' business or continue it in case of widowhood. The self-supporting spinsters were certainly the exception. The underlying assumption of colonial society was that women ought to occupy an inferior and subordinate position. The settlers had brought this assumption with them from Europe; it was reflected in their legal concepts, their willingness to exclude women from political life, their discriminatory educational practices. What is remarkable is the extent to which this felt inferiority of women was constantly challenged and modified under the impact of environment, frontier conditions, and a favorable sex ratio.

By 1840 all of American society had changed. The Revolution had substituted an egalitarian ideology for the hierarchical concepts of colonial life. Privilege based on ability rather than inherited status, upward mobility for all groups of society, and unlimited opportunities for individual self-fulfillment had become ideological goals, if not always realities. For men, that is; women were, by tacit concensus, excluded from the new democracy. Indeed their actual situation had in many respects deteriorated. While, as wives, they had benefitted from increasing wealth, urbanization, and industrialization, their role as economic producers and as political members of society differed sharply from that of men. Women's work outside of the home no longer met with social approval; on the contrary, with two notable exceptions, it was condemned. Many business and professional occupations formerly open to women were now closed, many others restricted as to training and advancement. The entry of large numbers of women into low status, low pay, and low skill industrial work had fixed such work by definition as "woman's work." Women's political status, while legally unchanged, had deteriorated relative to the advances made by men. At the same time the genteel lady of fashion had become a model of American femininity, and the definition of "woman's proper sphere" seemed narrower and more confined than ever.

Within the scope of this essay only a few of these changes can be more fully explained. The professionalization of medicine and its impact on women may serve as a typical example of what occurred in all the professions.

In colonial America there were no medical schools, no medical journals, few hospitals, and few laws pertaining to the practice of the healing arts. Clergymen and governors, barbers, quacks, apprentices, and women practiced medicine. Most practitioners acquired their credentials by reading Paracelsus and Galen and serving an apprenticeship with an established practitioner. Among the semi-trained "physics," surgeons, and healers the occasional "doctoress" was fully accepted and frequently well rewarded. County records of all the colonies contain references to the work of the female physicians. There was even a female Army surgeon, a Mrs Allyn, who served during King Philip's war. Plantation records mention by name several slave women who were granted special privileges because of their useful service as midwives and "doctoresses."

The period of the professionalization of American medicine dates from 1765, when Dr. William Shippen began his lectures on midwifery in Philadelphia. The founding of medical faculties in several colleges, the standardization of training requirements, and the proliferation of medical societies intensified during the last quarter of the 18th century. The American Revolution dramatized the need for trained medical personnel, afforded first-hand battlefield experience to a number of surgeons and brought increasing numbers of semi-trained practitioners in contact with the handful of European-trained surgeons working in the military hospitals. This was an experience from which women were excluded. The resulting interest in improved medical training, the gradual appearance of graduates of medical colleges, and the efforts of medical societies led to licensing legislation. In 1801 Maryland required all medical practitioners to be licensed; in 1806 New York enacted a similar law, followed by all but three states. This trend was reversed in the 1830s and 40s when most states repealed their licensure requirements. This was due to pressure from eclectic, homeopathic practitioners, the public's dissatisfaction with the "heroic medicine" then practiced by licensed physicians, and to the distrust of state regulation, which was widespread during the Age of Jackson. Licensure as prime proof of qualification for the practice of medicine was reinstituted in the 1870s.

In the middle of the 19th century it was not so much a license or an M.D. which marked the professional physician as it was graduation from an approved medical college, admission to hospital practice and to a network of referrals through other physicians. In 1800 there were four medical schools, in 1850, forty-two. Almost all of them excluded women from admission. Not surprisingly, women turned to eclectic schools for training. Harriot Hunt, a Boston physician, was trained by apprenticeship with a husband and wife team of homeopathic physicians. After more than twenty years of practice she attempted to enter Harvard Medical school and was repeatedly rebuffed. Elizabeth Blackwell received her M.D. from Geneva (New York) Medical College, an eclectic school. Sarah Adamson found all regular medical schools closed against her and earned an M.D. in 1851 from Central College at Syracuse, an eclectic institution. Clemence Lozier graduated from the same school two years later and went on to found the New York Medical College and Hospital for women in 1863, a homeopathic institution which was later absorbed into the Flower-Fifth Avenue Hospital.

Another way in which professionalization worked to the detriment of women can be seen in the cases of Drs. Elizabeth and Emily Blackwell, Marie Zakrzewska, and Ann Preston, who despite their M.D.s and excellent training were denied access to hospitals, were refused recognition by county medical societies, and were denied customary referrals by male colleagues. Their experiences were similar to those of most of the pioneer women physicians. Such discrimination caused the formation of alternate institutions for the training of women physicians and for hospitals in which they might treat their patients. The point here is not so much that any one aspect of the process of professionalization excluded women but that the process, which took place over the span of almost a century, proceeded in such a way as to institutionalize an exclusion of women, which had earlier been accomplished irregularly, inconsistently, and mostly by means of social pressure. The end result was an *absolute* lowering of status for all women in the medical profession and a *relative* loss. As the professional status of all physicians advanced, the status differential between male and female practitioners was more obviously disadvantageous and underscored women's marginality. Their virtual exclusion from the most prestigious and lucrative branches of the profession and their concentration in specializations relating to women and children made such disadvantaging more obvious by the end of the 19th century.

This process of pre-emption of knowledge, of institutionalization of the profession, and of legitimation of its claims by law and public acceptance is standard for the professionalization of the sciences, as George Daniels has pointed out. It inevitably results in the elimination of fringe elements from the profession. It is interesting to note that women had been pushed out of the medical profession in 16th-century Europe by a similar process. Once the public had come to accept licensing and college training as guarantees of up-to-date practice, the outsider, no matter how well qualified by years of experience, stood no chance in the competition. Women were the casualties of medical professionalization.

In the field of midwifery the results were similar, but the process was more complicated. Women had held a virtual monopoly in the profession in colonial America. In 1646 a man was prosecuted in Maine for practicing as a midwife. There are many records of well-trained midwives with diplomas from European institutions working in the colonies. In most of the colonies midwives were licensed, registered, and required to pass an examination before a board. When Dr. Shippen announced his pioneering lectures on mid-wifery, he did it to "combat the widespread popular prejudice against the man-midwife" and because he considered most midwives ignorant and improperly trained.

Yet he invited "those women who love virtue enough, to own their Igno-rance, and apply for instruction" to attend his lectures, offering as an induce-ment the assurance that female pupils would be taught privately. It is not known if any midwives availed themselves of the opportunity.

Technological advances, as well as scientific, worked against the interests of female midwives. In 16th-century Europe the invention and use of obstetrical forceps had for three generations been the well-kept secret of the Chamberlen family and had greatly enhanced their medical practice. Hugh Chamberlen was forced by circumstances to sell the secret to the Medical College in Amsterdam, which in turn transmitted the precious knowledge to licensed physicians only. By the time the use of the instrument became widespread it had become associated with male physicians and male midwives. Similarly in America, introduction of the obstetrical forceps was associated with the prac-tice of male midwives and served to their advantage. By the end of the 18th century a number of male physicians advertised their practice of midwifery. Shortly thereafter female midwives also resorted to advertising, probably in an effort to meet the competition. By the early 19th century male physicians had virtually monopolized the practice of midwifery on the Eastern seaboard. True to the generally delayed economic development in the Western frontier regions, female midwives continued to work on the frontier until a much later period. It is interesting to note that the concepts of "propriety" shifted with the prevalent practice. In 17th-century Maine the attempt of a man to act as a midwife was considered outrageous and illegal; in mid-19th-century America the suggestion that women should train as midwives and physicians was considered equally outrageous and improper.

Professionalization, similar to that in medicine with the elimination of women from the upgraded profession, occurred in the field of law. Before 1750, when law suits were commonly brought to the courts by the plaintiffs themselves or by deputies without specialized legal training, women as well as men could and did act as "attorneys-in-fact." When the law became a paid profession and trained lawyers took over litigation, women disappeared from the court scene for over a century.

A similar process of shrinking opportunities for women developed in business and in the retail trades. There were fewer female storekeepers and business women in the 1830s than there had been in colonial days. There was also a noticeable shift in the kind of merchandise handled by them. Where previously women could be found running almost every kind of retail shop, after 1830 they were mostly found in businesses which served women only.

The only fields in which professionalization did not result in the elimi-nation of women from the upgraded profession were nursing and teaching. Both were characterized by a severe shortage of labor. Nursing lies outside the field of this inquiry since it did not become an organized profession until after the Civil War. Before then it was regarded peculiarly as a woman's occupation, although some of the hospitals and the Army during wars employed male nurses. These bore the stigma of low skill, low status, and low pay. Generally, nursing was regarded as simply an extension of the unpaid services performed by the housewife—a characteristic attitude that haunts the profession to this day.

Education seems, at first glance, to offer an entirely opposite pattern from that of the other professions. In colonial days women had taught "Dame schools" and grade schools during summer sessions. Gradually, as educational opportunities for girls expanded, they advanced just a step ahead of their students. Professionalization of teaching occurred between 1820 and 1860, a period marked by a sharp increase in the number of women teachers. The spread of female seminaries, academies, and normal schools provided new opportunities for the training and employment of female teachers.

This trend, which runs counter to that found in the other professions, can be accounted for by the fact that women filled a desperate need created by the challenge of the common schools, the ever-increasing size of the student body, and the westward growth of the nation. America was committed to educating its children in public schools, but it was insistent on doing so as cheaply as possible. Women were available in great numbers, and they were willing to work cheaply. The result was another ideological adaptation: in the very period when the gospel of the home as woman's only proper sphere was preached most loudly, it was discovered that women were the natural teachers of youth, could do the job better than men, and were to be preferred for such employment. This was always provided, of course, that they would work at the proper wage differential—30 to 50 per cent of the wages paid male teachers was considered appropriate. The result was that in 1888 in the country as a whole 63 per cent of all teachers were women, while the figure for the cities only was 90.04 per cent.

It appeared in the teaching field, as it would in industry, that role expectations were adaptable provided the inferior status group filled a social need. The inconsistent and peculiar patterns of employment of black labor in the present-day market bear out the validity of this generalization.

There was another field in which the labor of women was appreciated and which they were urged to enter—industry. From Alexander Hamilton to Matthew Carey and Tench Coxe, advocates of industrialization sang the praises of the working girl and advanced arguments in favor of her employment. The social benefits of female labor particularly stressed were those bestowed upon her family, who now no longer had to support her. Working girls were "thus happily preserved from idleness and its attendant vices and crimes," and the whole community benefitted from their increased purchasing power.

American industrialization, which occurred in an underdeveloped economy with a shortage of labor, depended on the labor of women and children. Men were occupied with agricultural work and were not available or were unwilling to enter the factories. This accounts for the special features of the early development of the New England textile industry: the relatively high wages, the respectability of the job and relatively high status of the mill girls, the patriarchal character of the model factory towns, and the temporary mobility of women workers from farm to factory and back again to farm. All this was characteristic only of a limited area and of a period of about two decades. By the late 1830s the romance had worn off: immigration had supplied a strongly competitive, permanent work force willing to work for subsistence wages; early efforts at trade union organization had been shattered, and mechanization had turned semi-skilled factory labor into unskilled labor. The process led to the replacement of the New England-born farm girls by immigrants in the mills and was accompanied by a loss of status and respectability for female workers.

The lack of organized social services during periods of depression drove ever greater numbers of women into the labor market. At first, inside the factories distinctions between men's and women's jobs were blurred. Men and women were assigned to machinery on the basis of local need. But as more women entered industry the limited number of occupations open to them tended to increase competition among them, thus lowering pay standards. Generally, women regarded their work as temporary and hesitated to invest in apprenticeship training, because they expected to marry and raise families. Thus they remained untrained, casual labor and were soon, by custom, relegated to the lowest paid, least skilled jobs. Long hours, overwork, and poor working conditions would characterize women's work in industry for almost a century.

Another result of industrialization was in increasing differences in life styles between women of different classes. When female occupations, such as carding, spinning, and weaving, were transferred from home to factory, the poorer women followed their traditional work and became industrial workers. The women of the middle and upper classes could use their newly gained time for leisure pursuits: they became ladies. And a small but significant group among them chose to prepare themselves for professional careers by advanced education. This group would prove to be the most vocal and troublesome in the near future.

As class distinctions sharpened, social attitudes toward women became polarized. The image of "the lady" was elevated to the accepted ideal of femininity toward which all women would strive. In this formulation of values lower-class women were simply ignored. The actual lady was, of course, nothing new on the American scene; she had been present ever since colonial days. What was new in the 1830s was the cult of the lady, her elevation to a status symbol. The advancing prosperity of the early 19th century made it possible for middle-class women to aspire to the status formerly reserved for upper-class women. The "cult of true womanhood" of the 1830s became a vehicle for such aspirations. Mass circulation newspapers and magazines made it possible to teach every woman how to elevate the status of her family by setting "proper" standards of behavior, dress, and literary tastes. *Godey's Lady's Book* and innumerable gift books and tracts of the period all preach the same gospel of "true womanhood"—piety, purity, domesticity. Those unable to reach the goal of becoming ladies were to be satisfied with the lesser goal—acceptance of their "proper place" in the home.

It is no accident that the slogan "woman's place is in the home" took on a certain aggressiveness and shrillness precisely at the time when increasing numbers of poorer women *left* their homes to become factory workers. Working women were not a fit subject for the concern of publishers and mass media writers. Idleness, once a disgrace in the eyes of society, had become a status symbol. Thorstein Veblen, one of the earliest and sharpest commentators on the subject, observed that it had become almost the sole social function of the lady "to put in evidence her economic unit's ability to pay." She was "a means of conspicuously unproductive expenditure," devoted to displaying her husband's wealth. Just as the cult of white womanhood in the South served to preserve a labor and social system based on race distinctions, so did the cult of the lady in an egalitarian society serve as a means of preserving class distinctions. Where class distinctions were not so great, as on the frontier, the position of women was closer to what it had been in colonial days; their economic contribution was more highly valued, their opportunities were less restricted, and their positive participation in community life was taken for granted.

In the urbanized and industrialized Northeast the life experience of middle-class women was different in almost every respect from that of the lower-class women. But there was one thing the society lady and the mill girl had in common—they were equally disfranchised and isolated from the vital centers of power. Yet the political status of women had not actually deteriorated. With very few exceptions women had neither voted nor stood for office during the colonial period. Yet the spread of the franchise to ever wider groups of white males during the Jacksonian age, the removal of property restrictions, the increasing numbers of immigrants who acquired access to the franchise, made the gap between these new enfranchised voters and the disfranchised women more obvious. Quite naturally, educated and propertied women felt this deprivation more keenly. Their own career expectations had been encouraged by widening educational opportunities; their consciousness off their own abilities and of their potential for power had been enhanced by their activities in the reform movements of the 1830s; the general spirit of upward mobility and venturesome entrepreneurship that pervaded the Jacksonian era was infectious. But in the late 1840s a sense of acute frustration enveloped these educated and highly spirited women. Their rising expectations had met with frustration, their hopes had been shattered; they were bitterly conscious of a relative lowering of status and a loss of position. This sense of frustration led them to action; it was one of the main factors in the rise of the woman's rights movement.

The women, who at the first woman's rights convention at Seneca Falls, New York, in 1848 declared boldly and with considerable exaggeration that "the history of mankind is a history of repeated injuries and usurpations on the part of man toward woman, having in direct object the establishment of an absolute tyranny over her," did not speak for the truly exploited and abused working woman. As a matter of fact, they were largely ignorant of her condition and, with the notable exception of Susan B. Anthony, indifferent to her fate. But they judged from the realities of their own life experience. Like most revolutionaries, they were not the most downtrodden but rather the most status-deprived group. Their frustrations and traditional isolation from political power funneled their discontent into fairly utopian declarations and immature organizational means. They would learn better in the long, hard decades of practical struggle. Yet it is their initial emphasis on the legal and political "disabilities" of women which has provided the framework for most of the historical work on women.[1] For almost a hundred years sympathetic historians have told the story of women in America by deriving from the position of middle-class women a generalization concerning all American women. To avoid distortion, any valid generalization concerning American women after the 1830s should reflect a recognition of class stratification.

For lower-class women the changes brought by industrialization were actually advantageous, offering income and advancement opportunities, however limited, and a chance for participation in the ranks of organized labor.[2] They, by and large, tended to join men in their struggle for economic advancement and became increasingly concerned with economic gains and protective labor legislation. Middle- and upper-class women, on the other hand, reacted to actual and fancied status deprivation by increasing militancy and the formation of organizations for woman's rights, by which they meant especially legal and property rights.

The four decades preceding the Seneca Falls Convention were decisive in the history of American women. They brought an actual deterioration in the economic opportunities open to women, a relative deterioration in their political status, and a rising level of expectation and subsequent frustration in a privileged elite group of educated women. It was in these decades that the values and beliefs that clustered around the assertion "Woman's place is in the home" changed from being descriptive of an existing reality to becoming an ideology. "The cult of true womanhood" extolled woman's predominance in the domestic sphere, while it tried to justify women's exclusion from the public domain, from equal education and from participation in the political process by claims to tradition, universality, and a history dating back to antiquity, or at least to the *Mayflower*. In a century of modernization and industrialization women alone were to remain unchanging, embodying in their behavior and attitudes the longing of men and women caught in rapid social change for a mythical archaic past of agrarian family self-sufficiency. In pre-industrial America the home was indeed the workplace for both men and women, although the self-sufficiency of the American yeoman, whose economic well-being depended on a network of international trade and mercantilism, was even then more apparent than real. In the 19th and 20th centuries the home was turned into the realm of woman, while the workplace became the public domain of men. The ideology of. "woman's sphere" sought to upgrade women's domestic function by elaborating the role of mother, turning the domestic drudge into a "homemaker" and charging her with elevating her family's status by her exercise of consumer functions and by her display of her own and her family's social graces. These prescribed roles never *were* a reality. In the 1950s Betty Friedan would describe this ideology and rename it "the feminine mystique," but it was no other than the myth of "woman's proper sphere" created in the 1840s and updated by consumerism and the misunderstood dicta of Freudian psychology.

The decades 1800–1840 also provide the clues to an understanding of the institutional shape of the later women's organizations. These would be led by middle-class women whose self-image, life experience, and ideology had largely been fashioned and influenced by these early, transitional years. The concerns of middle-class women—property rights, the franchise, and moral uplift—would dominate the woman's rights movement. But side by side with it, and at times cooperating with it, would grow a number of organizations serving the needs of working women.

American women were the largest disfranchised group in the nation's history, and they retained this position longer than any other group. Although they found ways of making their influence felt continuously, not only as individuals but as organized groups, power eluded them. The mill girl and the lady, both born in the age of Jackson, would not gain access to power until they learned to cooperate, each for her own separate interests. It would take almost six decades before they would find common ground. The issue around which they finally would unite and push their movement to victory was the "impractical and utopian" demand raised at Seneca Falls—the means to power in American society—female suffrage.

Notes

1. To the date of the first printing of this article (1969).
2. In 1979, I would not agree with this optimistic generalization.

POSTSCRIPT

Did the Industrial Revolution Provide More Economic Opportunities for Women in the 1830s?

Professor Gerda Lerner was a pioneer in women's history. A European refugee and playwright, she entered the New School of Social Research at the age of 40 where she also taught the earliest course on women's history in 1962. At the same time, she developed an interest in African American history when she wrote the screen play for the film directed by her husband, *Black Like Me*, based on a best-selling memoir about a white man who dyed his skin black in order to experience what it was like to be non-white.

As a forty-three-year-old graduate student at Columbia University, she convinced her mentors that a dissertation about the Grimke sisters, who were southern abolitionists, was a viable subject. She published *The Grimke Sisters from South Carolina, Rebels Against Slavery* (Houghton Mifflin, 1967), though a number of major publishers rejected the manuscript because it lacked information about the psychological failings of the sisters.

Recognizing that women "are and always have been at least half of humankind and most of the time have been a majority," Lerner argued that women have their own history, which should not be marginalized by men nor forced to be subject to the traditional male framework of political/military/diplomatic/economic history. Along with other pioneers, she led the search for nontraditional sources that provided information about women: demographic records, census figures; parish and birth records, property taxes; organizational files of churches, schools, police, and hospital records; finally, diaries, family letters, and autobiographies that are more attuned to a women's point of view.

Lerner suggested that the writing of women's history could be divided into four parts: (1) "compensatory history" where historians search for women whose experiences deserve to be well known; (2) "contribution history" of women worthies to topics and issues deemed important to the American mainstream; (3) test familiar narratives and rewrite generalizations when they appear to be wrong; and (4) understand gender as a social construct, and rewrite and develop new frameworks and concepts to understand women's history.

The Lady and the Mill Girl is a classic article that uses the conceptual framework of the "cult of motherhood" to demonstrate how the experiences of middle-class and working-class women in the Jacksonian period was different from men because they were unable to vote and were driven out of the medical, legal, and business professions, which provided occupations of upward mobility for men. Written a decade before historians began to use the term "market revolution," Lerner's article argues that industrialization retarded women's attempts at economic advancements outside the home. The two professions dominated by women—teaching and nursing—were both poorly paid and were an extension of the family values carried outside the home.

Professor Dublin's article and subsequent books are based upon the two new approaches to women's history and labor history. Both fields are part of the new social history developed in the late 1960s, which looks at history from the bottom up rather than from the top down. Dublin's Lowell factory workers developed a collective consciousness because they spent all the leisure hours in boarding houses and their 72-hour workweek tending the looms. Their contact with the male owners was nonexistent. The modern corporation that separated owners and management was true at Lowell where the Boston capitalists who started the company rarely appeared. Usually the women tending the mills would have their only contact with their immediate male supervisors. Consequently, the women could enforce their moral standards in the boarding house and get rid of women whom they deemed promiscuous. Their collective consciousness also made it easier for the women to organize strikes when their owners cut the wages as they did in 1834 and 1836.

Dublin points out that the strikes did not succeed. He is unclear about the reasons for their failures. The major one could be that women viewed the work at Lowell as temporary, a chance to build up a dowry that they could use to get married. The cult of motherhood was strong even for female factory workers. Marriage was still their primary goal.

The Lowell experiment was short-lived. Though the female workers supported the Ten Hour Movement with men working in separate organizations, the early labor movement, like the protesters in the 1880s and 1890s, failed to achieve their objectives. By the 1850s, the "Daughters of Free Men" were replaced by Irish immigrants.

The bibliography on women's history since the 1960s is enormous. The starting points for reinterpreting the field are the oft reprinted articles by Barbara Welter, "The Cult of True Womanhood: 1820–1860," *American Quarterly* 18 (Summer 1966); Carol Smith-Rosenberg, "The Female World of Love and Ritual: Relations Between Women in Nineteenth-Century America," *Signs* 1 (1975); and the collection of essays including a brief autobiography by Gerder Lerner in *The Majority Finds Its Past: Placing Women in History* (Oxford, 1979). Also important for its primary research in Nancy F. Cott, *The Bounds of Womanhood: "Women's Sphere" in New England, 1780–1835* (Yale University Press, 1977).

Thomas Dublin's essay was drawn from his doctoral dissertation at Columbia University, which the press published in 1979 as *Women at Work: The Transformation of Work and Community in Lowell, Massachusetts, 1826–1860.* Dublin also published a primary source collection *From Farm to Factory: Women's Letters 1830–1860* (Columbia University Press, 1981 and 2nd ed., 1993). Other important works about women in the workforce include Alice Kessler-Harris, *Out to Work: A History of Wage-Earning Women in the United States* (Oxford University Press, 1982); Jeanne Boydston, *Home and Work:*

Housework, Wages and the Ideology of Labor in the Early Republic (Oxford University Press, 1990); and Ava Baron, ed., *Work Engendered: Toward a New History of American Labor* (Cornell University Press, 1992).

Issue 12 deals primarily with white working-class and middle-class women and does not treat the different experiences of western women, Native Americans, African Americans, Mexican Americans, or the white immigrants. For an example of the immigrants who succeeded the "Daughters of Freemen" at Lowell, see Hasia Diner, *Erin's Daughters in America: Irish Immigrant Women in the Nineteenth Century* (Johns Hopkins University Press, 1983).

ISSUE 13

Did Slavery Destroy the Black Family?

YES: Wilma A. Dunaway, from *The African-American Family in Slavery and Emancipation* (Cambridge University Press, 2003)

NO: Eugene D. Genovese, from *Roll Jordan Roll: The World the Slaves Made* (Random House, 1974)

ISSUE SUMMARY

YES: Professor Wilma A. Dunaway believes that modern historians have exaggerated the amount of control slaves exercised over their lives and underplayed the cruelty of the slave experience—family separations, nutritional deficiencies, sexual exploitation and physical abuse that occurred on the majority of small plantations.

NO: Professor Genovese argues that slaves developed their own system of family and cultural values within the Southern paternalistic and pre-capitalistic slave society.

$\mathbf{A}$ll the North American colonies had some slaves in the seventeenth century. But by the 1670s, slaves became the most important workforce in the southern colonies because of the intensive labor needed to cultivate the tobacco fields rice paddies. The enlightment philosophy that permeated the American Revolutionaries belief that "all men were created equal" might have caused slavery's eventual demise. But the invention of the cotton gin and the development of a "market revolution" of textile factories in Old and New England gave slavery a rebirth as millions of slaves were sold from the traditional tobacco-growing areas of the upper South to cotton-producing regions in Alabama and Mississippi and the sugar fields of Louisiana.

Until recently, historians debated the slavery issue with the same arguments used over a century ago by the abolitionists and plantation owners. Slavery had been viewed as a paternalistic institution that civilized and Christianized the heathen African who, though bought and sold by his masters, was better off than many free northern workers; he was, at least, cared for in his non-working hours and old age by his masters. The prodigious research of Georgia-born professor Ulrich B. Phillips and his followers, who mined the records of the large plantation owners, gave a picture of slavery that reflected the views of those slave masters. Because Phillips considered blacks intellectually inferior to whites, his books seem woefully outdated to the American student. But Phillips' book such as *American Negro Slavery* (New York, 1918; reprint, Louisiana State University Press, 1966) and those of his students dominated the field for over thirty years.

The climate of opinion changed after World War II. Hitler made the concept of "race" a dirty word that no respected biologist or social scientist would use. Assuming that "the slaves were merely ordinary human beings and that innately Negroes were, after all, only white men with black skins," Professor Kenneth Stampp wrote a history of slavery from a northern white liberal, or abolitionist, point of view. *The Peculiar Institution* (Vintage, 1956) utilized many of the same sources as Phillips's books but came to radically different conclusions; slavery was now considered an inhuman institution.

In 1959 Stanley Elkins synthesized these seemingly contradictory interpretations in his controversial but path-breaking study *Slavery: A Problem in American Institutional and Intellectual Life,* 3rd edition (University of Chicago Press, 1976). Elkins clearly accepted Stampp's emphasis on the harshness of the slave system by hypothesizing that slavery was a "closed" system in which masters dominated their slaves in the same way that Nazi concentration camp guards in World War II had controlled the lives of their prisoners. Such an environment, he insisted, generated severe psychological dysfunctions that produced the personality traits of Phillips's "Sambo" character type. Elkins book provoked an intense debate in the 1960s and 1970s. Although his image of the slave as "Sambo" was rejected by scholars, *Slavery* was an important work because it forced historians to reconceptualize and tell slavery from the point of view of the slave themselves.

In the second selection, Professor Eugene Genovese agreed with Elkins that it was important to view slavery through the eyes of the slave owners. But like many writers in the 1970s, Genovese disagreed with Elkins about the use of traditional sources to uncover slave culture. In his many books and articles, Genovese combined a search through the plantation records with a careful reading of slave autobiographies and the controversial records of the former slave interviews recorded in the 1930s by writers working for the federal Works Progress Administration (WPA). As a Marxist who defended Ulrich Phillips's conception of the plantation as a pre-capitalist feudal institution, Genovese's later writings reflected less concern for the economic aspects and more for the cultural interactions of blacks and whites in the antebellum South. He argues that southern slavery existed in a pre-capitalistic society dominated by a paternalistic ruling class of white slaveholders who ruled over their white and slave families. Under this system of paternalism, cultural bonds were forged between master and slave which recognized the slaves' humanity and enabled them to develop their own system of family and cultural values.

Have modern historians romanticized the ability of the slaves to maintain strong family ties? In the first selection, professor Wilma A. Dunaway argues that modern historians have exaggerated the amount of control slaves exercised over their lives and underplayed the cruelty of the slave experience–family separations, nutritional deficiencies, sexual exploitation, and physical abuse, which occurred on the majority of small plantations.

YES

Wilma A. Dunaway

Introduction

... The conventional wisdom is that owners rarely broke up slave families; that slaves were adequately fed, clothed, and sheltered; and that slave health or death risks were no greater than those experienced by white adults. Why have so many investigations come to these optimistic conclusions? U.S. slavery studies have been handicapped by four fundamental weaknesses:

- a flawed view of the slave family,
- scholarly neglect of small plantations,
- limited analysis of Upper South enslavement,
- academic exaggeration of slave agency.

The Flawed View of the Slave Family

U.S. slavery studies have been dominated by the view that it was not economically rational for masters to break up black families. According to Fogel and Engerman, households were the units through which work was organized and through which the rations of basic survival needs were distributed. By discouraging runaways, families also rooted slaves to owners. Gutman's work established the view that slave families were organized as stable, nuclear, single-residence households grounded in long-term marriages. After thirty years of research, Fogel is still convinced that two-thirds of all U.S. slaves lived in two-parent households. Recent studies, like those of Berlin and Rowland, are grounded in and celebrate these optimistic generalizations about the African-American slave family.

None of these writers believes that U.S. slave owners interfered in the construction or continuation of black families. Fogel argues that such intervention would have worked against the economic interests of the owners, while Gutman focuses on the abilities of slaves to engage in day-to-day resistance to keep their households intact. Fogel and most scholars argue that sexual exploitation of slave women did not happen very often. Moreover, the conventional wisdom has been that slaveholders discouraged high fertility because female laborers were used in the fields to a greater extent than male workers. Consequently, the predominant view is that most slave women did not have their first child until about age twenty-one and that teenage pregnancies were rare. To permit women to return to work as quickly as possible, owners protected children by providing collectivized child care.

Scholarly Neglect of Small Plantations

Those who have supported the dominant paradigm neglected small slaveholdings, the second methodological blunder of U.S. slave studies. Gutman acknowledged this inadequacy of his own work when he commented in passing that "little is yet known about the domestic arrangements and kin networks as well as the communities that developed among slaves living on farms and in towns and cities." Fogel stressed that "failure to take adequate account of the differences between slave experiences and culture on large and small plantations" has been a fundamental blunder by slavery specialists. Because findings have been derived from analysis of plantations that owned more than fifty slaves, generalizations about family stability have been derived from institutional arrangements that represented the life experiences of a small minority of the enslaved population. In reality, more than 88 percent of U.S. slaves resided at locations where there were fewer than fifty slaves.

Revisionist researchers provide ample evidence that slave family stability varied with size of the slaveholding. Analyzing sixty-six slave societies around the world in several historical eras, Patterson found that slavery was most brutal and most exploitative in those societies characterized by small-holdings. Contrary to the dominant paradigm, Patterson found that family separations, slave trading, sexual exploitation, and physical abuse occurred much more often in societies where the masters owned small numbers of slaves. There were several factors that were more likely to destabilize family life on small plantations than on large ones. According to Patterson, small slaveholdings allowed "far more contact with (and manipulation of) the owner" and "greater exposure to sexual exploitation." Compared to large plantations, slave families on small plantations were more often disrupted by masters, and black households on small plantations were much more frequently headed by one parent. Stephen Crawford showed that slave women on small plantations had their first child at an earlier age and were pregnant more frequently than black females on large plantations. Steckel argued that hunger and malnutrition were worse on small plantations, causing higher mortality among the infants, children, and pregnant women held there.

Scholarly Neglect of the Upper South

In addition to their neglect of small plantations, scholars who support the dominant paradigm have directed inadequate attention to enslavement in the Upper South. Instead, much of what is accepted as conventional wisdom is grounded in the political economy and the culture of the Lower South. Why is it so important to study the Upper South? In the United States, world demand for cotton triggered the largest domestic slave trade in the history of the world. Between 1790 and 1860, the Lower South slave population nearly quadrupled because the Upper South exported nearly one million black laborers. In a fifty-year period, two-fifths of the African-Americans who were enslaved in the Upper South were forced to migrate to the cotton economy; the vast majority were sold through interstate transactions, and about 15 percent were removed in relocations with owners.

Because of that vast interregional forced migration, Upper South slaves experienced family histories that contradict the accepted wisdom in U.S. slave studies. Though their arguments still have not altered the dominant paradigm, revisionist researchers offer evidence that slave family stability varied with southern subregion. Tadman contends that, after the international slave trade closed in 1808, the Upper South operated like a "stock-raising system" where "a proportion of the natural increase of its slaves was regularly sold off." As a result, the chances of an Upper South slave falling into the hands of interstate traders were quite high. Between 1820 and 1860, one-tenth of all Upper South slaves were relocated to the Lower South each decade. Nearly one of every three slave children living in the Upper South in 1820 was gone by 1860. Among Mississippi slaves who had been removed from the Upper South, nearly half the males and two-fifths of the females had been separated from spouses with whom they had lived at least five years. Stevenson contends that Virginia slave families were disproportionately matrifocal because of the slave trading and labor strategies of Upper South masters. Clearly, the fifty-year forced labor migration of slaves must be taken into account in scholarly assessments of family stability and of household living conditions.

Scholarly Preoccupation with Slave Agency

The fourth weakness in U.S. slavery studies has been a preoccupation with slave agency. As Kolchin has observed, most scholars "have abandoned the victimization model in favor of an emphasis on the slaves' resiliency and autonomy." Like a number of other scholars, I have grown increasingly concerned that too many recent studies have the effect of whitewashing from slavery the worst structural constraints. Because so much priority has been placed on these research directions, there has been inadequate attention directed toward threats to slave family maintenance. Notions like "windows of autonomy within slavery" or an "independent slave economy" seriously overstate the degree to which slaves had control over their own lives, and they trivialize the brutalities and the inequities of enslavement. Patterson is scathing in his criticism of the excesses of studies that assign too much autonomy to slaves.

> During the 1970s, a revisionist literature emerged in reaction to the earlier scholarship on slavery that had emphasized the destructive impact of the institution on Afro-American life. In their laudable attempts to demonstrate that slaves, in spite of their condition, did exercise some agency and did develop their own unique patterns of culture and social organization, the revisionists went to the opposite extreme, creating what Peter Parish calls a "historiographical hornet's nest," which came "dangerously close to writing the slaveholder out of the story completely."

In their haste to celebrate the resilience and the dignity of slaves, scholars have underestimated the degree to which slaveholders placed families at risk. Taken to its extreme, the search for individual agency shifts to the oppressed the blame for the horrors and inequalities of the institutions that enslaved them. If, for example, we push to its rhetorical endpoint the claim of Berlin and Rowland that slaves "manipulated to their own benefit the slaveowners' belief that regular family relations made for good business," then we would arrive at the inaccurate conclusion (as some have) that the half of the U.S. slave population who resided in single-parent households did so as an expression of their African-derived cultural preferences, not because of any structural interference by owners. If we push to its rhetorical endpoint the claim that there was an independent slave economy, then we must ultimately believe that a hungry household was just not exerting enough personal agency at "independent" food cultivation opportunities. Such views are simply not supported by the narratives of those who experienced enslavement. Nowhere in the 600 slave narratives that I have analyzed (within and outside the Mountain South) have I found a single slave who celebrated moments of independence or autonomy in the manner that many academics do. Some slaves did resist, but ex-slaves voiced comprehension that their dangerous, often costly acts of civil disobedience resulted in no long-term systemic change.

The Target Area for This Study

In sharp contrast to previous studies, I will test the dominant paradigm of the slave family against findings about a slaveholding region that was *typical* of the circumstances in which a majority of U.S. slaves were held. That is, I will examine enslavement in a region that was *not* characterized by large plantations and that did *not* specialize in cotton production. Even though more than half of all U.S. slaves lived where there were fewer than four slave families, there is very little research about family life in areas with low black population densities. Despite Crawford's groundbreaking finding that plantation size was the most significant determinant of quality of slave life, this is the first study of a multistate region of the United States that was characterized by small plantations.

This study breaks new ground by investigating the slave family in a slaveholding region that has been ignored by scholars. I will explore the complexities of the Mountain South where slavery flourished amidst a nonslaveholding majority and a large surplus of poor white landless laborers. In geographic and geological terms, the Mountain South (also known as Southern Appalachia) makes up that part of the U.S. Southeast that rose from the floor of the ocean to form the Appalachian Mountain chain 10,000 years ago. In a previous book, I documented the historical integration of this region into the capitalist world system. The incorporation of Southern Appalachia entailed nearly one hundred fifty years of ecological, politico-economic, and cultural changes. . . . Fundamentally, the Mountain South was a *provisioning zone*, which supplied raw materials to other agricultural or industrial regions of the world economy.

On the one hand, this inland region exported foodstuffs to other peripheries and semiperipheries of the western hemisphere, those areas that specialized in cash crops for export. The demand for flour, meal, and grain liquors was high in plantation economies (like the North American South and most of Latin America), where labor was budgeted toward the production of staple crops. So it was not accidental that the region's surplus producers concentrated their land and labor resources into the generation of wheat and corn, often in terrain where such production was ecologically unsound. Nor was it a chance occurrence that the Southern Appalachians specialized in the production of livestock, as did inland mountainous sections of other zones of the New World. There was high demand for work animals, meat, animal by-products, and leather in those peripheries and semiperipheries that did not allocate land to less-profitable livestock production.

On the other hand, the Mountain South supplied raw materials to emergent industrial centers in the American Northeast and western Europe. The appetite for Appalachian minerals, timber, cotton, and wool was great in those industrial arenas. In addition, regional exports of manufactured tobacco, grain liquors, and foodstuffs provisioned those sectors of the world economy where industry and towns had displaced farms. By the 1840s, the northeastern United States was specializing in manufacturing and international shipping, and that region's growing trade/production centers were experiencing food deficits. Consequently, much of the Appalachian surplus received in Southern ports was reexported to the urban-industrial centers of the American Northeast and to foreign plantation zones of the world economy. In return for raw ores and agricultural products, Southern markets— including the mountain counties— consumed nearly one-quarter of the transportable manufacturing output of the North and received a sizeable segment of the redistributed international imports (e.g., coffee, tea) handled by Northeastern capitalists.

Beginning in the 1820s, Great Britain lowered tariffs and eliminated trade barriers to foreign grains. Subsequently, European and colonial markets were opened to North American commodities. Little wonder, then, that flour and processed meats were the country's major nineteenth-century exports, or that more than two-thirds of those exports went to England and France. Outside the country, then, Appalachian commodities flowed to the manufacturing centers of Europe, to the West Indies, to the Caribbean, and to South America. Through far-reaching commodity flows, Appalachian raw materials—in the form of agricultural, livestock, or extractive resources—were exchanged for core manufactures and tropical imports.

Slavery in the American Mountain South

Peripheral capitalism unfolded in Southern Appalachia as a mode of production that combined several forms of land tenure and labor. Because control over land—the primary factor of production—was denied to them, the unpropertied majority of the free population was transformed into an impoverished *semiproletariat.* However, articulation with the world economy did not trigger only the appearance of free wage labor or white tenancy. Capitalist dynamics in the Mountain South also generated a variety of unfree labor mechanisms. To use the words of Phillips, "the process of incorporation . . . involved the subordination of the labor force to the dictates of export-oriented commodity production, and thus occasioned increased coercion of the labor force as commodity production became generalized." As a result, the region's land-holders combined *free* laborers from the ranks of the landless tenants, crop-pers, waged workers, and poor women with *unfree* laborers from four sources. Legally restricted from free movement in the marketplace, the region's free blacks, Cherokee households, and indentured paupers contributed coerced labor to the region's farms. However, Southern Appalachia's largest group of unfree laborers were nearly three hundred thousand slaves who made up about 15 percent of the region's 1860 population. About three of every ten adults in the region's labor force were enslaved. In the Appalachian zones of Alabama, Georgia, South Carolina, and Virginia, enslaved and free blacks made up one-fifth to one-quarter of the population. In the Appalachian zones of Maryland, North Carolina, and Tennessee, blacks accounted for only slightly more than one-tenth of the population. West Virginia and eastern Kentucky had the smallest percentage of blacks in their communities. The lowest incidence of slavery occurred in the *mountainous* Appalachian counties where 1 of every 6.4 laborers was enslaved. At the other end of the spectrum, the *ridge-valley* counties utilized unfree laborers more than twice as often as they were used in the zones with the most rugged terrain.

Consisting of 215 mountainous and hilly counties in nine states, this large land area was characterized in the antebellum period by nonslaveholding farms and enterprises, a large landless white labor force, small plantations, mixed farming, and extractive industry. Berlin's conceptualization of a *slave society* caused us to predict that slavery did not dominate the Mountain South because there were not large numbers of plantations or slaves. I contested that assumption in a previous book. A region was not buffered from the political, economic, and social impacts of enslavement simply because it was character-ized by low black population density and small slaveholdings. On the one hand, a Lower South farm owner was twelve times more likely to run a large plantation than his Appalachian counterpart. On the other hand, Mountain slaveholders monopolized a much higher proportion of their communities' land and wealth than did Lower South planters. This region was linked by rivers and roads to the coastal trade centers of the Tidewater and the Lower South, and it lay at the geographical heart of antebellum trade routes that connected the South to the North and the Upper South to the Lower South. Consequently, two major slave-trading networks cut directly through the region and became major conduits for overland and river transport of slave coffles. No wonder, then that the political economies of all Mountain South counties were in the grip of slavery. Even in counties with the smallest slave populations (including those in Kentucky and West Virginia), slaveholders owned a disproportionate share of wealth and land, held a majority of impor-tant state and county offices, and championed proslavery agendas rather than the social and economic interests of the nonslaveholders in their own communities. Moreover, public policies were enacted by state legislatures con-trolled and manipulated by slaveholders. In addition, every Appalachian county and every white citizen benefited in certain ways and/or was damaged by enslavement, even when there were few black laborers in the county and even when the individual citizen owned no slaves. For example, slaves were disproportionately represented among hired laborers in the public services and transportation systems that benefited whites of all Appalachian counties, including those with small slave populations. Furthermore, the lives of poor white Appalachians were made more miserable because slaveholders restricted economic diversification, fostered ideological demeaning of the poor, expanded tenancy and sharecropping, and prevented emergence of free public education. Moreover, this region was more politically divided over slavery than any other section of the South. Black and poor white Appalachians were disproportionately represented among the soldiers and military laborers for the Union Army. The Civil War tore apart Appalachian communities, so that the Mountain South was probably more damaged by army and guerilla activity than any other part of the country.

In an earlier work, I identified six indicators that distinguish the Mountain South from the Lower South.

- One of every 7.5 enslaved Appalachians was either a Native American or descended from a Native American. Thus, black Appalachians were 4.5 times more likely than other U.S. slaves to be Native American or to have Indian heritage, reflecting the presence of eight indigenous peoples in this land area.
- Mountain slaves were employed outside agriculture much more frequently than Lower South slaves. At least one-quarter of all mountain slaves were employed full time in nonagricultural occupations. Thus, slaves were disproportionately represented in the region's town commerce, travel capitalism, transportation networks, manufactories, and extractive industries.
- In comparison to areas of high black population density, mountain plantations were much more likely to employ ethnically mixed labor forces and to combine tenancy with slavery.
- Compared to the Lower South, mountain plantations relied much more heavily on women and children for field labor.
- Fogel argued that "the task system was never used as extensively in the South as the gang system." Except for the few large slaveholders, Mountain South plantations primarily managed laborers by assigning daily or weekly tasks and by rotating workers to a variety of occupations. Moreover, small plantations relied on community pooling strategies, like corn huskings, when they needed a larger labor force. Since a majority of U.S. slaves resided on holdings smaller than fifty, like those of the Mountain South, it is likely that gang labor did not characterize Southern plantations to the extent that Fogel claimed.
- Mountain slaves almost always combined field work with nonfield skills, and they were much more likely to be artisans than other U.S. slaves.

Several findings about the Mountain South cry out for scholarly rethinking of assumptions about areas with low black population densities and small plantations.

- On small plantations, slave women worked in the fields, engaged in resistance, and were whipped just about as often as men.

- Mountain masters meted out the most severe forms of punishment to slaves much more frequently than their counterparts in other Southern regions. Appalachian ex-slaves reported frequent or obsessive physical punishment nearly twice as often as other WPA interviewees. There was greater brutality and repression on small plantations than on large plantations. Moreover, areas with low black population densities were disproportionately represented in court convictions of slaves for capital crimes against whites. As on large plantations, small plantations punished slaves primarily for social infractions, not to motivate higher work productivity.
- As Berlin observed, "the Africanization of plantation society was not a matter of numbers." Thus, slaves on small plantations engaged in much more day-to-day resistance and counter-hegemonic cultural formation than had been previously thought. . . .

Methods, Sources, and Definitions

To research this complex topic, I have triangulated quantitative, archival, primary, and secondary documents. I derived my statistical analysis from a database of nearly twenty-six thousand households drawn from nineteenth-century county tax lists and census manuscripts. In addition to those samples, I relied on archived records from farms, plantations, commercial sites, and industries. A majority of the slaveholder collections utilized for this research derived from *small* and *middling* plantations. However, I did not ignore rich Appalachian planters, like Thomas Jefferson or John Calhoun. Never to quote or cite an Appalachian planter is to deny that they existed and to ignore that they were the richest, most politically powerful families in Appalachian counties. Indeed, I present information about them to demonstrate that they are similar to their Lower South counterparts and, therefore, very different from the typical farmers in their communities. It is also necessary to draw upon planter documents to show that larger plantations implemented different crop choices, surveillance strategies, and labor management practices than did smallholdings. Still, those rich planters account for less than 1 percent of all the citations and details provided in this study.

. . . I have used the term *plantation* consistently to refer to a slaveholding enterprise. I have purposefully done this to distinguish such economic operations from the nonslaveholding farms that characterized the Mountain South. Far too many scholars confront me at meetings with the mythological construct that the typical Appalachian slaveholder was a benign small farmer who only kept a couple of slaves to help his wife out in the kitchen. By using *plantation* to distinguish all slaveholding farms, I seek to erode the stereotype that small plantations might be the social, political, and economic equivalent of small nonslaveholding farms in their communities. On the one hand, small plantations could not have owned black laborers if those families had not accumulated surplus wealth far in excess of the household assets averaged by the majority of nonslaveholding Appalachians. On the other hand, planters and smallholders alike controlled far more than their equitable share of the political power and economic resources in their communities. Because small slaveholders aspired to be planters, they did not often align themselves with the political and economic interests of nonslaveholders. According to Berlin, "what distinguished the slave plantation from other forms of production was neither the particularities of the crop that was cultivated nor the scale of its cultivation. . . . The plantation's distinguishing mark was its peculiar social order, which conceded nearly everything to the slaveowner and nothing to the slave." That social order was grounded in a racial ideology in which chattel bondage and white supremacy became entwined. For that reason, it is crucial to distinguish a nonslaveholding farm from a slaveholding farm. In the Mountain South, a slaveholder did not have to reach planter status to be set apart from neighbors whose antagonism to enslavement would cause them to align themselves with the Union in greater numbers than in any other region of the American South. To distinguish plantations by size, I utilize the definitions that are typically applied by U.S. slavery specialists. A *planter* or *large plantation* held fifty or more slaves, while a *middling plantation* or slaveholder owned twenty to forty-nine slaves. Thus, a *small plantation* was one on which there were nineteen or fewer slaves. . . .

Slave Narratives from the Mountain South

I grounded this study in analysis of narratives of nearly three hundred slaves and more than four hundred white Civil War veterans. I spent many months locating Appalachian slave narratives within the Federal Writers Project, at regional archives, and among published personal histories. Beginning with Rawick's forty-one published volumes of the WPA slave narratives, I scrutinized every page for county of origin, for interregional sales or relocations that shifted slaves into or out of the Mountain South, and for occurrences during the Civil War that displaced slaves. After that process, I identified other archival and published accounts, finding several narratives in unusual locations, including archives at Fisk University and the University of Kentucky. In this way, I did not ignore the life histories of slaves who were born outside the Mountain South and migrated there or those who were removed to other regions. Ultimately, I aggregated the first comprehensive list of Mountain South slave narratives.

How representative of the region are these narratives? In comparison to the entire WPA collection, Appalachian slave narratives are exceptional in the degree to which they depict small plantations. By checking the slave narratives against census manuscripts and slave schedules, I established that the vast majority of the Appalachian narratives were collected from individuals who had been enslaved on plantations that held fewer than twenty slaves. Consequently, Blue Ridge Virginia is underrepresented while the Appalachian counties of Kentucky, North Carolina, and West Virginia are overrepresented. Thus, those areas that held the fewest slaves in this region are more than adequately covered. Appalachian slave narratives are not handicapped by the kinds of shortcomings that plague the national WPA collection. Large plantations, males, and house servants are overrepresented among the entire universe of respondents. In addition, two-fifths of the ex-slaves had experienced fewer than ten years of enslavement. The most serious distortions derived from the class and racial biases of whites who conducted the vast majority of the interviews. Most of the mountain respondents had been field hands, and very few were employed full time as artisans or domestic servants. In terms of gender differentiation, the Appalachian sample is almost evenly divided. In contrast to the entire WPA collection, three-quarters of the mountain ex-slaves were older than ten when freed. Indeed, when emancipated, one-third of the respondents were sixteen or older, and 12 percent were twenty-five or older. Thus, nearly half the Appalachian ex-slaves had endured fifteen years or more of enslavement, and they were old enough to form and to retain oral histories. Perhaps the greatest strength of this regional collection has to do with the ethnicity of interviewers. More than two-fifths of the narratives were written by the ex-slaves themselves or collected by black field workers, including many Tennessee and Georgia interviews that were conducted under the auspices of Fisk University and the Atlanta Urban League. Because the mountain narratives were collected over a vast land area in nine states, this collection offers another advantage. The geographical distances between respondents offer opportunities for testing the widespread transmission of African-Amemrican culture.

I have come away from this effort with a deep respect for the quality and the reliability of these indigenous narratives. When I tested ex-slave claims against public records, I found them to be more accurate than most of the slaveholder manuscripts that I scrutinized, and quite often much less ideologically blinded than many of the scholarly works I have consulted. Therefore, I made the conscious intellectual decision to engage in "the making of *history* in the final instance" by respecting the indigenous knowledge of the ex-slaves whose transcripts I analyzed. That means that I did not dismiss and refuse to explore every slave voice that challenged conventional academic rhetoric. In most instances, I triangulated the indigenous view against public records and found the slave's knowledge to be more reliable than some recent scholarly representations. In other instances, I perceived that Appalachian slaves are a *people without written history* and that it is important to document the oral myths in which they grounded their community building. Because mountain slave narratives present a view of enslavement that attacks the conventional wisdom, I recognized that they and I were engaging in a process that Trouillot calls "the production of alternative narratives." When contacted by a Fisk University researcher in 1937, one Chattanooga ex-slave comprehended that he possessed a knowledge about slavery that was different from the social constructions of the African-American interviewer. "I don't care about telling about it [slavery] sometime," he commented cynically, "because there is always somebody on the outside that knows more about it than I do, and I was right in it." Clearly, this poorly educated man understood that historical facts are not created equal and that knowledge construction is biased by differential control of the means of historical production. On the one hand, I set myself the difficult goal of avoiding the kind of intellectual elitism the ex-slave feared while at the same time trying to avoid the pitfall of informant misrepresentation. On the other hand, I heeded the advice of C. Vann Woodward and did not view the use of slave narratives as any more treacherous or unreliable than other sources or research methods. . . .

Toward a New Paradigm of the U.S. Slave Family

In his 1989 capstone study, Fogel argued that enslavement was morally reprehensible because owners denied to African-Americans freedom from domination, economic opportunity, citizenship, and cultural self-determination. It is disturbing that Fogel excluded from his moral indictment the forcible removal of kin and masters' disruptions of black households. While I strongly endorse his call for an "effort to construct a new paradigm on the slave family," I would hope to see writers assign greater priority to the human pain of family separations than has occurred over the last three decades. Celebration of resistance and cultural persistence to the exclusion of investigations of those forces that broke families will not advance a new school of thought in directions that are any more accurate and reliable than previous generalizations. As we move toward a new paradigm, we need to follow nine lines of new inquiry.

- We need new research that documents slave family life in institutional arrangements that represent the residential and work circumstances of a majority of African-Americans. That requires directing greater attention to plantations smaller than fifty, to the Upper South and slaveselling areas, and to nonagricultural laborers.
- We need to make realistic assessments of all labor migrations. Adherents to the dominant paradigm have been preoccupied with slave selling and have presumed that permanent separations were not caused by hireouts, migrations with owners, slave inheritance within the owner's family, and assignment to distant work sites. However, it is clear in the slave narratives that all these forced migrations severed kinship ties, threatened marriages, generated great numbers of female-headed households, and weakened bonds between children and fathers.
- New research needs to reevaluate the strengths and weaknesses of *abroad marriages* because scholars have tended to presume that such relationships were more stable than they actually were. Such arrangements left women to generate the survival needs of their households and to protect children without the daily support of husbands or other adult males. Moreover, masters withdrew family visits so routinely that households could not count on regular reunions of spouses or of parents and children.
- In future approaches, we need to define family disruption more broadly. Marriage breakups are only one indicator. Loss of children occurred much more frequently, breaking ties between parents and

offspring and between siblings. Moreover, few African-Americans maintained long-term connections with extended kin.

- Taking into account variations by size of slaveholding, by subregion, and by type of production, we need to reexamine threats to family persistence caused by inadequate nutrition, shortfalls in basic survival needs, and ecological conditions.

- Scholars need to abandon the myth that family stability is measured in terms of the presence of a *nuclear family*. First, such a family construct did not characterize antebellum white households, and it is doubtful that this ideal type has ever typified Americans. Second, stability characterizes nonnuclear family constructions in many nonwestern societies. Third, the absence of adult males was not a cultural choice because enslaved women were never in a structural position to control household composition without owners' intervention. Fourth, many enslaved women pooled survival resources by relying on support from other females.

- We need to learn from contemporary demographic trends in many poor countries where high infant mortality rates fuel population growth. On a different conceptual plane than has typified earlier discussions, we need to rethink the connection between high slave child mortality and fertility patterns of enslaved women.

- We need to investigate threats to slave families that occurred during the Civil War and the emancipation process. Families were separated, often permanently, by military labor impressments, enlistment of black soldiers, and the removal of kin to contraband camps. There was an increased incidence of Upper South slave selling and owner migrations throughout the war, magnifying the chances that a slave would be permanently separated from kin. Emancipation came slower in the Upper South, particularly in those counties with large numbers of pro-Union slaveholders or low black population densities. After liberation, most ex-slaves remained with former owners two years or longer, continuing to reside in the same cabins they had occupied during enslavement. Reconstruction labor policies worked against family rebuilding and increased the likelihood of new family disruptions (e.g., indenturement of children to former owners).

- Finally, scholars need to take a fresh look at the historical overlap between African and indigenous enslavement. First, the import of Africans did not trigger so abrsupt an end to Native American enslavement as historians have claimed. Second, researchers have ignored hardships for ethnically mixed slave families caused by forced removals of indigenous peoples from the U.S. Southeast. Third, there was a higher incidence of Native American heritage among southwestern African-Americans who were more often owned by or interacted frequently with Indians.

While Fogel stresses "the critical importance of quantitative consideration," I argue that integrating the perspective of the affected slaves is even more crucial. Even though the existing paradigm is heavily grounded in cliometrics, demography, and sophisticated economic projections, it has still failed to capture the diversity of slave family life on different sized plantations and in different sections of the American South. What we need in the future are approaches that triangulate quantitative analyses with slave accounts to draw comparisons between subregions of the American South, between different parts of the world, and between large and small plantations. The best rationale for a new paradigm can be heard in the painful voices of African-Americans. Elderly ex-slaves mourned the loss of parents, spouses, children, siblings, and grandparents. Even when they had been separated from kin at very early ages, they sensed that a significant element of their souls had been wrenched from them. A mountain slave says it best: "We never met again. . . . That parting I can never forget." In the minds of black Appalachians, poverty, illiteracy, and racial inequality were not the worst legacies of enslavement. Bad as those structural factors were, it was the forced removals of family that broke their hearts and generated a community wound that was not healed by liberation. Moreover, half the Appalachian ex-slaves carried into the twentieth century the structural impacts of past diasporas, exacerbated by new family separations borne of a chaotic war and an inhumane emancipation process.

The World of the Slaves

According to the slaveholders, slave men had little sense of responsibility toward their families and abused them so mercilessly that Ole Massa constantly had to intervene to protect the women and children. Skeptics might wonder how these allegedly emasculated men so easily dominated the strong-willed and physically powerful women of the matriarchal legend, but the slaveholders never troubled themselves about such inconsistencies.

"Negroes are by nature tyrannical in their dispositions," Robert Collins of Macon, Ga., announced, "and, if allowed, the stronger will abuse the weaker; husbands will often abuse their wives and mothers their children." Thus, he concluded, masters and overseers must protect the pace of the quarters and punish aggressors.

Life in the quarters, like lower-class life generally, sometimes exploded in violence. Court records, plantation papers and ex-slave accounts reveal evidence of wife-beating but do not remotely sustain the pretension that without white interference the quarters would have rung with the groans of abused womanhood. Too many black men did not believe in beating their wives, and too many black women, made physically strong by hard field work, were not about to be beaten. So, why should slaveholders, who thought nothing of stripping a woman naked and whipping her till she bled, express so much concern? The pontificating of the ideologues might be dismissed as politically serviceable rubbish, but the concern of the slaveholders who wrote in agricultural journals primarily for each other's eyes and who penned private instructions for overseers demands explanation.

The slaveholders needed order and feared that domestic abuse would undermine the morale of the labor force. By asserting himself as the protector of black women and domestic peace, the slaveholder asserted himself as *paterfamilias* and reinforced his claims to being sole father of a "family, black and white." In this light, the efforts of the drivers or plantation preachers or other prestigious slaves to restrain abusive husbands represented an attempt by the quarters to rule themselves.

The slaveholders intuitively grasped something else. A black man whose authority in the house rested on his use of force may have picked the worst way to assert himself, but in a world in which so much conspired to reduce

men to "guests in the house" and to emasculate them, even this kind of assertion, however unmanly by external standards, held some positive meaning.

Defending Their Own

The slave women did not often welcome Ole Massa's protection. They preferred to take care of themselves or, when they needed help, to turn to their
fathers, brothers or friend. As any policeman in a lower-class neighborhood,
white or black, knows, a woman who is getting the worst of a street fight with
her man and who is screaming for help usually wants relief from the blows;
she does not want her man subjected to an outsider's righteous indignation
and may well join him in repelling an attack.

When Ellen Botts' mother—the much respected Mammy of a sugar plantation—showed up with a lump on her head inflicted by her hot-tempered
husband, she told her master that she had had an accident. She would deal
with her husband herself and certainly did not want to see him whipped.
When James Redpath asked a slave woman in South Carolina if slave women
expected to leave their husbands when they fell out, he got the contemptuous
answer meddlers in other people's love lives ought to expect. "Oh, no, not all
us; we sometimes quarrel in de daytime and make all up at night."

The slaveholders, in their tender concern for black women who suffered
abuse from their husbands, remained curiously silent about those who fell
back on their husbands' protection. Laura Bell's father won her mother's hand
by volunteering to take a whipping in her place. Most slaveholders had the
sense to prohibit such gallantry, but no few black men braved their wrath by
interposing themselves between their wives or daughters and the white man
who sought to harm them. Not only husbands but male friends killed, beat or
drove off overseers for whipping their women.

Black women fell victims to white lust, but many escaped because the
whites knew they had black men who would rather die than stand idly by. In
some cases black men protected their women and got off with a whipping or
no punishment at all; in other cases they sacrificed their lives.

Even short of death, the pride of assertive manliness could reach fearful
proportions. An overseer tried to rape Josiah Henson's mother but was over-
powered by his father. Yielding to his wife's pleas and their overseer's promise
of no reprisal, the enraged slave desisted from killing him. The overseer broke
his promise. Henson's father suffered 100 lashes and had an ear nailed to the
whipping post and then severed.

"Previous to this affair my father, from all I can learn, had been a good-
humored and light-hearted man, the ringleader in all fun at corn-huskings
and Christmas buffoonery. His banjo was the life of the farm, and all night
long at a merry-making would he play on it while the other Negroes danced.
But from this hour he became utterly changed. Sullen, morose, and dogged,
nothing could be done with him."

Threats of being sold south had no effect on him. The thoughts running
through his mind as he came to prefer separation from the wife he loved to
enduring life there must remain a matter of speculation. His master sold him
to Alabama, and he was never heard from again.

Resisting Oppression

The slaveholders deprived black men of the role of provider; refused to dignify their marriages or legitimize their issue; compelled them to submit to physical abuse in the presence of their women and children; made them choose between remaining silent while their wives and daughters were raped or seduced and risking death; and threatened them with separation from their family at any moment.

Many men caved in under the onslaught and became irresponsible husbands and indifferent fathers. The women who had to contend with such men sometimes showed stubborn cheerfulness and sometimes raging bitterness; they raised the children, maintained order at home, and rotated men in and out of bed. Enough men and women fell into this pattern to give rise to the legends of the matriarchy, the emasculated but brutal male, and the fatherless children.

Many men and women resisted the "infantilization," "emasculation" and "dehumanization" inherent in the system's aggression against the slave family. How many? No one will ever know. At issue is the quality of human relationships, which cannot be measured. But there exists as much evidence of resistance and of a struggle for a decent family life as of demoralization. A brutal social system broke the spirit of many and rendered others less responsible than human beings ought to be. But enough men came out of this test of fire whole, if necessarily scarred, to demonstrate that the slaves had powerful inner resources. A terrible system of human oppression took a heavy toll of its victims, but their collective accomplishment in resisting the system constitutes a heroic story. That resistance provided black people with solid norms of family life and role differentiation, even if circumstances caused a dangerously high lapse from those norms. The slaves from their own experience had come to value a two-parent, male-centered household, no matter how much difficulty they had in realizing the ideal.

The role of the male slave as husband and father therefore requires a fresh look. If many men lived up to their assigned irresponsibility, others, probably a majority, overcame all obstacles and provided a positive male image for their wives and children. An ex-slave recalled his boyhood:

"I loved my father. He was such a good man. He was a good carpenter and could do anything. My mother just rejoiced in him. Whenever he sat down to talk she just sat and looked and listened. She would never cross him for anything. If they went to church together she always waited for him to interpret what the preacher had said or what he taught was the will of God. I was small but I noticed all of these things. I sometimes think I learned more in my early childhood about how to live than I have learned since."

Protective fathers appeared in the lullabies slave mothers sang to their children:

> Kink head, wherefore you skeered?
> Old snake crawled off, 'cause he's afeared.
> Pappy will smite him on de back
> With a great big club—Ker whack! Ker whack!

Many ex-slaves recalled their fathers as stern disciplinarians, and the slaveholders' complaints about fathers' abusing their children may be read as supporting evidence. Other slave men left their children a memory of kindness and affection that remained through life. Will Adams' father, a foreman on a Texas plantation, came in exhausted after a long day's work but never failed to take his son out of bed and to play with him for hours. The spirituals and other slave songs reflected the importance of the father in the lives of the children; many of them sang of the reunification of the family in heaven and of the father's return.

Middle-Class Norms

Men knew that they might have to part from their wives and children, but that knowledge did not engender indifference so much as a certain stoical submission to that which had to be endured. Under painful conditions, many did their best even while others succumbed. Mingo White's father, upon being sold, did nothing unusual when he charged a male friend with responsibility for looking after his son. A principle of stewardship had arisen in the quarters. Even in the absence of a father, some male would likely step in to help raise a boy to manhood. When the war ended, men crisscrossed the South to reclaim their families and to assert authority over their children.

Slave children usually did have an image of a strong blackolm man before them. Critical scholars have made the mistake of measuring the slave family by middle-class norms; naturally, they have found it wanting.

Even when a slave boy was growing up without a father in the house, he had as a model a tough, resourceful driver, a skilled mechanic or two, and older field hands with some time for the children of the quarters. Some of those men devoted themselves to playing surrogate father to all the children. They told them stories, taught them to fish and trap animals, and instructed them in the ways of survival in a hostile white world.

The norm in the quarters called for adults to look after children, whether blood relatives or not. Every plantation had some men who played this role. Under the worst of circumstances, one or two would have been enough; usually, however, there were a number. And there were the preachers. To the extent that the slaves heard their preachers, the children saw before them influential black men whose eloquence and moral force commanded the respect of the adults.

The slave children, like the ghetto children of later decades, saw a pattern of behavior that implied clear sexual differentiation and a notion of masculinity with its own strengths and weaknesses.

Don't Mess With Mammy

The daughters of the Confederacy suggested in 1923 that Congress set aside a site in Washington for a suitable memorial to the antebellum plantation Mammy. The good ladies had picked their symbol carefully, for no figure stands out so prominently in the moonlight-and-magnolias legend of the Old

South. The hostile reaction of so many blacks confirmed the judgment. As the old regime has come under increasingly critical scrutiny, Mammy has had a steadily worsening press. She remains the most elusive and important black presence in the Big House. To understand her is to move toward understanding the tragedy of plantation paternalism.

First, the white legend, Lewis H. Blair, attacking racial segregation in 1889, wrote:

"Most of us above 30 years of age had our mammy, and generally she was the first to receive us from the doctor's hands, and was the first to proclaim, with heart bursting with pride, the arrival of a fine baby. Up to the age of 10 we saw as much of the mammy as of the mother, perhaps more, and we loved her quite as well. The mammy first taught us to lisp and to walk, played with us and told us wonderful stories, taught us who made us and who redeemed us, dried our tears and soothed our bursting hearts, and saved us many a well-deserved whipping. . . ."

Word Had Force of Law

Mammy comes through the black sources in much the same way, but only so far. Lindey Faucette of North Carolina remembered her grandmother, Mammie Beckie, who "toted de keys," whose word had the force of law with Marse John and Mis' Annie, and who slept in the bed with her mistress when the master's law practice kept him in town all night. Alice Sewell of Alabama especially recalled the plantation Mammy's comforting the relatives of deceased slaves, arranging for the burial, and leading the funeral services. Ellen Botts of Louisiana noted: "All de niggers have to stoop to Aunt Rachel like they curtsy to Missy." And Adeline Johnson, who had served as a Mammy in South Carolina, spoke in her old age in accents that would have warmed the hearts of those Daughters of the Confederacy.

"I hope and prays to git to hebben. Whether I's white or black when I git dere, I'll be satisfied to see my Savior dat my old marster worshipped and my husband preached 'bout. I wants to be in hebben wid all my white folks, just to wait on them and love them and serve them, sorta lak I did in slavery time. Dat will be 'nough hebben for Adeline."

Who were these Mammies? What did they actually do? Primarily, the Mammy raised the white children and ran the Big House either as the mistress' executive officer or her de facto superior. Her power extended over black and white so long as she exercised restraint, and she was not to be crossed.

She carried herself like a surrogate mistress—neatly attired, barking orders, conscious of her dignity, full of self-respect. She played the diplomat and settled the interminable disputes that arose among the house servants; when diplomacy failed, she resorted to her whip and restored order. She served as confidante to the children, the mistress, and even the master. She expected to be consulted on the love affairs and marriages of the white children and might even be consulted on the business affairs of the plantation. She presided over the dignity of the whole plantation and taught the courtesies to the white children as well as to those black children destined to work in the Big House. On the small and medium-sized plantations she had to carry much of the house work herself, and her relationship to the field slaves drew closer.

In general, she gave the whites the perfect slave—a loyal, faithful, contented, efficient, conscientious member of the family who always knew her place; and she gave the slaves a white-approved standard of black behavior. She also had to be a tough, worldly-wise, enormously resourceful woman; that is, she had to develop all the strength of character not usually attributed to an Aunt Jane.

Mammy supposedly paid more attention to the white children than to her own. Even W. E. B. Du Bois, who was rarely taken in by appearances and legends, thought so. He described the Mammy as "one of the most pitiful of the world's Christs. . . . She was an embodied Sorrow, an anomaly crucified on the cross of her own neglected children for the sake of the children of masters who bought and sold her as they bought and sold cattle."

The Mammy typically took her responsibilities to the white family as a matter of high personal honor and in so doing undoubtedly could not give her own children as much love and attention as they deserved. House nannies, white and black, free and slave, have often fallen into this trap. But the idea that the Mammies actually loved the white children more than their own rests on nothing more than wishful white perceptions. That they loved the white children they themselves raised—hardly astonishing for warm, sensitive, generous women—in no way proves that they loved their own children the less. Rather, their position in the Big House, including their close attention to the white children sometimes at the expense of their own, constituted the firmest protection they could have acquired for themselves and their immediate families. Mammies did not often have to worry about being sold or about having their husbands or children sold. The sacrifices they made for the whites earned them genuine affection in return, which provided a guarantee of protection, safety, and privilege for their own children.

Barrier Against Abuse

The relationship between the Mammies and their white folks exhibited that reciprocity so characteristic of paternalism. "Of course," a planter in Virginia told a northern reporter in 1865, "if a servant has the charge of one of my little ones, and I see the child grow fond of her, and that she loves the child, I cannot but feel kindly towards her." Of course, Mom Genia Woodbury, who had been a slave in South Carolina, acknowledged that when white folks treat you kindly, you develop kind feelings toward their children.

The devotion of the white children, who regularly sought her as their protector, confidante, and substitute mother, established a considerable barrier against the abuse of Mammy or her family. "We would not hesitate about coming to see you," Laura S. Tibbets of Louisiana wrote her sister-in-law, "if I could bring my servants, but I could not bring my baby without assistance. She is a great deal fonder of her Mammy than she is of me. She nurses her and it would be a great trial to go without her."

The immunity that Mammy secured for herself did not fully cover husband and children, but it went far enough to shield them from the worst.

Mammy distraught, hurt, or angry was not to be borne. More than one over-seer learned to his cost to walk gingerly around her and hers. Ma Eppes of Alabama said that an overseer had whipped the plantation Mammy when the mistress was away:

"When Miss Sarah comed back and found it out she was the maddest white lady I ever seed. She sent for the overseer and she say, 'Allen, what you mean by whipping Mammy? You know I don't allow you to touch my house servants . . . I'd rather see them marks on my old shoulders than to see'em on Mammy's. They wouldn't hurt me no worse.' Then she say, 'Allen, take your family and git offen my place. Don't you let sundown catch you here.' So he left. He wasn't nothing but white trash nohow."

Another overseer made the incredible mistake of asking his employer for permission to punish Mammy. The reply: "What! What! Why I would as soon think of punishing my own mother! Why man you'd have four of the biggest men in Mississippi down on you if you even dare suggest such a thing, and she knows it! All you can do is to knuckle down to Mammy."

The plantation Mammy was not, as is so easily assumed, some "white man's nigger," some pathetic appendage to the powerful whites of the Big House. Her strength of character, iron will and impressive self-discipline belie any glib generalizations.

She did not reject her people in order to identify with stronger whites, but she did place herself in a relationship to her own people that reinforced the paternalist social order. Thus, she carried herself with courage, compassion, dignity and self-respect and might have provided a black model for these qualities among people who needed one, had not the constricting circumstances of her own development cut her off, in essential respects, from playing that role. Her tragedy lay not in her abandonment of her own people but in her inability to offer her individual power and beauty to black people on terms they could not accept without themselves sliding further into a system of paternalistic dependency.

Some Chose Freedom

The boldest slaves struck the hardest blow an individual could against the regime: they escaped to freedom. During the 1850s about a thousand slaves a year ran away to the North, Canada, and Mexico. Increased vigilance by the slaveholders and their police apparatus may have reduced the number from 1,011 in 1850 to 803 in 1860 as the census reports insist, but even so, the economic drain and political irritation remained serious.

The slaves in the border states, especially the extreme northern tier, had a much better chance to escape than did those in Mississippi or Alabama. But even in Texas, Arkansas and Louisiana, slaveholders had to exercise vigilance, for many slaves went over the Mexican border or escaped to friendly Indians.

Who ran away? Any slave might slip into the woods for a few days, but those whose departure rated an advertisement and organized chase—those who headed for freedom in the North, the Southern cities, or the swamps—fell into a pattern. At least 80 per cent were men between the ages of 16 and 35. At least one-third of the runaways belonged to the ranks of the skilled and privileged slaves—those with some education and with some knowledge of the outside world—and women occupied these ranks only as house servants.

The whip provided the single biggest provocation to running away. Many slaves ran in anticipation of a whipping or other severe punishment, and others in anger after having suffered it. In some cases—too many—slaves ran not simply from a particular whipping but from the torments regularly inflicted by cruel or sadistic masters or overseers.

A large if underdetermined number of slaves ran away to rejoin loved ones from whom they had been forcibly parted. Newspaper advertisements frequently contained such words as "He is no doubt trying to reach his wife." Slaveholders had great trouble with newly purchased slaves who immediately left to try to find parents or children as well as wives. In some instances the slaves had unexpected success when their masters, touched by the evidence of devotion and courage, reunited the family by resale.

In many more cases family ties prevented slaves from running away or kept them close to home when they did run. Frederick Law Olmsted reported from the lower Mississippi Valley that planters kept a sharp eye on mothers, for few slaves would leave permanently if they had to leave their mothers behind to face the master's wrath.

"The Thousands Obstacles"

Among the deterrents to making the long run to free states none loomed larger than the fear of the unknown. Most knew only the immediate area and often only a narrow strip of that. Even many skilled and relatively sophisticated slaves lacked an elementary knowledge of geography and had no means of transportation.

If most slaves feared to think about flight to the North, many feared even to think of short-term flight to the nearby woods or swamps. The slaves faced particularly difficult conditions in the swampy areas alongside the great plantation districts of Louisiana and the eastern low country. Solomon Northrup, a slave on a Louisiana cotton plantation in the 1840s, wrote:

"No man who has never been placed in such a situation can comprehend the thousand obstacles thrown in the way of the fleeing slave. Every whiteman's hand is raised against him—the patrollers are watching for him—the hounds are ready to follow on his track, and the nature of the country is such as renders it impossible to pass through it with any safety."

And yet, large numbers of slaves did brave the elements, the dogs, and the patrols; did swallow their fears; and did take to the woods. No plantation of any size totally avoided the runaway problem. Everywhere, the slaveholders had to build a certain loss of labor-time and a certain amount of irritation into their yearly calculations.

Slaves from one plantation assisted runaways from other plantations under certain circumstances. The slaves from neighboring plantations often knew each other well. They met for prayer meetings, corn shuckings, Christmas, and other holiday barbecues; often formed close attachments; and sometimes extended their idea of a plantation family to at least some of these friends and acquaintances. Within this wider circle, the slaves would readily help each other if they shunned those they regarded as strangers. But even strangers might find succor if they were fleeing the plantations of slaveholders known to be cruel.

Those who fled to freedom made an inestimable contribution to the people they left behind, which must be weighed against their participation in a safety-valve effect. These were slaves who, short of taking the path of insurrection, most clearly repudiated the regime; who dramatically chose freedom at the highest risk; who never let others forget that there was an alternative to their condition.

POSTSCRIPT

Did Slavery Destroy
the Black Family?

Major reinterpretations of slavery occurred in the 1970s. Professor John Blassingame was one of the first African American historians to challenge the Elkins thesis of the slave as "Sambo" and write a history of slavery from the point of view of the slaves themselves.

Blassingame centers his view of *The Slave Community: Plantation Life in the Antebellum South* revised and enlarged edition (Oxford University Press, 1972, 1979) around the slave family. Unlike other slave societies, Blassingame believes the even sex ration between males and females in the antebellum South contributed to the solidarity and generally monogamous relationships between husbands and wives. The author is no romantic, however, because he argues elsewhere that almost one-third of all slave marriages were broken up because of the sale of one partner to another plantation.

Blassingame was the first historian to make use of slave testimonies. A good example of Blassingame's use of sources—speakers, interviews, letters, and autobiographies—are collected in his *Slave Testimony: Two Centuries of Letters, Speeches, Interviews and Autobiographies* (Oxford University Press, 1979).

Several white historians such as Herbert Gutman and Eugene Genovese believed that careful usage of oral interviews greatly enhanced our view of nineteenth-century slavery. In his iconoclastic sprawling view of *The Black Family in Slavery and Freedom, 1750–1925* (Pantheon, 1976), Gutman argues that slaves were more monogamous, were less promiscuous, and did not marry kin as did the white slaveholding families. Furthermore Gutman argues somewhat controversially that the master had no influence on the slave family.

Professor Eugene Genovese has written dozens of journal articles, review essays, and books about the antebellum South. He views the antebellum South as a pre-capitalist agrarian society in which master and slave were bound together in a set of mutual duties and responsibilities similar to the arrangements of lords and serfs under the feudal system of middle ages Europe. Most of Genovese's contentions are rejected by modern historians of slavery. Robert W. Fogel and Stanley L. Engerman, in their controversial study of *Time on the Cross: The Economics of American Slavery*, 2 vols. (Hougton Mifflin, 1974), argued that planters were capitalists, ran plantations that were "35 percent more efficient than the northern system of family farms," and developed a system of rewards for the hardworking slaves who internalized the values of their masters.

In the *Taking Sides* selection from his major synthesis *Roll Jordan Roll* (Pantheon, 1974), Professor Genovese describes the important role men played on the plantation in defending women from advances by the owners at the risk of being beaten, killed, or sold to another plantation. When families were split, children would receive guidance from other males in the quarters. Genovese also explains how important "mammy" was to the "plantation mistress." At the same time, he notes that "mammy" made sure that her own family was treated well and remained intact because of her importance to the owner's family. Finally Genovese sketches the unhappiness that slaves felt about the institution in discussing the thousands of runaways—primarily single males—who attempted to escape under insurmountable odds to free states and Canada.

In the first selection, Professor Wilma Dunaway challenges the dominant paradigm that has celebrated the autonomy of the slave family in the histories of Professors Blassingame, Genovese, Gutman, Rawick, and others. Most of Professor Dunaway's generalizations come from an earlier study on *Slavery in the American Mountain South* (Cambridge University Press, 2003). Her research is rooted in a database of antebellum census returns and tax records from 215 Appalachian countries and almost 400 manuscript collections that range over nine states from Maryland and West Virginia to the deep South states of Georgia and Alabama. She also uses the oral history interviews of former slaves in the 1920s and 1930s by professional historians and New Deal government workers.

Her books demonstrated the strengths and weaknesses of local history. Dunaway argues that the Appalachian region with its medium and small plantations was more typical than the deep South regions with their large cotton-dominated plantations. According to Dunaway, Appalachian slaves were treated harshly by their masters. Whippings were standard practice, slaves sales to the plantations of the deep South were common without regard for family attachments, and fewer than 12 percent of mountain slaves grew market-based gardens because of exhaustion from 14-hour work days. Many slaves were engaged in industrial rather than agricultural jobs. Most grew corn and wheat for the "new global markets" rather than cotton. Slaves worked side by side with "landless tenants, croppers, wage workers, and unfree laborers." Interestingly there were a number of Cherokee Indian slave owners, but also Cherokee Indian slaves who worked with Afro-American slaves and slaves with mixed blood.

But local history has its limitations. Dunaway may also overgeneralize about the Appalachian experience as establishing a new or really pre-1970s paradigm for slavery. Perhaps, as Professor Berlin points out, the slave experience is too varied in terms of time, region, and size to lend itself to easy generalizations.

The two most important historiographical works on slavery are Mark Smith, *Debating Slavery: Economy and Society in the Antebellum American South* (Cambridge University Press, 1998) and Peter J. Parish, *Slavery: History and Historians* (Harper and Row, 1989). The best anthology of primary sources and secondary readings is *Slavery and Emancipation,* edited by Rick Halpern and Enrico Dal Lago (Blackwell Publishing, 2002). Three other useful anthologies of secondary readings are William Dudley, ed., *American Slavery* (Greenhaven Press, 2000), Lawrence B. Goodhart, et. al., eds., *Slavery in American Society,*

3rd ed. (D.C. Heath and Company, 1993) and the older but still useful Allen Weinstein, et al., eds., *American Negro Slavery,* 3rd ed. (Oxford University Press, 1979).

Finally, in addition to the works of Professor Berlin, *American Slavery 1619–1877* (Hill and Wang, 1993) by Peter Kolchin is an indispensable summary as well as the special issue on the "Genovese Forum" in the *Radical History Review* 88 (Winter 2004), 3–83, an analysis of the work of the "Marxian Conservative" scholar by several of his peers.

ISSUE 14

Was the Mexican War an Exercise in American Imperialism?

YES: Ramón Eduardo Ruiz, from "Manifest Destiny and the Mexican War," in Howard H. Quint, Milton Cantor, and Dean Albertson, eds., *Main Problems in American History,* 5th ed. (Dorsey Press, 1988)

NO: Norman A. Graebner, from "The Mexican War: A Study in Causation," *Pacific Historical Review* (August 1980)

ISSUE SUMMARY

YES: Professor of history Ramón Eduardo Ruiz argues that for the purpose of conquering Mexico's northern territories, the United States waged an aggressive war against Mexico from which Mexico never recovered.

NO: Professor of diplomatic history Norman A. Graebner argues that President James Polk pursued an aggressive policy that he believed would force Mexico to sell New Mexico and California to the United States and to recognize the annexation of Texas without starting a war.

As David M. Plecher points out in his balanced but critical discussion of *The Diplomacy of Annexation: Texas, Oregon and the Mexican War* (University of Missouri Press, 1973), the long-range effects on American foreign policy of the Mexican War were immense. Between 1845 and 1848, the United States acquired more than 1,200 square miles of territory and increased its size by over a third of its present area. This included the annexation of Texas and the subsequent states of the southwest that stretched to the Pacific coast incorporating California and the Oregon territory up to the 49th parallel. European efforts to gain a foothold in North America virtually ceased. By the 1860s, the British gradually abandoned their political aspirations in Central America, "content to compete for economic gains with the potent but unmilitary weapon of their factory system and their merchant marine." Meanwhile, the United States flexed her muscles at the end of the Civil War and used the Monroe Doctrine for the first time to force the French puppet ruler out of Mexico.

The origins of the Mexican War began with the controversy over Texas, a Spanish possession for three centuries. In 1821, Texas became the northernmost province of the newly established country of Mexico. Sparsely populated with a mixture of Hispanics and Indians, the Mexican government encouraged immigration from the United States. By 1835, the Anglo population had swelled to 30,000 plus over 2,000 slaves, while the Mexican population was only 5,000.

Fearful of losing control over Texas, the Mexican government prohibited further immigration from the United States in 1830. But it was too late. The Mexican government was divided and had changed hands several times. The centers of power were thousands of miles from Texas. In 1829, the Mexican government abolished slavery, an edict that was difficult to enforce. Finally General Santa Anna attempted to abolish the federation and impose military rule over the entire country. Whether it was due to Mexican intransigence or the Anglos' assertiveness, the settlers rebelled in September 1835. The war was short-lived. Santa Anna was captured at the battle of San Jacinto in April 1836, and Texas was granted her independence.

For nine years, Texas remained an independent republic. Politicians were afraid that if Texas were annexed it would be carved into four or five states, thereby upsetting the balance of power between the evenly divided free states and slave states that had been created in 1819 by the Missouri Compromise. But the pro-slavery president John Tyler pushed through Congress a resolution annexing Texas in the three days of his presidency in 1845.

The Mexican government was incensed and broke diplomatic relations with the United States. President James K. Polk sent John Slidell as the American emissary to Mexico to negotiate monetary claims of American citizens in Mexico, to purchase California, and to settle the southwestern boundary of Texas at the Rio Grande River and not farther north at the Nueces River, which Mexico recognized as the boundary. Upon Slidell's arrival, news leaked out about his proposals. The Mexican government rejected Slidell's offer. In March 1846, President Polk stationed General Zachary Taylor in the disputed territory along the Rio Grande with an army of 4,000 troops. On May 9, Slidell returned to Washington and informed Polk that he was rebuffed. Polk met with his cabinet to consider war. By chance that same evening, Polk received a dispatch from General Taylor informing him that on April 25 the Mexican army crossed the Rio Grande and killed or wounded 16 of his men. On May 11, Polk submitted his war message claiming "American blood was shed on American soil." Congress voted overwhelmingly for war 174 to 14 in the House and 40 to 2 in the Senate despite the vocal minority of Whig protesters and intellectuals who opposed the war.

In the following selections, Ramón Eduardo Ruiz argues that the United States waged a racist and aggressive war against Mexico for the purpose of conquering what became the American southwest. In his view Manifest Destiny was strictly an ideological rationale to provide noble motives for what were really acts of aggression against a neighboring country. Norman A. Graebner contends that President James Polk pursued the aggressive policy of a stronger nation in order to force Mexico to sell New Mexico and Texas to the United States and to recognize America's annexation of Texas without causing a war.

Ramón Eduardo Ruiz

Manifest Destiny
and the Mexican War

All nations have a sense of destiny. Spaniards braved the perils of unknown seas and the dangers of savage tribes to explore and conquer a New World for Catholicism. Napoleon's armies overran Europe on behalf of equality, liberty, and fraternity. Communism dictates the future of China and the Soviet Union. Arab expansionists speak of Islam. In the United States, Manifest Destiny in the 19th century was the equivalent of these ideologies or beliefs. Next-door neighbor Mexico felt the brunt of its impact first and suffered most from it.

What was Manifest Destiny? The term was coined in December 1845 by John L. O'Sullivan, then editor and cofounder of the *New York Morning News.* Superpatriot, expansionist, war hawk, and propagandist, O'Sullivan lived his doctrine of Manifest Destiny, for that slogan embodied what he believed. O'Sullivan spoke of America's special mission, frequently warned Europe to keep hands off the Weste Hemisphere, later joined a filibustering expedition to Cuba, and had an honored place among the followers of President James K. Polk, Manifest Destiny's spokesman in the Mexican War.

Manifest Destiny voiced the expansionist sentiment that had gripped Americans almost from the day their forefathers had landed on the shores of the New World in the 17th century. Englishmen and their American offspring had looked westward since Jamestown and Plymouth, confident that time and fate would open to them the vast West that stretched out before them. Manifest Destiny, then, was first territorial expansion—American pretensions to lands held by Spain, France, and later Mexico; some even spoke of a United States with boundaries from pole to pole. But Manifest Destiny was greater than mere land hunger; much more was involved. Pervasive was a spirit of nationalism, the belief that what Americans upheld was right and good, that Providence had designated them the chosen people. In a political framework, Manifest Destiny stood for democracy as Americans conceived it; to spread democracy and freedom was the goal. Included also were ideals of regeneration, the conquest of virgin lands for the sake of their development, and concepts of Anglo-Saxon superiority. All these slogans and beliefs played a role in the Mexican question that culminated in hostilities in 1846.

Apostles of these slogans pointed out that Mexicans claimed lands from the Pacific to Texas but tilled only a fraction of them, and then inefficiently.

From MAIN PROBLEMS IN AMERICAN HISTORY, 5th ed., Howard H. Quint, ed., pp. 254–260. Copyright © 1988 by Thomson Learning. Reprinted by permission.

"No nation has the right to hold soil, virgin and rich, yet unproducing," stressed one U.S. representative. "No race but our own can either cultivate or rule the western hemisphere," acknowledged the *United States Magazine and Democratic Review*. The Indian, almost always a poor farmer in North America, was the initial victim of this concept of soil use; expansionists later included nearly everyone in the New World, and in particular Mexicans. For, Caleb Cushing asked: "Is not the occupation of any portion of the earth by those competent to hold and till it, a providential law of national life?"

Oregon and Texas, and the Democratic Party platform of 1844, kindled the flames of territorial expansion in the roaring forties. Millions of Americans came to believe that God had willed them all of North America. Expansion symbolized the fulfillment of "America's providential mission or destiny"—a mission conceived in terms of the spread of democracy, which its exponents identified with freedom. Historian Albert K. Weinberg has written: "It was because of the association of expansion and freedom in a means-end relationship, that expansion now came to seem most manifestly a destiny."

Americans did not identify freedom with expansion until the forties. Then, fears of European designs on Texas, California, and Oregon, perhaps, prompted an identity of the two. Not only were strategic and economic interests at stake, but also democracy itself. The need to extend the area of freedom, therefore, rose partly from the necessity of keeping absolutistic European monarchs from limiting the area open to American democracy in the New World.

Other factors also impelled Americans to think expansion essential to their national life. Failure to expand imperiled the nation, for, as historian William E. Dodd stated, Westerners especially believed "that the Union gained in stability as the number of states multiplied." Meanwhile, Southerners declared the annexation of Texas essential to their prosperity and to the survival of slavery, and for a congressional balance of power between North and South. Others insisted that expansion helped the individual states to preserve their liberties, for their numerical strength curtailed the authority of the central government, the enemy of local autonomy and especially autonomy of the South. Moreover, for Southerners extension of the area of freedom meant, by implication, expansion of the limits of slavery. Few planters found the two ideas incompatible. Religious doctrines and natural principles, in their opinion, had ruled the Negro ineligible for political equality. That expansion favored the liberties of the individual, both North and South agreed.

In the forties, the pioneer spirit received recognition as a fundamental tenet of American life. Individualism and expansion, the mark of the pioneer, were joined together in the spirit of Manifest Destiny. Expansion guaranteed not just the political liberty of the person, but the opportunity to improve himself economically as well, an article of faith for the democracy of the age. Further, when antiexpansionists declared that the territorial limits of the United States in 1846 assured all Americans ample room for growth in the future, the expansionists-turned-ecologists replied that some 300 million Americans in 1946 would need more land, a prediction that overstated the case of the population-minded experts. And few Americans saw the extension of freedom in terms other than liberty for themselves—white, Anglo-Saxon, and Protestant. All these concepts, principles, and beliefs, then, entered into the expansionist creed of Manifest Destiny.

None of these was a part of the Mexican heritage, the legacy of three centuries of Spanish rule and countless years of pre-Columbian civilization. Mexico and the United States could not have been more dissimilar in 1846. A comparison of colonial backgrounds helps to bring into focus the reasons the two countries were destined to meet on the field of battle. One was weak and the other strong; Mexico had abolished slavery and the United States had not; Americans had their Manifest Destiny, but few Mexicans believed in themselves.

Daughter of a Spain whose colonial policy embraced the Indian, Mexico was a mestizo republic, a half-breed nation. Except for a small group of aristocrats, most Mexicans were descendants of both Spaniards and Indians. For Mexico had a colonial master eager and willing to assimilate pre-Columbian man. Since the days of the conqueror Hernán Cortés, Spaniards had mated with Indians, producing a Mexican both European and American in culture and race. Offspring of the Indian as well as the Spaniard, Mexican leaders, and even the society of the time, had come to accept the Indian, if not always as an equal, at least as a member of the republic. To have rejected him would have been tantamount to the Mexican's self-denial of himself. Doctrines of racial supremacy were, if not impossible, highly unlikely, for few Mexicans could claim racial purity. To be Mexican implied a mongrel status that ruled out European views of race.

Spain bequeathed Mexico not merely a racial attitude but laws, religious beliefs, and practices that banned most forms of segregation and discrimination. For example, reservations for Indians were never a part of the Spanish heritage. Early in the 16th century, the Spaniards had formulated the celebrated Laws of the Indies—legislation that clearly spelled out the place of the Indian in colonial society. Nothing was left to chance, since the Spanish master included every aspect of life—labor, the family, religion, and even the personal relations between Spaniard and Indian. The ultimate aim was full citizenship for the Indian and his descendants. In the meantime, the Church ruled that the Indian possessed a soul; given Christian teachings, he was the equal of his European conqueror. "All of the people of the world are men," the Dominican Bartolomé de las Casas had announced in his justly famous 1550 debate with the scholar Sepúlveda.

Clearly, church and state and the individual Spaniard who arrived in America had more than charity in mind. Dreams of national and personal glory and wealth dominated their outlook. Yet, despite the worldly goals of most secular and clerical conquerors, they built a colonial empire on the principle that men of all colors were equal on earth. Of course, Spain required the labor of the Indian and therefore had to protect him from the avarice of many a conquistador. Spaniards, the English were wont to say, were notorious for their disdain of manual labor of any type. But Spain went beyond merely offering the Indian protection in order to insure his labor. It incorporated him into Hispanic-American society. The modern Mexican is proof that the Indian survived: all

Mexicans are Indian to some extent. That the Indian suffered economic exploitation and frequently even social isolation is undoubtedly true, but such was the lot of the poor in the Indies—Indian, half-breed, and even Spaniard.

Spain's empire, as well as the Mexican republic that followed, embraced not just the land but the people who had tilled it for centuries before the European's arrival. From northern California to Central America, the boundaries of colonial New Spain, and later Mexico, the Spaniard had embraced the Indian or allowed him to live out his life. It was this half-breed population that in 1846 confronted and fell victim to the doctrine of Manifest Destiny.

America's historical past could not have been more dissimilar. The English master had no room for the Indian in his scheme of things. Nearly all Englishmen—Puritans, Quakers, or Anglicans—visualized the conquest and settlement of the New World in terms of the exclusive possession of the soil. All new lands conquered were for the immediate benefit of the new arrivals. From the days of the founding of Jamestown and Plymouth, the English had pushed the Indian westward, relentlessly driving him from his homeland. In this activity, the clergy clasped hands with lay authorities; neither offered the red man a haven. Except for a few hardy souls, invariably condemned by their peers, Englishmen of church and state gave little thought to the Indian. Heaven, hell, and the teachings of Christ were the exclusive domain of the conquerors.

Society in the 13 colonies, and in the Union that followed, reflected English and European customs and ways of life. It was a transplanted society. Where the Indian survived, he found himself isolated from the currents of time. Unlike the Spaniards, whose ties with Africa and darker skinned peoples through .seven centuries of Moorish domination had left an indelible imprint on them, most Englishmen had experienced only sporadic contact with people of dissimilar races and customs. Having lived a sheltered and essentially isolated existence, the English developed a fear and distrust of those whose ways were foreign to them. The Americans who walked in their footsteps retained this attitude.

Many American historians will reject this interpretation. They will probably allege that American willingness to accept millions of destitute immigrants in the 19th century obviously contradicts the view that the Anglo-Saxon conqueror and settler distrusted what was strange in others. Some truth is present here, but the weight of the evidence lies on the other side. What must be kept firmly in mind is that immigration to the English colonies and later to the United States—in particular, the tidal wave of humanity that engulfed the United States in the post–Civil War era—was European in origin. Whether Italians, Jews, or Greeks from the Mediterranean, Swedes, Scots, or Germans from the North, what they had in common far outweighed conflicting traits and cultural and physical differences. All were European, offspring of one body of traditions and beliefs. Whether Catholics, Protestants, or Jews, they professed adherence to Western religious practices and beliefs. The so-called melting pot was scarcely a melting pot at all; the ingredients were European in origin. All spices that would have given the stew an entirely different flavor were carefully kept out—namely, the Negro and the Indian.

It was logical that Manifest Destiny, that American belief in a Providence of special design, should have racial overtones. Having meticulously kept out the infidel, Americans could rightly claim a racial doctrine of purity and supremacy in the world of 1846. Had not the nation of Polk's era developed free of those races not a part of the European heritage? Had the nation not progressed rapidly? Most assuredly, the answer was yes. When American development was compared to that of the former Spanish-American colonies, the reply was even more emphatically in the affirmative. After all, the Latin republics to the south had little to boast about. All were backward, illiterate, and badly governed states. Americans had just cause for satisfaction with what they had accomplished.

Unfortunately for Latin America, and especially Mexico, American pride had dire implications for the future. Convinced of the innate racial supremacy which the slogan of Manifest Destiny proclaimed throughout the world, many Americans came to believe that the New World was theirs to develop. Only their industry, their ingenuity, and their intelligence could cope fully with, the continental challenge. Why should half-breed Mexico—backward, politically a waste-land, and hopelessly split by nature and man's failures—hold Texas, New Mexico, and California? In Mexico's possession, all these lands would lie virgin, offering a home to a few thousand savage Indians, and here and there a Mexican pueblo of people scarcely different from their heathen neighbors. Manifest Destiny simply proclaimed what most Americans had firmly believed—the right of Anglo-Saxons and others of similar racial origin to develop what Providence had promised them. Weak Mexico, prey of its own cupidity and mistakes, was the victim of this belief.

Manifest Destiny, writes Mexican historian Carlos Bosch García, also contradicts an old American view that means are as important as ends. He stresses that the key to the history of the United States, as the doctrine of Manifest Destiny illustrates, lies in the willingness of Americans to accept as good the ultimate result of whatever they have undertaken to do. That the red man was driven from his homeland is accepted as inevitable and thus justifiable. American scholars might condemn the maltreatment of the Indian, but few question the final verdict.

Equally ambivalent, says Bosch García, is the American interpretation of the Mexican War. Though some American scholars of the post–Civil War period severely censured the South for what they called its responsibility for the Mexican War, their views reflected a criticism of the slavocracy rather than a heartfelt conviction that Mexico had been wronged. Obviously, there were exceptions. Hubert H. Bancroft, a California scholar and book collector, emphatically denounced Polk and his cohorts in his voluminous *History of Mexico* (1883–88). Among the politicians of the era, Abraham Lincoln won notoriety—and probably lost his seat in the House of Representatives—for his condemnation of Polk's declaration of war against Mexico. There were others, mostly members of the Whig Party, which officially opposed the war; but the majority, to repeat, was more involved with the problem of the South than with the question of war guilt.

Most Americans, in fact, have discovered ways and means to justify Manifest Destiny's war on Mexico. That country's chronic political instability, its unwillingness to meet international obligations, its false pride in its military establishment—all those, say scholars, led Mexican leaders to plunge their people into a hopeless war. Had Mexico been willing to sell California, one historian declares, no conflict would have occurred. To paraphrase Samuel F. Bemis, distinguished Yale University diplomatic scholar, no American today would undo the results of Polk's war. Put differently, to fall back on Bosch García, American writers have justified the means because of the ends. Manifest Destiny has not only been explained but has been vindicated on the grounds of what has been accomplished in California and New Mexico since 1848. Or, to cite Hermann Eduard von Holst, a late 19th century German scholar whose writings on American history won him a professorship at the University of Chicago, the conflict between Mexico and the United States was bound to arise. A virile and ambitious people whose cause advanced that of world civilization could not avoid battle with a decadent, puerile people. Moral judgments that applied to individuals might find Americans guilty of aggression, but the standards by which nations survive and prosper upheld the cause of the United States. Might makes right? Walt Whitman, then editor of the *Brooklyn Daily Eagle,* put down his answer succinctly:

> We love to indulge in thoughts of the future extent and power of this Republic—because with its increase is the increase in human happiness and liberty. . . . What has miserable Mexico—with her superstition, her burlesque upon freedom, her actual tyranny by the few over the many—what has she to do with the great mission of peopling the New World with a noble race? Be it ours, to achieve that mission! Be it ours to roll down all of the up-start leaven of the old despotism, that comes our way.

The conflict with Mexico was an offensive war without moral pretensions, according to Texas scholar Otis A. Singletary. It was no lofty crusade, no noble battle to right the wrongs of the past or to free a subjugated people, but a war of conquest waged by one neighbor against another. President Polk and his allies had to pay conscience money to justify a "greedy land-grab from a neighbor too weak to defend herself." American indifference to the Mexican War, Professor Singletary concludes, "lies rooted in the guilt that we as a nation have come to feel about it."

American racial attitudes, the product of a unique colonial background in the New World, may also have dictated the scope of territorial conquest in 1848 and, ironically, saved Mexico from total annexation. Until the clash with Mexico, the American experience had been limited to the conquest, occupation, and annexation of empty or sparsely settled territories, or of those already colonized by citizens of the United States, as were Oregon and Texas. American pioneers had been reincorporated into the Union with the annexation of Oregon and Texas, and even with the purchase of Louisiana in 1803, for the alien population proved small and of little importance. White planters, farmers, and pioneers mastered the small Mexican population in Texas and easily disposed of the Indians and half-breeds in the Louisiana territory.

Expansionists and their foes had long considered both Indian and Negro unfit for regeneration; both were looked on as inferior and doomed races. On this point, most Americans were in agreement. While not entirely in keeping with this view, American opinions of Latin Americans, and of Mexicans in particular, were hardly flattering. Purchase and annexation of Louisiana and Florida, and of Texas and Oregon, had been debated and postponed partly but of fear of what many believed would be the detrimental effect on American democracy resulting from the amalgamation of the half-breed and mongrel peoples of these lands. Driven by a sense of national aggrandizement, the expansionists preferred to conquer lands free of alien populations. Manifest Destiny had no place for the assimilation of strange and exotic peoples. Freedom for Americans—this was the cry, regardless of what befell the conquered natives. The location of sparsely held territory had dictated the course of empire.

James K. Polk's hunger for California reflected national opinion on races as well as desire for land. Both that territory and New Mexico, nearly to the same extent, were almost barren of native populations. Of sparsely settled California, in 1845 the *Hartford Times* eloquently declared that Americans could "redeem from unhallowed hands a land, above all others of heaven, and hold it for the use of a people who know how to obey heaven's behests." Thus it was that the tide of conquest—the fruits of the conference table at Guadalupe Hidalgo—stopped on the border of Mexico's inhabited lands, where the villages of a people alien in race and culture confronted the invaders. American concepts of race, the belief in the regeneration of virgin lands—these logically ordered annexation of both California and New Mexico, but left Mexico's settled territory alone.

Many Americans, it is true, gave much thought to the conquest and regeneration of all Mexico, but the peace of 1848 came before a sufficiently large number of them had abandoned traditional thoughts on race and color to embrace the new gospel. Apparently, most Americans were not yet willing to accept dark-skinned people as the burden of the white man.

Manifest Destiny, that mid-19th-century slogan, is now merely a historical question for most Americans. Despite the spectacular plums garnered from the conference table, the war is forgotten by political orators, seldom discussed in classrooms, and only infrequently recalled by historians and scholars.

But Mexicans, whether scholars or not, have not forgotten the war; their country suffered most from Manifest Destiny's claims to California. The war of 1846–48 represents one of the supreme tragedies of their history. Mexicans are intimately involved with it, unlike their late adversaries who have forgotten it. Fundamental reasons explain this paradox. The victorious United States went to a post-Civil War success story unequaled in the annals of Western civilization. Mexico emerged from the peace of Guadalupe Hidalgo bereft of half of its territory, a beaten, discouraged, and divided country. Mexico never completely recovered from the debacle.

Mexicans had known tragedy and defeat before, but their conquest by Generals , Zachary Taylor and Winfield Scott represented not only a territorial loss of immense proportions, but also a cataclysmic blow to their morale as a nation and as a people. From the Mexican point of view, their pride in what they believed they had mastered best—the science of warfare—was exposed as a myth. Mexicans could not even fight successfully, and they had little else to recall with pride, for their political development had enshrined bitter civil strife and callous betrayal of principle. Plagued by hordes of scheming politicians, hungry military men, and a backward and reactionary clergy, they had watched their economy stagnate. Guadalupe Hidalgo clearly outlined the scope of their defeat. There was no success story to write about, only tragedy. Mexicans of all classes are still engrossed in what might have been *if* General Antonio López de Santa Anna had repelled the invaders, from the North.

Polk's war message to Congress and Lincoln's famous reply in the House cover some dimensions of the historical problem. Up for discussion are Polk's role in the affair, the responsibility of the United States and Mexico, and the question of war guilt—a question raised by the victorious Americans and their allies at Nuremberg after World War II. For if Polk felt "the blood of this war, like the blood of Abel, is crying to Heaven against him," as Lincoln charged, then not just the war but also Manifest Destiny stand condemned.

Norman A. Graebner  **NO**

The Mexican War:
A Study in Causation

On May 11, 1846, President James K. Polk presented his war message to
Congress. After reviewing the skirmish between General Zachary Taylor's dragoons and a body of Mexican soldiers along the Rio Grande, the president
asserted that Mexico "has passed the boundary of the United States, has
invaded our territory and shed American blood upon the American soil. . . .
War exists, and, notwithstanding all our efforts to avoid it, exists by act of
Mexico." No country could have had a superior case for war. Democrats in
large numbers (for it was largely a partisan matter) responded with the patriotic fervor which Polk expected of them. "Our government has permitted
itself to be insulted long enough," wrote one Georgian. "The blood of her citizens has been spilt on her own soil. It appeals to us for vengeance." Still,
some members of Congress, recalling more accurately than the president the
circumstances of the conflict, soon rendered the Mexican War the most
reviled in American history—at least until the Vietnam War of the 1960s. One
outraged Whig termed the war "illegal, unrighteous, and damnable," and
Whigs questioned both Polk's honesty and his sense of geography. Congressman Joshua R. Giddings of Ohio accused the president of "planting the standard of the United States on foreign soil, and using the military forces of the
United States to violate every principle of international law and moral justice." To vote for the war, admitted Senator John C. Calhoun, was "to plunge a
dagger into his own heart, and more so." Indeed, some critics in Congress
openly wished the Mexicans well.

For over a century such profound differences in perception have pervaded American writings on the Mexican War. Even in the past decade, historians have reached conclusions on the question of war guilt as disparate as
those which separated Polk from his wartime conservative and abolitionist
critics. . . .

In some measure the diversity of judgment on the Mexican War, as on
other wars, is understandable. By basing their analyses on official rationaliza-
tions, historians often ignore the more universal causes of war which transcend individual conflicts and which can establish the bases for greater
consensus. Neither the officials in Washington nor those in Mexico City ever

From Norman A. Graebner, "The Mexican War: A Study in Causation," *Pacific Historical Review,* vol. 49,
no. 3 (August 1980), pp. 405-426. Copyright © 1980 by The American Historical Association, Pacific
Coast Branch. Reprinted by permission of University of California Press Journals. Notes omitted.

acknowledged any alternatives to the actions which they took. But governments generally have more choices in any controversy than they are prepared to admit. Circumstances determine their extent. The more powerful a nation, the more remote its dangers, the greater its options between action and inaction. Often for the weak, unfortunately, the alternative is capitulation or war. . . . Polk and his advisers developed their Mexican policies on the dual assumption that Mexico was weak and that the acquisition of certain Mexican territories would satisfy admirably the long-range interests of the United States. Within that context, Polk's policies were direct, timely, and successful. But the president had choices. Mexico, whatever its internal condition, was no direct threat to the United States. Polk, had he so desired, could have avoided war; indeed, he could have ignored Mexico in 1845 with absolute impunity.

ぐ◎つ

In explaining the Mexican War historians have dwelled on the causes of friction in American-Mexican relations. In part these lay in the disparate qualities of the two populations, in part in the vast discrepancies between the two countries in energy, efficiency, power, and national wealth. Through two decades of independence Mexico had experienced a continuous rise and fall of governments; by the 1840s survival had become the primary concern of every regime. Conscious of their weakness, the successive governments in Mexico City resented the superior power and effectiveness of the United States and feared American notions of destiny that anticipated the annexation of Mexico's northern provinces. Having failed to prevent the formation of the Texas Republic, Mexico reacted to Andrew Jackson's recognition of Texan independence in March 1837 with deep indignation. Thereafter the Mexican raids into Texas, such as the one on San Antonio in 1842, aggravated the bitterness of Texans toward Mexico, for such forays had no purpose beyond terrorizing the frontier settlements.

Such mutual animosities, extensive as they were, do not account for the Mexican War. Governments as divided and chaotic as the Mexican regimes of the 1840s usually have difficulty in maintaining positive and profitable relations with their neighbors; their behavior often produces annoyance, but seldom armed conflict. Belligerence toward other countries had flowed through U.S. history like a torrent without, in itself, setting off a war. Nations do not fight over cultural differences or verbal recriminations; they fight over perceived threats to their interests created by the ambitions or demands of others.

What increased the animosity between Mexico City and Washington was a series of specific issues over which the two countries perennially quarreled—claims, boundaries, and the future of Texas. Nations have made claims a pretext for intervention, but never a pretext for war. Every nineteenth-century effort to collect debts through force assumed the absence of effective resistance, for no debt was worth the price of war. To collect its debt from Mexico in 1838, for example, France blockaded Mexico's gulf ports and bombarded Vera Cruz. The U.S. claims against Mexico created special problems which discounted their seriousness as a rationale for war. True, the Mexican government failed to protect the possessions and the safety of Americans in Mexico from robbery, theft, and other illegal actions, but U.S. citizens were under no obligation to do business in Mexico and should have understood the risk of transporting goods and money in that country. Minister Waddy Thompson wrote from Mexico City in 1842 that it would be "with somewhat of bad grace that we should war upon a country because it could not pay its debts when so many of our own states are in the same situation." Even as the United States after 1842 attempted futilely to collect the $2 million awarded its citizens by a claims commission, it was far more deeply in debt to Britain over speculative losses. Minister Wilson Shannon reported in the summer of 1844 that the claims issue defied settlement in Mexico City and recommended that Washington take the needed action to compel Mexico to pay. If Polk would take up the challenge and sacrifice American human and material resources in a war against Mexico, he would do so for reasons other than the enforcement of claims. The president knew well that Mexico could not pay, yet as late as May 9, 1846, he was ready to ask Congress for a declaration of war on the question of unpaid claims alone.

Congress's joint resolution for Texas annexation in February 1845 raised the specter of war among editors and politicians alike. As early as 1843 the Mexican government had warned the American minister in Mexico City that annexation would render war inevitable; Mexican officials in Washington repeated that warning. To Mexico, therefore, the move to annex Texas was an unbearable affront. Within one month after Polk's inauguration on March 4, General Juan Almonte, the Mexican minister in Washington, boarded a packet in New York and sailed for Vera Cruz to sever his country's diplomatic relations with the United States. Even before the Texas Convention could meet on July 4 to vote annexation, rumors of a possible Mexican invasion of Texas prompted Polk to advance Taylor's forces from Fort Jesup in Louisiana down the Texas coast. Polk instructed Taylor to extend his protection to the Rio Grande but to avoid any areas to the north of that river occupied by Mexican troops. Simultaneously the president reinforced the American squadron in the Gulf of Mexico. "The threatened invasion of Texas by a large Mexican army," Polk informed Andrew J. Donelson, the American chargé in Texas, on June 15, "is well calculated to excite great interest here and increases our solicitude concerning the final action by the Congress and the Convention of Texas." Polk assured Donelson that he intended to defend Texas to the limit of his constitutional power. Donelson resisted the pressure of those Texans who wanted Taylor to advance to the Rio Grande; instead, he placed the general at Corpus Christi on the Nueces River. Taylor agreed that the line from the mouth of the Nueces to San Antonio covered the Texas settlements and afforded a favorable base from which to defend the frontier.

Those who took the rumors of Mexican aggressiveness seriously lauded the president's action. With Texas virtually a part of the United States, argued the *Washington Union,* "We owe it to ourselves, to the proud and elevated character which America maintains among the nations of the earth, to guard our own territory from the invasion of the ruthless Mexicans." The *New York Morning News* observed that Polk's policy would, on the whole, "command a general concurrence of the public opinion of his country." Some Democratic leaders, fearful of a Mexican attack, urged the president to strengthen Taylor's forces and order them to take the offensive should Mexican soldiers cross the Rio Grande. Others believed the reports from Mexico exaggerated, for there was no apparent relationship between the country's expressions of belligerence and its capacity to act. Secretary of War William L. Marcy admitted that his information was no better than that of other commentators. "I have at no time," he wrote in July, "felt that war with Mexico was probable—and do not now believe it is, yet it is in the range of possible occurrences. I have officially acted on the hypothesis that our peace may be temporarily disturbed without however believing it will be." Still convinced that the administration had no grounds for alarm, Marcy wrote on August 12: "The presence of a considerable force in Texas will do no hurt and possibly may be of great use." In September William S. Parrott, Polk's special agent in Mexico, assured the president that there would be neither a Mexican declaration of war nor an invasion of Texas.

Polk insisted that the administration's show of force in Texas would prevent rather than provoke war. "I do not anticipate that Mexico will be mad enough to declare war," he wrote in July, but "I think she would have done so but for the appearance of a strong naval force in the Gulf and our army moving in the direction of her frontier on land." Polk restated this judgment on July 28 in a letter to General Robert Armstrong, the U.S. consul at Liverpool: "I think there need be but little apprehension of war with Mexico. If however she shall be mad enough to make war we are prepared to meet her." The president assured Senator William H. Haywood of North Carolina that the American forces in Texas would never aggress against Mexico; however, they would prevent any Mexican forces from crossing the Rio Grande. In conversation with Senator William S. Archer of Virginia on September 1, the president added confidently that "the appearance of our land and naval forces on the borders of Mexico & in the Gulf would probably deter and prevent Mexico from either declaring war or invading Texas." Polk's continuing conviction that Mexico would not attack suggests that his deployment of U.S. land and naval forces along Mexico's periphery was designed less to protect Texas than to support an aggressive diplomacy which might extract a satisfactory treaty from Mexico without war. For Anson Jones, the last president of the Texas Republic, Polk's deployments had precisely that purpose:

> Texas never actually needed the protection of the United States after I came into office. . . . There was no necessity for it after the 'preliminary Treaty,' as we were at peace with Mexico, and knew perfectly well that that Government, though she might bluster a little, had not the slightest idea of invading Texas either by land or water; and that nothing would provoke her to (active) hostilities, but the presence of troops in the immediate neighborhood of the Rio Grande, threatening her towns and settlements on the southwest side of that river. . . . But Donelson appeared so intent upon 'encumbering us with help,' that finally, to get rid of his annoyance, he was told he might give us as much protection as he pleased. . . . The protection asked for was only *prospective* and contingent; the *protection* he had in view was *immediate* and *aggressive*.

For Polk the exertion of military and diplomatic pressure on a disorganized Mexico was not a prelude to war. Whig critics of annexation had predicted war; this alone compelled the administration to avoid a conflict over Texas. In his memoirs Jones recalled that in 1845 Commodore Robert F. Stockton, with either the approval or the connivance of Polk, attempted to convince him that he should place Texas "in an attitude of active hostility toward Mexico, so that, when Texas was finally brought into the Union, *she might bring war with her.*" If Stockton engaged in such an intrigue, he apparently did so on his own initiative, for no evidence exists to implicate the administration. Polk not only preferred to achieve his purposes by means other than war but also assumed that his military measures in Texas, limited as they were, would convince the Mexican government that it could not escape the necessity of coming to terms with the United States. Washington's policy toward Mexico during 1845 achieved the broad national purpose of Texas annexation. Beyond that it brought U.S. power to bear on Mexico in a manner calculated to further the processes of negotiation. Whether the burgeoning tension would lead to a negotiated boundary settlement or to war hinged on two factors: the nature of Polk's demands and Mexico's response to them. The president announced his objectives to Mexico's troubled officialdom through his instructions to John Slidell, his special emissary who departed for Mexico in November 1845 with the assurance that the government there was prepared to reestablish formal diplomatic relations with the United States and negotiate a territorial settlement. . . .

⋅⟨⊙⟩⋅

Actually, Slidell's presence in Mexico inaugurated a diplomatic crisis not unlike those which precede most wars. Fundamentally the Polk administration, in dispatching Slidell, gave the Mexicans the same two choices that the dominant power in any confrontation gives to the weaker: the acceptance of a body of concrete diplomatic demands or eventual war. Slidell's instructions described U.S. territorial objectives with considerable clarity. If Mexico knew little of Polk's growing acquisitiveness toward California during the autumn of 1845, Slidell proclaimed the president's intentions with his proposals to purchase varying portions of California for as much as $25 million. Other countries such as England and Spain had consigned important areas of the New World through peaceful negotiations, but the United States, except in its Mexican relations, had never asked any country to part with a portion of its own territory. Yet Polk could not understand why Mexico should reveal any special reluctance to part with Texas, the Rio Grande, New Mexico, or California. What made the terms of Slidell's instructions appear fair to him was Mexico's military and financial helplessness. Polk's defenders noted that California was not a sine qua non of any settlement and that the president offered to settle the immediate controversy over the acquisition of the Rio Grande boundary alone in exchange for the cancellation of claims. Unfortunately, amid the passions of December 1845, such distinctions were lost. Furthermore, a settlement of the Texas boundary would not have resolved the California question at all.

Throughout the crisis months of 1845 and 1846, spokesmen of the Polk administration repeatedly warned the Mexican government that its choices were limited. In June 1845, Polk's mouthpiece, the *Washington Union,* had observed characteristically that, if Mexico resisted Washington's demands, "a corps of properly organized volunteers . . . would invade, overrun, and occupy Mexico. They would enable us not only to take California, but to keep it." American officials, in their contempt for Mexico, spoke privately of the need to chastize that country for its annoyances and insults. Parrott wrote to Secretary of State James Buchanan in October that he wished "to see this people well flogged by Uncle Sam's boys, ere we enter upon negotiations. . . . I know [the Mexicans] better, perhaps, than any other American citizen and I am fully persuaded, they can never love or respect us, as we should be loved and respected by them, until we shall have given them a positive proof of our superiority." Mexico's pretensions would continue, wrote Slidell in late December, "until the Mexican people shall be convinced by hostile demonstrations, that our differences must be settled promptly, either by negotiation or the sword." In January 1846 the *Union* publicly threatened Mexico with war if it rejected the just demands of the United States: "The result of such a course on her part may compel us to resort to more decisive measures. . . . to obtain the settlement of our legitimate claims." As Slidell prepared to leave Mexico in March 1846, he again reminded the administration: "Depend upon it, we can never get along well with them, until we have given them a good drubbing." In Washington on May 8, Slidell advised the president "to take the redress of the wrongs and injuries which we had so long borne from Mexico into our own hands, and to act with promptness and energy."

Mexico responded to Polk's challenge with an outward display of belligerence and an inward dread of war. Mexicans feared above all that the United States intended to overrun their country and seize much of their territory. Polk and his advisers assumed that Mexico, to avoid an American invasion, would give up its provinces peacefully. Obviously Mexico faced growing diplomatic and military pressures to negotiate away its territories; it faced no moral obligation to do so. Herrera and Paredes had the sovereign right to protect their regimes by avoiding any formal recognition of Slidell and by rejecting any of the boundary proposals embodied in his instructions, provided that in the process they did not endanger any legitimate interests of the American people. At least to some Mexicans, Slidell's terms demanded nothing less than Mexico's capitulation. By what standard was $2 million a proper payment for the Rio Grande boundary, or $25 million a fair price for California? No government would have accepted such terms. Having rejected negotiation in the face of superior force, Mexico would meet the challenge with a final gesture of defiance. In either case it was destined to lose, but historically nations have preferred to fight than to give away territory under diplomatic pressure alone. Gene M. Brack, in his long study of Mexico's deep-seated fear and resentment of the United States, explained Mexico's ultimate behavior in such terms:

President Polk knew that Mexico could offer but feeble resistance militarily, and he knew that Mexico needed money. No proper American would exchange territory and the national honor for cash, but President Polk mistakenly believed that the application of military pressure would convince Mexicans to do so. They did not respond logically, but patriotically. Left with the choice of war or territorial concessions, the former course, however dim the prospects of success, could be the only one.

⋯◉⋯

Mexico, in its resistance, gave Polk the three choices which every nation gives another in an uncompromisable confrontation: to withdraw his demands and permit the issues to drift, unresolved; to reduce his goals in the interest of an immediate settlement; or to escalate the pressures in the hope of securing an eventual settlement on his own terms. Normally when the internal conditions of a country undermine its relations with others, a diplomatic corps simply removes itself from the hostile environment and awaits a better day. Mexico, despite its animosity, did not endanger the security interests of the United States; it had not invaded Texas and did not contemplate doing so. Mexico had refused to pay the claims, but those claims were not equal to the price of a one-week war. Whether Mexico negotiated a boundary for Texas in 1846 mattered little; the United States had lived with unsettled boundaries for decades without considering war. Settlers, in time, would have forced a decision, but in 1846 the region between the Nueces and the Rio Grande was a vast, generally unoccupied wilderness. Thus there was nothing, other than Polk's ambitions, to prevent the United States from withdrawing its diplomats from Mexico City and permitting its relations to drift. But Polk, whatever the language of his instructions, did not send Slidell to Mexico to normalize relations with that government. He expected Slidell to negotiate an immediate boundary settlement favorable to the United States, and nothing less.

Recognizing no need to reduce his demands on Mexico, Polk, without hesitation, took the third course which Mexico offered. Congress bound the president to the annexation of Texas; thereafter the Polk administration was free to formulate its own policies toward Mexico. With the Slidell mission Polk embarked upon a program of gradual coercion to achieve a settlement, preferably without war. That program led logically from his dispatching an army to Texas and his denunciation of Mexico in his annual message of December 1845 to his new instructions of January 1846, which ordered General Taylor to the Rio Grande. Colonel Atocha, spokesman for the deposed Mexican leader, Antonio López de Santa Anna, encouraged Polk to pursue his policy of escalation. The president recorded Atocha's advice:

> He said our army should be marched at once from Corpus Christi to the Del Norte, and a strong naval force assembled at Vera Cruz, that Mr. Slidell, the U.S. Minister, should withdraw from Jalappa, and go on board one of our ships of War at Vera Cruz, and in that position should demand the payment of [the] amount due our citizens; that it was well known the Mexican Government was unable to pay in money, and that when they saw a strong force ready to strike on their coasts and border, they would, he had no doubt, feel their danger and agree to the boundary suggested. He said that Paredes, Almonte, & Gen'l Santa Anna were all willing for such an

arrangement, but that they dare not make it until it was made apparent to the Archbishop of Mexico & the people generally that it was necessary to save their country from a war with the U. States.

Thereafter Polk never questioned the efficacy of coercion. He asserted at a cabinet meeting on February 17 that "it would be necessary to take strong measures towards Mexico before our difficulties with that Government could be settled." Similarly on April 18 Polk told Calhoun that "our relations with Mexico had reached a point where we could not stand still but must treat all nations whether weak or strong alike, and that I saw no alternative but strong measures towards Mexico." A week later the president again brought the Mexican question before the cabinet. "I expressed my opinion," he noted in his diary, "that we must take redress for the injuries done us into our own hands, that we had attempted to conciliate Mexico in vain, and had forborne until forbearance was no longer either a virtue or patriotic." Convinced that Paredes needed money, Polk suggested to leading senators that Congress appropriate $1 million both to encourage Paredes to negotiate and to sustain him in power until the United States could ratify the treaty. The president failed to secure Calhoun's required support.

Polk's persistence led him and the country to war. Like all escalations in the exertion of force, his decision responded less to unwanted and unanticipated resistance than to the requirements of the clearly perceived and inflexible purposes which guided the administration. What perpetuated the president's escalation to the point of war was his determination to pursue goals to the end whose achievement lay outside the possibilities of successful negotiations. Senator Thomas Hart Benton of Missouri saw this situation when he wrote: "It is impossible to conceive of an administration less warlike, or more intriguing, than that of Mr. Polk. They were *men of peace, with objects to be accomplished by means of war*; so that war was a necessity and an indispensability to their purpose."

Polk understood fully the state of Mexican opinion. In placing General Taylor on the Rio Grande he revealed again his contempt for Mexico. Under no national obligation to expose the country's armed forces, he would not have advanced Taylor in the face of a superior military force. Mexico had been undiplomatic; its denunciations of the United States were insulting and provocative. But if Mexico's behavior antagonized Polk, it did not antagonize the Whigs, the abolitionists, or even much of the Democratic party. Such groups did not regard Mexico as a threat; they warned the administration repeatedly that Taylor's presence on the Rio Grande would provoke war. But in the balance against peace was the pressure of American expansionism. Much of the Democratic and expansionist press, having accepted without restraint both the purposes of the Polk administration and its charges of Mexican perfidy, urged the president on to more vigorous action. . . .

Confronted with the prospect of further decline which they could neither accept nor prevent, [the Mexicans] lashed out with the intention of protecting their self-esteem and compelling the United States, if it was determined to have the Rio Grande, New Mexico, and California, to pay for its prizes with something other than money. On April 23, Paredes issued a proclamation declaring a defensive war against the United States. Predictably, one day later the Mexicans fired on a detachment of U.S. dragoons. Taylor's report of the attack reached Polk on Saturday evening, May 9. On Sunday the president drafted his war message and delivered it to Congress on the following day. Had Polk avoided the crisis, he might have gained the time required to permit the emigrants of 1845 and 1846 to settle the California issue without war.

What clouds the issue of the Mexican War's justification was the acquisition of New Mexico and California, for contemporaries and historians could not logically condemn the war and laud the Polk administration for its territorial achievements. Perhaps it is true that time would have permitted American pioneers to transform California into another Texas. But even then California's acquisition by the United States would have emanated from the use of force, for the elimination of Mexican sovereignty, whether through revolution or war, demanded the successful use of power. If the power employed in revolution would have been less obtrusive than that exerted in war, its role would have been no less essential. There simply was no way that the United States could acquire California peacefully. If the distraught Mexico of 1845 would not sell the distant province, no regime thereafter would have done so. Without forceful destruction of Mexico's sovereign power, California would have entered the twentieth century as an increasingly important region of another country.

Thus the Mexican War poses the dilemma of all international relations. Nations whose geographic and political status fails to coincide with their ambition and power can balance the two sets of factors in only one manner: through the employment of force. They succeed or fail according to circumstances; and for the United States, the conditions for achieving its empire in the Southwest and its desired frontage on the Pacific were so ideal that later generations could refer to the process as the mere fulfillment of destiny. "The Mexican Republic," lamented a Mexican writer in 1848, " . . . had among other misfortunes of less account, the great one of being in the vicinity of a strong and energetic people." What the Mexican War revealed in equal measure is the simple fact that only those countries which have achieved their destiny, whatever that may be, can afford to extol the virtues of peaceful change.

POSTSCRIPT

Was the Mexican War an Exercise in American Imperialism?

According to Graebner, President James Polk assumed that Mexico was weak and that acquiring certain Mexican territories would satisfy "the long-range interests" of the United States. But when Mexico refused Polk's attempts to purchase New Mexico and California, he was left with three options: withdraw his demands, modify and soften his proposals, or aggressively pursue his original goals. According to Graebner, the president chose the third option.

Graebner is one of the most prominent members of the "realist" school of diplomatic historians. His writings were influenced by the cold war realists, political scientists, diplomats, and journalists of the 1950s who believed that American foreign policy oscillated between heedless isolationism and crusading wars without developing coherent policies that suited the national interests of the United States.

Graebner's views on the Mexican War have not gone unchallenged. For example, both David M. Pletcher's *The Diplomacy of Annexation* (University of Missouri Press, 1973), which remains the definitive study of the Polk administration, and Charles Seller's biography *James K. Polk*, 2 vols. (Princeton University Press, 1957–1966) are critical of Polk's actions in pushing the Mexican government to assert its authority in the disputed territory.

Professor Ruiz offers a Mexican perspective on the war in chapter 11 of his book *Triumphs and Tragedy: A History of the Mexican People* (W. W. Norton, 1992), in which he argues that while the United States went on to achieve great economic success after the Civil War, Mexico never recovered from losing half of her territories.

Ruiz also takes issue with Graebner, who considers Manifest Destiny to be mere political rhetoric with very limited goals. In Ruiz's view, Manifest Destiny was a reflection of the racist attitudes shown toward the non-white Native Americans, African Americans, and Mexican Americans who stood in the way of white America's desire for new land.

Both Graebner and Ruiz appear ethnocentric in their analysis of the origins of the war. Graebner neglects the emotionalism and instability of Mexican politics at the time, which may have precluded the rational analysis a realistic historian might have expected in the decision-making process. Ruiz also oversimplifies the motives of the Euroamericans, and he appears to neglect the political divisions between slaveholders and nonslaveholders and between Whig and Democratic politicians over the wisdom of going to war with Mexico.

The best two collections of readings from the major writers on the Mexican War are old but essential: see Archie McDonald, ed., *The Mexican*

War: Crisis for American Democracy (D. C. Heath, 1969) and Ramon Eduardo Ruiz, ed., *The Mexican War: Was It Manifest Destiny?* (Holt, Rinehart & Winston, 1963).

There are several nontraditional books that cover the Mexican War, including John H. Schroeder, *Mr. Polk's War: American Opposition and Dissent, 1846–1848* (University of Wisconsin Press, 1973). Robert W. Johannsen summarizes the ways in which contemporaries viewed the war in *To the Halls of the Montezumas: The Mexican War in the American Imagination* (Oxford University Press, 1985).

ISSUE 15

Were the Abolitionists "Unrestrained Fanatics"?

YES: C. Vann Woodward, from *The Burden of Southern History,* 3d ed. (Louisiana State University Press, 1993)

NO: Donald G. Mathews, from "The Abolitionists on Slavery: The Critique Behind the Social Movement," *Journal of Southern History* (May 1967)

ISSUE SUMMARY

YES: C. Vann Woodward depicts John Brown as a fanatic who committed wholesale murder in Kansas in 1856 and whose ill-fated assault on Harpers Ferry, Virginia, in 1859, while admired by his fellow abolitionists and many northern intellectuals, was an irrational act of treason against the United States.

NO: Donald G. Mathews describes abolitionists as uncompromising agitators, not unprincipled fanatics, who employed flamboyant rhetoric but who crafted a balanced and thoughtful critique of the institution of slavery as a social evil that violated the nation's basic values.

Opposition to slavery in the area that became the United States dates back to the seventeenth and eighteenth centuries, when Puritan leaders, such as Samuel Sewall, and Quakers, such as John Woolman and Anthony Benezet, published a number of pamphlets condemning the existence of the slave system. This religious link to antislavery sentiment is also evident in the writings of John Wesley as well as in the decision of the Society of Friends in 1688 to prohibit their members from owning bondservants. Slavery was said to be contrary to Christian principles. These attacks, however, did little to diminish the institution. Complaints that the English government had instituted a series of measures that "enslaved" the colonies in British North America raised thorny questions about the presence of *real* slavery in those colonies. How could American colonists demand their freedom from King George III, who was cast in the role of oppressive master, while denying freedom and liberty to African American bondsmen? Such a contradiction inspired a gradual emancipation movement in the North, which often was accompanied by compensation for the former slave owners.

In addition, antislavery societies sprang up throughout the nation to continue the crusade against bondage. Interestingly, the majority of these organizations were located in the South. Prior to the 1830s, the most prominent antislavery organization was the American Colonization Society, which offered a two-fold program: (1) gradual, compensated emancipation of slaves and (2) exportation of the freed men to colonies outside the boundaries of the United States, mostly to Africa.

In the 1830s, antislavery activity underwent an important transformation. A new strain of antislavery sentiment expressed itself in the abolitionist movement. Drawing momentum both from the revivalism of the Second Great Awakening and the example set by England (which prohibited slavery in its imperial holdings in 1833), abolitionists called for the immediate end to slavery without compensation to masters for the loss of their property. Abolitionists viewed slavery not so much as a practical problem to be resolved, but rather as a moral offense incapable of resolution through traditional channels of political compromise. In January 1831, William Lloyd Garrison, who for many came to symbolize the abolitionist crusade, published the first issue of *The Liberator*, a newspaper dedicated to the immediate end to slavery. In his first editorial, Garrison expressed the self-righteous indignation of many in the abolitionist movement when he warned slaveholders and their supporters to "urge me not to use moderation in a cause like the present. I am in earnest—I will not equivocate—I will not excuse—I will not retreat a single inch—AND I WILL BE HEARD. . . ."

Unfortunately for Garrison, relatively few Americans were inclined to respond positively to his call. His newspaper generated little interest outside Boston, New York, Philadelphia, and other major urban centers of the North. This situation, however, changed within a matter of months. In August 1831, a slave preacher named Nat Turner led a rebellion of slaves in Southampton County, Virginia, that resulted in the death of fifty-eight whites. Although the revolt was quickly suppressed and Turner and his supporters were executed, the incident spread fear throughout the South. Governor John B. Floyd of Virginia turned an accusatory finger toward the abolitionists when he concluded that the Turner uprising was "undoubtedly designed and matured by unrestrained fanatics in some of the neighboring states." Moreover, it would be charged, these abolitionists contributed to a crisis environment that degenerated over the next generation and ultimately produced civil war.

One such abolitionist was John Brown who became a martyr in the antislavery pantheon when he was executed following his unsuccessful raid on the federal arsenal in Harpers Ferry, Virginia in 1859. The late noted historian of the American South, C. Vann Woodward, explains that Brown had no qualms about using violence to conduct his fanatical war on slavery.

In the second selection, Donald Mathews insists that, although abolitionists often employed heated rhetoric in their condemnation of the slave system, they were neither irrational nor illogical. Instead, he concludes, the abolitionists were intelligent reformers whose opposition to slavery was presented in a thoughtful, balanced critique of slavery.

YES

C. Vann Woodward

John Brown's Private War

The figure of John Brown is still wrapped in obscurity and myth. . . . His fifty-nine years were divided sharply into two periods. The obscurity of his first fifty-five years was of the sort natural to a humble life unassociated with events of importance. The obscurity of his last four years, filled with conspiratorial activities, was in large part the deliberate work of Brown, his fellow conspirators, and their admirers. . . .

After 1855 John Brown abandoned his unprofitable business career when he was almost penniless and for the rest of his life was without remunerative employment. He depended for support upon donations from people whom he convinced of his integrity and reliability. Here and elsewhere there is strong evidence that Brown was somehow able to inspire confidence and intense personal loyalty.

The Kansas phase of Brown's guerrilla warfare has given rise to the "Legend of Fifty-six," a fabric of myth that has been subjected to a more rigorous examination than any other phase of Brown's life has ever received. [James C.] Malin establishes beyond question that "John Brown did not appear to have had much influence either in making or marring Kansas history," that his exploits "brought tragedy to innocent settlers," but that "in no place did he appear as a major factor." He also establishes a close correlation between the struggle over freedom and slavery and local clashes over conflicting land titles on the Kansas frontier, and he points out that "the business of stealing horses under the cloak of fighting for freedom and running them off to the Nebraska-Iowa border for sale" is a neglected aspect of the struggle for "Bleeding Kansas." John Brown and his men engaged freely and profitably in this business and justified their plunder as the spoils of war. Two covenants that Brown drew up for his followers contained a clause specifically providing for the division of captured property among the members of his guerrilla band.

It would be a gross distortion, however, to dismiss John Brown as a frontier horse thief. He was much too passionately and fanatically in earnest about his war on slavery to permit of any such oversimplification. His utter fearlessness, courage, and devotion to the cause were greatly admired by respectable antislavery men who saw in the old Puritan an ideal revolutionary leader.

One exploit of Brown in Kansas, however, would seem to have put him forever beyond the pale of association with intelligent opponents of slavery. This was the famous Pottawatomie massacre of May 24, 1856. John Brown, leading four of his sons, a son-in-law, and two other men, descended by night upon an unsuspecting settlement of four proslavery families. Proceeding from one home to another the raiders took five men out, murdered them, and left their bodies horribly mutilated. None of the victims was a slaveholder, and two of them were born in Germany and had no contact with the South. By way of explanation Brown said the murders had been "decreed by Almighty God, ordained from Eternity." He later denied responsibility for the act, and some of the Eastern capitalists and intellectuals who supported him refused to believe him guilty. In view of the report of the murders that was laid before the country on July 11, 1856, in the form of a committee report in the House of Representatives, it is somewhat difficult to excuse such ignorance among intelligent men. . . .

In the spring of 1858 plans for a raid on Virginia began to take definite shape. To a convention of fellow conspirators in Chatham, Canada, in May, John Brown presented his remarkable "Provisional Constitution and Ordinances for the People of the United States." It represented the form of government he proposed to establish by force of arms with a handful of conspirators and an armed insurrection of slaves. Complete with legislative, executive, and judicial branches, Brown's revolutionary government was in effect a military dictatorship, since all acts of his congress had to be approved by the commander-in-chief of the army in order to become valid. Needless to say, John Brown was elected commander-in-chief.

By July, 1859, Commander-in-Chief Brown had established himself at a farm on the Maryland side of the Potomac River, four miles north of Harpers Ferry. There he assembled twenty-one followers and accumulated ammunition and other supplies, including 200 revolvers, 200 rifles, and 950 pikes specially manufactured for the slaves he expected to rise up in insurrection. On Sunday night, October 16, after posting a guard of three men at the farm, he set forth with eighteen followers, five of them Negroes, and all of them young men, to start his war of liberation and found his abolitionist republic. Brown's first objective, to capture the United States arsenal at Harpers Ferry, was easily accomplished since it was without military guard. In the Federal armory and the rifle works, also captured, were sufficient arms to start the bloodiest slave insurrection in history.

The commander-in-chief appears to have launched his invasion without any definite plan of campaign and then proceeded to violate every military principle in the book. He cut himself off from his base of supplies, failed to keep open his only avenues of retreat, dispersed his small force, and bottled the bulk of them up in a trap where defeat was inevitable. "In fact, it was so absurd," remarked Abraham Lincoln, "that the slaves, with all their ignorance, saw plainly enough it could not succeed." Not one of them joined Brown voluntarily, and those he impressed quickly departed. The insurrectionists killed one United States Marine and four inhabitants of Harpers Ferry, including the mayor and a Negro freeman. Ten of their own number, including two of Brown's sons, were killed, five were taken prisoner by a small force of Marines commanded by Robert E. Lee, and seven escaped, though two of them were later arrested. John Brown's insurrection ended in a tragic and dismal failure.

When news of the invasion was first flashed across the country, the most common reaction was that this was obviously the act of a madman, that John Brown was insane. This explanation was particularly attractive to Republican politicians and editors, whose party suffered the keenest embarrassment from the incident. Fall elections were on, and the new Congress was about to convene. Democrats immediately charged that John Brown's raid was the inevitable consequence of the "irresistible-conflict" and "higher-law" abolitionism preached by Republican leaders William H. Seward and Salmon P. Chase. "Brown's invasion," wrote Senator Henry Wilson of Massachusetts, "has thrown us, who were in a splendid position, into a defensive position. . . . If we are defeated next year we shall owe it to that foolish and insane movement of Brown's." The emphasis on insanity was taken up widely by Wilson's contemporaries and later adopted by historians.

It seems best to deal with the insanity question promptly, for it is likely to confuse the issue and cause us to miss the meaning of Harpers Ferry. In dealing with the problem it is important not to blink, as many of his biographers have done, at the evidence of John Brown's close association with insanity in both his heredity and his environment. In the Brown Papers at the Library of Congress are nineteen affidavits signed by relatives and friends attesting the record of insanity in the Brown family. John Brown's maternal grandmother and his mother both died insane. His three aunts and two uncles, sisters and brothers of his mother, were intermittently insane, and so was his only sister, her daughter, and one of his brothers. Of six first cousins, all more or less mad, two were deranged from time to time, two had been repeatedly committed to the state insane asylum, and two were still confined at the time. Of John Brown's immediate family, his first wife and one of his sons died insane, and a second son was insane at intervals. On these matters the affidavits, signers of which include Brown's uncle, a half brother, a brother-in-law, and three first cousins, are in substantial agreement. On the sanity of John Brown himself, however, opinion varied. Several believed that he was a "monomaniac," one that he was insane on subjects of religion and slavery, and an uncle thought his nephew had been "subject to periods of insanity" for twenty years. . . .

"John Brown may be a lunatic," observed the Boston *Post*, but if so, "then one-fourth of the people of Massachusetts are madmen," and perhaps three-fourths of the ministers of religion. Begging that Brown's life be spared, Amos A. Lawrence wrote Governor Wise: "Brown is a Puritan whose mind has become disordered by hardship and illness. He has the qualities wh. endear him to our people." The association of ideas was doubtless unintentional, but to the Virginian it must have seemed that Lawrence was saying that in New England a disordered mind was an endearing quality. The Reverend J. M. Manning of Old South Church, Boston, pronounced Harpers Ferry "an unlawful, a foolhardy, a suicidal act" and declared, "I stand before it wondering and admiring." Horace Greeley called it "the work of a madman" for which he had not "one reproachful word," and for the "grandeur and nobility" of which he was "reverently grateful." And the New York *Independent* declared that while "Harpers Ferry was insane, the controlling motive of this demonstration was sublime." It was both foolhardy and godly, insane and sublime, treasonous and admirable.

The prestige and character of the men who lent John Brown active, if sometimes secret, support likewise suggest caution in dismissing Harpers Ferry as merely the work of a madman. Among Brown's fellow conspirators the most notable were the so-called Secret Six. Far from being horse thieves and petty traders, the Secret Six came from the cream of Northern society. Capitalist, philanthropist, philosopher, surgeon, professor, minister—they were men of reputability and learning, four of them with Harvard degrees.

With a Harvard Divinity School degree, a knowledge of twenty languages, and a library of sixteen thousand volumes, Theodore Parker was perhaps the most prodigiously learned American of his time. In constant correspondence with the leading Republican politicians, he has been called "the Conscience of a Party." What Gerrit Smith, the very wealthy philanthropist and one-time congressman of Peterboro, New York, lacked in mental endowments he made up in good works—earnest efforts to improve the habits of his fellow men. These included not only crusades against alcohol and tobacco in all forms, but also coffee, tea, meat, and spices—"almost everything which gave pleasure," according to his biographer. Generous with donations to dietary reform, dress reform, woman's rights, educational and "non-resistance" movements, Smith took no interest whatever in factory and labor reform, but he was passionately absorbed in the antislavery movement and a liberal contributor to John Brown. Dr. Samuel G. Howe of Boston, husband of the famous Julia Ward Howe, was justly renowned for his humanitarian work for the blind and mentally defective. In his youth he had gone on a Byronic crusade in Greece against the Turk. These experiences contributed greatly to his moral prestige, if little to his political sophistication. The most generous man of wealth among the conspirators was George L. Stearns of Boston, a prosperous manufacturer of lead pipe. In the opinion of this revolutionary capitalist, John Brown was "the representative man of this century, as Washington was of the last." Finally there were two younger men, fledgling conspirators. The son of a prosperous Boston merchant who was bursar of Harvard, Thomas Wentworth Higginson became pastor of a church in Worcester after taking his divinity degree at Harvard. Young Franklin B. Sanborn was an apostle of Parker and a protégé of Emerson, who persuaded Sanborn to take charge of a school in Concord.

The most tangible service the Secret Six rendered the conspiracy lay in secretly diverting to John Brown, for use at Harpers Ferry, money and arms that had been contributed to the Massachusetts-Kansas Aid Committee for use in "Bleeding Kansas." . . . By this means the Kansas Committee was converted into a respectable front for subversive purposes, and thousands of innocent contributors to what appeared to be a patriotic organization discovered later that they had furnished rifles for a treasonous attack on a Federal arsenal. . . .

The Secret Six appear to have been fascinated by the drama of conspiratorial activity. There were assumed names, coded messages, furtive committee meetings, dissembling of motives, and secret caches of arms. And over all the romance and glamor of a noble cause—the liberation of man. Although they knew perfectly well the general purpose of Brown, the Secret Six were careful to request him not to tell them the precise time and place of the invasion. The wily old revolutionist could have told them much that they did not know about the psychology of fellow travelers. Brown had earlier laid down this strategy for conspirators who were hard pressed: "Go into the houses of your most prominent and influential white friends with your wives; and that will effectually fasten upon them the suspicion of being connected with you, and will compel them to make a common cause with you, whether they would otherwise live up to their professions or not." The same strategy is suggested by Brown's leaving behind, in the Maryland farmhouse where they would inevitably be captured, all his private papers, hundreds of letters of himself and followers, implicating nobody knew how many respectable fellow travelers. . . .

The assistance that the Secret Six conspirators were able to give John Brown and his Legend was as nothing compared with that rendered by other Northern intellectuals. Among them was the cultural and moral aristocracy of America in the period that has been called a "Renaissance." Some of these men, Ralph Waldo Emerson and Henry Thoreau among them, had met and admired Brown and even made small contributions to his cause. But they were safely beyond reproach of the law and were never taken into his confidence in the way that the Secret Six were. Their service was rendered after the event in justifying and glorifying Brown and his invasion.

In this work the intellectuals were ably assisted by a genius, a genius at self-justification—John Brown himself. From his prison cell he poured out a stream of letters, serene and restrained, filled with Biblical language and fired with overpowering conviction that his will and God's were one and the same. These letters and his famous speech at the trial constructed for the hero a new set of motives and plans and a new role. For Brown had changed roles. In October he invaded Virginia as a conqueror armed for conquest, carrying with him guns and pikes for the army he expected to rally to his standard and a new constitution to replace the one he overthrew. In that role he was a miserable failure. Then in November he declared at his trial: "I never did intend murder, or treason, or the destruction of property, or to excite or incite slaves to rebellion, or to make an insurrection." He only intended to liberate slaves without bloodshed, as he falsely declared he had done in Missouri the year before. How these statements can be reconciled with the hundreds of pikes, revolvers, and rifles, the capture of an armory, the taking of hostages, the killing of unarmed civilians, the destruction of government property, and the arming of slaves is difficult to see. Nor is it possible to believe that Brown thought he could seize a Federal arsenal, shoot down United States Marines, and overthrow a government without committing treason. . . .

Emerson seemed hesitant in his first private reactions to Harpers Ferry. Thoreau, on the other hand, never hesitated a moment. On the day after Brown's capture he compared the hero's inevitable execution with the crucifixion of Christ. Harpers Ferry was "the best news that America ever had"; Brown, "the bravest and humanest man in all the country," "a Transcendentalist above all," and he declared: "I rejoice that I live in this age, that I was his contemporary." Emerson quickly fell into line with Thoreau, and in his

November 8 lecture on "Courage" described Brown as "the saint, whose fate yet hangs in suspense, but whose martyrdom, if it shall be perfected, will make the gallows as glorious as the cross." Within a few weeks Emerson gave three important lectures, in all of which he glorified John Brown.

With the Sage of Concord and his major prophet in accord on the martyr, the majority of the transcendental hierarchy sooner or later joined in— William E. Channing, Bronson and Louisa May Alcott, Longfellow, Bryant, and Lowell, and of course Wendell Phillips and Theodore Parker. Parker pronounced Brown "not only a martyr . . . but also a SAINT." Thoreau and Henry Ward Beecher frankly admitted they hoped Brown would hang. To spare a life would be to spoil a martyr. They were interested in him not as a man but as a symbol, a moral ideal, and a saint for a crusade. In the rituals of canonization the gallows replaced the cross as a symbol. . . .

The task to which the intellectuals of the cult dedicated themselves was the idealizing of John Brown as a symbol of the moral order and the social purpose of the Northern cause. Wendell Phillips expressed this best when he declared in the Boston Music Hall: "'Law' and 'order' are only means for the halting ignorance of the last generation. John Brown is the impersonation of God's order and God's law, moulding a better future, and setting for it an example." In substituting the new revolutionary law and order for traditional law and order, the intellectuals encountered some tough problems in morals and values. It was essential for them to justify a code of political methods and morals that was at odds with the Anglo-American tradition.

John Brown's own solution to this problem was quite simple. It is set forth in the preamble of his Provisional Constitution of the United States, which declares that in reality slavery is an "unjustifiable War of one portion of its citizens upon another." War, in which all is fair, amounted to a suspension of ethical restraints. This type of reasoning is identical with that of the revolutionaries who hold that class struggle is in reality a class war. The assumption naturally facilitates the justification of deeds otherwise indefensible. These might include the dissembling of motives, systematic deception, theft, murder, or the liquidation of an enemy class. . . .

The crisis of Harpers Ferry was a crisis of means, not of ends. John Brown did not raise the question of whether slavery should be abolished or tolerated. That question had been raised in scores of ways and debated for a generation. Millions held strong convictions on the subject. Upon abolition, as an *end,* there was no difference between John Brown and the American and Foreign Anti-Slavery Society. But as to the *means* of attaining abolition, there was as much difference between them, so far as the record goes, as there is between the modern British Labour Party and the government of Soviet Russia on the means of abolishing capitalism. The Anti-Slavery Society was solemnly committed to the position of nonviolent means. In the very petition that Lewis Tappan, secretary of the society, addressed to Governor Wise in behalf of Brown he repeated the rubric about "the use of all carnal weapons for deliverance from bondage." But in their rapture over Brown as martyr and saint the abolitionists lost sight of their differences with him over the point of means and ended by totally compromising their creed of nonviolence.

But what of those who clung to the democratic principle that differences should be settled by ballots and that the will of the majority should prevail? Phillips pointed out: "In God's world there are no majorities, no minorities; one, on God's side, is a majority." And Thoreau asked, "When were the good and the brave ever in a majority?" So much for majority rule. What of the issue of treason? The Reverend Fales H. Newhall of Roxbury declared that the word "treason" had been "made holy in the American language"; and the Reverend Edwin M. Wheelock of Boston blessed "the sacred, and the radiant 'treason' of John Brown."

No aversion to bloodshed seemed to impede the spread of the Brown cult. William Lloyd Garrison thought that "every slaveholder has forfeited his right to live" if he impeded emancipation. The Reverend Theodore Parker predicted a slave insurrection in which "The Fire of Vengeance" would run "from man to man, from town to town" through the South. "What shall put it out?" he asked. "The White Man's blood." The Reverend Mr. Wheelock thought Brown's "mission was to inaugurate slave insurrection as the divine weapon of the antislavery cause." He asked: "Do we shrink from the bloodshed that would follow?" and answered, "No such wrong [as slavery] was ever cleansed by rose-water." Rather than see slavery continued the Reverend George B. Cheever of New York declared: "It were infinitely better that three hundred thousand slaveholders were abolished, struck out of existence." In these pronouncements the doctrine that the end justifies the means had arrived pretty close to justifying the liquidation of an enemy class.

The reactions of the extremists have been stressed in part because it was the extremist view that eventually prevailed in the apotheosis of John Brown and, in part, because by this stage of the crisis each section tended to judge the other by the excesses of a few. "Republicans were all John Browns to the Southerners," as Professor Dwight L. Dumond has observed, "and slaveholders were all Simon Legrees to the Northerners." As a matter of fact Northern conservatives and unionists staged huge anti-Brown demonstrations that equaled or outdid those staged by the Brown partisans. Nathan Appleton wrote a Virginian: "I have never in my long life seen a fuller or more enthusiastic demonstration" than the anti-Brown meeting in Faneuil Hall in Boston. The Republican press described a similar meeting in New York as "the largest and most enthusiastic" ever held in that city. Northern politicians of high rank, including Lincoln, Douglas, Seward, Edward Everett, and Henry Wilson, spoke out against John Brown and his methods. The Republican party registered its official position by a plank in the 1860 platform denouncing the Harpers Ferry raid. Lincoln approved of Brown's execution, "even though he agreed with us in thinking slavery wrong." Agreement on ends did not mean agreement on means. "That cannot excuse violence, bloodshed, and treason," said Lincoln. . . .

Among the Brown partisans not one has been found but who believed that Harpers Ferry had resulted in great gain for the extremist cause. So profoundly were they convinced of this that they worried little over the conservative dissent. "How vast the change in men's hearts!" exclaimed Phillips. "Insurrection was a harsh, horrid word to millions a month ago."

Now it was "the lesson of the hour." Garrison rejoiced that thousands who could not listen to his gentlest rebuke ten years before "now easily swallow John Brown whole, and his rifle in the bargain." "They all called him crazy then," wrote Thoreau; "Who calls him crazy now?" To the poet it seemed that "the North is suddenly all Transcendentalist." On the day John Brown was hanged church bells were tolled in commemoration in New England towns, out along the Mohawk Valley, in Cleveland and the Western Reserve, in Chicago and northern Illinois. In Albany one hundred rounds were fired from a cannon. Writing to his daughter the following day, Joshua Giddings of Ohio said, "I find the hatred of slavery greatly intensified by the fate of Brown and men are ready to march to Virginia and dispose of her despotism at once." It was not long before they *were* marching to Virginia, and marching to the tune of "John Brown's Body." . . .

Donald G. Mathews  **NO**

The Abolitionists on Slavery: The Critique Behind the Social Movement

The abolitionists as agitators and moralists tried to change the mind of the American democrat. They appealed to his better nature and thundered against his fallen condition in pulpit, press, and petition in order to obtain for Negroes the same opportunity that white men had to participate in the nation's destiny. The goal was noble indeed, but the movement which tried to change American society was, as all human enterprises, compromised by the diverse motives, ideologies, and activities of its adherents.... Part of the ambiguity that supposedly shrouds antislavery history involves the assumption of many scholars that, since abolitionists were trying to destroy slavery, they could not have understood it. Careful investigation, however, will show that this assumption is untrue....

[I]n reading what abolitionists said about slavery and slaveholders, one gets the distinct impression of exaggerated rhetoric and elaborate condemnation on the one hand combined with astute insight, humane sympathy, and wide knowledge on the other. In fact, if one takes Herbert Butterfield's advice to practice "imaginative sympathy" in dealing with the past, he may almost conclude that abolitionists were right when they claimed to be able to understand slavery better than anyone else since they were "uncorrupted by a bribe." In any event, behind the flamboyant rhetoric and beyond the vicious allusions of popular oratory there was a legitimate critique of slavery. In order to discuss this critique it will not do to make distinctions between rational and irrational, sensible and nonsensical, sober and emotional abolitionists, since these categories are too vague and invidious for serious discussion. But it might be useful for the historian to make a distinction between the various functions of abolitionism, between its functions as a social movement, as a large-scale agitation, and finally as a legitimate and thoughtful critique of the institution of slavery. Once these distinctions are made, it may be easier to see that abolitionists held a balanced view of slavery even as they attempted to change prevalent attitudes towards it....

[T]housands of people joined the abolition movement in some capacity. They were encouraged to do so by itinerant organizers who built up a network

From the *Journal of Southern History* by Donald G. Matthew, vol. XXXIII, no. 2, May 1967, pp. 163–177, 180–182. Copyright © 1967. Reproduced with permission of the Southern Historical Association.

of local and state agencies and saw to it that the ideas of the movement were broadcast and perpetuated by subscription to one of the many antislavery periodicals. Slogans such as "immediate emancipation without expatriation" emerged from the endless discussions and articles which poured forth from the publicists who shaped the ideas of the movement. Along with the slogans often came the same lack of humor and viciousness of language which characterized the Great Revival's attack upon sin, the Democrat's attack upon Whig, and the rhetoric of many social movements which aimed at conversion either in religion or politics. Thus, when reading abolition literature, one is not called upon to explain away its exaggerations, but to understand them as a function of a movement which existed to perpetuate itself regardless of the value of its goals. As revivalists had been taught to be specific and harsh and to allow no "false comforts for sinners," so abolitionists acted in relation to slaveholders and slavery as they labored to build a movement. When they addressed those whom they hoped to convert they were as uncompromising as William Lloyd Garrison promised to be in the first edition of his *Liberator*. Unconditional attack was simply the approved method of the temperance reformation and the revivals; abolitionist crusaders saw no reason to discard weapons that had been so successful in previous sallies against evil. . . .

Nevertheless, when one takes into account how much abolitionist rhetoric had to accomplish and goes behind the functionally angry words to investigate what the historical evidence reveals, he finds a balanced, intelligent, and sometimes sophisticated understanding of the world which the antislavery radicals were trying to change. Historians divide abolitionists into Garrisonians, New Yorkers, denominationalists, and many more subgroups beloved of the specialist. But whether one does this or simply takes them straight as non-colonizationist, antislavery moralists (not politicians or nonextensionists), he will see that abolitionists (1) thought of slaveholders not merely as sinners but also as good men; (2) thought slavery a complex institution; but (3) understood it primarily as arbitrary and absolute power.

One of the basic charges leveled against abolitionists has been that they were morally simplistic in their condemnation of slaveholders. Repudiating social complexity as a legitimate vindication of slaveholding, they demanded that the abolition of slavery be begun at once. Years of waiting for conscientious Southerners to find a way to ease slavery out of existence had produced nothing to convince radical antislavery men that Negro servitude would die without purposeful action. The matter was made urgent for the revivalistically oriented abolitionists by their conviction that slavery was a sin: it was not a moral evil which everyone could regret and for which no one was responsible; it was not a political evil to be left to compromising politicians; it was not an economic evil to be left to self-interested slaveholders to manage—it was a sin. It broke the laws of God. It made man into merchantable property and deprived him of his humanity—his freedom to make of himself what he would. Thus, anyone involved in slavery as a master was culpably responsible to God. This conclusion put abolitionists in the position of calling decent, churchgoing Southerners sinners. Even though they worshiped three times a day, attended prayer meeting on Wednesday night, took their slaves with them to camp meeting, paid their debts, and gave money to foreign missions, slave-holders were sinners. This view became for many contemporaries as well as for historians the hallmark of abolitionist attitudes towards the South: abolitionists thought of slaveholders and their advocates as evil people.

In reaction to what they supposed was moralistic simplicity, antiabolitionists and later-day historians committed what could be called "the fallacy of misplaced righteousness." That is, by implication they attributed the personal moral respectability of individual Southerners to the institution of slavery. They pointed out that abolitionists were disastrously overstating their case by neglecting the complexities of the historical process, human motivation, and institutional entrenchment. Actually, the South was peopled, not by sinners as abolitionists so self-righteously assumed, but rather by good men caught in a difficult situation. Many Southern slaveholders were decent people, it was said, who secretly regretted the deep injustices of slavery, who treated their slaves well, and sent them to church on Sunday. Some Negroes even attained some status within the system. One ought not to curse good masters who were unfortunately involved in slavery, but praise them for responsibility in the midst of unjust institutions. These good men—reluctant and kindly slaveholders trying to make slavery as easy as possible for the slaves—were the tragic victims of a cruel and unjust fate. Furthermore, those people who believed the abolitionists irresponsible pointed out that slavery was not so bad as Theodore Dwight Weld claimed it to be in his pamphlet of 1839, *American Slavery as It Is.* As all sections, the South had its evil men (such as slave traders) who gave its peculiar institutions a bad name. The good, however, should not be confused with them and called sinners.

The "fallacy of misplaced righteousness" obscures what reformers are talking about in times of social change. Good men, abolitionists pointed out, were the chief vindicators of American Negro slavery. Had the antislavery vanguard been totally unaware of the moral character of slavery and its relationships, they could justly be accused of being irrelevant fanatics. But the abolitionists were not content with middle-class morality as some historians have been. The simple assumption that abolitionists thought of Southern slaveholders only as unregenerate sinners needs to be challenged to reveal what they did in fact say and simply to set the story straight.

The Missouri controversies had educated thoughtful Southerners to believe that Northern interest in slavery was primarily political. Therefore, they were in no mood to appreciate the care with which some abolitionists attempted to explain that slavery was a national problem and that sectional power or virtue was not really at issue. Abolitionists did maintain, however, that their not being from the South was an aid in gaining perspective. Mrs. Lydia Maria Child wrote in her pamphlet on slavery in 1833:

> It would be very absurd to imagine that the inhabitants of one State are
> worse than the inhabitants of another, unless some peculiar circum-
> stances, of universal influence, tend to make them so. Human nature is
> everywhere the same; but developed differently, by different incitements
> and temptations. . . . If we were educated at the South, we should no doubt
> vindicate slavery, and inherit as a birthright all the evils it engrafts upon

the character. If they lived on our rocky soil, and under our inclement skies, their shrewdness would sometimes border on knavery, and their frugality sometimes degenerate into parsimony. We both have our virtues and our faults, induced by the influences under which we live. . . .

Abolitionists were willing to admit the obvious: that people accustomed to slavery would be inclined to vindicate it.

In spite of this fact, there were Southerners to whom antislavery men thought they might effectively appeal—the responsible, churchgoing, humane slaveholders who would be sensitive to an honest discussion of slavery. Wrote a Methodist: "I sincerely sympathize with the slave, and as truly with many masters. I believe that northern men would be southern men in their circumstances; and that southern men would be northern men in ours, where moral principle was equally felt." The operative words were "where moral principle was equally felt." Abolitionists believed (or at least a great many of them did) that the moral regeneration of America institutionalized by steady increases in church membership would be the energizing force of abolition. They had seen this moral regeneration become moral action in the creation of new benevolent societies, and they saw no reason why slaves could not be helped just as much as drunkards, prostitutes, and the heathen. Thus they preached a new gospel because, as Orange Scott, the Methodist antislavery leader, wrote, it was "by preaching against great and destructive evils, *particularly, pointedly,* and *perseveringly,* that the world [was] to be reformed."

Preaching even to "good men" did not work. James G. Birney's special pilgrimage demonstrates what it did not take abolitionists everywhere long to find out: that the so-called good people of the South would not listen. As a colonization agent in the South in 1833, Birney, the owner of several slaves and heir to many others, found that the more he condemned slavery the less enthusiasm he engendered among his listeners. Nevertheless, he persisted in his efforts to convince the respectable portion of the community that it ought to think about abolishing slavery as soon as humanly possible. After his own conversion to abolitionism, Birney tried to convince the Kentucky Presbyterian clergy to urge abolition—but the result was a mild and evasive answer. He then tried to reach the community by reasonable discussion in an antislavery paper—but he was driven from Kentucky as a traitor. Even in the North, Birney's appeal to the churches as America's great moral institutions was repudiated by those whom he had hoped to convert. Not surprisingly, Birney and most of his abolitionist confreres were convinced that the good people were the bulwarks of slavery.

The morality ascribed to responsible people in the South did not impress abolitionists. Some conservative antislavery men tried to develop theories of moral responsibility which allowed for "moral men in immoral society," but most insisted that all slaveholders would have to be held responsible for their status. In this conclusion they denied the relevance of explanations deriving from the "fallacy of misplaced righteousness." Abolitionists admitted that slaveholders might be humanely motivated, that they might treat slaves well, that they might preach the Gospel (however mutilated) to them; but, in all cases, the Negroes were still slaves. This fact alone ran contrary to any concept of freedom, human dignity, and Christian love. Slavery was too evil in princi-ple to be vindicated by the heroic sadness of a conscience-stricken master or by the sympathy of the most gentle mistress. "In the hand of a good man or a bad man . . . *this principle is the same;*" wrote one abolitionist, "it [slavery] possesses not one redeeming quality." In other words, the fact that Southern slaveholders were good men was not relevant in the discussion of slavery. . . .

When abolitionists turned from the slaveholder to the system he repre-sented they were no more simplistic behind their bombastic rhetoric than when they were dealing with the Pollyanna propriety of the "fallacy of mis-placed righteousness." They could all agree that slavery was a complex, well-developed social and economic institution which could not be destroyed in one day. In fact, it would take so long to extinguish the psychological, moral, and cultural scars of slavery that its abolition should be begun immediately. Whether the abolitionist wanted "immediate emancipation gradually accom-plished" or "immediate unconditional emancipation," he had no intention of irresponsibly turning the slaves loose without some guidance. From the beginning of their agitation abolitionists could agree with William Lloyd Garrison's plea that Negro slaves be emancipated according to carefully worked out and equitably executed legal procedures which would in the end guarantee Negroes the equality they had been so long denied. The immediacy in immediate emancipation referred to the revivalist-agitator's desire to begin at once in order that something might be done eventually; but the formula in no way contradicted the abolitionist's belief that slavery was not a simple institution. . . .

They maintained that their agitation and ethical importunity was justi-fied because of slavery's effect upon the Negro and its ultimate character as absolute power. It was understood as absolute power because the slave had no legal claim upon the white man with which he could protect himself and because that most precious of American possessions, the right to one's own labor, was denied him. Slaves worked not because they would be better off if they did, but because they would be worse off if they did not. Force, fear, and fraud made slavery operate, abolitionists charged, and what they meant was that men's labor was extracted from them by an inherited system of bondage which ultimately relied upon brute force. They meant that men faced the future not with the hope and courage of the American Hercules but only with despair. And by fraud they meant that the church's Gospel had been used to enslave not free men's minds, that the law and planned ignorance which per-petuated slavery deprived Negroes of the same kind of advancement enjoyed by other Americans. They meant that the Negro was, for all intents and pur-poses, completely in the hands of the white man.

The best evidence of this fact, abolitionists thought, was the cruelties inflicted by whites on Negroes. Every discussion of the abolitionist attack on slavery includes an appropriate section for atrocities; and this was certainly a major aspect of antislavery propaganda. Everyone who has read this material is well acquainted with the vivid portrayal of all the infamies men can inflict upon their fellows, a striking method by which antislavery publicists could "clank the chains" of slavery in the ears of indifferent Americans. The atrocity stories, while possibly interesting in themselves to some abolitionists and historians, were printed not merely to arouse hatred of the kindly old slaveholder but also to demonstrate that slavery ultimately meant absolute and unchecked power. Abolitionists knew that some slaves were better treated than others—house servants and artisans were assumed to be safer than slaves less visible to the public—and they admitted that some slaveholders could be kind to their servants. But the significant aspect of slavery was not kind treatment. And cruelty was considered not as an exception to kind treatment, but as the natural result of the power to give or withhold kind treatment. With no effective way to defend themselves against the masters, Negroes bore mutilations, brands, and scars as identification not only of runaways in advertisements but also of the entire slave system. Men owned slaves not for altruistic purposes but to exploit their labor; and since the incentive to work was the thoroughly negative one of force not wages, since Negroes as men would intentionally frustrate the masters, and since men with absolute power used it, the natural result of slavery was cruelty. This was of course an abstract argument, but mutilated runaways seemed convincing empirical proof of its truth. Halos there were over the heads of some slaveowners; but scars on the backs of runaways were more significant. . . .

Corruption of people was a primary concern in the abolitionists' scheme of values, but slavery also corrupted the nation and the South. It became abstracted as diabolical power which stripped Americans of the security of their persons. It deprived them of their rights to petition Congress, to assemble peaceably, to publish freely, to dissent from majority opinion. And when the fugitive slave law was passed in 1850, the South's peculiar institution was interpreted as undermining the security of Northern legal processes. Southerners' fear of slaves, of new ideas, and of other white men was weakening the entire nation. Not only was this insecurity affecting freedom, but also the national defense. For if Americans were ever called to fight a strong foreign enemy, their efforts would be endangered by limiting available manpower to white men and limiting those whites' effectiveness by the necessity of policing slaves.

Slavery had corrupted the American economy even as it had its politics and security. It endangered all property by using arguments based upon property rights to defend holding men as slaves. The repugnancy men had for slavery could conceivably be transferred to property, thus devaluing the foundation of American wealth and stability. This consideration was overshadowed by the much more important concern for the economic disadvantages of slavery. Although an economic argument was never emphasized to the exclusion of others, it was usually present in abolitionist literature. Richard Hildreth was particularly eloquent in his *Despotism in America,* where he argued that slavery was a bad labor system which crippled American economic growth. Labor (the principal source of value) was not free to produce and consume at full capacity in a slave society. Slave laborers were presumed to be less productive than free because the former had no positive incentive. Only force and authority kept them at their tasks whereas wages and the hope of advancement would increase productivity if they were free.

Not only were the South and nation deprived of the full labor of the Negroes, but also of the whites. The low status of labor as being proper only to slaves supposedly paralyzed the poor whites as well as enervated the masters, whose disdain for work precluded the full utilization of labor resources. Slavery not only penalized the poor white man by devaluing labor, but also by requiring greater capitalization for expansion in the South than in the North. Since Southerners bought their laborers instead of hiring them, only the rich could increase their power appreciably. These supposed limitations on economic expansion were linked also with the fact that slaves did not consume as much as free laborers since their desires were so curtailed. With consumption at a low point, there was consequently less prosperity. This theory that slavery hindered optimum economic growth was complemented by other economic arguments. Most posited the superiority of industrial over agrarian society or accepted slavery as a single explanation of even those economic problems which derived from a one-crop economy. But in the economic and political sphere as in the personal, abolitionists understood slavery to be an unwarranted delimitation of freedom—arbitrary power.

There are many deficiencies in the arguments that abolitionists directed against slavery. Their data may have been faulty, but not the direction in which their understanding was taking them—towards an emphasis on social justice. Their objectivity was of course compromised by their partisan activity; but with all of the scientific knowledge of the twentieth century they would have come essentially to the same conclusions they reached a hundred years earlier. They would have admitted all the findings of historical investigation because they had a great appreciation for facts. But they would also have insisted that slavery, for all of its variety and complexity, still meant the white man's absolute power over the Negro.

Reflecting upon this view, one is struck by the contrast between the abolitionists' understanding of complexity and social determinism as opposed to their much-emphasized voluntarism. They were impressed by the effects of man's social situation in determining his values, goals, and general understanding, and yet they expected some men somehow to transcend their social context and by a sheer act of will break the chains binding their minds as well as their slaves. Frustrated in this, abolitionists retreated either to politics or to the mental and moral utopia of being "right" in a world that was wrong. Their "realism" in doing this is not so important as their pioneering attempt to understand social determinism and at the same time to thwart it. . . .

This kind of thinking about slavery, linked as it was with social agitation, personal frustration, civil war, and incomplete understanding was never fulfilled by a purposive and just transition from slavery to freedom. . . . But unlike most Americans, the abolitionists had at least tried to understand slavery in a new perspective even if with old formulae. And their attempt made them a vanguard in the fight to abridge the complexity of slavery by willful destruction of its absolute power.

POSTSCRIPT

Were the Abolitionists "Unrestrained Fanatics"?

One of the weaknesses of most studies of abolitionism, which is reflected in both of the preceding essays, is that they are generally written from a monochromatic perspective. In other words, historians typically discuss whites within the abolitionist crusade and give little, if any, attention to the roles African Americans played in the movement. Whites are portrayed as the active agents of reform, while blacks are the passive recipients of humanitarian efforts to eliminate the scourge of slavery. Students should be aware that African Americans, slave and free, also rebelled against the institution of slavery both directly and indirectly.

Benjamin Quarles in *Black Abolitionists* (Oxford University Press, 1969) describes a wide range of roles played by blacks in the abolitionist movement. The African American challenge to the slave system is also evident in the network known as the "underground railroad." Larry Gara, in *The Liberty Line: The Legend of the Underground Railroad* (University of Kentucky Press, 1961), concludes that the real heroes of the underground railroad were not white abolitionists but the slaves themselves who depended primarily upon their own resources or assistance they received from other African Americans, slave and free.

Other studies treating the role of black abolitionists in the antislavery movement include James M. McPherson, *The Struggle for Equality: Abolitionists and the Negro in the Civil War and Reconstruction* (Princeton University Press, 1964), Jane H. and William H. Pease, *They Who Would Be Free: Blacks' Search for Freedom, 1830–1861* (Atheneum, 1974), Benjamin Quarles, *Allies for Freedom: Blacks and John Brown* (Oxford University Press, 1974), R. J. M. Blackett, *Building an Antislavery Wall: Black Americans in the Atlantic Abolitionist Movement, 1830–1860* (Louisiana State University Press, 1983) and *Beating Against the Barriers: The Lives of Six Nineteenth-Century Afro-Americans* (Louisiana State University Press, 1986), Ronald K. Burke, *Samuel Ringgold Ward: Christian Abolitionist* (Garland, 1995), Nell Irvin Painter, *Sojourner Truth: A Life, A Symbol* (W. W. Norton, 1997), and Catherine Clinton, *Harriet Tubman: The Road to Freedom* (2004). Frederick Douglass' contributions are evaluated in Benjamin Quarles, *Frederick Douglass* (Atheneum, 1968; originally published 1948), Nathan Irvin Huggins, *Slave and Citizen: The Life of Frederick Douglass* (Little, Brown, 1980), Waldo E. Martin, Jr., *The Mind of Frederick Douglass* (University of North Carolina Press, 1984), and William S. McFeely, *Frederick Douglass* (W. W. Norton, 1991).

Conflicting views of the abolitionists are presented in Richard O. Curry, ed., *The Abolitionists: Reformers or Fanatics?* (Holt, Rinehart and Winston, 1965).

For general discussions of the abolitionist movement, see Gerald Sorin, *Abolitionism: A New Perspective* (Praeger, 1972), Lewis Perry, *Radical Abolitionism: Anarchy and the Government of God in Antislavery Thought* (Cornell University Press, 1973), James Brewer Stewart, *Holy Warriors: The Abolitionists and American Slavery* (Hill and Wang, 1976), Lawrence J. Friedman, *Gregarious Saints: Self and Community in American Abolitionism, 1830–1870* (Cambridge University Press, 1982), Stanley Harrold, *The Abolitionists in the South, 1831–1861* (University Press of Kentucky, 1995), Richard S. Newman, *The Transformation of American Abolitionism: Fighting Slavery in the Early Republic* (University of North Carolina Press, 2002), and John Stauffer, *The Black Hearts of Men: Radical Abolitionists and the Transformation of Race* (Harvard University Press, 2002). The lives of individual participants in the abolitionist movement are discussed in Henry Mayer, *All on Fire: William Lloyd Garrison and the Abolition of Slavery* (St. Martin's, 1998), Gerda Lerner, *The Grimké Sisters from South Carolina: Pioneers for Woman's Rights and Abolition* (Schocken Books, 1967), and Irving H. Bartlett, *Wendell and Ann Phillips: The Community of Reform, 1840–1880* (Harvard University Press, 1979). John Brown's controversial role in the movement is evaluated in Stephen B. Oates, *To Purge This Land With Blood: A Biography of John Brown* (Harper and Row, 1970), Louis A. DeCaro, Jr., *"Fire From the Midst of You": A Religious Life of John Brown* (New York University Press, 2002), and Merrill D. Peterson, *John Brown: The Legend Revisited* (University of Virginia Press, 2002).

Internet References . . .

AmericanCivilWar.com

The goal of this site is to provide a comprehensive source of Civil War information from the public domain or works published with the authors' permission. The sources are directed at students and Civil War buffs of all ages.

http://americancivilwar.com/index.html

The Valley of the Shadow Project

Developed under the direction of Edward Ayers and his graduate students at the University of Virginia, this site includes digital archives of thousands of primary source materials related to life in the Civil War–era communities in Augusta County, Virginia, and Franklin County, Pennsylvania.

http://valley.vcdh.virginia.edu/

Abraham Lincoln Online

Dedicated to the sixteenth president of the United States, this site offers educational links, Lincoln's speeches and writings, information on historic places, and much more.

http://www.netins.net/showcase/creative/lincoln.html

Reconstruction Era Documents

This page includes links to various Reconstruction era documents by such authors as Frederick Douglass, Booker T. Washington, and W. E. B. Du Bois.

**http://www.libraries.rutgers.edu/rul/rr_gateway/
research_guides/history/civwar.shtml**

PART 4

Conflict and Resolution

*T*he changing nature of the United States and the demands of its own principles finally erupted into violent conflict. Perhaps it was an inevitable step in the process of building a coherent nation from a number of distinct and diverse groups. The leaders, attitudes, and resources that were available to the North and the South were to determine the course of the war itself, as well as the national healing process that followed.

- Was the Confederacy Defeated Because of Its "Loss of Will"?

- Did Abraham Lincoln Free the Slaves?

- Was Reconstruction a "Splendid Failure"?

ISSUE 16

Was the Confederacy Defeated Because of Its "Loss of Will"?

YES: Richard E. Beringer, Herman Hattaway, Archer Jones, William N. Still, Jr., from *Why the South Lost the Civil War* (University of Georgia Press, 1986)

NO: James M. McPherson, from *The Illustrated Battle Cry of Freedom: The Civil War Era* (Oxford University Press, 2003)

ISSUE SUMMARY

YES: Professor of history Richard E. Beringer and his colleagues argue that the Confederacy lacked the will to win the Civil War because of an inability to fashion a viable southern nationalism, increasing religious doubts about the Confederate cause, and guilt over slavery.

NO: Pulitzer Prize–winning historian James M. McPherson maintains that either side might have emerged victorious in the Civil War but that the Union success was contingent upon winning three major campaigns between 1862 and 1864.

Over the past 125 years, contemporaries and historians have advanced dozens of explanations for the defeat of the Confederacy in the Civil War. Most of these can be divided into two categories: external and internal.

There are two external reasons for the Confederacy's failure: the Union's overwhelming numbers and resources and the uneven quality of leadership between the two sides. The North possessed two-and-one-half times the South's population, three times its railroad capacity, and nine times its industrial production. Given the statistical imbalance between the North and the South, it seems that the South lost the war even before the fighting had begun.

The Unionists also appear to have had better leadership. Lincoln is ranked as America's greatest president because he united his political objectives of saving the Union and freeing the slaves with a military strategy designed to defeat the Confederacy. Lincoln's generals—Ulysses S. Grant, William T. Sherman, and Philip H. Sheridan—outsmarted the Confederate leadership.

In 1864, for example, massive frontal attacks were made against the Confederates in the eastern and western theater. At the same time, Sherman destroyed much of the agricultural base of the Southerners as he marched his troops through South Carolina and Georgia.

Internal conflicts also spelled doom for the Confederacy, according to a number of historians. In his book *State Rights in the Confederacy* (1925), Frank Owsley maintained that the centrifugal forces of state rights killed the Confederacy. Owsley, a long-time Vanderbilt scholar, believed that governors in North Carolina and Georgia withheld men and equipment from the Confederate armies in order to build up their own state militias. On the Confederate tombstone, he said, should be inscribed: "Died of State Rights."

A second version of the internal conflict argument appeared in a 1960 essay in a symposium on *Why the North Won the Civil War*. In it, the editor, Pulitzer Prize–winning historian David Donald, argued that the resistance of Southerners to conscription, taxes, and limitations on speeches critical of the war effort fatally crippled the Confederacy's war effort. Instead of state rights, says Donald, the tombstone should read: "Died of Democracy."

A third variant of the internal conflict argument has recently been promoted by four Southern scholars: Richard E. Beringer, Herman Hattaway, Archer Jones, and William N. Still, Jr. Their main thesis is that the Confederacy lacked the will to win because of its inability to fashion a viable Southern nationalism, increasing religious doubts that God was on the Confederacy's side, and guilt over slavery. The first selection of this issue succinctly summarizes the "loss of will" thesis.

In a Gettysburg symposium, edited by Gabor S. Borritt, on *Why the Confederacy Lost* (Oxford University Press, 1992), James M. McPherson dismisses all the external and internal explanations for the South's defeat listed above. In his critique, McPherson applies the theory of reversibility. Briefly stated, the hindsight provided by knowing the outcome of the war allows the writer to attribute causes that explain the Northern victory.

But what if the South won the Civil War? Could the same external explanations be used to explain a Confederate win? Would Jefferson Davis's leadership emerge as superior to Abraham Lincoln's? Would the great military leaders be Robert E. Lee, Thomas "Stonewall" Jackson, and Braxton Bragg instead of Grant, Sherman, and Sheridan? Would one Confederate soldier be considered equal to four Union soldiers? Would a triumvirate of yeoman farmers, slaveholding planters, and small industrialists have proven the superiority of agrarian values over industrial ones?

McPherson rejects the traditional internal and external explanations as well as the theory of reversibility. In the second selection, McPherson advances the theory of contingency as an explanation for the Union victory. Of the four turning points in the war from the Union campaigns of 1863 through the Atlanta and western campaigns in 1864, the North won the latter three. In McPherson's view, chance or luck and not loss of will determined the outcome of the Civil War in favor of the Union.

YES    Richard E. Beringer et al.

Why the South Lost the Civil War

Why the South Lost

The immediate popular response to the question posed by this book and this chapter is usually that the North overwhelmed the South with its great numbers and resources. The Union possessed more than twice the population of the Confederacy, and the South endured an even greater disadvantage in military population, for the South included four million slaves, excluded from direct military participation on the Confederate side. But though numbers were certainly important, the inherent advantages of defense, illustrated by the virtual impossibility of destroying an enemy army unless it had an incompetent commander, required a greater disparity before the size and resources of the Union could explain Confederate defeat.

Many Confederates agreed that numbers or resources did not provide the margin, although they disagreed on what did. General Beauregard, for example, claimed that "no people ever warred for independence with more relative advantages than the Confederates; and if, as a military question, they must have failed, then no country must aim at freedom by means of war." "The South," Beauregard asserted, "would be open to discredit as a people if its failure could not be explained otherwise than by mere material conquest." To Beauregard, the Confederates did not owe their defeat to numbers but to faulty strategy and the poor leadership of Jefferson Davis, who attempted to defend all Confederate territory, thus dispersing Confederate strength and forbidding adequate concentration.

Some historians of our own generation agree with the thrust of Beauregard's remarks, though finding different flaws in Confederate military leadership. Clement Eaton, for example, aligned himself with T. Harry Williams, both of them maintaining that despite northern superiority in men and resources, the South had a good chance of success until Gettysburg and Vicksburg, "The chance was lost," says Eaton, because Davis "made the dubious decision of allowing [Lee] . . . to invade Pennsylvania instead of sending strong reinforcements from his army to defeat Grant at Vicksburg." But the ultimate cause of Confederate defeat, according to Eaton—and in agreement with a number of other historians cited earlier—was a loss of the will to fight. Both sides suffered from this problem, but after July 1863 it was worse for the South. Southerners' "morale rose and fell with victory and defeat, and also with their estimation of the northern will to persevere." At this point we should recall the biting comment of Confederate

From WHY THE SOUTH LOST THE CIVIL WAR, by Richard E. Beringer et al. (University of Georgia Press, 1986), pp. 424–440. Copyright © 1986 by University of Georgia Press. Reprinted by permission.

Senator Williamson S. Oldham, who maintained that the argument of numbers flattered one's vanity but that the Confederacy had everything it needed to fight in 1865, "morale alone excepted."

But the Confederates did lack morale, and their morale was sapped by uncertainty about their war aims. To fight to be left alone, as Davis and others put it, did not prove very inspiring. Most Confederates thought the war was fought to attain security of slave property and autonomous government, with independence as merely the means by which they would achieve the desired end. But the growth of power of the central government compromised autonomous government, and the exigencies of manpower policy and foreign policy jeopardized slave property. The authorization for enlistment of slaves in the army and the proposal to grant them freedom as a result of their service reflected a Confederate alteration in war aims whereby the means became an end. Secession to protect slavery had, ironically, led to a war by the end of which the Confederacy would arm slaves and even offer them their freedom. But in denying the original motive for the establishment of a separate country, the Confederacy undermined the fundamental basis of its tentative nationalism and deprived many of its citizens of their motive for continuing the conflict.

Lincoln's Emancipation Proclamation made it difficult for Confederates to feel entirely at ease with their assertion that they were fighting for liberty. It aggravated the misgivings of those who long had harbored quiet doubts about slavery and made many others even more uneasy about their isolation in a world in which the great powers of Europe, now joined by the United States, sought to extirpate slavery. Many southerners felt guilt over the institution or at least unease about their position. Thus, as the struggle drew to a close, the commitment to slavery of many southerners withered in the face of the contradiction it created and under the weight of world moral disapproval, which some Confederates felt acutely.

The change in the Confederacy's explanation for secession and war shows the seriousness of the cognitive dissonance created by the problem of slavery. To consider it merely a contest for the proper interpretation of the Constitution was to deny recent historical fact, but the constitutional question offered a far more comfortable explanation for the sacrifice of so much blood and treasure than the protection of slavery had. But to reject slavery as the cause for secession eliminated the characteristic that most distinguished the North from the South. Common history and language united the sections and so, too, in a lesser and more complex sense, did religion; only slavery truly separated them. By the end of the conflict many southerners had denied the basis of their distinctiveness and of their nationalism. Without a sufficiently distinctive history to undergird their weak sense of nationality, Confederates created their own mythic past to support the notion that the war was the logical outcome of a controversy over state rights, not slavery.

In any case, slavery had provided a very slender foundation for a distinguishing nationalism. When southerners' allegiance to slavery faltered, no ground for distinctiveness would remain. This lack of significant difference from the Union even applied to the emerging constitutional explanation of secession and war. Those who came to see state rights and a decentralized government as the cause for which they fought were very often the same people who denounced the centralized despotism of the Davis administration. Why, many asked, fight against one centralized government only to preserve another?

Thus the course of the conflict quickly exacerbated the weakness in the southern sense of separate identity and in the original cause of secession. Frank Owsley remarked that "the up-country people could easily fight a ninety-day war . . . but not a war that lasted over several years. Anger and enthusiasm are too transient to serve as a basis of war." What he said of the up-country people could reasonably have been said of the low-country people also, even though they, in fact, displayed much greater allegiance to the cause. But neither, as it turned out, had enough deep and enduring support for the struggle.

In fact, considering their fragile and insecure nationalism, one could almost ask what induced southerners to make such a powerful and prolonged resistance? Certainly the climate of opinion, which for two decades had reflected a consciousness of divergence between the sections and a hostility to Yankees, had much to do with magnifying grievances and strengthening the feeling of separateness. The churches contributed powerfully to fostering this climate of opinion, but they, too, like slavery and limited government, failed as the conflict wore on. In the same way that slavery was removed as a motive for continuing the struggle by the understanding that it was doomed regardless of who won, and development of centralized Confederate government mitigated state rights as a source of motivation, so, too, religion ceased to sustain Confederate morale and confidence in victory. Defeat in battle and loss of territory cast doubt on whether God truly favored the Confederacy and, for those who concluded that God did not, the cause seemed hopeless. The devout had no motive to keep struggling against God's will. A powerful prop initially, religion thus became a source of weakness in adversity.

As Confederates pondered the religious meaning of the Civil War, especially in the last dark months, they questioned why God had failed them. Southerners answered that question in various ways, most of which related to sin and punishment. But in identifying God's will with their own affairs on earth, Confederates unconsciously had been expanding their faith to the point that they created—in effect—a civil religion.

It is beyond the scope of this book to apply the concept of civil religion to the events of the Civil War. It is sufficient to our thesis to note that an American civil religion existed and that it was profoundly related to American nationalism. We suspect that it was also related to vague notions of Confederate nationalism. In his elemental study *Nationalism: A Religion,* Carlton J. H. Hayes has written about nationalism as a religion of sorts. Primarily a historian of the modern Western world, Hayes touched only lightly upon the American Civil War. But he did suggest that in addition to the primary nationalism of the United States, there were two others—the embryonic secondary nationalism of the Confederacy and the tertiary nationalism of the lost cause.

Our point is that the latter two never developed into the potent nation-building and nation-sustaining force that American nationalism, however weak or strong, eventually became. While Confederate nationalism, such as it was, crumbled away during the Civil War, American nationalism developed further and eventually emerged in the postwar period with Abraham Lincoln as its chief apostle, and he has been its figurehead ever since. As one historian remarked at a scholarly program commemorating the bicentennial of the American Revolution, in the American mind "Washington is but a monument, while Lincoln *lives.*" (It is no accident, we suspect, that the highway signs directing motorists to the Springfield, Illinois, exits give directions to the "Lincoln shrines.")

But what is it that makes Lincoln an American saint? We think Edmund Wilson in his essay "The Union as Religious Mysticism" correctly answered the question. Essentially, Lincoln himself "came to see the conflict in a more and more religious light," but beyond that there was a particular "interpretation of its meaning, that—influenced, of course, himself by the 'climate of opinion,' of the North—he fixed in the minds of the Union supporters." And as Martin Marty phrased it recently, "Lincoln did forge and use a new political religion for union," and thus Lincoln provided the North with an asset that the "Confederacy was missing." Was the American civil religion necessary for northern victory in the Civil War? Possibly not, but in all likelihood Kenneth S. Kantzer is correct in his characterization of American civil religion as "the cement holding our nation together."

And what of the South's civil religion, however embryonic: did it not exist? Yes, but only in embryo; it was aborted before birth. The reason is because its mother could not carry it to term: the philosophical and religious underpinnings of the Confederacy were not spawned in an atmosphere of nationalism but in one of racism and fear. And when at last it became obvious that even Confederate victory could not have resulted in a satisfactory continuation of white supremacy through the maintenance of slavery, white supremacy had to be nurtured in other ways. In a secular sense, this was done by salvaging the extant social structure in the nationalism of the lost cause, but the process also had its religious history because much of it occurred within the churches. Within those potent and significant institutions, a virile response to the Confederacy's change in war aims was forged.

Owsley's thesis "that the Confederacy collapsed more from internal than from external causes" certainly could find strong support in the embryonic nature of Confederate nationalism and the debilitating effects of southern civil religion in the face of God's apparent disfavor. But Owsley's original hypothesis, the crippling effect of state rights, does not, upon closer examination, suffice.

The tangible effects of state rights, as distinguished from the rhetoric, had little negative effect on the Confederate war effort. Even the total number of exempted men was small in relation to the Confederate armies, and most of them made significant economic contributions, served in local defense forces, or become. The protection of ports and the production of such important items as salt had an importance that military authorities and President Davis both recognized, and state local defense forces therefore contributed materially to this effort. Further, state endeavors to supply and equip local defense forces and to meet the needs of their own men in the Confederate service provided a major supplement to the national war effort. State uniforms and blankets did not come from stocks accessible to the Confederate government; rather, they constituted an addition to the total available. If Governor Vance in truth had ninety-two thousand uniforms at the end of the war, as he claimed, they did not belong to the Confederate government but were an addition to the total stock of uniforms in the Confederacy, a supply made ready by the state's funds, enterprise, and concern for its fighting men. On balance, state contributions to the war effort far outweighed any unnecessary diversion of resources to local defense.

State-rights attempts to obstruct the Confederate government by resisting conscription or the suspension of habeas corpus, for example, also had a negligible effect. State rights in writing and oratory provided a rallying cry for opposition that already existed in any case. Just as in England under the early Hanoverians the association of the Prince of Wales with the group out of power showed the opposition's loyalty to the king and dynasty, so an appeal to the universally accepted notion of state rights provided a legitimacy to the opposition and protected it from accusations of disloyalty during a struggle for national existence. Thus state rights made a political contribution, one probably necessary in the absence of organized political parties.

In view of the rhetoric of state rights and the long, disputatious correspondence between Governor Brown and the Richmond government, Frank L. Owsley made a natural mistake in choosing state rights as the internal cause of Confederate collapse. But in placing the blame on disunity caused by state rights, he did not show that military causes inadequately explained defeat. Considering the still continuing flow of books and articles about Civil War military operations, he displayed wisdom in avoiding a topic on which he would have had difficulty securing agreement. But in view of the harmony of Clausewitz and Jomini on the relevant strategic variables, it is possible to use them effectively as authorities to provide a fairly firm basis for settling the military questions about the Confederacy. Their essential consensus says that an invader needs more force than the North possessed to conquer such a large country as the South, even one so limited in logistical resources.

In making this judgment Clausewitz and Jomini assumed a national resistance. This the Confederacy made, so far as its limited national will permitted, as the Union's difficulties protecting its railroads from guerrillas amply attest. Sherman's complaint about invading a country populated by the "meanest bitterest enemies" illustrates the strength of the national opposition that the Union armies initially confronted.

Clausewitz and Jomini also assumed a competent defense. Using their principles and criteria, the South clearly provided an excellent army, very capably led. Examples of Confederate bungling, such as Pemberton's losing his army at Vicksburg or Bragg's ineffective campaigning, are counterbalanced by Burnside's fairly reliable mismanagement and the pessimism and slow execution of such generals as McClellan and Buell. Both sides wasted lives in frontal attacks, sometimes because they knew no better and other times because commanders and their subordinates lacked the ability or experience to catch their opponent at a disadvantage.

Since the Confederate army clearly did not have a significantly worse command than the Union forces, Clausewitz's and Jomini's strategic variables of space and supply must control. In view of the experience of the operationally superior French armies in Spain and Russia, one must respect their sophisticated conclusion from appropriate historical experience as well as their authority as experts on the kind of war the Union and Confederacy fought. They might well have added the American Revolution to their example of the virtual impossibility of overcoming a national resistance in a vast space without overwhelming forces, and Jomini did include it in his list of national wars.

T. Harry Williams said Jomini preached cities and territory, rather than enemy armies, as the objective in military operations. If this was the case, and it certainly was not in the instance of the strategic turning movement which Jomini liked so well, it proved a realistic doctrine for both armies. Jomini's fondness for the strategic turning movement does fit with Williams's idea that Jomini favored maneuvering over fighting. As to Williams's idea that Jomini advocated one big effort at a time in a single theater, the precept of the use of interior lines to concentrate on a single line of operations also fits Williams's interpretation. The Confederates practiced this strategy successfully in the Shiloh and Chickamauga campaigns and on a lesser scale in the Seven Days' Battles. The Union did the same after the battles of Lookout Mountain and Missionary Ridge and in a different way by their earlier concentration on the Mississippi. But the Union relied more on concentration in time, advocated by Clausewitz, as well as on Jomini's concentration in space.

Williams and some other historians in this country seem to have misunderstood Jomini enough to overlook his essentially Napoleonic viewpoint and to attribute to him some of the views held by Bülow and others in an essentially pre-Napoleonic tradition. Williams also noted a differential effect in Jomini's influence on each combatant that is hard to discern in the West Point officers, many of whom served apprenticeships under Winfield Scott and Zachary Taylor in the Mexican War.

Thus both armies seemed to have followed Jomini while they fairly consistently, though unconsciously, responded to Clausewitz's perception of the difficulties of executing decisive campaigns in view of the power of the defense, the lack of overwhelming numerical superiority, and the huge extent of the Confederacy. Clausewitz, who had considerable knowledge of the French campaign in Russia, stressed the obstacle of the size of an invaded country, whereas Jomini, who had served with the French in Spain, predicted most clearly the trouble Confederate guerrillas caused the Union invaders. These difficulties, foreseen by the authorities and present in abundance in the Civil War, adequately explain the slow progress of Union armies. It is not necessary to look to Jomini, or elsewhere, to find a reason for the protracted character of the Civil War.

In spite of Lee's blunder in attacking the Union center on the third day of the Battle of Gettysburg, and Grant's seriously mistaken assault at Cold Harbor, they and the majority of other generals on both sides adhered more to Clausewitz than to Jomini in their recognition of the power of the defense. Grant best exemplified Jomini's ideal with his victories at Vicksburg and Appomattox, but the failure of other generals to achieve similar successes justified Clausewitz's observation that such maneuvers rarely would succeed. And the ideas of Bülow proved not archaic but ahead of their time, though not because of the author's foresight. Unconsciously, Hood used them in a manner approved by Clausewitz, as did Lee in his Second Manassas, Antietam; and Gettysburg campaigns. Grant's strategy of raids also had an indirect relation to Bülow's concept of attacking the enemy's communications rather than his army.

Thus we have difficulty following T. Harry Williams in discriminating between Jomini's possible influence on either side or seeing Jomini as a potential inhibitor of action on the part of Union or Confederate generals. That Jomini and Clausewitz have so little difference in their prescriptions and that Jomini had more faith in the offensive makes it hard to single out Jomini as hampering offensive action or as an advocate of a pre-Napoleonic form of warfare when no authorities so classify Clausewitz.

So Confederate military competence that capably managed its armies and consciously, and skillfully, used cavalry raids to aid guerrillas in destroying Union supply lines provided the means of validating Clausewitz's and Jomini's judgment about the impossibility of the Union attaining its strategic objective by military means if faced with a determined, unremitting national resistance. If, then, the Confederacy had the means to resist military conquest, one must find the cause of defeat within. If state lights was not this cause, what alternatives are there to the thesis of insufficient nationalism as the internal cause of defeat?

In spite of the blockade and the steady decline of the railways, Confederate supply did not fail. After each apparently catastrophic shock, such as the closure of communication with the trans-Mississippi or the loss of key railroad lines, the ramshackle Confederate logistic organization, displaying an amazing resilience, continued to make adequate provision for the armies. The accumulation in Richmond during the winter of 1865 of a week's reserve of rations for Lee's army illustrates the South's capability. Lee still had this reserve available in early April, in spite of the earlier closure of Wilmington, the presence of Sherman's army in North Carolina, and Sheridan's devastating raid against supply and communications northwest of Richmond. The Confederacy provided its armies with food and clothing, albeit often in barely adequate and sometimes inadequate quantities, and with a sufficiency of weapons and ammunition. And all the while it kept a higher proportion of the population under arms than did the Union.

As Stanley Lebergott has shown, the Confederate Congress did not prohibit the export of cotton, a measure many believed would bring intervention on the South's behalf by France and the United Kingdom in an effort to save their cotton textile industries. This failure, like the failure to restrict cotton planting during the war, reflects a lack of appreciation of the nature of total economic mobilization and a concern for the pecuniary interests of the growers of cotton. But the production of so much cotton between 1861 and 1865 (the 1864 inventory equaled twice the exports during the war) also indicates a debilitating confidence in a short conflict and an early return to unimpeded cotton exports. Significantly, the 1862 cotton crop was the second largest on record.

But the production of too much cotton and not enough food crops, like the decline in railway service and the constraints of the blockade, severely affected the home front, already heavily taxed through inflation and diminished in man-power because of the needs of the army and of war production. These costs and hardships, like the casualties in battle and the gloom occasioned by defeats, depressed civilian morale. Many of the deficiencies of Confederate supply affected civilians more than the armies and aggravated hardships inseparable from such a bloody and costly war. And the depressed morale of the home front communi-cated itself to the soldiers through newspapers and the Confederate postal service, which continue to function throughout the war in spite of numerous obstacles, including a constitutionally mandated requirement that postal expenses not exceed postal income.

The defeats, shortages, reduced standard of living, and change of war goals, as well as the war's length, obviously placed a severe strain on the Confederates' dedication to their cause. The high degree of dependence of Confederate morale on military events meant that setbacks on the battle front usually had a significance far beyond the military importance of the loss of a battle or a frag-ment of territory. A succession of defeats and territorial losses, though not representing militarily consequential conquests of the South's vast land area, worked steadily to depress morale and confidence in victory. With fewer such military disappointments and less hardship for civilians, or with a shorter war, Confederate nationalism, weak though it was, would have equaled the demands placed upon it and might well have developed real strength after the war; in any case, a greater measure of nationalism during the conflict certainly would have enabled the Confederates to resist longer.

In addition, planters felt alienated from a government that seemed to threaten their privileges and property and, in spite of the exemplary relief efforts of Georgia and North Carolina, and the similar, if not so extensive, mea-sures in other states, the yeomen, too, felt disaffection with the Confederacy. Both planter and yeoman paid economically for the immense war effort, but too many yeomen lived too close to the margin of existence not to feel the hard-ships acutely; the costs of the war deprived them of the means to meet their basic needs, or threatened to do so. At the same time they felt that, with such perquisites as the exemption of the overseers of twenty slaves and the right to purchase substitutes for military service, the rich did not bear their fair share of the burdens. Paul Escott stressed that throughout the struggle the planters gave primacy to their own rather than national interests. He points out that "a selfish and short-sighted ruling class had led its region into secession and then proven unwilling to make sacrifices or to surrender its privileges for independence." These class differences in the demands of the war effort created another drain on the limited supply of Confederate nationalism.

But the resulting decline in commitment to the struggle did not begin to affect the war effort very seriously until after the middle of 1864. Then soldiers began to leave the army in increasing numbers. The fall of Atlanta in early September and Sheridan's victories over Early in the Shenandoah Valley, victo-ries that significantly improved Lincoln's chances of reelection, also signaled the beginning of a marked rise in desertion from the Confederate army. Soldiers left not only from discouragement at these defeats but also from a realization that Union victories increased the likelihood of Lincoln's continuation in office and his policy of prosecuting the war to victory. As the fall elections confirmed this apprehension, the augmented stream of deserters continued unabated. The soldiers were voting for peace with their feet, and the few disaffected conscripts sent to the Confederate army probably hurt morale and effectiveness more than their small numbers could have added to its strength. By the early spring of 1865 the Confederate armies east of the Mississippi had shrunk to barely half their size the previous August.

Adventitiously, Grant's strategy began to play some part in this Confederate decline soon after the Union presidential contest of 1864, when Sherman marched from Atlanta to Savannah, breaking railways, destroying factories, stripping the countryside of slaves, and subsisting an army of sixty thousand men on the country. Sherman perceived the effect of this devastation on southerners when he wrote that his march would show the falsity of Davis's "promise of protection. If we can march a well-appointed army right through his territory, it is a demonstration to the world, foreign and domestic, that we have a power which Davis cannot resist." He believed that there were "thousands of people abroad and in the South who will reason thus: If the North can march an army right through the South, it is proof positive that the North can prevail in this struggle." But Sherman's raid occurred well after the exodus from the army began. His raids through Georgia and later into the Carolinas only reinforced a discouragement that already had begun to manifest itself in a dramatic rise in the desertion rate.

Since Lee's army and the other main armies remained sufficiently supplied until the end of the war, one reasonably can conclude that Grant's military strategy influenced the outcome of the conflict but did not determine it. The Confederacy's forces dwindled and surrendered before Grant's raids could deprive them of supplies. The strategy of raids had, of course, considerable political and psychological significance, reinforcing the effect on southern will of the defeats of September and October and the return of Lincoln to the Executive Mansion.

In any event, Grant's strategy alone could not have won a war against a people sufficiently determined to maintain their independence. Grant aimed only to break up the Confederacy's main armies by severing the railroads that connected them to their supplies of food, shoes, uniforms, weapons, and ammunition. He provided no means of dealing with these armies should they disperse and thereafter continue offering organized resistance as units ranging in size from a division of several brigades down to independent companies. These units would have dominated the country, reducing Federal control to the immediate vicinity of the Union armies, as Jomini had learned in Spain. Such forces, aided by guerrilla activity, could have found some food and other supplies in the country they controlled and secured more from the invader's always vulnerable supply columns.

But Confederate armies surrendered rather than dispersing into small but formidable groups, and the soldiers went home for the same reason that many had already deserted—they did not want an independent Confederacy badly enough to continue the struggle, and they placed the welfare of their loved ones ahead of the creation of a new nation. But even if they had wished to continue, slavery would have inhibited the usual war waged by small units and guerrillas against invading armies. Indeed, many slaves already had become sympathizers and recruits for the Union. The same bitter experience of Santo Domingo might have come to the South, just as southerners always had feared.

As old Confederates resolved their dissonance in one way or another, they indicated directly or indirectly that what Ulrich B. Phillips called the central theme of southern history inevitably had dictated their actions. Whether pro-Union or prosecession, in favor of the war or opposed, pushing for peace or desiring to fight to the bitter end, willing to accept Radical Reconstruction or challenging it, white southerners had "a common resolve indomitably maintained—that it [the South] shall be and remain a white man's country." The South could give up slavery with more relief than regret, as events proved. But it could not surrender white supremacy, "especially," notes Carl Degler, "when it was imposed by a North whose hands in this respect were far from clean." To be sure, slavery supplied an instrument of racial adjustment, and Independence constituted a long-shot effort to ensure freedom of action on racial as well as other issues; but state rights and honor remained, state rights to provide a political ideology that permitted local control of racial relations, and honor to require that southerners shape their own institutions without outside pressure. Thus today's historian, like Henry James on his southern tour early in the twentieth century, must come to the realization that "the negro had always been, and could absolutely not fail to be, intensely 'on the nerves' of the South, and that as, in the other time [before the war], the observer from without had always, as a tribute to this truth, to tread the scene on tiptoe, so even yet, in the presence of the immitigable fact, a like discretion is imposed on him.

In the antebellum era and throughout most of the war, the desire to preserve slavery exemplified this constant concern. And slavery turned out to have a far-reaching effect on the strategy of the Civil War, for it made unlikely a Confederate resort to its most promising means of resistance, "general insurrection." Clausewitz and Jomini made a strong case that a resort to guerrilla warfare constituted an inefficient means of defense because the results of such a total effort were "not commensurate with the energies" expended. More relevant, such a strategy incurred high nonmilitary costs. Clausewitz noted one of these costs when he pointed out that guerrilla warfare could be considered "a state of legalized anarchy that is as much a threat to the social order at home as it is to the enemy." When that social order included race relations, it would have been dangerous for the Confederacy to have resorted to it, as some Confederate Unionists had realized in 1861.

Further, by 1863 the black population had proved itself willing to enlist in the Union army and had surprised skeptics by its military effectiveness when adequately trained. In any guerrilla resistance the black population in the Confederacy would constitute a resource for an enormously powerful indigenous counterinsurgency force. The turmoil introduced into the countryside would have made slavery more precarious, not less, and would have provided slaves with even more opportunity to subvert the Confederate war effort, perhaps by sabotage and espionage, but more likely by escape and enlistment in the Union army. The Union would certainly have used this formidable weapon, and its use would have changed race relations well beyond the point that the actual events did change them, even beyond the possibility of recognition or restoration.

By surrendering without resort to wholesale use of guerrillas, southerners had, as John Shy has pointed out, "saved the basic elements—with the exception of slavery itself—of the Southern social, that is to say racial, order. The social order could not possibly have survived the guerrilla warfare which a continued resistance movement would have required." Thus slavery brought on the conflict, but, with the underlying problem of race relations, it paradoxically ended it as well, by making fainthearted southerners too fearful to employ their one, otherwise invincible, military weapon. Under such circumstances, it is unreasonable to expect that a people not fully committed to the war would run the risk of creating another Santo Domingo, or at least breaking down remaining social controls. Doubtless, the reasoning of many southerners did not reach that far. The wholesale desertion that took away 40 percent of the Confederate armies east of the Mississippi in the fall and early winter of 1864-65 showed that, before a full-scale resort to guerrilla warfare loomed as the alternative, a critical number of Confederates had given to the cause all that their commitment warranted.

Clausewitz excoriated such behavior. Although he did not use the word "honor," he demanded that a people fight to preserve it. "No matter how small and weak a state may be in comparison with its enemy," he wrote, "it must not forego these last efforts, or one would conclude that its soul is dead." "There will always be time enough to die," he continued. "Like a drowning man who will clutch instinctively at a straw, it is a natural law of the moral world that a nation that finds itself on the brink of an abyss will try to save itself by any means." Clausewitz felt that a failure to fight to the last shows that the nation "did not deserve to win, and, possibly for that very reason was unable to." But Clausewitz did not take into sufficient account moral and religious factors, such as those that made some Confederates more than willing to surrender slavery. For, when the institution faced severe pressure, a multitude of Confederates were willing to see it go, having "discovered" that they were not fighting for slavery at all, or even for state rights, but for white supremacy, independence, and honor.

But Clausewitz's caustic criticism has relevance only if one assumes that the Confederacy was a nation—that it was sufficiently separated from the Union and the glory of their common history to make it a distinct nationality. Analyzing conflict "between *states of very unequal strength*," Clausewitz noted that "inability to carry on the struggle can, in practice, be replaced by two other grounds for making peace: the first is the improbability of victory; the second is its unacceptable cost." Powerful Union armed forces and sophisticated and innovative strategy supplied the first ground; the insufficiency of a nationalism based on slavery, state rights, and honor meant that the cost of continuing the struggle ran too high. Perhaps no white southerners could contemplate such a war. Slavery, the cause of secession and four years of military conflict, would thus have limited the extent and persistence of the Confederacy's resistance even had it wished to carry on beyond the defeat of the principal armies; but desertion and surrender showed that few Confederates had any such desire.

So the Confederacy succumbed to internal rather than external causes. An insufficient nationalism had to survive the strains imposed by the lengthy hostilities. Necessary measures alienated planters, who, by planting cotton and husbanding their slaves, already had limited the national effort. Privation affected many yeomen, soldiers, and their families as the costs and shortages of the contest reduced their already meager standards of living. These hardships and the perception of inequitable and unwise actions placed an added strain on a nationalism already taxed by the duration and bloodshed of the conflict. Slavery, in a sense the keystone of secession, became a liability as the Union's fight against slavery and the South's own religious beliefs induced more guilt among more southerners. After three years of essentially successful defense against powerful invading forces, these prolonged strains proved more than Confederate nationalism could bear and, frequently encouraged by a sense that defeat must be the Lord's work, Confederates, by thousands of individual decisions, abandoned the struggle for and allegiance to the Confederate States of America.

The transformation southerners made in identifying the causes of the struggle well illustrates the South's essentially ephemeral allegiance to slavery and devotion to independence, and the rapid development of a powerful central government indicated the slender cord that bound some state-righters to the concept of state rights until they appealed to state rights once again after the war was over. Only the determination to hold fast to honor, and the concomitant desire to dictate the terms of racial adjustment, proved constant.

And yet, in a very real sense, the answer to the question posed by the title of this book is that in some respects the South did not lose the Civil War. Southerners eventually resolved the dissonance between the world as it was and the world as they had wanted it to be by securing enough of their war aims—state rights, white supremacy, and honor—to permit them to claim their share of the victory.

Battle Cry of Freedom:
The Civil War Era

The weeks after Booth fulfilled his vow on Good Friday passed in a dizzying sequence of events. Jarring images dissolved and re-formed in kaleidoscopic patterns that left the senses traumatized or elated: Lincoln lying in state at the White House on April 19 as General Grant wept unabashedly at his catafalque; Confederate armies surrendering one after another as Jefferson Davis fled southward hoping to reestablish his government in Texas and carry on the war to victory; Booth killed in a burning barn in Virginia; seven million somber men, women, and children lining the tracks to view Lincoln's funeral train on its way back home to Springfield; the steamboat *Sultana* returning northward on the Mississippi with liberated Union prisoners of war blowing up on April 27 with a loss of life equal to that of the *Titanic* a half-century later; Jefferson Davis captured in Georgia on May 10, accused (falsely) of complicity in Lincoln's assassination, imprisoned and temporarily shackled at Fortress Monroe, Virginia, where he remained for two years until released without trial to live on until his eighty-first year and become part of the ex-Confederate literary corps who wrote weighty tomes to justify their Cause; the Army of the Potomac and Sherman's Army of Georgia marching 200,000 strong in a Grand Review down Pennsylvania Avenue on May 23–24 in a pageantry of power and catharsis before being demobilized from more than 1,000,000 soldiers to fewer than 80,000 a year later and an eventual peacetime total of 27,000; weary, ragged Confederate soldiers straggling homeward begging or stealing food from dispirited civilians who often did not know where their own next meal was coming from; joyous black people celebrating the jubilee of a freedom whose boundaries they did not yet discern; gangs of southern deserters, guerrillas, and outlaws ravaging a region that would not know real peace for many years to come.

The terms of that peace and the dimensions of black freedom would preoccupy the country for a decade or more. Meanwhile the process of chronicling the war and reckoning its consequences began immediately and has never ceased. More than 620,000 soldiers lost their lives in four years of conflict—360,000 Yankees and at least 260,000 rebels. The number of southern civilians who died as a direct or indirect result of the war cannot be known;

what *can* be said is that the Civil War's cost in American lives was almost as great as in all of the nation's other wars combined through Vietnam. Was the liberation of four million slaves and the preservation of the Union worth the cost? That question too will probably never cease to be debated—but in 1865 few black people and not many northerners doubted the answer.

In time even a good many southerners came to agree with the sentiments of Woodrow Wilson (a native of Virginia who lived four years of his childhood in wartime Georgia) expressed in 1880 when he was a law student at the University of Virginia: "*Because* I love the South, I rejoice in the failure of the Confederacy. . . . Conceive of this Union divided into two separate and independent sovereignties! . . . Slavery was enervating our Southern society. . . . [Nevertheless] I recognize and pay loving tribute to the virtues of the leaders of secession . . . the righteousness of the cause which they thought they were promoting—and to the immortal courage of the soldiers of the Confederacy." Wilson's words embodied themes that would help reconcile generations of southerners to defeat: their glorious forebears had fought courageously for what they believed was right; perhaps they deserved to win; but in the long run it was a good thing they lost. This Lost Cause mentality took on the proportions of a heroic legend, a southern *Götterdämmerung* with Robert E. Lee as a latter-day Siegfried.

But a persistent question has nagged historians and mythologists alike: if Marse Robert was such a genius and his legions so invincible, why did they lose? The answers, though almost as legion as Lee's soldiers, tend to group themselves into a few main categories. One popular answer has been phrased, from the northern perspective, by quoting Frederick the Great's aphorism that God was on the side of the heaviest battalions. For southerners this explanation usually took some such form as these words of a Virginian: "They never whipped us, Sir, unless they were four to one. If we had had anything like a fair chance, or less disparity of numbers, we should have won our cause and established our independence." The North had a potential manpower superiority of more than three to one (counting only white men), and Union armed forces had an actual superiority of two to one during most of the war. In economic resources and logistical capacity the northern advantage was even greater. Thus, in this explanation, the Confederacy fought against overwhelming odds; its defeat was inevitable.

But this explanation has not satisfied a good many analysts. History is replete with examples of peoples who have won or defended their independence against greater odds: the Netherlands against the Spain of Philip II; Switzerland against the Hapsburg Empire; the American rebels of 1776 against mighty Britain; North Vietnam against the United States of 1970. Given the advantages of fighting on the defensive in its own territory with interior lines in which stalemate would be victory against a foe who must invade, conquer, occupy, and destroy the capacity to resist, the odds faced by the South were not formidable. Rather, as another category of interpretations has it, internal divisions fatally weakened the Confederacy: the state's-rights conflict between certain governors and the Richmond government; the disaffection of non-slaveholders from a rich man's war and poor man's fight; libertarian opposition to necessary measures such as conscription and the suspension of habeas corpus; the lukewarm commitment to the Confederacy by quondam Whigs and unionists; the disloyalty of slaves who defected to the enemy whenever they had a chance; growing doubts among slaveowners themselves about the justice of their peculiar institution and their cause. "So the Confederacy succumbed to internal rather than external causes," according to numerous historians. The South suffered from a "weakness in morale," a "loss of the will to fight." The Confederacy did not lack "the means to continue the struggle," but "the will to do so."

The "internal division" and "lack of will" explanations for Confederate defeat, while not implausible, are not very convincing either. The problem is that the North experienced similar internal division, and if the war had come out differently the Yankees' lack of unity and will to win could be cited with equal plausibility to explain that outcome. The North had its large minority alienated by the rich man's war/poor man's fight theme; its outspoken opposition to conscription, taxation, suspension of habeas corpus, and other war measures; its state governors and legislatures and congressmen who tried to thwart administration policies. If important elements of the southern population, white as well as black, grew disaffected with a war to preserve slavery, equally significant groups in the North dissented from a war to abolish slavery. One critical distinction between Union and Confederacy was the institutionalization of obstruction in the Democratic party in the North, compelling the Republicans to close ranks in support of war policies to overcome and ultimately to discredit the opposition, while the South had no such institutionalized political structure to mobilize support and vanquish resistance.

Nevertheless, the existence of internal divisions on both sides seemed to neutralize this factor as an explanation for Union victory, so a number of historians have looked instead at the quality of leadership both military and civilian. There are several variants of an interpretation that emphasizes a gradual development of superior northern leadership. In Beauregard, Lee, the two Johnstons, and Jackson the South enjoyed abler military commanders during the first year or two of the war, while Jefferson Davis was better qualified by training and experience than Lincoln to lead a nation at war. But Lee's strategic vision was limited to the Virginia theater, and the Confederate government neglected the West, where Union armies developed a strategic design and the generals to carry it out, while southern forces floundered under incompetent commanders who lost the war in the West. By 1863, Lincoln's remarkable abilities gave him a wide edge over Davis as a war leader, while in Grant and Sherman the North acquired commanders with a concept of total war and the necessary determination to make it succeed. At the same time, in Edwin M. Stanton and Montgomery Meigs, aided by the entrepreneurial talent of northern businessmen, the Union developed superior managerial talent to mobilize and organize the North's greater resources for victory in the modern industrialized conflict that the Civil War became.

This interpretation comes closer than others to credibility. Yet it also commits the fallacy of reversibility—that is, if the outcome had been reversed some of the same factors could be cited to explain Confederate victory. If the

South had its bumblers like Bragg and Pemberton and Hood who lost the West, and Joseph Johnston who fought too little and too late, the North had its McClellan and Meade who threw away chances in the East and its Pope and Burnside and Hooker who nearly lost the war in that theater where the genius of Lee and his lieutenants nearly won it, despite all the South's disadvantages. If the Union had its Stanton and Meigs, the Confederacy had its Josiah Gorgas and other unsung heroes who performed miracles of organization and improvisation. If Lincoln had been defeated for reelection in 1864, as he anticipated in August, history might record Davis as the great war leader and Lincoln as an also-ran.

Most attempts to explain southern defeat or northern victory lack the dimension of *contingency*—the recognition that at numerous critical points during the war things might have gone altogether differently. Four major turning points defined the eventual outcome. The first came in the summer of 1862, when the counteroffensives of Jackson and Lee in Virginia and Bragg and Kirby Smith in the West arrested the momentum of a seemingly imminent Union victory. This assured a prolongation and intensification of the conflict and created the potential for Confederate success, which appeared imminent before each of the next three turning points.

The first of these occurred in the fall of 1862, when battles at Antietam and Perryville threw back Confederate invasions, forestalled European mediation and recognition of the Confederacy, perhaps prevented a Democratic victory in the northern elections of 1862 that might have inhibited the government's ability to carry on the war, and set the stage for the Emancipation Proclamation which enlarged the scope and purpose of the conflict. The third critical point came in the summer and fall of 1863, when Gettysburg, Vicksburg, and Chattanooga turned the tide toward ultimate northern victory.

One more reversal of that tide seemed possible in the summer of 1864, when appalling Union casualties and apparent lack of progress especially in Virginia brought the North to the brink of peace negotiations and the election of a Democratic president. But the capture of Atlanta and Sheridan's destruction of Early's army in the Shenandoah Valley clinched matters for the North. Only then did it become possible to speak of the inevitability of Union victory. Only then did the South experience an irretrievable "loss of the will to fight."

Of all the explanations for Confederate defeat, the "loss of will" thesis suffers most from its own particular fallacy of reversibility—that of putting the cart before the horse. Defeat causes demoralization and loss of will; victory pumps up morale and the will to win. Nothing illustrates this better than the radical transformation of *northern* will from defeatism in August 1864 to a "depth of determination . . . to fight to the last" that "astonished" a British journalist a month later. The southern loss of will was a mirror image of this northern determination. These changes of mood were caused mainly by events on the battlefield. Northern victory and southern defeat in the war cannot be understood apart from the contingency that hung over every campaign, every battle, every election, every decision during the war. This phenomenon of contingency can best be presented in a narrative format—a format this book has tried to provide.

Arguments about the causes and consequences of the Civil War, as well as the reasons for northern victory, will continue as long as there are historians to wield the pen—which is, perhaps even for this bloody conflict, mightier than the sword. But certain large consequences of the war seem clear. Secession and slavery were killed, never to be revived during the century and a quarter since Appomattox. These results signified a broader transformation of American society and polity punctuated if not alone achieved by the war. Before 1861 the two words "United States" were generally rendered as a plural noun: "the United States *are* a republic." The war marked the transition of the United States to a singular noun. The "Union" also became the nation, and Americans now rarely speak of their Union except in an historical sense. Lincoln's wartime speeches betokened this transition. In his first inaugural address he used the word "Union" twenty times and the word "nation" not once. In his first message to Congress, on July 4, 1861, he used "Union" thirty-two times and "nation" three times. In his letter to Horace Greeley of August 22, 1862, on the relationship of slavery to the war, Lincoln spoke of the "Union" eight times and of the "nation" not at all. Little more than a year later, in his address at Gettysburg, the president did not refer to the "Union" at all but used the word "nation" five times to invoke a new birth of freedom and nationalism for the United States. And in his second inaugural address, looking back over the events of the past four years, Lincoln spoke of one side seeking to dissolve the *Union* in 1861 and the other accepting the challenge of war to preserve the *Nation*.

The old federal republic in which the national government had rarely touched the average citizen except through the post office gave way to a more centralized polity that taxed the people directly and created an internal revenue bureau to collect these taxes, drafted men into the army, expanded the jurisdiction of federal courts, created a national currency and a national banking system, and established the first national agency for social welfare—the Freedmen's Bureau. Eleven of the first twelve amendments to the Constitution had limited the powers of the national government; six of the next seven, beginning with the Thirteenth Amendment in 1865, vastly expanded those powers at the expense of the states.

This change in the federal balance paralleled a radical shift of political power from South to North. During the first seventy-two years of the republic down to 1861 a slaveholding resident of one of the states that joined the Confederacy had been president of the United States for forty-nine of those years—more than two-thirds of the time. In Congress, twenty-three of the thirty-six speakers of the House and twenty-four of the presidents pro tem of the Senate had been southerners. The Supreme Court always had a southern majority; twenty of the thirty-five justices to 1861 had been appointed from slave states. After the war a century passed before a resident of an ex-Confederate state was elected president. For half a century only one of the speakers of the House and none of the presidents pro tem of the Senate came from the South, and only five of the twenty-six Supreme Court justices appointed during that half-century were southerners.

These figures symbolize a sharp and permanent change in the direction of American development. Through most of American history the South has seemed different from the rest of the United States, with "a separate and unique identity . . . which appeared to be out of the mainstream of American experience." But when did the northern stream become the mainstream? From a broader perspective it may have been the *North* that was exceptional and unique before the Civil War. The South more closely resembled a majority of the societies in the world than did the rapidly changing North during the antebellum generation. Despite the abolition of legal slavery or serfdom throughout much of the western hemisphere and western Europe, most of the world—like the South—had an unfree or quasi-free labor force. Most societies in the world remained predominantly rural, agricultural, and labor-intensive; most, including even several European countries, had illiteracy rates as high as or higher than the South's 45 percent; most like the South remained bound by traditional values and networks of family, kinship, hierarchy, and patriarchy. The North—along with a few countries of northwestern Europe—hurtled forward eagerly toward a future of industrial capitalism that many southerners found distasteful if not frightening; the South remained proudly and even defiantly rooted in the past before 1861.

Thus when secessionists protested that they were acting to preserve traditional rights and values, they were correct. They fought to protect their constitutional liberties against the perceived northern threat to overthrow them. The South's concept of republicanism had not changed in three-quarters of a century; the North's had. With complete sincerity the South fought to preserve its version of the republic of the founding fathers—a government of limited powers that protected the rights of property and whose constituency comprised an independent gentry and yeomanry of the white race undisturbed by large cities, heartless factories, restless free workers, and class conflict. The accession to power of the Republican party, with its ideology of competitive, egalitarian, free-labor capitalism, was a signal to the South that the northern majority had turned irrevocably toward this frightening, revolutionary future. Indeed, the Black Republican party appeared to the eyes of many southerners as "essentially a revolutionary party" composed of "a motley throng of Sans culottes . . . Infidels and freelovers, interspersed by Bloomer women, fugitive slaves, and amalgamationists." Therefore secession was a preemptive counterrevolution to prevent the Black Republican revolution from engulfing the South. "*We* are not revolutionists," insisted James B. D. DeBow and Jefferson Davis during the Civil War, "We are resisting revolution. . . . We are conservative."

Union victory in the war destroyed the southern vision of America and ensured that the northern vision would become the American vision. Until 1861, however, it was the North that was out of the mainstream, not the South. Of course the northern states, along with Britain and a few countries in northwestern Europe, were cutting a new channel in world history that would doubtless have become the mainstream even if the American Civil War had not happened. Russia had abolished serfdom in 1861 to complete the dissolution of this ancient institution of bound labor in Europe. But for Americans the Civil War marked the turning point. A Louisiana planter who returned home sadly after the war wrote in 1865: "Society has been completely changed by the war. The [French] revolution of '89 did not produce a greater change in the 'Ancien Régime' than this has in our social life." And four years later George Ticknor, a retired Harvard professor, concluded that the Civil War had created a "great gulf between what happened before in our century and what has happened since, or what is likely to happen hereafter. It does not seem to me as if I were living in the country in which I was born." From the war sprang the great flood that caused the stream of American history to surge into a new channel and transferred the burden of exceptionalism from North to South.

What would be the place of freed slaves and their descendants in this new order? In 1865 a black soldier who recognized his former master among a group of Confederate prisoners he was guarding called out a greeting: "Hello, massa; bottom rail on top dis time!" Would this new arrangement of rails last? Will a nation "conceived in liberty and dedicated to the proposition that all men are created equal" continue to evolve in accordance with that fundamental "proposition"? This is a question that can be answered only by generations yet to come.

POSTSCRIPT

Was the Confederacy Defeated Because of Its "Loss of Will"?

Beringer et al. give a new twist to the old argument that the Confederacy lost because it lacked the will to win. Rather than blaming Jefferson Davis's political failures or General Robert E. Lee's strategy of attacking Gettysburg, the authors argue that Southern guilt over slavery and inability of Southern political and religious leaders to fashion a viable nationalism caused the Confederacy to collapse.

Beringer et al. also believe that the internal dissension among the Confederate states and their central government was not an important factor in the South's defeat. The authors maintain that the states made positive contributions to the Confederate war effort through the organization of state militias and provisions for the coastal defenses. The economies of the states, say the authors, also provided enough uniforms and equipment for the military, even though the planters continued to overproduce cotton.

The Civil War was fought between two sections that had been united under the same government for 85 years. Southerners controlled the presidency, the Supreme Court, and the major offices in Congress during much of this time. Could it be that the South left the Union, as McPherson and others have pointed out, because the northern and western states, with their free labor ideology of an industrial-based economy, were to dominate nationally once Lincoln was elected president in 1860?

McPherson, now the acknowledged dean of the Civil War scholars, rejects all prior internal and external arguments for the defeat of the Confederacy as hindsight arguments. In his view, historians could have cited economic power, military brilliance, political leadership, internal dissension, and loss of will to explain a Confederate victory had the South emerged victorious.

McPherson argues that chance or contingency best explains why the North won. He points out that victories at Antietam in 1862, Gettysburg in 1863, and the total war campaigns of Grant and Sherman in 1864 led to political victories for the Republicans in Congress in 1862 and for Lincoln's reelection in 1864. Victories at Antietam and Gettysburg in particular were not foregone conclusions. If the South had won these battles, the outcome of the war might have been different.

Students who wish to pursue the causation question should compare the essays in David Donald, ed., *Why the North Won the Civil War* (Louisiana State University Press, 1960) with a more recent collection edited by Gabor S. Borritt on *Why the Confederacy Lost* (Oxford University Press, 1992).

ISSUE 17

Did Abraham Lincoln Free the Slaves?

YES: Allen C. Guelzo, from *Lincoln's Emancipation Proclamation: The End of Slavery in America* (Simon & Schuster, 2004)

NO: Vincent Harding, from *There Is a River: The Black Struggle for Freedom in America* (Vintage Books, 1981)

ISSUE SUMMARY

YES: Allen Guelzo insists that Abraham Lincoln was committed to freeing the nation's slaves from the day of his inauguration and that, by laying the foundation for liberating some four million African Americans held in bondage, the Emancipation Proclamation represents the most epochal of Lincoln's writings.

NO: Vincent Harding credits slaves themselves for engaging in a dramatic movement of self-liberation while Abraham Lincoln initially refused to declare the destruction of slavery as a war aim and then issued the Emancipation Proclamation, which failed to free any slaves in areas over which he had any authority.

In April 1861, less than a month after his inauguration, President Abraham Lincoln attempted to send provisions to Fort Sumter, a federal military installation nestled in the harbor of Charleston, South Carolina, part of the newly formed Confederate States of America. Southern troops under the command of General P. G. T. Beauregard opened fire on the fort, forcing its surrender on April 14. The American Civil War had begun.

Numerous explanations have been offered for the cause of this "war between the states." Many contemporaries and some historians saw the conflict as the product of a conspiracy housed either in the North or South, depending upon one's regional perspective. For many in the northern states, the chief culprits were the planters and their political allies who were willing to defend southern institutions at all costs. South of the Mason-Dixon line, blame was laid at the feet of the fanatical abolitionists (see Issue 13) and the free-soil architects of the Republican party. Some viewed secession and war as the consequence of a constitutional struggle between states' rights advocates and defenders of the federal government, while others focused upon the economic rivalries or the cultural differences between North and South. Embedded in each of these interpretations, however, is the powerful influence of the institution of slavery.

Abraham Lincoln fully understood the role slavery had played in the outbreak of the Civil War. In March 1865, as the war was nearing its end, he presented the following analysis: "One eighth of the whole population [in 1861] was colored slaves, not distributed generally over the Union, but localized in the southern part of it. These slaves constituted a peculiar and powerful interest. All knew that this interest was somehow the cause of the war. To strengthen, perpetuate, and extend this interest was the object [of the South] . . . , while the [North] . . . claimed no right to do more than to restrict the territorial enlargement of it."

In light of Lincoln's recognition of the role slavery played in the clash between North and South, none should find it surprising that the Emancipation Proclamation, which the President issued, established a policy to end slavery. Hence, the demise of slavery became a war aim, and Lincoln seemed to have earned his place in history as "the Great Emancipator." Upon learning of the president's announcement, the fugitive slave and abolitionist Frederick Douglass was ecstatic. "We shout for joy," he declared, "that we live to record this righteous decree."

But Douglass had not always been so encouraged by Lincoln's commitment to freedom. Lincoln was not an abolitionist by any stretch of the imagination, but Douglass was convinced that the Republican victory in the presidential election of 1860 had brought to the White House a leader with a deserved reputation as an antislavery man. That confidence declined, however, in the early months of Lincoln's presidency as Douglass and other abolitionists lobbied for emancipation during the secession crisis and, when the war began, as a military necessity only to have their demands fall on deaf ears. Lincoln consistently avoided any public pronouncements that would suggest his desire to end slavery as a war aim. The priority was preserving the Union, and Lincoln did not view emancipation as essential to that goal.

Until the president changed his course, it appeared that the slaves would have to free themselves. This is precisely what some scholars insist happened. Southern slaves, they argue, became the key agents for liberation by abandoning their masters, undermining the plantation routine, serving as spies for Union troops, and taking up arms against the Confederacy. Black northerners pitched in as well by enlisting in the United States Army to defeat the Confederacy and end slavery.

The question "Who freed the slaves?" is the focus of the following essays. Allen Guelzo portrays Lincoln as a president deeply committed to ending slavery. The Emancipation Proclamation was drafted as an emergency measure to substitute for the slower process of a long-term legislative solution in the midst of the Civil War. Coupled with the Thirteenth Amendment, which had Lincoln's support prior to his assassination, this action laid a firm foundation for sounding the death knell to the slave system in the South.

For Vincent Harding, credit for the end of slavery belongs to the masses of slaves who sought self-liberation by running away from their masters, undermining plantation operations, engaging in local insurrections, and offering their services to the Union army and navy.

YES

Allen C. Guelzo

Introduction

The Emancipation Proclamation is surely the unhappiest of all of Abraham Lincoln's great presidential papers. Taken at face value, the Emancipation Proclamation was the most revolutionary pronouncement ever signed by an American president, striking the legal shackles from four million black slaves and setting the nation's face toward the total abolition of slavery within three more years. Today, however, the Proclamation is probably best known for what it did *not* do, beginning with its apparent failure to rise to the level of eloquence Lincoln achieved in the Gettysburg Address or the Second Inaugural. Even in the 1860s, Karl Marx, the author of a few proclamations of his own, found that the language of the Proclamation, with its ponderous *whereas*es and *therefore*s, reminded him of "ordinary summonses sent by one lawyer to another on the opposing side." When the Lincoln Memorial was dedicated in 1922, quotations from the Second Inaugural and the Gettysburg Address flanked the great Daniel Chester French statue of the seated Lincoln, but there was no matching quotation from the Proclamation, only a vague, elliptical representation in Jules Guerin's mural, *Emancipation of a Race,* which was mostly lost to sight near the ceiling of one of the memorial's side chambers.

But the unkindest cut at the Proclamation came from the hands of Columbia University historian Richard Hofstadter, in his essay on Lincoln in *The American Political Tradition and the Men Who Made It* (1948). A onetime member of the circle of American Marxist intellectuals around *Partisan Review,* Hofstadter repudiated the traditional Progressive view of American political history as a struggle between the legacies of the liberal Thomas Jefferson and the conservative Alexander Hamilton. Instead, Hofstadter viewed American politics as a single, consistent, and deeply cynical story of how capitalism had corrupted Jeffersonians and Hamiltonians alike and turned the United States into "a democracy of cupidity rather than a democracy of fraternity." But he reserved his angriest words for Lincoln and for the Emancipation Proclamation. Lincoln's opposition to slavery, in Hofstadter's reckoning, was kindled only by the threat it posed to free white labor and the development of industrial capitalism. Lincoln "was, as always, thinking primarily of the free white worker" and was "never much troubled about the Negro." No one, then, should be fooled by the Proclamation. Its motives were entirely other than had been advertised, and that fact explained its stylistic flaccidity. "Had the political strategy of the moment called for a momentous human document of the stature of the Declaration of Independence, Lincoln could have risen to the occasion." Instead, what he composed on New Year's Day, 1863, "had all the moral grandeur of a bill of lading." It accomplished nothing because it was intended to accomplish nothing "beyond its propaganda value."

The influence of Hofstadter's easily repeatable quip about "the moral grandeur of a bill of lading" has had long innings, and even the most favorably disposed of modern Lincoln biographers have found themselves forced to concede that the Proclamation "lacked the memorable rhetoric of his most notable utterances." And perhaps for that reason, no serious study of the Proclamation has appeared since John Hope Franklin's brief *The Emancipation Proclamation* in 1963, written for its centennial. (That centennial itself was a disappointing affair, capped by President John F. Kennedy's refusal to give the principal address at ceremonies at the Lincoln Memorial on September 22, 1963, for fear of suffering deeper losses of Southern Democrats in his reelection bid the next year.) As the Proclamation's negative symbolic power has risen, efforts to interpret the text have diminished, and examination of the Proclamation's contents has subsided into offhand guesswork and angry prejudice. The Proclamation has become a document (as Garry Wills once described the Declaration of Independence) "dark with unexamined lights." As with Jefferson's Declaration, we have lost in the cultural eddies of the last hundred and forty years the assumptions that would make the Emancipation Proclamation readable.

Recapturing at least some of those assumptions will begin, I think, with recognizing in Abraham Lincoln our last Enlightenment politician. The contours of Lincoln's mind—his allegiance to "reason, cold, calculating, unimpassioned reason"; his aversion to the politics of passion; the distance he maintained from organized religion; his affection for Shakespeare, Paine, and Robert Burns; and his unquestioning belief in universal natural rights—were all shaped by the hand of the Enlightenment. But the most important among the Enlightenment's political virtues for Lincoln, and for his Proclamation, was prudence.

Prudence carries with it today the connotation of "prude"—a person of exaggerated caution, bland temperance, hesitation, a lack of imagination and will, fearfulness, and a bad case of mincing steps. This view would have surprised the classical philosophers, who thought of prudence as one of the four cardinal virtues and who linked it to shrewdness, exceptionally good judgment, and the gift of *coup d'oeil*—the "coup of the eye"—which could take in the whole of a situation at once and know almost automatically how to proceed. Among political scientists, it has more specific meanings, but those meanings are usually just as repellent—of cunning, *realpolitik,* and in some quarters, an unhealthy preoccupation with the neo-classicism of Leo Strauss. (So let me say, for the benefit of the hunters of subtexts, that I can cheerfully confess to never having read Leo Strauss, nor, for that matter, to possessing much aptitude for the peculiar dialect spoken by my political science friends.) It is an ironic rather than a tragic attitude, in which the calculus of costs is critical rather than crucial or incidental. It prefers incremental progress to categorical solutions and fosters that progress through the offering of motives rather than expecting to change dispositions. Yet, unlike mere moderation, it has a sense of purposeful motion and declines to be paralyzed by a preoccupation with process, even while it remains aware that there is no goal so easily attained or so fully attained that it rationalizes dispensing with process altogether. Montesquieu found the origins of political greatness in "prudence, wisdom, perseverance," since prudence would "guard the passions of individuals for the sake of order and guard the guardians for the sake of freedom." In the new American republic, James Madison argued (in the forty-third of the *Federalist Papers*) for ratification of the 1787 Constitution on the grounds of "the rights of humanity," the "considerations of a common interest," and on "prudence." So also for Lincoln: The practice of politics involved the rule of prudence, and "obeying the dictates of prudence" was as important for Lincoln as obeying "the obligations of law." He hoped, as president, that "it will appear that we have practiced prudence," and in 1861, he promised that the management of the Civil War would be "done consistently with the prudence . . . which ought always to regulate the public service" and without allowing the war to degenerate "into a violent and remorseless revolutionary struggle."

It is this politics of prudence which opens up for us a way to understand Lincoln's strategy in "the mighty experiment" of emancipation. The most salient feature to emerge from the sixteen months between his inauguration and the first presentation of the Proclamation to his cabinet on July 22, 1862, is the consistency with which Lincoln's face was set toward the goal of emancipation from the day he first took the presidential oath. Lincoln was not exaggerating when he claimed in 1858 that he "hated" slavery:

> I hate it because of the monstrous injustice of slavery itself. I hate it because it deprives our republican example of its just influence in the world—enables the enemies of free institutions, with plausibility, to taunt us as hypocrites—causes the real friends of freedom to doubt our sincerity, and especially because it forces so many really good men amongst ourselves into an open war with the very fundamental principles of civil liberty—criticising the Declaration of Independence, and insisting that there is no right principle of action but self-interest.

But in Lincoln's case, prudence demanded that he balance the integrity of *ends* (the elimination of slavery) with the integrity of *means* (his oath to uphold the Constitution and his near-religious reverence for the rule of law). Lincoln understood emancipation not as the satisfaction of a "spirit" overriding the law, nor as the moment of fusion between the Constitution and absolute moral theory, but as a goal to be achieved through prudential means, so that worthwhile consequences might result. He could not be persuaded that emancipation required the headlong abandonment of everything save the single absolute of abolition, or that purity of intention was all that mattered, or that the exercise of the will rather than the reason was the best ethical foot forward.

Far too often, Lincoln's apologists hope to give the lie to Hofstadter's scalding attack by pulling apart means and ends, either apologizing for the former or explaining away the latter, a sure sign that they have no better grasp on the politics of prudence than Hofstadter. Most often, this pulling apart happens whenever we are tempted to plead that Lincoln was either a man in *progress* or a man of *patience*. That is, Lincoln was (as Horace Greeley put it) "a growing man," growing in this case from a stance of moral indifference and ignorance about emancipation at the time of his election in 1860, toward deep conviction about African-American freedom by the time of the Emancipation Proclamation less than two years later. Or else that Lincoln already had all the racial goodwill necessary for emancipation but had to wait until the right moment in the war or the right moment in the growth of Northern acceptance of the idea of emancipation. These are both generous sentiments, but I am not sure that generosity is quite what is needed for understanding Lincoln's proclamation. Rather than needing to develop *progress,* I believe that Abraham Lincoln understood from the first that his administration was the beginning of the end of slavery and that he would not leave office without some form of legislative emancipation policy in place. By his design, the burden would have to rest mainly on the state legislatures, largely because Lincoln mistrusted the federal judiciary and expected that any emancipation initiatives which came directly from his hand would be struck down in the courts. This mistrust is also what lies behind another curiosity: Lincoln's rebuffs to the covert emancipations that Congress constructed under the cover of the two Confiscation Acts (of August 1861 and July 1862), the "contraband" theory confected by the ingenious Benjamin Butler, and the two martial-law emancipation proclamations attempted by John Charles Frémont and David Hunter. Lincoln ignored the Confiscation Acts, showed no interest in Butler's "contraband" theory, and actually revoked the martial-law proclamations—not because he was indifferent to emancipation, but because he was convinced (and with good reason) that none of these methods would survive challenges in federal court.

But why, if he was attuned so scrupulously to the use of the right legal means for emancipation, did Lincoln turn in the summer of 1862 and issue an Emancipation Proclamation—which was, for all practical purposes, the very sort of martial-law dictum he had twice before canceled? The answer can be summed up in one word: time. It seems clear to me that Lincoln recognized by July 1862 that he could not wait for the legislative option—and not because he had patiently waited to discern public opinion and found the North readier than the state legislatures to move ahead. If anything, Northern public opinion remained loudly and frantically hostile to the prospect of emancipation, much less emancipation by presidential decree. Instead of exhibiting *patience,* Lincoln felt stymied by the unanticipated stubbornness with which even Unionist slaveholders refused to cooperate with the mildest legislative emancipation policy he could devise, and threatened by generals who were politically committed to a negotiated peace. (We usually underrate the menace posed by the generals, largely because, in the end, it did not materialize, but on at least some level, Lincoln feared that emancipation risked triggering a military coup d'etat by General George McClellan and the Army of the Potomac.) Thus Lincoln's Proclamation was one of the biggest political gambles in American history.

But gambles are not necessarily inconsistent with prudence, and Lincoln's gamble may be considered a prudent one for the role that providence came to play in it. For a man with such a vague religious profile, Lincoln nevertheless understood that a significant part of the politics of prudence involved a deference to providence—whether one defined *providence* as the work of an active and interventionist God or merely the forces of history, economics, or ideas.

Lincoln was raised in an environment saturated with notions of providential determinism, beginning with his upbringing among the "hard-shell" Separate Baptists. As he did with so much else in his upbringing, Lincoln lost what little faith he might have had, and he acquired more notoriety than was good for an ambitious young politico in Illinois as an "infidel." It was an Enlightenment infidelity, a rationalistic deism stoked in equal parts by the smile of Voltaire and the arguments of Tom Paine. But even then, Lincoln's unbelief had this much still in common with the Calvinism he had forsaken— both subscribed alike to the notion that all events were determined by forces beyond human power.

This is not the most optimistic way of looking at the world, but it can lend a certain confidence to one's plans if the direction in which determinism is pointing also happens to be the upward path you are following. Lincoln, like so many other secular determinists shaped by the Enlightenment's delight with the idea of a mechanically predictable universe—Thomas Henry Buckle, Karl Marx, Adolphe Quetelet, Pierre Laplace—thought that progress, improvement, and invention were written into the script of human affairs beyond the power of human effacement. And that meant, from Lincoln's vantage point, that an institution as hateful and retrograde as slavery had to be as inalterably doomed as superstition and tyranny. Whatever the occasional wrong moves— the economic surge of the cotton South, the overthrow of the safeguards against slavery's expansion by the Kansas-Nebraska Act, even the Civil War itself—the fundamental direction of events was inevitable and required only a certain amount of machinery-tending to put things back on the rails.

The carnage, the stalemate, and the incomprehensible rebel victories of the War's first year conspired to strip Lincoln of his optimism in the natural, pleasant ascent of progress, but not of his fundamental belief in providence. Instead, the war saw him veer away from a providence defined by indifference and the iron law of cause and effect, and back toward the providence of a mysterious and self-concealing God whose will for the human future did not necessarily move according to the sweet and logical processes of progress. And in the case of emancipation, Lincoln came to see the Proclamation as the only alternative God had left to emancipation being swept off the table entirely.

All the same, Lincoln never intended the Proclamation to be a substitute for a long-term legislative solution, and in fact, that hope for a legislative solution eventually bore fruit as the Thirteenth Amendment. The Proclamation was an emergency measure, a substitute for the permanent plan that would really rid the country of slavery, but a substitute as sincere and profound as the timbers that shore up an endangered mine shaft and prevent it from collapsing entirely.

Understanding prudence as the key to Lincoln's political behavior gives us the "big picture" behind the Emancipation Proclamation. It does not speak automatically to four very specific questions about the Emancipation Proclamation that I am asked nearly everywhere I go. First and most frequent is the Hofstadter question: *Why is the language of the Proclamation so bland and legalistic?* The answer, I think, really should be obvious, and it was not because Lincoln wrote the Proclamation grudgingly and of necessity. Very simply: The Proclamation is a legal document, and legal documents cannot afford very much in the way of flourishes. They have work to do. In this instance, we are dealing with a document with a very great deal of it to do, and one which had to be composed with the understanding that every syllable was liable to the most concentrated legal parsing by the federal court system. If it falls short of the eloquence of the Gettysburg Address, I only have to point out that the Gettysburg Address was not a document anyone could take into court, and at least in legal terms, it was not intended to accomplish anything. In other words, Lincoln could afford eloquence at Gettysburg; he could not in the Proclamation.

The second question is linked to the Hofstadter question, if only because Hofstadter believed, wrongly, that a linkage between the two existed: *Did the Proclamation actually do anything?* Because the Proclamation limited emancipation only to the states or parts of states still in rebellion and did not include the slaves in the four loyal slave states—Delaware, Maryland, Kentucky, and Missouri—it has been easy to lampoon the Proclamation as a puff of political air. But laws are not the less laws merely because circumstances render them inoperative at a given time or place. I should be ashamed to offer myself as an example, but I do so only because it will force Lincoln's critics to examine their own terms: Every day that I traveled between Paoli and Princeton, I took liberties with the speed limit which the Commonwealth of Pennsylvania and the State of New Jersey forbid. (Judging from the abandon with which other drivers flew past me, most of my readers, it is safe to say, are doubtless implicated in similar offenses.) The guardians of the turnpike might have lacked the energy, the technology, or even the power to enforce the legislated speed limits, but they certainly possessed the perfect and unimpaired authority to do so, as I would have discovered if ever once they had gotten me to stop. The same is true with Lincoln and the Proclamation. Lincoln may not have had the *power* available to him to free every slave in the Confederacy, but he certainly had the *authority,* and in law, the authority is as good as the power. The proof is in the pudding: No slave declared free by the Proclamation was ever returned to slavery once he or she had made it to the safety of Union-held territory.

This raises a related question: *Did the slaves free themselves?* In 1979, Leon Litwack laid the foundations for an alternative view of emancipation when he urged historians to regard emancipation not as an event beginning and ending with Lincoln but as a process in which pressure was exerted on Lincoln and Congress by the slaves themselves. By running away, by labor sabotage, and by volunteering to serve the Union armies, the slaves forced Lincoln's hand toward emancipation. But looked at in the larger context of nineteenth-century

American race relations, the "self-emancipation" thesis asks for too great a suspension of disbelief. Without the legal freedom conferred first by the Emancipation Proclamation, no runaway would have remained "self-emancipated" for very long. The files on the first year and a half of the war bulge with accounts of thwarted slaveowners with court papers in their hands and sheriffs at their sides, stalking through the camps of Union regiments in pursuit of slave runaways as though a barbecue rather than a war was in progress. Without the Proclamation, the Confederacy even in defeat would have retained legal title to its slaves, and there is little in the oppressive patterns of coercion Southerners employed before the Civil War or afterward in Reconstruction to suggest that they would not have been willing to reclaim as many of their self-emancipated runaways as they could; and if the record of the federal courts in the post—Civil War decades is any proof, the courts would probably have helped them.

In the same skeptical spirit, a fourth question is frequently aimed at the intentions behind the Proclamation: *Did Lincoln issue the Proclamation only to ward off European intervention or inflate Union morale?* To this, I can only say that if intervention and morale were Lincoln's primary concerns, then an Emancipation Proclamation was probably the worst method, and at the worst time, with which to have met them. Abroad, there was as much danger that an Emancipation Proclamation would trigger foreign intervention as there was that the Proclamation would discourage it. At home, Pennsylvania politician Alexander McClure warned Lincoln that "political defeat would be inevitable in the great States of the Union in the elections soon to follow if he issued the Emancipation Proclamation." Significantly, Lincoln agreed "as to the political effect of the proclamation." He knew that the Proclamation, for all that he hoped it would forestall the generals and put the Union cause unreservedly on the side of the angels, might just as easily convince them to accelerate plans for an intervention or put Lincoln's administration on the side of the losers. To his surprise, McClure found that this made no dent in Lincoln's determination. Those who have sung in Richard Hofstadter's choir need, as McClure needed, to take a new measure of that determination.

But it is not simply the complexities of Lincoln's mental habits or the difficulty involved in piecing together the circumstances and chronology of Lincoln's decision to emancipate which make the Proclamation so difficult for us to grasp. A good deal of our befuddlement is wrapped up in the way that our notions of political ethics have changed since Lincoln's day. Even as Lincoln emerged onto the national political scene in the 1850s, the politics of prudence that had guided Enlightenment political theory was being devalued in favor of a Romantic politics of ethical absolutism. One source of that absolutism lay close to home for Americans in the radical perfectionism of evangelical Protestant revivalism; another was the influence of Immanuel Kant, mediated through English and American Romantics such as Emerson, Samuel Taylor Coleridge, Frederick Augustus Rauch, and James Marsh, the "Vermont Transcendentalist." What the American Romantics particularly admired in Kant was his attempt to locate a source for ethical judgments within men (instead of imposed externally, through divine revelation or natural law), in a "categorical imperative" that yields absolute and universal answers to ethical dilemmas. "We do not need science and philosophy to know what we should do to be honest and good, yea, even wise and virtuous," argued Kant in his *Fundamental Principles of the Metaphysic of Morals*. What we need to do is obey the imperative. Kant's hope was to be able to isolate moral decisions from the flux of circumstance, culture, and individual experience, and thus escape the threat of moral relativism. He was, in other words, looking for a way out of the mechanistic universe, where ethics is simply a pretty name we give to justify whatever decisions circumstances force upon us. Kant sought to base the right or wrong of things solely on the principle that moved the will to choose one thing over another. Purifying the will trumps the claims of all other values, and willing purely is all that is necessary to overcome injustice. As much as Kant believed in universal rational criteria for ethical behavior, those criteria spoke in (as Isaiah Berlin put it) "the language of inner voices."

It is the convergence of American evangelical absolutism and the ethic of the imperative that, more than anything else, erects a translucent shield between our habits of mind and Lincoln's, passing enough light to make us think we see but not enough to allow us to understand. This is not to say that Lincoln, as a man of the Enlightenment, possessed a superior morality or always did well and right. Nor does it mean that Lincoln was untinged by certain elements of Romanticism himself or that he conforms in precise anticipation to all our American anxieties about race and reconciliation at the beginning of the twenty-first century. It would be special pleading to claim that Lincoln was in the end the most perfect friend black Americans have ever had. But it would also be the cheapest and most ignorant of skepticisms to deny that he was the most significant. And if the Emancipation Proclamation was not, as Richard Hofstadter so mordantly complained half a century ago, the most eloquent of Lincoln's writings, it was unquestionably the most epochal. It may have had little more "moral grandeur" than a "bill of lading," but Lincoln's Emancipation Proclamation was still a bill that itemized the destinies of four millions of human beings, bound in the way of danger for the port of American freedom.

The Blood-Red Ironies of God

Although the destruction of the oppressors God may not effect by the oppressed, yet the Lord our God will surely bring other destructions upon them—for not infrequently will he cause them to rise up against one another, to be split and divided, and to oppress each other, and sometimes to open hostilities with sword in hand.

— David Walker, 1829

On certain stark and bloody levels, a terrible irony seemed to be at work. For those who interpreted the events of their own times through the wisdom and anguish of the past, the guns of Charleston certainly sounded like the signal for the fulfillment of David Walker's radical prophecies. Here at last was the coming of the righteous God in judgment, preparing to bring "destructions" upon America. Here was the divine culmination of the struggle toward freedom and justice long waged by the oppressed black people. From such a vantage point, the conflict now bursting out was the ultimate justification of the costly freedom movement, a welcome vindication of the trust in Providence. And yet the war was not simply an ally. Like all wars, it brought with it a train of demoralizing, destructive elements, deeply affecting even those persons and causes which seemed to be its chief beneficiaries. In the case of black people, the guns broke in upon their freedom struggle at many levels, diverted and diffused certain of its significant radical elements, and became a source of profound confusion and disarray among its most committed forces. This was especially the case where independent radical black struggle for justice and self-determination was concerned. . . .

When the war broke out, black men and women were convinced that it had to destroy slavery. Especially in the North, this inner certainty flooded their consciousness, buoyed up their hopes. Now it appeared that God was providing a way out of the darkness of slavery and degradation, a way which would release some of the frightening tension of the previous decade. Because they wanted a way out so desperately, because it was hard to be driven by a fierce urgency, fearsome to experience the personal honing in spite of one's own softer and blunter ways, the children of Africa in America clutched at a solution which would not cause them to be driven into the depths of radicalism. For they must have realized that the chances were good that they might not survive without being seriously, unpredictably transformed. Therefore,

From Vincent Harding, THERE IS A RIVER: THE BLACK STRUGGLE FOR FREEDOM IN AMERICA (Vintage Books, 1981). Copyright © 1981 by Vincent Harding. Reprinted by permission of Harcourt, Inc. Notes omitted.

when the guns began, black people shunted aside the knowledge of certain fierce realities.

In that mood their men surged forward to volunteer for service in the Union cause, repressing bitter memories. In spite of their misgivings, disregarding the fact that it was not the North which had initiated this righteous war, they offered their bodies for the Northern cause, believing that it was—or would be—the cause of black freedom. If the excited, forgetful young volunteers sought justification, they could find it in the *Anglo-African:* "Talk as we may, we are concerned in this fight and our fate hangs upon its issues. The South must be subjugated, or we shall be enslaved. In aiding the Federal government in whatever way we can, we are aidin g to secure our own liberty; for this war can end only in the subjugation of the North or the South." When hard pressed, the journal, like the young men it encouraged, knew very well the nature of the "liberty" they had found so far in the unsubjugated North, and the writer admitted that the North was not consciously fighting for black rights. However, the *Anglo-African* chose to see a power beyond the councils of the North: "Circumstances have been so arranged by the decrees of Providence, that in struggling for their own nationality they are forced to defend our rights." . . .

And what of the South? What of those sometimes God-obsessed black believers who had long lifted their cries for deliverance in songs and shouts, in poetry filled with rich and vibrant images? Did they sense the coming of Moses now? Was this finally the day of the delivering God, when he would set his people free? Did they hear Nat Turner's spirit speaking in the guns? Did they believe he was calling them to freedom through all the lines of skirmishers who left their blood upon the leaves? Did they have any difficulty knowing which of the white armies was Pharaoh's?

The answers were as complex as life itself. In many parts of the nation and the world there had been predictions that secession, disunion, and war would lead to a massive black insurrection which would finally vindicate Turner and Walker, and drown the South in blood. Such predictions were made without knowledge of the profound racism and fear which pervaded the white North, and certainly without awareness of the keen perceptions of black people in the South. For most of the enslaved people knew their oppressors, and certainly realized that such a black uprising would expose the presence of Pharaoh's armies everywhere. To choose that path to freedom would surely unite the white North and South more quickly than any other single development, making black men, women, and children the enemy—the isolated, unprepared enemy. For anyone who needed concrete evidence, Gen. George B. McClellan, the commander of the Union's Army of the Ohio, had supplied it in his "Proclamation to the people of Western Virginia" on May 26, 1861: "Not only will we abstain from all interferences with your slaves, but we will, with an iron hand, crush any attempt at insurrection on their part."

So, heeding their own intuitive political wisdom, the black masses confirmed in their actions certain words which had recently appeared in the *Anglo-African.* Thomas Hamilton, the editor, had heard of Lincoln's decision to countermand an emancipation order issued by one of his most fervent Republican generals, John C. Fremont, in Missouri. Hamilton predicted: "The forlorn hope of insurrection among the slaves may as well be abandoned. They are too well informed and too *wise* to court destruction at the hands of the combined Northern and Southern armies—for the man who had reduced back to slavery the slaves of rebels in Missouri would order the army of the United States to put down a slave insurrection in Virginia or Georgia." He was right, of course, and the enslaved population was also right. Therefore, instead of mass insurrection, the Civil War created the context for a vast broadening and intensifying of the self-liberating black movement which had developed prior to the war. Central to this black freedom action, as always, was the continuing series of breaks with the system of slavery, the denials of the system's power, the self-emancipation of steadily increasing thousands of fugitives. Thus, wherever possible, black people avoided the deadly prospects of massive, sustained confrontation, for their ultimate objective was freedom, not martyrdom.

As the guns resounded across the Southern lands, the movement of black folk out of slavery began to build. Quickly it approached and surpassed every level of force previously known. Eventually the flood of fugitives amazed all observers and dismayed not a few, as it sent waves of men, women, and children rushing into the camps of the Northern armies. In this overwhelming human movement, black people of the South offered their own responses to the war, to its conundrums and mysteries. Their action testified to their belief that deliverance was indeed coming through the war, but for thousands of them it was not a deliverance to be bestowed by others. Rather it was to be independently seized and transformed through all the courage, wisdom, and strength of their waiting black lives.

This rapidly increasing movement of black runaways had been noted as soon as the reality of Southern secession had been clearly established. Shortly after the guns of April began to sound in Charleston harbor, large companies of fugitives broke loose from Virginia and the Carolinas and moved toward Richmond. Again, one day in Virginia in the spring of 1861, a black fugitive appeared at the Union-held Fortress Monroe. Two days later eight more arrived, the next day more than fifty, soon hundreds. The word spread throughout the area: there was a "freedom fort," as the fugitives called it, and within a short time thousands were flooding toward it. Similarly, in Louisiana two families waded six miles across a swamp, "spending two days and nights in mud and water to their waists, their children clinging to their backs, and with nothing to eat." In Georgia, a woman with her twenty-two children and grandchildren floated down the river on "a dilapidated flatboat" until she made contact with the Union armies. In South Carolina, black folk floated to freedom on "basket boats made out of reeds," thus reviving an ancient African craft. A contemporary source said of the black surge toward freedom in those first two years of the war: "Many thousands of blacks of all ages, ragged, with no possessions, except the bundles which they carried, had assembled at Norfolk, Hampton, Alexandria and Washington. Others . . . in multitudes . . . flocked north from Tennessee, Kentucky, Arkansas, and Missouri."

This was black struggle in the South as the guns roared, coming out of loyal and disloyal states, creating their own liberty. This was the black movement toward a new history, a new life, a new beginning. W. E. B. Du Bois later said,

"The whole move was not dramatic or hysterical, rather it was like the great unbroken swell of the ocean before it dashes on the reefs." Yet there was great drama as that flowing movement of courageous black men and women and children sensed the movement of history, heard the voice of God, created and signed their own emancipation proclamations, and seized the time. Their God was moving and they moved with him.

And wherever this moving army of self-free men and women and children went, wherever they stopped to wait and rest and eat and work, and watch the movement of the armies in the fields and forests—in all these unlikely sanctuaries, they sent up their poetry of freedom. Some of them were old songs, taking on new meaning:

> Thus said the Lord, Bold Moses said
> Let my people go
> If not I'll smite your first-born dead
> Let my people go.
> No more shall they in bondage toil
> Let my people go.

But now there was no need to hide behind the stories of thousands of years gone by, now it was clearly a song of black struggle, of deliverance for their own time of need. Now the singers themselves understood more fully what they meant when they sang again:

> One of dese mornings, five o'clock
> Dis ole world gonna reel and rock,
> Pharaoh's Army got drownded
> Oh, Mary, don't you weep.

They were part of the drowning river. Out there, overlooking the battlefields of the South, they were the witnesses to the terrible truth of their own sons, to the this-worldliness of their prayers and aspirations. Remembering that morning in Charleston harbor, who could say they were wrong? "Dis ole world gonna reel and rock . . ."

Every day they came into the Northern lines, in every condition, in every season of the year, in every state of health. Children came wandering, set in the right direction by falling, dying parents who finally knew why they had lived until then. Women came, stumbling and screaming, their wombs bursting with the promise of new and free black life. Old folks who had lost all track of their age, who knew only that they had once heard of a war against "the Redcoats," also came, some blind, some deaf, yet no less eager to taste a bit of that long-anticipated freedom of their dreams. No more auction block, no more driver's lash, many thousands gone.

This was the river of black struggle in the South, waiting for no one to declare freedom for them, hearing only the declarations of God in the sound of the guns, and moving.

By land, by river, creating their own pilgrim armies and their own modes of travel, they moved south as well as north, heading down to the captured areas of the coast of South Carolina. *Frederick Douglass's Monthly* of February 1862 quoted the report of a *New York Times* correspondent in Port Royal: "Everywhere I find the same state of things existing; everywhere the blacks hurry in droves to our lines; they crowd in small boats around our ships; they swarm upon our decks; they hurry to our officers from the cotton houses of their masters, in an hour or two after our guns are fired. . . . I mean each statement I make to be taken literally; it is not garnished for rhetorical effect." As usual, black people were prepared to take advantage of every disruption in the life of the oppressing white community. When they heard the guns, they were ready, grasping freedom with their own hands, walking to it, swimming to it, sailing to it—determined that it should be theirs. By all these ways, defying masters, patrols, Confederate soldiers, slowly, surely, they pressed themselves into the central reality of the war.

. . . By the end of the spring of 1862, tens of thousands [of self-liberated fugitives] were camped out in whatever areas the Northern armies had occupied, thereby making themselves an unavoidable military and political issue. In Washington, D.C., the commander-in-chief of the Union armies had developed no serious plans for the channeling of the black river. Consequently, in the confusion which all war engenders, his generals in the field made and carried out their own plans. They were badly strapped for manpower, and the black fugitives provided some answers to whatever prayers generals pray. The blacks could relieve white fighting men from garrison duties. They could serve as spies, scouts, and couriers in the countryside they knew so well. They could work the familiar land, growing crops for the food and profit of the Union armies. But as the war dragged on and Northern whites lost some of their early enthusiasm, many Union commanders saw the black men among them primarily as potential soldiers. Many of the black men were eager to fight, but Lincoln was still not prepared to go that far.

Nevertheless, some Union commanders like Gen. David Hunter in South Carolina were again issuing their own emancipation proclamations and beginning to recruit black soldiers. In places like occupied New Orleans it was the unmanageable and threatening movement of the blacks themselves which placed additional pressures on the Union's leader. Reports were pouring into Washington which told not only of the flood of fugitives, but of black unrest everywhere. Black men were literally fighting their way past the local police forces to get themselves and their families into the Union encampments. There was word of agricultural workers killing or otherwise getting rid of their overseers, and taking over entire plantations. Commanders like Gen. Ben Butler warned that only Union bayonets prevented widespread black insurrection. (In August 1862, to preserve order and satisfy his need for manpower, Butler himself had begun to recruit black troups in New Orleans, beginning with the well-known Louisiana Native Guards.) The dark presence at the center of the national conflict could no longer be denied. Lincoln's armies were in the midst of a surging movement of black people who were in effect freeing themselves from slavery. His generals were at once desperate for the military resources represented by the so-called contrabands, and convinced that only through military discipline could this volatile, potentially revolutionary black element be contained. As a result, before 1862 was over, black troops were being enlisted to fight for their own freedom in both South Carolina and Louisiana.

In Washington, Congress was discussing its own plans for emancipation, primarily as a weapon against the South, hoping to deprive the Confederacy of a major source of human power and transfer it into Union hands. Their debates and imminent action represented another critical focus of pressure on the President. While Lincoln continued to hesitate about the legal, constitutional, moral, and military aspects of the matter, he was also being constantly attacked in the North for his conduct of the war. The whites were weary and wanted far better news from the fronts. The blacks were angry about his continued refusal to speak clearly to the issue of their people's freedom and the black right to military service. In the summer of 1862 Frederick Douglass declared in his newspaper: "Abraham Lincoln is no more fit for the place he holds than was James Buchanan. . . . The country is destined to become sick of both [Gen. George B.] McClellan and Lincoln, and the sooner the better. The one plays lawyer for the benefit of the rebels, and the other handles the army for the benefit of the traitors. We should not be surprised if both should be hurled from their places before this rebellion is ended. . . . The signs of the times indicate that the people will have to take this war into their own hands." But Frederick Douglass was not one to dwell on such revolutionary options. (Besides, had he considered what would happen to the black cause, if the white "people" really did take the war into their own hands?) Fortunately, by the time Douglass's words were published, he had seen new and far more hopeful signs of the times.

In September 1862 Abraham Lincoln, in a double-minded attempt both to bargain with and weaken the South while replying to the pressures of the North, finally made public his proposed Emancipation Proclamation. Under its ambiguous terms, the states in rebellion would be given until the close of the year to end their rebellious action. If any did so, their captive black people would not be affected; otherwise, the Emancipation Proclamation would go into effect on January 1, 1863, theoretically freeing all the enslaved population of the Confederate states and promising federal power to maintain that freedom.

What actually was involved was quite another matter. Of great import was the fact that the proclamation excluded from its provisions the "loyal" slave states of Missouri, Kentucky, Delaware, and Maryland, the anti-Confederate West Virginia Territory, and loyal areas in certain other Confederate states. Legally, then, nearly one million black people whose masters were "loyal" to the Union had no part of the emancipation offered. In effect, Lincoln was announcing freedom to the captives over whom he had least control, while allowing those in states clearly under the rule of his government to remain in slavery. However, on another more legalistic level, Lincoln was justifying his armies' use of the Confederates' black "property," and preparing the way for an even more extensive use of black power by the military forces of the

Union. Here, the logic of his move was clear, providing an executive confirmation and extension of Congress's Second Confiscation Act of 1862: once the Emancipation Proclamation went into effect, the tens of thousands of black people who were creating their own freedom, and making themselves available as workers in the Union camps, could be used by the North without legal qualms. Technically, they would no longer be private property, no longer cause problems for a President concerned about property rights.

It was indeed a strange vessel that the Lord had chosen, but black folk in the South were not waiting on such legal niceties. Not long after the preliminary proclamation, an insurrectionary plot was uncovered among a group of blacks in Culpepper County, Virginia. Some were slaves and some free, and the message of their action carried a special resonance for South and North alike, and perhaps for the President himself. For a copy of Lincoln's preliminary proclamation was reportedly found among the possessions of one of the conspirators. Though at least seventeen of the group were executed, their death could not expunge the fact that they had attempted to seize the time, to wrest their emancipation out of the hands of an uncertain President. On Nat's old "gaining ground" they had perhaps heard the voice of his God and, forming their own small army, were once again searching for Jerusalem.

Such action symbolized a major difference in the movement of the Southern and Northern branches of the struggle. In the South, though most of the self-liberating black people eventually entered the camps, or came otherwise under the aegis of the Northern armies, they were undoubtedly acting on significant, independent initiatives. During the first years of the war, the mainstream of the struggle in the South continued to bear this independent, self-authenticating character, refusing to wait for an official emancipation.

In such settings black hope blossomed, fed by its own activity. Even in the ambiguous context of the contraband communities the signs were there. In 1862–63, in Corinth, Mississippi, newly free blacks in one of the best of the contraband camps organized themselves under federal oversight, and created the beginnings of an impressive, cohesive community of work, education, family life, and worship. They built their own modest homes, planted and grew their own crops (creating thousands of dollars of profit for the Union), supported their own schools, and eventually developed their own military company to fight with the Union armies. It was not surprising, then, that black fugitives flocked there from as far away as Georgia. Nor was it unexpected that, in 1863, federal military plans demanded the dismantling of the model facility. Nevertheless, the self-reliant black thrust toward the future had been initiated, and Corinth was only one among many hopeful contraband communities.

Such movement, and the vision which impelled it, were integral aspects of the freedom struggle in the South. Meanwhile, to aid that struggle, by 1863 Harriet Tubman had entered the South Carolina war zone. Working on behalf of the Union forces, she organized a corps of black contrabands and traveled with them through the countryside to collect information for army raids, and to urge the still-enslaved blacks to leave their masters. Apparently the intrepid leader and her scouts were successful at both tasks, though Tubman complained that her long dresses sometimes impeded her radical activities.

In the North the situation was somewhat different. Word of Lincoln's anticipated proclamation had an electrifying effect on the black community there, but at the same time further removed the focus from the black freedom-seizing movement in the South. The promised proclamation now gave the Northerners more reason than ever to look to others for release, to invest their hope in the Union cause. Now it seemed as if they would not need to be isolated opponents of an antagonistic federal government. Again, because they wanted to believe, needed to hope, yearned to prove themselves worthy, they thought they saw ever more clearly the glory of the coming; before long, in their eyes the proclamation was clothed in what appeared to be almost angelic light. As such, it became an essentially religious rallying point for the development of a new, confusing mainstream struggle: one which, nervous and excited, approached and embraced the central government and the Republican Party as agents of deliverance. Doubts from the past were now cast aside, for their struggle was unquestionably in the hands of Providence and the Grand Army of the Republic. The voice of God was joined to that of Abraham Lincoln.

. . . [F]rom a certain legal point of view it could be argued that the Emancipation Proclamation set free no enslaved black people at all. Since by December 31, 1862, no Confederate state had accepted Lincoln's invitation to return to the fold with their slaves unthreatened, and since Lincoln acknowledged that he had no real way of enforcing such a proclamation within the rebellious states, the proclamation's power to set anyone free was dubious at best. (Rather, it confirmed and gave ambiguous legal standing to the freedom which black people had already claimed through their own surging, living proclamations.)

Indeed, in his annual address to Congress on December 1, 1862, Lincoln had not seemed primarily concerned with the proclamation. Instead, he had taken that crucial opportunity to propose three constitutional amendments which reaffirmed his long-standing approach to national slavery. The proposed amendments included provisions for gradual emancipation (with a deadline as late as 1900), financial compensation to the owners, and colonization for the freed people. In other words, given the opportunity to place his impending proclamation of limited, immediate emancipation into the firmer context of a constitutional amendment demanding freedom for all enslaved blacks, Lincoln chose another path, one far more in keeping with his own history.

But none of this could dampen the joy of the black North. Within that community, it was the Emancipation Proclamation of January 1, 1863, which especially symbolized all that the people so deeply longed to experience, and its formal announcement sent a storm of long-pent-up emotion surging through the churches and meeting halls. It was almost as if the Northern and Southern struggles had again been joined, this time not through wilderness flights, armed resistance, and civil disobedience, but by a nationwide, centuries-long cord of boundless ecstasy. In spite of its limitations, the proclamation was taken as the greatest sign yet provided by the hand of Providence. The river had burst its boundaries, had shattered slavery's dam. It appeared as if the theodicy of the Northern black experience was finally prevailing. For the freedom struggle, especially in the South, had begun to overwhelm the white man's war, and had forced the President and the nation officially to turn their faces toward the moving black masses. Wherever black people could assemble, by themselves or with whites, they came together to lift joyful voices of thanksgiving, to sing songs of faith, to proclaim, "Jehovah hath triumphed, his people are free." For them, a new year and a new era had been joined in one.

On the evening of December 31, 1862, Frederick Douglass was in Boston attending one of the hundreds of freedom-watch-night services being held across the North in anticipation of the proclamation. That night, a line of messengers had been set up between the telegraph office and the platform of the Tremont Temple, where the Boston meeting was being held. After waiting more than two hours in agonized hope, the crowd was finally rewarded as word of the official proclamation reached them. Douglass said: "The effect of this announcement was startling beyond description, and the scene was wild and grand. Joy and gladness exhausted all forms of expression, from shouts of praise to sobs and tears . . . a Negro preacher, a man of wonderful vocal power, expressed the heartfelt emotion of the hour, when he led all voice in the anthem, 'Sound the loud timbrel o'er Egypt's dark sea, Jehovah hath triumphed, his people are free.'"

Such rapture was understandable, but like all ecstatic experiences, it carried its own enigmatic penalties. Out of it was born the mythology of Abraham Lincoln as Emancipator, a myth less important in its detail than in its larger meaning and consequences for black struggle. The heart of the matter was this: while the concrete historical realities of the time testified to the costly, daring, courageous activities of hundreds of thousands of black people breaking loose from slavery and setting themselves free, the myth gave the credit for this freedom to a white Republican president. In those same times when black men and women saw visions of a new society of equals, and heard voices pressing them against the American Union of white supremacy, Abraham Lincoln was unable to see beyond the limits of his own race, class, and time, and dreamed of a Haitian island and of Central American colonies to rid the country of the constantly accusing, constantly challenging black presence. Yet in the mythology of blacks and whites alike, it was the independent, radical action of the black movement toward freedom which was diminished, and the coerced, ambiguous role of a white deliverer which gained pre-eminence.

POSTSCRIPT

Did Abraham Lincoln
Free the Slaves?

Abraham Lincoln's reputation as "the Great Emancipator" traditionally has been based upon his decision in 1862 to issue the Emancipation Proclamation. While Harding stresses that Lincoln was forced to act by the large number of slaves who already had engaged in a process of self-liberation, he and other scholars point out the limited impact of Lincoln's emancipation policy. Announced in September 1862, the measure would not go into effect until January 1, 1863, and it would apply only to those slave states still in rebellion against the Union. In other words, emancipation would become law in states where the federal government was in no position to enforce the measure. Also, the status of slaves residing in states that had not seceded (Missouri, Kentucky, Maryland, and Delaware) would not be altered by this fiat. Theoretically, then, the Proclamation would have few benefits for those held in bondage in the Confederacy.

Critics of Lincoln's uncertain approach to ending slavery in particular and to the rights of African Americans, slave and free, in general also cite a number of other examples that draw Lincoln's commitment to freedom into question. During the presidential campaign of 1860, candidate Lincoln had insisted that he had no desire to abolish slavery where the institution already existed. There was, of course, the President's statement that he would be willing to keep slavery intact if that was the best means of preserving the Union. His alternative claim that he would be willing to free all the slaves to maintain the sanctity of the Union appeared as just so much rhetoric when compared to his policies as president. For example, Lincoln initially opposed arming black citizens for military service, he countermanded several of his field generals' emancipation orders, and he consistently expressed doubts that blacks and whites would be able to live in the United States as equal citizens. Then, in December 1862, between his announcement of the preliminary emancipation proclamation and the time that the order was to go into effect, the President proposed a constitutional amendment that would provide for gradual emancipation, with compensation to the slave owners followed by colonization of the liberated blacks to a site outside the boundaries of the United States.

In assessing Lincoln's racial attitudes and policies, care should be taken not to read this historical record solely from a twenty-first century perspective. Lincoln may not have been the embodiment of the unblemished racial egalitarian that some might hope for, but few whites were, including most of the abolitionists. Still, as historian Benjamin Quarles has written, Lincoln "treated Negroes as they wanted to be treated—as human beings." Unlike most white Americans of his day, Lincoln opposed slavery, developed a policy that held out hope for emancipation, and supported the Thirteenth Amendment.

Lincoln is the most written-about president. Students should consult Carl Sandburg, *Abraham Lincoln*, 6 vols. (Harcourt, Brace & World, 1926–1939), a poetic panorama that focuses upon the mythic Lincoln. Benjamin Thomas, *Abraham Lincoln: A Biography* (Alfred A. Knopf, 1952), Stephen B. Oates, *With Malice Toward None: The Life of Abraham Lincoln* (Harper & Row, 1977), Philip Shaw Paludan, *The Presidency of Abraham Lincoln* (University Press of Kansas, 1994), and David Donald, *Lincoln* (Simon & Schuster, 1995) are excellent one-volume biographies. David Donald, *Lincoln Reconsidered: Essays on the Civil War Era* (Alfred A. Knopf, 1956) and Richard N. Current, *The Lincoln Nobody Knows* (McGraw-Hill, 1958) offer incisive interpretations of many aspects of Lincoln's political career and philosophy. George B. Forgie, in *Patricide in the House Divided: A Psychological Interpretation* (W. W. Norton, 1979), and Dwight G. Anderson, in *Abraham Lincoln: The Quest for Immortality* (Alfred A. Knopf, 1982), offer psychoanalytical approaches to Lincoln. Lincoln's responsibility for the precipitating event of the Civil War is explored in Richard N. Current, *Lincoln and the First Shot* (Lippincott, 1963). T. Harry Williams, *Lincoln and His Generals* (Alfred A. Knopf, 1952), looks at Lincoln as commander in chief and remains one of the best Lincoln studies. Gabor S. Boritt, ed., *The Historian's Lincoln: Pseudohistory, Psychohistory, and History* (University of Illinois Press, 1988) is a valuable collection. For Lincoln's role as "the Great Emancipator" and his attitudes toward race and slavery, see Benjamin Quarles, *Lincoln and the Negro* (Oxford University Press, 1962), James M. McPherson, *Abraham Lincoln and the Second American Revolution* (Oxford University Press, 1990), and Mark E. Neely. Jr., *The Fate of Liberty: Abraham Lincoln and Civil Liberties* (Oxford University Press, 1991). John Hope Franklin's *The Emancipation Proclamation* (Anchor, 1965) was the key study of this presidential policy prior to the publication of Guelzo's recent analysis.

In addition to the work of Vincent Harding, the self-emancipation thesis is developed in Ira Berlin, Barbara J. Fields, Thavolia Glymph, Joseph P. Reidy, and Leslie S. Rowland, eds., *Freedom: A Documentary History of Emancipation, 1861–1867*, 4 vols. (Cambridge University Press, 1982–1993). Lerone Bennett's *Forced Into Glory: Abraham Lincoln's White Dream* (Johnson Publishing Company, 2000) is highly critical of Lincoln's racial attitudes and commitment to emancipation. The role of African Americans in the Civil War is the subject of James McPherson, ed., *The Negro's Civil War* (Pantheon, 1965). Black military experience is treated in Benjamin Quarles, *The Negro in the Civil War* (Little, Brown, 1969), Dudley Cornish, *The Sable Arm: Black Troops in the Union Army, 1861–1865* (Longmans, 1956), Joseph Glatthaar, *Forged in Battle: The Civil War Alliance of Black Soldiers and White Officers* (Free Press, 1990), Ervin L. Jordan, Jr., *Black Confederates and Afro-Yankees in Civil War Virginia* (University Press of Virginia, 1995), and James G. Hollandsworth, Jr., *The Louisiana Native Guards: The Black Military Experience During the Civil War* (Louisiana State University Press, 1995).

ISSUE 18

Was Reconstruction a "Splendid Failure"?

YES: Eric Foner, from "The New View of Reconstruction," *American Heritage* (October/November 1983)

NO: LaWanda Cox, from *Lincoln and Black Freedom: A Study in Presidential Leadership* (University of South Carolina Press, 1981)

ISSUE SUMMARY

YES: Eric Foner asserts that although Reconstruction did not achieve radical goals, it was a "splendid failure" because it offered African Americans in the South a temporary vision of a free society.

NO: LaWanda Cox explores the hypothetical question of whether Reconstruction would have succeeded had Lincoln lived and concludes that, despite his many talents, not even Lincoln could have guaranteed the success of the full range of reform for African Americans.

Given the complex issues of the post–Civil War years, it is not surprising that the era of Reconstruction (1865–1877) is shrouded in controversy. For the better part of a century following the war, historians typically characterized Reconstruction as a total failure that had proved detrimental to all Americans—northerners and southerners, whites and blacks. According to this traditional interpretation, a vengeful Congress, dominated by radical Republicans, imposed military rule upon the southern states. Carpetbaggers from the North, along with traitorous white scalawags and their black accomplices in the South, established coalition governments that rewrote state constitutions, raised taxes, looted state treasuries, and disenfranchised former Confederates while extending the ballot to the freedmen. This era finally ended in 1877 when courageous southern white Democrats successfully "redeemed" their region from "Negro rule" by toppling the Republican state governments.

This portrait of Reconstruction dominated the historical profession until the 1960s. One reason for this is that white historians (both northerners and southerners) who wrote about this period operated from two basic assumptions: (1) The South was capable of solving its own problems without federal government interference, and (2) the former slaves were intellectually inferior to whites and incapable of running a government (much less one in which some whites would be their subordinates). African American historians, such as W. E. B. Du Bois, wrote several essays and books that challenged this negative portrayal of Reconstruction, but their works seldom were taken seriously in the academic world and rarely were read by the general public. Still, these black historians foreshadowed the acceptance of revisionist interpretations of Reconstruction, which coincided with the successes of the civil rights movement (or "Second Reconstruction") in the 1960s.

Without ignoring obvious problems and limitations connected with this period, revisionist historians identified a number of accomplishments of the Republican state governments in the South and their supporters in Washington, D.C. For example, revisionists argued that the state constitutions that were written during Reconstruction were the most democratic documents that the South had seen up to that time. Also, while taxes increased in the southern states, the revenues generated by these levies financed the rebuilding and expansion of the South's railroad network, the creation of a number of social service institutions, and the establishment of a public school system that benefited African Americans as well as whites. At the federal level, Reconstruction achieved the ratification of the Fourteenth and Fifteenth Amendments, which extended significant privileges of citizenship (including the right to vote) to African Americans, both North and South. Revisionists also placed the charges of corruption leveled by traditionalists against the Republican regimes in the South in a more appropriate context by insisting that political corruption was a *national* malady. Although the leaders of the Republican state governments in the South engaged in a number of corrupt activities, they were no more guilty than several federal officeholders in the Grant administration, or the members of New York City's notorious Tweed Ring (a Democratic urban political machine), or even the southern white Democrats (the Redeemers) who replaced the radical Republicans in positions of power in the former Confederate states. Finally, revisionist historians sharply attacked the notion that African Americans dominated the reconstructed governments of the South. They pointed out that there were no black governors, only two black senators, and fifteen black congressmen during this period.

In the essays that follow, Eric Foner and LaWanda Cox present thought-provoking analyses of the Reconstruction period. In the first selection, Foner concedes that Reconstruction was not very radical, much less revolutionary. Nevertheless, he argues, it was a "splendid failure" (a phrase coined by Du Bois) because it offered African Americans a vision of how a free society could look.

LaWanda Cox approaches this question from the counterfactual premise that Abraham Lincoln lived to oversee the political, economic, and social experiment that was Reconstruction. If anyone could have met the challenges of the post–Civil War era, she states, it was Lincoln. On the other hand, however, even had Lincoln gained broad consent from the white South during his second presidential term, Republican lawmakers' commitment to state responsibility for the rights of citizens, coupled with deeply entrenched racism in the South, would have derailed the more progressive aspects of Reconstruction legislation.

YES

Eric Foner

The New View of Reconstruction

In the past twenty years, no period of American history has been the subject of a more thoroughgoing reevaluation than Reconstruction—the violent, dramatic, and still controversial era following the Civil War. Race relations, politics, social life, and economic change during Reconstruction have all been reinterpreted in the light of changed attitudes toward the place of blacks within American society. If historians have not yet forged a fully satisfying portrait of Reconstruction as a whole, the traditional interpretation that dominated historical writing for much of this century has irrevocably been laid to rest.

Anyone who attended high school before 1960 learned that Reconstruction was an era of unrelieved sordidness in American political and social life. The martyred Lincoln, according to this view, had planned a quick and painless readmission of the Southern states as equal members of the national family. President Andrew Johnson, his successor, attempted to carry out Lincoln's policies but was foiled by the Radical Republicans (also known as Vindictives or Jacobins). Motivated by an irrational hatred of Rebels or by ties with Northern capitalists out to plunder the South, the Radicals swept aside Johnson's lenient program and fastened black supremacy upon the defeated Confederacy. An orgy of corruption followed, presided over by unscrupulous carpet-baggers (Northerners who ventured south to reap the spoils of office), traitorous scalawags (Southern whites who cooperated with the new governments for personal gain), and the ignorant and childlike freedmen, who were incapable of properly exercising the political power that had been thrust upon them. After much needless suffering, the white community of the South banded together to overthrow these "black" governments and restore home rule (their euphemism for white supremacy). All told, Reconstruction was just about the darkest page in the American saga.

Originating in anti-Reconstruction propaganda of Southern Democrats during the 1870s, this traditional interpretation achieved scholarly legitimacy around the turn of the century through the work of William Dunning and his students at Columbia University. It reached the larger public through films like *Birth of a Nation* and *Gone With the Wind* and that best-selling work of myth-making masquerading as history, *The Tragic Era* by Claude G. Bowers. In language as exaggerated as it was colorful, Bowers told how Andrew Johnson "fought the bravest battle for constitutional liberty and for the preservation of

From Eric Foner, "The New View of Reconstruction," *American Heritage*, vol. 34, no. 6 (October/November 1983). Copyright © 1983 by *American Heritage*. Reprinted by permission.

our institutions ever waged by an Executive" but was overwhelmed by the "poi-sonous propaganda" of the Radicals. Southern whites, as a result, "literally were put to the torture" by "emissaries of hate" who manipulated the "simple-minded" freedmen, "inflaming the negroes' egotism" and even inspiring "lustful assaults" by blacks upon white womanhood.

In a discipline that sometimes seems to pride itself on the rapid rise and fall of historical interpretations, this traditional portrait of Reconstruction enjoyed remarkable staying power. The long reign of the old interpretation is not difficult to explain. It presented a set of easily identifiable heroes and villains. It enjoyed the imprimatur of the nation's leading scholars. And it accorded with the political and social realities of the first half of this century. This image of Reconstruction helped freeze the mind of the white South in unalterable opposition to any movement for breaching the ascendancy of the Democratic party, eliminating segregation, or readmitting disfranchised blacks to the vote.

***

Nevertheless, the demise of the traditional interpretation was inevitable, for it ignored the testimony of the central participant in the drama of Reconstruction—the black freedman. Furthermore, it was grounded in the conviction that blacks were unfit to share in political power. As Dunning's Columbia colleague John W. Burgess put it, "A black skin means membership in a race of men which has never of itself succeeded in subjecting passion to reason, has never, there-fore, created any civilization of any kind." Once objective scholarship and modern experience rendered that assumption untenable, the entire edifice was bound to fall.

The work of "revising" the history of Reconstruction began with the writings of a handful of survivors of the era, such as John R. Lynch, who had served as a black congressman from Mississippi after the Civil War. In the 1930s white scholars like Francis Simkins and Robert Woody carried the task forward. Then, in 1935, the black historian and activist W. E. B. Du Bois pro-duced *Black Reconstruction in America,* a monumental reevaluation that closed with an irrefutable indictment of a historical profession that had sacrificed scholarly objectivity on the altar of racial bias. "One fact and one alone," he wrote, "explains the attitude of most recent writers toward Reconstruction; they cannot conceive of Negroes as men." Du Bois's work, however, was ignored by most historians.

It was not until the 1960s that the full force of the revisionist wave broke over the field. Then, in rapid succession, virtually every assumption of the tra-ditional viewpoint was systematically dismantled. A drastically different por-trait emerged to take its place. President Lincoln did not have a coherent "plan" for Reconstruction, but at the time of his assassination he had been cautiously contemplating black suffrage. Andrew Johnson was a stubborn, rac-ist politician who lacked the ability to compromise. By isolating himself from the broad currents of public opinion that had nourished Lincoln's career, Johnson created an impasse with Congress that Lincoln would certainly have avoided, thus throwing away his political power and destroying his own plans for reconstructing the South.

The Radicals in Congress were acquitted of both vindictive motives and the charge of serving as the stalking-horses of Northern capitalism. They emerged instead as idealists in the best nineteenth-century reform tradition. Radical leaders like Charles Sumner and Thaddeus Stevens had worked for the rights of blacks long before any conceivable political advantage flowed from such a commitment. Stevens refused to sign the Pennsylvania Constitution of 1838 because it disfranchised the state's black citizens; Sumner led a fight in the 1850s to integrate Boston's public schools. Their Reconstruction policies were based on principle, not petty political advantage, for the central issue dividing Johnson and these Radical Republicans was the civil rights of freedmen. Studies of congressional policy-making such as Eric L. McKitrick's *Andrew Johnson and Reconstruction,* also revealed that Reconstruction legislation, ranging from the Civil Rights Act of 1866 to the Fourteenth and Fifteenth Amendments, enjoyed broad support from moderate and conservative Republicans. It was not simply the work of a narrow radical faction.

⋯◈⋯

Even more startling was the revised portrait of Reconstruction in the South itself. Imbued with the spirit of the civil rights movement and rejecting entirely the racial assumptions that had underpinned the traditional interpretation, these historians evaluated Reconstruction from the black point of view. Works like Joel Williamson's *After Slavery* portrayed the period as a time of extraordinary political, social, and economic progress for blacks. The establishment of public school systems, the granting of equal citizenship to blacks, the effort to restore the devastated Southern economy, the attempt to construct an interracial political democracy from the ashes of slavery, all these were commendable achievements, not the elements of Bowers's "tragic era."

Unlike earlier writers, the revisionists stressed the active role of the freedmen in shaping Reconstruction. Black initiative established as many schools as did Northern religious societies and the Freedmen's Bureau. The right to vote was not simply thrust upon them by meddling outsiders, since blacks began agitating for the suffrage as soon as they were freed. In 1865 black conventions throughout the South issued eloquent, though unheeded, appeals for equal civil and political rights.

With the advent of Radical Reconstruction in 1867, the freedmen did enjoy a real measure of political power. But black supremacy never existed. In most states blacks held only a small fraction of political offices, and even in South Carolina, where they comprised a majority of the state legislature's lower house, effective power remained in white hands. As for corruption, moral standards in both government and private enterprise were at low ebb throughout the nation in the postwar years—the era of Boss Tweed, the Credit Mobilier scandal, and the Whiskey Ring. Southern corruption could hardly be blamed on former slaves.

Other actors in the Reconstruction drama also came in for reevaluation. Most carpetbaggers were former Union soldiers seeking economic opportunity in the postwar South, not unscrupulous adventurers. Their motives, a typically American amalgam of humanitarianism and the pursuit of profit, were no more insidious than those of Western pioneers. Scalawags, previously seen as traitors to the white race, now emerged as "Old Line" Whig Unionists who had opposed secession in the first place or as poor whites who had long resented planters' domination of Southern life and who saw in Reconstruction a chance to recast Southern society along more democratic lines. Strongholds of Southern white Republicanism like east Tennessee and western North Carolina had been the scene of resistance to Confederate rule throughout the Civil War; now, as one scalawag newspaper put it, the choice was "between salvation at the hand of the Negro or destruction at the hand of the rebels."

At the same time, the Ku Klux Klan and kindred groups, whose campaign of violence against black and white Republicans had been minimized or excused in older writings, were portrayed as they really were. Earlier scholars had conveyed the impression that the Klan intimidated blacks mainly by dressing as ghosts and playing on the freedmen's superstitions. In fact, black fears were all too real: the Klan was a terrorist organization that beat and killed its political opponents to deprive blacks of their newly won rights. The complicity of the Democratic party and the silence of prominent whites in the face of such outrages stood as an indictment of the moral code the South had inherited from the days of slavery.

By the end of the 1960s, then, the old interpretation had been completely reversed. Southern freedmen were the heroes, the "Redeemers" who overthrew Reconstruction were the villains, and if the era was "tragic," it was because change did not go far enough. Reconstruction had been a time of real progress and its failure a lost opportunity for the South and the nation. But the legacy of Reconstruction—the Fourteenth and Fifteenth Amendments— endured to inspire future efforts for civil rights. As Kenneth Stampp wrote in *The Era of Reconstruction,* a superb summary of revisionist findings published in 1965, "If it was worth four years of civil war to save the Union, it was worth a few years of radical reconstruction to give the American Negro the ultimate promise of equal civil and political rights."

As Stampp's statement suggests, the reevaluation of the first Reconstruction was inspired in large measure by the impact of the second—the modern civil rights movement. And with the waning of that movement in recent years, writing on Reconstruction has undergone still another transformation. Instead of seeing the Civil War and its aftermath as a second American Revolution (as Charles Beard had), a regression into barbarism (as Bowers argued), or a golden opportunity squandered (as the revisionists saw it), recent writers argue that Radical Reconstruction was not really very radical. Since land was not distributed to the former slaves, they remained economically dependent upon their former owners. The planter class survived both the war and Reconstruction with its property (apart from slaves) and prestige more or less intact.

Not only changing times but also the changing concerns of historians have contributed to this latest reassessment of Reconstruction. The hallmark of the past decade's historical writing has been an emphasis upon "social history"—the evocation of the past lives of ordinary Americans—and the downplaying of strictly political events. When applied to Reconstruction, this concern with the "social" suggested that black suffrage and officeholding, once seen as the most radical departures of the Reconstruction era, were relatively insignificant.

❦

Recent historians have focused their investigations not upon the politics of Reconstruction but upon the social and economic aspects of the transition from slavery to freedom. Herbert Gutman's influential study of the black family during and after slavery found little change in family structure or relations between men and women resulting from emancipation. Under slavery most blacks had lived in nuclear family units, although they faced the constant threat of separation from loved ones by sale. Reconstruction provided the opportunity for blacks to solidify their preexisting family ties. Conflicts over whether black women should work in the cotton fields (planters said yes, many black families said no) and over white attempts to "apprentice" black children revealed that the autonomy of family life was a major preoccupation of the freedmen. Indeed, whether manifested in their withdrawal from churches controlled by whites, in the blossoming of black fraternal, benevolent, and self-improvement organizations, or in the demise of the slave quarters and their replacement by small tenant farms occupied by individual families, the quest for independence from white authority and control over their own day-to-day lives shaped the black response to emancipation.

In the post–Civil War South the surest guarantee of economic autonomy, blacks believed, was land. To the freedmen the justice of a claim to land based on their years of unrequited labor appeared self-evident. As an Alabama black convention put it, "The property which they [the planters] hold was nearly all earned by the sweat of *our* brows." As Leon Litwack showed in *Been in the Storm So Long,* a Pulitzer Prize–winning account of the black response to emancipation, many freedmen in 1865 and 1866 refused to sign labor contracts, expecting the federal government to give them land. In some localities, as one Alabama overseer reported, they "set up claims to the plantation and all on it."

In the end, of course, the vast majority of Southern blacks remained propertyless and poor. But exactly why the South, and especially its black population, suffered from dire poverty and economic retardation in the decades following the Civil War is a matter of much dispute. In *One Kind of Freedom,* economists Roger Ransom and Richard Sutch indicted country merchants for monopolizing credit and charging usurious interest rates, forcing black tenants into debt and locking the South into a dependence on cotton production that impoverished the entire region. But Jonathan Wiener, in his study of postwar Alabama, argued that planters used their political power to compel blacks to remain on the plantations. Planters succeeded in stabilizing the plantation system, but only by blocking the growth of alternative enterprises, like factories, that might draw off black laborers, thus locking the region into a pattern of economic backwardness.

≈◉≈

If the thrust of recent writing has emphasized the social and economic aspects of Reconstruction, politics has not been entirely neglected. But political studies have also reflected the postrevisionist mood summarized by C. Vann Woodward when he observed "how essentially nonrevolutionary and conservative Reconstruction really was." Recent writers, unlike their revisionist predecessors, have found little to praise in federal policy toward the emancipated blacks.

A new sensitivity to the strength of prejudice and laissez-faire ideas in the nineteenth-century North has led many historians to doubt whether the Republican party ever made a genuine commitment to racial justice in the South. The granting of black suffrage was an alternative to a long-term federal responsibility for protecting the rights of the former slaves. Once enfranchised, blacks could be left to fend for themselves. With the exception of a few Radicals like Thaddeus Stevens, nearly all Northern policy-makers and educators are criticized today for assuming that, so long as the unfettered operations of the marketplace afforded blacks the opportunity to advance through diligent labor, federal efforts to assist them in acquiring land were unnecessary.

Probably the most innovative recent writing on Reconstruction politics has centered on a broad reassessment of black Republicanism, largely undertaken by a new generation of black historians. Scholars like Thomas Holt and Nell Painter insist that Reconstruction was not simply a matter of black and white. Conflicts within the black community, no less than divisions among whites, shaped Reconstruction politics. Where revisionist scholars, both black and white, had celebrated the accomplishments of black political leaders, Holt, Painter, and others charge that they failed to address the economic plight of the black masses. Painter criticized "representative colored men," as national black leaders were called, for failing to provide ordinary freedmen with effective political leadership. Holt found that black officeholders in South Carolina mostly emerged from the old free mulatto class of Charleston, which shared many assumptions with prominent whites. "Basically bourgeois in their origins and orientation," he wrote, they "failed to act in the interest of black peasants."

In emphasizing the persistence from slavery of divisions between free blacks and slaves, these writers reflect the increasing concern with continuity and conservatism in Reconstruction. Their work reflects a startling extension of revisionist premises. If, as has been argued for the past twenty years, blacks were active agents rather than mere victims of manipulation, then they could not be absolved of blame for the ultimate failure of Reconstruction.

Despite the excellence of recent writing and the continual expansion of our knowledge of the period, historians of Reconstruction today face a unique dilemma. An old interpretation has been overthrown, but a coherent new synthesis has yet to take its place. The revisionists of the 1960s effectively established a series of negative points: the Reconstruction governments were not as bad as had been portrayed, black supremacy was a myth, the Radicals were not cynical manipulators of the freedmen. Yet no convincing overall portrait of the quality of political and social life emerged from their writings. More recent historians have rightly pointed to elements of continuity that spanned the nineteenth-century Southern experience, especially the survival, in modified form, of the plantation system. Nevertheless, by denying the real changes that did occur, they have failed to provide a convincing portrait of an era characterized above all by drama, turmoil, and social change.

Building upon the findings of the past twenty years of scholarship, a new portrait of Reconstruction ought to begin by viewing it not as a specific time period, bounded by the years 1865 and 1877, but as an episode in a prolonged historical process—American society's adjustment to the consequences of the Civil War and emancipation. The Civil War, of course, raised the decisive questions of America's national existence: the relations between local and national authority, the definition of citizenship, the balance between force and consent in generating obedience to authority. The war and Reconstruction, as Allan Nevins observed over fifty years ago, marked the "emergence of modern America." This was the era of the completion of the national railroad network, the creation of the modern steel industry, the conquest of the West and final subduing of the Indians, and the expansion of the mining frontier. Lincoln's America—the world of the small farm and artisan shop— gave way to a rapidly industrializing economy. The issues that galvanized postwar Northern politics—from the question of the greenback currency to the mode of paying holders of the national debt—arose from the economic changes unleashed by the Civil War.

Above all, the war irrevocably abolished slavery. Since 1619, when "twenty negars" disembarked from a Dutch ship in Virginia, racial injustice had haunted American life, mocking its professed ideals even as tobacco and cotton, the products of slave labor, helped finance the nation's economic development. Now the implications of the black presence could no longer be ignored. The Civil War resolved the problem of slavery but, as the Philadelphia diarist Sydney George Fisher observed in June 1865, it opened an even more intractable problem: "What shall we do with the Negro?" Indeed, he went on, this was a problem *"incapable* of any solution that will satisfy both North and South."

As Fisher realized, the focal point of Reconstruction was the social revolution known as emancipation. Plantation slavery was simultaneously a system of labor, a form of racial domination, and the foundation upon which arose a distinctive ruling class within the South. Its demise threw open the most fundamental questions of economy, society, and politics. A new system of labor, social, racial, and political relations had to be created to replace slavery.

The United States was not the only nation to experience emancipation in the nineteenth century. Neither plantation slavery nor abolition were unique to the United States. But Reconstruction was. In a comparative perspective Radical Reconstruction stands as a remarkable experiment, the only effort of a society experiencing abolition to bring the former slaves within the umbrella of equal citizenship. Because the Radicals did not achieve everything they wanted, historians have lately tended to play down the stunning departure represented by black suffrage and officeholding. Former slaves, most fewer than two years removed from bondage, debated the fundamental questions of the polity: What is a republican form of government? Should the state provide equal education for all? How could political equality be reconciled with a society in which property was so unequally distributed? There was something inspiring in the way such men met the challenge of Reconstruction. "I knew nothing more than to obey my master," James K. Greene, an Alabama black politician later recalled. "But the tocsin of freedom sounded and knocked at the door and we walked out like free men and we met the exigencies as they grew up, and shouldered the responsibilities."

✑◈✑

You never saw a people more excited on the subject of politics than are the negroes of the south," one planter observed in 1867. And there were more than a few Southern whites as well who in these years shook off the prejudices of the past to embrace the vision of a new South dedicated to the principles of equal citizenship and social justice. One ordinary South Carolinian expressed the new sense of possibility in 1868 to the Republican governor of the state: "I am sorry that I cannot write an elegant stiled letter to your excellency. But I rejoice to think that God almighty has given to the poor of S. C. a Gov. to hear to feel to protect the humble poor without distinction to race or color. . . . I am a native borned S. C. a poor man never owned a Negro in my life nor my father before me. . . . Remember the true and loyal are the poor of the whites and blacks, outside of these you can find none loyal."

Few modern scholars believe the Reconstruction governments established in the South in 1867 and 1868 fulfilled the aspirations of their humble constituents. While their achievements in such realms as education, civil rights, and the economic rebuilding of the South are now widely appreciated, historians today believe they failed to affect either the economic plight of the emancipated slave or the ongoing transformation of independent white farmers into cotton tenants. Yet their opponents did perceive the Reconstruction governments in precisely this way—as representatives of a revolution that had put the bottom rail, both racial and economic, on top. This perception helps explain the ferocity of the attacks leveled against them and the pervasiveness of violence in the postmancipation South.

The spectacle of black men voting and holding office was anathema to large numbers of Southern whites. Even more disturbing, at least in the view of those who still controlled the plantation regions of the South, was the emergence of local officials, black and white, who sympathized with the plight of the black laborer. Alabama's vagrancy law was a "dead letter" in 1870, "because those who are charged with its enforcement are indebted to the vagrant vote for their offices and emoluments." Political debates over the level and incidence of taxation, the control of crops, and the resolution of contract disputes revealed that a primary issue of Reconstruction was the role of government in a plantation society. During presidential Reconstruction, and after "Redemption," with planters and their allies in control of politics, the law emerged as a means of stabilizing and promoting the plantation system. If Radical Reconstruction failed to redistribute the land of the South, the ouster of the planter class from control of politics at least ensured that the sanctions of the criminal law would not be employed to discipline the black labor force.

⎯⎯⎯⎯

An understanding of this fundamental conflict over the relation between government and society helps explain the pervasive complaints concerning corruption and "extravagance" during Radical Reconstruction. Corruption there was aplenty; tax rates did rise sharply. More significant than the rate of taxation, however, was the change in its incidence. For the first time, planters and white farmers had to pay a significant portion of their income to the government, while propertyless blacks often escaped scot-free. Several states, moreover, enacted heavy taxes on uncultivated land to discourage land speculation and force land onto the market, benefiting, it was hoped, the freedmen.

As time passed, complaints about the "extravagance" and corruption of Southern governments found a sympathetic audience among influential Northerners. The Democratic charge that universal suffrage in the South was responsible for high taxes and governmental extravagance coincided with a rising conviction among the urban middle classes of the North that city government had to be taken out of the hands of the immigrant poor and returned to the "best men"—the educated, professional, financially independent citizens unable to exert much political influence at a time of mass parties and machine politics. Increasingly the "respectable" middle classes began to retreat from the very notion of universal suffrage. The poor were no longer perceived as honest producers, the backbone of the social order; now they became the "dangerous classes," the "mob." As the historian Francis Parkman put it, too much power rested with "masses of imported ignorance and hereditary ineptitude." To Parkman the Irish of the Northern cities and the blacks of the South were equally incapable of utilizing the ballot: "Witness the municipal corruptions of New York, and the monstrosities of negro rule in South Carolina." Such attitudes helped to justify Northern inaction as, one by one, the Reconstruction regimes of the South were overthrown by political violence.

⎯⎯⎯⎯

In the end, then, neither the abolition of slavery nor Reconstruction succeeded in resolving the debate over the meaning of freedom in American life. Twenty years before the American Civil War, writing about the prospect of abolition in France's colonies, Alexis de Tocqueville had written, "If the Negroes have the right to become free, the [planters] have the incontestable right not to be ruined by the Negroes' freedom." And in the United States, as in nearly every plantation society that experienced the end of slavery, a rigid social and political dichotomy between former master and former slave, an ideology of racism, and a dependent labor force with limited economic opportunities all survived abolition. Unless one means by freedom the simple fact of not being a slave, emancipation thrust blacks into a kind of no-man's land, a partial freedom that made a mockery of the American ideal of equal citizenship.

Yet by the same token the ultimate outcome underscores the uniqueness of Reconstruction itself. Alone among the societies that abolished slavery in the nineteenth century, the United States, for a moment, offered the freedmen a measure of political control over their own destinies. However brief its sway, Reconstruction allowed scope for a remarkable political and social mobilization of the black community. It opened doors of opportunity that could never be completely closed. Reconstruction transformed the lives of Southern blacks in ways unmeasurable by statistics and unreachable by law. It raised their expectations and aspirations, redefined their status in relation to the larger society, and allowed space for the creation of institutions that enabled them to survive the repression that followed. And it established constitutional principles of civil and political equality that, while flagrantly violated after Reconstruction, planted the seeds of future struggle.

Certainly, in terms of the sense of possibility with which it opened, Reconstruction failed. But as Du Bois observed, it was a "splendid failure." For its animating vision—a society in which social advancement would be open to all on the basis of individual merit, not inherited caste distinctions—is as old as America itself and remains relevant to a nation still grappling with the unresolved legacy of emancipation.

LaWanda Cox

Reflections on the Limits of the Possible

. . . Lincoln's presidential style, at odds with that forthrightness which stands high in twentieth-century criteria for presidential leadership, was not inappropriate to the situation he faced. The manner in which he unveiled the crucial, controversial element of his Reconstruction policy—some measure of suffrage for blacks—was designed to crystallize support and minimize opposition. At the time only the most minimal suffrage proposal could command an intraparty consensus; this was all that he asked, actually less than his supporters had sought in Louisiana. Yet he managed to open the door to future enfranchisement for more blacks than the relatively few, Union soldiers and the "very intelligent," whose qualifications he commended. In phrasing that avoided a definite formulation of either means or goal he suggested the desirability of a fuller franchise, one that would meet what "the colored man" "desires." In the same address he stated that "the sole object of the government" was to get the secession states back into "their proper practical relation with the Union" and asked that "all join in doing the acts necessary" to restore them. He refrained from defining the "acts necessary." To counter criticism that he had set up the reconstructed state government, Lincoln minimized his role in Louisiana, but he did not disavow his authority as commander in chief to shape the Reconstruction process. By virtue of that power he had just sent General Banks back to New Orleans with military authority to perform an essentially civil mission—to promote the kind of Unionist government and racial policy the administration desired.

Although his statements could be otherwise interpreted, Lincoln's purpose, like that of his party, went beyond the readmission of the secession states. In early 1865 he was in an excellent position to implement a larger purpose by combining a minimum of direct force with a maximum use of other means of asserting the power and influence of the presidency. Lincoln's election victory the previous November had greatly strengthened his hand with Congress and with the northern public. Final military victory could only have increased the public esteem and congressional respect he had won. In the summer and fall that followed, Lincoln would have found additional support in a mounting sense of indignation in the North as reports from the South confirmed warnings that the freedom of blacks would be in peril if left in the

From LINCOLN AND BLACK FREEDOM: A STUDY IN PRESIDENTIAL LEADERSHIP by LaWanda Cox, pp. 172–183. Copyright © 1981 by University of South Carolina Press. Reprinted by permission.

hands of southern whites. A widespread perception of injustice can be a powerful political force, as indeed it became in 1866.

It would have been uncharacteristic of Lincoln not to have recognized the opportunity. In his pragmatic fashion, advancing step by step as events permitted, with caution but when necessary with great boldness, it is just possible that Lincoln might have succeeded in making a policy of basic citizenship rights for blacks "acceptable to those who must support it, tolerable to those who must put up with it." The challenge to presidential leadership was formidable. If any man could have met the challenge, that man was Lincoln.

⚜

Had Lincoln in the course of a second term succeeded in obtaining a far broader consent from the white South to terms that would satisfy northern Republican opinion than did Congress in 1867–1869, ultimate victory in the battle over the ex-slave's status as free man would not necessarily have followed. There would still have been the need to build institutions that could safeguard and expand what had been won—laws that the courts would uphold, an economy offering escape from poverty and dependency, a Union-Republican party in the South recognized by its opponents as a legitimate contestant for political power. The opportunities open to Lincoln for institutionalizing gains made toward equal citizenship irrespective of color were limited.

A fatal weakness of Reconstruction, constitutional historians have argued, arose from the constitutional conservatism of Republican lawmakers, particularly their deference to the traditional federal structure embodied in the Constitution. This led them to preserve the primacy of state responsibility for the rights of citizens, thereby denying to the national government effective power to protect the rights of blacks. It has been contended that Reconstruction required "a major constitutional upheaval," that it "could have been effected only by a revolutionary destruction of the states and the substitution of a unitary constitutional system." Part of the argument is unassailable. The new scholarship has demolished the old stereotype of Republican leaders as constitutional revolutionaries. They had, indeed, been waging a war for constitution as well as for nation with every intent of maintaining both. And the concern of Republicans for state and local government was no superficial adulation of the constitution; it was deeply rooted in their commitment to self-government. Yet unlike Democrats who denounced as unconstitutional any amendment to the constitution that enlarged federal authority at the expense of the states, Republicans did not uphold state rights federalism without qualification. They believed that they had found a way to protect freedmen in their new citizenship status by modifying, rather than destroying, the traditional federal structure.

What is questionable in the case against "respect for federalism" as fatally compromising Reconstruction is the assumption that the state rights federalist approach to the problem made a solution impossible. Not all scholars would agree. Some believe that the Reconstruction amendments needed only to have been more carefully framed. Others hold that as written they were adequate to the task. The Supreme Court, of course, seemed to disagree, overturning much of the legislation Congress passed under the amendments. Beginning with the Slaughterhouse decision of 1873, which did not directly affect blacks but carried ominous implications for them, a Republican Court handed down a series of constrictive decisions described in retrospect as "vacuous" and as "a major triumph for the South." Concern to preserve the functions of the states strongly influenced those decisions. Some authorities hold that without destroying federalism the Court could have devised a workable new division of authority between state and nation which would have enabled the latter to protect the rights of blacks against violation by either states or individuals. The Court did not foreclose all avenues of congressional action to protect black rights. However, by 1875 when it rendered the first adverse decision directly relating to the national enforcement effort, further legislation to meet the Court's criteria of adequacy was politically impossible because of the strength in Congress of the Democratic political opposition.

The Supreme Court seemed to have denied to congressional Reconstruction much needed legitimacy and legal sanctions. Without them, it is questionable that the Reconstruction effort could have been successfully defended during the postemancipation decades. The Court's narrow interpretation of which civil rights pertained to national as distinct from state citizenship added to the difficulties the Court had raised for the exercise of power to protect rights recognized as subject to the nation's authority. The decisions presented monumental obstacles to the enforcement of black rights. Better drafted amendments, laws, and indictments, more resourceful judicial reasoning, or less concern in the early decisions for technicalities might have avoided or remedied them. Lincoln's presence was unlikely to have increased those possibilities directly. Yet had he been president in the immediate post-Appomattox period he might have succeeded in dissipating southern resistance, in unifying Republicans on the preconditions for restoration, and in inducing reconstructed state governments to accept those conditions—a tall order. The resulting climate of opinion could have led the Court to play a positive role in the nineteenth-century Reconstruction effort. A possibility, but a very tenuous possibility.

Similarly circumscribed was any potential role for Lincoln in helping shape economic developments to assure freedmen an escape from poverty and dependence. No explanation for the tragic outcome of the postwar decades for black America has been more generally accepted in modern scholarship than that Reconstruction failed because the national government did not provide land for the freedman. The thesis has been sharply challenged, and the challenge has not been met. The work of historians and economists in exploring afresh the roots of poverty, particularly of black poverty, in the postbellum South afford some relevant perspectives. Between 1974 and 1979 six book-length studies appeared with significant bearing on the problem of black poverty, and others were in progress; conference papers and published articles also reflected the vigor of scholarly interest in the question.

No consensus has developed either as explanation for the continuing dependence and poverty of southern blacks or as an analysis of the potential economic effect of land distribution. However, four of five econometricians who addressed the latter question concluded that grants of land, while desirable and beneficial, would not have solved the predicament of the freedmen and their children. Robert Higgs has written that "historians have no doubt exaggerated the economic impact of such a grant." Gavin Wright holds that "the tenancy systems of the South cannot be assigned primary blame for Southern poverty," that a more equitable distribution of land "would not have produced dramatic improvements in living standards" or "generated sustained progress." In their book, *One Kind of Freedom,* Roger Ransom and Richard Sutch appear to accept what Heman Belz has characterized as the "new orthodoxy" of the historians, but they dramatically qualified that position in a subsequent paper. They argued that confiscation and redistribution would have resulted in little improvement in the postbellum situation, which they characterize as one of economic stagnation and exploitation, unless accompanied by federally funded compensation for landowners thereby providing liquid capital for rein vigorating agriculture and possibly developing manufactures. This retrospective prescription is restrained as compared to the requirements outlined by twentieth-century experts who seek land distribution as an avenue out of rural poverty. They see successful land reform as requiring supplementary government programs providing credit, seed and fertilizer distribution, marketing facilities, rural and feeder transportation, pricing mechanisms affecting both what the farmer buys and what he sells, technical research, and agricultural education.

More than a land program was needed to insure the freedman's economic future. Although areas of land with high fertility prospered, it seems doubtful that income from cotton between the close of the war and the turn of the century, even if equitably distributed, could have sustained much beyond a marginal level of existence for those who worked the cotton fields whether as wage earner, cropper, tenant, or small owner. And the lower South because of its soils and climate, as Julius Rubin has convincingly shown, had no viable alternative to cotton as a commercial crop until the scientific and technological advances of the twentieth century. Nor could nonmarket subsistence farming offer much by way of material reward. The "more" that was needed can be envisaged in retrospect, and was glimpsed by contemporaries, but it is not clear how it could have been achieved. Gavin Wright has concluded that the postbellum South "required either a massive migration away from the region or a massive Southern industrial revolution." Both in the North and the South there was enthusiasm for promoting southern industry, but only the future could reveal how elusive would be that "New South" of ever-renewed expectations. Despite scholarship, new and old, there is no certain explanation of why the South failed to catch up with the North. If historians and economists should agree upon a diagnosis, it is unlikely that they will uncover a remedy that could have been recognized and implemented a century ago. The heritage of slavery most certainly will be part of the diagnosis. It left behind an underdeveloped, overwhelmingly rural economy tied to the world market and bereft of adequate foundations for rapid economic growth. Recovery and growth had to be attempted in a period of initial crop disasters, of disadvantage for primary products in terms of world trade, and by the mid-1870s of prolonged and recurrent economic crises. There were high hopes for southern industrialization in the

1880s, but the effort substantially failed. With opportunity drastically limited in the South and industry expanding in the North, there was yet no great out-migration of blacks until the twentieth century. The reasons for this also are not altogether clear. Neither the restraints placed on southern agricultural labor by law and custom nor the discrimination blacks faced in the North is sufficient explanation. The ways in which European immigrants blocked black advance deserve further study, as does the attitude of blacks themselves both toward leaving the South and toward the unskilled, menial labor which alone might have afforded them large-scale entry into the northern labor market.

Lincoln was a man of his age. The concepts and perceptions then dominant, although not unreasonable on the basis of past experience, were inadequate to meet the challenge of transforming the South. Postwar expectations were buoyant. King Cotton was expected to regain his throne with beneficent results for all. Freed from the incubus of slavery, the South would be reshaped after the image of the bustling North, with large landholdings disintegrated by natural forces, village and school house replacing plantation quarters, internal improvements and local industry transforming the economy. The former slave would share the bright future through diligence and thrift, and the forces of the marketplace. There were, of course, dissenters, both radicals like George W. Julian and Thaddeus Stevens who would confiscate the great estates and conservatives such as those cotton manufacturers, by no means all, who would perpetuate the plantation in some form. Neither had sufficient influence at war's end to shape national policy. Republican leaders who did make postwar policy would have reached beyond prevailing concepts of self-help, the law of supply and demand, and the danger of "class legislation" to enact a modest land program had not President Johnson vetoed it with an appeal to all the economic verities of the day.

In the interest of the emancipated, Lincoln could have been expected to approve and encourage such deviations from the doctrinaire. And it would have been completely out of character for Lincoln to have exercised his power of pardon, as did President Johnson, with ruthless disregard for the former slave's interest and justifiable expectations. Indeed, there are intimations that Lincoln considered using that power to obtain from former masters grants of land for former slaves. Whatever support the national government might have given to the freedman's quest for land would have been a psychological boon, more symbol than substance of equal citizenship and independence, but not without some economic advantage. A land program more effective than the southern homestead act was a real possibility, lost due to President Johnson's opposition. With Lincoln, a Whiggish heritage, as well as humanity and a sense of responsibility for the emancipated, reinforced a pragmatic approach to the relationship between government and the future of the freedmen. Nor was he inhibited by the anxiety felt by many, including Thaddeus Stevens, over the unprecedented debt incurred in fighting the war. In early 1865 he calmly contemplated adding to the war's cost by indemnifying southerners for property seized and not restored. Whatever sums Congress might have appropriated to finance land purchase for freedmen could only have helped alleviate the South's postwar paucity of capital and credit. Its economic recovery would also have benefited from the lesser turbulence of the immediate postwar years had there been no war between president and Congress. Limited gains would have been possible and probable, but there existed neither the power nor the perception necessary to forestall the poverty that engulfed so many southerners, black and white, during the last decades of the nineteenth century.

There were limits to the possible. Yet the dismal outcome for southern blacks as the nation entered the twentieth century need not have been as unrelieved as it was in fact. More than a land program, the civil and political rights Republicans established in law, had they been secured in practice, could have mitigated the discrimination that worsened their condition and constricted whatever opportunities might otherwise have existed for escape from poverty. Moreover, the extraordinary effort black men made to vote—and to vote independently in the face of white cajolery, intimidation, and economic pressure—strongly suggests that for the emancipated to cast a ballot was to affirm the reality of freedom and the dignity of black manhood.

The priority Republicans gave to civil and political rights in their fight to establish a meaningful new status for ex-slaves has been too readily discounted by historians. Small landholdings could not have protected blacks from intimidation, or even from many forms of economic coercion. They would not have brought economic power. In the face of overwhelming white opposition, they could not have safeguarded the new equality of civil and political status. Where blacks voted freely, on the other hand, there was always the potential for sharing political power and using it as a means to protect and advance their interests. There is considerable evidence that this did happen. Local officials elected by black votes during the years of Republican control upheld blacks against planters, state legislators repealed Black Codes, shifted the burden of taxation from the poor, granted agricultural laborers a first lien on crops, increased expenditures for education. Eric Foner has concluded that at least in some areas Republican Reconstruction resulted in subtle but significant changes that protected black labor and prevented planters from using the state to bolster their position. Harold D. Woodman's study of state laws affecting agriculture confirms the generalization that a legislative priority of the Redeemer governments was passage of measures to give landowners greater control over the labor force. By the end of the century legal bonds had been so tightened that as prosperity returned to cotton culture neither cropper nor renter but only their employer was in a position to profit. In a study of rural Edgefield County, South Carolina, Vernon Burton has found that black voting made possible real gains in economic position and social status between 1867 and 1877. Howard Rabinowitz's examination of the urban South discloses that Republican city governments brought blacks a greater share of elected and appointed offices, more jobs in construction work, in fire and police departments. And beyond immediate gains, black votes meant support for educational facilities through which blacks could acquire the literacy and skills essential for advancement.

Security for black civil and political rights required acceptance by white southerners. An acquiescence induced by a judicious combination of force and consent needed for its perpetuation reinforcement by self-interest. The most effective vehicle of self-interest would have been a Union-Republican party able to command substantial continuing support from native whites. The Republican party that gained temporary dominance through the congressional legislation of 1867 enfranchising blacks failed to meet the test of substantial white support. Despite a strong white following in a few states, its scalawag component from the start was too limited to offset the opposition's attack on it as the party of the black man and the Yankee. And white participation diminished as appeals to race prejudice and sectional animosity intensified.

The potential for a major second party among southern whites existed in the aftermath of Confederate defeat. The Democratic party was in disarray, discredited for having led the South out of the Union and having lost the war. Old Whig loyalties subsumed by the slavery issue had nonetheless endured; southern unionism had survivied in varying degrees from wartime adherence to the Union to reluctant support of the Confederacy. Opposition to Jefferson Davis' leadership and willingness to accept northern peace terms had grown as the hope for southern victory diminished. Such sources of Democratic opposition overlapped with the potential for ready recruits to Union-Republicanism from urban dwellers, from men whose origins had been abroad or in the North, from those whose class or intrasectional interests created hostility to the dominant planter leadership of the Democracy. A "New South" of enterprise and industry presented an attractive vision to many a native son. And there were always those who looked to the loaves and the fishes dispensed from Washington.

Had party recruitment and organization, with full presidential support, begun at the end of hostilities and escaped the period of confusion and bitterness that thinned the ranks of the willing during the conflict between Johnson and Congress, the result could have been promising. Greater white support and the accession of black voters by increments might have eased racial tension and lessened deadly factionalism within the party. Lincoln's political skill and Whig background would certainly have served party-building well, as would the perception of presidential policy as one of moderation and reconciliation. The extent to which southern whites did in fact support the Republican party after 1867 despite its image as Radical, alien, and black-dominated, an image that stigmatized and often ostracized them, suggests the potency of a common goal, or a common enmity, in bridging the chasm between the races.

Even under the guidance of a Lincoln, the building of a permanent biracial major party in the South was by no means assured. A broad enduring coalition of disparate elements would face the necessity of reconciling sharply divergent economic interests. Agricultural workers sought maximum autonomy, more than bare necessities, and an opportunity for land ownership while planter-merchants strove to control labor and maximize profit. The burden of increased taxation to meet essential but unaccustomed social services, particularly for blacks, meant an inescapable clash of class and racial interests. Concessions by the more privileged were especially difficult in a South of limited available resources and credit, impoverished by war and enmeshed in inflated costs, crop disasters, and falling cotton prices. By the mid-1870s a nationwide depression intensified regional problems. Efforts to promote a more varied and vigorous economy by state favor, credit, and appropriation became a political liability as the primary effect appeared to be the proliferation of civic corruption and entrepreneurial plunder.

Outside the South a vigorous Republican party and two-party system managed to endure despite the clash of intraparty economic interests. A similar development in the South faced the additional and more intractable conflict inherent in the new black-white relationship. Within the Republican party that took shape after 1867, factionalism often cut between blacks and carpetbaggers, on the one hand, and scalawags on the other; but there was also a considerable amount of accommodation, not all of it from blacks. A study of the voting record of 87 Republicans, 52 of them native whites, who served in the North Carolina House of Representatives in the 1868 to 1870 session shows scalawags trailing carpetbaggers and blacks in voting on issues of Negro rights and support for public schools, yet compiling a positive overall record, a score of 61.2 and 55.9 respectively. On the few desegregation questions that came to a roll call, however, only a small minority of native whites voted favorably. In Mississippi when the black-carpetbagger faction gained control, they quietly ignored the platform calling for school integration even though black legislators were sufficiently numerous and powerful to have pressed the issue. Black officeholding was a similar matter where fair treatment held danger, and black leaders often showed restraint. Such issues were explosive. They not only threatened the unity of the party but undermined its ability to attract white votes or minimize opposition demagoguery and violence. A Lincolnian approach to building an interracial party would have diminished the racial hazard, but could hardly have eliminated it.

The years of political Reconstruction, to borrow an apt phrase from Thomas B. Alexander's study of Tennessee, offered no "narrowly missed opportunities to leap a century forward in reform." Not even a Lincoln could have wrought such a miracle. To have secured something less, yet something substantially more than blacks had gained by the end of the nineteenth century, did not lie beyond the limits of the possible given a president who at war's end would have joined party in an effort to realize "as nearly as we can" the fullness of freedom for blacks.

Possible is not probable. To the major obstacles must be added the hazards disclosed by the Louisiana story. Lincoln's Louisiana policy had been compromised by Banks' blunders of execution and attacked by Durant and fellow Radicals in part because they distrusted Lincoln's intent. The effective implementation of a president's policy by his surrogates is a problem to plague any administration. Distrust by those otherwise allied in a common goal pertained more distinctively to the man and his style of leadership. Yet Radical distrust of Lincoln may also have reflected dilemmas inherent in presidential leadership—the need for candor and for persuasion, for vision and for practicality, for courage and for flexibility, for heeding while leading a national consensus. Obscured by his characteristic self-effacement, after his own fashion Lincoln as president was both lion and fox. . . .

POSTSCRIPT

Was Reconstruction a "Splendid Failure"?

In *Nothing But Freedom: Emancipation and Its Legacy* (Louisiana State University Press, 1984), Eric Foner advances his interpretation by comparing the treatment of ex-slaves in the United States with that of newly emancipated slaves in Haiti and the British West Indies. Only in the United States, he contends, were the freedslaves given voting and economic rights. Although these rights had been stripped away from the majority of black southerners by 1900, Reconstruction had, nevertheless, created a legacy of freedom that inspired succeeding generations of African Americans.

C. Vann Woodward, in "Reconstruction: A Counterfactual Playback," an essay in his thought-provoking *The Future of the Past* (Oxford University Press, 1988), shares Cox's pessimism about the outcome of Reconstruction. For all the successes listed by the revisionists, he argues that the experiment failed. He challenges Foner's conclusions by insisting that former slaves were as poorly treated in the United States as they were in other countries. He also maintains that the confiscation of former plantations and the redistribution of land to the former slaves would have failed in the same way that the Homestead Act of 1862 failed to generate equal distribution of government lands to poor white settlers. Finally, Woodward contends that reformers who worked with African Americans during Reconstruction and native Americans a decade or two later were often the same people and that they failed in both instances because their goals were out of touch with the realities of the late nineteenth century.

Thomas Holt's *Black Over White: Negro Political Leadership in South Carolina During Reconstruction* (University of Illinois Press, 1977) is representative of state and local studies that employ modern social science methodology to yield new perspectives. While critical of white Republican leaders, Holt (who is African American) also blames the failure of Reconstruction in South Carolina on freeborn mulatto politicians, whose background distanced them economically, socially, and culturally from the masses of freedmen. Consequently, these political leaders failed to develop a clear and unifying ideology to challenge white South Carolinians who wanted to restore white supremacy.

The study of the Reconstruction period benefits from an extensive bibliography. Traditional accounts of Reconstruction include William Archibald Dunning's *Reconstruction, Political and Economic, 1865–1877* (Harper & Brothers, 1907); Claude Bowers' *The Tragic Era: The Revolution after Lincoln* (Riverside Press, 1929); and E. Merton Coulter's, *The South During Reconstruction, 1865–1877* (Louisiana State University Press, 1947), the last major work written from the Dunning (or traditional) point of view. Early revisionist views are presented in W. E. B. Du Bois, *Black Reconstruction in America: An Essay Toward a History of the Part Which Black Folk Played in the Attempt to Reconstruct Democracy in America, 1860–1880* (Harcourt, Brace, 1935), a Marxist analysis; John Hope Franklin, *Reconstruction: After the Civil War* (University of Chicago Press, 1961); and Kenneth M. Stampp, *The Era of Reconstruction, 1865–1877* (Alfred A. Knopf, 1965). Foner's *Reconstruction: America's Unfinished Revolution, 1863–1877* (Harper & Row, 1988) includes the most complete bibliographies on the subject. Brief overviews are available in Forrest G. Wood, *The Era of Reconstruction, 1863–1877* (Harlan Davidson, 1975) and Michael Perman, *Emancipation and Reconstruction, 1862–1879* (Harlan Davidson, 1987). One of the best-written studies of a specific episode during the Reconstruction years is Willie Lee Rose's *Rehearsal for Reconstruction: The Port Royal Experiment* (Bobbs-Merrill, 1964), which describes the failed effort at land reform in the sea islands of South Carolina. Richard Nelson Current's *Those Terrible Carpetbaggers: A Reinterpretation* (Oxford University Press, 1988) is a superb challenge to the traditional view of these much-maligned Reconstruction participants. Heather Cox Richardson, *The Death of Reconstruction: Race, Labor, and Politics in the Post–Civil War North, 1865–1901* (Harvard University Press, 2001) is a significant post-revisionist analysis of the failure of Reconstruction. Finally, for collections of interpretive essays on various aspects of the Reconstruction experience, see Staughton Lynd, ed., *Reconstruction* (Harper & Row, 1967); Seth M. Scheiner, ed., *Reconstruction: A Tragic Era?* (Holt, Rinehart and Winston, 1968); and Edwin C. Rozwenc, ed., *Reconstruction in the South*, 2d ed. (Heath, 1972).

Contributors to This Volume

EDITORS

LARRY MADARAS is a professor of history and political science at Howard Community College in Columbia, Maryland. He received a B.A. from the College of the Holy Cross in 1959 and an M.A. and a Ph.D. from New York University in 1961 and 1964, respectively. He has also taught at Spring Hill College, the University of South Alabama, and the University of Maryland at College Park. He has been a Fulbright Fellow and has held two fellowships from the National Endowment for the Humanities. He is the author of dozens of journal articles and book reviews.

JAMES M. SoRELLE is a professor of history and former chair of the Department of History at Baylor University in Waco, Texas. He received a B.A. and M.A. from the University of Houston in 1972 and 1974, respectively, and a Ph.D. from Kent State University in 1980. In addition to introductory courses in United States and world history, he teaches upper-level sections in African American, urban, and late nineteenth- and twentieth-century U.S. history and a graduate seminar on the civil rights movement. His scholarly articles have appeared in the *Houston Review, Southwestern Historical Quarterly,* and *Black Dixie: Essays in Afro-Texan History and Culture in Houston* (Texas A&M University Press, 1992), edited by Howard Beeth and Cary D. Wintz. He also has contributed entries to *The Handbook of Texas, The Oxford Companion to Politics of the World,* and *Encyclopedia of the Confederacy.*

STAFF

Larry Loeppke	Managing Editor
Jill Peter	Senior Developmental Editor
Susan Brusch	Senior Developmental Editor
Beth Kundert	Production Manager
Jane Mohr	Project Manager
Tara McDermott	Design Coordinator
Nancy Meissner	Editorial Assistant
Julie Keck	Senior Marketing Manager
Mary Klein	Marketing Communications Specialist
Alice Link	Marketing Coordinator
Tracie Kammerude	Senior Marketing Assistant
Lori Church	Pemissions Coordinator

AUTHORS

IRVING BRANT (1885–1976) was a newspaper journalist and writer for several major newspapers, including the *St. Louis Star-Times* and the *Chicago Sun*. He is the author of over a dozen books, including *The Bill of Rights: Its Origin and Meaning* (Bobbs-Merrill, 1965) and *Impeachment: Trials and Errors* (Alfred A. Knopf, 1972).

JON BUTLER is the Howard R. Lamar Professor of American History and Dean of the Graduate School of Arts and Sciences at Yale University. He is the author of *Awash in a Sea of Faith: Christianizing the American People* (Harvard University Press, 1990) and is currently writing a book on religion in modern New York City.

COLIN G. CALLOWAY is professor of history and Samson Occom Professor of Native American Studies at Dartmouth where he chairs the Native American Studies Program. He recently published *The Scratch of a Pen: 1763 and the Transformation of North America* (Oxford University Press, 2006).

LaWANDA COX is professor emeritus of history at Hunter College. She is the author, with John H. Cox, of *Politics, Principle, and Prejudice, 1865–1866: Dilemma of Reconstruction America* (Macmillan, 1963). Her most important scholarly writings can be found in Donald E. Nieman, ed., *Freedom, Racism, and Reconstruction: Collected Writings of LaWanda Cox* (University of Georgia Press, 1997).

THOMAS DUBLIN is professor of history and codirector of the Center for the Historical Study of Women and Gender at The State University of New York at Binghamton. He is the author of *Women at Work: The Transformation of Work and Community in Lowell, Massachusetts, 1826–1860* (Columbia University Press, 1979) and *Transforming Women's Work: New England Lives in the Industrial Revolution* (Cornell University Press, 1994).

WILMA A. DUNAWAY is associate professor of sociology at Virginia Polytechnic Institute and State University. Her first book, *The First American Frontier: Transition to Capitalism in Southern Appalachia, 1700–1860* (University of North Carolina Press, 1996) won the 1996 Weatherford Award for the best book about Southern Appalachia.

DAVID HACKETT FISCHER is University Professor and Warren Professor of History at Brandeis University. Among his most recent books are *Paul Revere's Ride* (Oxford University Press, 1994), *Bound Away: Virginia and the Westward Movement* (University of Virginia Press, 2000), and the Pulitzer Prize–winning *Washington's Crossing* (Oxford University Press, 2004).

ERIC FONER is the DeWitt Clinton Professor of History at Columbia University in New York City. He earned his B.A. and his Ph.D. from Columbia in 1963 and 1969, respectively, and he was elected president of the American Historical Association in 2000. His many publications include *A Short History of Reconstruction, 1863–1877* (Harper & Row, 1990) and *America's Reconstruction: People and Politics After the Civil War,* coauthored with Olivia Mahoney (HarperPerennial, 1995).

EUGENE D. GENOVESE, a prominent Marxist historian and Civil War scholar, is president of the Historical Society, a professional organization of historians, and a former president of the Organization of American Historians. His many publications include *A Consuming Fire: The Fall of the Confederacy in the Mind of the White Christian South* (University of Georgia Press, 1998) and *The Southern Front: History and Politics in the Cultural War* (University of Missouri Press, 1995).

NORMAN A. GRAEBNER is the Randolph P. Compton Professor Emeritus of History at the University of Virginia in Charlottesville, Virginia. He has held a number of other academic appointments and has received distinguished teacher awards at every campus at which he has taught. He has edited and written numerous books, articles, and texts on American history, including *Foundations of American Foreign Policy: A Realist Appraisal From Franklin to McKinley* (Scholarly Resources Press, 1985) and *Empire on the Pacific: A Study in American Continental Expansion,* 2d ed. (Regina Books, 1983).

ALLEN C. GUELZO is Henry R. Luce Professor of the Civil War Era at Gettysburg College. His book *Abraham Lincoln: Redeemer President* (Eerdmans, 1999) won the Lincoln Prize for best book in the field of Civil War history. He is also the author of *Edwards on the Will: A Century of American Theological Debate* (Wesleyan University Press, 1989) and *For the Union of Evangelical Christianity: The Irony of the Reformed Episcopalians* (Pennsylvania State University Press, 1994).

OSCAR HANDLIN is professor emeritus of history at Harvard University. He is the author of numerous books, including *The Uprooted: The Epic Story of the Great Migrations That Made the American People* (Little, Brown, 1951), *Boston's Immigrants, 1790–1880: A Study in Acculturation* (rev. and enl. ed., Belknap Press, 1991), and with Lilian Handlin, *Liberty in America,* 4 vols. (Harper & Row, 1986–1994).

VINCENT HARDING is a professor of religion and social transformation at the Iliff School of Theology in Denver, Colorado, and has long been involved in domestic and international movements for peace and justice. He is the author of *Hope and History: Why We Must Share the Story of the Movement* (Orbis Books, 1990) and coauthor, with Robin D. G. Kelley and Earl Lewis, of *We Changed the World: African Americans, 1945–1970* (Oxford University Press, 1997).

NATHAN O. HATCH currently serves as president of Wake Forest University following a distinguished teaching and administrative career at Notre Dame University. A specialist in American religious history, he is the author of *The Sacred Cause of Liberty: Republican Thought and the Millennium in Revolutionary New England* (Yale University Press, 1977), *The Search for Christian America* (Helmers and Howard, 1983), and *The Democratization of American Christianity* (Yale University Press, 1989).

DONALD R. HICKEY is professor of history at Wayne State College in Nebraska. He is also the author of *Nebraska Moments: Glimpses of Nebraska's Past* (University of Nebraska Press, 1992).

DAVID S. JONES is an assistant professor in the History and Culture of Science and Technology at MIT. He also works as a staff psychiatrist in the Psychiatric Emergency Center at Cambridge Hospital. He is the author of *Rationalizing Epidemics: Meanings and Uses of American Indian Mortality since 1600* (Harvard University Press, 2004).

LYLE KOEHLER was an instructor of history at the University of Cincinnati where he held several other administrative positions. He is the author of numerous scholarly articles in the fields of colonial American history and ethnic studies.

GERDA LERNER is Robinson-Edwards Professor of History Emerita at the University of Wisconsin at Madison. One of the foremost historians of women in America, she is the author of numerous books, including *The Grimké Sisters from South Carolina* (Houghton Mifflin, 1967) and *The Creation of Patriarchy* (Oxford University Press, 1986).

GLORIA L. MAIN is professor of history at the University of Colorado, Boulder. She is also the author of *Tobacco Colony: Life in Early Maryland, 1650–1720* (Princeton University Press, 1983) and *Peoples of a Spacious Land: Families and Cultures in Colonial New England* (Harvard University Press, 2001).

DONALD G. MATHEWS is professor of history at the University of North Carolina, Chapel Hill. He is the author of *Slavery and Methodism: A Chapter in American Morality, 1780–1845* (Princeton University Press, 1965) and *Religion in the Old South* (University of Chicago, 1977).

ERNEST R. MAY is professor of history at Harvard University. He is the author of numerous distinguished studies in diplomatic history, including *The World War and American Isolation, 1914–1917* (Harvard University Press, 1959), *Imperial Democracy: The Emergence of the United States as a Great Power* (Harcourt, Brace & World, 1961), and *Lessons of the Past: The Use and Misuse of History in American Foreign Policy* (Oxford University Press, 1973).

RICHARD P. McCORMICK (1916–2006) was professor emeritus of history at Rutgers University at the time of his death. He was the author of several influential works on American political history, including *The Second American Party System* (W. W. Norton, 1966 and *The Presidential Game: The Origin of American Presidential Politics* (Oxford University Press, 1982).

FORREST McDONALD, Distinguished University Research Professor of History Emeritus at the University of Alabama, was the 1980 recipient of the George Washington medal from Freedom's Foundation in Valley Forge, Pennsylvania. He is also the author of *Alexander Hamilton: A Biography* (W. W. Norton, 1982) and *Novus Ordo Seclorum: The Intellectual Origins of the Constitution* (University Press of Kansas, 1985).

WILLIAM H. McNEILL is professor emeritus of history at the University of Chicago where he was the Robert A. Milliken Distinguished Service Professor prior to his retirement. He is the author of *The Rise of the West: A History of the Human Community* (University of Chicago, 1970), which received the National Book Award, *Plagues and Peoples* (Anchor Press, 1976), and *A World History* (4th ed., Oxford University Press, 1998).

RUSSELL R. MENARD is professor of history at the University of Minnesota. He is the author of dozens of articles on the colonial Chesapeake as well as *Economy and Society in Colonial Maryland* (Garland, 1985) and *Migrants, Servants and Slaves: Unfree Labor in Colonial British America* (Ashgate, 2001).

EDMUND S. MORGAN is the Sterling Professor Emeritus of history at Yale University and the author of sixteen books on the colonial period. These works include *The Puritan Family: Religion and Domestic Relations in Seventeenth-Century New England* (Harper & Row, 1966), *The Puritan Dilemma: The Story of John Winthrop* (2d ed., Longman, 1998), and *Benjamin Franklin* (Yale University Press, 2002). His most recent book, *The Genuine Article: A Historian Looks at Early America* (W. W. Norton, 2004), is a collection of his review essays that appeared in *The New York Review of Books*. In 2000, he received the National Humanities Medal.

GARY B. NASH is professor emeritus of history at UCLA and director of the National Center for History in the Schools. Considered one of the nation's foremost social historians, his work focuses on race, class, and power dynamics in early America. The author of 20 major works, his most recent book is *First City: Philadelphia and the Forging of Historical Memory* (University of Pennsylvania Press, 2001).

DEXTER PERKINS (1889–1984) was professor emeritus of history at the University of Rochester and University Professor Emeritus at Cornell University. The author of many books on American diplomatic history, his *Hands Off: History of the Monroe Doctrine* (Little Brown, 1941) remains the standard on this subject.

JOHN P. ROCHE (1923–1993) was the Olin Distinguished Professor of American Civilization and Foreign Affairs at the Fletcher School of Law and Diplomacy in Medford, Massachusetts, and director of the Fletcher Media Institute. His many publications include *Shadow and Substance: Essays on the Theory and Structure of Politics* (Macmillan, 1964).

RAMÓN EDUARDO RUIZ is professor emeritus of Latin American history at the University of California–San Diego. He is the author of *Triumphs and Tragedy: A History of the Mexican People* (W. W. Norton, 1993).

SEAN WILENTZ is Dayton-Stockton Professor of History and director of the Program in American Studies at Princeton University. His book *Chants Democratic: New York City and the Rise of the American Working Class, 1788–1850* (Oxford University Press, 1984) won the prestigious Frederick Jackson Turner Award and the Albert J. Beveridge Award.

C. VANN WOODWARD (1908–1999), considered the dean of historians of the South prior to his death, was Sterling Professor of History at Yale University. He won the Pulitzer Prize in 1982 for *Mary Chesnut's Civil War* (Yale University Press, 1981). His other most distinguished books include *Origins of the New South, 1877–1913* (Louisiana University Press, 1951), *The Future of the Past* (Oxford University Press, 1989), *Reunion and Reaction: The Compromise of 1877 and the End of Reconstruction* (rev. ed., Oxford University Press,

1991), and *The Strange Career of Jim Crow* (3d rev. ed., Oxford University Press, 1979).

HOWARD ZINN is professor emeritus of political science at Boston University. A political activist and prolific writer, he is the author of *SNCC: The New Abolitionists* (Beacon Press, 1964), *Postwar America: 1945–1971* (MacMillan, 1973), and *A People's History of the United States* (Harper & Row, 1980).

Index